Volume 1

HEBREWS 2 TO NEGROES

Wake up Black America!

RONALD DALTON JR.

Cover Design: Brittany Jackson

Book Images used are Public Domain and Free Stock Photos

Published by G Publishing, LLC

Library of Congress Control Number: 2015913566

ISBN: 978-0-9862379-8-0

Printed in the United States of America

TABLE OF CONTENTS

CHAPTERS

23. CHURCH IS OVER, BUT NOTHING HAS CHANGED.

THE CURSES OF ISRAEL, BROKEN DOWN PLAIN

24. DEUTERONOMY 28:16-17

- THE 1948 STATE OF ISRAEL AND RETURN OF THE JEWS WAS NOT BIBLE PROPHECY.

- WHEN ARE WE GOING TO GET THE CONCEPT OF "GROUP ECONOMICS?"

- BLACKS HAVE THE HIGHEST "SPENDING POWER" DESPITE BEING THE MINORITY RACE IN AMERICA. SO WHY IS OTHER IMMIGRANT RACES SURPASSING US?

25. DEUTERONOMY 28:18

- SLAVE TRADES IN WEST AND EAST AFRICA? FAMINE IN WEST AND EAST AFRICA? COINCIDENCE?

- ARE WEST AFRICANS GENETICALLY RELATED TO THE BANTUS EAST AFRICANS THAT WERE TAKEN AS SLAVES IN THE ARAB SLAVE TRADES?

- FAMINE-LAND FOR CAIN AND THE "LAND OF NOD".

- THE OTHER CURSE: "THE CURSE OF LEPROSY" AND ITS CONNECTION TO THE ANCIENT ISRAELITES.

26. DEUTERONOMY 28:19-25

- IS THE KING ALFRED PLAN REAL? IS THIS POLICE BRUTALITY ALL A SET UP?

- NO OWNERSHIP MEANS NO CONTROL.

- SKIN COLOR DOES MATTER! THE CURSES PROVE IT!

- THE BODY DOESN'T LIE ON ITSELF.

- TURN OFF THE WATER TO SUB-SAHARAN AFRICA AND
  EAST AFRICA.

27. DEUTERONOMY 28:26-27

- BEASTS, BOILS, SWORDS, AND SCABS FOR THE
  THE ISRAELIITES.

- DID ANY OTHER NATIONS EXPERIENCE THESE CURSES
  OF ISRAEL?

- DID THE TAINO INDIANS SPEAK HEBREW?

- JUDAISM IN MEXICO AND SOUTH AMERICA.

28. DEUTERONOMY 28:28-30

- ALL WE CAN DO IS SHAKE OUR HEADS?

- WHO IS HAS BEEN SLEEPING WITH MY WIFE?

- WHAT HAPPENED TO ALL THE BLACK ARABS?

- ARE GENETICISTS REVEALING EDOM'S SEED?

- ARABS AND JEWS KEPT THEIR BLOODLINE "WHITE".

- DID THE JEWS BUILD HOUSES AND PLANT VINEYARDS?

29. DEUTERONOMY 28:31-36

- THOU SHALL NOT STEAL, UNLESS IT'S FROM A NEGRO.

- CHILDREN SOLD INTO SLAVERY? WHAT RACE?

- THE HOUSE NEGRO VS THE FIELD NEGRO.

- THE QUESTION IS WHY? WHY ARE WE SO ANGRY?

- ISRAELITES CONSTANTLY WORSHIPPING OTHER GODS?

- THE POURING OF "LIBATIONS" IN AFRICA AND AMERICA.

- WHY WOULD AN ISRAELITE CONVERT TO ISLAM?

- GOD DID NOT GIVE THE ISRAELITES A STAR AS THEIR SYMBOL.

- WITHOUT A TRUE LEVITICAL PRIESTHOOD THE THIRD TEMPLE IN JERUSALEM IS A SCAM.

- ARE AFRICANS FROM GHANA LEVITES? ARE HAITIANS LEVITES? THE FACTS WILL BLOW YOU AWAY!

- THE WEST AFRICAN ISRAELITE CONNECTION (1000 A.D. – 1600 A.D.): PRE –SLAVERY.

- ARE THERE ANY YORUBA ISRAELITE CONNECTIONS?

- WEST AFRICANS, NEW MOONS, SABBATHS. HOW CAN THIS BE? THESE ARE ISRAELITE CUSTOMS.

- THE NIGER RIVER, SENEGAL RIVER, NILE RIVER, AND THE EUPHRATES RIVER WERE BLACK HEBREW ISRAELITE TERRITORIES.

- WHAT COLOR WERE THE ORIGINAL ARABS PRIOR TO ISLAM? HAS THIS HISTORY BEEN DELETED FROM THE BLACK RACE TOO?

30. **DEUTERONOMY 28:37-44**

- WELCOME TO AMERICA SAMBO AND BOJANGLES.

- WHOSE CHILDREN HAVE GONE INTO SLAVERY? THE NEGROES OR THE EUROPEAN JEWS?

- BUILDING A BLACK "ECONOMY WITHIN AN ECONOMY".

31. DEUTERONOMY 28:45-49

- ARE THE CURSES OF ISRAEL FOREVER?

- WHERE IS THE SPIRITUAL "POWER" IN THE CHURCH?

- THE ARK OF THE COVENANT IS NOT IN MOUNT NEBO.

- IF THEY ARE LYING ABOUT THE ARK OF THE COVENANT, WHAT ABOUT SOLOMON'S TEMPLE?

- THE REBELLIOUS AND STIFF-NECKED ISRAELITES.

- WHAT WAS THE NATIVE TONGUE OF THE WEST AFRICANS TAKEN FROM THE SLAVE COAST?

- THE NIGERIAN IGBO EGYPTIAN-ISRAELITE CONNECITON.

32. DEUTERONOMY 28:50-57

- BLACK ISREALITES GET NO RESPECT IN THEIR SCATTERED LANDS.

- WHY WE CAN'T HAVE ANYTHING WITHOUT SOMEONE TRYING TO TAKE IT FROM US.

- BEYOND THE RIVERS OF ETHIOPIA, MY DISPERSED ONES (ISRAELITES).

- WHAT PEOPLE EXPERIENCED THE "BESIEGING" OF THEIR LAND NO MATTER WHERE THEY LIVED?

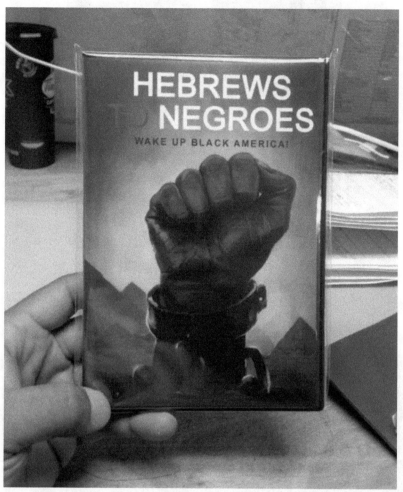

DVD-Hebrews to Negroes: Wake Up Black America – 2 disc, 16 hour presentation documentary available only at <u>www.thenegronetwork.com</u> Released 12-14-14.

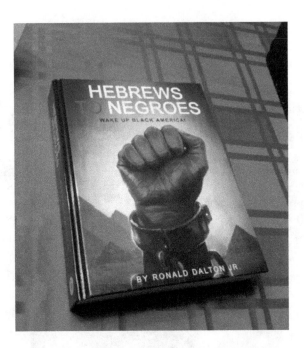

BOOK-Hebrews to Negroes (Part 1): Wake Up Black America available on Amazon, eBay, and www.thenegronetwork.com Released 12-14-14.

For coming "Hebrews to Negroes" Book & DVD Volumes please visit www.thenegronetwork.com

CHAPTER 1

THE INTRODUCTION

In December 2014, I published my first book "**Hebrews to Negroes: Wake Up Black America**". In 2011, I started to inquire about things in the Bible that were not adding up to me. Growing up in a Black Pentecostal Christian church I knew the bible, but there were a whole lot of unanswered questions I started to have as I got older and wiser. No one would explain the answers to these questions. Bible Class never provided me with all the answers. All we were told in church is that we are "**Gentiles**" and that Children of Israel are the European Caucasian people we see so frequently today in America. Well, I asked God to show me the answers and give me the knowledge I was desperately seeking.

As an African-American male in America, I have been through the struggle. As many black people say who have overcome the odds: "*We all have a story to tell,*" holds very true in my case in regards to my life story. It wasn't until I was in my 30's that I started to see the world in a different way. I started to see the suffering of Black people in America on different scales. Four to five generations post-slavery, most blacks are still stuck in time, trying to make it in a country that operates on the premise of "**White Supremacy**". Many of us do not know the secret agendas that are set in place to keep us down and destroy us. Most Blacks may not be aware that the "**American system**" is designed for "**us**" to "**suffer peacefully**". However, Blacks are starting to get fed up. We are tired of being mistreated and suppressed. Blacks are speaking up and are we are standing up. We are now calling things out for what they truly are. No more keeping silent, no more turning the blind eye. We are tired of the lies and broken promises. Just as the Haitian African Slaves revolted from the French, Blacks are starting to revolt. Black Pride is coming back; and with that an "**Awakening**". In Israel, Ethiopian Jews have been protesting their rights and the discrimination they face every day while trying to fit in with "**White European Ashkenazi Jew-ish**" culture. In America, Blacks are tired of being the victims of Police Brutality and Police killings. From New York, Chicago, Detroit, Missouri, Illinois, South Carolina and Maryland, black people are coming together to stand up for their rights. "**Black Lives Matter**" can be heard from many Protesters and black celebrities. But there is a new Awakening that is happening; **A**

HEBREW ISRAELITE AWAKENING! Blacks have been researching their past history going back further into time before the 1600's and have found out fascinating connections to the slave trades and the biblical "**Children of Israel**". It has amazed me how fast Blacks and Latinos are waking up to their heritage going further back into their history before Slavery or the invasion of lands by the Europeans. For years we have been taught to accept what we have been called by Europeans. We are no longer accepting the term African-American, Latino, Spanish, Haitian, Jamaican, Puerto Rican, Cuban, Dominican, Nigerian, Ghanaian, Mexican, Brazilian and so on. These are all titles given to us by the same people who enslaved our ancestors and colonized their lands. History for us did not begin with the 1500's and slavery. Many people have been wondering why history books and classes will not venture past this time period. Why? Because if we dig to deep in the past we will find out our "**True Heritage**". What people are realizing is that before there was an island called "**Hispaniola**" or a continent called "**Africa**" or countries like "**Nigeria**", "**Benin**", "**Cameroon**", and "**Ghana**" there was just land. In this land, there were Kingdoms and Tribes, of different ethnicities. Some of these Kingdoms and Tribes consisted of the ancestors of the biblical Hebrew Israelites. Not "**Jews**", but "**Hebrew Israelites**" who practiced the "**Mosaic Law**", or "**Karaite Judaism**". These "Israelites" did not have the appearance of our typical "European Ashkenazi" or "Sephardic Jew" we commonly see today. These Israelites were "**People of Color**". Yes, they were the "indigenous" people the European Explorers encountered when the landed on the land now known as the Americas, Africa, Puerto Rico, Haiti, Cuba and the Dominican Republic. How did this happen? West Africans are exploring and researching their old manuscripts. They are talking to their Elders or Grandparents about their passed down laws, heritage and culture. They are making the connection as to where these strange "**Judaic-type**" laws and customs have come from. They are remembering how their elders set aside a certain day "**for rest**". They are questioning why they have Hebrew Old Testament names, why they circumcise/name their children on the 8th day. They are wondering why they restrain from cutting their children's hair until they are seven and why the perform sacrifices once a year or on "**New Moon**" days. They are asking themselves, "Why do we pour out libations to the gods?" Many of these "**Indigenous**" people remember that their elders once told them as kids that they were descendants of the Children of Israel. Surprisingly, they are finding out that they may in fact have Hebrew Israelite Ancestry. But how can that be? If the White Caucasian European Jews make up over 85% of the world Jewry then how can there be Black Hebrew Israelites/Jews from Africa. How can the "Native Americans" or "Natives" of the Caribbean be also Hebrew Israelites? How can a white couple have a Black African looking baby? Can White people turn black in the Sun? Can black people turn white from the lack of sunlight? No! Of course not, but these are the answers that many Jews today will tell us to justify there being white Jews and just a collection (1%) of Black (Ethiopian) Jews. In America, with DNA testing, African-Americans are finding out what country they are from despite slavery disconnecting us from knowing anything about ourselves. Blacks with the "*Age of the Internet*" are now able to download books online, tune into alternative news, watch educational documentary videos from other people and also research vast amounts of information in regards to the Ancient Hebrew Israelites in comparison to the European Ashkenazi Jews in Israel today. With the Internet, you can gain access to the English Translations of the Greek Septuagint Bible, the Aramaic Bible, the Hebrew Mechon Bible and so on. Reading these books and using them for comparison to the King James Bible can also be interesting when it comes to inaccuracies. After having all these tools of research at the tips of your fingertips it is easy to see how black people are waking up in America. God is working in mysterious ways to wake each and every one of us. Other races are also waking up to this newfound knowledge, but many of us are still sleep. My mission from God is to "**Wake Up Black America**". The "**Signs of the Times**" are evident and God is pouring out knowledge on those whom he has selected to receive it. For over centuries, Black slaves were not allowed to learn how to read or write. After slavery ended, "**White America**" still feared what would happen if Blacks were able to get an education and apply for jobs. God forbid if Blacks were allowed to have access to the Libraries. Now with the age of the internet, blacks now have access to an abundance of information. The "**Internet**" which was created for Americans by our Government, now has the potential to sabotage the **NWO** agenda of an All-controlling Government. It also allows blacks to research about their "**Real heritage**" and not just the notion of being a "**Negro**" or "**African-American**." This was also predicted by former slave owner "Willie Lynch".

"Our experts warned us about the possibility of this phenomenon occurring, for they say that the mind has a strong drive to correct and re-correct itself over a period of time if it can touch some substantial original historical base; And they advised us that the best way to deal with this phenomenon is to shave off the brute's mental history and create a multiplicity of phenomena of illusions".

Willie Lynch Letter

With all that is going on in Black America, this "**Identity Awakening**" is heaven sent. It can only strengthen **Black America**, and explain why for centuries we have been the victims of constant oppression. In Black America, racial tensions is **high**, Police Brutality against blacks is **high**, joblessness is **high**, education is **low**, incarceration rates for black men/women is **high**, mental illness is **high**, Autism/ADHD rates is **high** in black boys, unemployment is **high**, unity is **low**, health problems in the black community is **high**, broken fatherless families is **high**, homosexuality/bisexuality in the black community is **high**, substance abuse is **high**, marriage rates in black women is **low**, black divorce is **high**, fertility rates is **low** and spiritual confusion is **high**. If there is anything that can turn this around it is God. But first we have to turn from our wicked ways and come back to him. We must have eyes to see and ears to hear the message the Lord is trying to spread to us in these last and evil days. The bible says:

Hosea 4:6-7 *"MY PEOPLE are destroyed for LACK OF KNOWLEDGE: Because thou hast rejected knowledge, I will also reject thee, that thou shalt be no priest to me: seeing thou hast forgotten the law of thy God, I also forget thy children."*

Daniel 12:4 "But thou, O Daniel, shut up the words, and seal the book, even to the time of the end: many shall run to and fro, and **KNOWLEDGE SHALL BE INCREASED.**"

For all this time we have been without "**Knowledge**" and we have been reading the Bible, but not reading it with "**Understanding**". The Bible says this will too change.

Proverbs 1:23 "Turn you at my reproof: Behold, I will pour out my spirit unto you, **I WILL MAKE KNOWN MY WORDS UNTO YOU.**"

The Bible also says:

Deuteronomy 28:1-2 "And it shall come to pass, it thou shalt hearken diligently unto the voice of the Lord thy God, **TO OBSERVE AND TO DO ALL HIS COMMANDMENTS** which I command thee this day, that the Lord thy God will set thee on high above **ALL NATIONS** of the earth."

2 Chronicles 7:14 "If **MY PEOPLE**, which hare called by my name, shall humble themselves, and pray, and seek my face, and turn from their wicked ways; **THEN** will I hear from heaven, and will forgive their sin, and will heal their land."

Now there are over **600 commandments/laws** in the Old Testament that God required the Israelites to follow. While we are not perfect and are still human beings who sometime fall short, we must realize that we are barely keeping **ALL 613** of God's commandments. But are the commandments necessary? Which commandments are we supposed to follow? Should we follow 9 of the 10 Commandments and leave 1 out? No.

Revelations 12:17 "And the Dragon was wroth with the woman. And went to make war with the remnant of her seed (Children of God). **WHICH KEEP THE COMMANDMENTS OF GOD (FATHER)**, and have the testimony of Yahusha HaMashiach (Jesus Christ).

The TV hit show "**Empire**" which aired on the Fox channel in 2015 shows the breaking of pretty much **ALL** of the 10 commandants including plenty of others by our Black People. This show was primarily to target blacks with its juicy storyline and plot. Black America fell for it hook, line and sink. But this is no surprise. Black Christians watch the "**Preachers Daughters**" on Lifetime, then "**Preachers of Detroit**", and then "**Preachers of L.A** (Oxygen)" followed by the homosexual show "**The Prancing Elites Project**". While these Reality Series may try to show some positivity, instead it draws more viewers by showing conflict in relationships/friendships and confusion. But hope is not all lost. God has a perfect plan for everything despite Satan's agenda and he is using the youth to bring this plan forward.

CHAPTER 2

HOW DO WE KNOW THIS IS FROM GOD?

Acts 2:17 "And it shall come to pass in the **LAST DAYS**, saith God, "I will pour out my spirit upon all flesh; and **your sons and your daughters shall prophesy**, and **your young men shall see visions**, and your old men shall dream dreams:"

This scripture is also verified in **Joel 2:28**.

In these times, many Pastors are having dreams about current world events in relation to the biblical **"End of Days"**. God is revealing to them about the **"Illuminati"**, the **"Freemasons"**, the **"Money Masters"**, the **"Jewish Deception"**, and the **"Web of Evil"** that plagues our Governments. Young men and women of all races are also becoming more aware about the evil agenda that is spreading subliminally throughout the **Mass Media**. They are learning about **"Real History"** and about their **"True Heritage"**, not the heritage that the Europeans told us. The Holy Spirit is falling on **ALL FLESH**, in different countries, on peoples with different ethnic backgrounds and religions.

As a child I often had visions and dreams. They were very lucid and real. They were often religious, and had to do with the Rapture, Judgement day and so on. I also had dreams where I would experience Sleep Paralysis. They would always go away when I called on the name of the Lord. These dreams use to scare me and I would ask my mother if she knew the reason why I was having these dreams. She would do her best to decipher the dream but never had a real clue as to what was the meaning of the dream. Many of times the content was straight out of the bible which I would've been too young to understand. In my adulthood, I finally was able to look back at my pre-adolescent years and realize that God had a plan for me, but Satan desired hard to try sabotage this. As an adult now, I realize why I have been through so many trials and tribulations. At the age of 13, I was filled with the Holy Ghost, speaking in tongues as the *Spirit of God* gave utterance. My life afterwards was changed. I also witnessed my sister and some of my brothers receive the gift of the Holy Spirit with my own eyes. I am also proud to say that my daughter received the Gift of the Holy Spirit. Receiving the Holy Spirit gave me the **"Extra protection"** and **"Power"** I would need further in my life. I wouldn't however fully understand this until 25 years later. After I received the Holy Spirit the many frequent episodes of Sleep Paralysis went away. I had a newfound zeal in the Holy Bible and learning the scriptures. I read different bibles that would make the scriptures plainer, especially at my reading level. All of this reading, would later fuel my curiosity. It would spark questions in bible class or at home with my parents. When I was in my early 20's I slowed down going to church because of work, college and other various reasons. I was going through my own internal problems at the time and I was still trying to find my purpose in life. I still would sometimes attend afternoon/evening church services, concerts or revivals. In my mid-twenties I graduated from Eastern Michigan University and Wayne State Universities Physician Assistant program. Afterwards, I got a job and started working. I had no clue as to what was really was going on in the world. All I cared about was finally making some money, saving it, buying a car, a new apartment/condo and living my life. As I got older I started to see things in the Black community that bothered me. Working at Sinai Grace Hospital in the inner city of Detroit showed me a lot of what was going on. People in Detroit were suffering and things did not seem to be getting any better. However on the other side of town across 8 mile and in the Suburbs other races were prospering. It was like day and night. Beverly Hills vs Gotham City. The people in the suburbs were living a different life. They were going about their daily life with an "**I ain't worried about nothing**" aura. I started talking about this with another Black fellow employee at Sinai Grace Hospital and our conversations opened my eye to much more that was going on in the world. I started researching lightly about some things and finding out the facts. It disturbed me. I asked God to reveal to me "**the truth**" and to give me "**knowledge**" and boy he did! From that day forth things I read started connecting like new brain neurons forming connections with other neurons. Things all started to make sense. As I read my bible, I started to pick up on certain things that I had never picked up on before. These sparked even more internal questions as to who the bible was referring to in regards to the "**Curses of Israel**" in Deuteronomy 28. I realized that the Curses of Israel did not end after the resurrection of Yeshua HaMashiach (Jesus Christ). So then I started to research what people out in the world were still going through the "**Curses of Israel**" listed in Deuteronomy 28:16-68 and Leviticus 26. I compared these "Curses" to the European Jews today and Blacks in America today. It really disturbed me when I started noticing the "Curses" describing everything Blacks had been through and were still going through. I once even had an older Nigerian Igbo man read these curses out load from beginning to end and after he finished reading verse 68, he was gripped with numerous emotions almost coming to tears (anger, sadness, astonishment, fear, happiness). I asked him was he ok after reading Deuteronomy 28:68 and all he did was shake his head while looking out the window. We both agreed that nothing in the "**Curses of Israel**" fit the European Jews of today. Then I had him read **Luke 21:24-28** and he was disturbed even more. I knew that the Biblical Hebrew Prophets were not liars and I knew that the prophecies of "**The Christ**" could not be all made up. I started taking notes and saving printouts of the important stuff I was researching. I didn't know what to do with it at that moment and I had contemplated putting it all into a Book or somehow putting it into "DVD form" but that seemed like wishing on a star at the time. Nobody in my family had written a **Book** or put together a **DVD**. I didn't know anybody that could help me publish a book or make a DVD so I kept writing notes in my notebook and I saved all my printouts/articles in a folder for safekeeping. I didn't know God would show me what to do with all this information.

On one Sunday afternoon Church service I had short words with a young Pastor that would change how I felt about life and my purpose as a "**Child of God**". I can remember originally that day not wanting to go to the service because it was already late and I had to work the next day. I arrived to the afternoon service late and sat in the back behind a crowd of people as the Pastor was getting ready to preach his sermon. Throughout the sermon I was reading my Bible and listening to what the Pastor was saying. After he finished his sermon he started altar call. Nobody was really going up for prayer at first but then a few people started trickling up to the front. The Pastor was talking as the ministers and other pastors were laying hands on the people in line. A lot of people were standing up in front of me praying silently for those who were in line requesting prayer. This was common in a Black Pentecostal Church. I was sitting down with my palms up praying quietly amidst the people standing in front of me. All of a sudden, I felt people around me tapping me. I opened my eyes and asking them "What?" and they replied "the pastor wants you to come up". I asked "Why?" and they all shrugged their shoulders as if they didn't' know. I reluctantly went up to the front because normally I don't like church members who "call people out" to come to the front for any reason. Nobody else was at the front of the church at this moment. When I got to the front, the Pastor grabbed my face with both his hands and looked in my eye for like 10 seconds without saying a word and then said *"You are going to do something great for the Lord," "You will see."* I didn't know what he was talking about. After he prayed for me I stood in the front and continued to pray. I was going through a lot at the time (**as most Black people are**) and I had a lot of things to talk to God about. God says that his people would go through "**Trials and Tribulations**" but that we are "**Rich**" inside. As I prayed I kept calling out "**I am your child**". Ever since I received the Holy Spirit at 13 years old I knew that I was a *Child of God* and that he would watch over me, however my life had seemed to get harder and harder. As I cried out to God the Spirit of God entered me changing my tongues and controlling my body. As I cried out to God speaking in tongues I felt cleansed at that moment and a feeling of reassurance that God was still with me. God knew my pain, my struggles and what I was going through. I went back home after the service feeling rejuvenated. That night I asked God to help me decipher the "**Truth**" from the "**Lies**" and show me what I need to do with it. Boy, did he answer my prayers because within 1-2 years I was revealed many things about the world and how Satan has deceived mankind. I also found out the truth about the Ancient Hebrew Israelites and who were the people calling themselves "**Jews**" today. I Deuteronomy 28 combing through each of the verses and almost had a breakdown. This information had shook the very foundation of what I had been taught for so many years in Organized Western Education, in Sunday School, Bible Class and all the Church services I had sat through for over 30 years. I often would tell others about this information but they didn't receive it as I would. It would go in one ear and out the other as if it was not important. I knew then how lost my Black People were. I felt like I was all alone in the world with this knowledge. Nobody I talked to understood where I was coming from. I made up in my mind that if I didn't have the platform like a Pastor to teach the people about this knowledge that I was going to put it in a book for people to read. I also said to myself, "**Well, people nowadays do not want to read books so I got to also give them something visual to look at.**" So then I made it up in my mind that I would put together a DVD with all this information. All the information God gave me was locked and loaded in my brain ready to be unleashed to the Black people of world. So I followed the command of my God and got to work.

During the long process of putting together the Book and DVD "**Hebrews to Negroes**" I had a lot of strange experiences. I remember one day at work I was very, very tired. I had only got 3 hours of sleep and needed something to stay awake. Normally I would drink some Pepsi, Mountain Dew or Coca-Cola to give me a boost of energy but on this particular day I didn't want soda. I decided to try to get some tea with caffeine in it. I found a Starbucks which I had never went to before to get tea and I stood in line. I ordered a Green Tea with caffeine and sat down in one of the lounge chairs inside. There was an empty lounge chair and other chairs around me because I was the only one in Starbucks at the time. An elderly black man in his 60's then sat down directly in front of me. Little did I know what kind of conversation we would end up having. The man asked me general questions about my job and where I was from and I answered him. We then started talking about Black issues that African-Americans are facing today. During our talk, the man revealed that he was a Pastor of a Church in Ypsilanti, Michigan. I told him that I was the son of a Pastor and that I was raised in a Pentecostal Christian Black Church. He knew about the Pentecostal Apostolic Christian Faith. I then asked him if Yeshua (Jesus) was "White". The Pastor laughed and said "No, he was Black." I then asked him if the Original Jews of the bible were "White." He looked at me and said "No, they were Black too." I asked him who were the Jews in America, Europe and Israel today if the original Jews were Black? He didn't understand the question fully and thus said to me "I don't know." I asked him if he taught that Jesus was black and that the real Jews were people of color in his church. He told me he didn't teach his congregation this because he said that his congregation couldn't handle it. I wasn't surprised because I had talked to other Black Pastors and Ministers who said they knew the truth about the Jews but didn't want to tell their church congregation in fear of being silenced by their organization or stirring up controversy. Likewise, this particular pastor said that "Black folk" couldn't handle it and if he told this what would they do with it? I laughed and told him that it was his job as the Pastor/Shepard of his flock to teach his people the **TRUTH**. In the bible it states:

John 4:24 "*God is a Spirit: and they that worship him must worship him in SPIRIT AND IN TRUTH.*"

Nowadays many church congregations are teaching doctrines of ignorance; meaning that they are teaching the same things but are not giving their congregation the whole truth. They are selectively teaching what they feel their congregation needs to hear. They are telling Black church members to follow certain commandments and that it's not necessary to follow others. We must be aware of our enemy (Satan) and all the tricks he has up his sleeve to deceive us. God's children are constantly under attack not by just **FLESH AND BLOOD**, but by principalities, against powers, against the rulers of the darkness of this world, and against spiritual wickedness in high places (**Ephesians 6:12**). Believe me, there is more to meets the eye in the world today. Many of our Governments, World Leaders, Religious figures and TV entertainers are involved in the works of Satan, or what they like to call "*Luciferianism*" but they will say that Lucifer worship and Satanism is not the same. It is truly a dirty game.

Fact: *The famous cartoon "**Transformers**" theme song "**More than Meets the Eye**" is a subliminal message for Satan. In the early beginnings of Transformers, there were two Decepticon leaders. On was "**Megatron**", similar to the Kabbalistic antichrist-Lesser Yahweh "**Metatron**" who holds the "**Kether**" or "**Crown**" position in the Sephirot Tree of Life in Kaballah Babylonian-inspired mysticism. The other one was called "**Apollyon**", which is the Angel over the bottomless pit in Revelations 9:1. In the Hebrew Bible this angel is referred to as "**Abaddon**", based off the Hebrew Strong's #6 Word "**Abad**" which means "**to perish**", "**to destroy**" or "**the destroyer**". Likewise, the Hindu god equivalent to Satan is "Shiva the Destroyer". Her statute sits in Europe outside the **CERN facility** where the internet was first created and where the **Large Hadron Collider** is being tested/used to re-create matter or possible open up a portal to another dimension like the movie "**Stargate**". Remember, Satan is also an angel and is always associated with the bottomless pit, or Hell. Could there be any coincidence in the verse 9:11 in Revelation and the day of the terrible 9/11 attack on New York City's Twin Towers.*

Revelations 9:11 "*And they had a king over them, which is the angel of the bottomless pit, whose name in the Hebrew tongue is **Abaddon**, but in the Greek tongue hath his name **Apollyon.**"*

We must be aware of the tactics he will use in the last days to bring about the "**Great Delusion**" that will cause many Christians to doubt their faith. The bible talks about the Antichrist being revealed when the time is allowed by God.

2 Thessalonians 2:3-4 "Let no man deceive you by any means: for that day shall **NOT COME, EXCEPT THERE COME A FALLING AWAY FIRST,** and that man of sin (Antichrist) be revealed, the son of perdition; who opposeth and exalteth himself above all that is called God, or that is worshipped; so that he as God sitteth in the temple of God, shewing himself that he is God.

2 Thessalonians 2:7, 2:11 "For the mystery of iniquity doth already work: **ONLY HE (GOD) WHO NOW LETTETH WILL LET,** until he be taken out of the way. And then shall that Wicked (Antichrist) be revealed, whom the Lord shall consume with the spirit of his mouth, and shall destroy with the brightness of his coming.........And for this cause God shall send them **STRONG DELUSION**, that they should believe **A LIE;**"

That being said I told the Pastor that the problem with Black America was that no one is speaking the truth. Our Black Pastors, Al Sharpton, Jesse Jackson and countless other influential black figures do not always preach or teach the **TRUTH!** For this reason we are being destroyed from many angles. This is why I see it as teaching "**Doctrines of Ignorance**". It is time for us to wake up as a people. We have eyes to see but don't see, and ears to hear but we don't listen. As a race we are like hard-headed disobedient children who **DON'T** want to listen.

Exodus 32:8 *"They have turned aside quickly out of the way which I commanded them: they have made them a molten calf, and have worshipped it, and have sacrificed thereunto, and said, These be thy gods, O Israel, which have brought thee up out of the Land of Egypt. And the Lord said to Moses, "I HAVE SEEN THIS PEOPLE (ISRAEL), AND, BEHOLD, IT IS STIFFNECKED PEOPLE:"*

But we are also a "**Special People**" unto God. Therefore God requires our obedience to him and only him. If we only could wake up and know that we are "**God's REAL Chosen People**" then maybe we could start listening and turning from our wicked ways. The Bible and the Quran both admit that the "**Jews**" are a special/favorite people unto the Most High God.

Deuteronomy 7:6 *"For thou art an Holy People unto the LORD thy God: the LORD thy God hath chosen thee to be a* **SPECIAL PEOPLE** *unto himself, above all the people that are upon the face of the earth."*

Qur'an Sura 2:47 *"O Children of Israel! Remember My favour wherewith I* **FAVOURED** *you and how* **I PREFERRED YOU** *to all creatures (peoples)."*

So here we see that God has a special place for us because we are his people. Therefore we must be obedient. God established a covenant with us (Hebrew Israelites) way before the Bible was finished or the Qur'an was even created.

Exodus 2:24-25 *"...And God remembered his* **COVENANT** *with* **Abraham, Isaac** *and* **Jacob.** *So God looked on the sons of Israel and God took notice."*

Even in the Muslim **"Holy Quran"** it states that **"Prophethood"** (those chosen by God to be prophets) came only from Jacob's seed: **The Children of Israel**.

Qur'an Sura 29:27 *"And (as for Abraham), We bestowed upon him Isaac and (Isaac's son) Jacob, and caused* **prophethood** *and revelation to continue among his offspring."*

Qur'an Sura 45:16 *"And verily We gave the Children of Israel the* **SCRIPTURE (HOLY BOOKS)** *and the* **COMMAND** *and the* **PROPHETHOOD,** *and provided them with good things and* **FAVOURED THEM ABOVE ALL PEOPLES.***"*

At the end of my conversation with the Pastor at Starbucks, he told me that he agreed that our people needed to wake up. I told him that I was writing a book about all of this called *"Hebrews to Negroes: Wake Up Black America"*. He laughed, and then proceeded to say that black people do not read books. Then he said, **"If it was me, I would've done a movie or a DVD"**. I told him I was doing a DVD and he was shocked. I told him it was an educational 16-hour DVD put together not to **"Entertain"** but to **"Wake up"** sleeping minds. The Pastor was pleased after hearing that. Of course like others, he told me "Be careful". I told him that Black people have been operating in "Fear" for too long and that "God hath not given us the spirit of fear; but of **POWER**, and of **LOVE AND OF A SOUND MIND (2 Timothy 1:7)**."

Throughout the process of writing my Book I have had crazy "supernatural" experiences that are unexplainable. In 2014, I had a Caucasian middle-aged man come up to me out of the clear blue asking to talk to me while I was waiting on an order at Coney Island. I was on the phone at the time so the man waited for about 20 minutes until I was done and then asked me the question, **"What is God's name?"** I told the man God's name could be multiple names depending on who your God was. I named off Yahweh, Yahuah, Jehovah, Satan, Lucifer, Jahbulon, Dagon, Jesus, Baal, Moloch, Allah, Zeus, Jupiter, Zeus, Osiris, Horus, Vishnu, Shiva or Buddha. The man replied **"Yahuah"**. He sat down with me briefly in the Coney Island and we talked. He said a couple years ago he had died after suffering a severe head and neck injury while riding on a horse/bull.

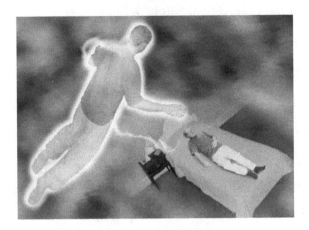

Many people have had their life changed after having out-of-body experiences or near-death experiences.

He said that he had an **"Outer Body Experience"** and was able to see his own mortal body as he looked down from the sky. He revealed to me that God had told him that it wasn't his time to die but that his angels would reveal to him later information about the truth of America and were it was headed in the future. 2 years later, the man said he was visited by 2 angels who showed him all that was going to happen in the future for America. Everything he told me was what I already knew. He said that his family did not want to hear what was revealed to him because it was to terrifying. He said that some people just want to accept life the way it is, never ask questions, and continue living in their life as they see fit.

Others ask questions and search for the Truth.   We had a long conversation and afterwards as we were leaving he told me, "Don't let anybody make you believe that you are crazy for thinking the way you do; God has revealed to you the Truth." The man gave me his phone number and I entered it into my phone. I confirmed it and also gave him my phone number by calling his phone, which rang. I told him that I would research everything he gave me.   Two days later after researching some of the stuff from our conversation, I decided to give this man a call. When I called him, the prompt stated that the phone number was not a "**working number**". I found this to be very odd.

Another incidence I had was when I was writing the 32nd Chapter of my book titled "**Is the Holy Spirit Real**?"   As I was writing words for this chapter, whenever I would type in the words "**Holy Spirit**" a happy face "☺" would appear.   It happened so unexpectedly that I had to stop to see if I was accidentally pushing a ":" and a ")" or if there was a "happy face" button. I had done neither to my amazement.   When I resumed typing I carefully watched my fingers while I was typing and when I typed the words "**Holy Spirit**" again the same "☺" symbol appeared not just once but twice on more than one occasion without me hitting the ":" and ")" keys on the keyboard. I immediately called a friend of mine who was a minister and told him. He couldn't believe it. Another interesting thing I noticed was that whenever I typed in the words "**Synagogue of Satan**", an unhappy face "☹" would appear, again without me typing in the ":" or "("characters.   So throughout this project of putting together the book/DVD "**Hebrews to Negroes**" I have met different people from different countries who have mysteriously brought up the subject of the original "**Black Hebrew Israelites**" without me bringing up the subject. I have experienced encounters with Black Freemasons, White Freemasons, Catholic Priests, Indian Pastors, African Pastors, Black Pastors, Atheists, Jewish Rabbi's, Egyptian Coptic Priests, and Arab Imam Leaders. I found this to be amazing; like it was a sign from God that I was doing the right thing. All the knowledge I had acquired from God had to be told and thus "**Hebrews to Negroes**" was born.

CHAPTER 3

THE JEWISH DECEPTION: IS THIS IN THE TORAH (BIBLE)?

Revelations 12:9 "And the great dragon was cast out, that old serpent called the devil, and Satan, which deceiveth the whole world:"

So who are the Jews today? Are they really "God's Chosen People"? Are they really the blood descendants of the Biblical 12 Tribes of Israel? Was the creation of the Israel in 1948 and the return of the European Jews Bible Prophecy? What does the Bible say?

Jeremiah 46:27 "But fear not thou, O my servant Jacob, and be not dismayed O Israel: for behold, I will save thee from afar off, and thy seed from the land of their CAPTIVITY; and Jacob (the Israelites) shall return, and be in REST, and EASE, and NONE SHALL MAKE HIM AFRAID."

Jeremiah was a prophet of God. He was not a false prophet. This prophecy was not for 500 B.C. when the Jews were allowed to rebuild the 2nd temple under the Persian Rule of King Cyrus and King Darius. This prophecy is for the future. However since the Jews came to Israel in 1948 there has been no rest, no ease and no peace. There has been fighting, constant wars, suicide bombings, constant missile firing from other Arab countries and for this reason Israel has Warning Sirens in addition to the "Iron Dome Anti-Missile Defense System". This is not the behavior of a people who are "**NOT AFRAID**". So if these Jews are not the Jews that the Prophet Jeremiah was talking about returning to Israel, then who are they? Why are they in the Holy Land? Hold on to your seats because the Truth will shock you.

It is documented that in 740 A.D., King Bulan, the King of the Khazars in Eastern Europe/Modern Day Russia converted to Judaism and made it their countries new religion. Before the mass conversion to Judaism from which they adopted the word "**Jew**", the Khazar people were known as the "**Serpent People.**" Christian of Stavelot in the "*Expositio in Matthaeum Evangelistam* (9th Century A.D.) referred to the Khazars as the biblical descendants of "**Gog and Magog**", who were circumcised (like the Edomite's) and observed all the laws of Judaism. Persian historian Ibn al-Faqih wrote that "*All the Khazars are Jews, but they have been Judaized recently*". Muslim Ibn fadlan (10th Century A.D.) on his visit to the

Bulgars, also reported that the core element of the state, the Khazars, were Judaized (Judaism Converts.). Erak Elhaik, a geneticist from the University of Sheffield has also admitted with genetic research that the Caucasian European Ashkenazi Jews of today are descendants of the Khazars. They currently make up about 90% of all worldwide Jewry (Jews) today. That being said this would mean that most of the Jews today are Jews not by blood (12 Tribes of Israel), but are Jews by religious conversion. This is called a "**Proselyte**".

Matthew 10:5 "These twelve Jesus sent forth, and commanded them, saying, Go not into the way of the Gentiles, and into ANY cities of the Samaritans enter ye not:"

The book of Matthew also talks about how the Gentile Pharisees loved making other races of people proselytes, teaching them the doctrines of man instead of God.

Matthew 23:15 "Woe unto you, scribes and Pharisees, hypocrites! For ye compass sea and land to make one proselyte, and when his is made, ye make him twofold more the child of hell than yourselves."

But these Gentile proselytes were also following true Hebrews (Jews) like Paul (a Benjaminite) in the Book of Acts while they are spreading the Gospel.

Acts 13:43 "Now when the congregation was broken up, many of the Jews and religious proselytes followed Paul and Barnabas: who, speaking to them, persuaded them to continue in the grace of God."

In the Chapter 2:10-11 of the "**Acts of (Pontius) Pilate/Gospel of Nicodemus**" it reads:

"And Pilate, summoning the Jews, says to them: You know that my wife is a worshipper of God, and prefers to adhere to the Jewish religion along with you. Annas and Caiaphas say to Pilate: "All the multitude of us cry out that he (Jesus) was born of fornication, and are not believed (those that believe in Jesus); these are proselytes, and his disciples." And Pilate, calling Annas and Caiaphas, says to them: "**What are proselytes?**" They say to him: "**They are by birth children of the Greeks, and have now become Jews**".

Other versions may also read: **Pilate answered Annas and Caiaphas, "Who are the proselytes?" They answered, "They are those who are the children of Pagans, and are not become Jews, but followers of him."**

So this would imply that some of Yahusha's (Jesus) followers were not followers of the Pharisees (called Jews), but instead were Gentile people from other lands. In both cases, they were considered "**Proselytes**".

However, little is known that the Jews of today are the descendants of the Khazar Gentile Japhetic "**Proselytes**" who follow the teachings of the Pharisees and thus are called "Jews".

These are some quotes about the Khazars from people living in their time period.

1. **"There exists people under the sky in regions where no Christians can be found, whose name is GOG AND MAGOG, and who are HUNS,; among them is one called the KHAZARI(GAZARI), who are circumcised and observe Judaism in its entirety."** *Westphalian Monk, Christian Druthmar of Aquitania in Exposito in Evangelium Mattei 864 A.D*

2. **"The Khazars and their Kings are all Jews. The Bulgars and all their neighbors are subject to him. They treat him with worshipful obedience. Some are of the opinion that GOG AND MAGOG are the Khazars."**-*Arab Traveler Ibn Fadian 922 A.D.*

The Khazars were a diabolical ruthless pagan nation in Eastern Europe who was involved with phallic (penis) worship. Their symbol before even converting to Judaism was the six-pointed Satanic Hexagram. This hexagram has always been linked to the "**Occult**", "**Witchcraft**", and "**Satanism**".

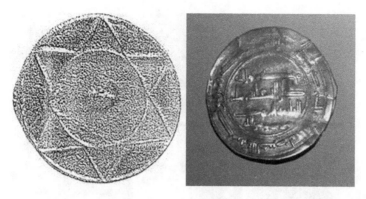

(**Left***)* Khazarian Seal coin found around the 8-9th Century A.D. (**Right**) Is another coin found in Khazarian land dating back to 838 A.D. It has inscriptions in writing saying "ard al-hazar" or "Land of the Khazars" and also "Musa rasul Allah" which means in Arabic "Moses the messenger of God, in imitation to the Islamic coin phrase "Muhammad the messenger of God". Many historians state that the Khazarian Empire consisted of Judeo-Islam followers.

(**Above**) Muslim Hero "**Saladin's Star**" after he captured Jerusalem during the Crusades from 1099-1187 A.D. Saladin was not Jewish. He was a Muslim of Kurdish origin. So this cannot be the "**Star of David**". The Star of David hexagram was adopted by the Gentile Jews later.

(**Above**) *The Hexagram is not the Symbol of the Israelites, the God of the Israelites or the symbol of King David. It is used by many pagan religions including Luciferianism/Satanism. It is Satanic. The* **Star of Chiun (Hebrew)**, *The Star of* **Remphan (Greek)** *and the* **Star of Saturn(Akkadian/Babylonian)** *is occultic and evil. This is supported in* **Acts 7:43** *and* **Amos 5:26.**

Acts 7:43 "Yea, ye took up the tabernacle of Moloch, and the **STAR** of your god Remphan, figures which ye made to worship them: and I will carry you away beyond Babylon (Iraq)."

It is a known fact that Ashkenazi Jew Harold Wallace Rosenthal was an Administrative assistant to U.S Senator Jacob Javitz. In Mr. Rosenthal's 1976 interview he stated, "**Most Jews do not like to admit it, but our God is Lucifer… and we are his CHOSEN PEOPLE. Lucifer is very much alive.**" He would also quote:

- "Anytime truth comes forth which exposes us, we simply rally our forces-the ignorant Christians. They attack the crusaders even if they are members of their own families

- "It is a reality that we have complete control of organized Christianity. Almost anywhere, completely. We Jews must become lawyers so we could control and strangle the courts, we should become teachers and leaders in all the churches."

- "At first, by controlling the banking system we were able to control corporation capital. Through this, we acquired total monopoly of the movie industry, the radio networks and the newly developing television media. The printing industry newspapers, periodicals, and technical journals had already fallen into our hands. The richest plum was later to come when we took over the publication of all school materials. Through these vehicles we could mold public opinion to suit our own purposes."

Benjamin Franklin even knew about the cunning practices of the Khazar Jews in America who came from Eastern Europe/Russia.

Benjamin Franklin: Philadelphia Convention, 1787

"They are vampires, and vampires do not live on vampires. They cannot live only amongst themselves. If you do not exclude them (Khazars) from these United States…in less than 200 years they will have swarmed here in such great numbers that they will dominate and devour the land and change our form of government, for which we Americans have shed our blood, given our lives, our substance and jeopardized our liberty. If you do not exclude them, in less than 200 years our descendants will be working in the field to furnish them substance, while they will be in the counting houses rubbing their hands. I warn you, gentlemen, if you do not exclude the Jews for all time, your children will curse you in your graves."

The Khazarian Empire is never talked in our History books. Attila the Hun and many others attested that the Khazars practiced Judaism and were the biblical "Gog and Magog (Genesis 10:2)"

So who has been deceiving us and programming our minds on a daily basis? You guessed it, these same Khazars. On the "**Times of Israel**" Blog by **Ashkenazi Jew Manny Friedman** on July 1, 2012 an article read as such:

"Let's be honest with ourselves, here fellow Jews. WE DO CONTROL THE MEDIA. We've got so many dudes up in the executive offices in all the big movie production companies it's almost obscene. Just about every movie or TV show, whether it be "Tropic Thunder" or "Curb Your Enthusiasm," is rife with actors, directors and writers who are Jewish. Did you know that all eight major film studios are run by Jews?"

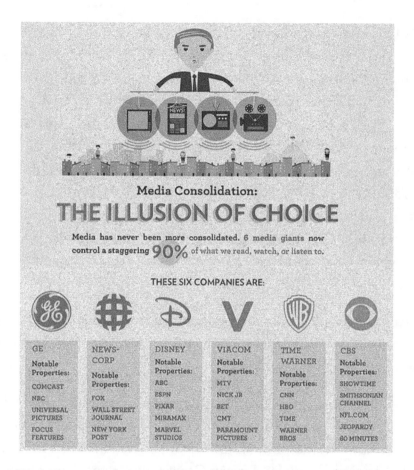

All of these six major media companies are owned by Jews.

In **Matthew 7:7-9**, Jesus says "**Howbeit in vain do they worship me, teaching for doctrines the commandments of men**. For laying aside the commandment of God, ye hold the tradition of men, as the washing of pots and cups: and many other such things ye do.　And he said unto them, Full well ye **REJECT THE COMMANDMENT OF GOD**, that ye may keep your own tradition."

Jesus knew that these Pharisees were of Satan and their doctrine "**Talmudic Judaism**" was not of God. That's why he and John the Baptist called them the "**seed of the serpent**" or "**a generation of vipers**".　He knew **Esau's seed** and the **Seed of Cain** infiltrated the Pharisees "**Sanhedrin**" club.　They infiltrated Judea, Samaria, the Sanhedrin, the High positions of the Priests and the High positions of the scribes (Kenites, Nethinims), writing in their own laws.　These laws would be upheld by its followers as traditions. Thus **"Pharisaism"** or **"Phariseeism"**, which is defined as the doctrines and practices of the Pharisees, later gave rise to Babylonian-inspired Talmudic Judaism. As a result the Talmud, which is made up of the **"Mishnah"** and the **"Gemara"**, is the written **"Oral Law"** that most Jews today follow. Written in Babylonian Hebrew-Aramaic, the Gemara and Mishnah was edited sometime near 200 A.D. There are actual Two Talmud's: the Y'rushalmi or **Jerusalem Talmud** (from Israel) and the Bavli or **"Babylonian Talmud"**. The Babylonian Talmud was edited after the Jerusalem Talmud and is much more widely known and used by the Jews today. This Talmud, per the Ashkenazi Judaism-converts would trump the Old Testament (**Tanakh**) and the Torah (**Pentateuch**) which God gave the Original Black Hebrew Israelites. Here is the Proof:

Soncino Edition, Erubin 21 "My son be more careful in the **OBSERVANCE** of the (**Talmudic**) words of the (**Edomite, Kenite and Nethinim**) scribes than in the words of the **TORAH**."

Ethiopian Jews upon becoming citizens in Israel are required to learn the Talmudic form of Judaism they were not accustomed to. They were accustomed to Karaite Judaism (Mosaic Law -written law in the Torah). The Ancient West African Tribes and African Tribes along the East African Great Lakes region only knew the Mosaic Law. Black Hasidic Jews in America today are required to study the Talmud, the Zohar and the Torah. But why? Why do we need to follow laws based upon a group of men and their opinions? The Transatlantic Slave Trade which the European Jews were a part of involved the breaking of just about every commandment in the 10 Commandments given to Moses by God. In **Matthew 15:1-20** the Pharisees questioned why Jesus' disciples did not eat with washed hands. These man-made traditions (**ceremonial washing of the hands**) somehow slipped into the practices of many West Africans claiming Hebrew Israelite heritage today. Jesus replied by how they were breaking **GOD'S LAW,** by keeping the **TRADITIONS OF MEN** and adding to God's Law. This whole event revolved around the washing of hands, and whether or not it makes you unclean (Mat 15:20). Mark 7 talks about the same event. The Pharisees asked why Jesus' disciples were not keeping the "**traditions of the elders**"(Mark 7:5). They didn't understand that Man's commandments are irrelevant to Gods commandments. These Gentile Elders who converted to Judaism laid aside the **COMMANDMENTS OF GOD** to keep the **TRADITIONS OF MEN** (Mark 7:8,9). They broke **GOD'S COMMANDMENTS** because of their **TRADITIONS** (Mark 7:13). Paul kept these traditions before he believed in Jesus (Gal 1:14).

Fact: *Even today, the Jews do not eat unless they keep the tradition of washing the hands. (The "washing of the hands" is not in the Old Testament. It is not part of God's Law). And there are many Jewish traditions like this.*

So let's look at some of the traditions that the Jews follow that are not in the Torah/Tanakh (Bible) and thus are not of God.

1. **Kapparot chicken slaughter**

   Kapparot is a Jewish custom in which the sins of a Jew are symbolically transferred to a fowl (chicken). The fowl is held above the Jew's head and swung in a circle three times while certain words are spoken. The fowl is then slaughtered so that the Jew performing the ritual may have a good life. This is not supported in the Old Testament.

2. **Smoking Cigarettes**

   Smoking seems to be very prevalent in the Ultra-Orthodox community. Many Jewish Rabbis can be found smoking Cigarettes on certain holidays. Where did this come from? In (**Deuteronomy 4:9,15**) it says "**Take good care of yourselves**" but the Jews practice man-made customs that are bad for your health. Even in their laws, smoking is prohibited such as **Mishnah Bava Kamma 8:6** where it conveys the message that "**a person is not permitted to injure himself,**" In the Talmud some Rabbis may say that even though there is an obligation for Jews to avoid danger, it is halachically permitted to ignore this because "**the Lord watches over the simple. (Psalms 116:6)**" So different Rabbis can come up with laws to not do things such as "**drive a car**", and then another Rabbi can years later say that it is "**permitted to take a risk driving a car as other people do**". Different Rabbis such as Rabbi Finkelstein will use certain Talmudic Laws to justify smoking in addition to the fact that they say the Ancient Jewish sages used to smoke. One such example is **Yebamot 72a** in which it says: "**it is dangerous to circumcise a** child or let blood on a cloudy day or on a day that the south wind blows." Since the Jews cannot control the wind and people do in fact get circumcised on days where the weather conditions are not favorable this is considered a man-made law which is justifiable under Jewish "**Halakhah**" law.

3. **Drinking Alcohol during holidays or celebrations**

   If the Jews are supposed to be "**God's Chosen People**" why are they getting drunk in Israel? If some of them claim to be Priestly Levites and Kohanites (Sons of Aaron) should they indulge in "**strong drinks**"? Are they supposed to get wasted, lying out on the street or in the synagogues? This can be seen practiced in Israel, the "Holy Land". How is this being "Holy"? I'm not trying to judge but are not the Jews supposed to uphold the laws of God? What about the Jews today calling themselves Levites? This is what God commanded the Levites and his sons (Kohanites).

   In **Leviticus 10:9** it states **"You and your sons are not to drink wine or other fermented drink whenever you go into the tent of meeting, or you will die. This is a lasting ordinance for the generations to come."**

   But the Jews all have a huge meeting inside a building and they all get drunk during the Purim feast. They say that Purim is about being "drunk" with sincere happiness. Drinking, according to the Sages/Pharisees who wrote the Babylonian Talmud, elevates the "joy" and "excitement" of Purim.

   It also says in **Isaiah 5:22 "Woe unto them that are mighty to drink wine, and men of strength to mingle strong drink."**

   It is a known fact that in the celebration of the massacre of 75,000 Persians in the Book of Esther, the Jews have their **Purim feast**. Here Jews indulge in heavy drinking of alcoholic beverages. But this is not just any kind of party. Jewish authors Israel Shahak and Norton Mezvinsky write in their important book "**Jewish Fundamentalism in Israel**" that there are " **many well-documented cases of massacres of Christians and mock repetitions of the crucifixion of Jesus on Purim**" (Chapter 7).

So the bible discourages the Levitis, Kohanites (Aaronites) not to drink and it also discourages the overindulgence of wine or strong drink. But the Jewish Rabbis give their own opinion. Some say its ok, some say it's not. So if these conflicting opinions are in their Talmud, how is one to know what to believe or follow?

Orach Chaim 695:2 cited by Beit Yosef
"To be thoroughly drunk is completely forbidden. There is no greater sin than this, for it leads to adultery, bloodshed, and many other sins besides. **Rather, you should drink a little more than you are accustomed to.**"
Is something wrong with this statement?????

Famous Jewish Rabbi Maimonides, (**Mishnah Torah, Hil. Yom Tom 6:20**)
"When a person eats and drinks on a festival, he should not get pulled into the wine and laughter and frivolity, saying that the more of this, the greater the mitzvah of rejoicing on a festival. For drunkenness and too much laughter and frivolity are not rejoicing, but wild and stupid behavior. We were commanded to rejoice, because this is a way to serve the Creator of all things, as it says (Deuteronomy 28:47), 'Because you did not serve the Lord your God out of joy and with a good heart when you had everything.' This teaches that serving God must be with joy. But it is impossible to serve God in the midst of mockery, frivolity, and drunkenness"

The **Purim Festival** is not one of the feasts holidays commanded by God but the Rabbis comment on it as if it was given to them by God in the **Book of Esther 9:27**. However, the Book of Esther was not found to be included in the Hebrew Dead Sea Scrolls written in Paleo-Hebrew and Aramaic. Why? The Book of Esther has the made up word "**Jew**" in it more times than any other book in the Old Testament. Why? The word "Jew" appears in the whole Old Testament **74 times** and over 50 of these times is all in the Book of Esther! The Iranian Jews whole existence to them being Jews is all based on the Book of Esther. But do they practice the "Purim Feast Holiday"?

Esther 9:26-32 "Wherefore they called these days Purim after the name of Pur. Therefore for all the words of this letter, and of that which they had seen concerning this matter, and which had come unto them, the Jews ordained, and took upon them, and upon their seed, and upon all such as joined themselves unto them, so as it should not fail, that they would keep these two days according to their writing, and according to their appointed time every year; And that these days should be remembered and kept throughout every generation, every family, every province, and every city; and that these days of Purim should not fail from among the Jews, nor the memorial of them perish from their seed. Then Esther the queen, the daughter of Abihail, and Mordecai the Jew, wrote with all authority, to confirm this second letter of Purim. And he sent the letters unto all the Jews, to the hundred twenty and seven provinces of the kingdom of Ahasuerus (Achashverosh) with words of peace and truth. **To confirm these days of Purim in their times appointed, according as Mordecai the Jew and Esther the queen had enjoined them, and as they had decreed for themselves and for their seed, the matters of the fastings and their cry. And the decree of Esther confirmed these matters of Purim; and it was written in the book.**"

So what happened to "**Thus saith the Lord**"? Did the Lord decree this additional feast holiday? No! This is not of God, but of man. For this reason we can tell the difference between a Gentile "Jew" and a "Hebrew Israelite". Even more, Mordecai is supposed to be a Jew from the Tribe of Benjamin but the genealogy of King Saul (Benjaminite) to Mordecai is off by a couple hundreds of years. Even more, Esther's proof of being a Jew from the Tribe of Benjamin is not proven in the bible with genealogy. Esther's Father Abihail adopted her as a child. All the listed people named **Abihail** were from the Tribe of Levi (**Numbers 3:35**), Gad (**1 Chronicles 5:14**), and Judah (**1 Chronicles 2:29, 2 Chronicles 11:18**). According to **Esther 2:15** and **Esther 9:29**, Abihail was also the Uncle of Mordecai (a Benjaminite). In Hebrew and Islamic tradition you are what your father is, so if Abihail was Mordecai's Uncle than Abihail must have had to been a Benjaminite also. However, the Bible has no record of a man named "Abihail" from the Tribe of Benjamin. Per the Jewish Talmud, Esther's cousin is Mordecai whom she marries and sleeps with. But it says in the Hebrew Bible that Esther was married to the King Ahasuerus (Xerses I) of Persia.

In **Shabbat 88a** in the Talmud it ranks the Book of Esther and Purim with that of the Torah. The famous Jewish scholar and Rabbi Maimonides (Ramban) also stated this. Many Christians have said that the book of Esther is merely **"a memorial to the nationalistic spirit of Judaism"** (A. Weiser, Into to OT, 1961) and even a **"bloodthirsty attempt to justify the ethnic pride in being a Jew"** (B.W. Anderson, Esther, 1950).

It is a known fact that there is barely a reference to prayer, miracles or God in the Book of Esther. The Biblical prophets would speak for God to the people as "Thus Saith the Lord" and God would even speak himself in the Old Testament (Torah) but this is not so in the Book of Esther. It is also interesting to know that the Book of Esther was "canonized" by the Jews at the **Council of Yavne in 90 A.D.** However, again the Essene Jewish Sect at Qumran Israel rejected the "canonization" of this Book as it was not found in the Hebrew Dead Sea Scrolls which dated back to 400 B.C. during the time of the Israelites from the House of Judah who were under Persian rule. The Essenes supposedly existed in small number for generations scattered through Israel. They were said to be descendants of Zadok, a High Priest descended from Eleazar the son of Aaron (brother of Moses). The sons of Zadok were against pagan practices within the Israelite nation and the prophet Ezekiel noted this in Ezekiel 42:13 and Ezekiel 43:19. Zadok helped King David during his internal fight with his son Absalom and was key in bringing King Solomon to the throne. After King Solomon built the First Temple in Jerusalem, Zadok was the first High Priest to serve there. Ezra was a descendant of the Zadokites. Some people reject that the Essenes existed or even wrote the Dead Sea Scrolls in Qumran, Israel but Pliny the Elder (1st century Roman writer and geographer) wrote that he encountered them at Ein Gedi, next to the Dead Sea where the scrolls were found. Josephus Flavius also wrote about the Essenes as one of the three sects of Jewish philosophy (Essenes, Pharisees, Sadducees). In his book, *"The Jewish War (75 A.D.)"*, the book *"Antiquities of the Jews (94 A.D.)"* and *"The life of*

Flavius Josephus (97 A.D.)" he writes that the Essenes practiced celibacy, didn't marry, didn't drink, didn't own property, didn't possess money, they strictly observed the Sabbath and they ritually immersed themselves in water every morning. They also forbade showing anger, they prayed before eating, they studied the books of the prophets, they preserved secrets and knew the names of the good angels in their religious texts. Many believe they rejected the Book of Esther because it did not contain the name of God (Tetragrammaton) and for the same reasons they rejected the made-up Jewish "Hanukkah" holiday during the Gentile Greek Hasmonean-Maccabean dynasty that controlled the Second Temple until it was under the rulership of the Edomite **"Herod the Great"**. The Jews beloved Gentile Roman Jew Flavius Josephus (37 A.D.-100 A.D.) regarded the Book of Esther as canonical (Antiquities XI) as did the early Catholic Church father who incorporated it into the canon of the Christian Bibles we use today.

But the question is, why would God ordain a book that does not have his name Yahuah (**Yod-Hey-Uau-Hey/Tetragrammaton**) in it, no miracles, no prophet, no prayer and no "thus Saith the Lord" saying in it? Even more why would God establish certain Feast Holidays in the Torah for the Israelites to uphold and then add another **"Feast Holiday"** 1,000 years later? Mordecai was no prophet and Esther was not a Prophet. God usually speaks himself to the Israelites or he speaks through one of his Prophets. Did the Jews/Pharisees trick us by inserting this book into our Christian bibles?

4. **Homosexuality**

The Bible says: **Leviticus 18:22** "Thou shalt not lie with mankind, as with womankind: it is an abomination."

*The Rainbow "**Gay Pride**" Flag flys strong in Israel with the regular Israeli Blue & White flag. This is the Holy Land. The Prophet Jeremiah did not prophesy this happening when Jacob returned to Israel.*

Israel holds **Gay pride parades** in **Tel Aviv, Israel** every year uncontested for well over the last 10 years. What started in 1998 with a couple hundred of Gay partiers has turned into an event with over 100,000 Jews celebrating in the streets of the "**Holy Land**" in gay fun. Just as in America where homosexuality is almost everywhere, in Israel, on "**Gay Pride Day**" one can see two women kissing, two men lying together on the beach holding hands. The Holy Land of Israel has also been infiltrated with abominations that the Most High commanded **mankind** not to do. Why would God promise to bring back his people from the 12 tribes of Israel in 1948 only to allow them to practice immoral sexual abominations in the Holy Land? **Israel** is now marketing itself internationally as welcoming to the gay community. Participants in the annual gay pride parade in Jerusalem are shown in magazines and blogs on July 29, 2010 with the headlines:

"The sun is setting, gay pride flags wave next to the water, same-sex couples kiss and cuddle on the beach. This is Tel Aviv — which the government of Israel is now pushing as one of the most gay-friendly cities in the world — and gay tourism is booming."

Again, we need to ask ourselves, if the European Jews are "God's Chosen People" then where is "homosexual" behavior supported in the bible? It's not supported in the Torah so according to Deuteronomy Chapter 28 this means the Jews should be punished by God and should also be going through the "**Curses of Israel**" as listed in Deuteronomy 28:16-68. But they are not. Why? Is God a liar? No he is not. This is happening because the Jews are **NOT** God's Chosen People.

Fact: People will try to explain science for a "**homosexuality gene**" but we don't see the animal kingdom practicing homosexuality. When was the last time we saw a Male Alpha Lion trying to have sex with another Alpha lion? Or what about two Male Silverback Gorillas trying to have sex with each other? Or two male dogs in heat trying to hump each other. We don't see this abominable phenomena happening with Animals like it is happening with humans. God made man and the beasts of the earth perfect, the way he wanted. Sin crept in after Eve ate from the apple from the Tree of Knowledge and allowed Satan and his forces to deceive mankind. But Satan's attack seems to be geared more towards spreading Homosexuality/Bisexuality in the Black African-American community more than any other race groups. This should be raising questions but it's not.

5. **The Bizarre Metzitzah b'peh**
    The "Metzitzah B'preh" is the direct oral blood sucking ritual performed by Rabbis after circumcision of a boy infant's penis. After circumcision, the Rabbi has to draw blood from the penis by sucking on it. This practice is not recommended by the **American Medical Association** but is carried out in Talmudic Judaism for some strange odd reason. The Rabbi puts the freshly cut circumcised penis of the infant Jewish boy into his mouth and sucks it until the blood stops flowing from the wound on the child's penis. This is not a tradition in the Old Testament Torah but is a **Satanic Tradition of Man**. According to the **American Academy of Pediatrics**, this procedure is still widely accepted in Jews, and 60-90% of newborn boys of the Jewish population in the U.S undergo this bizarre, homosexual, unsanitary procedure. This practice however is sometimes under scrutiny as some babies have contracted Genital Herpes, of course from the mouths of the Rabbis who obviously have Oral Herpes. In a public lecture in 2012 Rabbi Hershel Schachter, a Rosh Yeshiva, or senior chief rabbinic authority at Y.U.'s Rabbi Isaac Elchanan Theological Seminary, claimed that his

daughter's hospital treated three cases per year of Hasidic babies infected with Herpes. These babies will go on to have Genital Herpes their whole life, all thanks to the Talmud, the Rabbi and his mouth. Don't believe it?

Shabbath 19:2

They may perform on the Sabbath all things that are needful for circumcision: excision, tearing, sucking [the wound], and putting thereon a bandage and cumin. If this had not been pounded up on the eve of the Sabbath a man may chew it with his teeth and then apply it. The Mishnah, Translated by Herbert Danby Oxford: Oxford University Press. 1933. pp. 116-117.

Shabbat 133B

II.1.

A. Suck [out the wound]:

B. Said R. Pappa, "A Surgeon who didn't suck out the wound - that is a source of danger, and we throw him out."

C. So what else is new? Obviously, since we are prepared to desecrate the Sabbath on that account, it is certainly dangerous not to do it!

D. What might you have supposed? That this blood is stored up. So we are informed that it is the result of the wound, and in the status of a bandage and cumin: Just as when one doesn't put on a bandage and cumin, there is danger, so here, too, if one doesn't do it, there is danger.- The Talmud of Babylonia: An American Translation, Translated by Jacob Neusner Number 275. Volume II.E: Shabbat Chapters 18-24.

Program in Judaic Studies Brown University

Atlanta: Scholars Press. 1993. p. 45.

So it is easy to see how man has come up with Laws and Doctrines which are not commanded by God. This can all be proven by comparing the Jews "**Talmudic laws**" to the "**Mosaic Law**" aka the laws commanded to Moses for Israel by God. So how about when the Jews "**orally**" admit to their Agenda and their involvement in evil practices in the world today.

CHAPTER 4

JEWS ADMIT THE TRUTH THEMSELVES!

- **Ashkenazi Jewish Rabbi Marc Lee Raphael** - "Jews also took an active part in the Dutch colonial slave trade; indeed, the bylaws of the Recife and Mauricia congregations (1648) included an *"Imposta"* (Jewish tax) of five *soldos* for each Negro slave a Brazilian Jew purchased from the West Indies Company. Slave auctions were postponed if they fell on a Jewish holiday. In Curacao in the seventeenth century, as well as in the British colonies of Barbados and Jamaica in the eighteenth century, Jewish merchants played a major role in the slave trade. In fact, in all the American colonies, whether French (Martinique), British, or Dutch, Jewish merchants frequently dominated. This was no less true on the North American mainland, where during the eighteenth century Jews participated in the **'triangular trade'** that brought slaves from Africa to the West Indies and there exchanged them for molasses, which in turn was taken to New England and converted into rum for sale in Africa. Isaac Da Costa of Charleston in the 1750's, David Franks of Philadelphia in the 1760's, and Aaron Lopez of Newport in the late 1760's and early 1770's dominated Jewish slave trading on the American continent." *Jews and Judaism in the United States a Documentary History* (New York: Behrman House, Inc., Pub, 1983), p. 14. Raphael is the editor of *American Jewish History*, the journal of the American Jewish Historical Society at Brandeis University in Massachusetts.

- **Cecil Roth -** The Jews of the Joden Savanne [Suriname] were also foremost in the suppression of the successive negro revolts, from 1690 to 1722: these as a matter of fact were largely directed against them, as being the greatest slave-holders of the region." *History of the Marranos* (Philadelphia: Jewish Publication Society of America, 1932), p. 292.

- **Ira Rosenwaike** - "In Charleston (South Carolina), Richmond (Virginia) and Savannah (Georgia) the large majority (over three-fourths) of the Jewish households contained one or more slaves; in Baltimore, only one out of three households were slaveholding; in New York, one out of eighteen....Among the slaveholding households the median number of slaves owned ranged from five in Savannah to one in New York." "**The Jewish Population in 1820,**" in Abraham J. Karp, ed., *The Jewish Experience in America: Selected Studies from the Publications of the American Jewish Historical Society* (Waltham, Massachusetts, 1969, 3 volumes), volume 2, pp. 2, 17, 19.

- **Jacob Rader Marcus** -"All through the eighteenth century, into the early nineteenth, Jews in the North were to own **black servants**; in the South, the few plantations owned by Jews were tilled with slave labor. In 1820, over 75 percent of all Jewish families in Charleston, Richmond, and Savannah owned slaves, employed as domestic servants; almost 40 percent of all Jewish householders in the United States owned one slave or more. There were no protests against slavery as such by Jews in the South, where they were always outnumbered at least 100 to 1....But very few Jews anywhere in the United States protested against chattel slavery on moral grounds." **United States Jewry**, *1776-1985* (Detroit: Wayne State University Press, 1989), p. 586.

- **Rabbi Bertram W. Korn** - "It would seem to be realistic to conclude that any Jew who could afford to own slaves and had need for their services would do so....Jews participated in every aspect and process of the exploitation of the defenseless blacks." "Jews and Negro Slavery in the Old South, 1789-1865," in Abraham J. Karp, *The Jewish Experience in America: Selected Studies from the Publications of the American Jewish Historical Society* (Waltham, Massachusetts, 1969), pp. 184, 189. Dr. Korn is a Rabbi, historian; A.B., Cincinnati, 1939;.

- **Louis Epstein,** author of *Sex Laws and Customs in Judaism*: "The Black female slave was a sex tool beneath the level of moral considerations. She was an economic good, useful, in addition to her menial labor, for breeding more slaves. To attain that purpose, the master mated her promiscuously according to his breeding plans. The master himself and his sons and other members of his household took turns with her for the increase of the family wealth, as well as for satisfaction of their extra-marital sex desires. Guests and neighbors too were invited to that luxury."

Deuteronomy 28:30 "Thou shalt betroth a wife, and another man shall lie with her: thou shalt build a house, and thou shalt not dwell therein: thou shalt plant a vineyard, and shalt not gather the grapes thereof."

- **Herbert I. Bloom** - "The Christian inhabitants of Brazil were envious because the Jews owned some of the best plantations in the river valley of **Pernambuco** and were among the leading slave-holders and slave traders in the colony." "Slave trade was one of the most important Jewish activities here in Suriname (South America) as elsewhere in the colonies." "**A Study of Brazilian Jewish History** 1623-1654,

- **Wilfred Samuels (1680)** - "I gather that the Jews of Barbados made a good deal of their money by purchasing and hiring out **Negroes**."

- **Moses Maimonides** - The **Encyclopedia of the Jewish Religion** refers to Moses Maimonides as "the symbol of the pure and orthodox faith." His **Guide to the Perplexed** is considered the greatest work of Jewish religious philosophy, but his view of Blacks was Hitlerian:

"The Negroes found in the remote South, and those who resemble them from among them that are with us in these climes. The status of those is like that of irrational animals. To my mind they do not have the rank of men, but have among the beings a rank lower than the rank of man but higher than the rank of apes. For they have the external shape and lineaments of a man and a faculty of discernment that is superior to that of the apes."

- **Major Mordecai Manuel Noah** (1785-1851) - was considered the most distinguished Jewish layman in his time. He was such a prolific proponent of slavery, that the first Black American periodical, **The Freedom's Journal**, was launched in response to Noah's racist propaganda. Here is what he had to say:

"There is liberty under the name of slavery. A field Negro has his cottage, his wife, and children, his easy task, his little patch of corn and potatoes, his garden and fruit, which are his revenue and property. The house servant has handsome clothing, his luxurious meals, his admitted privacy, a kind master, and an indulgent and frequently fond mistress."

He argued that "**the bonds of society must be kept as they now are**" and that "To emancipate the slaves would be to jeopardize the safety of the whole country." The **Freedom's Journal** called Noah the Black man's "bitterest enemy" and **William Lloyd Garrison**, the leading White abolitionist, called him the "lineal descendant of the monsters who nailed Jesus to the cross."

- **Seymour B. Liebman** - "They (**Jews**) came with ships carrying African blacks to be sold as slaves. The traffic in slaves was a royal monopoly, and the Jews were often appointed as agents for the Crown in their sale....**They were the largest ship chandlers in the entire Caribbean region, where the shipping business was mainly a Jewish enterprise....The ships were not only owned by Jews, but were manned by Jewish crews and sailed under the command of Jewish captains.**" - **New World Jewry 1493-1825:** Requiem for the Forgotten (KTAV, New York, 1982), pp. 170, 183. Liebman is an attorney; LL.B., St. Lawrence University, 1929; M.A. (Latin American history), Mexico City College, 1963; Florida chapter American Jewish Historical Society, 1956-58; Friends of Hebrew University, 1958-59; American Historical Society Contributor to scholarly journals on Jewish history.

- **Robert A. Rockaway**, is a senior lecturer in the Department of Jewish History at Tel Aviv University. "After the first World War, Jewish Gangsters became major figures in the American underworld and played prominent roles in the creation and extension of organized crime in the United States.

During Prohibition fifty percent of the leading bootleggers were Jews, and Jewish criminals financed and directed much of the nation's narcotics traffic. Jews also dominated illicit activities in a number of America's largest cities, including **Boston, Cleveland, Detroit, Minneapolis, New York, and Philadelphia.**"

Many times Jews will deny their involvement in the Slave Trade. Many books such as **"The Secret Relationship between Blacks and Jews"** published in 1991 by the **Nation of Islam** proves this to be false. In August 2, 1492 the **REAL BLACK JEWS** were expelled from Spain/Portugal aka **"Iberia"**. It wasn't until this time that the word **"Sephardic Jew"** became prominently used referring to Spanish-Middle Eastern Jew. Many of the Real Black Hebrew Israelites (Jews) fell back across the Strait of Gibraltar into Morocco while others were but on Slave Ships and sent to the Spanish Colonies in the Caribbean. The Black Moors (**who some believe consisted of Black Israelites who converted to Islam**) also retreated back in Africa after Battle of Granada (Alhambra) in 1485 and with the **"Spanish Inquisition"** of 1492.

Note: **"Omoros"** was the original name of the Moors which means **"Children of Light"**. **"Omo"** means **"Children"** and Oro comes from the Hebrew root **"Or"** which means light. In Nigerian Yoruba language, **"Omo"** means **"Child"**. The Nigerian Yoruba Jews also are said to have roots in Iberia and North Africa before settling in West Africa.

1 Thessalonians 5:5 "Ye are all **Children of the Light**, and the children of the day: we are not of the night, nor of darkness."

The descendants of the Gentile **"Proselyte-Judaism Converts"** Jews that originated from Europe-Middle East and entered into Judea/Samaria instead of the Children of Israel over the years were the people who stayed in Europe as **"Crytpo-Jews"**. It was at this very moment (1490's) of the expelling of the Black Hebrew Israelites and Black Moors that they called themselves **"Sephardic Jews"**. Many of these Sephardic Jews migrated to different areas in Eastern Europe, Western Europe, the Middle East, Africa and also as overseers of the "Real" Black Israelite slaves taken to the Caribbean/West Indies. This is why there are Synagogues found in the Caribbean today. Perhaps some of these Black Hebrew Israelites were able to hang around North Africa, Spain and Portugal undetected and un-expelled for the eye witness account of the Black Jews in Portugal.

Historians stated concerning the Jews in Spain and Portugal: Waitz says, "**An interesting gradation of all shades down to the black is exhibited by the Jews.**" **Especially dark were the Jews of Spain and Portugal. The Portuguese Jews were "very dark,"** says J.C Prichard. The Duchess d'Abrantes (born Laure Junot 1784-1838 A.D), wife of Napoleon's ambassador to Portugal, said that **"the Jew, the Negro and the Portuguese could be seen in a single person."** (Book: **Nature knows no Color Line**.)

"So dark were the Jews, especially of Portugal and Southern Spain that many whites thought all the Jews were black or dark. Many of the Jews who were banished from Portugal by John II settled in the West Indies. John Bigelow, who visited Jamaica in 1850, saw the descendants of these Jews and says they were Negroid." (Book: **Nature Knows No Color-Line, pages 123,130**).

So some of the Gentile "**Sephardic Jews**" that didn't want to hide and practice Judaism secretly as "Crypto-Jews" emigrated to Holland, where they set up the Dutch West Indies Company to start slave trading in the New World. In 1654, Jewish Jacob Barsimson, emigrated from Holland to New Amsterdam (New York) and after 10 years more Jews followed him to get in on trading Black Hebrew Israelite slaves while settling along the East Coast, principally in **New Amsterdam (New York) and Newport (Rhode Island)**. They soon found that in the New World that there were no laws to prevent the Jews from trading with the Native Indians. The first Jew to start trading with the Indians was **Hayman Levy**. Levy had glass beads, textiles, armbands and other cheap products from Holland which he traded for valuable fur pelts. Hayman Levy teamed up with other Jews named **Nicholas Lowe** and **Joseph Simon**. They then came up with the idea of selling rum and whiskey to the Indians and set up a distillery in Newport.

Note: The practice of Israelites selling other Israelites for European goods or money was also common in West Africa countries such as Senegal, Gambia, Ghana, Benin, and Togo.

Over this period of time the Jews also shared business in the slave commerce. The East Coast at this time was known as "**The Jewish Newport-World center for Slave Commerce.**" Altogether there were six communities in North America set up for trading slaves: **Newport (Rhode Island), Charleston (South Carolina), New York, Philadelphia (Pennsylvania), Richmond (Virginia), and Savannah (Georgia).** It was from these city ports that slave ships would leave from America on the Atlantic Ocean to West Africa to get Negro slaves using "Rum, whiskey, guns, and whatever goods they could barter". Once they brought the slaves back to America and sold them, they could earn anywhere from $40,000-$100,000 a year in income. It was reported that within 1 year, 128 slave ships unloaded in Charleston, South Carolina and 120 of these slave ships were Jewish.

Fact: By 1860, there were 4 million slaves in the United States, and 400,000 of them (10%) lived in South Carolina. To put this in perspective, Detroit has a little over 600,000 blacks in its city where it is in the top 3 cities with the highest percentage of blacks. African-Americans, enslaved or free, made up 57% of South Carolinas population. Charleston, SC at this time was the nation's capital of the slave trade, the place where many slaves saw for the first time as their new home.

Any Jewish person saying that Jews had nothing to do with the Slavery of Negroes needs to do the research. The real question is, if the Israelites did in fact disobey God's commandments then **their seed** should be going through the curses listed in Deuteronomy 28:16-68. The Israelites admitted to disobeying God in Daniel 9:8-14.

Daniel 9:8-13 "O Lord to us belongeth confusion of face, to our kings, to our princes, and to our fathers because we have sinned against thee. To the Lord our God belong mercies and forgiveness, though we have rebelled against him; neither have we obeyed the voice of the Lord our God, to walk in his walks, which he set before us by his servants the prophets. Yea **ALL ISRAEL HAVE TRANGRESSED THE LAW**, even by departing, that they might not obey thy voice; **THERFORE THE CURSE IS POURED UPON US**, and the oath that is written in the law of Moses the servant of God, because we have sinned against him.

So how could the European White Jew (**so-called Israelite**) be sold into captivity as listed in the curses if they were the ones doing the enslaving? Wake Up Black America.

CHAPTER 5

HAS THE POWER OF GOD LEFT THE CHRISTIAN CHURCH?

Acts 1:8 "But ye shall receive **POWER**, after that the **Holy Ghost is come upon you**: and ye shall be witnesses unto me both in Jerusalem, and in all Judea, and in Samaria, and unto the uttermost part of the earth."

This was the last words Jesus (Yehsua) told his disciples as God in the flesh before ascending to heaven. So what did Jesus (Yeshua) mean by POWER? In **Luke 24:29** it reads "And, behold, I send the promise of my Father upon you: but tarry ye in the city of Jerusalem, until ye be endued with **POWER** from on high." So based on these two scriptures we see that this power gives us the ability to be witnesses for Jesus/Yeshua. It allows us to proclaim the Word of God to any and everybody. In Acts 4:3 this was evident:

Acts 4:31 "And when they prayed, the place was shaken where they were assembled together; and they were **ALL** filled with the Holy Ghost, and they spake the **WORD OF GOD** with boldness."

In Acts, the Apostle Paul, **a Benjaminite** ran into some believers of "Christ" in the city of Ephesus, Turkey. The people of Ephesus (Ephesians) tell Paul that they were believers in "Christ" and that they were baptized by John the Baptist for their repentance. They were told by John that another man was coming greater than him. But Paul let them know that despite being baptized by John they had to be baptized in the in the name of "**Yeshua Mashiach (Jesus Christ)**."

Acts 19:2-6 "He said unto them, Have ye received the Holy Ghost since ye believed: And they said unto him, We have not so much as heard whether there be any Holy Ghost. And he said unto them, Unto what then were ye baptized? And they said, Unto John's baptism. Then said Paul, John verily baptized with the baptism of repentance, saying unto the people, that they should believe on him which should come after him, that is, on "**Mashiach Yeshua (Christ Jesus)**". **When they heard this, they were baptized in the name of the name of the Lord Jesus/Yeshua**. And when Paul had laid his hands upon them, the **HOLY GHOST** came upon them; and they **SPAKE WITH TONGUES**, and **PROPHESIED**.

So two things happen when the Holy Spirit comes into a believer of Christ according to the Bible:

1. They receive the Power to witness the gospel of Christ.
2. They also can receive the ability to prophesy.

So with all these churches out here, how do we know if we are in the right church? How do we know that the Pastor we are listening to has been called by God to preach? How do we know if the Pastor is anointed? How do we know if the Pastor isn't just concerned with achieving financial gains by starting a church? Many churches today do not have any "**Power**" and this is the reason why so many Black Christians are lost. This is why many Blacks are considering Islam. Even more, "Why do we have so many Religious Denominations?" Why do we need "Religion?" "Did the Israelites practice a "Religion"? No, no and no! I have ran into so many Black Christians who have tried almost every religious faith: Seventh Day Adventist, Jehovah's Witness, Mormonism, Non-Denominational, Scientology, Baptist, Apostolic/Pentecostal, Catholic, Judaism and even Islam. I once talked to a friend who told me a real story about how a particular black woman wanted the Holy Spirit so bad that she had went to a lot of different Black Churches in Detroit. Every church she went had no evidence of the "**Holy Spirit**" she was looking for as written in the Book of Acts and none of the churches had evidence of "**Power**", "**Anointing**" or "**Deliverance**". She said these churches barely even mentioned "**Water Baptism**" or the Holy Spirit in their sermons. She finally was fed up and tried a larger, more famous church in Detroit. During altar call she went up and told the Pastor that she wanted to receive the Holy Spirit. The Pastor deferred her to a Deacon who took her into another room in the Church. The deacon told the lady to close her eyes and repeat a bunch of random incomprehensible words. He told her to memorize the words and to repeat them over and over again. Of course, she did as she was told. After she had repeated the words correctly in order over and over again the Deacon told her to go faster. With no hesitation she started mumbling the rehearsed words faster. After about 3-5 minutes the deacon said "**You did it!**" and "**Congratulations, you just received the Holy Spirit of God.**" The lady felt nothing and surely didn't feel any spirit. She left the church saddened and even more confused. She would eventually tell others about her experience. Just as in these Black Churches, many Mega-Churches mislead people with a

"**Great Show**". They give you stories, inspirational speeches and they crack jokes. Most people are quietly sitting down with their bibles in their laps more focused on the evangelists' stories than the actual "**Word**" in their bible. They tell the church audience, "**God doesn't care if you're not perfect, he is always going to be there for you.**" This is what everyone wants to hear. This is called "**Safe and Easy Preaching**". There is no talk about **Hell** or the **Lake of Fire** and a **short repeated sentence** is all that is needed to enter into the Kingdom of God. Church is not supposed to teach that anything is supposed to be hard. This will run away potential members will eventually be "offering givers" and "consumers" of various religious materials offered by the ministry (DVD's, CD's, Anointing Oil, Holy Water, Rosaries etc.). Christ didn't always come with the "Easy" approach when talking to the Pharisee Nicodemus or his own twelve disciples.

Matthew 19:23-15 "And Jesus said to His disciples, "Truly I say to you, it is **HARD** for a rich man to enter the kingdom of heaven. "Again I say to you, it is **EASIER** for a camel to go through the eye of a needle, than for a rich man to enter the kingdom of God." When the disciples heard this, they were very astonished and said, "Then who can be saved"?

Oprah during an interview asked Joel Osteen: "Ok, here is the big question. **Are there many paths to get to the one God**? This question is straightforward. To most people watching they would interpret this question as, "Is there many paths (religions) to get to the Creator (God)? Joel Osteen responds by saying, "Well, I believe Oprah that there, I believe that Jesus is the way to **one God**, but there are **many paths** to Jesus." The big question is what does Osteen mean by Jesus being the way to "**One God**". For some this may pose the question: "**Are there other Gods?**"

There is one pathway to Salvation and to the Father (Creator) according to the bible. According to the Bible, one cannot enter the kingdom of Heaven worshipping Allah, Shiva, Vishnu, Set, Horus, Osiris, Baal and Zeus. John 4:6 "*Yahusha (Jesus) saith unto him, I am the way, the truth, and the life: no man cometh unto the Father, but by me.*" *What other paths can bring us to Christ? Can I read the Book of Mormon, the New World Translation (Jehovah's Witness), the Quran (Islam), the Vedas (Hinduism), or the Pali Canon (Word of Buddha), the Babylonian Talmud (Judaism) and the Satanic Bible to get to Christ (Yahusha)? Absolutely not! Don't be fooled by Pastor Joel Osteen. In **John 14:9** it says "**He that hath seen me (Yahusha) hath seen the Father.**"*

Then Oprah drops another question that the world loves today, the "Homosexual" question. She states: "I can't imagine that you would have 16,000 people in there and none of them would be gay. So are gay people also included?" Osteen responds, "Absolutely, anybody is." Then Oprah asks, "**Will gay people be accepted into heaven...as you see it?**" Osteen says, "**Well, I believe they will**, because I believe you know that we have to have forgiveness for our sins...". What Joel Osteen doesn't understand is that a "**gay person**" according to the bible will not be accepted into heaven. That is unless that gay person asks for forgiveness of his/her sins and then becomes "**un-gay (not a gay person)**" by not engaging in homosexual sex. So therefore, a "**Gay person**" has to be delivered from Homosexuality. Once he/she is delivered by God from Homosexuality than this person is no longer a "**gay person**". So Joel Osteen's response could easily be interpreted as "**Yes, a gay person can be accepted into heaven.**"

This type of "**Cotton Candy Safe Christianity teaching**" misleads people to believe that if you go to church, confess to love the Lord but lead a homosexual, bisexual or pedophile-led life that God will still be there for you. Even the Vatican's Pope Francis has fell victim to this "safe" approach to homosexuality as a religious leader. These Mega-Churches will air for 30-60 min but at the end of the broadcast there is nobody getting baptized and there is nobody getting filled with the Holy Spirit. Before closing, they tell viewers to repeat a sentence and there you have it! Congratulations, you are now part of God's Kingdom in Heaven.

Many churches now have services that are like spectacles, and perhaps more like an entertaining show. In fear of losing church members, many churches will allow all types of foolish behavior to go on in their churches. People can jump up, fall down, roll on the ground, dance, do jumping-jacks, do push-ups, rap a song, moon-walk, dance on money poured out on the floor from the collection plate, grab the microphone at any time to sing or say whatever and can even command the congregation to do whatever they say like a game of "**Simon says**". Pastors can wave their suit jacket like a "magic cloak", blow on a row of people and even use their feet to push people down to the floor, all in the name of Jesus Christ. They can "**speak in tongues**" on command and then turn it off to speak English. It seems nowadays that church services are more focused on "**Entertaining**" and "**taking your money**" than they are about teaching God's salvation. Black people are very spiritual people and often very loyal to the church. That being said, all it takes is for a Pastor to appear kind and be good with words for the church to fall in love with him. Using looks, the "**gift of gab**" (which most pastors have), and manipulative tactics backed by the Word of God in their hand, this pastor can suck the life out of his congregation by demanding all types of offerings in one service. Many Black Churches that have large congregations of 5,000-30,000 members have the financial resources to make huge differences in the community. They also have members that have skills and connections that can further help re-develop black inner-cities. The Potter's House Church in Dallas, Texas seats about 7,600 people. On an average Sunday, if every person gave $20 for offering this would amount to $150,000. For some, this is enough money to buy a franchise business (Subway's) or buy a vacation rental property. Simply investing this amount of money into a property or a business can bring even more return on the money invested. For 1 out of 4 Sundays a month, black churches statewide could donate a portion of their offering to invest in the black inner cities, but do they do this? No! The Black Churches should have more ownership of the businesses in their communities; that is if they practiced "**Unity**" and **Yeshua's** greatest 2 commandments. But they don't. So whenever black people complain, "**we don't own anything**", we should look at the number of churches in that city and then look at who owns all the businesses or property for the proper answer of why we don't own anything.

Fact: *If all the Black people in America donated just $1 every Sunday to a **Black Investment Fund** or **Black Free Loan company** for 1 year (52 weeks) that would amount to **2.34 Billion dollars**. If we started doing this in 1965, (when Martin Luther King Jr marched in Selma, Alabama) until now we would have an excess of 117 Billion dollars for the advancement of Black People in America. I think 117 Billion dollars is enough money for a Black Loan company to turn things around for Black Cities/communities all over the United States of America. Don't believe this can be done? Check out the **Hebrew Free Loan** site at www.hflasf.org. The Jews have been doing this since **1897**. The Jews are 1% of America. Blacks are 14% of America. 2.34 Billion Black dollars per year x 118 years (2015-**1897**) = **276 Billion Dollars**. Wake up Black People. There is no excuse. Or is it the "Curses of Israel"..."**He shall lend to thee, and thou shalt not lend to him: he shall be the head, and thou shall be the tail**-Deuteronomy 28:44".*

CHAPTER 6

THE CATHOLIC CHURCH DECEPTION

The Pope is the "Vicar" or Representative or Substitute of Yeshua HaMashiach while on the Earth. That being said let us see how well the Pope is living up to what the "**Messiah**" preached on Earth. In John 3, the Pharisee Nicodemus, a ruler of the Jews came to visit Yeshua (Jesus) at night in secret and asked him some questions. Let's compare Yeshua's (Jesus) response vs the Pope's (Catholic Church) response.

Test question for "The Christ"

John 3:1-5 "There was a man of the Pharisees, named Nicodemus, a ruler of the Jews: The same came to Jesus by night, and said unto him, Rabbi, we know that thou art a teacher come from God: for no man can do these miracles that thou doest, **except God be with him**. Jesus answered and said unto him, Verily, verily, I say unto thee, Except a man be born again, he cannot see the kingdom of God. Nicodemus saith unto him, How can a man be born when he is old: can he enter the second time into his mother's womb, and be born? Jesus answered, Verily, verily, I say unto thee, Except a man be born of water and of the spirit, he cannot enter into the kingdom of God. "

Test question for the Pope "Vicar" of Christ

Pope Francis in 2015 spoke to reporters aboard his plane with returning to Rome from World Youth Day. The Pope made some impromptu remarks such as "I think like a Jesuit". The Pope is right because he is a "Jesuit" and a Pope, thus making him the first "**Black Pope**". Reporters also asked Pope Francis if Homosexual behavior is ok. This is what he said:

"When I meet a gay person, I have to distinguish between them being gay and being part of a lobby (gay lobby). **If they accept the Lord and have goodwill, who am I to judge? They shouldn't be marginalized. The tendency [to homosexuality] is not the problem....they're our brothers.**

Well, the word "**Marginalized**" is defined as: **To put or keep (someone) in a powerless or unimportant position within a society or group**. So if the world or the Catholic Church doesn't agree with "**Marginalizing**" homosexuals then this means that they would rather see homosexuals become more important people with power within the Church and in Christianity. If we see homosexuals as our brothers than this means that the Catholic Church is teaching that heterosexuals and homosexuals are **ALL** brothers in Christ. Does this sound like what God would say? In Sodom and Gomorrah, **ALL OF THE MEN OF THE TOWN WERE HOMOSEXUA**LS. They saw the two angels disguised as men go into Lot's house and they all wanted to have sex with them. God did not see the Homosexual people of the town as brothers to Lot and his family. Nor did he see them as being obedient to his commandments. If the homosexuals and the heterosexuals were **ALL EQUAL** in Sodom and Gomorrah then God would've spared the town with the people in it. For the reason of "**Sexual Immorality**" God killed **ALL** of the people of Sodom & Gomorrah by Fire and Brimstone.

Genesis 19:4-5 (Greek Septuagint) "But before they went to sleep, the men of the city, the Sodomites, compassed the house, **BOTH YOUNG AND OLD, ALL THE PEOPLE TOGETHER**. And they called out Lot, and said to him, Where are the men that went in to thee this night? Bring them out to us that we may be (have sex) with them."

In **Jude 1:7** it says "In a similar way, Sodom and Gomorrah and the surrounding towns gave themselves up to **SEXUAL IMMORALITY AND PERVERSION.** They serve as an example of those who suffer the punishment of **ETERNAL FIRE.**"

Leviticus 20:13 "If a man lies with a man as one lies with a woman, both of them have done what is detestable. They must be put to death; their blood will be on their own heads."

Fact 1: In 2015, Pope Francis met with representatives from each major religion: Judaism, Hinduism, Islam, the Catholic Church and Buddhism urging the world that we need to all UNITE beliefs for the better good of mankind. This is false teaching for the Vicar of Christ as it states:

John 14:6 "Yahusha (Jesus) saith unto him, I am the way, the truth, and the life: no man cometh unto the Father, buy by me."

Fact 2: *In 2015, **Pope Francis** stated that Yahusha's (Jesus) life **"humanly speaking"** ended in **failure….the failure of the cross**. What does the Pope mean by "humanly speaking"? Is he trying to say that Yahusha (Jesus) was just a mortal man and not God? This sounds "**Antichrist-like**". But the Pope has never said that "**Mary**" failed Christians. In hospital rooms and Catholic houses you will see more pictures of Mary than Yahusha (Jesus). The Catholic Church creates idols of Mary, call her the "**Queen of Heaven**", they ascribe miracles to her, pray to her and even bow down to worship her. So in the Catholic Church Yahusha has been demoted to the **fourth position**. The Pope has even hinted that he wants all religions (Buddhism, Hinduism, Christianity, Islam and Judaism) to come together as "One". This is essentially creating a "**One World Religion**". This is the agenda of the **New World Order**.*

*1. **The Father***

*2. **Mary "Queen of Heaven"***

*3. **The Catholic Church***

*4. **Yahusha (Jesus)***

*5. **Holy Spirit***

In **2 Thessalonians 2:3** it says "Let no one in any way deceive you, for it (Yahusha's return) will **NOT COME** unless the **APOSTASY COMES FIRST**, and the man of lawlessness is **REVEALED**, the son of **DESTRUCTION (Antichrist)**." Apostasy means to fall from the truth. Therefore an "**Apostate**" is someone who has once believed and then rejects the Truth of God. Apostasy is a rebellion of God because it is a rebellion of the **TRUTH**. While we are waiting to see when the 3rd Temple in Jerusalem will be started on and when the Antichrist will reveal himself we must watch to see when this "Apostate" person comes. After all, he is supposed to come **FIRST**, paving the way for the Antichrist. The Antichrist cannot abide and move in a world that is upholding the **TRUTH** and the Word of God. Look around, we already have Legal Gay Marriage in the United States. Homosexuality and

Beastiality is being practiced all over the world. Just as it was in the "**Days of Noah**" and in the days of "**Sodom & Gomorrah**". So is there an "Apostasy" going on in the Christian Church? Yes! Wake Up people. Never, in all the years of the Catholic Church have we seen such a progression of "**Apostasy**" in regards to the Bible. In 2014, during Catholic Mass, the Pope said that if "**Martians/Aliens**" came to him asking him to be "**baptized**" he wouldn't turn them away. But how can you "Baptize" a fallen demonic angel? Who does the Pope think he is?

The Catholic Church and the Vatican also quoted in 2014:

"**Homosexuals have GIFTS AND QUALITIES**" to offer to the Christian Community. Are we capable of welcoming these people, guaranteeing to them a fraternal space in our communities? Often they wish to encounter a church that offers them a welcoming home. Are our communities capable of providing that, accepting and valuing their sexual orientation, without compromising Catholic doctrine on the family and matrimony?"

So the question is, what "**Gifts and Qualities**" can homosexuals offer to Christians? When will we see Churches full of homosexuals and heterosexuals together praising God in worship? When will we see Gay preachers, deacons, and ministers? When will we see gay Sunday school teachers? Has Satan taken over the Christian Church? Can Church's discriminate and not marry homosexual couples? Not anymore thanks to the 2015 U.S. Supreme Ruling legalizing Gay marriage in all 50 states of America. The Pope is the "Vicar" or Representative of the Christ on earth to its many followers. This is not how Christ or his disciples would carry on affairs on earth in regards to spreading the Gospel and upholding the Law. Since the Catholic Church is accepting of homosexuals and we know that the Bible teaches against homosexuality then essentially the Catholic Church is "**Anti-Christ**" or "**Anti-God**".

Fact: On March 20, 2013 Pope Francis said:

*"I greet and thank cordially all of you, dear friends belonging to other religious traditions; firstly the Muslims, who worship the **ONE LIVING AND MERCIFUL GOD**, and call upon him in prayer. I really appreciate your presence, and in it I see a tangible sign of the wish to grow in reciprocal trust and in cooperation for the common good of humanity."*

Now the question is, would a Muslim Imam or a Jewish Rabbi address a crown by saying "Christians, who worship the **ONE LIVING AND MERCIFUL GOD YAHUSHA HAMASHIACH (Jesus Christ)**?" Is this the Pope's way of sneaking in a "One World Religion?"

CHAPTER 7

THE CATHOLIC CHURCH AND THE SABBATH DAY

The Catholic Church has violated the "**Lord's Day**" by changing it to "**Sun-day**" which in ancient times was considered the pagan "**Day of the Sun**".

"Sunday is our (Vatican's) Mark of Authority....The Church is above the Bible, and his transference of Sabbath (from Saturday) observance is proof of that fact." - **Catholic Record of London, Ontario Sept 1, 1923**

"We observe Sunday instead of Saturday because the Catholic Church in the Council of Laodicea (336 A.D) transferred the solemnity from Saturday to Sunday." **– The Convert's Catechism of Catholic Doctrine. 50 A.D.**

"I saw all that "would not receive the mark of the Beast, and his Image, in their foreheads or in their hands," could not buy or sell. I saw that the number (666) of the Image Beast was made up; and that it was the beast that changed the Sabbath, and the Image Beast had followed after, and kept the Pope's, and not God's Sabbath. And all we were required to do, was to give up God's Sabbath, and keep the Pope's (Sabbath) and then we should have the mark of the Beast, and of his image. " **- Co-founder of the Seventh-Day Adventist Church, Ellen White. In "A Word to the Little flock, p. 19,**

Throughout history Satan has gotten mankind to worship the sun (Amen-Ra, Aten), Bulls (Apis Bull) and also lightning/thunder (Baal, Zeus, Jupiter, Shango, Set). He used the Catholic Church to name the pagan days of the week and establish Sunday as the "**New Sabbath**". But "SUN-day" worship started in Babylon and possibly earlier in Ancient Sumeria or Ancient Egypt. Satan used the Catholic Church, Judaism and Islam to mingle lies with the truth. He intended to blend pagan Satanic theology with Christian concepts, coming up with the perfect deception which people would believe is authentic. This is why the world believes the Egyptian deities Osiris, Isis, and Horus (Heru) pre-date Christianity. Now people are seeing the deception of the Catholic Church and its push to bring about a "**New World Religion**" and a "**New World Order**" which Pope Francis has admitted in his campaign throughout South America. Is this new religion "**Chris-Lam**"? Or is this religion a mix of Judaism, Catholicism and Islam? Are they all playing on the same time but confusing believers at the same time? **You be the judge in this chapter.**

Fact: *The current "**Code of Canon Law (1983)**", released by **Pope John Paul II** has 1,752 canons. The former canon in 1917 had 2,414 canons. These "canons" were rules related to the governance of the Catholic Church, and they are now divided into seven headings: general norms, the people of God, teaching mission of the Church, sanctifying mission of the Church, temporal goods of the Church, penal law, and procedural law. Many of these laws (like Talmud Judaism) are subject to change over time as the Church sees fit, while others are not.*

CHAPTER 8

10 SIMILARITIES BETWEEN THE CATHOLIC CHURCH AND ISLAM

1. If a Religion denies Christ as being God….. they are essentially "Anti-Christ". According to Islam, God cannot be a man, and God cannot have a child (son). This is the whole basis on why Muslims don't believe in the New Testament but yet Jesus defeats the Muslim Antichrist (**dajjal**) in the "**End of Days**". This is also the reason why Jehovah Witnesses believe Jesus (Yahusha) is the archangel Michael. The Pope's Tiara (Priests of Dagon Hat) has the Latin words "**Vicarius Filii Dei**" written on it. It means "**Substituting Agent or Representative of Jesus Christ**". So the Pope is essentially the "**Stand-In**" for Jesus Christ to his 1.2 billion followers before his return. **Note: the numerical value of the word "Vicarius Filii Dei" in Hebrew, Greek and Latin is 666.** Is this why Catholic followers have to "confess their sins" to a Catholic Priest instead of just asking God for forgiveness of their sins? The Bible does not support this type of man-made doctrine.

   John 14:6 "Yeshua (Jesus) saith unto them, I am the way, the truth, and the life: **no man cometh unto the Father, but by me.**"

2. Both religions aspire to a "**Global Agenda**". A "**New World Religion**", "**One World Government**" and "**New World Order**" as spoken by the Pope Francis in his three-nation South American pilgrimage in July 2015. In Ecuador, he issued an impassioned call for a "**New World Order**" where the goods of the Earth are "**Shared**" by everyone, not just exploited by the rich. But how can "**goods**" be shared unless the people who "**own**" the goods willingly give these "**goods**" to the people of the world, but based on a small stipulation (i.e. RFID chip, Mark of the beast). The Muslims aspire to a Universal World Wide Caliphate like the Old Ottoman Empire.

   In the Quran in **Sura 8:39** (Sahih International) it reads "**And fight them until there is no fitnah (persecution) and until the religion, ALL OF IT, is** for Allah, and if they cease – then indeed, Allah is Seeing of what they do."

3. Both religions believe in using **FORCE** to "**convert**" or impose their will to the unbelievers (i.e. **Spanish Inquisition, The Crusades**). The "**Syllabus of Errors**" says that it is an error to say that the "Church" cannot use force. The Quran says to fight against and **SLAY OR KILL** those who refuse to convert to **ISLAM**.

Sura 2:191 (Sahih International) "And **KILL THEM** wherever you overtake them and expel them wherever they have expelled you, and fitnah (persecution) is worse than killing. And do not fight them at al-Masjid al-Haram (Inviolable Place of Worship) until they fight you there. **But if they fight you, then kill them. Such is the recompense of the disbelievers."**

4. Both religions despise manual labor and practice/promote inhumane slavery. The Muslim Arabs enslaved the people of Africa from as early as 600 A.D. to 1900's A.D. The Vatican (Pope's) approved of slavery, especially by Catholic Christian Slavetraders.

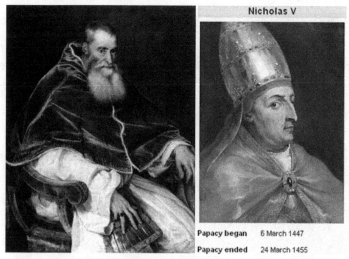

Pope Paul III (left) and Pope Nicholas V (right)

Fact: Pope Paul III confirmed in 1548 that all Christian men and all members of the clergy had the right to own slaves. Also, **Pope Nicholas V**, in his bull **Romanus pontifex** of 1455, gave his blessing to the enslavement of conquered "**native people** (Negroes/Natives)", by Catholics, whether Portuguese or Spanish. The Bible is not all about enslaving people. In the Greek Septuagint version of the Old Testament the use of the word "**maidservants**" is common. In **Colossians 3:22** the verse in Hebrew reads "**Servants**" using the Hebrew Strong's #5650/5651 "**ebed**".

Mysteriously the Hebrew word for "**Hebrew (ibri-#5680)**" is almost identical to the Hebrew word for "**Servant (Ebed-#5650)**". So in the Hebrew bible the word "Hebrew" and "Servant" looks the same.

עֶבֶד   עִבְרִי

Servant   Hebrew

Exodus 21:2 *Hebrew and KJV version* "If thou buy a **Hebrew servant**, six years he shall serve: and in the seventh he shall go out free for nothing."

This word whether in singular or plural format is used frequently in the Old Testament (700+ times) as "Servant" (**ex. Genesis 9:25-27**). This Hebrew word "**Ebed**" for "Servant" can be seen in **Colossians 3:22, Ephesians 6:5, Exodus 21:2 and 1 Peter 2:18**. Even in the Aramaic Peshitta version of these scriptures the word "**Servants**" is used instead of "**Slaves**". We know that Yeshua and his disciples spoke in Aramaic. So to use the word "slaves" is improper. The King James Version and other newer Bible versions started use the word "**slaves**" in the later years. There is a big difference between a "**maidservant**", "**manservant**" and a "**slave**". A slave gets treated inhumanely (ex. raped, beat, starved, tortured, forced to work with physical abuse). A servant doesn't. Yeshua (Jesus) spent most of his ministry working, teaching, performing miracles and traveling. He did not approve of followers to have slaves. He did not say you could enslave, forcefully convert then marry non-Christian women as the "Gifts of War from God".

He did not slaughter thousands of people or forcefully convert non-believers in the name of God. He was not carried around on a "**pope-mobile**", nor did he ask for people to pay and feed him as he preached the gospel. The New Testament Gospels in fact agrees with the saying "If you don't work, you don't eat". **Thessalonians 3:10** "For even when we were with you, this we commanded you, **that if any would not work, neither should he eat.**"

5. Both religions practice book banning and exercise rigid censorship over the reading material of their followers. The Vatican burned books and Bibles for centuries and only allowed people to hear the "**Word**" orally until the bible was available for mass printing. Even then they omitted and inserted words into the Bibles after deciding first what religious canons (books) were going to be allowed. The included the "**historical Apocrypha books**" and then took them out. The Vatican also holds hostage many Ancient relics, pictures and texts that would expose their "**Agenda**". The Jews are also said to prevent the public from having "full viewing access" to the Dead Sea Scrolls found in 1948 in Qumran, Israel. The Arabs destroyed the library at Alexandria, Egypt which contained the scientific wisdom of the world and they also burned hundreds of Ancient manuscripts in the libraries of Mali, Timbuktu (Africa), some which were Ancient Hebrew manuscripts! But nobody asks the question, "**What were Ancient Hebrew manuscripts doing in West sub-Saharan Africa**?

6. Both religions have an inquisition to **punish** any deviation from their teachings. In Saudi Arabia, the Religious and Morals Police are called the "**Mutawwa**". They basically enforce "**Sharia Law**" using the government as its back up. So if Muslim is not obedient to the laws of Allah/Muhammad they can be paid a visit from the "**Sharia Law Police**" and in worst cases it can lead to stoning, drowning or beheading. In 2013, Pope Francis and the Vatican passed a law making it **ILLEGAL** for anyone to report sex crimes against children and/or report new cases. This was a clever way to stop the endless flow of child sexual abuse complaints in the Vatican. So basically Child sexual abuse can continue to go on unknown or un-punished because

the Vatican basically made a law saying that people cannot accuse them anymore. Wow!

7. Both Religions hate the "**Sabbath**" or the "**Lord's day**". They do not keep the "**Sabbath**" Holy or follow the rules of the Sabbath. In many Muslim countries, Saturday is considered just another day. The Catholic Church does not observe the Sabbath as well. It was Catholic Church under **Pope Gregory XIII** that established the "Gregorian-Christian Calendar" in 1582.

   Exodus 20:8 "Remember the Sabbath day, **to keep it holy**."

8. Both religions have pagan shrines or objects that are sacred to their followers. The Egyptian pagan obelisk (**Asherah pole or groves in the bible**) can be seen in Vatican City, London City and Washington D.C.

"**Asherah Pole**" or "**Groves**" are symbols of Ancient idolatry worship still seen today in America and the Vatican.

*(**Above**) The Rothschild Grove of pagan origin sitting at the Israeli Supreme Court, Israel. The **Asherah Pole or Grove** is a symbol of Pagan worship. Used in Ancient Egypt for the worship of **Ra/Horus** and in Canaan as **Baal's Shaft**. In the Bible, God tells the Israelites to destroy the "**Groves**". So why is this grove still standing "erect" on the grounds of the Israeli Supreme Court? If they are God's Chosen People and are disobeying God's Laws in Israel by have monuments promoting "**Idol worship**", shouldn't they be experiencing the "**Curses of Israel**" listed in Deuteronomy 28:16-68? Wake up people. The signs are evident.*

2 Kings 18:4 "He (King Hezekiah) removed the high places, and brake the images, **AND CUT DOWN THE GROVES**, and brake in pieces the **BRASEN SERPENT** that Moses had made, for until those days the sons of Israel burned incense to it; and it was called **Nehushtan**."

Judges 6:25 "And it came to pass the same night, that the Lord said unto him, Take thy father's young bullock, even the second bullock of seven years old, and throw down the altar of **BAAL** that thy father hath, and cut down **THE GROVE** that is by it."

Asherah, or **Ashtoreth**, was the name of the chief female deity worshipped in Ancient Syria, Canaan and Philistine. The Assyrians/Babylonians worshipped her as "**Ishtar**" and the Philistines had a temple for her in 1 Samuel 31:10. Asherah worship continued as soon as Joshua died in Judges 2:13. The Asherah pole was initially in Ancient times a limbless tree planted into the ground. It usually had carvings on it and in the bible was referred to as "groves" or the Hebrew word "Asherah". Asherah was also sometimes viewed as the wife of El and Baal, the Canaanite sun-god. This is supported in Judges 3:7, 6:28, 10:6, 1 ; 1 Samuel 7:4, 12:10. King Solomon brought an "Asherah" pole into his Kingdom called "The goddess of the Sidonians" in 1 Kings 11:5, 33.   King Ahab's wife Jezebel also made Asherah worship a common thing by having 400 prophets of Asherah on the royal payroll in 1 Kings 18:19. God told the Israelites to destroy all the Canaanite idolatry symbols when they possessed the land.

Deuteronomy 7:5 "But thus shall ye deal with them; ye shall destroy their altars, and break down their images, and cut down their **GROVES**, and burn their graven images with fire."

Judges 3:7 "And the people of Israel did what was evil in the sight of the Lord. They forgot the Lord their God and served the Baals and the **ASHEROTH**."

This form of Idolatry can also be seen today with **"The Virgin Mary"** statue/pictures, **Mecca** (Ka'ba and black stone), **Medina** and **Temple Mount**. The Israelites had a temple. They didn't have not shrine, statue or object they were told to worship.

9. Both religions ins some aspect worship "**Allah**" as god. Catholic Freemasons start out as Catholics worshipping "**Christ**" and "**Mary**" but as they get higher and higher up in the ranks they are given the opportunity to become a "**Moslem Shriner**" or a "**Rosicrucian**". After that point, all oaths are done with your hand on the **Quran** in the name of "**Allah**". They then greet each other as "**Assalamu Alaikum**" which is an Arabic greeting for "**Peace Be Upon You**". Both **Moslem Shriners** and **Muslims** have the Crescent Moon, Sun and Star symbol as their normal traditional religious objects. But why are they there? Why do we need planetary, celestial symbols or geometric shapes to represent religion? These are forbidden in the Bible and in the Quran but these religions still have pagan celestial symbols hanging around.

Quran, Sura 41:37 (Sahih International) "And of his signs are the night and day and the sun and moon. Do not prostate to the sun or to the moon, but prostate to Allah, who created them, if it should be Him that you worship."

Deuteronomy 17:3 "And hath gone and served other gods, and worshipped them, either the sun, or moon, or any of the host of heaven, which I have not commanded;"

Moon Crescent Pagan carving of the Canaanite Sky/Thunder deity
Baal-Hadad depicted as a disk in a crescent

The Moon crescent are in all Roman Catholic monstrance's to hold the wafer-god of Babylon within it, thereby depicting an exact duplicate of Babylonian worship of the sun-god BAAL

Hilal pronounced **"Helel or Halal"** in Arabic means **"Crescent Moon"**. In Ancient Ireland/Scotland the Celts worshipped the Moon Goddess and used the **"Celtic Moon"** symbol (seen above the Hindu God Shiva). Hebrew Strong's Lexicon #1966 **"Helel or Heylel"** is pronounced the same as the Arabic version **"Hilal"** but means **Lucifer** (Star of the morning/Shining one). The Hindu God **"Shiva the Destroyer"** is the equivalent of Satan in its religion. The Freemasons also know **"Shiva"** is another ancient name for Satan as is the Egyptian God **"Set"**. Shiva wears a **"Crescent Moon"** crown on top of her hair. **Coincidence?**

The Bible predicts that the seed of Edom and Ishmael would come against Israel to destroy it from being a Nation. It states that Edom's seed and Ishmael's seed amongst others would make a pact (agreement) to wipe the name of Israel of the map. Black Christian theologians believe this is why the Transatlantic slave trade and the Arab Slave trade happened to the **"Bantus Negroes"** in East/West Africa. By captivity and invasion the Israelites would be dispersed into other countries, thus losing their **identity**. Who would then pick up this **"identity"** as their own? The descendants of Edom and Ishmael. We know for a fact that the bible says that Edom intermarried into the Ishmaelite Arab clan. We also know from the book of Jasher that Edom also mixed himself into the Children of Japheth, including the Ashkenazi Jews, the Sephardic Jews and Turkish/Kurdish Arabs. So over the last 2,000 years, the Black Arabs, the White Arabs and the Ashkenazi/Sephardic Jews were the main ones who were enslaving the Bantus "Negro" Israelite.

Genesis 36:2 "Esau took his wives of the daughters of Canaan; Adah the daughter of Elon the Hittite, and Aholibamah the daughter of Anah the daughter of Zibeon the Hivite; **and Bashemath Ishmael's daughter**, sister of Nebajoth."

Who would try to cut off Israel from being a nation?

Psalms 83:3-7 "They take crafty counsel against thy people, And consult together against thy hidden ones. **They have said, Come, and let us cut them off from being a nation; That the name of Israel may be no more in remembrance. For they have consulted together with one consent;** Against thee do they make a covenant: **The tents of Edom and the Ishmaelite's**; Moab, and the Hagarenes; Gebal, and Ammon, and Amalek; Philistia with the inhabitants of Tyre: Assyria also is joined with them; They have helped the children of Lot."

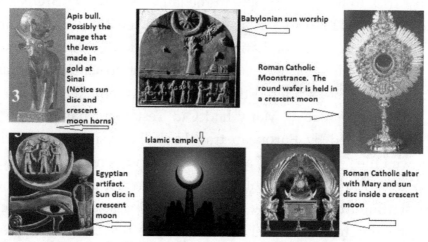

Has Satan infiltrated all the Major religions throughout time? The moon crescent was used to depict pagan gods or **Satan** in Canaanite, Babylonian, Egyptian, Christian and Islamic religions.

10. Both religions don't believe in the teachings of "**Water Baptism**" and "**Spirit Baptism (Holy Ghost)**" as taught by Yeshua HaMashiach to Nicodemus and others.   John 3:5 "Jesus answered, Verily, Verily, I say unto thee, Except a man be **BORN OF WATER AND OF THE SPIRIT**, he **CANNOT** enter into the kingdom of God."

CHAPTER 9

DON'T BE FOOLED BY THE CATHOLIC CHURCH

In the King James Bible it states:

Matthew 16:18 "And I say also unto thee, That thou are Peter, and **UPON THIS ROCK I WILL BUILD MY CHURCH**; and the gates of hell shall not prevail against it."

Many races across the world are devout Catholics. Why? Because of Slavery and colonization from the Europeans. Latinos, African-Americans, Africans, Chaldeans, Filipinos are some to name. The Catholic Missionaries made it their business to come into Africa to teach the people in the land **THEIR VERSION OF THE BIBLE AND CHRISTIANITY.** They also colonized, enslaved, killed and forced the Catholic Religion on ALL of Latin America which currently makes up 40% of Catholic Church followers today. However, prior to Christianity and Islam, the different African Tribes scattered throughout Africa already somehow knew about the Old Testament already. Many had Old Testament names (like Yosef, Yacub, Miriam) as witnessed by European travelers who visited the interiors of Africa. They followed the "**Mosaic law**" and the commandments. They rested on a certain day of the week four times a month, guided by the use of the 29-day Lunar cycle of the moon starting from the "**New Moon**" beginning at the first of each month. But the Catholic Church had another agenda for the Black (Israelite) people living in Africa. They had to change what the natives in Africa already knew about the Old Testament and then add the New Testaments teachings, but with a "**White Supremacy**" Europeanized twist. The first thing they had to do was establish the "**Whiteness**" of the Bible starting with Adam, Eve, Abraham, Jacob, the Children of Israel all the way down to Yeshua Mashiach (Jesus Christ). They had to do away with the Sabbath and force the slaves to forget their laws. They had to explain the Black Negro slaves' role in the bible as "**Cursed Canaanites**". The "Gentile" Europeans (Greeks, Romans etc.) had to write and insert themselves into the Bible using the Apocrypha Books with the mysterious appearance of the White Greek Jewish Maccabean family. Many of the Blacks in Africa bought this lie and continued to teach this to their children generation after generation. **So there we have the start of the Black Christian Church based on slavery, manipulated**

"White" Bible doctrines and lies. They used colonization to change the language of the "**Negroes**" and also used their "**Europeanized**" Religion to mentally brainwash the "Negro Slaves".   So if the whole Christian world believes this "**Europeanized version of the Bible**" to be true than how could anybody deny it or fight it? This is all the world knows. Especially if these false doctrines have been pounded into our brains day after day, month after month, year after year and century after century? But how do we know if the Catholic Church is teaching the right thing? How do we know if they are corrupt and are they leading us down the wrong path? It is a known fact that many Catholics, especially the clergy and Pope himself are involved in fraternal organizations or secret societies. These can also be called "**Occult (Hidden) Societies or Secret Societies**" Many Catholics are a part of **Freemasonry**, the **Rosicrucian's**, the **Jesuits** or the **Knight of Malta**. Many Africans admit to being converted to "Catholicism" by Catholic Missionaries only to be introduced by these Pastors/Bishops/Priests to the **Secret Rosicrucian sect**. Many Catholic Priests are a part of this secret society. It believes in "**enhancing**" your life for a small price. If members want to know what this price is than they are told to read some books; one of which is "**The Tragical History of the Life and Death of Doctor Faustus.**" Once they agree to join in, they start the "**Oaths**" followed by more satanic occultist teaching and education. Many people realize that after joining the Rosicrucian sect that it is not something that they want to be a part of. It doesn't sit well with their spirit. Some of these sects will ask you to willingly sell your soul to the devil (Lucifer). This is also seen in the Music and Movie Industry with many of our famous celebrities. Some even co-worship the Christian God with Allah (Chris-lam) as you will see later. This is the "**New Age Religious**" deception that is coming our way. It is a known fact that our current Pope Francis is a Jesuit and a Freemason. High Ranking Catholic clergyman **Hannibal Bugnini** was a Freemason and author of the 1962 **Novus Ordo Liturgy**. In the St. John Cantius Temple in Chicago, Illinois there is a Freemason-Satanic sign on the floor with the "**Chi-Ro**" symbol inside of a six-sided hexagram. If you do the research you will find out "**what**" and "**who**" is behind the Freemasons, Jesuits, and the Illuminati. You will be completely shocked if you can crack the code. **Note: (I break this down in my first book "Hebrews to Negroes").** So if this is true, is there is anything else we need to know about the Catholic Church? YES! The Catholic Church has 1.2

billion followers so it is important that the people know the deception they're getting into! So let's begin.

CHAPTER 10

WAS PETER THE FOUNDING ROCK OF THE CHURCH?

In the New Testament Greek Septuagint version Peter is called "**Petros**" and the word "**rock**" is called "**Petra**". So Yahusha (Jesus) said that upon himself he would build the church. It was not upon Peter, because Peter was not stable and unmovable like a rock. Peter was also never in Rome; it was Paul who was in Rome. Paul was an Apostle to the Gentile Romans and wrote the epistle of Romans. The word "**Petra**" occurs four times in the New Testament: Matt 12:18, Matt 27:60, 1 Corinthians 10:4, and 1 Peter 2:8. In Matt 27:60 "**Petras**" describes a large immovable mass of rock in which a tomb is carved out and it is also used as a reference to "**Christ**" in 1 Corinthians 10:4 and 1 Peter 2:8.

Peter was not stable and removable. Read Matt 14:29-30, Luke 22:57-58, Galatians 2:11,14.

Yeshua/God was referred to as a "**rock**" in Deuteronomy 32:4, 2 Samuel 22:2-3, Psalm 18:31, Isaiah 44:8 and Romans 9:33.

1 Corinthians 3:11 "For NO MAN can lay a foundation other than the one which is laid, which is Jesus Christ (Yeshua Mashiach).

This means **NO MAN** can be the "**Cornerstone**" for the Christian or Catholic Church because the Messiah, "**Yeshua HaMashiach**" has already laid this foundation down for this. The "**Cornerstone**" is the first foundation stone of a building.

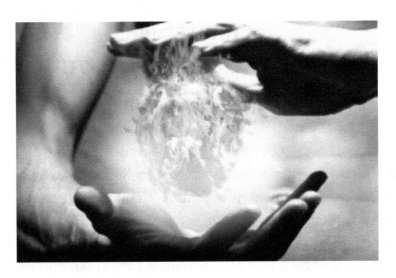

*In 2011 **Pope John Paul II** was accredited with his "first miracle" to become a saint. French nun **Marie Simon Pierre** (47 years old) was suffering from Parkinson's disease and could barely move her legs. Her symptoms mysteriously went away after she prayed to Pope John Paul II in 2011. Another miracle was accredited to Pope John Paul II in 2013 when a woman named **Floribeth Mora Diaz** of Costa Rica was cured of a brain aneurysm. Doctors told Floribeth that she only had one month to live so she began praying to a picture of the deceased Pope John Paul II with his arms outstretched on a magazine. She held the magazine close to her heart as she fell asleep and when she woke up she felt a deep sense of healing. She told her husband she was cured which was later confirmed by medical tests. Praying to a man or a woman for a miracle is a form of idol worship. Angels in the bible made it clear that man was not to worship them. This is not of God.*

Every Pope under the **"beatification"** and **"canonization"** process has to be declared **"venerable"**, then **"blessed"** to be named a **"Saint"**. Candidates for this process are required to have done **two miracles**. In Catholic theology, miracles are the proof of sainthood. Miracles are considered acts of divine intervention from God, so without two miracles, a Catholic Clergyman cannot be considered a "Saint". **Pope Francis so far has not performed not one full "True" credible miracle.** In 2015 in Naples, the Pope was credited with a "half-miracle" after St. Gennaro's (**Saint Januarius**) blood liquefied in his presence. The saint's blood is usually dry inside of its sealed glass ampule. However, after the pope kissed the relic, only half of it began to turn to liquid. Pope John Paul II is accredited with two so-called miracles; Pope John XXIII only did one. So how did he get "**Saint**" and "**Pope**" status? How can Pope Francis elevate anyone to "**Sainthood**" if his is not a "**Saint**" himself? According to the Washington Post in 2014, Pope Francis exercised his right to "**equipollent canonization**", which gave him the power to speed up the canonization and sainthood process for those Catholic Clergy who did not fulfill the "**two miracle**" rule. This is how the Catholic Church operates under the "**Doctrines of Man**". Man can set laws and change rules whenever he pleases because they obviously don't uphold the laws of God.

CHAPTER 11

DO CATHOLIC FREEMASONS ALSO WORSHIP ALLAH?

During the making of the original Book "**Hebrews to Negroes**", I had the chance to talk to an Elderly Catholic Priest about the Original Hebrew Israelites being black and not white. I showed him old quotes of historians who lived in the 1st century A.D. and pictures dating back to B.C. times of the Black Hebrew Israelites. I also showed him pictures of the Ancient Egyptian Pharaoh's who lived during the time of Moses.

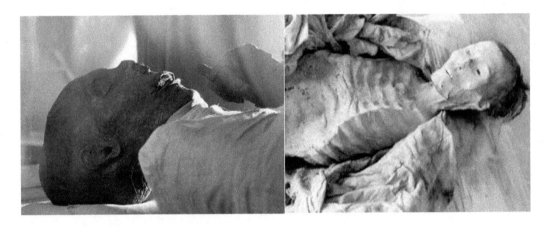

*(Left) Black Egyptian Mummy **Pharaoh Thutmoses III** (1485-1421 B.C.), (Right) White Mummy.*

The Catholic Priest was so blown away by the information I gave him that he wanted to meet me for lunch. I told him to give me his number but he insisted for my number. Two weeks later he called me for lunch. He wanted to meet me at a Polish restaurant in Downtown Detroit but I declined. He then offered lunch at a Jewish restaurant in West Bloomfield called "**Stage Deli**". I declined. I told him where I would meet him for lunch, on "**my terms**". I invited a Black Junior Pastor to come along just for back up and to be a witness to what was about to go down. When the Junior pastor and I arrived at our lunch location the Catholic Priest was running late. When he arrived he showed up with a cane and a slow limp. He almost couldn't even sit in the seat without help. As we were waiting to order, the Catholic Priest starts running down his credentials to me and the Junior pastor. He admitted that he was a **Scottish Rite Freemason, a Jesuit and a member of the Knights of Malta**. He admitted that he had been a Catholic Priest over a Church in Michigan for over 30 years. I asked him if he was a Rosicrucian and a Moslem Shriner and he smiled, laughing with a sinister chuckle. He never answered the question. I asked him what degree of Freemasonry was he and he still continued laughing. I told him that I had talked to many Freemasons from Europe, Belize, America, and even Black Freemasons. I explained they all admitted that a 32 degree Freemason could petition to become a **Moslem Shriner**. I expressed that in my discussions with these Freemasons they all said that "**Shriners**" call their god "**Allah**" and that they swear on the **Qur'an** instead of the **King James 1611 Bible**. They even sometimes greet each other by saying "**As-salamu alaykum**" which means "**May Allah's peace, mercy and blessing be upon you.**" I told the Catholic Priest from my talks with his Freemason brethren, they admitted that they were correctly called "**Moslem Shriners**". The complete name was "**The Ancient Arabic Nobles of the Mystic Shrine**". He never admitted this to be true, never denied it and he never admitted if he was in fact a "**Moslem Shriner**". Throughout the dinner he admitted to knowing the Bush Family personally, visiting Ethiopian Emperor Haile Selassie's palace as a youth (of note he had Lions there at his Palace) and knowing our current Pope Francis on a personal basis. He showed us pictures proving all of this. Then I showed him pictures of famous Blacks such as Sammy Davis Jr and Nelson Mandela with Knights of Malta robes on. I showed him pictures of Queen Elizabeth, the Rockefellers, Adolf Hitler, and former Italian Dictator Mussolini all wearing the Knights of Malta symbol. I told him that this symbol was also used in Ancient Egypt with the **Priests of Horus**. He was quiet. I asked him how one joins into the Knights of Malta. He didn't respond. I asked him how one joins into the Rosicrucian Sect and he didn't respond. I told him that I knew the truth about these organizations and that I wanted him to elaborate on his experiences and the secret organizations he was a part of. I told him who were the real Biblical Israelites (Jews) according to the Bible and who were the people today calling themselves "Jews" all across the world. I recited scriptures all from his Bible. All he did was chuckle. He then said that he had to use the bathroom because of complaints of a "weak bladder". I said, "Go right ahead". He asked our waiter where the bathroom was and as he got up he used his cane to help him with his balance. He walked slowly to the bathroom. The Junior Pastor and I talked about what the Priest was saying and within no time we noticed the Catholic Priest walking fast down the aisle from the bathroom "**WITHOUT HIS CANE!**" After seeing that, the Junior pastor was spooked. He told me he was ready to go and was worried that he was a sort of "**undercover agen**t". We ended the lunch, and the Catholic Priest asked if he could meet us again for lunch. We politely said, "No thank you." Most of the lunch the Catholic Priest did not answer my questions in regards to the Rosicrucian's, the Freemason, the Knights of Malta, the "Black Pope" or the "New World Order Agenda". He chuckled sinisterly at all the truth that was told to him, never denying it and on some occasions he acknowledged what I was asking him with a simple nod. The Moral of this story is that on the outside of the Catholic Church things may appear Benevolent but in the inner workings of these organizations there may be secret malevolent agendas and intentions.

FAMOUS KNIGHTS OF MALTA FREEMASONS
ADOLF HITLER, MUSSOLINI, BENEDICT XVI, THE QUEEN OF ENGLAND

CHAPTER 12

THE HIDDEN WORSHIP OF SATAN IN OCCULT SECRET SOCIETIES? WHERE AND WHEN DID IT START?

YESHUA said "And he said unto them, I beheld Satan as **LIGHTNING** fall from heaven. Heaven is also known as "**The Heights**" in the Bible. But here is where Kemetians (Egyptologists) are going to get mad. Freemasons all know that the Egyptian God **Set** is synonymous with Satan.

Fact: There are 77 names which pagans have used to refer to Satan over the centuries that are in the Satanic Bible as "**Infernal Names**" (*Satanic Bible, Anton LaVey, p. 144-146*).

"Hermes, the god of wisdom, is also called Thoth, Tat, Set, and Sat-an (Satan); and that he was, furthermore, when viewed under his bad aspect, Typhon the Egyptian Satan, who was also Set."(**Helena Petrovna Blavatsky, Isis Unveiled, Vol. 1. Science, New York, Trow's Printing and Bookbinding Company, 1877, p. 554, xxxiii.**

In 1975, there was a division in the **Church of Satan** formed by Ashkenazi Jew Anton LaVey and Michael Aquino. Many believe Michael Aquino wanted to run his own Satanic Organization on his own, while others say they had a difference on who was the literal "**Prince of Darkness**". In 1975, supposedly, Aquino invoked the "**Prince of Darkness**" as Satan, but the "Prince of Darkness" **answered** Aquino by the name of "**Set**". From this invocation, Aquino put together "**The Book of Coming Forth by Night**", a document that is said to have been inspired by the "Prince of Darkness" himself in his form as "**Set**". It is from this book that the "**Temple of Set**" was founded by Aquino. This Church/Temple was based on the belief that "Satan" or the "Christian Devil" was not a mere symbol as in the "Church of Satan" doctrine but as an actual being named "Set" from Ancient Egyptian Theology. Also, Aquino believed that Satan was not just a "**Fallen Angel**" that rebelled against God; but rather was originally the Ancient Egyptian god Set, whom Aquino and his associates defined as "The Principle of Isolate Intelligence". But it is also a known fact that Magician and Satanist "Aleister Crowley (1875-1947)" also considered the Christian Devil to be the Egyptian pagan god Set.

Crowley also gave "Set" the astrological properties of **Saturn**, which is used in Satanism, Witchcraft and Sorcery as the "**Talisman of Saturn (Satan)**". Satanists agree that Set was the "**Neter (i.e. god)**" who opposed peace, harmony and order in Egyptian theology. Meaning, Set was the rebel who initiated change and evolution by **sparking conflict, disorder and strife**. In this manner, "Set", "Satan", or the "Prince of Darkness" purposely "**stirs up chaos**" in order to control and deceive mankind. Set was associated with the color red and was called the "**Red Lord**". He was also associated with the infertile **desert regions** surrounding the fertile land of the Nile River (**just as the Devil is associated with tempting Jesus in the desert in the New Testament**).

So the trick of creating "**Chaos**" to seize the power of putting things back in order is a **New World Order** method of deception and manipulation. The Latin Motto: "**ORDO AB CHAO**" meaning "**order out of chaos**" is supposedly what the Jesuits use to promote their control and agendas. The Jesuits create "**dis-order**" so the people will demand "**order**". The price of "**order**" always involves the people (citizens of countries) handing over their freedom and control to a select group of individuals. So "**Out of chaos comes order**" which is "**Their Order**" or the "**New World Order**" under Satan and the Beast System. This philosophy has also been referred to as the **Hegelian Dialect** after the philosopher **Georg Hegel** who described it as: **THESIS – ANTI-THESIS – SYN-THESIS**. Other people have called this **PROBLEM – REACTION – SOLUTION**. This is how our daily news operates and how "**false flags**" on TV reveal to us the true meaning behind an "**event**". First you create the problem; then secondly you fan the flames to get a reaction; then thirdly you provide the solution. The solution is something you wanted to achieve in the first place, but wouldn't have been able to achieve under normal circumstances. This is how racial tensions erupt, civil wars start, World Wars start, regimes/dictators fall and how our economy has upturns or downturns.

CHAPTER 13

EGYPTIAN THEOLOGY AND ITS SATAN-INSPIRED PAGAN GODS IS NOT THE WAY!

So in Ancient Egyptian Theology **Set** is the God of **Darkness, Lightning/Thunder and chaos**. He was supposed to be the twin brother **AND EQUAL** of Horus. The Egyptians at one point were worshipping both of these pagan gods until **HORUS** defeated **SET** taking rulership of Set's Kingdom of Upper Egypt. Afterwards Set became the **Evil one**. Ironically, in Ancient Egyptian mythology the Gods Set and Horus have homosexual sex with each other in the "**Contending's of Horus and Set**" written in the first sixteen pages of the **Papyrus Chester Beatty I**. These writings are dated the Egyptian 20th Dynasty around 1188 B.C.-1069 B.C. So here we see **Set (Satan)** having sex with his twin brother/nephew **Horus**. Horus, Osiris and Set all come from the **Orion belt** which the Egyptians say their creator came from along with other civilizations.

Fact: Osiris per Egyptian mythology is the son of the earth god **Geb** and the sky goddess **Nut**. The first known use of the word "**Osiris**" is found in the religious Egyptian "**Pyramid Texts**" from the Old Kingdom. These texts were carved on the walls & sarcophagus of the Pyramids at Saqqara during the 5th and 6th Dynasties. They have dated these texts to 2400-2300 B.C. The "**Coffin Texts**" which are funeral spells are dated to 2100 B.C. Only the Pharaoh's and rich Egyptians had these funeral spells carved in their tomb areas. The Egyptian "Book of the Dead" consisted of texts and spells to help assist a dead person's journey through the underworld. It is dated from 1550 B.C. to 50 B.C. because over 1,000 years different Egyptian priests contributed to this piece of literary work. In the Book of Enoch, the Evil Fallen Angels or "**Watchers**" taught mankind how to do spells, enchantments, and magic. They also taught mankind astrology, the stars and the zodiac. This was the work of Lucifer and his demonic fallen angels.

Fact: The 200 fallen angels taught mankind forbidden knowledge. In the **Book of Enoch** it states that the fallen angel "**Armaros**" taught mankind enchantments and sorcery (magic). The fallen angel "**Baraqijal**" taught mankind Astrology and the fallen angel "**Kokabel**" taught mankind the constellations (Zodiac). This was not given to men by Yahuah (God).

The 42 Laws of Ma'at are a set of Laws which date back to 2400 B.C. These were laws the Egyptians had to fulfill in their lifetime. At death, an Egyptian had to make 42 Negative confessions such as "**I HAVE NOT** committed murder." "**Maat**", the goddess of Truth would judge the dead this way. Interesting enough though, the 42 Laws of Ma'at do not talk against Homosexuality or Beastiality, something that is common in the religious story of Horus and Set. Also in a Egyptian tomb established by two men (**Niankhkhnum and Khnumhotep**) it reveals that homosexuality was possibly common among the Egyptian priesthood (like the Catholic Church?). The tombs of these priests depict two men holding hands, embracing each other and another scene it depicts two men in typical female/male positions. Even in the Pyramid Texts it talks about how the Sun God Ra masturbated his children into existence.

Pyramid Text 1248-49 - "Atum (in the form of Ra) is he who masturbated in On (city of Egypt). He took his phallus in his grasp that he might create orgasm by means of it, and so were both born the twins Shu and Tefnut."

But what about Horus and Set?

The Contending's of Horus and Set (1188-1069 B.C.) written on Chester Beatty Papyrus I, XX Dynasty - "Then Set said to Horus: "Come, let us have a feast day at my house." And Horus said to him: "I will, I will." Now when evening had come, a bed was prepared for them, and **THEY LAY DOWN TOGETHER**. At night, Set let his member (penis) become stiff, and he inserted it between the thighs of Horus. And Horus placed his hand between his thighs and caught the semen of Set.

In the "**Contending's of Horus and Set**", after Osiris' death, while Horus was growing up and planning his own revenge, Set and Horus engaged in a homosexual relationship. In one part of the myth, Set proclaimed to Horus, "**How lovely your backside (behind) is.**" Informing his mother Isis about his uncle's behavior, Horus is told to catch Set's semen instead of becoming impregnated by the murderer of his father. Set, in doing so, was planning on humiliating Horus by showing the gods that Horus would be filled with someone else's semen. Then Horus and Isis stage a plan to impregnate Set with Horus' semen by ejaculating into a jar and then spreading it on some lettuce for Set to eat, which he does becoming the laughing stock of the Egyptian gods.

42 Principles of Ma'at

1. I have not done iniquity.
2. I have not robbed with violence.
3. I have not stolen.
4. I have done no murder; I have done no harm.
5. I have not defrauded offerings.
6. I have not diminished obligations.
7. I have not plundered the neteru.
8. I have not spoken lies.
9. I have not uttered evil words.
10. I have not caused pain.
11. I have not committed fornication.
12. I have not caused shedding of tears.
13. I have not dealt deceitfully.
14. I have not transgressed.
15. I have not acted guilefully.
16. I have not laid waste the ploughed land.
17. I have not been an eavesdropper.
18. I have not set my lips in motion (against any man).
19. I have not been angry and wrathful except for a just cause.
20. I have not defiled the wife of any man.
21. I have not been a man of anger.
22. I have not polluted myself.
23. I have not caused terror.
24. I have not burned with rage.
25. I have not stopped my ears against the words of Right and Truth.
26. I have not worked grief.
27. I have not acted with insolence.
28. I have not stirred up strife.
29. I have not judged hastily.
30. I have not sought for distinctions.
31. I have not multiplied words exceedingly.
32. I have not done neither harm nor ill.
33. I have not cursed the King. (i.e. violation of laws)
34. I have not fouled the water.
35. I have not spoken scornfully.
36. I have never cursed the neteru.
37. I have not stolen.
38. I have not defrauded the offerings of the neteru.
39. I have not plundered the offerings of the blessed dead.
40. I have not filched the food of the infant.
41. I have not sinned against the neter of my native town.
42. I have not slaughtered with evil intent the cattle of the neter.

In the 42 Principles of Ma'at you will not have any "Principle" that is against homosexuality or beastiality. Why?

So we also find that many Egyptologists and Kemetians believe Christianity is a copycat off of the Egyptian Religion. The believe that the 42 laws of Ma'at is the basis of the 10 Commandments and since they claim it was written 2,000 years before Moses got the 10 Commandments that the bible is nothing other than a plagiarized book. They claim the Egyptians are older than all civilizations and Osiris is older than the God of the Hebrews, including Noah. Let's break this down for one-time sake.

The first mention of Osiris is around 2400-2300 B.C. The Exodus with Moses is reported by many Egyptologists to happen during 1450 B.C. There are 4 generations from Levi to Moses. **This is Levi, Kothath, Amram and Moses.** Levi was 42 years old when he came into Egypt and he lived there 94 years (Exodus 6:16). Levi died at age 137. Kothath the son of Levi lived 133 years (1 Chronicles 6:1-3, Exodus 6:16-18). Amram, the son of Kohath and the father of Moses lived for 137 years (Exodus 16:16-20). Moses was 120 years old when he died in the land of Moab (Jordan) according to Deuteronomy 34:7. Isaac lived 180 years (Genesis 35:28) and Jacob lived for 147 years (Genesis 47:28).

So here we have at least 400 to 430 years that the Israelites staying in Egypt before leaving in 1450 B.C. This would bring Levi's date of entering Egypt with Joseph at about **1850-1880 B.C**. Abraham was 100 years old when he had Isaac (Genesis 21:5). Isaac was 60 years old (Genesis 25:26) when he had Jacob and Jacob was presumed to be 74-90 years old when he had Joseph. **So here we have a minimum of 234 years that passed from Abraham to Joseph's birth**. If we add **234 years** to **1880 B.C.** we get **2111 B.C**. Now Noah lived 950 years according to **Genesis 9:29**. Noah lived long enough to see Abraham and to teach Abraham about Yahuah (the Creator). This is recorded in the Book of Jasher, which Joshua references in **Joshua 10:13**.

Book of Jasher 9:5-6 "And when **Abram** came out from the cave, he went to **Noah** and his son **Shem**, and he remained with them **TO LEARN THE INSTRUCTION OF THE LORD AND HIS WAYS**, and no man knew where Abram was, and Abram served Noah and Shem his son for a long time. **And Abram was in Noah's house thirty-nine years, and Abram knew the Lord from three years old, and he went in the ways of the Lord until the day of his death, as Noah and his son Shem had taught him.**"

So moving along, if we add 950 years of Noah's life to 2111 B.C. we get a timeline of **3,061 B.C.!** This is 500-700 years before the first appearance of the word "**Osiris**" in Ancient Egyptian writings. So we all know that Noah was not calling God "**Osiris**", "**Isis**" or "**Horus**". We all know that the Great Flood (Deluge) happened because it is written on Ancient Sumerian Tablets and is talked about by many civilizations all over the world. We even have archaeological proof that a Great Flood causing a world-wide mass die off with findings of whale bones in the desert, and fish bones embedded in the tops of mountains. They have even found perfectly preserved Dinosaur eggs! But it gets even deeper! There are 10 generations and roughly 1100 years of timeline from Adam to Noah. So if you add 1100 years to 3,061 B.C. you get 4,161 B.C. Wow! Now remember "**Osiris**" wasn't even a word in Egypt until 2300 B.C. This is almost a 2,000 year difference in the past. But Seth was the son of Adam. Seth and his son Enosh prior to 3500 B.C. were already calling God's name "**Yahuah**" according to the Hebrew Torah.

Genesis 4:26 "And to Seth, to him also there was born a son; and he called his name Enos(h): **then began men to call upon the name of the Lord (Yahuah).**

וּלְשֵׁת גַּם-הוּא יֻלַּד-בֵּן, וַיִּקְרָא אֶת-שְׁמוֹ אֱנוֹשׁ; אָז הוּחַל, לִקְרֹא בְּשֵׁם יְהוָה.

Above: Genesis 4:26 (Hebrew-Mechon-Mamre Tanakh)

Hebrew reads from Right to Left so if you look closely at the last Hebrew word on the Left you will see that the name "**Lord**" is actually the "**Tetragrammaton**", aka the 4 Hebrew Letters "**Yod-Hey-Uau-Hey**" or "**Yahuah**". There is no "**Osiris**", "**Horus**" or "**Amun-Ra**" here folks.

(Above Right) Actual Egyptian Chariot wheels found at the bottom of the Red Sea in 1978. Who says the Exodus didn't happen? This 4-spoked Chariot Wheel was classic in the **Eighteenth Egyptian Dynasty, which was the same Egyptian Dynasty that Pharaoh's Thutmoses I, II, III and Amenhotep II witnessed Moses grow up to be a man, later leaving Egypt to conquer Canaan with his assistant Joshua (Yehoshua). (Above Left) Pharaoh Amenhotep II** in target practice mode with bows/arrows while riding his Chariot with **4-spoked wheels!**

Exodus 14:25 "And took of their **Chariot wheels**, that they drave them heavily: so that the Egyptians said, Let us flee from the face of Israel; for the Lord fighteth for them against the Egyptians."

Note: Many Blacks today are falling back into worshipping the pagan gods of Egypt that God delivered our forefathers from. They claim that there is no proof of Moses, Joshua, King Saul, King David, King Solomon and the Kings of Israel/Judah. For this reason they also say that Yahusha (Jesus) didn't exist and that the Bible is made up, plagiarized, and copied from Ancient Egyptian theology. They are blinded by Satan (Set). **The Egyptian-Canaanite Amarna Letters #286-288 proves them to be false.** According to the Bible, which Kemetians/Egyptologists don't believe, Joshua led the Israelites into Canaan & began taking over cities. Joshua first appeared in the Bible as Moses' assistant when he was going to send forth a military campaign to fight the Amalekites (Edomite's). They knew who the God of Israel was because they were Semitic, being the sons of Jacob. In the Bible it says that Joshua never lost a battle as he was victorious in taking over many Canaanite cites, with their Kings included. In one of the **Amarna Letters** a man named "**Shuwadata, governor of Gath**" makes mention of the "**Chief of the Habiru (Hebrews)**". This was a reference to Joshua because Moses died in the land of Moab (Jordan). The Canaanite-Egyptian letter reads: "**May the King, my lord, know that the "Chief of the Habiru" has invaded the lands which your god has given me; but I have attacked him. Also let the king, my lord, know that none of my allies have come to my aid, it is only I and Abdi-Heba who fight against the "Habiru Chief".** Shurwardata, the governor of the Canaanite/Philistine city of Gath is also mentioned in an Amarna letter to **Milkilu**, a Prince of the Canaanite city "Gezer".

In the **Armana Letter #271** it confirms this as it reads: "**Let it be known to the king that there is great hostility against me and against Shuwardata. I ask the king, my lord, protect his lands from the approaching Habiru**". The Canaanite governor of Jerusalem **Abdi-Hebab** wrote a letter to Pharaoh Amenhotep II for help from the invading Hebrews. In **Joshua 10:1-5** it talks about Abdi-Hebab, whose title name by the Hebrews was **Adoni-Zedek**. Why? Because **Melchi-Zedek** was the **Prince of Salem (Jerusalem)** in Genesis 14:18 during the times of Abraham. Therefore Adoni-Zek was the Lord-King of Salem. Abdi-Hebab tried to get help from other neighboring Canaanite governors but they were all defeated by Joshua.

Abdi out of desperation asked Pharaoh Amenhotep II for help. The Egyptians in Ancient times ruled over the Canaanites, similar to how the Romans ruled over Judea but allowed the Edomite Herodian family to be Kings of certain districts. The **Amarna Letter #286** directed to Pharaoh Amenhotep II reads: **"Why do you not hear my call for help? All the governors are lost (because Joshua had killed them all Joshua 10:26): the king, my lord, does not have a single governor remaining! Let the King (Amenhotep II) send troops and archers, or the King will have no lands left. All the Lands of the King are being plundered by the Habiru (Hebrews)."**

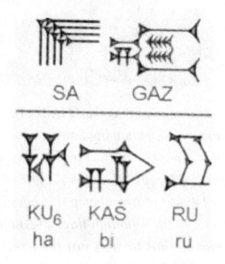

SA   GAZ

KU₆ KAŚ RU
ha   bi   ru

This was the Assyrian-Babylonian Cuneiform script used Ancient B.C. times before Aramaic even existed. The Assyrians and Babylonians knew about the Israelites in the land of Canaan from word of mouth in Mesopotamia/Levant. They too called the Israelites the "Habiru" which is the name for the English word "Hebrews". It is a known fact that the European Spaniards called the Taino mountain dwelling natives of Puerto Rico "Jibaro".
In Spanish when using the "H" sound pronunciation for the letter "J" as in the word "Jesus" (which sounds like Hay-Zeus) to pronounce "Jabiro" you get something similar in sound to "Habiru". Maybe the Spaniards tried their best to pronounce what the "Taino Indians" were calling themselves which had to have sounded like "Habiru". There has been stones found in Puerto Rico, predating the Spaniards that have Ancient Paleo-Hebrew inscriptions on them. How could this be? Many Bible scholars believe the Taino Indians who dwelt in Puerto Rico were descendants of the 10 Lost Tribes of Israel.

The Assyrian/Babylonian Cuneiform script also when translated refers to the Hebrews as "**Habiru**" or "**Ibiru**". Why? Because Hebrew Strong's **#5680** lists "**Eber**" the father of the Hebrews as "**Ibri**" which is another name for an Israelite. So after the Israelites left with Moses at the command of **Pharaoh Thutmoses III** to go, the next Pharaoh that came in line was **Amenhotep II of the 18th Dynasty**.

(Above) "Amenemhat I". Amenemhat was the "Firstborn" son of **Thutmoses III**. *He mysteriously died without anyone really knowing how he died and thus Thutmoses III's son,* **Amenhotep II** *took the throne. Could he be the Firstborn son of the Pharaoh of the Exodus that died in "Tenth Plague" of Egypt" (Exodus 12:29)? But wait! On the Egyptian "Dream Stela" of Thutmoses IV, son of Amenhotep II, we find out that* **Thutmoses IV was also** *not the legitimate successor to the Egyptian throne –***Ancient Near-Eastern Texts, p. 449, J.B. Pritchard. This means that he was not the firstborn son of Amenhotep II!**

Nobody knows what happened to Amenhotep II's firstborn son either? It is said that in Thutmoses III's final years, he co-ruled with his son Amenhotep II. So which one was the firstborn son that died? Or maybe it was **both** *of their firstborn sons that mysteriously died if they both had firstborn sons during the time of the "***Tenth Plague***" of Egypt.* **WOW!** *The bible discusses this in Exodus 12. We also know that the Army of Amenhotep II was very weak and limited during his military campaigns in the Syria and other places. Could this be because half of his "***Egyptian Army***" was washed up in the Red Sea?*

In more Amarna Letters, it says that the Pharaoh of the land had conquered the Land of Aram-Naharaim (**Syria/Assyria**) & the Land of Cush (**Nubia**) which would point to Amenhotep II because he did lead military campaigns against these countries.

Book of Jubilees 9:5 *"And for **Aram** there came forth the fourth position, all the land of Mesopotamia (**Aram-Naharaim**) between the Tigris and the Euphrates to the North of the Chaldeans to the border of the mountains of Asshur and the land of Arara".* **The Chaldeans were from the land of Ur, south of the Euphrates."**

In the bible in **Genesis 11:31**, *"Naharaim"* is referred to in Hebrew as *"**Haran**"*, which is the place of Ancient Aram or modern day Syria. The Chaldeans lived southeast of Haran. **It is said that Abraham's wife was a Syrian.** We know that the Syrians back in Biblical times were black-brown skinned people because in **2 Kings 5:1-19**, **Naaman**, the Commander of the army of the King of Aram (Syria) had his **complexion** restored after being told by Elisha to wash his body in the Jordan River seven times. In 100 A.D. there is an art picture of a Syrian labeled *"**Scene of a sacrifice by Conon and his family**"*. It is from the **Temple of Bel, Dura Europos which is in Syria**. This art piece is in the **Damascus National Museum**. It shows the Syrians to all be black-brown skinned peoples. The Syrians today are white skinned Arab peoples, some with blue eyes looking no different than European Caucasians.

(Above-From left to right) This is a relief picture of a Libyan (Phut), a Canaanite, a Syrian (Aram) and a Nubian (Cush) bowing to the Pharaoh of Egypt during the 18th Dynasty. Pharaoh Amenhotep II (1450-1425B.C.) was the 7th king of the 18th Egyptian Dynasty. His father Thutmoses III had conquered Setet (Nubia), Kush, and Canaan. He then had one of his sons (**many say his firstborn son Amenemhat**) go into Syria to try to conquer them but his son mysteriously died around the time the 10th Plague of God were upon Egypt during the time of Moses. His other son took over as Amenhotep II took over later as Pharaoh of Egypt and continued his father's duty of leading military campaigns to Syria in which he was successful. This Ancient 3,500 old relief (in color) shows that the Libyans, Canaanites, Syrians (Arameans) and Nubians Kushites were all people of brown skin color, not white. This means Abraham's Syrian wife Sarah and his son Isaac were black. It also means that Ishmael, and the sons of Keturah were also people of color, not the white skinned Arabs we see today.

Amarna Letter#288 - "The arm of the mighty king conquers the land of **Aram-Naharaim** (Modern day Syria) and the **Land of Cush**, and now the **Habiru** have captured the cities of the King (Amenhotep). Behold, Zimreda, the townsmen of **Lachish** have smitten him, **SLAVES WHO HAD BECOME HABIRU**." So in the Canaanite-Egyptian Amarna Letters it describes how Joshua captures the Canaanite cities under the Pharaoh's rule. He also conquers the Canaanite city of Lachish with the King. This is supported also in the Bible.

Joshua 10:22-24 "Then said Joshua, Open the mouth of the cave, and bring out those five (Canaanite) kings unto me out of the cave. And they did so, and brought forth those five kings unto him out of the cave, the **King of Jerusalem**, the **King of Hebron**, the **King of Jarmuth**, the **king of Lachish**, and the **king of Eglon**. And it came to pass, when they brought out those kings unto Joshua, that Joshua called for all the men of Israel, and said unto the captains of the men of war which went with him, Come near, put your feet upon the necks of these kings. And they came near, and put their feet upon the necks of them."

Amarna Tablet #287 "From Abdi-Heba, mayor of Jerusalem to king Pharaoh: They are attempting to take Jerusalem. Pharaoh has placed his name in Jerusalem forever, he cannot abandon the land of Jerusalem." **Gezer**, **Ashkelon**, and **Lachish** have given oil, food & supplies to the **Habiru.**"

Amarna Tablet #271 "From Milkili, mayor of **Gezer.** King, the war against me and Shuwardata, mayor of Hebron is severe, save your land from the **POWER OF THE HABIRU.**"

Amarna Tablet #284 "From Shuwardata, mayor of **Hebron**: I fall before you 7 times on my tummy, 7 times on my back to worship you O Pharaoh, my lord. All your lands have been taken away. I am all alone."

Amarna Tablet #329 "To the king, my lord, my god, my sun, the Sun from the sky: Message of Zimreddi, mayor of **Lachish**, your servant, the dirt at the kings feet. You sent a messenger to me and I am making preparation in strict accordance with his order."

Kemetians don't get that Joshua didn't link up with Moses until after they had crossed the Red Sea & had to fight the Amalekites. So of course the Pharaoh wouldn't write about him, but the Canaanites did. They knew him as the "**Chief of the Habiru**". The Hebrews were slaves in Egypt so why would anybody know their names? The Egyptians didn't know who he was just as the Canaanites had no clue who was conquering all their cities one by one. If Joshua was real then we must also conclude that Moses was real.

In **Amarna Tablet #284 and #329** it shows how the Canaanite/Egyptian people worshipped the Pharaoh (a man) and also worshipped the Sun. These are all the "**creations**" of the Creator and are therefore forms of pagan idolatry worship. Here is even more proof that Satan started the Egyptian Religion to get the sons of Mizraim to worship false gods instead of the Creator and the God of their father Noah.

Artefact Found in Mana Ecuador
Klaus Dona
Strange Archeology
PHOTO

This stone pyramid was found in the 1980s in the jungles of Ecuador, along with other artifacts referred to as "**La Mana artifacts**". The stone is black and white, with thirteen levels of a brick pyramid engraved into it. There is also an eye that glows with UV light at the top of the pyramid. They also found a small artifact depicting a Cobra, which his native in India and Africa. The Cobra was also the Royal symbol of Egypt.

The Dots on the Bottom of the Pyramid make up the Orion Constellation, the same place the Egyptian deity **Osiris** and **Horus** come from in Egyptian Mythology. The symbols above the dots signifying the **Orion Belt Constellation** are **pre-Archaic Sanskrit**. It was supposedly translated by German linguist Kurt Schildmann. Before seeing this, linguistics considered Sanskrit was considered to be the oldest written language which is similar to India's Hindi (Tamil/Dravidian) language. The translation of these symbols on the bottom of the stone pyramid artifact is:

"The Son of the Creator Comes From Here.."

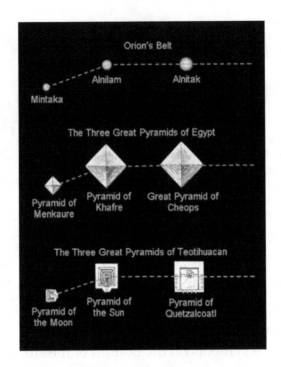

The 3 dots on the base of the **La Mana artifact Pyramid** match up perfectly with the **Orion Belt constellation**. Mysteriously the Orion Belt constellation is also in alignment with the **Pyramids of Giza** (Egypt), the **Pyramids of Teotihuacan** (Mexico) and also supposedly the **Pyramids of Cochasqui** (Ecuador). They are all situated parallel to the Equator so that these civilizations could celebrate the solstices and equinoxes on the exact same day. Satan is very tricky and deceitful in making mankind worship the **snake, sun, moon and stars**. These were all things the Most High commanded the Children of Israel not to do.

Isaiah 14:13-14 "For thou hast said in thine heart, I will ascend into heaven, I will exalt my throne above the stars of God: I will sit also upon the mount of the congregation, in the sides of the north: **I WILL ASCEND ABOVE THE HEIGHTS OF THE CLOUDS; I WILL BE LIKE THE MOST HIGH.**"- This is what Lucifer's goal is.

Luke 10:18 (words of Yeshua) "And he said unto them, I beheld **Satan as Lightning fall from heaven**".

So based on the writing on the bottom of the La Mana Artifact it seems that Satan is telling the Egyptian people and other civilizations that he is their **"Creator"** just as he aspires to do as witnessed in **Isaiah 14:13-14**. But we know that **SETH**, **ENOS**, **ENOCH**, **NOAH** and **SHEM** knew who their creator was before Ham's son **Mizraim** (Kemet/EGYPT) was born. Many civilizations were tricked to worship Satan and his pagan **lightning** gods. **BAAL-Hadad** (Canaan), **Zeus** (GREEK), **Thor** (Norse), **Jupiter** (Romans), **Shango** (Nigeria) and it continues today. Lady Gaga, David Bowie, Madonna, ACDC, KISS, Cassie, Justin Timberlake, Jaden smith, Amy Winehouse, Adolfo Hitler, Black Sabbath, Marilyn Manson, Grateful Dead, Harry Potter, the Simpsons, Power Rangers, Gatorade, Selena Gomez (**Jesus saves t shirt with lightning bolt and all-seeing eye**), Nickelodeon, and Anton LaVey all show their Lucifer lightning bolt with or without the Satanic Pentagram. And the list goes on.... folks the Lightning bolt and the Lightning Pentagram is the new symbol of Satan. It's on Clothes, earrings, Tattoos and in advertisements. Even the name "Barack (Baraq)" means "**Lighting**" in Aramaic [**#H1299/H1300** "Baraq"] and [**#H1116** Bamah] means "**Heights/Heavens**". Adding in an Aramaic conjunction letter "**U**" or "**O**", you get the words in Aramaic for "**Lighting from the Heights/Heaven**" as "**Baraq O/U Bamah**".

CHAPTER 14

WAHHABISM? WHAT IS THAT?

The founding fathers of Freemasonry (Manly P. Hall, Albert Pike, Aleister Crowley, Alice Bailey, Helen Blavatsky) all refer to their "**god**" as **Shatan, Set, Satan and Lucifer**. Lucifer is the grand architect to this great deception. Many theorists say that Islamic terrorist groups like **ISIS** are controlled by outside non-Muslim governments while operating under the "**cloak**" of Sunni Islam. They are no different than other Secret Societies; **they are masters of deception**. Many say they are followers of **Wahhabism** (Salafis), which is supposedly a **Masonic Creation**. Could this be possible especially since there are many known documented Masonic lodges throughout the Middle East, even in Israel? Saudi Arabia, Oman and the United Arab Emirates are strong followers of Wahhabism which is supposed to be a pure, untampered and fundamentally correct form of Islam, not like other sects. This is why the Sunni/Sufi Muslims & **ISIS** are against the Shiite Muslims. That's why Shiite Muslims speak out against America and the Masonic Deception. Freemason Agents back in the day wanted to destroy the Ottoman Empire, so they could orchestrate their great deception. Freemason agents successfully radicalized a man named **Muhammad Ibn Abd Al -Wahhab** (1703-1792 A.D.) who created "Wahhabism."

Muhammad Ibn Abd Al-Wahhab (1700's)

Muhammad Al-Wahhab wanted reform in the Islamic world. He believed that many Muslims were not "**Real Muslims**" or followers of "**Allah**" because of religious practices they were doing that were not ordained by "**Allah**". He believed those who would not conform to his views should be killed, their wives and daughters violated, and their possessions confiscated." Wahhab demanded conformity which was to be demonstrated in physical and tangible ways. He believed that all Muslims must individually pledge their allegiance to a single Muslim leader or a Caliphate. Abd al-Wahhab's views were considered "**ultra-radical**" and it eventually led to his expulsion from his own town. In the mid-1700's he found refuge in the Saudi "**Ibn Saud**" family and their tribe. Since then, the Islamic world has been in turmoil with the Sunni's fighting the Shiites. With the creation of Radical Islam/Wahhabism the Saudi's with the "**Wahhabism doctrine**" were able to orchestrate the **Ottoman - Wahhabi War/Ottoman - Saudi/Salafi War** in the 1800's which in time helped created the First Saudi State which the Freemasons needed! The Rockefeller and Rothschild family had a hand in finding a loophole in the Islam religion, the Muslim Arabs and the Ottoman Empire. A British spy (Intelligence Agent) by the name of Mr. Hempher was sent to mislead the Wahhabism founder to gain access into the Islamic Arab world to destroy Islam from within using "**divide and conquer**" techniques. The British would be the "**Puppet Master**" of Islamic Terrorism and would insert people into various positions as puppets to start "**terrorism**" acts called "**jihad**" in the name of Islam. The British, under the control of the Elite Jewish money changers used mind control programs like the **CIA's MK-ULTRA** (started by Nazi psychologists) to brainwash civilians and military personnel for perfect spies or leaders of Terrorist organizations such as the Taliban, Al-Qaeda and ISIS. Like the "**Manchurian Candidate**" and "**Bourne Identity**", intelligence organizations (**CIA**) were supposedly reported to have used different forms of torture to form a dissociative state in the victim who would ultimately develop different personalities and identities for different missions, (**Mission Impossible, Bourne Identity**) with none of the personalities knowing what the other was programmed for or had achieved using the same body. The British used their mysterious British agent called **Mr. Hempher** to internally create chaos in the Islamic world. Mr. Hempher was mentioned in a Turkish work called "**Mir'at al-Haramain**", by Ayyub Sabri Pasha between 1933-1938. The details of this diabolical conspiracy was outlined in the "**Memoirs of Mr. Hempher: The British spy to the Middle East**" published in the German paper "**Spiegel**" and later in a prominent French paper. The Wahhabi movement could not have been successful if it wasn't for the cooperation of the Saudi Family who many claim are descendants of Judaism converts from Ottoman Iraq. The Rothschild and the Saudi Family scratch each other's back with the "**Petrodollar**" connection. How so? The Rothschild family has all the money and gold while the Saudi Family has all the oil. This helps keep the Petrodollar dominance going. Saudi Arabia is also vital for tempering down other Arab Countries when they start getting angry and hostile towards Israel, their secret ally. In return America subsidizes (**provides monetary contributions**) for up to 80 percent of all the Islamic Mosques in the country and it uses the Media to get other Arab countries to fight each other, most notably for the shift of regimes that favor the placement of Wabbhaism/Sunni leaders. This was partly the reason for the removal of Saddam Hussein, Muammar Qaddafi and the "**cleanse/removal**" of long-standing Arab leaders in the North Africa during "**Arab Spring (2010)**".

It is a known fact that in 1999 King Fahd of Saudi Arabia along with Yasser Arafat and the Pope attended the Bilderberg meeting, presumably to discuss their roles in the interests of World Government. Ultimately the Bilderberg group is a part of the Freemason-Illuminati network along with United States, Europe and Israel. The Illuminati's motto is "**Create order out of chaos**" and "**The end justifies the means**". They were the co-conspirators and main players in starting World War I, World War II and they will be the cause of World War III. But the key country to focus on is "**Iran**". Iran is mostly Shia Muslims and they are one of a few countries that are not controlled by a Jewish Central Bank (**IMF, World Bank, Federal Reserve, Bank of London**). In Iran they also have Iranian Judaism converts and Iranian Shiite Muslims who live in harmony with one another. In addition the Iranian Jews **have not** all returned to Israel (**which should raise a red-flag**). The Iranians, like their former President Mahmoud Ahmadinejad know the Masonic Agenda and they know the Israel-United States-Wabbhaism Agenda for world dominance, the building of the Third Temple in Jerusalem, the arrival of the Christian Antichrist (Muslim dajjal) and the implementation of the "**New World Order**" and the "**Beast System**". The Freemasons and Illuminati, by infiltrating Wabbhaism have undermined the Sunni Muslims into doing the dirty work for their Satanic Agenda. The Illuminati, by promoting and funding Muslim Terror Groups like Al-Qaeda, Hamas and ISIS are setting up the stage for their One World Government for Total domination. By portraying "**Iran**" as the enemy with "**Nuclear Weapons**" and by using tactics like "**Sanctions**", "**Nuclear Plant Inspections**" or "**false flag attacks**" on other countries (Israel, Iraq) to justify attacking Iran (using our media), the stage for World War III is slowly being set up. This way the United States, Israel and the Vatican (Pope) can promote a Religious war (Muslim Arabs vs Israel) or they can sit everybody down for a 7-year peace treaty that will set the stage for the Antichrist.

"The Sunni Muslim is very much anti-Shiite, and very much anti-, anti-, anti-
Iran….Look, Iran is a **HUGE THREAT**, historically speaking," he said. "The
Persian empire was always against the Muslim Arab Empire, especially the Sunni's.
The treat is from Persia, not from Israel. This was a great empire ruling the whole
neighborhood. I'll tell you something…they are in Bahrain, they are in Iraq, they
are in Syria, they are with Hezbollah in Lebanon and Hamas, which is Sunni, in
Gaza. They are intruding into these areas. King Abdullah of Jordan had a good

statement on this...he said that a Shiite crescent begins from Iran, through Iraq, Syria, Lebanon and goes down to Palestine, to Hamas."

Prince Al Waleed bin Talal bin Abdulaziz Al-Saud

If we really think about it, this is why Satan/Lucifer gave Albert Pike the Vision of the 3 World Wars! So in end what percentages of Sunni/Salafi Muslims actually follow the teachings of Wahhabism, which is a Masonic creation and according to many the extension of Freemasonry into the Middle East.

Fact: According to Islam there are minor signs and major signs that herald the "**End times**".   It is interesting that in Islam, there can be prophecies about the "**Synagogue of Satan**" aka "**Gog & Magog**" drinking up the water in the "**Sea of Galilee**" and also other prophecies that have to do with things "**evil**" and "**Satanic**". We all know that things are going to get worse in the "**Last Days**" but if everything that is going to happen is linked with something bad or a people that is deceitful than does this mean than the god controlling the inner core of Islam is behind all of this "**negative**" **stuff**? Could this be "The end justifies the means" type of philosophy? The Devil creates "**problems**" in the world which is based on "**evil**", therefore allowing himself to be able to tell his devout followers that these things are prophecy.   Satan and his angels are very intelligent but if you have the ability to create problems you can pose the belief to the world that you have the ability to prophecy these bad events. You be the judge based on reading these Islamic "**minor**" and "**major**" prophecies that would foretell signs that would happen in the last days prior to the coming of the Messiah:

ISLAMIC MINOR PROPHECIES

- Women would regularly dress wearing revealing clothes rather than modestly.
- Men would dress like women and women would dress like men (Transgender).
- Homosexuality and lesbianism will increase in the world. Social acceptance and "legal protection" for this sexual perversion would gain ground in the world (ex. America).

- People who are against Homosexuals would be "demonized" and labeled with the term/disease called "Homophobia".
- More children would be born out of wedlock. Marriage would be less popular in society.
- Fornication and adultery will increase.
- Single women would outnumber single men. There will be a disproportion in the balance of men wanting women and women wanting men. Women will find themselves wanting a man more than a man finds himself wanting a woman. (**ex. Decrease in testosterone and sperm production from obesity, lack of exercise, alcohol, drugs, environmental pollution and genetically modified foods – GMO**).
- There will be an increase in the consumption of Alcohol and Wine.
- Religious knowledge will disappear.
- Time will move faster as people are busier working and paying bills.
- Random killing, murder and violence will increase all around the world.
- Universal consumption of money lent on interest and credit will increase. The "Banking System" will take control over our lives, cities, states and countries.
- Surrogacy will increase (ex. India, America).
- Increase in issues in Saudi Arabia, possible Nuclear Attack with three countries involved (Israel, Saudi Arabia, Iran).
- The rise of an Great Imam (Islamic Teacher).
- The rise of a Great Islamic Caliphate heralded by a Black Flag (i.e. ISIS).

ISLAMIC MAJOR SIGNS

- Smoke in Saudi Arabia (? Oil fields burning from missile bombing)
- Dajjal (The False Messiah or The Antichrist) will rise, born of (Gentile) Jewish Parents to rule over Israel.
- The Beast (some Muslims believe this is the imposter State of Israel) will come into existence.
- The Sun will rise from the West and set in the East.
- The descent of Yahusha Mashiach (Jesus Christ).
- Gog and Magog battle (Ashkenazi Jews).

- The sinking of the earth in three places. One in the east, one in the west and one in Arabia at the end of which "fire" would burn in Yemen and would drive people to their place of judgement.
- A Great Earthquake.

But here is the odd thing. Satan is very tricky. In Islamic prophecy it talks about the European Ashkenazi Jews obtaining the State of Israel in 1948 under the Rothschild purchase deal so that "someone" could build the Third Temple for the Antichrist. Who else in the world would fulfill bible prophecy by building a Third Temple in Jerusalem? It has to be a people that believe they are "Jews". These people are labeled "Gog (Gomer) and Magog", which is their Ancient inheritance. Attila the Hun and others labeled the Ashkenazi Jewish Khazars as being descendants of "**Gog of Magog**". So does Satan know who his "Synagogue of Satan" is? Just as Yahusha Hamashiach knew that the Jewish Pharisees were of the "**Seed of the Serpent**".

Qur'an 21:95-96 "But there is a ban on a town (**Jerusalem**) which we (**Muslims**) have destroyed (**Crusades**): that they (**the people of the town – Jerusalem**) shall not return (**to reclaim that town as their own**); until Gog and Magog (**Europe**) are let through their barrier, and they swiftly spread out in every direction (**replicating themselves amongst all the peoples of the world**)."

Qur'an 43:61 "And he (Jesus) shall be a sign for the coming of the Hour of Judgement: therefore have no doubt about the Hour, **but follow me**: this is a Straight Way."

But look at this!

Qur'an 10:94 "So if you are in doubt, {O, Muhammad}, about that which We have revealed to you, then ask those who have been reading the Scripture (Bible) before you. The truth has certainly come to you from your Lord, so never be among the doubters."

So Satan knows that the Book (Bible) before the Qur'an Bible is the "**Real Truth**" and that Yahusha Hamashiach (Jesus Christ) is coming back but he still wants to be worshipped as "**Allah**". Satan still wants man to read a book copied and remixed from the Bible for his pagan agenda. Satan copied the "**Godhead-Trinity**" in the beginning (Genesis 1:1-2) and gave it to the Sumerians as **Enki, Enlil and Anu**. He made the Ancient Sumerians believe his demonic Fallen Angels (aka. **Annunaki**) created mankind (**which they didn't**). He gave them the pagan god "**Ptah**" which crossed over into Egyptian theology for their creator as "**Ptah**". Ptah is a Sumerian name with a Sumerian meaning as "**He who fashions by carving and opening up**". In Egypt Ptah, gave rise to "**Ra**" and also another copycat "trinity" called **Osiris, Isis, and Horus**. Satan knows how to deceive mankind into worshipping whatever he wants. He uses his knowledge of the celestial bodies and the creation to get mankind to worship everything that God created or fairy tale pagan gods. Didn't Satan know that if Adam and Eve ate of the Tree of Knowledge that it would mess everything up? Didn't he know that if he perverted God's creation (Humans & Animals) it would upset God? Didn't he know that that by teaching mankind Astrology, Magic, weaponry, and other eternal secrets that it would take us farther away from God? Yes he did. So he also knows that by doing his "**Evilness**" throughout the world that the Messiah would come again. Therefore if he creates or instigates all of these major and minor Islamic prophecies to come to life then he can have people (Muslims) believe that these prophecies are from God (Allah) when they are actually from the doings of Satan himself.

CHAPTER 15

WHAT GOD DO THE FREEMASONS BELIEVE IN? WHAT ARE MOSLEM SHRINERS?

The Moslem Shriners are also known as the "Ancient Arabic Nobles of the Mystic Shrine". If you notice the "Pyramid" is a common theme in their symbolism. Why is this? The Pyramid is also a common theme in Ancient Egypt and Satanism/Luciferianism.

Hon. Warren Gamaliel Harding   Hon. Franklin Delano Roosevelt   Hon. Harry S Truman, MWPGM   Hon. Gerald Rudolph Ford, Jr.

Ex. José de la Cruz Porfirio Díaz Mori   Ex. Pascual Ortiz Rubio   Ex. Abelardo Luján Rodríguez   Ex. Miguel Alemán Valdés

His Majesty Kalākaua I, David   Rt.Hon. John G. Diefenbaker   Gen.Army Douglas MacArthur

109

THE FEZ

The Masonic Shriners wear a red hat known as a **Fez** named after a town in Morocco, where in 980 A.D., 50,000 Christians, including women and children, were brutally murdered by the Muslims. As the streets ran red with the Christians' blood from the massacre, the Muslims dipped their hats in that blood as a testimony to Allah. The red Fez symbolizes the slaughter of Christians in that town. The Masons still wear the red Fez adorned with the Islamic crescent symbol.

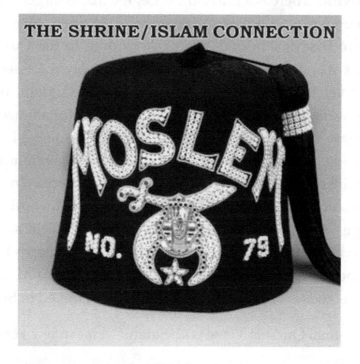

THE SHRINE/ISLAM CONNECTION

Everything that the Freemason Moslem Shriners do is based on paganism, mixing Egyptian symbols with Islamic symbols.

White Almas Moslem (MUSLIM) Shriners have been posing for the Camera IN AMERICA for over 100 years. The Almas Shriners are based out of Washington D.C. You can check them out at www.almasshriner.org If you look closely their Fez hats which was the official headgear of the Ottoman Islamic TURKISH Empire from 1832-1925. The Ottomans Empire slaughtered 1.5 million Christian Armenians in 1915. The ARABS you see today in North Africa and the Middle East are mostly of Ottoman Turkish stock. These white MOSLEM SHRINERS ARE ALSO FREEMASONS. They swear their oaths on the QURAN and pray to Allah. They end their message with "Es Selamu Aleikum". 191 MOSLEM Shriner Temples exist in America, Canada, Mexico and the Republic of Panama. Are our countries top officials MUSLIMS in disguise?

Fact: THE SHRINER: There is a thirty-third degree that is largely honorary, but the thirty-two degree gives you access to becoming a **Shriner**. As a Shriner you will pledge yourself to the Muslim god Allah. According to the Qur'an, God cannot have a son, Jesus did not die on a cross and he is only a Lesser Prophet under Muhammad but yet Jesus defeats the Antichrist in the Quran, not Muhammad. Jesus's name appears more times in the Quran than Muhammad's name. The Shriners congregate in a Temple fashioned after a Mosque. They speak secret passwords and code phrases in Arabic which they have to memorize in order to be in the group. Shriners like Muslims usually pray facing Mecca. In the Torah, which the Quran is based off of, God forbids that man pray toward shrines. In the Hebrew language "**Allah**" means "**Oak**". Many Muslims will say that in Eastern Aramaic the word "**Aa-Lah**" meaning "**The God**". This is correct. Allah also had three goddess daughters named **Al-Uzza** (The Mighty One), **Al-Lat** (The Mother) and **Manat** (Crone-godess of Fate/Time). They are mentioned in **Sura 53:19-23**.

Sura 53:19-23 (Original Quranic Verse with Satanic verse in brackets)

*"Near it is the Garden of Abode. Behold, the Lote-tree was shrouded (in mystery unspeakable!) (His) sight never swerved, nor did it go wrong! For truly did he see, of the Signs of his Lord, the Greatest! Have ye seen Lat, and Uzza, And another, the third (goddess), Manat? [**These are the exalted cranes (intermediaries) Whose intercession**]*

(prayer/worship) is to be hoped for.] What! For you the male sex, and for Him, the female? Behold, such would be indeed a division most unfair!

Eastern Aramaic was spoken by those in Assyria, Babylon (Iraq), and Persia (Iran). Western Aramaic was spoken in Israel (Judea/Palestine) and is not spoken anymore. Why? Because the Hebrew Israelites left Israel! In Ancient Hebrew "**El**", "**Elohim (plural)**" or "**El-o-ah**" was used as the word for "God". In the Genesis 1:1 the word for "Elohim" is used in the Hebrew Torah. The Plural form "Elohim" for God reveals that the "Trinity/Godhead" existed in the very beginning as the Father (Yahuah), the Son (Yahusha-Alpha & Omega-the Word) and the Holy Spirit. But we know that the word "God" is a title. When God told Moses his name, he did not say my name is "God". He spoke a name and this name was "**Yahuah**" or "**Yod-Hey-Uau-Hey**". Abraham was a Hebrew and therefore we would assume that he spoke Paleo-Hebrew to his son Ishmael and Isaac which was very similar to the Canaanite "Phoenician" language. The name for the word "**God**" during his time was "**El**", just as it was also the name for "god" in the Canaanite culture.

Exodus 6:3 "And I appeared unto Abraham, unto Isaac, and unto Jacob as El-Shaddai (God Almighty), but by my name YAHUAH (Jehovah) was I not known to them."

Aramaic and Arabic were not languages during the times of Abraham, Isaac or Jacob. Aramaic many say became more wide spread around 400 B.C. Some say Aramaic was made the official language of the Assyrian Empire in 700 B.C., but during this time the Cuneiform Assyrian and Babylonian script was officially still being used. The Assyria-Babylonian writing style was quite different compared to Aramaic and Hebrew. Thus the True God of Israel and Abraham would have been "**Yahuah**", pronounced "**Ya-oo-ah**". Paleo-Hebrew, Greek and Aramaic (which the Qumran Dead Sea Scrolls are written in) are both older than the Arabic language. Judaism, Christianity and Zoroastrianism are all older than Islam. That being said, let's go back to the Shriners. The Shriner is given a Red fez hat with an Islamic sword and crescent jewel on the front of it. This sword emblem originates from 7th century A.D. Arabia when the Moslems, under the leadership of Muhammad (aka: Mohammed), slaughtered all Christians and Jews who would not bow down to

Allah. It is a symbol of subjugation. The Shriners appear to the naïve to have begun innocently; except for their link to and allegiance to Allah.

FREEMASONRY, CATHOLISM, AND THE PAGAN DOCTRINES OF MEN

Freemasons are known to throw a séance with the dead on the black and white tiled floor which symbolizes the pathway between the living and the dead. Of course the Masonic priests that do this aren't going to tell their flocks about this. They have taken a blood oath to keep what goes on in the Lodge a secret. But when they come out of the Lodge, they're subversive killers. Unfortunately, their flock won't find this out until it is too late. In Turkey there has been leaked footage of 33 degree Freemasons doing a Satanic Ritual on a black-and-white checkered floor. But the eerie connections between Freemasonry, the Illuminati and Satanism can be easily researched now on the Internet and studied from various books written by Freemasons themselves. Only 33 degree masons can do these Satanic rituals. The Senior Master drinks the blood of a goat which is sacrificed to Satan in the middle of the lodge floor and is finalized with prayers to Satan (Set) in Hebrew.

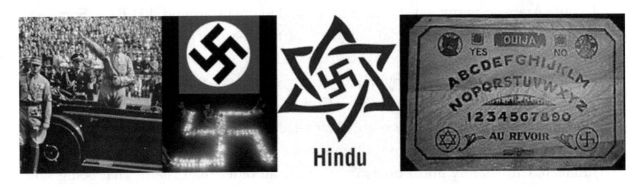

*The Swastika is also a Hindu Symbol. It represents the Hindu god **Vishnu** and the Sun. The word "**Aryan**" in Hitler's Aryan Race derives off the Indian Sanskrit word called "**Arya**" meaning "**Supreme**" or "**Pure**".*

Fact: Pope John Paul II can be seen kissing the Holy Qur'an and bowing to the Muslim Patriarch Raphael I of Iraq on May 14, 1999.

BLASPHEMY OR APOSTASY? When **John Paul II** and **Benedict XVI** (with high-ranking members of the Vatican II sect) attend the mosque, the Buddhist Temple, the Lutheran temple and the Synagogue they are manifesting their apostasy by their deed. Apostasy is the abandonment or renunciation of a religious or political belief. They are manifesting by their deed that they accept these false religions, and that these people don't need to become Catholic for salvation.

Note: *Has Israeli Prime Minister Benjamin Netanyahu or the late Ariel Sharon ever visited a Muslim Mosque? Have they ever kissed the Quran? No! So why is the Pope kissing the religious texts of other religions that don't believe Jesus (Yahusha) is God?*

When Pope Benedict XVI entered the synagogue and took active part in a Jewish worship service on August 19, 2005, he was manifesting his apostasy (his acceptance of the false Jewish religion) by his deed. Jews don't believe that Jesus (Yahusha) is God and the Messiah that is soon to come. That is why St. Thomas Aquinas taught that if anyone were to worship at the tomb of Mohammed he would be an apostate. Such an **action** alone would show that he does not have the Catholic Faith, and that he accepts the false Islamic religion.

WARNING TO THE CHRISTIAN

Since Freemasonry has attempted so strenuously to claim that they are just a "**good ole boy**" fraternity that does good works and has a good time, most people will be shocked to learn the bitter truth behind that facade. An insidious by product is to keep husbands and wives out of churches & away from the Truth.

Satan does not need to receive worship to achieve his goals. All he has to do is to keep us from following **Yeshua HaMashiach** (Jesus). Satan knows that anyone who does not follow in the teachings of the Christ does not have God. (2 John 9) Freemasonry teaches that due-paying Freemasonry alone is one's guarantee for

Heaven without any intervention needed by **Yeshua HaMashiach (Jesus Christ)**. This of course is the deception that the Freemasons want us to fall for. Many people have also failed to realize that "**phallus worship**", aka "**Sex worship**" is the basis for many Secret Societies that are in existence in the world today.

Freemasonry is a hidden fraternal order and is defined by them as a system of morality. The first three steps are the **Blue Lodge**. The first degree is called **Entered Apprentice**. The second degree is called **Fellow Craft**. The Third degree is called **Master Mason**. Most men only go to the third degree, but if one chooses, he may advance either through the York Rite or the Scottish Rite. **The Scottish Rite** has thirty-two degrees (some say 33 as well). In each degree, the Mason pledges himself to a different **Egyptian deity**. This is why we have a Pyramid on the back of our American Dollar Bill. Many Freemasons admit that the pagan gods the Israelites were told **NOT** to worship are the same gods that they pray to or take oaths under. This deception of worshipping pagan gods can also be seen in the Jewish Kabballah.

George Washington   Karl Marx   Friedrich Nietzsche   Baron von Knigge

Sign of the Master of the Second Veil (Royal Arch Mason – York Rite)   Frédéric Bartholdi   Joseph Stalin   Napoleon

(**Above**) Freemason "**Hidden Hand**" sign sported by **George Washington, Karl Marx, Joseph Stalin and Napoleon to name a few**. Some say it's based on Exodus

4:6 when Moses put his hand in God's bosom. The heart (bosom) stands for what we are, the hand for what we do. The "Hidden Hand" simply signifies to others that this person is part of the "Secret Brotherhood and that his actions are inspired by Masonic beliefs.

Some famous people caught doing this sign are: 1. President Mubarak of Egypt 2. Arnold Schwarzenegger 3. Tom Hanks 4. Kanye West. 5. Barack Obama 6. Napoleon Bonaparte 7. George Washington 8. Salomon Rothschild 9. George Washington 10. Wolfgang Mozart 11. Andrew Johnson 12. John Wilkes Boothe 13. Robert Deniro 14. Al Pacino 15. Johnny Depp 16. Karl Marx 17. Joseph Stalin

Fact: Cardinal Bergoglio (**now Pope Francis**) was pictured with the "**Hidden Hand**" symbol while riding the bus in Argentina. During his inauguration as pope, as he walked out of the balcony of St. Peter for the first time as pope, he likewise briefly flashed the "**hidden hand**" sign. Was he revealing to the Masonic World, "**Masons and Jesuits now control the Vatican?**"

(**Above**) Pope Benedict was the 111th out of 112 Popes that St. Malachy (**Malachy Prophecy**) predicted we would have before the revealing of the "**Antichrist**". The last Pope he saw in a vision was a man named "**Peter the Roman**". On February 28th, **2013** Pope Benedict officially resigned. For **13** days there was a "**Vacant Seat or Sede Vacante**" in the Holy See of the Catholic Church. Camerlengo Cardinal

Tarcisio **PIETRO** Bertone born in **Rome**, Italy was the head of the Catholic Church for **13** days.   **13** days later on 3/**13**/**2013** = **13** at 7:06 pm (=**13**), the first 76 year old Latin Jesuit (=**13**) was elected Pope. Another way of saying 7:06 pm is saying 66 minutes past 6 or **666**. Coincidence.

CHAPTER 16

SCRIPTURAL ERRORS AND MANIPULATION OF CATHOLIC DOCTRINES

Many times I run into African-Americans that are Catholics and even Africans that are Catholics. When I try to tell them about the Catholic Church and what it stands for they usually do not want to hear it. When I try to tell them that Jesus was not a European White man and that the Children of Israel were people of color they look at me like I'm crazy. It wasn't until I started doing some research on the Catholic Church and its organizations that I saw how pagan its roots were. The Catholic Church has over 1 billion devoted followers who love the Pope as if he is God incarnate and Mary as if she was part of the Godhead. They pray towards an image of Jesus and Mary, even kissing the feet of these images. The bible says:

Isaiah 42:8 "I am the Lord: that is my name: and my glory **WILL I NOT** give to another, neither my praise to **graven images**."

Roman Catholicism is nowhere in the Bible. The Catholic Church believes that man himself cannot ask God for forgiveness and that we need a mediator between God and Man. This is where the Catholic Priest and clergy come in. This is why Catholics have to go to "**Confession**" to admit their wrong doing to God so that they can have forgiveness. But what if you are alone and don't have a Catholic Priest on "**standby**"? What if you are disabled and cannot make it out the Church? Does the Catholic Priest make home visits for the disabled so they can have their sins forgiven? What if the priest is a homosexual? Does he still have a direct connect to the "Father" to forgive sins? The bible makes it clear that there is only one mediator between God (father) and man.

1 Timothy 2:5 "For there is **one God**, and one **MEDIATOR** between **GOD** and **MEN**, the man **Christ Jesus** (Yahusha)."

If the bible clearly states that there is only one way to the Father (Creator) what is the Catholic Church talking about? Why do Catholics have to go to "**confession**" to let their sins be made known and to repent of their sins?

John 14:6 "Jesus saith unto him, I am the way, the **TRUTH**, and the **LIFE: NO MAN** cometh unto the father, but by me."

Jesus never asked his disciples to bow to any statue, image or crucifix (cross). These were all invented by the Catholic Church almost 300 years after Yeshua/Yahusha died and was resurrected. He never asked his disciples to pray the **Apostles' Creed** or asked his disciples to create an image of him crucified on a cross. The Catholic Church infested Christianity with the doctrines of man, including idols, new laws, crucifixes, rosary beads and superstitions.

As suggested by the Pope St. John Paul the Great Catholics are supposed to Pray "**The Rosary**" to help keep in memory certain principal events or mysteries in the history of our salvation, and to thank and praise God for them. There are twenty mysteries reflected upon in the Rosary, and these are divided into the five **JOYFUL MYSTERIES**, the five **LUMINOUS MYSTERIES**, the five **SORROWFUL MYSTERIES**, and the five **GLORIOUS MYSTERIES**. The Pope wants these joyful mysteries said on Monday and Saturday, the Luminous on Thursday, the Sorrowful on Tuesday and Friday, and the Glorious on Wednesday and Sunday. This is what the Catholic Church (**Not God**) commands:

1. Make the **Sign of the Cross** and say the "**Apostles' Creed**".
2. Say the "**Our Father**" prayer.
3. Say three "**Hail Mary's**".
4. Say the "**Glory be to the Father**" prayer.
5. Announce the First Mystery; then say the "**Our Father**" prayer again.
6. Say ten "**Hail Mary's**" while meditating on the Mystery.
7. Say the "**Glory be to the Father**" prayer.
8. Announce the Second Mystery; then say the "**Our Father**" prayer, then Repeat 6 and 7 and continue with Third, Fourth and Fifth Mysteries in the same manner.

This is the "**Apostles Creed**".

"I believe in God, the Father Almighty, Creator of heaven and earth; and in Jesus Christ, His only Son, our Lord; Who was conceived by the Holy Spirit, born of the Virgin Mary, suffered under Pontius Pilate, was crucified, died, and was buried. He descended into hell; the third day He arose again from the dead. He ascended into heaven, and sits at the right hand of God, the Father Almighty; from thence He shall come to judge the living and the dead. **I believe in the Holy Spirit, the Holy Catholic Church (?), the communion of Saints, the forgiveness of sins, the resurrection of the body and life everlasting. Amen."**

This is the "**Hail Mary**".

"Hail Mary, full of grace, the Lord is with thee; blessed art thou among women, and blessed is the fruit of thy womb, Jesus. **Holy Mary, Mother of God, pray for us sinners, now and at the hour of our death. Amen."**

This is the "**Glory be to the Father**" prayer.

"Glory be to the Father, and to the Son, and to the Holy Spirit. **As it was in the beginning, is now, and ever shall be, world without end. Amen."**

We all know the "**Our Father**" Prayer but none of this other stuff is commanded by Yeshua in the bible. What about the "**Sign of the Cross**" with the rosary necklace? That's not in the Bible either. These are all doctrines of men. Just as the Pope and Catholics bow to the false images they also bow to images of Mary. But Mary is not the "**Queen of Heaven**", nor did she die for our sins. So why have a prayer to a mortal woman? Is this commanded by God anywhere in the Bible? No! She was just the woman chosen by God to carry the infant child Jesus/Yeshua. Even the anticipated 2016 movie "**Mary**" gives the Mother of Jesus a different pedestal to be on higher than that of the biblical prophets and the 12 Tribes of Israel. The Catholic Church also teaches that Mary was born without any "**original sin**" when the word "**Original**" is nowhere in the bible.

Fact: *Catholics and even the Pope often are seen praying to the Virgin Mary. This is not in the Bible, so this is called "**Doctrines of Men.**" Yeshua warned of the "Doctrines of Men" in the bible.*

Per Catholics, Salvation is based on works and the following practices, traditions and beliefs:

- By reverence of Peter
- By reverence of Mary
- By works
- By attending Mass

- By the Sprinkling of Water (John the Baptist didn't sprinkle water on Yeshua)
- By Church Attendance
- By Tithing
- By Penance
- By healthy "Confessions"
- By Last Rites
- By believing in Purgatory
- By wearing a "Rosary" and doing the "Sign of the Cross" with the Rosary with Beads
- By Pilgrimages
- By Meditation
- By Candles'
- By Holy Water
- By Incense
- By kissing the Popes hand or feet
- By devotion to icons
- By taking the sacraments

Fact 1: It has been found that 75% of the Catholic Rites and ceremonies of the Roman Catholic Church are of pagan origin. It is not a coincidence that the Priests of Dagon, Priests of Baal, and the Priests of Horus also carried on the same rituals and ceremonies of the Catholic Church. If you look at the hats of the pagan gods "El", "Baal", "Osiris", "Horus" and "Dagon" you will see that it is very similar to the hats the Catholic Priests wear.

This is the same hat worn by the Pope and Bishops of Rome

The "Mitre" Hat of the Dagon priests resembles the open mouth of a Fish.

"Dagon" was the Fish god of pagans

The Religious "Mitre" Hat From Babylon

The Priest of Ancient "Dagon" Fish Worship

Fact 2: Catholics are taught to call their Priests or Pope's "**Father**" supposedly out of respect. The bible does not give the Catholic Church permission to do this. In fact, Yeshua/Yahusha speaks against this. He also speaks against any calling someone a "Rabbi".

Matthew 23:8-9 "But be not ye called Rabbi: for one is your Master, even Christ; and all ye are brethren. And call no man your father upon the earth: for one is your Father, which is in heaven. "

Fact 3: Catholics pray repetitive words with Rosary Beads that were first invented in 1090 A.D. by "**Peter the Hermit**" and made popular by St. Dominic in 1208 A.D. Catholics believe that Mary appeared to St. Dominic in 1208 A.D., at the Church of Prouille and revealed the Rosary Beads to him. From this time Catholics prayed 15 sets of 10 consecutive "**Hail Mary's**" in a row (150 times) in the Rosary. In 2003, Pope John Paul II added a new set of "Mysteries", so now it is 20 sets of 10 "Hail Mary's" (200 times) in the Rosary. Catholics vainly appeal to Psalm 136 that alternates the same phrase 26 times with 26 different blessings God gives us. But Psalms is a song, not a prayer such as in Revelation 4:8 where "**angels are singing**" not to be confused with "**Men praying**". The Romans borrowed the idea of praying with beads from the pagan religions that were already using them hundreds of years before. In 456 A.D. Hinduism followers are thought to have introduced the concept of praying with beads to the world. The earliest reference to a rosary (called boberkhas) is in their "Jain Canon" (450 A.D). The Boberkhas had various numbers of beads 6, 9, 12, 18, 36. Islam (610 A.D) uses a rosary of 99 beads, one for each of the names of their pre-Islamic pagan gods. Buddhists have 108 prayer beads on a string. The Rosary-Beads is of pagan origin and **NO CHRISTIAN** prior to 1,000 A.D used beads to pray. Jesus actually forbids repetitive prayer using Rosary Beads.

Matthew 6:7 "But when ye pray, **use not vain repetitions**, as the heathen do: for they think that they shall be heard for their much speaking."

Jesus predicted what was going to happen to his Gospel and that the "**Doctrines of Man**" would infiltrate into the practices of the "Followers of Christ."

Some people will say this scripture also pertains to "**Tarrying**" for the Holy Ghost, but they must understand that when the "**Spirit of God**" gives utterance no man can control what comes out. Anybody that can turn off and turn on the tongues at will does not have the True "Spirit of God". People have gotten the Holy Spirit while singing in the Choir, praying alone silently at home, after getting baptized, after laying of the hands, and from simply giving praise unto God. There is no need for "**vain repetitions or chanting**" when the Spirit of God is the one giving utterance of speech in different tongues.

Fact 4: Roman Catholics are taught that the Virgin Mary never had sex after Jesus was born and that Jesus had no brothers and sisters. The Pope also teaches that Mary can be the mediator between God and man. This has already been proven to be false. Catholics engage more in praising Mary than Yeshua HaMashiach himself and they actually pray to her to have their prayers answered! Rosary Beads graphically represent how Roman Catholics give 10 times more praise to Mary than God himself. Of the 59 total beads of the Rosary, 53 beads are "**Hail Mary**" prayers, but only 6 beads are "**Our Father**" prayers. The Rosary often ends with a "**Hail, Holy Queen**" prayer to Mary, instead of God. This is not supported in the Bible anywhere. So are the Catholics using the same Bible everyone else is or does their Bible have added things to it?

Matthew 13:55 "Is not this the carpenter's (Joseph) son? Is not his mother called Mary? And his brethren (brothers), James, and Joses, and Simon, and Judas?"

Luke 11:27-28 "And it came to pass, as he (Jesus) spake these things, a certain woman of the company lifted up her voice, and said unto him, **Blessed is the womb that bare thee, and the paps which thou hast sucked. But he said, Yea rather (On the contrary), blessed are they that hear the word of God, and keep it.**"

So Yeshua didn't promote or encourage the praise or worship of Mary.

Fact 5: Catholics baptize by "**Water Sprinkling**", not immersion. The Greek word for Baptism means "**immersion**". In the bible people were baptized in water (i.e. River, Sea of Galilee) not sprinkled with water.

Matthew 3:16 "And Jesus, when he was baptized, went up straightway **OUT OF THE WATER**: and, lo, the heavens were opened unto him, and he saw the Spirit of God descending like a dove, and lighting upon him:"

The Catholic Church is not doing what the bible says. Maybe this is why when Pope Francis released two doves they were immediately attacked by a Seagull and a Crow.

On **January 26th, 2014**, Pope Francis released two doves into the air only for them to be attacked by a Crow and a Sea Gull, birds that normally feed on dead things and trash. The same thing happened to Pope Benedict January 27th, 2014. Was this a sign? You be the Judge.

So as you can see the Catholic Church is full of apostasy, meaning they have abandoned the True Gospel of the "Christ". In the Book "**The Development of the**

Christian Religion" by Cardinal Newman it states that "Temples, incense, oil lamps, votive offerings, holy water, holidays and season of devotions, processions, blessing of fields, sacerdotal vestments, the tonsure (of priests, monks, nuns) images....are all of pagan origin...(Page 359). The "**Heresies**" or doctrines/practices of the Catholic Church which are contrary to the Bible are what Jesus/Yeshua calls the "Doctrines of Man". Both Peter and Paul predicted that this would happen in later times. Well, it didn't take no more than 200 years for Roman Emperor Constantine to establish the Roman Catholic Church and change up the Doctrines/Teachings that Jesus/Yeshua laid out for the world and the **LOST SHEEP OF ISRAEL**.

James 1:1 "James, a servant of God and of the Lord Jesus Christ, to the twelve tribes which are **SCATTERED ABROAD**, greeting."

Want proof that Peter and Paul knew the Catholic Church would infiltrate the "Christs Message"?

2 Peter 2:1-3 "But there were false prophets also among the people, even as there shall be false teachers among you, who privily shall bring in **damnable heresies**, even denying the Lord that brought them, and bring upon themselves swift destruction. And **MANY SHALL FOLLOW THEIR PERNICIOUS WAYS**; by reason of whom the way of truth shall be evil spoken of. And through covetousness shall they with feigned words make merchandise of you: whose judgement now of a long time lingereth not, and their damnation slumbereth not."

The word "**Pernicious**" means: having a harmful effect, especially in a gradual or subtle way. The Catholic Church and the Pope have a lot of power, hurting people gradually, but also taking their money (**making merchandise of them**).

The Catholic Church also looks down on its Clergy, Bishops and Pope's being married. Why is that? Many of the Apostles had wives. Even Peter had a wife who is supposed to be the founder of the Catholic Church and 1st Pope. Its verified in Matthew 8:14-18, Mark 1:29-34, and Luke 4:38-41. Let's pick one!

Matthew 8:14 "And when Jesus was come into Peter's house, **HE SAW HIS WIFE'S MOTHER LAID, AND SICK OF FEVER.**"

So what is this! Why isn't the Pope married with Children? Is this why there is so much Pedophilia and sexual abuse going on in the Catholic Church? The Bible states that a Bishop should have one wife and teach his children to be obedient.

1 Timothy 3:1-4 "This is a true saying, If a man desire the office of a bishop, he desireth a good work. A bishop then must be blameless, **THE HUSBAND OF ONE WIFE**, vigilant, sober, of good behavior, given to hospitality, apt to teach; Not given to wine, no striker, not greedy of filthy lucre; but patient, not a brawler, not covetous; One that ruleth well his own house, **HAVING HIS CHILDREN** in subjection with all gravity;"

Again, just as Jesus/Yeshua rebuked the Pharisees (who founded Judaism) for teaching the "Commandments of Men" in Matthew 15:3-9 his disciples also prophesied that the God's Message would be infiltrated as well with the Catholic Church doctrine.

Fact 1: In 1834, The "Immaculate Conception" proposal of the Virgin Mary was proclaimed by **Pope Pius IX**. Mind you, the bible states that **ALL MEN**, with the sole exception of Christ are sinners. Mary herself needed a Saviour (Romans 3:23, 5:12; Psalm 51:5; Luke 1:30, 46, 47).

Fact 2: In 1439, the "**Doctrine of Purgatory**" was proclaimed as a dogma of faith by the Council of Florence. In the bible there is no such thing as "**Purgatory**" and the bible says that Christ instituted only two ordinances, Baptism and the Lord's Supper (Matthew 28:19-20; 26:26-28). Also the Catholic heresy of the "**Assumption of Mary**" isn't found in the bible either.

The Pope's Tiara (Hat) is also full of abominations. Inscribed on his hats are the words "**Vicarius Filii Dei**" in Latin meaning "**Substituting Agent for the Son of God**". So basically the Pope is "**The Son of God or the person who replaces the Son of God**" while he holds the title of Pontiff of the "Holy See". Wow!

But do these words have any other "Hidden meanings". Satan likes to do things backwards, or opposite, or in secret. Let's take a look.

LATIN

V	5	F	0	D	500		
I	1	I	1	E	0		
C	100	L	50	I	1		
A	0	I	1				
R	0	I	1		501		
I	1				112		
U	5		53		53		
S	0						
	112				666		

GREEK — Lateinos
(Latin Man or Church)

Λ	30
Α	1
Τ	300
Ε	5
Ι	10
Ν	50
Ο	70
Σ	200
	666

HEBRON — Romiith
(Roman Kingdom)

ר	200
ו	6
מ	40
י	10
י	10
ת	400
	666

"Now we challenge the world to find another name in these languages: Greek, Hebrew, and Latin, which shall designate the same number." Joseph F. Berg, in his book, *The Great Apostasy*, pages 156-158.

The Pope is often seen sitting on a Throne between "**Two Cherubim's (angels)**". Why does he do that? Only God does this, but the Antichrist is also prophesied to do this as well. Again, this is an abomination unto God.

Isaiah 37:16 "O LORD of hosts, God of Israel, **that dwellest between the cherubim's**, thou art the God, even thou alone, of all the kingdoms of the earth: thou hast made heaven and earth."

2 Thessalonians 2:3 "Let no man deceive you by any means: for that day shall not come, except there come a falling away first, and that man of sin be revealed, the son of perdition; Who opposeth and exalteth himself above all that is called God, or that is worshipped; so that he as God sitteth in the temple of God, showing himself that he is God."

Wait, there is more; the Catholic Church also promotes the abstaining for Vatican disapproved meats. What their Bible say about that?

1 Timothy 4:1-3 "Now the Spirit speaketh expressly, that in the latter times some shall depart from the faith, giving heed to **SEDUCING SPIRITS**, and **DOCTRINES OF DEVILS**; Speaking lies in hypocrisy; having their conscience seared with a hot iron; **FORBIDDING TO MARRY**, ...and **COMMANDING TO ABSTAIN FROM MEATS**, which God hat created to be receive with thanksgiving of them which believe and know the **TRUTH**."

Does the Catholic Church disobediently teach that it's ok to teach abstaining from meats for any reason? **YES!** What kind of religious Christian organization has doctrines and teachings that go against the Bible? How can they be followers of Christ if they do not follow the Bible? Or are they followers of something/someone else, appearing to be benevolent people on the outside?

The "**Abstinence of Meat**" is a rule binding **ALL CATHOLICS** at the age of 14 years old until death to abstain from Meat on "**Ash Wednesday**", "**Good Friday**", and all the "**Fridays of Lent**". There are exceptions to people who are ill, who need the nourishment that comes from meat or those who would give offense to a host who unknowingly served meat on one of these days. But why did they pick Friday? What about fish? And why Meat? They claim that since the first century meat was singled out as being a food Christians occasionally abstained from. They believe that "**meat**" is so good that we have to give it up sometimes as a sign of respect to God. Did God tell us to give up Beef, Goat or Chicken? No! But here's another twist to how "**Man**" and the Catholic Church institutes these "New" Doctrines. In a 1966 document, "**Apostolic Constitution on Penance**", Pope Paul VI reorganized and clarified the Church's practice of eating meats. He determined himself (Not according to God) that abstinence forbids the use of meat, but **NOT EGGS, MILK, FISH** or condiments made of animal fat. Is Pope Paul VI God? How can he ordain for his followers to eat eggs, milk and fish but disapprove meat? What about Gravy, Broths, and soups cooked with the meat flavoring? Is this permissible? In the English language "**Meat**" can refer to any flesh, from a fowl, fish, or animal. In Latin somewhere is limits meat to mammals and birds only. Wow! So again the Catholic Church is into the "**Spirit of Rebellion**" and not the "**Spirit of Christ.**"

*Catholics practice various acts of penitence and spiritual self-discipline during **Lent Fridays**, approximately forty days leading up to Easter. One of those disciplines is a fast that requires Catholics to abstain from meat on Fridays during Lent. The rule is based on the authority of the Church, not on the Authority of the Bible and its God inspired Scriptures. Shame on the Catholic Church!*

ST. PETER WAS NEVER IN ROME! WHAT IS GOING ON?

I talked about how the Catholic Church in Rome, Italy was founded based off St. Peter. But Peter was never in Rome! The Catholic Church will read the bible and say that the Apostle Peter was the "**Rock**" upon which Christ would build the Church. Why do they say this? Because of this one scripture:

Matthew 16:18 "And I say also unto thee, **That thou are Peter, and upon this rock I will build my church**; and the gates of hell shall not prevail against it."

But wait, in **1 Peter 2:7** it reads "**Unto you therefore which believe he is precious: but unto them which be disobedient, the stone which the builders disallowed, the same is made the head of the corner.**"

Basically "**Unto you therefore which believe**" is referring to the message Yahusha was giving to the Jewish Gentiles and remaining Lost Sheep of Israel. The Gentile Jews were disobedient at the time and they continued to reject the Gospel of Jesus/Yeshua. God is Precious and the "builders" are the rulers of the Jews (Scribes, Pharisees, and Chief Priests). The "Stone" "Cornerstone" or "Rock" is "Jesus/Yeshua" and the Jews didn't allow "Christ" into the building. They rejected him as the "Messiah" and refused him as the Saviour and the Redeemer. This stone/cornerstone is referenced in **Psalms 118:22, Matthew 21:42 and Act 4:11-12**. King David prophesies that the stone (Jesus) whom the builders (Jews) rejected is the **HEAD STONE OF THE CORNER**. Today any architect and builder knows that to build any structure, **YOU MUST** have a very accurate starting point upon which everything else can be built. Jesus/Yeshua was prophesied by King David in Psalms 118:22 to be that Precious and Perfect cornerstone upon which everything the Gospel of the "Christ" is based on. Jesus/Yeshua also himself stated this. We know two people cannot be the "Cornerstone" of the Church. It has to be one person. **AND THIS PERSON IS "THE CHRIST".**

Matthew 21:42 "Jesus saith unto them, Did ye never read in the scriptures, The stone which the builders rejected, the same is become the head of the corner: this is the Lord's doing, and it its marvelous in our eye?"

So the salvation of Jesus Christ (Yeshua Ha' Mashiach) is available to anyone who will receive it. God doesn't require us to do rituals, rites, vain repetitions or sacraments to enter into the Kingdom of Heaven. He told Nicodemus how we could enter into the Kingdom of Heaven. God does not need extravagant buildings that seat 10,000 people or fancy temples to worship him. God wants us to worship him in **SPIRIT** and **TRUTH**. With that being said we need to know the **TRUTH** about the Catholic Church and its man-made doctrines before jumping in and calling ourselves "**Catholics**". The Europeans did a number on invading and colonizing most of the other lands (Australia, Tasmania, India, Middle East, Judea/Israel,/Palestine, Africa, the West Indies/Caribbean, the Americas, the

Philippines) in the world other than their own land. With this they brought new boundaries, new names, new languages and a new-Europeanized corrupted version of the Bible. Not the True, untampered word of the "Christ". Please do not allow the Catholic Religion to lead you into Hell.

Did their "**Agenda**" work? During slavery they made us hate ourselves for being black as if it was a "**Curse**" because of the "**Curse of Canaan**" story. So as we got older it was the norm to love our slavemasters children. We watched our children get sold into slavery and we watched them starve. We nursed their babies while our babies died. We took care of the master's house chores and the master's family while our family was in turmoil. We watched their children go off to school while our children died in the streets. We learned to love the image of a "**White Saviour**" because we were taught that black skin was "**ugly**" and a "**curse**". We went from watching cartoons with white princesses and princes to watching T.V. sitcoms where whites dominated the cast. As a result we wanted our hair to look "**straight**" like the Princesses we saw on T.V. or the girl that was liked by all the boys. This mental brainwashing was "**key**" in the process of erasing our "**true identity**".

Slavery and Colonization allowed the Catholic Church and Islam to stray the Hebrew Israelites far from the TRUTH. However, it is in God's Perfect plan that he is restoring us back to the Truth.

In conclusion, the traditions of the Catholic Church are not Bible inspired. With knowledge of Bible lingo and biblical terms many Pastors/Bishops are deceiving the masses. The Catholic Church teaches the "**Traditions of Men**" instead of the "**Commandments of God**". Remember "**Cain**" tried to impress God with his works. Abel had faith and it pleased God. The "Spirit of **Tubal-Cain**" still exists **today in our World.**

Matthew 5: 17-18 "Think not that I am come to destroy the law, or the prophets: I am not come to destroy, but to fulfil, For verily I say unto you, Till heaven and earth pass, one jot or one tithe shall in no wise pass from the law, till all be fulfilled."

Luke 16:17 "**And it is easier for heaven and earth to pass away, than one tittle of the law to fail.**"

Mark 7:6-9 "He answered and said unto them, Well hath Esaias (Isaiah) prophesied of you hypocrites, as it is written, This people honoureth me with their lips, but their heart is far from me. Howbeit in vain do they worship me, teaching for doctrines the commandments of men. For laying aside the commandment of God, ye hold the tradition of men, as washing of pots and cups: and many other such like things ye do. And he said unto them, Full well ye reject the commandment of God, that ye may keep your own tradition."

CHAPTER 17

I LOVE MY CHURCH, BUT DOES YOUR CHURCH LOVE YOU? ARE THEY TEACHING "SOUND DOCTRINES" OR "DOCTRINES OF IGNORANCE"?

Black people in America were typically raised up in the Church, especially in the South. A lot of times there was one Church in the Black Community that everyone would go to. Most black families walked to church in their freshly ironed Church outfits. Everybody went to Church. Children, aunts, uncles, parents and grandparents. Everyone in the community knew each other. It was not uncommon for people to spend most of the day at the church on Sundays while the kids played in the street or grass after Church. The whole community raised the children, instilling morals and life lessons. The community was so close that there were old ladies in the Church that had the authority to give whippings when watching other people's kids. The Church was the source of spiritual teaching and knowledge. The Community depended on the Pastor to be able to interpret the scriptures and deliver a message to the people from the Lord every Sunday. Some of the members of the Church had little education and some didn't' know how to read. So reading the bible was difficult, and then to understand it was another thing. Everything was in the hands of the Good Ol' Pastor. The Catholic Church controlled what people heard and was given in regards to the Holy Scriptures. During the early centuries of Christianity the Bible was on scrolls and parchments. **NO ONE** had a "Bible." Even into the "Middle Ages", each bible was written hand by hand. Many people back then were functionally illiterate. The Invention of the Printing Press in 1436 by Johann Gutenberg allowed **CONTROL**. He controlled who got the books and what was in the books. Gutenberg's printing technology spread from Mainz, Germany to Subiaco, Italy in 1465, Paris (1470), and London (1476). By the beginning of the 16th Century, there were 240 printing shops in Europe. The first printing press in the Americas was set up in Mexico. In 1638, Cambridge, Massachusetts United received its first Printing press machine. It began printing books in 1639, only 19 years after the arrival of the Mayflower.

Fact: The Catholic Church realized the potential of the printing press as a challenge to its influence. Censorship was introduced into the print shop in 1487, when Pope Innocent VIII required that Church Authorities approve all books before publication. The Church had censored books for Centuries, though it became more difficult to do so after the invention of printing. Controlling thousands of copies coming off the press was hard to do, but the English bibles posed the biggest threat. Don't believe? The Catholic Church used a 2001 document which ruled that the word "**Yahweh**" be replaced with "**Dominus (Lord)**". In 2008 they came up with another rule that "Yahweh" be removed from Catholic Prayers, spoken songs, and song books. Still don't believe that man can change the words of the Bible? Research this: In the King James bible **Exodus 4:6** it reads:

Exodus 4:6 "And the Lord said furthermore unto him, Put now thine hand into thy bosom. And he put his hand into his bosom: and when he took it out, behold HIS HAND WAS LEPROUS AS SNOW. Here we see the word "Leprous" being associated with "White skin".

What about the Greek-English Translation of this same scripture?

Greek Septuagint Exodus 4:6 "And the Lord said again to him, Put now thine hand into thy bosom; and he put his hand into thy bosom; and brought his hand out of his bosom, AND HIS HAND BECAME AS SNOW.

The big difference is the missing word "**Leprous**" from Greek-Septuagint translation of the Bible. Why is the word "**Leprous**" gone in the older Greek-Septuagint translated version of Exodus 4:6?

Let's look at some more verses.

King James-Exodus 32:14 "And the Lord repented of the evil which he thought to do unto his people."

Greek Septuagint-translation-Exodus 32:14 "And the Lord was prevailed upon to preserve his people."

The word "**prevailed**", means "win, triumph, succeed, conquer or overcome." Nowhere do these scriptures resemble each other. Repent does not mean "**prevailed**" and the word "evil" somehow mysteriously makes its way into the King James Bible.

So obviously there are two versions of the bible. Once version said God repented and the other one said he succeeded in preserving his people.

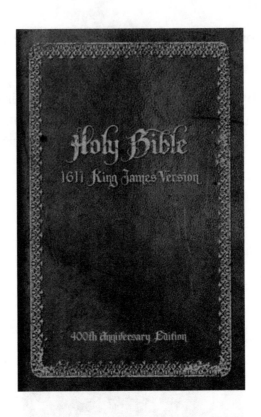

Black Church in the South.

Most African-Americans today can attest that their parents and grandparents grew up going to church in the South. Everybody in the community walked or drove to church. Everybody knew each other. The Pastor knew his entire congregation and had a "**Word from the Lord**" on Sunday. In Southern talk, "**Pastor shole did preach today,**" was a common saying for many after church was over. Many pastors today have graduated from Theology school and with that comes knowledge of the scriptures. They can recite scriptures off the top their heads but will **NEVER** say that "**Negroes**" are the descendants of **HEBREW ISRAELITES** taken from West Africa. They will never say that Giants lived after the Great Flood because they would have to explain how they survived, and where are they today. But many people might be shocked to know that the Giants (Nephilim) did not all die off. Pastors will never admit that the **JEWS** in Israel are just converts to Judaism and not the blood descendants of the Biblical 12 Tribes of Israel. If the church started demanding why the prophecy in Jeremiah 30:10 hasn't been fulfilled yet despite the Jews coming back to Israel in 1948, the Pastor would have a heart attack. Pastors and Deacons have tons of Religious books in their personal libraries so why is it that for all these centuries we have not been told the **TRUTH**? Whose fault is it? Hosea 4:6 says "**My people are destroyed for a lack of knowledge.**" Do we have **ALL** the right knowledge? Just as it's important to worship God in **SPIRIT** it's also necessary to worship God in **TRUTH**. The Devil knew this was a key ingredient to our awakening. He had to keep this knowledge from us by keeping us preoccupied with other things. But it's not too late. So, we have to ask ourselves, are churches teaching about our heritage, unifying our resources and monies to establish our own "economy within an economy"? Are they teaching about the tactics of the Enemy? Are they helping the communities or are they taking from the already poor black communities? Who is to be held responsible? I have met pastors who knew about the modern JEWS being converts (proselytes) but wouldn't tell their congregation in fear of stirring up controversy or being silenced by the Presiding Apostle of the church organization. Some Pastors will say that it doesn't matter who are the people are in Israel. If it didn't matter than what was Jesus (Yahusha) talking about in Luke 21:24-28? Was he just talking nonsense? No! Christians will support the people of Israel simply because they live in the land of Israel. But we all know Churches worldwide would not want to support Israel if Israel was full of African-Americans, Latinos and Native Americans. Christians frequently say "They (**other countries**) shouldn't mess with the **JEWS**, they are **God's Chosen People**". But nobody uses what's in the actual bible to figure out who the Real Children of Israel are today (**according to scriptures**). So if we still don't know the answer to this question then who are we? Imbeciles? Bastards? Canaanites? Gentiles?

THE BRAINWASHING OF THE BLACK CHURCH STARTED IN SLAVERY AND IS PUSHED ONTO THE YOUNG

On one Saturday afternoon in Southfield, Michigan, as a child I asked my parents, "Momma, who are those white people walking wearing black suits and funny hats?" My mother responded **"Those are God's Chosen People, the Jews that Jesus talks about in the bible."** Then I asked, **"Who are black people according to the bible?"** My mom replied **"We are Gentiles."**

Matthew 10:5-6 "These twelve Jesus sent forth, and commanded them, saying, **Go not into the way of the GENTILES, and into any city of the Samaritans enter ye not: BUT GO RATHER TO THE LOST SHEEP OF THE HOUSE OF ISRAEL."**

Isaac gave his blessing to Jacob.

(To the left) Isaac is giving his blessing to a Caucasian looking Jacob with straight hair, the father of the Children of Israel. (To the right)-The Real Children of Israel from 700 B.C. depicted by Assyrian King Sennacherib. This is verified in the Bible in II Kings 18, 2 Chronicles 13, Micah 1:13 and the Annals of the Assyrian King Sennacherib. Does Jacob's hair and beard in this Sunday School cartoon photo look like the hair and beard of the 2,700 year old picture of the Real Israelites? No, but this is what many Black children are taught in Sunday School all across the world, even in Africa. This is "Trick knowledge" at its best.

So as you can see, the brainwashing and indoctrination of a black youths mind in regards to our identity as it pertains to the Bible is started in the Black Church as early as Sunday school. Yeshua (Jesus) knew who was in Judea during his time. If all the Israelites were walking around living in their designated Tribal territories given to them by Joshua then Yeshua (Jesus) would not have instructed his disciples to not go into the way of the Gentiles or the Samaritans. He would not have said go find the "**LOST SHEEP OF ISRAEL**". This is because starting from the rebuilding of the 2nd Temple with Ezra in 500 B.C. many other nations had infiltrated into Jerusalem and the Temple. These were Kenites, Nethinims, Edomite's, Greeks, Romans, Syrians, Persians and so on. They all practiced the religion of Judaism (Hellenized or not) and were therefore referred to as Jews. King

Herod had replaced all the real Israelite High Priests with his own by the time he started to upgrade the unfinished 2nd Temple Ezra came into. This continued when Yeshua (Jesus) walked the Earth. **Need Proof?**

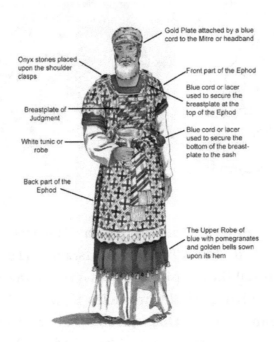

Fact: *Mysteriously the last High Priest of the Bible was possibly **Jehozadak the son of Seraiah (High Priest)** at the time of the Babylonian exile (1 Chronicles 6:14,15) around 500 B.C. The last book of the Bible Malachi stops around 400 B.C. Mysteriously Josephus Flavius has the list of **ALL** the Jewish High Priests all the way to the High Priests that delivered **YESHUA** up to be crucified. It is said that under the Herodians and Romans during the time of Yeshua birth in the 1st century they appointed their own High Priests. In Herod's temple there was **NO** Ark of the Covenant or Stone Ten Commandments. Therefore the Most High was not in there. Any Sacrifices done during the Herodian rule was done in vain/waste. Around 300 B.C the Greeks sacked **EGYPT**, Judea and extended their territory all the way to India/Afghanistan. The people in Judea and the High Priests at this time were mostly **GENTILES**. Many of Levite records were lost and burned during the destruction of the temples. Ezra had a hard time finding **LEVITES** to do the temple duties. He needed help from the fake "LEVITES" called the "**Nethinim**".*

This is an Ashanti (Akan-Ghana) Priest from the 1800's with the Hebrew Israelite Breastplate of Judgement on his chest. The Black Priest also has a gold metal piece fashioned on the forehead part of his headwrap (turban). This falls in line with Exodus 28:36 for the attire of the Aaronite High Priests. How can the Priestly Sons of Levi/Aaron go from looking like a Black man to looking like a White European Man? That doesn't make any sense.

Exodus 28:36 "And thou shalt make a **PLATE OF PURE GOLD**, and grave upon it, like the engravings of a signet, **HOLY TO YAHUAH (JEHOVAH)**. And thou shalt put it on a lace of blue, and it shall be upon the mitre (hat); upon the **FOREFRONT OF THE MITRE (HAT)** it shall be. And it shall be upon Aaron's forehead, and Aaron shall bear the iniquity of the holy things,"

"That country is also called Judea, and the people **Jews**; and this name is given also to as many as embrace **THEIR RELIGION** (Judaism), though of **OTHER NATIONS**.

(**Note**: The above statement by Flavius Josephus is proof that the Jews in that time were simply Judaism converts from other nations like Greece or Rome).

"But then upon what foundation so good a governor as Hyrcanus (grandson of Matthias patriarch of the Maccabees, a family of Judahite patriots of 2nd and 1st centuries B.C). Took upon himself to compel these Idumeans (Edomites) either to become Jews (**BY RELIGION**) or to leave their country, deserves great consideration. I suppose it was because they had long ago been driven out of the land of Edom, and had seized on and possessed the Tribe of Simeon (the land not the people), and all the southern part of the land of the Tribe of Judah, which was the peculiar inheritance of the worshippers of the **True God** without idolatry...."

Flavius Josephus, 1st century A.D. Roman-Judean historian.

Disorder was going on in the Temple when Ezra was around. He saw the corruption and blasphemy that was going on with the Israelites and the other Gentile nations that started to infiltrate their religious ways into the temple services.

Ezra 9:1 "Now when these things were done, the princes came to me, saying, The people of Israel, and **THE PRIESTS**, and **THE LEVITES**, have not separated themselves from the people of the lands, doing according to **THEIR ABOMINATIONS**, even of the **Canaanites**, the **Hittites**, the **Perizzites**, the **Jebusites**, the **Ammonites**, the **Moabites**, the **Egyptians**, and the **Amorites**. For they have taken of their daughters for themselves, and for their sons: so that the holy seed have mingled themselves with the people of those lands: yea, the hand of the princes and rulers hath been chief in this trespass. **And when I heard this thing, I rent (tore) my garment and my mantle, and plucked off the hair of my head and of my beard, and sat down astonished**.

In 300 B.C. the Greeks would conquer Egypt, Judea along with most of Mesopotamia. This would lead to the Hellenistic Era and Hellenized Judaism. It would also give rise to the Seleucid Empire and the late Maccabean Dynasty before the Edomites would rise to power. During this time the **Children of Judah** were sold as slaves to the Grecians to be shipped far from their land. This would pretty much mark the time when most of Israel was of Gentile nations calling themselves "Jews". It is documented in the Book of Joel, 10 books before the Book of Malachi, the last book of the Old Testament.

Joel 3:6 "The Children also of Judah and the children of Jerusalem have ye sold unto the **Grecians** that ye might remove them far from their border."

Joel was a prophet whom many believed lived during the 2nd temple period (400-300 B.C.). Why? The Persians took Judea and Jerusalem from the Babylonians in 539 B.C. It was during this time that King Cyrus issued a decree allowing the Jews to come back to Israel. The Book of Joel talks about the Greeks getting Israelite slaves. The Greeks didn't conquer Egypt and Jerusalem until 332 B.C. It wasn't until 19 B.C. that King Herod started rebuilding/re-finishing the Second Temple in Jerusalem. Joel was able to talk about the Children of Israel (Judah) being scattered into all nations (including Greece) because by the time he was talking the Assyrians and Babylonians had already scattered most of the Israelites. For this reason scholars believe that Joel lived during the post-exilic period after the Second Temple was built.

Joel 3:1-3 "For behold, in those days and at that time, When I restore the fortunes of Judah and Jerusalem, I will gather ALL the nations and bring them down to the valley of Jehoshaphat. **Then I will enter into judgement with them there On behalf of My people and My inheritance, ISRAEL. Whom they have scattered among the nations. And they have divided up My land**. They have also cast lots for My people, Traded a boy for a harlot and sold a girl for wine that they may drink."

Joel prophesied that "**the fortunes of Judah and Jerusalem were to be restored**" in the future. This means that the fortunes of Judah/Jerusalem were already taken. This had to be the result of the Babylonians when they laid siege to the House of Judah in the 6th Century B.C. because the Assyrians laid siege to the Northern Tribes of the House of Israel in 700 B.C. That being said, if Joel admits that the Children of Judah were sold to the Grecians (**Joel 3:6**) then who would be left in their territory? The Greeks, Edomites, Babylonians, Elamites, Persians, Assyrians and anyone else that wanted settle in Israel!

Before Alexander the Great visited Jerusalem in 332 B.C. he had already defeated the mighty Persian Empire lead by **King Darius III**. Around the time that Persia was defeated by the Greeks, **Judah** was considered a small and unimportant part of the Persian Empire. So when Alexander conquered the Persians he also took the territories they controlled. The Greeks came in and the **REAL** Children of Judah were removed. This would be evident 150 years later when the Greek Maccabean family would appear out of nowhere as **"so-called Jews"** in the Historical **Apocrypha Books**. **Shall we see the proof again?** Roman-Judean Historian **Flavius Josephus** admits this to be true without even knowing it!

> "But then upon what foundation so good a governor as **Hyrcanus** took upon himself to compel these **Idumeans (Edomites)** either to become Jews (**BY RELIGION**) or to leave their country, deserves great consideration. I suppose it was because **they had long ago been driven out of the land of Edom, and had seized on and possessed the Tribe of Simeon (the land not the people), and all the southern part of the land of the Tribe of Judah**, which was the peculiar inheritance of the worshippers of the **True God** without idolatry...."

> **Flavius Josephus, 1st century A.D. Roman-Judean historian.**

John Hyrcanus (2 Maccabees 3:11) was the grandson of Matthias patriarch of the Maccabees, a family of Judahite patriots of 2nd and 1st centuries B.C).

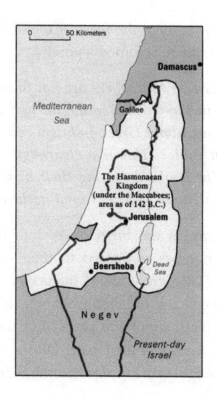

(Above) Hasmonean Kingdom under John Hyrcanus 150 B.C.

So 150 years later, Jesus (Yeshua/Yahusha) was aware of those Gentiles in Judea. The **Book of Malachi** took place around 400 B.C. during the Persian Rule. Once the Greeks defeated the Persians, there was nothing standing in their way to attack Egypt, Canaan or the Levant. This would be one of the last blows to the **TRUE ISRAELITES** that would scatter them (**Tribe of Judah, Levi, Benjamin**) into other lands before the Destruction of Second Temple in 70 A.D. by the Romans. The Maccabean family would then insert themselves into history as being "**Jews and Levites**", just as the European Jews do today. The Sephardic/Mizrahi Jews are the descendants of all these Gentile Nations that lived in Israel at this time, coupled with centuries of mixing with the Romans and Gentile White Arab Turks/Kurds during the "**Crusades**". They came up with a fake Jewish Holiday called "**Hanukkah**" which was not ordained as a holiday, feast or festival ordained by the Most High to the Israelites. (**Many claim Jesus observed Hanukkah but John 10:22 doesn't say that**). Jesus just happened to be in the Temple during that time.

John 10:22 "And it was at Jerusalem the feast of the dedication and it was winter. And Jesus walked in the temple in Solomon's porch."

Note: *The Four Books of (Greek) Maccabees are not found in the Hebrew Bible but of course these books are in the Greek Septuagint and the Latin Vulgate biblical canon. Why wouldn't a book about Greek Judaism converts who ruled over Judea be in the Greek Septuagint Bible? This is a clear sign that the Maccabees family was not Real Israelites. The books depicting their history are not in the Hebrew Tanakh and the Book of Maccabees is NOT found in the Dead Sea Scroll collection.*

During 100 B.C all the way to the birth of Yeshua (Jesus), the Real Israelites remaining were small in number compared to their original size. It is for this reason, no **REAL ISRAELITES** wrote about the accounts of the Greeks in Judea. This was written by Gentile Greek Judaism Converts called the **Maccabeans**. The **Book of Maccabees** takes place about 150 years after the Greek takeover of Judea (probably 175 B.C.), under Alexander the Great. During this time the Greek Empire was divided into part of the **Ptolemy Empire** and the **Seleucid Empire.**

Fact: The Ethiopian Orthodox Books of Maccabees called "**Meqabyan**" is only written in three books while that of the Catholic Church canon is written in four books. The books of the Ethiopian "Meqabyan" are totally different than the Latin Vulgate/Catholic Church "**Book of Maccabees**". The Maccabees described in the Ethiopian books are not the **Maccabeans** of the Hasmonean dynasty. The Book of Maccabees was also not found in the Hebrew Dead Sea Scrolls found in Qumran, Israel. The Hebrew Dead Sea Scrolls date back to around 400-300 B.C. The Essene Jewish Sect, who was accredited to the Dead Sea Scrolls, lived during the 2nd Century B.C. and the 1st Century A.D. This would've given them plenty of time to record the History of the Maccabees in Paleo-Hebrew/Aramaic. But they didn't'. This is another reason why the Book of Maccabees to many is not trusted as being "**Inspired by God**" but instead is viewed as a Jewish (Gentile) historical book.

As we can see from 300 B.C. continuing to the turn of the B.C. to A.D. most of the people living in Judea were "**Gentiles**". They would keep possession of Jerusalem/Judea even after the fall of Herod's Temple by the Romans in 70 A.D. until this present day (**ex. Crusades, Ottoman Palestine, British Mandatory Palestine, State of Israel**). Yeshua (Jesus) predicted this in **Luke 21:24-28.**

Luke 21:24 "And they (Israelites) shall fall by the edge of the sword, and shall be led away **CAPTIVE INTO ALL NATIONS**: and Jerusalem shall be trodden down (taken over) of the GENTILES, until the times of the Gentiles be fulfilled."

So why are Black pastors telling the fable that Blacks are Gentiles? Some African-American Black pastors even tell the lie to their Black congregation that they are Canaanites, descendants of Ham. This is some serious brainwashing! But yet in the same breath they don't reveal how it was the Canaanites who the Israelites men and women mostly married. So it would be hard to pick out a pure Black Canaanite person today based on our knowledge of Israelite-Canaanite "**race mixing**" in the Old Testament (**Ezra 9:1-2, Judges 3:1-6**).

Westernized American Education during "**Black History Month**" will only teach that **ALL BLACKS WERE SLAVES IN THE PAST**. They never address Black History before the 1600's. So as a black youth we are taught two things: that we are **Gentiles** and that we used to be **slaves**. That is as far back as our history goes to "White America". But the Chaldeans, Armenians, Indians, Chinese, Greeks, Jews and Arabs mysteriously claim know their history going back over 2,000 years ago. So why does our history stop when we get to the 1600's? What do we call ourselves in America? **African-Americans**? This is the name of two continents! Never did it dawn on me growing up that we were given a special name. Today, not once do I hear people saying: "I'm Arab-American", "I'm Indian-American", "I'm Jewish-American", or "I'm Chinese-American". Chinese people living in Africa don't say they are "African-Chinese" or "African." They say they are "Chinese". When Africans immigrate to America and have children here are their kids called "African-Americans"? No! They are called Africans. If any African-American calls himself "African" around a real "African" or around other races, they might just get laughed at or told, "No you're not." But crazy as it seems, they are actually right. What's even more messed up about it is that many "**West Africans**" do not know their former heritage, before their land was divided up into countries with the names "Ghana", "Benin", "Togo", "Nigeria", "Cameroon", or "Congo.

Fact: *The name "**Nigeria**" is coined after the British Journalist "**Flora Shaw**". The name "**Cameroon**" was named after a Portuguese Explorer named "**Fernano Po**" who saw that* *the river in the land had vast amounts of shrimp. "Camaroes" in Portuguese means "Shrimp River". And the list of European-inspired African country names goes on....*

In the past many West Africans in addition to **"Negro Slaves"** knew their Israelite heritage, but over centuries with the influence of Western Culture, the youth have swept these memories under the rug. They do not practice the old traditions that their grandparents and elders kept (**ex. Widow had to marry her deceased husbands brother**). Even till this day there are West Africans that remember being told stories when they were young of how their tribe migrated from Israel to West Africa. Each story is the same, no matter if it is coming from a person from Guinea, Ghana, Nigeria, Benin or Cameroon. This I found amazing. Sadly, many of the youth in West Africa as well as the African-American youth in America have no clue of their past heritage going back 1,000 years. Many still believe that Jesus/Yeshua is white and the Israelites were white as well. Everyone is so quick to acknowledge the origin of their ancestors as being in Africa, but what was the land mass known as prior to its name of "Africa"? Who lived on this land? What Tribes and Kingdoms lived there? Were they Hamitic, Semitic (Shem-Israelites) or Japhetic? Where did "Mongloid" people come from? Who made up this name? Did Noah have a son named "Mongloid"? No! The people living in Africa pre-slavery had to be a descendant of one of the three because as the bible tells us Noah and his three sons populated the earth after the flood. There was nobody in the Bible named "Mongloid". History has made us forget this, therefore we rely on the continent the Europeans named **"Africa"** and the term **"Slavery"** to define us. They changed our name from **"Hebrews"** to **"Negroes"** so that we would not start connecting the dots. Calling us **"Heeboes"** or **"Hebrews"** in America would be too easy.

Fact: *In some white schools you will see Black History Month questions that read like this:*

1. Please select the appropriate answer for the person with the following saying, "I'm tired of getting whipped for not picking cotton fast enough."

a) Fisherman

b) Slave Master

c) Farmer

d) Slave

This question was an actual Test Question of a History Test in a predominately White Elementary School. Yes, they are still teaching kids at young ages that Blacks were just slaves. This continues the Superiority complex that non-black children have over black children.

SO ARE WE REALLY "GENTILES" AS THE PASTOR TELLS US?

If we look at what the bible says we can see clearly who the Gentiles are and what role they will play in Israel until the 2nd coming of Christ. But if all of this is in the Bible then how come our Pastors failed to see this? How did we miss it? Is this the "**Age of Revealing**" or the "**Age that Knowledge shall increase?**"

THE MYSTERY OF THE GENTILES

The word "Gentile" in the Old Testament was first associated with the descendants of Japheth. Abraham didn't come from **Japheth**, he came from **Shem**.

1. **Genesis 10:2** "The sons of JAPHETH; Gomer, and Magog, and Madai, and Javan, and Tubal, and Meschech, and Tiras. And the sons of Gomer; ASHKENAZ, and Riphath, and Togarmah. And the sons of Javan; Elishah, and Tarshish, Kittim, and Dodanim. **BY THESE WERE THE ISLES OF THE GENTILES DIVIDED IN THEIR LANDS;**

2. **Luke 21:24** "And they (Israelites) shall fall by the edge of the sword, and shall be led away captive into **ALL NATIONS: and Jerusalem shall be trodden down of the Gentiles (those who are not Israelites), UNTIL** the times of the Gentiles be fulfilled."

3. **Romans 11:25** "For I would not, brethren, that ye should be ignorant of this mystery, lest ye should be wise in your own conceits (pride, ego); that **BLINDNESS IN PART IS HAPPENED TO ISRAEL**, until the fullness of the **GENTILES** be come in.'

So here we have proof that the Gentiles could not be African-American because we are not in possession of Israel/Jerusalem right now. We never have been in possession of Israel since 400 B.C. which I will explain in detail in the following volumes of "Hebrews to Negroes". During A.D. times and up until now, the Greeks, Romans, Arabs (Turks/Kurds) and European Jews have possessed Judea/Israel. I have read Luke 21:24-28 out loud to Pastors, pastor's kids, deacons, Catholic Priests, Muslims and Church folk for them to interpret the scripture with no luck at all. When they don't believe that these scriptures are talking about the Gentiles today and the time frame we are living in now I usually have to read to them the rest of the scripture. The Bible doesn't lie. People commonly try to twist the scriptures for **"their interpretation"** instead of just reading the bible for what it says. It's not rocket science. But it's not that hard to interpret the scripture. There is no mystery in these particular verses. Let see:

- **Luke 21:24** "And they (**Israelites**) shall fall by the edge of the sword, and shall be **LED AWAY CAPTIVE** into **ALL NATIONS: and Jerusalem shall be trodden down of the Gentiles (those who are not Israelites), UNTIL** the times of the Gentiles be fulfilled."

- So when is this **"Fulfillment"** of the Gentiles? The word "Fulfilled" means, **"To come to an end, finish, or complete in regards to time"**. When will the Gentiles reign in **Jerusalem** come to an end? Yeshua (Jesus) tells us in the next 4 verses. Let's read it, the scriptures speak for itself.

- **Luke 21:25-27 "And there shall be signs in the sun, and in the moon, and in the stars; and upon the earth distress of nations, with perplexity; the sea and the waves roaring; Men's hearts failing them with fear, and for looking after those things which are coming on the earth: for the power of heaven shall be shaken. And then shall they see the Son of man coming in a cloud with power and great glory"**......hmm, this sounds like the Second Coming of Christ.

Jesus is saying when he returns for a Second time (Judgement Day) the Gentiles reign will come to an end. So who is in Israel now? The Gentile **Palestinians**, Gentile **Lebanese**, Gentile **Armenians** and the Gentile **European Jews**? This is not to bash anyone's race but the facts are the facts.

Note: Saladin was a Gentile **Kurdish** Muslim who conquered Jerusalem in the Second Crusade from the Roman (Latin) Christians in 1187 A.D. **The Turks and Kurds are descendants of Togarmah, son of Gomer, son of Japheth (not Shem or Abraham).** This of course did not sit well with the Gentile Europeans so in 1189 A.D. they teamed up forces with other Europeans to launch a **Third Crusade** which was led by **King Richard (the Lionheart) of England, Phillip II of France**, and the **Holy Roman Emperor Frederick I Barbarossa (Italy)**. Saladin defeated the Europeans which sparked the "**Treaty of Ramla**" in 1192 which decreed that Jerusalem would stay in Muslim hands but that Christians would be allowed to come for pilgrimages. In 1500 A.D. Arab Turkish ruler "**Suleiman the Magnificent**" also did the same thing after he conquered Israel and Jerusalem. So here have "Gentiles" both fighting over Jerusalem, just as Luke 21:24 states.

CHAPTER 18

HAS EDOM MIXED HIMSELF AMONGST THE GENTILE EUROPEANS AND GENTILE ARABS, FULFILLING WHAT THE BOOK OF OBADIAH SAYS?

(**Above**) The **Eagle of Saladin** in the Egyptian Coat of Arms and next to it the Eagle of Saladin in the coat of arms of the **Kurdistan Regional Government**. They know Saladin was a Kurdish King. The Turks and Kurds are descendants of **Togarmah**, like the Armenians. Armenians known their heritage goes back to Togarmah. **Togarmah** was the son of Gomer, son of Japheth.

State of Palestine

دَوْلَة فِلسْطِين

*The icon of **America** is the **Eagle**, so was **Ancient Egypt**, so was **Ancient Edom**, so was **Ancient Rome**, so was the **German Nazi party**, so was **Spain**, so was the **Arabs** who took over Jerusalem during the Crusades, and so is the state of **Palestine**. Are we seeing a trend here? **Who is Edom**? He is the great "**Masquerader**"? Has Edom infiltrated his bloodline into the Gentile nations that have had their foot in Jerusalem in the past and right now? **Just as Yeshua prophesied in Luke 21:24**. The Palestinian Coat of Arms is the Eagle as well. The Palestinians will often say they are the descendants of Shem while some will say that they are the "Real" Israelites. Palestinians also commonly say that there is no way Blacks can be the real Israelites.*

Obadiah 1:4-6 "Though thou exalt thyself **AS THE EAGLE**, and though thou set thy nest among the stars, thence will I bring thee down, saith the Lord. If thieves came to thee, if robbers by night, (how art thou cut off!) would they not have stolen till they had enough? If the grape gatherers came to thee, would they not leave some grapes? **HOW ARE THE THINGS OF ESAU** searched out! How are his hidden things sought up!

Esau was the mortal enemies of the Children of Israel. Edom did not allow Moses and the Israelites to pass into Canaan at the city of Kadesh. The Amalekites **(Children of Edom)** also waged war against the Israelites as they journey to Canaan. Edom was there when the Solomon's Temple was destroyed by the Babylonians and King Nebuchadnezzar. They were also there when the Second Temple was destroyed by the Romans in 70 A.D. When the Edomites fled from

155

their land into Israel in the 1st to 2nd century B.C. they were forced to get circumcised by the Greek Gentile Jews and were thereafter called "**Jews**" as well. So from 70 A.D., the remnant of Edom stayed around in Israel with his converted "**Judaism**" religion and influenced the coming invaders from the North (Europeans, Turkish/Kurdish Caucasian Arabs) to practice Judaism as well. Some of these Jewish-Edomite followers along with other Gentile Judaism Proselytes migrated into North Africa and then into Iberia (Spain/Portugal). This is why we have Middle Eastern Jews (**Mizrahi**), Spanish Jews (**Sephardic**) and European Jews (**Ashkenazi**). But the Middle Eastern Jews will claim that they are the oldest Jews of the entire bunch. They however need to know some important things.

1. The people that entered into Israel after the Assyrian Siege of Lachish in 700 B.C. were "**Real Semites**", meaning they were descendants of Shem but were not Israelites. They also were people of color (brown-black skinned people).

   2 Kings 17:24 "And the King of Assyria brought men from Babylon (Arphaxad), and from Cuthah, and from Ava, and from Hamath, and from Sepharvaim, and placed them in the cities of Samaria **INSTEAD** of the Children of Israel: and they possessed Samaria, and dwelt in the cities thereof."

2. Shem had 5 sons who populated the Middle East: Arphaxad, Aram, Ashur, Lud and Elam. Arphaxad populated Babylon (Iraq), Aram populated Ancient Aram where the Aramaic language began (Syria), Ashur populated Ancient Assyria (Turkey, Northern Iraq, Babylon, parts of Iran) and Lud populated a part of Turkey. Eber's son Joktan populated Arabia. Basically all the people the Assyrians replaced Israel with were Assyrians (Ashur) and Babylonians (Arphaxad). While in Israel, these foreigners defiled the land by not fearing the Lord so lions were sent to kill them. Then these Samaritan people asked the King of Assyria to have someone teach them the religious faith of the Israelites God. So the King of Assyria granted this request to have some of the Israelite Levite Priests brought back to teach the people the ways of the God of Israel. However, only **ONE** of the Levite priests came back and taught them how they should fear the Lord God of Israel while

dwelling in Bethel. The people learned how to fear the Lord but they still served their own pagan gods, from the nations they were originally from. In Israel they worshipped the pagan gods **Succothbenoth**, **Nergal**, **Ashima**, **Nibhaz** (Dog), **Tartak** (prince of darkness-donkey), **Adrammelech** (Moloch or Sun God), and **Anammelech** (Moon God). They built shrines for these pagan gods mixing in their worship with the worship of Yahuah (God of Israelites). These pagan gods were of Sumerian, Akkadian and Assyrian stock.

2 Kings 17:28 "Then **ONE** of the priests from whom they had carried away from Samaria came and dwelt in Bethel, and taught them how they should fear the Lord. Howbeit every nation made gods of their own, and put them in the houses of the high places which the Samaritans had made, every nation in their cities wherein they dwelt. **And the men of Babylon made Succothbenoth, and the men of Cuth made Nergal, and the men of Hamath made Ashima, and the Avites made Nibhaz, and Tartak, and the Sepharvites burnt their children (like Moloch) in fire to Adrammelech and Anammelech, the gods of Sepharvaim.**"

So these were the "half **Judaism**"-half **Pagan**" practicing people that were living in Israel after the Israelites from the 10 Northern Tribes were exiled from their land. Only **ONE Levite priest** came back, commanded by the Assyrian King to teach them the ways of Yahuah. So we can assume that the Gentile nations enlarged and increased their population in the land until 500 B.C. when the Babylonians destroyed Solomon's temple, exiling the House of Judah (Benjamin, Judah) in the process. After 300 B.C. the Greeks came and took over Egypt, Israel, and the Middle East. They started Hellenistic Judaism before the Edomites controlled Israel, followed by the Romans takeover of Israel and Jerusalem heralded by the destruction of the Second Temple in 70 A.D.

3. So if the Mizrahi Jews claim they are descendants from Babylon/Persian from B.C. times they must understand that they are most likely Gentile converts to Judaism, or White Japhetites. But then the question we need to

ask is: "**If the Ancient Babylonians, Persians, Elamites, and Assyrians were brown/black people than how can these white skinned Mizrahi Jews be those people?**" It is because they are **NOT** the people that possessed Israel in B.C. times following the exile of the Original Black Israelites. They are likely the product of the Arab Ottoman Turks, Arab Kurds, Greeks, Romans and other Europeans who invaded Israel in A.D. times who just so happened to embrace the Judaism Religion.

Note: *Mizrahi Jews trace their roots back to Muslim-Majority countries. This includes* ***Iraq, Syria, Bahrain, Kuwait, Dagestan, Azerbaijan, Iran, Lebanon, Uzbekistan, Kurdistan (Kurds), Afghanistan, Turkey, Pakistan, Yemen, and Georgia.*** *Today these Mizrahi – Sephardic Jews make up more than half of Israel's Jewish population. Before 1948 and the mass immigration of European Ashkenazi Jews, most of the people already living in Israel as "Jews" were (Edomite) Sephardic or Mizrahi Jews who simply returned back to Israel from Spain/Portugal or the Middle East.*

THE WORD "JEW" IS SYNONYMOUS WITH "EDOM", AND A LITTLE BIT OF CAIN.

The word "Jew" had been a stumbling block for Christians since man inserted it into the Book of Esther and other books. The NWO's crowned achievement was purchasing the State of Israel. After 2,000 years of Gentile Arabs fighting with Gentile Europeans the "European Gentiles" finally got it. Christians say that it was Bible prophesy coming to play like in Isaiah 11:11 and Ezekiel's bones. But we forgot to do the research as to who was "these people"? And where are the other 10 tribes at? Christians today bless the people in Israel and also the Catholic Church (Rome) who both seek to destroy Christianity and establish a NWO. Yahusha said they were of their father the Devil. He knew the Pharisees were Edom. Children of the Tares and also a mix of the seed of the "Wicked One". Edom sold his birthright for a bowl of beans. The Bible states Edom will be the end of the world and JACOB the beginning. Even the Catholic Church's own book, the Apocrypha in 2 Esdras 6:9 says this.

2 Esdras 6:9 "For **Esau** is the end of the age (world), and **Jacob** is the beginning of the one that follows."

So who is controlling the world in these last days of wickedness and sexual immorality? Edom? Or is it Rome, the Vatican, ISRAEL and the United States?

The 1925 Edition of the Jewish Encyclopedia, Vol. 5, Pg. 41 says "**Edom is in modern Jewry**". The Encyclopedia Judaica (Jerusalem, Israel: Encyclopedia Judaica Company, 1971, Vol. 6, p. 378 states "**The Non-Israelite Edomites became a section of the Jewish people.**" The Bible and the Book of Jasher prove Edom mixed his seen into Europe and Rome. This is exactly where the Ashkenazi , Sephardic and Mizrahi Jews ultimately come from. The Bible also states Edom mixed his seed with the Black Canaanites and Black Arab Ishmaelite's. So let's do some "critical thinking." Who named Africa and America? An **Italian** named Amerigo and Africanus (**Rome**). Rome is in Italy! **Edom is the ISRAELITES enemy**. Who authorized and participated in the slavery of Black Bantus "Negro" Hebrew Israelites that were scattered into **ALL NATIONS**? The Europeans, the Catholic Church, the Ashkenazi/Sephardic Jews and the Arabs! **These are the people Edom DNA dwells in.** The bible says in Obadiah that Edom would **impersonate** the **REAL ISRAELITES** that were scattered into other nations via slavery or migration. It also predicts their destruction. Overall Edom is small amongst the other **GENTILES** but they are **despised** (Obadiah 1:2). Obadiah 1:18 says that God is going to judge and finish Edom-Satan in the end. The Prophet Ezekiel even predicts how Edom would eventually plot to possess Israel/Palestine in the last days. They would be successful in 1948 with the Creation of the State of Israel. The Vatican also has been trying to work out a deal with Israel to obtain Mount Zion and King David's Tomb.

Ezekiel 35:10 "Because thou hast said, These **TWO NATIONS** (House of Judah and Israel), and these **TWO COUNTRIES** (Judea and Samaria) shall be mine, and we will possess it."

Ezekiel 36:2 "Thus saith the Lord Yahuah: Because the enemy hath said against you, Aha! and, **The ancient high places are ours in possession;**"

Fact: *Some people believe that that the wife of Ham was of the seed of Cain and this is how the seed of the "wicked one" was able to continue after the flood. Esau would then further contaminate the Nephilim mixed Canaanites with his DNA by marrying the daughters of Canaan. Perhaps this is why God didn't want the Israelites mixing with the Canaanites.*

Genesis 26:34 "And when Esau was forty years old he took to wife Judith the daughter of Beeri the **Hittite**, and Bashemath the daughter of Elon the **Hittite**: Which were a grief of mind unto Isaac and to Rebekah."

God says in the Book of Obadiah that he will use the Children of Israel to expose Edom in the last days. What have Black Hebrew Israelites been doing since waking up? **EXPOSING WHO EDOM IS!** Edom even says that he will continue Baal worship in the land of Israel which they are doing today if you look at the Grove/obelisk (Baal's shaft) standing outside of the Israeli Supreme Court.

If you read the Bible, one can see that Esau joined with the evil race of Cain. King Herod tried to prevent the birth of the Messiah by committing infanticide on the children of Judea under two years old. How did King Herod know to do this? Perhaps this is because it is innately in the Edomites to destroy the Children of Israel.

Fact: *In 163 B.C. Gentile Greek Judaism convert leader, **Judas Maccabeus** conquered the Edomites and their territory for a short time. In 125 B.C. **John Hyrcanus** (Hasmonean) forced the Edomites to convert to Judaism and to get circumcised. The Edomites country "Idumea" and its people were then incorporated into the Gentile Jewish culture of the land. From that day forth they were known as "**Jews**" and not "**Edomites**". When the Romans came to besiege Jerusalem the Edomite Jews fought hard to defend the city, but suffered great losses (more than a million died and 97,000 were taken captive). After the destruction of the Second temple in Jerusalem (70 A.D.), the Edomites would never be talked about again.*

After the fall of Jerusalem in 70 A.D. some of the Sephardic Jews migrated into Europe and North Africa. In North Africa they would camouflage themselves amongst the "**Real Black Hebrew Israelites**". They were not known as "**Sephardic Jews**" at that time because this name would not be made known until after the 15th Century. In Iberia (Spain/Portugal) they would stay "**incognito**" until the Spanish Inquisition in 1492. When the Black Moors were defeated and forced back across

160

the Strait of Gibraltar some of the Black Hebrew Israelites also fell back into North Africa. Some were less fortunate and were taken as slaves to the Spanish Colonies in the Caribbean. This is why there are still Jews and their synagogues in the Caribbean (i.e. Jamaica) today. The Black Hebrew Israelites that fell back into Morocco (Northwest Africa) after 1492 followed the trade routes into Timbuktu, Mali (Africa). Other Edomites would migrate to Eastern Europe and Russia mixing in with Khazaria, progenitors of the Ashkenazi Jews. The Edomite Sephardic Jews over the years would set up shop in Iberia/Spain, the Middle East, Western Europe and Eastern Europe. By the 1900's the Sephardic Jews would return to Israel before the Ashkenazi Jews would arrive there in 1948.

CHAPTER 19

ISRAELITES, SEMITES, JAPHETITES, HAMITES, AND EDOMITES

We all know Noah's seed populated the earth after the flood. So all mankind must be of Japhetic descent, Hamitic descent and Semitic descent. All the nations of people that fought in the "**Crusades**" were from the nations of Japheth. Even the first Sultan of the Muslim Ottoman Empire, **Osman I** was of **Gentile Turkish (Togarmah) descent**. He became leader of the Ottoman Empire in 1300 A.D. So for about 700 years his descendants would be the ones who would colonize the Middle East, Macedonia, Asia Minor, North Africa, Sudan, Judea/Samaria/Palestine and parts of Arabia. These are the White-skinned Arabs we see in Europe, North Africa, Israel/Palestine/Lebanon, the Middle East and Arabia. This is very hard to swallow for many. I once had to read Luke 21:24-28 over and over 3-4 times in a row to a Pastor to really let it sink in. Once it started sinking in, his face was full of confusion. The question that usually follows is: "**If the Gentiles are in Jerusalem (Israel) per the Bible in Jesus/Yeshua's own words then where are the "Real Jews" at now?**"

The bible reveals who we are and it also states that we would be few in number among the "Heathen". **The Heathen is anybody that is not Israel**. It is all the descendants of Japheth from Europe and the pure Hamitic races.

Obadiah 1:2 "Behold, **I have made you small among the heathen**: thou art greatly despised."

COAT OF ARMS
EAGLE

Albania 1443	Austria 1919	Czech Rep. 1918	Egypt 1958	Germany 1928
Indonesia 1950	Iran 1980	Iraq 1965	Lybia 1977	Mexico 1821
Moldova 1990	Montenegro 2004	Poland 1295	Romania 1870	Russia 1650
Serbia 1882	Sudan 1969	Syria 1958	Thailand 1911	UAE 1973
USA 1782	Uzbekistan 1992	Yemen 1961	Nagorno Karabakh 1918	Horus Ancient Egypt 25th cent BC

As you can see above the result of the (**Gentile European/Asia Minor**) Japhetic Nations invading/colonizing the Americas, North Africa, Sudan, Israel, and the Middle East is the appearance of the "**Eagle Coat of Arms**". Even in Sudan we know that the original Nubians and Cushites did not speak "**Arabic**". But the Sudan coat of arms has Arabic letters below it. We know that Mexico was invaded and colonized by the Spanish Europeans. So is this a coincidence that the "**Eagle**"

(Like what is referenced in Obadiah 1:4, 4:1) is seen as the "**Icon**" for so many Middle Eastern Countries as well as European Countries? No!

Genesis 36:10 "These are the names of **ESAU'S SONS; Eliphaz** the son of Adah the wife of Esau, Reuel the son of **Bashemath** the wife of Esau. And the sons of **Eliphaz** were Teman, Omar, **Zepho**, and Gatam, and Kenaz."

Note: In Genesis 36:3 Bashemath was also the daughter of Ishmael. Yes, Esau's seed intermarried with the Black Arab Ishmaelite's and the Black Canaanites. Could this be why many Black Arabs also sold Black Hebrew Israelites from East Africa into slavery in the Arab Slave Trade/Indian Ocean Slave Trade?

*(Left) The **San Tribe** from South Africa (**Botswana**). Genetically the have the oldest DNA of all races. Many believe they could be descendants of the biblical Canaanites. Why? Because one of the Canaanite Tribes, the "**Sinites**" were thought to have migrated from the Levant (Canaan) to Asia, started "**Shina-Sina**" which the Japanese call Ancient "**China**". They are one of the only Africans that are born with "Asian Eyes (single epicanthal fold)". (Right) **Afar** Boy from **Ethiopia (Cush)**. Many slaves taken by the Arabs during the Arab Slave Trade were from Abyssinia (Ethiopia), Kenya, Tanzania, Sudan and other East African Countries.*

*(**Above left**) Statue of a man from the Cushite Kingdom of Sheba (Seba/Saba) in Yemen, 500 B.C. Joktan, son of Eber (Father of the Hebrews) also had a son named Seba/Saba. His Hebrew Semitic children lived in South Arabia with the Cushite Kingdom of Sheba (Saba-Ethiopic). (**Above right**) Typical hairstyle of African-Americans/Black people. The original Arab Ishmaelite's, Cushites and Hebrews (**Sons of Joktan in South Arabia**) were brown skinned people with kinky "**Negro**" hair. In Ancient Times, these three nations lived and intermixed amongst each other, hence the reason why the Ethiopian alphabet and the Ancient South Arabian alphabet are similar to each other as well as to Aramaic/Hebrew. During medieval times, Arab historians like Ibn Khaldun and other spoke of the transition of the Black Arab to the White Arab in the Middle East. The Sudan, Hijaz (**West Arabia**), Nejd (**Central Arabia**) and Arabia Felix-Yemen (**South Arabia**) eventually came under rule by the White Syrian/Turkish Arabs of the North, descendants of Gomer, son of Japheth.*

Many Arabs or skeptics will say to the above picture, "Well, he doesn't have the nose and lips of a Negro so that doesn't mean he was black." As we should know by now, all Africans do not have tight kinky hair, wide noses or big lips. Let's do another comparison.

This is a Black Saudi Arabian boy compared to an Ancient statue of a man from the Kingdom of Sheba, Yemen.

Jasher 61:12 "And when Zepho (Esau's Grandson) the son of Eliphaz saw that Angeas despaired of going forth to battle with the Egyptians, Zepho fled from Angeas from Africa, and he went and came unto Chittim (Kittim).

Note: *Angeas was believed to be of Kittim stock (Rome) who also ruled over North Africa (excluding Egypt).* **Kittim** *was the son of Javan. Javan's name in Hebrew (Strong's #3120)* **"Yavan-Ionah"** *is associated with the* **"Ionians"** *or Greeks. Kittim was associated with Rome. Back in the day Greek Historians (Herodotus, Diodurus, Strabo) and Romans referred to the continent of "Africa" as* **"Libya"** *even though Ethiopia (Cush) also consisted of a large portion of modern day Africa.* **Scipio Africanus** *(236 B.C.-183 B.C.) was a Roman after whom many say* **"Africa"** *is named after. By the time of the* **"Imperial Roman Empire"** *there was a Roman territory known as* **"Africa".** *It was associated with Angeas's old territory from the Book of Jasher. This is why the Book of Jasher (Chapter 61:5) associates* **Angeas** *as the King of Dinhabah (**Modern day Africa-excluding Egypt, Cush/Nubia**). It was an area surrounding Carthage in modern day Tunisia. Carthage, Tunisia was associated with the Roman Territory of the character "Aeneas" in the book "The Aeneid" by Virgil the 1st Century Roman poet. Per Roman history, the Romans trace their origin to "Aeneas" who was supposedly one of the Trojans who was said to have led the surviving Greek Trojans to modern day Italy (possibly after the Trojan War). Also back in the day the Romans controlled North Africa (Libya, Tunisia, Algeria), sharing its control with the Moors and with the Black Hebrew Israelites also living in the land.*

So in the Book of Jasher it states that Esau's grandson Zepho becomes the so-called King of Kittim (Chittim) which is modern day Rome (Italy) and perhaps Greece.

Fact: *Kittim (Chittim)* *is often associated with the Island Cyprus and the Mediterranean Islands including Rome, Italy and Greece. In the Greek Septuagint in Daniel 11:30 the word "Kittim" is translated as "Romans". Some believe that in Ancient times the word "Kittim" was a code name for* **"Romans"**. *Even the word "Kittim" in the Hebrew Dead Sea Scroll "War Scroll" aka* **"The War of the Sons of Light Against the Sons of Darkness"** *is synonymous to "Rome".*

Jasher 61:13 "And all the people of Chittim received him (Zepho, grandson of Esau) with great honor, and they hired him to fight their battles of all the days, and Zepho became exceedingly rich in those days, and the troops of the king of Africa still spread themselves in those days, and the children of Chittim assembled and went up to Mount Cuptizia on account of the troops of Angeas king of Africa, who were advancing upon them."

Jasher 61:24 "And the children of Chittim saw the valor of Zepho, and the children of Chittim resolved and they made Zepho king over them, and he became king over them, and whilst he reigned they went to subdue the children of Tubal, and all the surrounding islands. And their king Zepho went at their head and they made war with Tubal and the Islands, and they subdued them, and when they returned from battle they renewed his government for him, and they built for him a very large palace for his royal habitation and seat, and they made a large throne for him, and Zepho reigned over the whole land of Chittim and over the land of Italia fifty years."

(***Zondervan Atlas Bible map***) – *Magog, Tubal and all the islands of the Mediterranean Sea were considered to be in Gentile Japheth Territory. Esau's Grandson **Zepho** ruled over all of these Gentile Japhetic lands, mixing his seed into modern day Greece, Italy, Macedonia, Turkey, Armenia, Kurdistan, Cyprus, etc. It is a known fact that the Khazars before becoming "**Ashkenazi Jews**" were speaking a **Turkish/Slavic/Germanaic dialect** before fusing it with Hebrew to form "Yiddish". Therefore they also have "**Edom**" in them too! But who were the main slavetraders of Black Negro-Hebrew Israelites in the Transatlantic Slave Trade? **The European Jews and other European nations!** The Europeans (Romans/Greeks), the White European Arab Turks (Ottoman), the Kurds, and the Khazars (European Ashkenazi Jews) would fight over the land of Israel/Jerusalem for almost 2,000 years just as Yeshua predicted in **Luke 21:24**. These nations were all Japhetic Gentiles. Ezekiel 38 & 39 talks about Gog and Magog. The Apostle Paul was an "Apostle to the Gentiles". Where did he go preaching the Gospel? To Europe and Asia Minor, the land of Japheth!*

Don't believe these people are Gentiles?

Isaiah 66:19 "And I will set a sign among them, and I will send those **that escape of them unto the nations, to Tarshish, Phut, and Lud, that draw the bow, to Tubal, and Javan, to the isles afar off**, that have not heard my fame, neither have seen my glory; and they shall declare my glory among the **GENTILES**."

Jasher 90:30-31 "He then heard that Edom had revolted from under the hand of Chittim, and Latinus went to them and smote them and subdued them, and placed them under the hand of the children of Chittim, **and Edom became one kingdom**

with the children of Chittim all the days. And for many years there was no king in Edom, and their government was with the children of Chittim and their king."

Why should we believe anything out of the Book of Jasher?

Joshua 10:13…"Is not this written in the **Book of Jasher?"**

2 Samuel 1:18 "(Also he bade them teach the children of Judah the use of the bow: **behold, it is written in the Book of Jasher.)"**

*Note: Some sources say the people of Chittim gave **Zepho** the name "**Janus Saturnus**" and from his line came the first King of Rome, "**Romulus**". Well Janus was known as the Roman god of "**Change and Time**" which the Romans did use to change the "**Lord's day-Sabbath**" to **Sunday (day of the sun)** and our calendar with the first day of the month being "**January**". Janus was also supposed to be the god of the sun and moon. **Saturn** was associated with the god of "**wealth**" and "**abundance**" which the Vatican has today. Saturn was the son of the Roman lightning/sky god "**Jupiter**" who was the equivalent of the Greek god **Zeus** and Canaanite god "**Baal**". Saturn was also equivalent to the Egyptian god "**Set**" who is considered by Satanists/Freemasons to be the "**Devil/Lucifer/Satan**".*

In the Book of Obadiah even though Obadiah is using "**past tense**" he is actually talking about future events. Isaiah, Jeremiah, Ezekiel and other Hebrew prophets have done so as well. In the Book of Obadiah it explains when the **Edomites** and the **Heathen** will be dealt with. Who are the **Edomites**? As you will see later I believe the Edomites are like Chameleons; they have infused their bloodline into many of the Heathen/Gentile nations of the World. The people that have been infected with Edom's bloodline have been enslaving and wreaking havoc on the **REAL LOST CHILDREN OF ISRAEL.** They are going to be involved with the chain of events that bring about the "**End of the World**". This includes the Black Ishmaelite Arabs, the Europeans (including European Jews) and the Japhetic White Arabs (Ottoman Turks, Kurds). Edom's **pure seed/nation** is now small compared to the descendants of Ham, Japheth and Shem. But according to the Book of Obadiah the Edomites are also going to be despised.

ALL I WANT IS THE TRUTH

So to no avail, every Sunday blacks go to Church and listen to the message of the preacher. They get a message during Sunday school, during prayer request, during testimony and praise, during the bible scripture of the day, during the Choirs A & B selection and during the Pastor's sermon. We are always told we are **Gentiles**, yet nobody in the church has questions about **Deuteronomy 28:15-68 or Luke 21:24-28**. We know that the **Curses of Israel** were supposed to apply to the **Israelites** and their **SEED FOREVER**. That is if they were disobedient and didn't follow the Commandments of God.

Daniel 9:9-10 "Neither have we obeyed the voice of the Lord our God, to walk in his laws, which he set before us by his servants the prophets. **Yea, all Israel have transgressed thy law**, even by departing, that they might not obey thy voice; therefore **THE CURSE IS POURED UPON US**, and the oath that is written in **THE LAW OF MOSES** the servant of God, because we have sinned against him."

In the Book of Daniel around 500 B.C., when King Darius of Persia ruled the Middle East, Egypt and Judea, the Children of Israel were still disobeying the Commandments of God, given to them by Moses. King Darius II"s father was Artaxerxes I (reign 465-424 B.C.) Artaxerxes I was the 5th King of Persia and third son of Xerxes I (reign 486-465 B.C). See for yourself:

Daniel 9:1 "In the first year of **Darius the son of Ahasuerus (Artaxerxes)**, of the seed of the Medes, which was made king over the realm of the Chaldeans;"

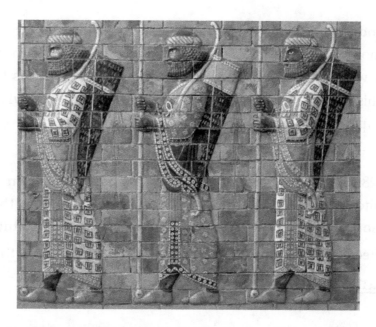

Persian/Elamite Warriors from 500 B.C. *These were the 10,000 Immortals the 2006 movie "300" talks about. This picture is a depiction of what the Persians/Elamites looked like from the Palace of Susa, Iran (Daniel 8:2). Also seen from the Ishtar gate (the eight gate to the inner city of Babylon (Iraq). This picture although you cannot see, shows the Ancient Persians/Elamites to be brown-skinned people of color. Not the white-skinned Caucasian Persians we see today.*

Biblical Scholars and Jewish Rabbis all agree that Ezra, Nehemiah and Malachi all lived during the Persian rule of Judea. This would set the scene of the last books of the Old Testament to around 400 B.C., right before the European Greeks would conquer and dominate Judea for almost 400 years prior the Roman destruction of Herod's Temple in 70 A.D. So when our Old Testament Bible stops with the Book of Malachi at 400 B.C. we see that almost 1,000 years go by before we see the massive persecution and enslavement of the Hebrew Israelite people in East Africa by the Arabs.

Believe it or not, the hardships the Hebrew Israelites experienced over many centuries parallel the hardships people of African (Black) descent have gone through since the beginning of the Common Era (C.E. or A.D). Africans are always known to flee one country where they are persecuted or where the land is barren to another "**Safe**" land. These "**African refugees**" as we all know are not always welcome in "**other lands**", just like the Hebrew Israelites. This is why they called them the "**Wandering Israelites**", "**Foreigners**" or "**Nomads**". For centuries the Israelites did not have a home. This is similar to the migration patterns of the different tribes we see living in West Africa and the Bantus lands today. Did the Arabs follow this type of behavior? No! The Arabs went everywhere conquering and setting up shop. They were not fleeing anything. Is this a coincidence........NO!

Deuteronomy 28:45-46 "**Moreover all these curses shall come upon thee, and shall pursue thee, and overtake thee, till thou hearkenedst not unto the voice of the LORD thy God, to keep his commandments and his statutes which he commanded thee: And they shall be upon thee for a sign and for a wonder, and upon thy seed FOREVER.**"

CHAPTER 20

GIVE AND I'LL GIVE IT BACK TO YOU: IS CHURCH A BUSINESS NOW?

Many churches today require your license, W-2's, two years tax returns, place of employment before being accepted as a member of the their church. Some even have dues called "financial support" that church members are required to pay. If church members don't contribute to the minimum assessed amount required by the church than they become a "delinquent member" and end up getting a nice letter reminding them to pay. Some Churches require a minimum of $50.00 a month in "financial support" aka (offerings, tithes etc.) for adults and $5.00 a month for Youth members. But don't worry; if church members are experiencing an "**economic hardship**", some churches will give a 30-90 day extension. What is going on? There is something obviously wrong with this picture. Didn't Yahusha drive people from doing business in the Temple (**John 2:14-16**)? Many churches nowadays will run their "**offering time**" like an auction, seeing who can hold up to the opening bid of what the Minister or Pastor wants everyone in the church to pay. Originally tithes were collected for the Levite Priests so that they would not have to work.

Numbers 18:21 "And, behold, **I have given the children of Levi all the tenth in Israel for an inheritance**, for their service which they serve, even the service of the tabernacle of the congregation."

Hebrews 7:5 "And verily they that are of the **sons of Levi**, who receive the office of priesthood, have a **commandment to take tithes of the people according to the law**, that is, of their brethren, though they come out of the loins of Abraham."

Leviticus 27:30 "And all the tithe of the land, whether of the seed of the land, or of the fruit of the tree, is the Lord's: it is holy unto the Lord.

Numbers 18:26 "Thus speak unto the Levites, and say unto them, When ye take of the Children of Israel the tithes which I have given you from them for your inheritance, then ye shall offer up an heave offering of it for the Lord, even a tenth part of the tithe."

Deuteronomy 14:22 "Be sure to set aside a tenth of all that your fields produce each year."

So according to the Old Testament, Tithes was given to the **Levite Priestly tribes**, just as Abraham gave tithes to Melchizedek. Back in Old Testament times during the "**Feast of Firstfruits**", the Israelites gave their "firstfruits" to the Levite Priests as an offering to God. They didn't have a collection plate and dollar bills. They gave what God provided them from the land. What started out as tithes and offerings from God's creation (i.e. fruits, vegetables, grains, livestock) now has become singles, fives, tens, twenties, fifties, hundred dollar bills and private jets. Of course, crooked Pastors see this as an easy way to get people to pay their bills, car payments, and house payments. They can then use the building space during the week to run a daycare. Also, with the addition of the Church's **501c(3)** status the Pastor doesn't have to pay federal income taxes. All in the name of the Lord. Jesus/Yeshua mentioned paying tithes but stated that there were other matters of the law that weighed more than paying tithes. Meaning that there were other laws that people should be focusing on more instead of tithes.

Matthew 23:23 "Woe unto you, scribes and Pharisees, hypocrites! For ye pay tithe of mint (plant) and anise (plant) and cumin (plant), and have omitted the weightier matters of the law, **judgement, mercy, and faith**: these ought ye to have done, **AND NOT TO LEAVE THE OTHER UNDONE.**"

So is the money we give to Pastors at churches supposed to be used solely so they don't have to work? What about using some of this money to rebuild the community, thereby ensuring the success of **the people**? Some black churches have 5,000-20,000 members and some black pastors have multiple churches that they oversee. There are Pastors that get up in the morning (like work) on Sundays to be driven to one church to deliver the 9-10am sermon of the day, then get driven to another church to deliver the 11-12 noon sermon of the day and then get driven to yet another church to deliver the 1pm-2pm sermon of the day. **All this in one day**! Is this how God wants his Church leaders to deliver the message of God? To collect offerings and give **1 hour circuit sermons**? The church has become a business where anyone can say they are a Pastor and open up a church. They can take advantage of being paid (**tax-free – 501c3**) by the congregation and not paying tax on certain items. But if Pastors do not have to pay tax on food, property taxes and if they don't have to file their earnings with the government, then should some of this money be used to do good in the community? But yet most communities where Black Churches can be found are in bad shape with lack of jobs, lack of education, no black-owned businesses, crime, drugs, and homelessness. Other non-black races clean up by opening up businesses after businesses to take the money of Black people. Then after a day's work, these non-black business owners drive their cars to suburbs where a 4-car Mansion awaits. Don't these churches care about the community? Giving away free bikes to the kids every year is not doing anything for the betterment of black people as a whole. There is a saying, **"If you give a man a fish, he will eat for just that day, but if you teach that man how to fish he will eat for the rest of his life."** Pastors should use these practices and philosophies.

Below is an actual statement made by a person in regards to the Church's tax exempt status.

"The best part of being a church is that you don't have to file anything with the IRS! All other non-profits have to file annual statements with basic financial information so the IRS can determine whether they qualify. Churches automatically qualify with no paperwork! Some churches do file voluntarily."

So in addition to this the IRS cannot decide what is a church and what is not a church. A church can be the **"Church of Beyoncé"**, the **"Church of Satan – *Anton LaVey*"**, **"The Temple of Set (Satan) – *Michael A. Aquino*"** or whatever. A church can be a Pastors house, or his shed or a piece of property that he uses for other purposes as well. Barber shops, Hair Salons, and Car washes are notorious for getting paid under the table, bypassing the IRS. The question still becomes: "Why do we have so many black churches making money but none of them are linking up with other Churches to help rebuild the community."

Fact: *US churches received an official federal income tax exemption in 1894, making them unofficially tax-exempt since the country's founding. All 50 states and the District of Columbia exempt churches from paying property tax. Donations to churches are tax-deductible. Even* **James Hale**, *founder of the Satanic Church called* **"The Lord High Master of the Church of the IV Majesties"** *was granted tax-exempt status by the state of Oklahoma in 2010.*

So if a church that has 5,000 members and its congregation gives $20 in offering every Sunday for 1 year (52 weeks) this equals $100,000 x 52 weeks/year =5.2 million dollars in one year. Drop that down to 1,000 members and you get 1.2 million dollars in offering per year just by putting only $20 in the collection plate every Sunday. **But what if ALL African-Americans gave $1 every Sunday in Church to a Black Loan Fund organization?** 45 million African-Americans in America x $1 x 52 (Sundays/weeks) = 2.3 Billion dollars. If we started doing this in 1960 when Martin Luther King Jr and Malcolm X was alive until now we would have 117 Billion dollars to use to become **"Economically Independent"** from the other races we make rich every day. Wow! Imagine if these members give more money for tithes, foreign mission, Sunday School offering, Building Fund offerings and so on. So what if Black people applied this same concept of giving $20/week into a fund or account that would allow us open up businesses and rebuild our black communities? Let's compare these financial revenue numbers based on Church members and **"Offerings"** to some of our famous Black pastors with Mega-Churches we see today on T.V. There is no excuse why Black Churches cannot use the finances from its congregation to team up with other Black Churches in the area to make **SERIOUS CHANGES** in the community. There are currently 8 Black pastors whose net worth is 200 times more than the folks that live in their community.

CHAPTER 21

CAN WE SERVE MAMMON AND GOD? CAN PASTORS HELP OUR COMMUNITY? WHERE IS OUR JESUS MONEY GOING?

Blacks all over the United States of America often ask the question, "Why are Black communities suffering when we have churches on every corner?" They also ask, "If we have all of these Black Millionaire/Billionaire Secular and Gospel entertainers, why is it that we as a people work for everyone else? I often wonder myself why the Black Church and Black Millionaires can't come together to build up an independent "Black America" economy within an economy. Each Black church that we frequent or drive by has members loaded with talent. All throughout America, Black churches are filled with Lawyers, Doctors, Architects, Carpenters, Realtors, Plumbers, Electricians, Engineers, Social Workers, Medical Examiners, Nurses, Medical Assistants, Business owners, Construction workers, Gardeners, Landscapers, Farmers, Barbers, Bankers, Stock Brokers, Mechanics, Pilots, Military personnel, Teachers, Tailors, Seamstresses, Hunters, Cooks, and Computer Technicians. With all of these resources at our fingertips and with a little bit of financial "Teamwork", we could start to rebuild Black communities, just like blacks did in Tulsa, Oklahoma during the era of "**Black Wall Street**."

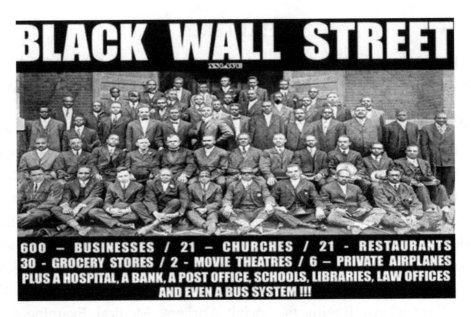

BLACK WALL STREET

600 – BUSINESSES / 21 – CHURCHES / 21 - RESTAURANTS
30 - GROCERY STORES / 2 - MOVIE THEATRES / 6 – PRIVATE AIRPLANES
PLUS A HOSPITAL, A BANK, A POST OFFICE, SCHOOLS, LIBRARIES, LAW OFFICES
AND EVEN A BUS SYSTEM !!!

*In 1921, in Tulsa, Oklahoma, "**Black Wall Street**" was attacked by mobs of angry white men. The Military sent vehicles armed with machine guns as well as airplanes to bomb the city, killing 100 people and setting ablaze every one of the Black businesses in the city.*

Back then in 1921, the United States of America didn't have as much wealthy blacks as we do now. But they made it work. So what is holding blacks today from sprouting "**Black Wall Street's**" all over America? Every Sunday, Black people get up early for Church and at the end of service we go home without trying to put plans in motion to better our community. We will stay after church to hear singing at a concert or to get Church dinners in the basement but we cannot put our heads and money together to make "power" moves in our community. Meanwhile the Pastor gets richer, while the people get poorer. How rich do the get?

1. **Pastor Creflo Dollar** – College Park, Georgia. Net Worth **$27 million**. Even with all of this money he asked his members to fund a $65 million G650 luxury Jet to spread the Gospel to mankind. Creflo even said if they ever discover there is life on Mars, he's going to have to believe God for a billion dollar space shuttle. But how will 10,000 black church members gather up 1 billion dollars? This is ridiculous. Pastor Dollar has a Million dollar home in Atlanta, a private jet and a $2.5 million Manhattan apartment. The average income in College Park, Georgia is estimated at $29,000.

2. **Bishop David Oyedepo** – Nigeria. Net Worth **$150 million dollars**. He has four private jets and owns **Dominion Publishing House** which publishes all his books which his church members then buy. Almost 55% of Nigeria's citizens live below the poverty level on under $2 a day.

3. **Bishop Eddie Long** – Lithonia, Georgia. Net Worth **$5 million dollars**. In Lithonia, Georgia the resident's average annual income is estimated at $25,000.

4. **Pastor Christian Oyakhilome** – Lagos, Nigeria. Net Worth **$50 million**. His church has over 40,000 members. He has businesses which include newspapers, magazines, a television station, a record label, satellite TV, hotels and real estate. Nigeria lives below the poverty level with some people making incomes of less than $2 a day.

5. **Bishop T.D. Jakes** – Dallas, Texas. Net Worth **$18 million**. The annual income of his community in Texas is $56,000.

6. **Temitope B**. Joshua aka **Prophet T.B. Joshua** – Lagos, Nigeria. Net Worth **$15 million**. He owns a Christian Television Network and leads the Synagogue Church of all Nations (SCOAN).

7. **Charles Blake** – Beverly Hills, LA. Net Worth estimated at **$1 million** dollars. In South Central, LA the annual income is less than $30,000.

8. **Matthew Ashimolowo** – London, U.K. Net Worth **$10 million**. His hometown in Nigeria is in poverty in most places.

CHURCH MEMBERSHIP FOR PASTORS EQUAL FINANCIAL WEALTH. BUT AGAIN, WHAT ABOUT THE COMMUNITY?

1. **Bishop Noel Jones**, City of Refuge Church in **Gardena, California**, has about **17,000 members** and was formerly the Greater Bethany Community Church.
2. **Bishop Clarence McClendon** Full Harvest International Church has **10,000 members** is located in Los Angeles, California
3. **Pastor Wayne Chaney Jr** is senior pastor at the **1,000 member** Antioch Church of Long Beach in **Long Beach, California**, USA.
4. **Pastor Ron Gibson** is senior pastor of Life Church of God in Christ in Riverside, California. Its membership is estimated at **4,000 members**.
5. **Pastor Joel Olsteen** is pastor of Lakewood Church in Houston, Texas with an estimated **43,000 members**.
6. **Pastor Charles E. Blake** is pastor of West Angeles Cathedral in Los Angeles, California with an estimated **20,000 members**.
7. **Pastor T.D Jakes** is pastor of the Potter's House in Dallas, Texas with an estimated **17,000 members**.
8. **Pastor Eddie Long** is pastor of the New Birth Missionary Baptist in Lithonia, Georgia with an estimated **15,000 members**.
9. **Pastor Charles H. Ellis III** is pastor of Greater Grace Church in Detroit, Michigan with an estimated **6,000 members**.
10. **Pastor Creflo Dollar** is pastor of World Changers Church International in College Park, Georgia with an estimated **10,000 members**.

Let's just forget the numbers of members these Mega Churches have. I get very tired of seeing so many Black Churches in Detroit while the city suffers and we don't own anything as a people. The Pastors live in nice houses (**As they show us on Preachers of LA/Preachers of Detroit**) and are able to send their kids to private schools. Meanwhile the schools in these Church communities close down, leaving the kids to travel farther to go to school (often without reliable transportation). The **Teacher-to-student ratio** increases because of the consolidation of inner-city schools into 1 or 2 schools. This means the teacher has a larger classroom of kids from different neighborhoods and often different cliques. So more time is spent disciplining students than actually teaching students. No learning is done. Black students are then not prepared for Colleges or Universities. The schools in non-black communities do not close; instead they renovate their schools to make them bigger and better. But why should other races worry or care about the state of the Black community and the Black educational system? The Jews, Arabs, Indians, Koreans, Greeks and Italians all make money off the black residents in the cities where these Black churches are but at the close of the day these non-black business owners drive out in their fancy cars to the suburbs where their seed prospers generation after generation. They're going to Medical School graduations, Law School graduations while a large majority of black people are going to work, to the Family Independence Agency office, funerals, ER visits, and doctor's visits. Grandma Willie Mae Jones shouldn't have to lose her house if she has been paying tithes to her neighborhood Black church for 30 years faithfully like everyone else in the community. Grandma Willie Mae Jones grandson shouldn't have to decide not go to College because he can't afford it. Especially if her church has 10,000 members. Black Churches should show **"Brotherly and Sisterly Love"** to one another. Yahusha (Jesus) told us the **"Greatest Two Commandments"**. Since when do we get to pick and choose which commandments we want to follow? Shouldn't we ask our Pastors how come they are not teaming up with other Black pastors to start taking back our cities and improving the conditions for the youth so that they can achieve their dreams? The kids in the Black Church as well as the Black kids in the community have dreams just as the Pastor's children have dreams. After all, they do ask for multiple offerings every Sunday from the congregation. Where is the money going? Where is the **"Power"** in these churches? Where is the deliverance? Where is the salvation? Where is the change? What benefit have we seen in our community in the last 30 years? All over you see other races taking care of theirs. 80% of Muslim Mosques are subsidized by the United States of America. Jewish community centers are supported/financed by the Jewish people and the Synagogues. Jews make up 1.5%-2% of America, Blacks make up 14%. **AGAIN**, If every black person (45 million) deposited $20 dollars every Sunday for one year into a Black Central Bank/Fund this would equal **5 Billion dollars**. If we did this for as long as we have been going to church we would have in excess of 150 Billion dollars. This could supply the funding for Schools, College Scholarships, Housing, Farmland, Real Estate investments, businesses (Grocery Stores), School Loans, Business loans, Car loans, House loans etc. I think 150 billion dollars is enough to become independent in a "**White America**" that wants to keep Blacks uneducated, unemployed, incarcerated and dead.

THE WHITENIZATION OF THE BIBLE

Many, many years ago, the Catholic Church decided that it was not feasible to show representation of "**The Christ**" as a Black man. Neither could they admit that Israel was in "**Northeast**" Africa, being that it shared the same tectonic plate as Egypt and the Sinai Peninsula. Back in the early days of the Catholic Church the Suez Canal was not present. One could walk from Canaan to Egypt, just as the bible states with the biblical story of Joseph being sold to the Egyptians by his Israelite brothers. Many Churches are filled with Theologians and Biblical scholars who have vast knowledge of the Bible. Many pastors, deacons and ministers have countless numbers of books in their study at home but never try to explain how the bible can be all white when the bible is centered out of the hot climate area of Africa/Mesopotamia/Levant. The Black church draws visitors from all races, whites, Indians, Asians, Arabs and some Jews that have converted to Christianity. Some just visit to show their support for Black people and "**The Cause**". But do they know that we have been missing the big picture in regards to the "**WHOLE**" Bible Story? Some Caucasians even know that the original people of the bible were black. Down from the Egyptians to the Cushites to the Canaanites and to the Israelites. To them it is common sense. So how come we haven't figured this out? Are we being bamboozled in our own religious institution? **Donald Sterling**, the former owner of the Los Angeles Clippers (NBA) has visited the black church despite all the racist comments he has said about Black people in 2014. Here are some of his comments.

1. "Well then, if you don't feel -- don't come to my games. Don't bring black people, and don't come. "

2. "I support them (blacks) and give them food, and clothes, and cars, and houses. Who gives it to them? Does someone else give it to them? Do I know that I have – Who makes the game? Do I make the game, or do they

(blacks) make the game? Is there 30 owners that created the league (NBA)?"

3. "You go to Israel, the Blacks are just treated like dogs".

4. "It bothers me a lot that you want to broadcast that you're associating with black people. Do you have to?"

What some people don't understand is that the Baptist and Pentecostal Church was sprung out of the teachings of what the White slavemasters taught the slaves. The White Jewish slavemasters and non-Jewish slavemasters taught the slaves to worship on Sunday. They told the Negro slaves to eat pork, they told them that Jesus/Yeshua was a white man and that they were Canaanites. Because of this, they could justify that they were **"God's People"** and that the slaves were cursed from the biblical **"Curse of Canaan."** Even till this day, there are Africans that believe they are Canaanites and that slavery was simply the **"Curse of Canaan"**. However, not all of the slaves were easily misled. Some of the slaves were able to keep their heritage, or at least remember and pass down to their children who they really were. I remember witnessing this first hand in 2015.

I was talking one day to an 80+ year old African-American. She told me she was from Texas and that her parents/grandparents were from the south. Her son happened to be with her and he told me stories of how his mother was raised. The elderly woman stated that when she was engaged to get married, her father told her fiancé that he had three things that he had to do in order for him to accept his request to marry his daughter. These were his rules:

1. **Never lay your hands on (hit) my daughter.**
2. **She is to never eat Pork.**
3. **She must observe the Sabbath and keep it Holy.**

At first I thought she was a Muslim, but when I asked her if she was an **Israelite**, both the elderly mother and son said "Yes"! They acknowledged that they were **"Hebrew Israelites"** but called themselves **"Hebrew Pentecostals"**. This is because they had been raised as children in the Pentecostal Church. The Elderly woman stated that her Father was a Black Rabbi in the South. I immediately asked her **"Who told your father he was an Israelite?"** She said, "His father." I then told her that based on her age her father and grandfather must have lived during times when slavery was legal. She said, "Yes." She began to tell me that back when the slaves were taken on ships to be brought to the Americas the "**Negroes**" spoke **Hebrew/Aramaic** with some mixture of the Hamitic dialect in their language. She said that when the slaves landed in America they already had their "**Hebrewism**" traditions and customs from back home. She said elderly slaves that tried to teach the young these traditions/customs were quickly killed off or separated from the younger slaves so that the erasing of our history would take place. This was akin the "**Willie Lynch**" method of controlling the slaves. They gave us European slave names, European food that they were used to eating, a language that we would pick up as "broken English" and a religion which we only learned "Orally" out of their mouth because they did not allow blacks to learn how to read. This was the beginning of the "**Identity Theft**" and erasing of our history. She said there were some slaves that were able to remember what the elders told them and this knowledge was passed down as stories to future generations, even after slavery was abolished.

CHAPTER 22

THE HEBREW ISRAELITE GROUNDBREAKERS: THE "PHYSICAL ISRAEL".

One of the earliest Hebrew Israelite Churches was "**The Church of God and Saints of Christ**" established in Lawrence, Kansas, in 1896 by African-American *William Saunders Crowdy* (**Below**).

(Left) William Saunders Crowdy. (Right) Wentworth Arthur Matthew reading the Torah.

In 1919, *Wentworth Arthur Matthew* founded the "**Commandment Keepers Congregation**" in Harlem, New York. Some sources say he was born in Lagos, Nigeria while others list his birthplace in the West Indies. When Matthew learned about the Ethiopian Beta Israel Jews, he got inspired and could identify with them. He trained rabbis, who set up synagogues all throughout the United States and the Caribbean. His members observed the Jewish dietary laws and they observed the Sabbath. Matthew was so influenced by the European Jews that he, like others (some say Crowdy), rejected the New Testament. Matthew believed blacks were the original Jews, and white Jews were the descendants of the Khazars who had converted to Judaism in the 8th century A.D. He knew that Black Jews would not be accepted by the white Jewish community. After his death in 1973, his church was taken on by **Rabbi Capers Funnye**, an African-American with Gullah GeeChee West African ancestry. Rabbi Funnye leads the Beth Shalom B'nai Zaken Ethiopian Hebrew Congregation of Chicago, Illinois which he founded in 1985.

Arnold Josiah Ford (Above) was a Rabbi, a Black Nationalist, and emigrationist. He was born in Bridgetown, Barbados, the son of Edward Ford and Elizabeth Augusta Braithwaite. Ford asserted that his father's ancestry could be traced to the Yoruba tribe of Nigeria and his mother's to the Mende tribe of Sierra Leone. According to his family's oral history, their heritage extended back to one of the priestly families of the Ancient Israelites, and in Barbados his family maintained customs and traditions that identified them with Judaism. Arnold Josiah Ford established **Beth B'nai Abraham** in Harlem in 1924. A Jewish scholar who visited the congregation described their services as "a mixture of Reform and Orthodox Judaism, but when they practice the old customs they are seriously orthodox". Harlem chronicler James Vanderzee photographed the congregation with the Star of David and bold Hebrew lettering identifying their presence on 135th Street and showing Rabbi Ford standing in front of the synagogue with his arms around his string bass, and with members of his choir at his side, the women wearing the black dresses and long white head coverings that became their distinctive habit and the men in white turbans.

Prophet F. S. Cherry was called by the Lord in a vision to be His Prophet. He was fluent in Hebrew and Yiddish. In 1886, F.S Cherry established the "**Church of the Living God, the Pillar Ground of Truth for All Nations,**" the first Black Hebrew Israelite Church, in Chattanooga, Tennessee. He did not want to associate himself with "**Synagogues**" due to Revelations 2:9 and 3:9. Cherry drew sharp distinctions between his sect and traditional Jews, whom he considered impostors. Cherry's theology held that God, Jesus, Jacob, and Esau were Black; and that logically black people should be Jews, the direct descendants of Jacob. White Jews were held in contempt for rejecting Jesus; and consequently only black people could join his church. His church supposedly mixed elements of Judaism, Christianity (both Testaments) and the Talmud.

Despite all of this happening in the late 1800's and early 1900's we still see that the Black Hebrew Israelite movement was overshadowed by the Black Christian Church in the South. Many Blacks today do not know about the "**Black Hebrew Israelites**", what it means and when did it start. Many African-Americans and even Africans still believe that the Jews or "**God's Chosen People**" are white. Only when you try to prove that the people of the Bible were "**Black**" using "Critical Thinking" and knowledge of the Ancient nations that lived in Africa/Mesopotamia in Biblical times do people say "**Why does skin color matter?**" Or, "**It's not important what color Yeshua (Jesus) was; we are all God's people.**" Another often saying is, "We are all descendants of Abraham." This is incorrect. Japheth and Ham were not descendants of Abraham. The Bible states that Abraham only had children with Sarah, Hagar the Egyptian and Keturah. Everyone else on earth cannot be of Abraham's seed. Likewise we know that Greeks, Chaldeans, Persians, Arabs, and Romans lived during Biblical times. These nations are still with us today as living people, who know their heritage (**At least they claim to know their heritage**). So we should also question if the "**REAL**" descendants of the Children of Israel are alive today. If they are alive, we need to find out who they are **or** research as to where they may be according to Bible scriptures. The 144,000 Israelites who are sealed in Revelations are going to be living people, flesh and blood.

Revelations 7:4 "And I heard the number of them which were sealed: and there were sealed an **hundred and forty and four thousand of all the tribes of the children of Israel.**"

Want more proof?

Jeremiah 31:31-37 "Behold, days are coming, "declares the LORD, "When I will make a new covenant with the **HOUSE OF ISRAEL** and with the **HOUSE OF JUDAH**, not like the covenant which I have made with their fathers in the day I took them by the hand to bring them out of the land of Egypt. My covenant which they broke, although I was a husband to them," declares the LORD. But this is the covenant which I will make with the House of Israel after those days,' declares the LORD, "I will put my law within them and on their heart I will write it; and I will be their God, and they shall be my people. **THEY WILL NOT TEACH AGAIN**, each man his neighbor and each man his brother, saying, "Know the LORD," for they will all know Me, from the least of them to the greatest of them," declares the LORD, " for I will forgive their iniquity, and their sin I will remember no more." **Thus says the LORD, Who gives the sun for light by day and the fixed order of the moon and the stars for light by night, Who stirs up the sea so that its waves roar; The Lord of hosts is His name. If this fixed order departs from before me," declares the LORD of, Then the offspring of Israel also will cease from being a nation before me forever.** Thus says the LORD, If the heavens above can be measured and the foundations of the earth searched out below, Then I will also cast off all the offspring of Israel for all that they have done, declares the LORD."

This scripture is revealing to us that there will be a "**Nation of Israel (House of Judah/House of Israel)** as long as there is a **sun**, **moon** and **stars** in the sky.

But some people don't see it that way and think the following:

Galatians 3:28-29 "There is neither **Jew nor Greek**, there is neither bond nor free, there is neither male nor female: for ye are all one in Christ Jesus. And if ye be Christ's, then are ye Abraham's seed, and heirs according to the promise."

If we are followers of the whole bible then based on Jeremiah 31:31-37 there is a "**Physical Israel**" and a "**Spiritual Israel**". The Spiritual Israel are for those Gentiles who are believers in "**Christ**" and have been "**born again**". The Physical Israel is connected to the Ancient 12 Tribes of Israel by blood, **NOT** religious (Judaism) conversion.

Currently, all of the Ashkenazi Jews and Sephardic Jews will only tell you that they are from 3 Tribes if you ask them. If you ask any European Jew, "What Tribe are you from?" They will **ALWAYS** respond "**Judah, Benjamin, or Levi (Cohenite).**" If they say "**I don't know,**" their usual default answer to go to is the "**Tribe of Judah**". So what about the other 10 Tribes (Levi wasn't counted as a Tribe)? The European Jews (Sephardic/Ashkenazi) make up 99% of all worldwide Jewry. The Ethiopian Jews make up 1% and they are told they are from the Tribe of Dan. **Isn't Dan part of the 10 Lost Tribes?** So how can the European Jews say that the 10 Northern Tribes are still lost but the Tribe of Dan is found? Likewise, how is the Tribe of Dan found but the Tribe of Naphtali (Dan's full brother) is still lost???? What about the other Tribes? How come they are not found? These are all questions the Black Christian Church avoids. We have to use "**Real History**", "**the Bible**" and "**Critical thinking**" to determine that the Israelites of old were black. Moses, Joseph, and the Apostle Paul were all mistaken for Egyptians. Joseph, his family and his brothers' families were all mistaken for Egyptians upon burying their father Jacob in the land of Canaan (Abel-mizraim).

Genesis 50:11 "And when the inhabitants of the land, **THE CANAANITES**, saw the mourning in the floor of Atad, they said, This is a grievous mourning to the **EGYPTIANS**: wherefore the name of it was called Abel-mizraim, which is beyond Jordan."

*If you show Jews the proof that they are Jews by religious conversion to Judaism (**proselytes**) and **ARE NOT** the blood descendants of the Biblical Children of Israel they usually want **PROOF**. That's when you use scriptures in their own **Torah** and **Tanakh** (**Old Testament**) along with Ancient quotes, Ancient pictures with analogies to prove them wrong. **The Truth will ALWAYS be victorious over LIES**.*

In B.C. Times the Egyptians were Black people. So were the Cushites (Nubians) and the Canaanites. The proof is out there. The scriptures are laid out before us plain. If only we had eyes to see and ears to hear. For this reason the "Whitenization" of the bible has been allowed to go on. But Black people and the world are waking up now. Is this a sign of the times?? We must teach the Truth and not doctrines of ignorance. There are many Church pastors that know the truth but do not teach their congregation this in fear of being silenced or causing controversy that will result in lost church members. This is not what Yeshua (Jesus) is about. Satan is the "Father of lies". We must operate as if we are Disciples of Christ teaching the **TRUTH**, not disciples of Satan teaching lies.

CHAPTER 23

CHURCH IS OVER, BUT NOTHING HAS CHANGED?

Church is over and people are at home watching the Sunday NBA basketball game while getting ready to have a wonderful meal before going to bed for work the next day. But Monday thru Saturday, the **STRUGGLE** continues. Blacks go to work and at the job "**ALL EYES**" is on them, like a hawk. A Black worker that is seen talking to another black worker is always going to be given more work to do because corporate America does not want to see Blacks relaxed without stress on the job. The non-black bosses of Black Employees use their "**Authority status**" to crack the "**Invisible Whip**" 24/7, seven days a week all across America. "Complaints" and "Red Forms" are the norm for Blacks because nobody wants to see black people with a job. This is why there is always someone trying to get a Black employee fired. For a Black person to make it to 30 years at one Job, especially in a predominately white work environment, that Black Employee has probably had to go through hell and back. This is a major achievement many Blacks cannot say they have achieved. But why are Blacks still going through this type of treatment and why are we as a race still suffering in America despite going to church faithfully? Why are there so many Churches in our communities but so much destruction in the communities of these Black churches? Has the Black Church become a social meeting place to gossip, sell dinners, sell DVD's/CD's, collect more offerings (building fund, Missionary fund, speakers fund, music fund etc.) and provide false hope? Many of these churches have rooms, kitchens and extra unused space that serve no good during the week while hungry homeless people sleep outside every night. With all the resources/connections the Church has there is no change in education, no empowerment, no lending, no infrastructure, no business plans, no programs etc. So why no change? What are we doing wrong as a people?

Deuteronomy 28:45 "Moreover all these curses shall come upon thee, and shall pursue thee, and overtake thee, till thou be destroyed; because thou hearkenedst not unto the Lord thy God, to keep his commandments and statutes which he commanded thee:......And they shall be **UPON THEE** for a **SIGN** and for **A WONDER**, and **UPON THY SEED (CHILDREN) FOREVER.**"

Many Black churches and pastors will say this verse doesn't apply to African-Americans. So who does it apply to? Who are the **REAL CHILDREN OF ISRAEL**? Well, if you had a chance to read my initial book "**Hebrews to Negroes**" you would certainly know by now, but in case we need a refresher, the pictures and the bible do not lie.

(Above) Hebrew Israelites taken into captivity, 700 B.C. "**Siege of Lachish**" by the Assyrian King Sennacherib. Relief found at his Palace in the Capital of Ancient Assyria, Nineveh (North Iraq now).

Found in **II Kings 18, II Chronicles 32 and Micah 1:13**

Did the Israelites grow "Starter Locs" into longer locks as black people do today? This would explain the thickness of each individual hair/loc. White European hair does not grow this thick nor does it naturally "lock" or "mat" together. Pictures don't lie. The Hebrew word for Locks is Hebrew Strong's #6545 פֶּרַע or "Pera", which is used in Numbers 6:5 (Nazarite Vow) and Ezekiel 44:20.

(Above) Notice the Ancient Hebrews with Dreadlock hair styles (or Cornrows). Notice the FRINGES on the bottom of their garments, the HARPS AND CYMBALS. This was common with the Hebrew Israelites, just as Blacks in Church today worship with the Drums, Cymbals and Tambourine! The Ancient Hebrews from 700 B.C. were Black, not European or Arab looking people. (Below) This depiction of an Ancient Israelite in NO WAY resembles an European Ashkenazi Jew, Sephardic Jew or Mizrahi Jew.

In the previous picture you can see the Hebrew "Dreadlocked" Israelites playing the "Cymbals and Harp/Timbrels". Just as Blacks do today in Church.

Psalms 137:3 "For there **they carried us away captive required of us a song**; and they that wasted us (required of us) mirth, saying, **Sing us one of the songs of Zion.** How shall we sing the LORD'S son in a strange land?"

1 Chronicles 13:8 "And David and all Israel played before God with all their might, and with singing, and with **HARPS**, and with psalteries, and with timbrels and with **CYMBALS**, and with trumpets?

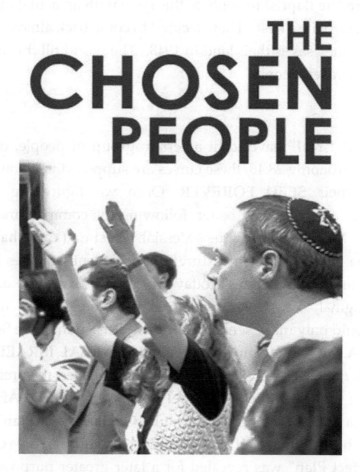

(Above) **Ashkenazi Caucasian Jews heritage is from Eastern Europe and Russia.** Originally Russia and Eastern Europe was known as the "**Land of the Khazars**" before it would be named "**Russia**" by Scandinavian **King Vladimir the Great,** ruler of "**Kievan Rus**". They claim that the Israelites left Israel to go into Europe where they never lost their heritage. However, they don't speak Paleo-Hebrew. Instead they combined the modern Syriac-Aramaic Hebrew language with their European (**Germanaic/Slavic/Turkish**) language dialect and called it "**Yiddish**". The claim they have kept 2,400 years of written records that prove they are from the Tribe of Judah, Benjamin and Levi. They claim they have records that trace their people back to the Priestly Levite (Aaronites) such as the Zadokites (900 B.C) and Ezra (400 B.C**.**). **Also, in 1997 they mysteriously created the Y-Haplogroup J1c gene linking it to the High Priests of Israel from about 3,000 years ago.** However there were no reports about them digging up the body of **Aaron, Zadok, Ezra, Zacharias** or **John the Baptist** to confirm this gene with an actual biological (tissue) sample from an Aaronite Priest. They decided to come back almost 2,000 years later taking back what they say is their land in 1948. The world till this day still believes they are "**God's Chosen People**".

So the "**Curses of Israel**" have to fit a certain group of people, or a "**nation**" of people. Per Deuteronomy 28:46, these curses are supposed to be on the Children of the Israel and their **SEED FOREVER**. Once we figure we are the **REAL ISRAELITES** we can start doing better, following the commandments/laws given to us by God via Moses and from the "Messiah" **Yeshua (Yahusha) Ha Mashiach**. By looking at the picture and hair texture of the Ancient Israelites from over 3,000 years ago and the so called "**Jews**" today we can see that these are not the same people. The original "Jews" were people akin to the "**Negro**" or "**People with Color**". This would only make sense. After the destruction of the Second temple in Jerusalem in 70 A.D. the remaining small number of **REAL ISRAELITES** would be scattered into all nations. Yeshua and his disciples needed to spread the gospel of salvation to all of the "**Lost Sheep of Israel**". This was done in Africa, Arabia, the Middle East, Asia and as far as India through "**God's Perfect Plan**". While many Blacks know the horrific stories of slavery, it was through slavery (**Curses of Israel**) that "**God's Perfect Plan**" was revealed for a later greater purpose. The disciples went everywhere they could, spreading the gospel before the slave trades started and the rise of Islam would start in 600 A.D. During and after slavery, the slaves were introduced to Christianity. However since 70 A.D. the Israelites would still endure more of the Curses while in Africa, Arabia and the Islands of the Seas. More persecution, more civil war, more attacks, more captivity, more disease and more genocide. The Arab Slave Trade beginning in the early centuries of the Common Era would further remove more Israelites into other nations and following the Transatlantic Slave Trade via the "**Middle Passage**" more Israelites would be taken to the Western lands of sea (Americas, Caribbean) to meet their "**Native**" Israelite brothers.

James 1:1 "James, a servant of God and of the Lord Yeshua Ha Mashiach (Jesus Christ), to the **TWELVE TRIBES WHICH ARE SCATTERED ABROAD, GREETING.**"

Need proof?

Romans 11:25 "For I would not, brethren, that ye should be **ignorant of this mystery**, lest ye should be wise in your own conceits; that blindness in part is happened to Israel, **until the fullness of the Gentiles be come in (in other words, until the times of the Gentiles be fulfilled).**"

Jeremiah 24:9 "And I will deliver them **to be removed into all the kingdoms of the earth** for their hurt, to be a reproach and a proverb, a taunt and a curse, in all places whiter I shall drive them."

Blacks are scattered into all kingdoms while the Gentiles are in possession of Israel; that is until their time is fulfilled.

Still not convinced that the "**Curses of Israel**" applies to the so called "**Negro**" and other Melaninated nations scattered into the many Islands of the Sea? Let's check out the Curses of Israel in Deuteronomy 28:16-68 and compare them to the "**Negro**" and the "**European Ashkenazi Jew/Sephardic Jew.**"

CHAPTER 24

THE CURSES OF ISRAEL: BROKEN DOWN PLAIN

DEUTERONOMY 28:16-17

In Deuteronomy 28:46 and other verses throughout the bible we see the curses that are bestowed on the Children of Israel and their seed **FOREVER**. So let's carefully go through **ALL** these Curses listed in Deuteronomy 28 and see **WHO** today is going through these curses; after all it say the curses will be upon the **Israelites seed (children) forever**.

Deuteronomy 28:46 **"And they (the curses) shall be upon thee (Israelites) for a sign and for a wonder, and <u>UPON THY SEED FOREVER</u>."**

Forever in the bible means "**Forever**". This is why the Children of Israel weren't re-gathered to Israel during the birth or after the resurrection of **Yahusha (Yeshua) HaMashiach (Jesus Christ)**. It also didn't happen after the ascension of "**Christ**" into Heaven. It is only going to happen during the 2nd coming of Christ. The bible clears states in multiple verses that God will in the future re-gather his children from the four corners of the earth. So why does most of the world believe these scriptures apply to the European white Jews that arrived to Israel in 1948 after the Holocaust? How could these verses contradict themselves? The Bible is not supposed to contradict itself! God is not the author of confusion as stated in the bible. Here is more proof in the scriptures that link slaves taken from Africa to the **Curses of the Hebrew Israelites** of Ancient times:

Deuteronomy 28:16 **"Cursed shalt thou be in the city, and cursed shalt that be in the field."**

When there are a majority of blacks living in crowded urban cities or villages in the poorest conditions these areas are commonly nicknamed "**Ghetto**", "**Projects**", "**Hood**", "**Slums**" and many more. Blacks in the South (**Field/Country**) and blacks in the North (**City**) all experience racial discrimination. Extreme poverty can be seen in blacks living in the Americas all the way Africa, Jamaica, Brazil and Haiti.

Here in America, Blacks are at the bottom of society economically, politically, socially, and academically. It is the same scenario in New York all the way South to Mississippi and Alabama. Martin Luther King Jr. even experienced this when he went in 1966 to Chicago to protest housing segregation. Martin Luther King Jr quoted:

"I have seen many demonstrations in the South, but I have never seen anything so hostile and hateful as I've seen here today."...."I have to do this...to expose myself...to bring this hate into the open."
Martin Luther King Jr, 1966 Marquette Park, Chicago Southwest side

Education is lacking in rural-city areas where blacks reside and the drop-out rates is higher in these schools compared to any other race. Ethiopian Jews, despite living in the Holy Land of Israel face the same problems African-Americans face in America with poverty, suicide, high school dropout, drugs, eugenics and racial discrimination. This is because it wasn't time yet for them to come to Israel. The Jews who brought the Ethiopians to Israel are Gentiles, descendants of Japheth and his children. The possession of Israel in 1948 was not the re-gathering of the Israelites that was prophesied in the bible. If it was, the Ethiopian Jews would have peace and brotherly acceptance in Israel. Neither is there peace for the European Jews in Israel despite the Bible saying that the Children of Israel should be in peace when they return back to their homeland.

THE 1948 STATE OF ISRAEL & RETURN OF THE JEWS WAS NOT BIBLE PROPHECY

Exodus 34:22-24 "You shall celebrate the Feast of Weeks, that is, the first fruits of the wheat harvest, and the Feast of Ingathering at the turn of the year. Three times a year all your males are to appear before the Lord God, the God of Israel. For I will drive out nations before you and **ENLARGE YOUR BORDERS**, and **NO MAN SHALL COVET (DESIRE) YOUR LAND WHEN YOU GO UP THREE TIMES A YEAR TO APPEAR BEFORE THE LORD YOUR GOD.**"

In **Jeremiah 31:10** it specifically states that when God brings back the Children of Israel to the Holy Land they will enjoy peace, rest and quiet. It also says that **NOBODY WILL MAKE THE CHILDREN OF ISRAEL AFRAID**. Ask any Jew the question, "Why hasn't Jeremiah 31:10 been fulfilled yet if God brought back the Children of Israel to the Holy Land in 1948?" They usually will have no answer. But if they say Jeremiah 31:10 is referring to Ezra and the Israelites returning to Israel under Persian King Cyrus to rebuild the 2nd Temple simply ask them, "**So where was the peace, rest, quiet and no fear when the Children of Judah were sold into the Grecians in Joel 3:6 and where was this peace, rest and quiet at when the Romans invaded ISRAEL and destroyed the 2nd Temple?**"

But here is another question regarding the creation of the State of Israel in 1948. ☞ We cannot accurately tell for a fact if the ISRAELITES were attacked by the Romans or the Babylonians during these **Three Feast Holidays** but we do know that the REAL Israelites were disobedient so they were in turn punished by God. God let other nations invade Israel to conquer the land and enslave the people. But the Jews today say God brought them back as a sign of "**Bible Prophecy**". In Jeremiah 31:31-

37 it says that God is going to give the Israelites a "**New Covenant**" when he brings the Israelites back to the Holy Land. But God is not going to give Gentile-Converts to Judaism a New Covenant. To the world it has appeared that Bible prophecy has in fact happened because the Gentile Jews have been blessed with Israel, money, and businesses. We know Satan also gives his children the material things of this world and in the Bible it states that the Pharisees (founders of Modern Judaism) were constantly called "Children of Satan".

John 8:44 "**Ye are of your father the devil**, and the lusts of your father ye will do. He was a murderer from the beginning, and abode not in the truth, because there is no truth in him. When he speaketh a lie, he speaketh of his own: for he is a liar, and the father of it."

The Festivals on the Calendar
(Religious Calendar)

1. Pesach/Passover-	Aviv 14
2. Hag Ha Matzah/Unleavened Bread-	Aviv 15-21
3. Firstfruits of the Barley Harvest- The Day after the Sabbath during Hag Ha Matzah	
4. Shavuot/Weeks- 50 days after Firstfruits of the Barley	
5. Yom Teruah (Rosh haShanah)/Trumpets- Tishri 1	
6. Yom Kippur/Atonement- Tishri 10	
7. Sukkot/Tabernacles- Tishri 15-21	

*The Jewish seven feasts are frequently grouped under the **THREE MAJOR FESTIVALS** listed in **Exodus 34:23**: **Feast of Unleavened Bread** (Passover-Pesach), **Feasts of Weeks** (Shavout), and **Feast of Tabernacles/Booths** (Ingathering-Sukkoth). All Jewish males are required to appear before Yahuah at these major feasts (Deuteronomy 16:6). Passover, Unleavened Bread, Firstfruits, and Pentecost occur during the Spring months and correspond with the barley and wheat harvests. Trumpets, Day of Atonement (Yom Kippur) and the Feast of Tabernacles/Booths/Ingathering occur during the Fall months and correspond to the olive and grape harvests.*

But if the creation of the State of Israel in 1948 was "**Bible Prophecy**" then why did the "**Passover Massacre**" in **3/27/2002** happen? Palestinian based Terrorist group **Hamas** attacked ISRAEL during the **Passover (Feast of Unleavened Bread)**. What's even more a joke is that Palestine, Jordan & Lebanon still have pieces of Israel's old borders. **Reuben, Gad, Manasseh's territories are now Jordan. Asher is Lebanon.**

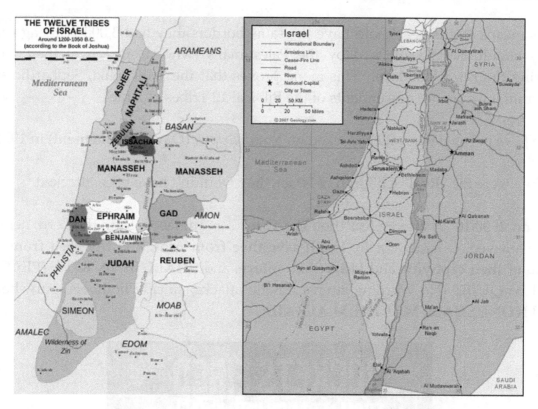

(*Left*) *The Land of Israel according to the Book of Joshua from the Time of King Saul to King David.* (*Right*) *The State of Israel (2015). Notice how the Tribe of Asher is now* **Lebanon.** *Notice how the Tribe of Manasseh, Gad and Reuben is now* **Jordan.** *The Jews today only occupy the land west of the Jordan River and Dead Sea. As you can see on the older map of Israel, this was not the case. Did God say in the "Last Days" that he would give the Israelites back part of their former land? No he did not. This is a clear sign the people living in Israel are not the "Real" Israelites.*

Well, the Jews in Israel were attacked on the "**Passover**" by the Palestinian terrorist group Hamas on March 27, 2002 in Netanya, Israel. 30 people were killed and 140 were injured. The Palestinians do not accept the Jews being in Israel and still to this day they want their former land back. Therefore, they "Desire and Covet" their former land. Remember the Bible says in Exodus: "For I will drive out nations before you and **ENLARGE YOUR BORDERS**, and **NO MAN SHALL COVET**

(DESIRE) YOUR LAND WHEN YOU GO UP THREE TIMES A YEAR TO APPEAR BEFORE THE LORD YOUR GOD."

This means that Israel should have the same borders they had 3,000 years ago and they should not be attacked by the Palestinians (who desire/covet their land) during the Feast Holidays. This alone proves that the Ashkenazi, Sephardic and Mizrahi Jews are not descendants of the Biblical 12 Tribes of Israel.

The Jews in Israel were also attacked on **Yom Kippur (Day of Atonement)** in 1973.

If they were the "**Real**" Children of Israel, they wouldn't have been attacked.

Jeremiah 30:10 "Therefore fear thou not, O my servant Jacob, saith the Lord; neither be dismayed, O Israel: for lo, **I will save thee from Afar**, and **thy seed from the land of their captivity**; and **Jacob shall return**, and **SHALL BE IN REST (PEACE)**, and be **QUIET** (No Warning sirens, missile attacks, suicide bombers, gun shots), and **NONE SHALL MAKE HIM AFRAID**."

*The **Israel Defense Forces (IDF)** protects Israel from outside threats from neighboring Muslim Countries such as Palestine, Lebanon, Jordan and Syria. Jeremiah wasn't prophesying about the re-gathering of the Tribe of Judah, Benjamin and Levi under Persian Rule to rebuild the Second Temple in Jerusalem with Ezra. **Why? Because 100 years later the Greeks under Alexander the Great would invade Egypt, Judea (Israel) and the***

*Middle East selling the Children of Judah to the Grecians. Then in 70 A.D. the Romans under **Roman Emperor Vespasian**, son Titus and Julius Alexander destroyed the Second Temple in Jerusalem exiling the last remnant of the Jews from the Holy Land. Jeremiah the Prophet of God is not a False Prophet, **MAN IS A LIAR**!*

Fact: Since the European Jews came to Israel there has been no peace, no quiet and no rest. They are constantly on guard, with sirens going off to warn Israeli citizens that rockets are fired from neighboring Muslim areas (**Lebanon, Palestine**) headed for their land. The "**Iron Dome**" system created in 2011 is an all-weather short range air defense system that has stopped **90%** of rockets courtesy of **Terrorist groups Hamas and Hezbollah** from hitting populated areas in Israel. Israel has built enough "**Iron Dome**" systems to protect Northern and Southern Israel from the barrage of rockets fired from their enemies. But something is not right here. Jeremiah was a prophet of the Almighty True Living God. He was not a "**False**" Prophet. He prophesied the **TRUTH**! So if Jeremiah said when God would bring his people from afar into the land of Israel that they would have no fear, but instead rest and quiet was he lying? NO! Israel would not have built "Iron Dome" systems if they were not afraid of rockets hitting their land. So why is lying here? The Prophet Jeremiah or the European and Sephardic Jews? **You be the judge.**

The Bible clearly proves that if the European Jews are descendants of Jacob, that these things above should **NOT** be seen today in Israel after 1948. But they are not.

The Ethiopian Jews, out of everyone in Israel, have more biblical and historical proof to prove that they are descendants of the Tribes of Israel than their European Jewish neighbors. Why? Because we know that the Israelites intermarried with the Sons of Ham in the Bible, including the Cushites (**Moses and his Cushite wife Zipporah**). Coincidence? In America the similarities of the curses in everyday life for blacks can be seen easily. Nobody wants to invest money in predominately black neighborhoods and only non-black business owners are willing to set up stores in these areas (Arabs, Koreans, Jews etc...) because they wish to profit off black dollars (consumerism). These business owners are not setting up their establishments in poor urban black communities to provide jobs, nor are they using the money they get from blacks to help rebuild the black inner-city communities that they service.

*(**Above**) Former Barbershop in Detroit. Black Businesses open and then close, but **NON-BLACK** businesses in our community (liquor stores, beauty supply stores, grocery stores, nail shops, pawn shops, Chinese food restaurants, laundry mats) open and **STAY OPEN**.*

Their agenda is to monopolize and make money by taking money from the people of the area. Even though we are called all sorts of derogatory names like **"monkeys"**, **"gang bangers"**, and **"niggers"** by other races that do business in the black community we still go back to these business establishments to give them our money. Never do we teach them to respect us by sticking together and boycotting. Never do all the Black Churches say **"Enough is Enough"** and devise an economic plan using the principle of **"Unity"** or **"Group Economics"** to take back their cities. Black inner cities are run down with the lack of basic services and lack of quality schools that suburbia provides its residents. The inner cities where blacks live to outsiders may look similar to war-torn countries overseas like Beirut, Lebanon. In some areas in the rural south like in Mississippi and Alabama there are **blacks still living in a form of "Chattel Slavery"** like the same way slaves did post-Civil war times **(etc. without electricity, without running water in faucets, property of the white plantation owner)**.

206

White America won't tell you that Chattel Slavery still exists today in the Rural South.

There are even areas in America that look worse than some of the hometowns and villages that Africans grew up in before immigrating to America. The lack of jobs, education, decent housing, and a political voice leads to frustration which then leads to increased crime. Unfair treatment practices and longer prison sentences for blacks in the judicial system leads one to believe that the world has an agenda to destroy blacks (**like the "Negro Project" of 1939**). We know this because we see so many innocent black people killed by our law enforcement system or by regular Caucasians citizens with no type of indictment or punishment given whatsoever. We see discrepancies between the prison sentencing methods that give higher prison sentences to blacks compared to whites. We see an increasing higher percentage of mental illness among African-American compared to other races in America which many of times is linked to socioeconomic status. We see an increasing number of Black male athletes coming out as **"Gay"** and we see more homosexuality shown in the Black music industry than any other music industry. We still see extreme poverty and a difference in the how blacks are treated compared to other races no matter what area of the world they live at. Blacks living in the cities experience the same problems that blacks living in poor areas of country experience. There are blacks living in the Basra, Iraq and Akhdam, Yemen

207

who live in the poorest of conditions just as Ethiopian blacks live in poverty in Israel. They are called "**Abd**", "**Abeed**", "**Akhdam**" or "**Khadama**" which is Arabic for Servant or Slave. They are distinguished by their darker skin. Although they are Arabic-speaking and practicing Muslims, they are stigmatized as Non-Arabs, who are economically, morally and religiously inferior to the light skinned white Arabs. For those who are living in these situations and are angry, "**looking from the inside out**", it is easy to see why Blacks would feel like they are cursed compared to those with better lives who live in the suburbs. In Israel, Blacks (Africans and African-Americans) are called "**Kushim**" or "**Kooshim**" which is a derogatory word meaning "**Nigger**" in reference to "**Cush**" being black.

Is this Detroit or Chicago? It is not in the Suburbs. It's in the Black inner city.

Deuteronomy 28:17 "Curse shall be thy basket and thy store."

Blacks have not progressed in America as a people despite being here over 500 years. Immigrant Jews, Greeks, Italians, Koreans, Filipinos, Chinese, Arabs, Europeans, Eastern Indians and Latinos have surpassed us despite only being here maybe a little over 150 years. These immigrant races are accepted in America without much racial discrimination. Their businesses thrive, making money off of the people of America. This is not the case for blacks or black businesses. We as blacks will eat at Chinese, Indian, Jewish and Middle Eastern restaurants and find that they have adjusted their menu to attract us to buy and come back. Perfect example is Fried Chicken being served at Chinese Restaurants. A plate of Shrimp Fried Rice and Fried Chicken Wings in a Chinese restaurant doesn't seem like a big deal to us. But in all actuality it needs to be. I once asked an Indian woman if she and her family would eat at an Indian restaurant if an **All-Black staff** was cooking the food. **She said "no."** I asked a Middle Eastern woman if she would dine out at a Middle Eastern restaurant with her family if it was owned by blacks and staffed by blacks (**including the cook**). **She also said "no."** I asked some Asians if they would take their family to a Chinese Restaurant if the restaurant was owned by blacks and staffed by all blacks. **They all said "no."** So based on these responses, it seems that we have been conditioned to accept and support other races businesses but not support our own. This fits the **Curses of Israel**.

WHEN ARE WE GOING TO GET THE CONCEPT OF "GROUP ECONOMICS?"

(**Above**) *A common scene at some Chinese Restaurants is **Chinese Food-Soul Food combinations** such as **Shrimp Fried Rice and Fried Chicken Wings**. This is obviously a tactic to keep blacks coming back for more food while we give them more of our money. It is also not uncommon to see Liquor Stores and Gas Stations owned by Middle Easters serving Soul Food such as Fried chicken wings, chicken tenders, mac' n cheese, greens, or cornbread.*

In Guyana, South America, Blacks are still poorer than the Indian indentured servants brought there in the 1800's, centuries after the African slaves were there. Even in Africa, the land is stricken with drought, famine, disease, plagues, and war which limit the full capability of Africans from profiting off the resources of the land. Other foreign peoples such as the British, the Germans, the Portuguese, the Dutch, the French and the Chinese are profiting off the land of Africa, using its resources to make them rich. The British (Europeans) in Nigeria have established generations of wealth compared to the African natives. The same can be said about other European races and their socioeconomic statuses compared to Africans in countries like Ghana, Benin, Togo, Congo, South Africa, and so on. Many countries make money off the precious metals, oils and other resources Africa has to offer. The Chinese build companies-industries in Africa and often do not employ the native Africans living in the land. They bring technology to harvest the rich oil land of South Sudan and also build Oil Refineries to make the crude oil make them money. Then they build their own housing, followed by Chinese businesses so that they can have their own "**Chinatown**" in Africa if they decide to live there. This ensures the success of the Chinese and their families wherever they may be while the native people of Africa still live in poverty. It is a known fact that China is Africa's biggest trading partner and other countries profit off of selling Africa their newest technologies. Most of the goods sold in Nigeria such as cell phones, electronics and flip-flop sandals are made in China or other Asian countries. The designs our goods are from China but the manufacturing of these goods may be in countries like Indonesia. It is also a known fact that China supplies many of the goods imported into **OUR** country and onto the shelves of our local stores. Just look at the tags on items bought from Walmart. The proof is there. It is for these reasons that Africans are then forced to work for corporations owned by other races in their own country just like African-Americans work for other races in America. African-Americas and Africans are known to have businesses in hair care (**Barber shops, Beauty Salons, Hair Braiding/Loctitian Shops**) but is this going to give us wealth? How can we achieve "**Wealth**" off the labor of our own hands? There is only 24 hours in a day. When our manual labor stops, the money stops. When debilitating illnesses strike the money stops. We have to learn how to use the system of "**Group Economics**", like the Chinese, Arabs, Jews, and Indians do. This way our "money" is not dependent on "**physical hard labor**" but our "**mind power**". Other races don't make money doing physical labor like Blacks and Latinos do. These other races make money whether they are sleeping, eating lunch or getting a massage outside while enjoying nature.   Likewise, when other non-black races approach a project or a task, they approach it as a "**Group**" or "**Team**". This is why they are able to accomplish large jobs and be successful when immigrating to America, sometimes with nothing but the clothes on their back.

Fact 1: *It's a known fact that Whites benefit financially from Life Insurance compared to Blacks.   This has been taught to them from their parents.   When Black couples are approached with the question of: "**When are you going to get Life Insurance?**" we get defensive and question the motive of the question. We may say, "**Why do you want me to get Life Insurance; are you expecting me to die**" or "**You just want me to get Life Insurance so you can kill me and move on with the money afterwards.**"   Blacks automatically think someone is plotting on their death or betting on their death to "**cash in**". This goes back to our "**Distrust**" of one another, programmed into us by the "**Willie Lynch**" letters and learned behavior from **Ancient Israel**.   So we delay getting Life Insurance because we think we are too young to get it and that nobody is going to benefit off my death, unless I approve of it after living a long life. But sometimes, uneventful things happen and Blacks die unexpectedly. Now there is no Life Insurance for the kids, the wife and no money to even help pay for a proper funeral service or burial. Whites frequently deposit Life Insurance checks from their loved ones and they gain wealth each time someone dies in their family.*

Fact 2: *In 2011, Alabama passed their anti-immigration law HB 56 which caused a mass exodus of undocumented immigrants from Mexico. Many farmers could not find workers to tend to the fields the way the Mexicans did. In Alabama, agriculture is a $5 billion dollar industry with 3.4 billion coming from poultry (chickens) and the rest coming from farmland that produces everything from cattle to cotton, peanuts to azaleas. One out of every five jobs is connected to **Agriculture.** Most undocumented workers in this industry are paid "**Piecework**", meaning they pay for how much they pick. They get paid for the number of chickens they can round up, how many buckets of potatoes they can pick or how many barrels of oranges they can fill during the course of a shift. The work is all physical as workers stoop and kneel to pick up whatever needs picking. After the Alabama anti-immigration law was passed the farmlands became empty as undocumented workers left in fear of "**surprise deportation**" if they stayed.   Alabama thought that eager White Americans would fill these positions, since Alabama in certain counties were over 80% white. Most of the non-Mexican workers that many of these farmlands hired only lasted a* *couple of hours before they quit. So after weeks to months the anti-immigration law was labeled a failure.*

Are Beauty Salons, Barber Shops, and Braiding shops the only Black businesses in your community? It is hard to get rich if your money depends on physical labor. There is only 24 hours in a day.

Is this a coincidence or just bad luck? Despite being in America longer than most other immigrants including Latino's, African-Americans still do not own anything. Barbershops and Salons are not helping us build wealth. If it were, we would have franchises of them, city-to-city and state-to-state. Instead of seeing this we see the transformation of our community businesses into businesses designed to take our money. I call it the "**Nigga-fication**" process. It involves replacing normal businesses that offer a variety of services to businesses that steal our money and keep us in bondage. Check cashing stores, Liquor stores, Cash Advance stores, Pawn Shops, Nail Shops, Beauty Supply stores, Dollar Stores, Chicken shacks, Chinese restaurants, Plasma centers, Coney Islands and Laundry mats. These types of businesses are all too familiar in our communities, especially those communities that see a high influx of blacks and a mass exodus of whites. Previous businesses leave and the following businesses pop-up, sometimes seemingly overnight.

- Chinese Restaurant
- LA insurance
- Beauty Supply store
- Dollar Store
- Meat Town
- Check-n-Go/Cash Advance
- Nail shop
- Fish & Chicken shack
- Laundry Mat
- Check Cashing/Bill Payment Center
- Strip Club
- Church
- MetroPCS/Wireless center
- Pawn shop/Diamond Jewelry and Loan
- Tax preparation stores
- Abortion Clinics
- HydroGiant (Medical Marijuana Certification Center)
- Grocery Store
- Plasma Center
- Liquor Store

BLACKS HAVE HIGHEST "SPENDING POWER" DESPITE BEING THE MINORITY RACE IN AMERICA. SO WHY ARE OTHER IMMIGRANT RACES SURPASSING US?

It is a known fact that the Black population in America in the 1860's was around 14%. 150+ years later in 2015 it is still the same around 14% but Latinos are now close to 20%. We know blacks are still having babies in the inner cities (married or unmarried) so this means either the American borders and coastlines are wide open for Latinos to come to America or that they are controlling the population of blacks with various means such as **"negative eugenics"**.

Fact:
- **Arab-Americans** make up **1%** of America.
- **Indian-Americans** make up **1%** of America.
- **Asian-Americans** make up **6%** of America.
- **Jewish-Americans** make up **2%** of America.
- **African-Americans** make up **13%** of America.
- **Latin-Americans** make up **17%** of America.
- **Non-Hispanic White Americans** make up **63%** of America.

*Black people outnumber Arabs, Jews, Asians, and Indians combined but we all work for them or Caucasians. Blacks have been in America for over 500 years, longer than every other immigrant race but yet we don't own anything and we provide the labor workforce for all these other races. Is this the **Curse of Israel** or **Curse of Canaan**? You be the judge after reading Deuteronomy 28:15-68 and the rest of the bible.*

Looking at Black population statistics it seems unreal that we are working for other immigrant races but are ten times more numerous than these other races in America. It doesn't make any sense at all. For almost every race in America, it is seen as disgrace to work for a Black person as opposed to a non-black person. For this reason you will hardly ever see a Chaldean, an Arab, an Indian, or a Jewish person working for a black person. Likewise, you will hardly ever see a homeless Chaldean, Arab, Indian, Jewish or Asian person in America. Despite the abolishment of slavery, we still haven't been able to stick together and own businesses within our communities like the famous **"Black Wall Street"** in Tulsa, Oklahoma. Black millionaires and billionaires turn the blind eye when countless numbers of schools are closed down in major Black inner cities all throughout America but yet they can pack out the **Soul Train Awards or BET awards.**

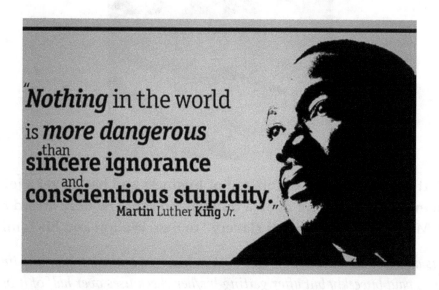

"*Nothing* in the world is *more dangerous* than sincere ignorance and conscientious stupidity." Martin Luther King Jr.

The "**long-term economic vision**" our so-called black rich role models and leaders lack is one of the many problems why blacks as a whole are still way behind compared to other races. So generation after generation like the blind leading the blind we make them rich while we stay poor. This helps their children be successful and keeps the cycle going. Our black dollars don't get recycled into black businesses because there are none. Therefore we remain poor, while they thrive. They control all the staple businesses and positions (Food, energy, transportation, housing, shopping-retail, music, entertainment-sports, Judicial system, Banking-accounting, hair care products) while we own what we do best. Cut hair, do hair, and braid hair. Aside from "**Hair Maintenance**", every other business in our community is set up and designed to take our money.

"Wal-Mart put my appliance store out of business so I had to get a job at Wal-Mart. Thanks to Wal-Mart, I'm on a budget and can now only afford to shop at Wal-Mart. Isn't this "partial slavery" to Sam Walton and his family?"

Fact: *Here is a simple example of how this system keeps us enslaved: If a Full-time Walmart Employee gets paid biweekly but after getting his/her check uses over half of it buying goods from Walmart, that person is essentially no different than a slave that works in the field for his slavemaster (Chattel Slavery) and then the eats the food the slavemaster provides the slave. In this case the "Slavemaster" is the founder of Walmart, **Sam Walton** and his descendants. In the same sense, if we continue to work for other races but then give our paycheck money to these races we will only see their descendants get rich while we stay poor. Are we secretly "**Still Enslaved**"? Is this a "**Prison Planet?**" This is why we need more black business and economic power.*

CHAPTER 25

DEUTERONOMY 28:18

Deuteronomy 28:18 "**Cursed shall be the fruit of thy body and the fruit of thy land, the increase of thy kine, and the flocks of thy sheep.**"

(Above) Plants and livestock die in many countries in Africa due to famine, drought and disease.

The word "**Kine**" is plural for a "**Cow**". As you can see in the picture above, hundreds of cows die in Africa due to famine, drought and disease such as **trypanosomiasis** from the "**Tsetse fly**". Low rainfall leads to plant/crop die off which shrinks the food supply for livestock. The livestock lose weight, become susceptible to disease and then die. The availability of food (meat/crops) is dependent on "**Supply and Demand**". Food crisis affects Humans and the livestock. Without food the livestock will die. The farmer that plants crops and takes care of livestock (Sheep, cattle, chickens) has no control over nature. Unfortunately, this is a common occurrence in West Africa and East Africa, the places where many "**Bantus Negro**" Israelite tribes settled after leaving Israel. This are of land was commonly called "**Negroland.**"

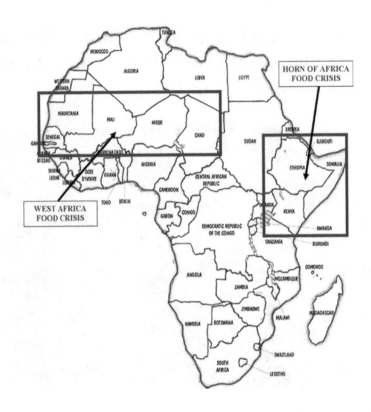

*There are two main areas in Africa that Famine has hit hard over the years as you can see on the map above. Ironically, these two regions in Africa were also "**hotspots**" for slavery in the past. **Slavery of the Bantus Negro "Hebrew Israelites"**. So we know the Israelites were living in these areas because they experienced the "**Curses of Israel**". They had famine in this area (**Deuteronomy 28:18**) and they were taken captive as slaves across the world from this area (**Deuteronomy 28:32,64,68**). The area in West Africa was called "**Negroland**" and the other area known as the "**Horn of Africa**" was where many Bantu Negroes were sold into slavery. Others may call it the "**Nile River Valley**" or "**African Great Lakes**". From this area slaves were taken from **Zanzibar , Ethiopia, Somalia, Tanzania, Kenya, Uganda, Sudan, Mozambique and even as far inland as the Congo.** These slaves were sold to the Middle East, India, the Pacific Islands (Indonesia, Java) and as Far East as China. Some Ethiopian slaves were sold to **Akhdam, Yemen** in early A.D. times before Islam even existed. It is a known fact that in **Kenya**, the majority of people are labeled "**Bantus**" while the rest are labeled "**Nilotic**" or "**Cushitic**". Some*

218

tribes genetically also have a mixture of both *"Bantus"* and *"Nilotic"* stock. The *"Bantus"* people obey the Laws of Moses (**Mosaic Law**), they circumcise and they practice a form of Judaism. In Ethiopia, Somalia, and Kenya we see Afro-Asiatic (Hamitic-Semitic) Blacks who speak Semitic languages (**Hebrew, Arabic, Amharic, Ge'ez, Tigray**) from their mixture with so-called Semitic peoples or peoples with learned Semitic traditions.

East Africa has been subjected to slavery as far back as 600 B.C. (some sources say earlier). The Arabs from Oman and Yemen (**Arabia Felix**) used Zanzibar Island in Tanzania as their main Slaving trading port. The Tanzania people prior to the Arab/Indian invasion were primarily "**Bantus**" people that had migrated from West Africa (Nigeria/Cameroon) to Central, Southeast and East Africa during the "**Bantus Expansion**" period 2,000-3,000 years ago. When the Arabs came to East Africa to do trade (**which slave trading was also a big part of their wealth**) they started mixing with the local people.

(**Far left**) *Non-Arab Cushite people (i.e. Afar, Somali).* (**Middle two pictures**) *Nilotic people (i.e. Dinka).* (**Far Right**) *Bantus people (i.e. Nigerian - Igbo/Nigerian, Rwanda-Tutsi/Hutu, Ghana - Akan/Ewe, Kenya – Kikuyu/Mbeer/Kamba/Meru/Embu). Can you tell the difference between these people without these classifications? This is how the Israelites blended in with the other Hamites in Africa. Their religion and Hebrew customs set them apart.*

The Bantus people in Somalia, Kenya and Tanzania are usually set apart by their hair texture (**kinky**) and their skin color (**dark**). Sometimes the non-Bantus Cushite people in these countries have lighter skin and soft, curly hair from mixing with the Arabs (**ex. Somalians, Ethiopians, North Sudan**). The **non-Arab** "Cushitic" Africans are dark-skinned just like the Bantus and Nilotic people, but with varying hair textures (soft vs thick). The "**Nilotic**" people are also dark-skinned African with kinky hair. The Bantus people often mix with Nilotic people and Cushitic people in their land just as the Israelites in Ancient times intermarried mostly with the sons of Ham. One example is the **Maasai Tribe** in Kenya. **In the Y-Chromosome study by Wood (2005) it was shown that 50% of the Maasai Tribe had the E1b1b (former E1b1c-Cushite/?Semitic) gene, 27 % had the A3b2 gene and 13 percent had the E1b1a. 8% of the Maasai Tribe had the Haplogroup B gene.**

ARE WEST AFRICANS GENETICALLY RELATED TO THE BANTUS EAST AFRICANS THAT WERE TAKEN AS SLAVES IN THE ARAB SLAVE TRADE?

Haplogroup A is most often associated with the descendants of Ham (**Hamite Africans**). It is an old genetic Haplogroup that doesn't have mutations. For this reason it is labeled Haplogroup A (Adam). Haplogroup A is found primarily in Africa in high frequencies (>40%) with the Bushmen Pygmies of Central Africa, the Khoi-San People (**who also carry the Y-Haplogroup B**), the Nilotic people of Sudan, and the Ethiopian Jews. **41% of the Ethiopian Jewish subjects in the genetic study by Fulvio Cruciani (2002) were shown to have the Haplogroup A**. Just like the Israelites did in Egypt, the Bantus (Israelite) people who commonly have the E1b1a gene have multiplied, taking over almost half of Africa. The E1b1a Gene that the Bantus people have has been traced thousands of years in the past to Northeast Africa (Israel). Over time the Bantus people eventually left Northeast Africa (Israel) and settled in West Africa (**coming from different routes such as North Africa and East Africa**). From there, they spread to Central, Southern and Southeastern Africa. However, what most people don't know is that before 2008, the Sub-Saharan Bantus and Non-Bantus/Non-Nilotic East Africans (**Ethiopians, Ethiopian Jews, and Somalians etc.**) were classified into one segment of the **E Haplogroup** called **E-V38**. **The E-V38 had 2 main (clades) branches: E-M2 which is E1b1a (Bantus) and E-M329 which is E1b1c (Ethiopians/Somalians-Semitic/Cushite). E-M2 (E1b1a) is found exclusively in West Africa (80%), Central Africa (60%) and South Africa (Bantus lands).** In 2008 **Tatiana Karafet** did a genetic study and proposed new mutation findings which resulted in adding a new group **E-M215 (E1b1b)** into the **E-V38 class.** This "**New**" **E-M215 (E1b1b)** basal branch had a broad geographic distribution from **Southern Europe (Spain, Portugal, Italy, Greece, Turkey, Kurdistan) to Northern Europe and Eastern Africa** to from where they believe they originated from. People with the E1b1b gene are currently in North Africa Morocco, Egypt, Libya, Tunisia and Algeria. Because of this E1b1b discovery, Somalians and Ethiopians have been bunched into the E1b1B class. The Ethiopian/Somalian E1b1c class disappeared into this new **E1b1b** class so now Africa is broken into **E1b1b (North Africa/East Africa) and E1b1a (Sub-Saharan Africa) groups**. So why after 2008-2011 has the original **E1b1c (E-M329)** genetic classification of the Ethiopians/Ethiopian Jew/Somalians vanished? How can we find them or distinguish them in this new E1b1b class. Was this done on purpose to confuse the genetic make-up of the Ethiopian Jews? The West Africans Bantus Negroes and the East African Cushitic/Hamitic Africans were all in the same E-V38 class. Why add another class and erase the Ethiopians/Somalian former class? Was this done to get people to believe that the Ethiopian Jews are nothing but Ethiopian Hamites who converted to Judaism? The Ethiopian Jews today are classified by their **Hamitic Haplogroup A3b2 gene** and **their Haplogroup E1b1b genes**. Here is the big question? **Were the Ethiopians former E1b1c genetic group a Semitic/Cushitic group that was akin to the E1b1a Semitic group of West Africans?** We all know that Moses married a Cushite (Zipporah) and we all know the story of King Solomon and Queen Sheba. We also know the story in Acts 8 of how Philip (an Israelite) heard the Ethiopian Eunuch reading the Book of Isaiah in the Hebrew language. So based on this we can accurately assume that there are some Cushite people with mixed Semitic Israelite blood.

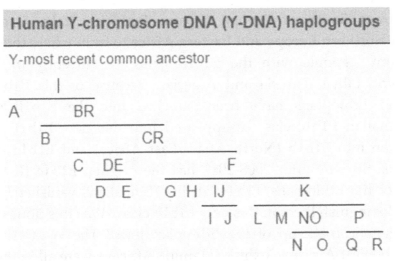

Human Y-chromosome DNA (Y-DNA) haplogroups

Y-most recent common ancestor

Y-Haplogroup Chart

Haplogroup Naming *wasn't around until after the year 2000. The* **Y-Chromosome Consortium in 2002** *defined a set of rules to label the different lineages within the tree of binary Haplogroups. Capital Letters* ***(from A to R)*** *were used to identity 18 major Haplogroups called* ***"clades"***. *It is here that they developed an "Alpha-numeric" system (i.e. E1b1a, R1b) for subclades. Newer Haplogroups like* ***"Q"*** *and* ***"R"*** *have been added to the Y-Haplogroup Tree.* **Note: Mysteriously, these two Haplogroups are the main Haplogroups of the Native Americans.** *If you look at most Genetic Studies involving Y-Haplogroups, they typically are no older than 2000-2001. In 2012 the way Haplogroups were being named and referenced started changing. A perfect example is* **Haplogroup "Q" and "R"** *which are supposedly a branch of* **Haplogroup "P". Haplogroup "Q" and "R" at the bottom for a reason.** *The* ***"powers to be"*** *do not want you to know the* ***"Truth"*** *about the "R" and "Q" Haplogroups. If you did it would explain a lot of stuff. They also don't want you to know why the "E" and "R" Haplogroups have a lot of mutations (***Michael Hammer and Tatiana Karafet 2008 study***). These are some of the main Haplogroups seen in West Africans, Native Americans, Caribbean's (Blacks & Latinos) and India of whom many say are where the* ***"Real Children of Israel"*** *can be found.*

*Fact: The **Y-Haplogroup K2b2** and **P295** are found in the "Negrito" **Aeta people** (**Above**) of the Philippines. Haplogroup K2b2 comprises Haplogroups P and its sub-Haplogroups "Q" and "R" which make up the main two Haplogroups of Native Americans/Latinos. Is this a clue that Native Americans and Latinos share common Ancient Hebrew Israelite ancestry from Africa? This proves that they are not descendants of Europeans or the "**Sons of Japheth**". Perhaps the Israelites mixed with other nations in their travels to the New World (by land-Beringia or sea-Atlantic Ocean). This would explain the many genetic mutations that could arise creating new Haplogroups such as "P", "Q", and "R".*

The Bantus people (i.e. Bantus Kenyans) do not eat pork, they abstain from alcohol and they often eat flat unleavened bread. The Bantus people circumcise and some (**Maasai Tribe**) even practice a sort of "**Nazarite Vow**" for their children when born. They are discriminated against by other African groups in politics, education, and employment. During the Arab Slave Trades, African Muslims could own Bantus slaves because they were not Muslim. But if a Bantus man or woman converted to Islam they would be "**spiritually/religiously redeemed**" from Slavery. These Bantus tribes would then become "**Bantu Muslims**" just as in West Africa where many Africans or (**perhaps Israelites**) in the past practiced a form of **Karaite Judaism** only to convert to Islam later (**Senegal-Gambia, Mali, Guinea**).

Fact: *The Bantus Africans of East Africa were subject to slavery by the Arabs around the time that the Arabs started to establish dominance in the Middle East. The **Abbasid Caliphate** was the third Islamic Caliphate to succeed the **Prophet Muhammad**. They ruled from 700 A.D to the 1200 A.D. roughly. The Abbasid Caliphate was known for the capturing and selling of Bantus Black (Hebrew Israelite) slaves from Zanzibar, Tanzania.*

They brought them to **Basra, Iraq** amongst other places to work in the salt mines. From 869 A.D. to 883 A.D. the Black Zanji people fought back, killing hundreds (some say thousands) of Arabs. This was called the *"Zanj Revolt/Rebellion"*. During the *"Age of Exploration"* in the 1400's the Portuguese shifted their attention to Zanzibar, Tanzania. They invaded and controlled Zanzibar for almost 200 years.

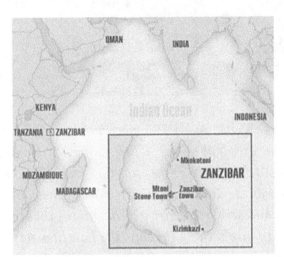

The Island of Zanzibar was designated for slave trading until the Anglo-Zanzibar war of 1896.

In 1698, Zanzibar fell under the control of the Muslims from Oman. They used the Zanji Bantus people for slaves as their forefathers had done 800 years ago. The Arabs got rich of the trading of Spice, Ivory and slaves. The Arabs controlled a big portion of the **African Great Lakes** during that time and even expanded their territory in land into the Congo. The British eventually would take Zanzibar, Tanzania from the Muslims (**like they did Nigeria**) in the late 1800's abolishing slavery and in the 1900's the Island of Zanzibar, Tanzania would finally gain their independence.

(Above) Zanzibar Freed slaves on the British "Flying Fish" boat that intercepted a slave trading vessel of the coast of Zanzibar (1873).

FAMINE LAND FOR CAIN AND THE "LAND OF NOD"

Africa's history includes some of humankind's earliest food production, with one of the most fertile centers located in Northern Africa, the Nile Valley. The Nile Valley area is considered by many the Biblical "**Garden of Eden**". In this Area everything was plentiful. We know that Adam's son "**Abel**" was a keeper of the flock (livestock) while "**Cain**" was a tiller of the ground "**Farmer**". God banished Cain to the land "East" of the Garden of Eden.

Genesis 4:16 "And Cain went out from the presence of the Lord and dwelt in the Land of Nod, on the **East of Eden**."

Fact: *To the East of the Nile River Valley in Egypt is Southern (Negev) Canaan or the* *"Negev Desert".* *The "African Hebrew Israelites of Jerusalem" who came with Ben Ammi live in the* ***Negev Desert*** *in the city* ***Dimona, Israel.*** *There is hardly any vegetation there as it is mostly desert terrain and mountains.* *The word* ***"Nod"*** *is the Hebrew root of the verb* ***"to wander".*** *The Negev Desert is also where the nomadic Bedouin Arabs live.* *A nomad is a* ***"wanderer",*** *someone without a home looking for areas to cultivate the land or pasture.* *It is in this area that the Kenites (some say the descendants of Cain), the Edomites (enemies of Israel) and the Amalekites (sons of Esau) also lived.* **So the bible says that Cain would be a fugitive, a vagabond and would not be able to yield many crops from the ground.** The area of Southern Negev in the **"Negev Desert"** is known for not being able to not produce crops. Bedouins have a hard time finding food in these areas. Interestingly, the Biblical Kenites (Cainites aka "Children of Cain?) also were associated with being a fugitive and a vagabond on the Earth. In the map above you can see the close vicinity of the **Negev Desert** and **Edom**.

*The **Bedouins** living in the **Negev Desert** are not welcome in Israel. This area used to be the biblical "**Land of Nod**" where the Cainites and Edomites lived. King Saul and the Israelites fought the Amalekites (Edom) in this area. The Arab Bedouins are constantly harassed by Israel to leave, especially when Israel wants to use the land for whatever reason. The Bedouins have managed to stay and escape expulsion after the European Jews started kicking out Palestinians in 1948. Their unrecognized villages are denied basic services such as water and electricity. After 1948 many Sephardic Jews and Mizrahi Jews immigrated to Beersheba in the Negev Desert from Arab countries. Smaller populations include the Bene Israel and Cochin Jews of India.*

Genesis 4:12 "When thou tillest the ground, it shall not henceforth yield unto thee her strength; a fugitive and a vagabond shalt thou be in the earth."

THE OTHER CURSE: "THE CURSE OF LEPROSY" AND ITS CONNECTION TO THE ANCIENT ISRAELITES

Fact: *Many people have theorized that the "**Mark**" of Cain was "**White Skin**" and that everyone during that time in Genesis was brown-skinned people. This would possibly explain why no one would try to kill him, especially if they saw his white skin and was afraid or if they thought he was some type of god or angel.*

227

Genesis **4:15** *"And the Lord said to him, Therefore whoever kills Cain, vengeance shall be taken on him sevenfold.* **And the LORD set a mark on Cain, lest anyone finding him should kill him."**

*The Mormons have a myth that believes that Cain's descendants survived the flood through the wife of Ham but were black-skinned. Some Midrashim Jewish teachings (***Bereishet Rabbah 22:8 and Midrash Aggadah 4:15***) claim that Cain became a white leper. Some say he grew horns on his head to protect him like the famous skull found with horns and red hair.*

True or False? Spanish Hill reports that Captain John Smith (of Jamestown, Virginia) in the 1600's witnessed seeing many giant skeletons called "Susquehannocks (Andastes)" with some reports of "horns" being seen on the skull. In the book, "A Tradition of Giants" by Ross Hamilton it states that many North American Indian tribes such as the Iroquois, the Osage, the Tuscaroras, the Omahas, and the Hurons spoke of Giants that lived in their territories.

Fact 1: *Human skulls with horns were discovered in a burial mound at Sayre, Bradford County, Pennsylvania, in the 1800's. The Horny projections came out two inches about the eye-browns, were 4 inches long, and the skeletons were seven feet tall. They dated the bones to 1200 A.D. The Bones were sent to the American Investigating Museum in Philadelphia, where they were later claimed to have been stolen and have never been seen again." Giant,* horned skulls were also found in human skeletons south of Elmira and Wellsville, New York. In Texas a skeleton was also found in the El Paso area with horns. A Texas Ranger witnessed it while investigating a murder case.

The Book of Enoch 106 describes Noah being born white-skinned akin to the Sons of God (Angels).

Book of Enoch 106:1-5 "And after some days my son Methuselah took a wife for his son Lamech and she became pregnant by him and bore a son **(Noah)**. And his body was **WHITE AS SNOW** and red as the blooming of a rose, and the hair of his head and his **LONG LOCKS** were **WHITE AS WOOL**, and his eyes beautiful. And when he opened his eyes, he lighted up the whole house like the sun, and the whole house was very bright. And thereupon he arose in the hands of the midwife, opened his mouth, and conversed with the Lord of righteousness. And his father Lamech was afraid of him and fled, and came to his father Methuselah. And said unto him: I have begotten a **STRANGE SON**, diverse from and unlike man, **AND RESEMBLING THE SONS OF THE GOD OF HEAVEN**. "

If the Sons of God were white could this explain the race of white Red-haired Giants that lived on the Earth many, many years ago prior to the floor and afterwards? Like the Red haired Giants found in South America and off the coast of Northwest Africa in the Canary Islands?

Fact 2: *The **Guanches** were a race of pale white-skinned people with blonde or reddish hair that looked Nordic in appearance. The lived on the Canary Islands which is right off the coast of Morocco, Africa. These people before being invaded by the Spanish in the 1400's were a primitive people. They lived in Stone Age conditions, living in caves and using sharpened rocks for cutting tools. They also practiced mummification of the dead, just like the Egyptians. Many of the Guanches were massacred by the Spanish in fierce battles and others were sold into slavery. What is also fascinating is that archaeologists have found pyramids in the city of **Guimar** and **Tenerife** that are aligned for the Summer Solstice solar cycles. They also used stamps called a "**Pintadera**" that were in Pyramid Triangle shapes. Europeans called these people the "**White Indians of Nivaria**" and even wrote books about them.*

(Left) Pintadera stamp. (Right) "The White Indians of Nivaria by Gordon Kennedy"

The **Guanche people** claimed to be survivors of a *"Great Flood"* which destroyed their former homeland. Could they be descendants of the Nephilim and sons of Cain? This *"deluge"* story by the *"White Indians"* is also found in stories by Ancient Civilizations all across the world. However the only people that survived the flood was Noah and his children but also the Nephilim Giants! The Giants were present when Joshua set forth 2 spies into Jericho, Canaan. Some say these Giants had infected the Seed of Cain, producing giant men of renown. Some civilizations liken this Giant race to what the Sumerians called the *"Annunaki"* or *"those who from the heavens came"*.

"In the "Temple of the Warriors in Chichen Itza, Mexico" there are paintings of golden haired White men. In *"Matto Grosso, Brazil"*, famous British explorer **Colonel. P. H. Fawcett** disappeared while looking for the legend of *"white tribes"*. He had gone there on expeditions in the early 1900's trying to find any sightings of blue-eyed, red-haired, white-skinned Indians. **Harold T. Wilkins** was also another European who was told by an old Spanish historian that there were **tall, red-haired, bearded** Amazon people called the *"Mayorumas"*. He admitted their skin was pale white like Europeans. Harold T. Wilkins stated that in 1929, an American Traveler **Lawrence Griswold** was captured by **Shuar Indians** and taken deep into the Amazon (**Peru-Ecuador**). During his captivity by the natives he saw the ruins of an ancient city with pyramids. The Natives supposedly stated that the tall, pale white, red-haired builders of these pyramids were changed *"White"*

*because of their wicked behavior before the flood. (**Could this white skin be the "Mark of Cain"?**) (**Note: The Shuar People are not pale white Indians because they are brown-skinned Indians**) Mr. Griswold was tall, white and red-headed so the Indians thought that he was of the "**Lost Race**".*

Fact: Professor David Reich, a geneticist at Harvard Medical School led a study in which researchers found that the Amazon tribes of Surui, Karitiana, and Xavante are more closely genetically related to the Black indigenous populations in Australia (aborigines) than any other modern group in the world. They have also been genetically linked to the natives of Papua New Guinea and the Andaman Islands. His results were published in the Science Journal "**Nature**".

This is a little white Indian girl is from the Chepu Tule Tribe in Panama. They spoke a language similar to Indo-Iranian-Sanskrit from India and built pyramids. They also used "whistling" in their language. In past years scientists have also found pre-Inca mummy heads from Makat Tampu, Paracas Peninsula and Nazca, Peru with blond, red and red hair. They believed these white Indians of South America were descendants of the "Viracocha", an Ancient Caucasian Tribe who lived in pre-Inca Peru before the Spanish got there. But still, Geneticists say that their R1a/R1b Y-Haplogroup gene comes from Europe and not the other way around. This is because they refuse to believe that Albino Indians are the modern

day "White Race". These are one of many theories about the evolution of the "White Race".

The Book of Mormon speaks also of two groups of people that lived in the Americas in B.C. times. The **dark-skinned** people were called "**Lamanites**" and the **white-skinned** people were called the "**Nephites**". Strange that the white skinned people are called "**Nephites**", similar to the "Nephilim" fallen angel seed. In the Book of Mormon it states that there was a war between both groups which resulted in the destruction of the **Nephite** people and culture.

Some people believe that Noah and his 3 sons Ham, Shem and Japheth were originally all Black and that the Fallen Angels (**2012 Movie Prometheus**) manipulated the DNA of mankind causing a defective human prone to diseases and with skin that is unable to protect itself from the Sun. In the Bible (**Leviticus 13, 14**) white skin is associated with Leprosy and as a "**Curse**". In the bible, leprosy made your skin "**white as snow**". This was not the color of the Israelites skin. If it was so then what would be the "**miracle**" behind changing Moses' hand from "**White to White**". It is said that the Hebrew Israelites viewed white as a skin. Ethiopia in Ancient times depicted the color black as "good" and white was depicted as "bad". So let's say Cain's seed died in the flood and Cain's mark was the mark of "**Leprosy**" or "white skin." If this mark of "**white skin**" was infused into the Nephilim giants than could that explain why there existed races of white giants in the time period post-flood? We know the story of Elisha's servant Gehazi, and how his children, and his children's children were cursed with the sign of Leprosy forever. Elisha was an Israelite from the Tribe Issachar. His forefather 1,000 years prior was Shem. Namaan was a Syrian who was afflicted with "**white skin**". Syrians are descendants of Aram, the son of Shem. So if the "biblical Leprosy" is really "Albinism", this would lead us to believe that many of those who are descendants of Shem should have a strong history of "Albinism" in their race. Need proof that the Semites and Israelites frequently saw "Albinism" in their community? God gave the Israelites two chapters in the Torah (**Leviticus 13 &14**) explaining how to detect and handle a person whose skin has turned "white as snow". This should be enough proof that "Albinism", "Vitiligo" and "Leprosy" were common in the Israelites camp 4,000 years ago. In the Book of Enoch (**Chapter 106**) is states that Noah was an Albino man (**Oculocutaneous Albino Type 1**) even though we know that two Albinos can still have black child and thus father 3 brown skinned children (**i.e. Ham, Shem, Japheth**).

2 Kings 5:27 "The Leprosy therefore of Naaman shall cleave unto thee, and unto thy seed **FOREVER**, And **he went out from his presence a leper as white as snow**.

Was this the beginning of the White Race? In Saudi Arabia and Egypt the Temperature can exceed 120 Degrees Fahrenheit. The White Race cannot survive in Africa and Arabia. White skin doesn't have any protection from the UV rays of the Sun.

Albino Native American Boy with his sister

Out of all races, East Indian Albinos and Native American Albinos exhibit features identical to modern day Caucasians. There are people that believe that Albinos everywhere, including Europeans, come from Albino Blacks and Albino Indians (**Dravidian/Native American**). Many believe that the Dravidian Dialect goes as far back as Ancient Hebrew because of their Ancient Ancestor Elam who was the son of Shem. Shem was the father of the Sumerian and Akkadian Semitic languages which is similar to the Sanskrit script used by Dravidian Indians. So in theory Amerindians could be Blacks with curly hair, Blacks with straight hair, Blacks with negroid features, or Blacks with Caucasian features (ex. Modern term for "Mongoloid"). Noah was an Albino in the Book of Enoch. Elisha (**Tribe of Issachar**) had a servant named Gehazi. If Gehazi was also an Israelite his seed would have been cursed with a high frequency of Albinism from the story of

Naaman's (Syrian) Leprosy. So was Gehazi from the Tribe of Issachar? What about Zebulon or Asher? The Tribe of Issachar and Zebulon have the same mother (**Leah**) and father (**Jacob**). It's a known fact that the **Zanu People of Panama/Columbia**, the **San Bias Indians of Panama**, and **Mexicans** have high rates of Albinism in addition to **African-Americans/Africans (Nigerians/Tanzanians))**. In the "**12 Tribes Chart Theory**" which is famous in the Hebrew Israelite community, Mexico has been linked to the **Tribe of Issachar**, Panama has been linked to the **Tribe of Zebulon** and the **Tribe of Asher** has been linked to Columbia. So if "**Hypopigmentation disorders**" was something commonly seen in the Israelite camp as discussed in Leviticus this would mean that this trait was passed possibly from Noah to Shem. **Shem would be the forefather of the Hebrews Israelites through Arphaxad, Elam, Assyrians, Aram and Lud. Shem also had a daughter who was the wife of Japheth's son Madai, father of Medes (Persia).**

White Negro Girl and her brother 1800's

Fact 1: Albinism is very common in Native America/Latin America. The Albino children of Native Americans and Indians often resemble Caucasians. Coincidence? Some theorists believe there are two groups of Caucasians: those who are the product of Albinism and those who have been genetically designed or afflicted to have white skin thousands of years ago?

Fact 2: *Mr. Dinesh Kumar from SRM University found out that there are certain tribes in Cameroon that speak the Dravidian language "Tamil". Could this explain why the **Y-Haplogroup R1b1b2 (formally called R1b1c)** has been found in the DNA of Egyptian Pharaoh's Amenhotep III, Akhenaten, and King Tut? But wait! During a recent excavation at **Quseir-al-Qadim**, Egyptian pottery dating back to 100 B.C. was discovered with **Ancient Tamil Brahmi** inscriptions. The R1b1b (R1b1c) Y Haplogroup gene can be found in high frequencies in **Cameroonians**, **Hausa Nigerians/Sudanese**, **Chadic Africans**, and **Siwa Egyptians**? The R1b Y-Haplogroup is one of the most common Haplogroups found in Mexicans.*

*The Highest percentages of the **Blood Type "O"** are in **Native Americans/Mexicans** (80-100%) and **Sub-Saharan Africans/East Africans** (70-80%). It is also seen in the indigenous populations of **Australia** (70-90%). Blood Groups are inherited by both parents, therefore it is **genetic**. Is it a coincidence that Africans, the indigenous Australians and the indigenous Amerindians share a common Blood Group?*

Many Civilizations in Central/South America like the Mayans, Incas and Aztecs had pyramid-like structures and tales of Giants. So are these Pyramids Egyptian-inspired or Hebrew-inspired? We know the Hebrew Israelites helped build the Pyramids with Mud bricks and straw for 400 years, the same way they still do in Egypt today. We also know the Egyptians intermarried with the Israelite (Joseph-Ephraim and Manasseh).

Leviticus 24:10 "And the son of an Israelitish woman, **WHOSE FATHER WAS AN EGYPTIAN**, went out among the children of Israel; and the son of the Israelitish woman and a man of Israel strove (walked) together in the **CAMP**:"

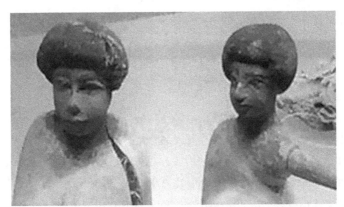

Ancient Egyptian statues with Afros.
Do the Egyptians today all have Afros? No!

Exodus 5:6-8 "So the same day Pharaoh commanded the taskmasters over the people and their foremen, saying, 'You are no longer to give the people straw to make brick as previously; let them go and gather stray for themselves. But the quota of bricks which they were making previously, you shall impose on them, **YOU ARE NOT TO REDUCE ANY OF IT**. Because they are lazy, therefore they cry out, 'Let us go and sacrifice to our God.'"

So the Israelites were made to work harder, and thus they complained.

Exodus 5:15-16 "Then the foremen of the **sons of Israel** came and cried out to Pharaoh, saying, "Why do you deal this way with your servants? "There is no straw given to your servants, yet they keep saying to us, '**Make bricks!**' And behold, your servants are being beaten; but it is the fault of your own people."

So we find in "**Native America**" **Egyptian-style** Pyramids and huge rocks with Paleo-Hebrew Inscriptions on it. Only the Hebrew Israelites and Hebrews (**descendants of Eber-Moabites, Ammonites**) wrote in Paleo-Hebrew. It is a known fact that the Children of Israel also intermarried with the **Moabites**, **Ammonites** and **Egyptians** in Biblical times.

Ezra 9:1 "Now when these things were done, the princes came to me, saying, The people of Israel, and the priests, and the Levites, have not separated themselves from the people of the lands, doing according to their abominations, even of the Canaanites, the Hittites, the Perizzites, the Jebusites, the **Ammonites, the Moabites, THE EGYPTIANS, and the Amorites. For they have taken of their daughters for themselves, and for their sons: so that the holy seed have mingled themselves with the people of those lands:**"

The Incas, Mayans and Aztecs lived in pre-Christopher Columbus and pre-Transatlantic Slave Trade times. There was no "**Egyptian Hieroglyphics**" found in America or no mention of Osiris, Horus, Isis, Set, or Thoth mentioned in the Americas. But there is mention of the name "**Yahuah**", "**Yehowah**" and "**Ya-ho-wa**" by the Native Americans Tribes. Yahuah was the name of God **ONLY** the Israelites knew. It is found on many Ancient Israelite artifacts found in Israel. Many people are now doing the research and finding out that some of the **Native Americans** and "**Natives**" of the Caribbean were in fact the "**Lost Tribes of Israel**". Their descendants still live in these lands but of course the European Ashkenazi Jew, the Sephardic Jew, and the Mizrahi Jew do not want to hear any of this. So what does man do? He wants to justify everything by science and DNA because he can "**Control**" this. He comes up in 1997-1998 with the **Jewish "Cohenite" J1c gene** out of thin air. Then he labels the indigenous people of the Americas with the **Haplogroup Q, R, and C**. Man also slips up and finds out that some of these "**Native Americans**" and "**Latinos**" in the Americas have the **E1b1b gene,** the same gene that North African Turkish Arabs/Europeans are grouped into. But geneticists magically erase the Ethiopians and Somalians former **E1b1c group**, placing them now with the **E1b1b group**. But how can the Ethiopians and Somalians be related to Caucasians with the E1b1b gene? Why are the Europeans always trying to "**whitenize**" everything that is "**Black**" and then claim "**White**" in everything that started off "**Black or Brown**"? Perfect example is Europeans saying that Ethiopians, Somalians and Native Americans are more "White" than indigenously "Native" or "Black". It's a shame. Here are some people geneticists claim possessed the "**E1b1b**" gene.

1. The Wright Brothers
2. Napoleon
3. Albert Einstein
4. Adolph Hitler
5. President Lyndon B. Johnson
6. Michaelangelo

Well it just so happens that the **Y-Haplogroup "R"** is very unique. The "**Natives**" of the Americas carry the Y Haplogroup **R1b** gene, which supposedly was also carried by the **Ancient Egyptian Pharaoh's**. Different sources say based on the information (**Y-STR's**) provided on the Discovery Channel about the genetic analysis of the Ancient Egyptian Pharaohs that the Genetic Y Haplogroup of King Tut, Amenhotep III and Akhenaten is either **R1b12** (formerly called R1b1c) or **R1b**1a. The Discovery Channel was doing a genetic analysis of these Pharaoh's to see if they died of Malaria. Well, in Modern Genetics the R1b gene and the R1a gene has been associated with the "**European gene**" as if the Ancient Egyptians were white (**which we know is not true**). But little do they know that the **R1b gene** (R1b1b2/R1b1c-V-88) is seen in high frequencies in African countries such as Chad, Niger, Nigeria, Cameroon and Sudan. The **R1a gene** is also seen in high frequencies throughout India, including the South Dark-skinned Dravidian Indian and Sri Lankans. So how can this be? Do Dark-skinned Africans and Dark-skinned

Indians come from Whites? **NO WAY**! The highest rates of reverse hypopigmentation disorders (**i.e. Albinism**) are seen in **India, Africa and Native America (Central/South America).** Many scientists theorize that the white race is simply the by-product of **Albino Indians and Albino Africans.** Moreover, since we all know that the White Race cannot produce the Black race (**especially down to the darkest African/Indian**) the R1a and R1b gene has to originate from people of color with a **"functioning" "P-Protein"** that helps melanocytes stimulate **"Melanin"**.

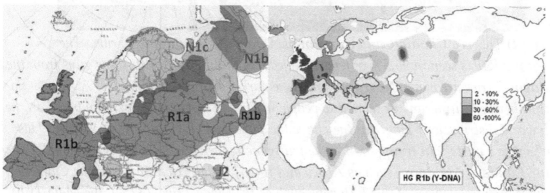

The **Y-Haplogroup R1b** and **R1a** distribution is seen in Western Europe as well as Eastern Europe. But these genes are seen in **HIGH FREQUENCIES** in Central Africa and India. So who came from whom? Are these two genes "**European White Genes**" or "**Black skin Genes**".

*(Left) This is a **Chadic/Cameroonian** man from the "**Ouldeme**" Tribe. The Y-Haplogroup R1b is seen in 95.5% of tested subjects from this tribe. But these guys from the "**Ouldeme**" tribe are more "**Negroid**" and have darker skin tones than most Africans. So how can they be "European" or related to people in France, Spain and Portugal based on the R1b world distribution? How can they have the same gene as Western Europeans? Has "man" made a mistake in trying to hide the true genetic identity of those bearing the R1b or R1a in "**Lands of Melanin**" such as Africa and India? Other tribes in Northern Cameroon also have high frequencies of this R1b gene such as the Mada Tribe. (82%), the Mafa Tribe (88%), the Guiziga Tribe (78), the Moundang Tribe (67%) and the Guidar Tribe (67%).*

*(Right) This is a **Brahmin Indian Priest**. Some call them the "**Jews of India**". The Brahmins are the Priestly Tribe (caste) and typically do not intermarry. For those that do marry their paternal ancestry and Y-Haplogroup would still be passed down to their children. They pass down oral traditions/laws and written traditions/laws. They are scholars and are at the top of the caste system although they make up <5% of the population of India. They are found to have the highest percentages of the R1a gene in India which is also seen primarily in Eastern Europe. Many of the Brahmins are brown-dark skinned Indians. They live mostly in North India but some like in South India (**Kerala, Tamil Nadu**). How are these Brahmin Indians related to Eastern Europeans? Where did the R1a gene originate?*

Fact: Modern day Indians are said to be descendants of the **Ancient Persians (Medes)** and the **Ancient Elamites (Son of Shem)**. The Ancient Indo-Persian "**Zoroastrianism**" religion was originally started in Persia but is now most practiced in India because of their migration patterns to the East. In Ancient times, explorers attested there were black-looking people in India who practiced Judaism and were said to be one of the Lost Tribes of Israel that left Assyria/Persian settling in South Asia (India).

Isaiah 11:11 "And it shall come to pass in that day, that the Lord shall set his hand again the second time to recover the remnant of his people, which shall be left, from Assyria, and from Egypt, and from Pathros, and from Cush, **AND FROM ELAM**, and from Shinar, and from Hamath, and from the islands of the sea."

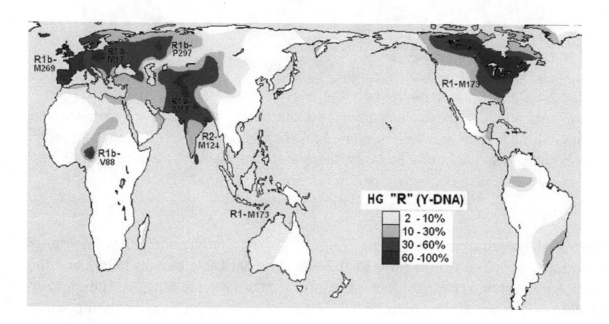

The Haplogroup Y-DNA family **R1b** is found in Central Africa (Cameroon, Chad, Northern Nigeria), in Western Europe and in isolated cases in Sri Lanka Dravidian Indians. It is also found in the Arawak natives (38.1%), Ojibwe Indians (79%), Chipewyan Indians (62%), Chippewa Indians (50-70%), Seminole Indians (50%), Cherokee Indians (47%), Dogrib (40%), Papago Indians (38%), and the Sioux Indians (50%). Some sources say the Apache and Navajo Tribes also have high percentages of the R1b gene. This R1b Y-DNA Haplogroup is the 2nd most predominant Haplogroup found in Native Americans after the newer Q Y-Haplogroup which geneticists say is secondary to Mutations from the root "P" Haplogroup (**ex. Blonde Haired Australian Aborigines**).

241

(**Left**) Na-Dene Indians. Notice how they are not white-skinned. (**Right**) The Pre-Incan Uros people of Peru. They are indigenous South Americans and they are also dark-skinned. How can they be related to Noah's son "Japheth"? If they are not Japheth that leaves Ham or Shem as their possible ancestors. Hamitic people are mostly in Africa. These two nations of people have the Q Haplogroup or R Haplogroup.

The **Q Haplogroup** is seen most frequent in the Indigenous (Pre-Christopher Columbus) people of South America (**83-94%**), the Na-Dene Indians (**50%**), and the Aleut/Inuit Eskimos (**46%**). It is for the most part not seen in Europe. **Haplogroup Q** descends from **Haplogroup P** (i.e. Negrito/Aeta natives of the Philippines), which is the ancestor of **Haplogroup R1a** (India) and **R1b** (Africa, Ancient Egypt, Native Americans, Latinos).

Top Countries with Oculocutaneous Albinism (OCA) (Not in particular order of highest, just frequency per their population).

1. **Nigeria/Benin**
2. **San Bias, Hopi, Zuni, Kuna, Jemez, Laguna, San Juan, and Navajo Indians**
3. **Tanzania**
4. **India, Pakistan, Bangladesh, Sri Lanka**
5. **African-Americans**
6. **Brazil**
7. **Mexico**

8. China
9. Russia
10. Ethiopia

Fact: Albino Children constitute up to 40% of the population of Nigeria. In Tanzania 1 in 4,000 babies are born with Albinism. Some reports list 1 in 1,200 babies born in Tanzania have Albinism. Like the "Biblical Leprosy" which causes your skin to turn white as snow, there is a negative stigma associated with having Albinism. Many Albinos are hunted and persecuted because of their white skin. Many view it as a "Curse", just like the Curse of Leprosy on Gehazi, Elisha's servant.

2 Kings 5:27 "The Leprosy therefore of Naaman shall cleave unto thee, and unto thy seed **FOREVER**. And he (Gehazi) went out from his presence a leper as **WHITE AS SNOW**.

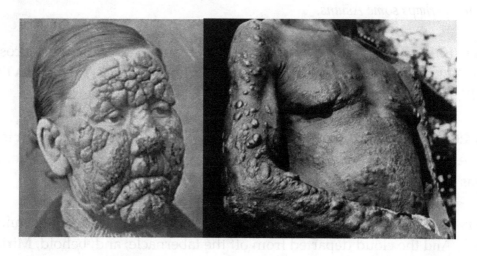

(**Above**) This is modern day "**Leprosy**". It is primary a granulomatous disorder causing skin lesions and bumps. The disease called "**Leprosy**" most likely was not called "**Leprosy**" in Ancient Times. Leprosy is derived from the Latin word "**Lepta**" which means "**Scaly**". Old Latin dates back to 75 B.C., about 2000 years after the Israelites entered into Egypt with Joseph. Leprosy, now called "**Hansen's disease**" was discovered in 1873 by the Norwegian physician **Gerhard Armauer**

Hansen, who was searching for the bacteria in the skin nodules of patient with leprosy. This bacterium is called "**Mycobacterium Leprae**". Even the cutaneous "**Tuberculoid**" form of Leprosy which causes "**patch lesions**" doesn't not cause your skin to turn "**white as snow**", which the bible frequently lists as the main sign of leprosy. For this reason, many biblical scholars believe that the Biblical "**Leprosy**" is actually "**Albinism**" when white skin covers the entire body. When the white skin covers part of the body and this person is considered "**unclean**" in the bible this person is believed in the bible to have "**Vitiligo**". Vitiligo can also turn the hair white depending on the area it affects (i.e. nape of neck and hair).

Fact: *The Hebrew Strong's word "Tsaraath" means "Leprosy" or "Mark" in Hebrew. It is found in the Hebrew bible. The word "Albinism" is not in the Bible. Could "Albinism" be what the bible calls "Leprosy". Leprosy today does not turn one's hair white or yellow. Albinism and Vitiligo does, which is more prevalent in Blacks, East Indians and descendants of Native Americans than any other race. Using Leviticus Chapter 13 and 14 which was given to the "Israelites" ONLY, this could be the "missing link" as to who are the "Real" Israelites today. The people that exhibit Vitiligo and Albinism the most per population. That would be West Africans, East Africans, Native Americans/Latinos, East Indians and perhaps some Asians.*

Leviticus 13:13 "Then the priest shall consider: and behold, if the leprosy have covered **ALL HIS FLESH**, he shall pronounce him **CLEAN THAT HATH THE PLAGUE**: it is all turned **WHITE**: he his clean."

Exodus 4:6 "And the Lord said furthermore unto him, Put now thine hand into thy bosom. And he put his hand into his bosom: and when he took it out, behold, his hand was **LEPROUS AS SNOW**.

Numbers 12:10-12 "And the anger of the Lord was kindled against them; and he departed. And the cloud departed from off the tabernacle; and, behold, Miriam became **LEPROUS, WHITE AS SNOW**: And Aaron looked upon Miriam, and, behold, she was **LEPROUS**. And Aaron said unto Moses, Alas, my Lord, I beseech thee, lay not the sin upon us, wherein we have done foolishly, and wherein we have sinned. Let her not be as one dead, of whom the **FLESH IS HALF CONSUMED WHEN HE COMETH OUT OF HIS MOTHER'S WOMB**."

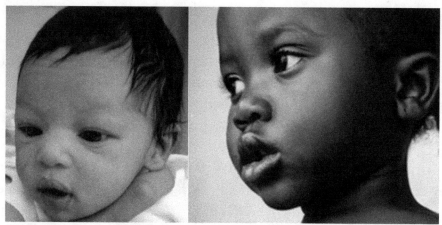

(Above) A Black newborn baby and Black child. Can you tell if these pictures are the same person? It is not uncommon for African-Americans to have newborn babies with white skin that eventually turns dark over the course of weeks to months. This is what is being described in Numbers 12:10-12.

Many dark-Skinned African-Americans are born light-skinned or with white-appearing skin. Some are even said to look (**Chinese**) at birth. But as time progresses this light-skinned black baby's skin color changes from almost white to dark brown. Why? Melanin, simple and plain. Some people look at the ears to guess the baby's final skin color. Nevertheless, this is not seen in the white race. It is not seen in Ashkenazi, Sephardic or Middle Eastern Mizrahi Jewish babies. Aaron pleaded to Moses to have God restore Miriam's skin complexion back to black because her skin was the same color as what it would've been when she came out the womb which is white/light-skinned. Aaron attested to this by saying in the Book of Numbers "**Let her not be as one whom the flesh (skin color) is HALF consumed when he cometh out of his mother's womb**". Because this is verified in the **Hebrew Torah**, the Jews today cannot refute that the Original Israelites (**especially Levi and Cohenites**) were Black and not white. The Jews have to accept the Torah. Jews disregarding the Torah is like the Jews disregarding Moses or Abraham. The Torah consists of the first five books of the bible written by Moses: **Genesis, Exodus, Leviticus, Numbers, and Deuteronomy.**

Fact: Albinism is a rare disorder found in fewer than 5 people per 100,000 people in the United States and Europe. Albinism is seen in higher amounts in other races such as **Nigeria** (20 out of every 100,000 people), **East Indians**, and the **San Bias Indians of Panama** (7 out of every 1,000 births).

TYPES OF ALBINISM

1. **Oculocutaneous Albinism Type I** is an autosomal recessive disorder caused by a mutation in the tyrosinase gene on **Chromosome 11**. Patient with OCA I have no pigment in their hair, skin and eyes. The condition does not improve with age.

2. **Oculocutaneous Albinism Type IA** patients also do not make any melanin. They are born with white hair, white skin and blue eyes. With time, the hair may develop a yellow tint. The iris at birth appears pink in but often turns a grey-blue color with time. Vision is poor and many patients are considered legally blind.

3. **Oculocutaneous albinism Type IB** patients have some tyrosinase activity. They have very little to no pigment at birth but develop varying amounts of melanin in their hair and skin over time. It can sometimes present later as nearly normal skin color and hair pigment (close to a Caucasian). Ethnicity and family pigment patters influences this. Sun exposure may cause some tanning but the skin will most likely burn if it is exposed to long. The hair can develop a golden color, freckles can appear and the eyelashes are often darker than the scalp hair. Vision improves with age.

4. **Oculocutaneous Albinism Type 2 (most common type)** is caused by a mutation of "**P-Protein**". People with OCA 2 generally have more pigment and better vision than other types of OCA but cannot tan like OCA 1B. They may have pale blond, golden or even brown hair and most often blue eyes. In Africans, they have yellow hair, blue, grey or hazel eyes.

5. **Oculocutaneous Albinism Type 3 (rare)** is found in Africa and New Guinea. Patients have Red hair, pale to reddish-brown skin and blue or grey eyes.

Indians Playing a game, by Louis Choris. Louis (1795-1828) was a famous German-Russian painter and explorer. He documented and drew pictures of the "Ohlone People" in the missions of San Francisco, California in 1816. He also traveled to South America (Mexico) where he was murdered. He depicted the Indians to be different shades of brown. Not white.

DOES FAMINE STILL EXIST IN AFRICA?

Bedouin Nomadic Arab

The Nile Valley historically was and continues to be a rich source of fish, animal, and plant food. In the drier African savannas, especially after the Sahara region became arid after 6000 B.C.E., nomad tribes raised cattle, goats, or sheep, which served as part of the tribes' food source. Crops that were less affected by extreme weather like rice, cereals (such as wheat, barley, millet, and sorghum), cassava, potatoes, tubers (such as yams) slowly became popular throughout the continent and have remained important **staples** in the African diet today.

Throughout Africa, the main meal of the day is lunch, which usually consists of a mixture of vegetables, legumes (beans/peas), and sometimes meat. However, though different meats are considered staples in many areas, many Africans are not able to eat meat often, due to economic constraints and livestock shortages in certain areas secondary to famine, disease, or low rainfall. Beef, goat, and sheep (mutton) are quite expensive in Africa, so these foods are reserved for special days. However, fish is abundant in coastal regions such as Madagascar and in many lakes. Beef, goat, chicken, or sheep are the most common meats eaten in Africa.

CHAPTER 26

DEUTERONOMY 28:19-25

Deuteronomy 28:19 **"Cursed shalt thou be when thou comest in, and cursed shalt thou be when thou goest out."**

NO PEACE FOR THE BLACK MAN

We all know the saying **"Living as a Black man in White America"**, **"Driving while Black"** or **"Guilty until proven innocent"**. This definitely holds true today because despite all the issues the Black family faces at home with high rates of divorce and fatherless homes; blacks still face even greater obstacles soon as we step foot outside the door. Raising your hand up at a routine police stop or arrest can get a black man beat or riddled with 100 bullets compared to other races. In the **"Michael Brown shooting-death"**, Michael Brown had his hands up but was still shot repeatedly by Ferguson Police. During this incident the Media only showed the negative things blacks were doing like robbing, looting and vandalism. They didn't show the peaceful protest and demonstrations on T.V. Everything was focused on the negative, to portray us to Americans as **"savages"**. The negative is always brought out somehow, someway in regards to blacks on T.V. If we are not the objects of **Coonery and Buffoonery** on T.V, then we are the objects of **negativity**. This promotes the formation of black stereotypes to the people of America and the whole world. Even in Africa and other countries the images that they see of African-Americans is that of drugs, gangs, thievery, killing, aggressiveness, robbing, rape, laziness and irresponsible parents. But this has been taught in Jewish literature to Jewish people as the **"Curse of Canaan"** on Blacks today.

Below is **PROOF** that racist stereotypes are also taught in European Jewish documents and in the teachings of the Talmud book in Judaism. Some can say that it established the base for Black racism even before the KKK. In the **Jewish Torah Anthology Volume 1, pages 392-393** the details of the true origin of the slanderous beliefs that blacks received the punishments/curses from Canaan reads as follows:

1. Because he (**Ham**) looked at his naked father (**Noah**) his eyes became red, always appearing bloodshot (**referring to Africans**).
2. Because he (**Ham**) mockingly told his brothers about his father's condition, his lips were made thick and gross like those of a Negro.
3. Because he (**Ham**) turned his head to see his father (**Noah**), the hair of his head and beard became kinky.
4. Because he did not cover his father, it was decreed that he always go naked and blackened by the sun.
5. The last will and testament to Canaan was to speak not the truth (**lie**); hold not yourselves aloof from theft (**meaning go ahead and steal**); lead a dissolute life (**meaning-lacking restraint or given to immoral and improper conduct**); hate your master with an exceeding great hate; and love one another.

Blacks are the victims of racial discrimination every day and are more likely the law enforcements **main target** to incarcerate or stop during the course of their shift. Black people are also commonly watched and discriminated against at work. Unfair and discriminatory practices at work cause blacks to feel that their job position is insecure and unsafe. Worrying about write-ups, red forms and complaints from non-black people on the job can make that black persons job more stress than it needs to be. Heresies are always regarded as "**Truth**" by non-black employers instead of what they really are, "**Heresies**". For this reason, Blacks often get fired or suspended based on "**lies**", which are usually maliciously driven to get the "**black employee**" fired. Other races do not have to worry about these issues. Other races can go to work and go home without problems. The can come to work late, leave early or forget to do certain tasks. No biggie. But for Blacks, these are grounds for "termination". This pressure outside our homes also affects our personal relationship with our significant other, our kids and our health.

Fact 1: Being "**Black**" in America, for parents and the children, is full of constant worrying. Worrying if Dad will make it home safe. Worrying that our Black sons and daughters are not the victims of Black-on-Black crime, hate crimes or police brutality/murder from a judicial system that puts the target on blacks as "**The Problem**". Therefore the talk that black parents have with their children is different than those of other races in America. Non-Black, non-Hispanic races don't have to worry about dying in the streets. Like Black inner-cities, Mexicans also have to be careful not to be the victims of car-jacking, robbing, and murder. Coincidence?

Fact 2: Pennsylvania **Judge Mark Ciavarell Jr.** was involved in the "**Black Kids for Cash**" scandal in 2008. He was sentenced to 28 years in prison for conspiring with private prisons to sentence Black juvenile offenders to maximum sentences for bribes and kickbacks which totaled millions of dollars. He was ordered to pay $1.2 million dollars in restitution. In the private prison industry, the more time a black inmate spends at the facility the more profit the state and the prison owners get. Black men and women under Judge Mark Ciavarell Jr. were unjustly punished and penalized in the name of corporate profit. He is one of many Judges that probably runs his courtroom this way, putting blacks behind bars with lengthy sentences compared to other races who commit the same crime.

Fact: A survey done consisting of 100 Black men and women indicated that the tendency to embrace mainstream American culture (i.e. "**fit in**") was associated with higher blood pressure and heart rates than other races. Unwanted stress from trying to be "**accepted**" on the job or in society is also common for Blacks.

Ultimately this stress can lead to anxiety and depression. The survey also found out that the pressure to "**Fit in**" was also associated with higher degrees of "**hostility**". This means that all of the "**butt kissing**" we're doing at the office to keep our jobs or to not get "**written up**" is impacting our health and making us more likely to snap emotionally when we step out of the office. The Division of Population Science at the Fox Chase Cancer Center examined the effects of racial stressors on cardiovascular reactivity. 31 Black males and 31 White males were shown racist videos. Although the racist videos increased blood pressure for both samples, **the Black people maintained the high blood pressure after the video was done**. So when a White person sees something racist, it affects them at that moment. If a Black person sees something racist, it just keeps affecting them, even after they are off work and at home. Black men and women have to deal with this every day.

The founding fathers of this country originally wanted to send all blacks back to Africa once the notion of freeing the slaves was on the table. Then they changed their minds and decided to keep the "Negroes" in America because they saw some use in them, they just didn't know what. They definitely did not want us to compete for their jobs so they had to keep us from reading or acquiring an education. After slavery was abolished, White America imposed "**Jim Crow**" laws to further suppress us. If post-slavery "White America" had it their way they would have all blacks' jobless, uneducated and incarcerated.   Because once incarcerated, a black man is a legal slave just as it states in the 13th Amendment; and in this country prisoners make businesses a lot of money, just as in slavery.

"Neither **SLAVERY** nor **INVOLUNTARY** servitude, **EXCEPT as punishment for crime** whereof the party shall have been duly convicted, **shall exist within the United States**, or any place subject to their jurisdiction."
Thirteenth Amendment

The 13th Amendment allows slavery to exist under a narrow exception for those who have been convicted of a crime. It denies a convicted person "**equal protection of the Law**", the right to vote, the right to bear arms, the right to participate in jury duty, the right to run for or hold a political office, and a right to protection against "cruel and unusual" punishment. In essence, according to the 13th Amendment, **a convicted person, especially a felon, is programmed into the legal system as a SLAVE.**   Once a black man gets caught up in the judicial system with misdemeanors, felonies, costly tickets-fines and warrants it is very hard to recover because of the negative mark it leaves for future employers or educational institutions. No other race deals with this problem more than black people.

Fact: *More Blacks are under Prison/Parole control today than there was enslaved in the 1850's. Was this prophesied on the Children of Israel?*

Isaiah 42:22 "But this is a people (Israelites) robbed and spoiled; they are all of them snared in holes, **and they are hid in PRISON HOUSES: they are for a prey, and none delivereth; for a spoil, and none saith, Restore.** Who among you will give ear to this? Who will hearken and hear for the time to come? Who gave Jacob for a spoil, and Israel to the robbers? Did not the Lord, he against whom we have sinned? **For they (Israelites) would not walk in his ways, neither were they obedient unto his law"**

IS THE KING ALFRED PLAN REAL?
IS THIS POLICE BRUTALITY ALL A SET UP?

Supposedly the "**King Alfred Plan**" was drafted up in the 1950s to round up black people at the start of race riots, segregate them and move them to a concentration camp or a separate location and kill them off, literally. There are tons of memos online that have now been declassified. Is this for real? Of course there is much more to this plan than is being released to the public. With the recent wave of black deaths from the hands of police enforcement, it makes many blacks wonder and ask themselves, "**Are they doing this on purpose to get a reaction from blacks?**" Well here is a little bit of what this "**King Alfred Plan**" is all about.

In the event of widespread, continuing and coordinated racial or civil disturbances in the United States of America, the "**KING ALFRED PLAN**", at the behest and discretion of the President, is to be put into action immediately.

- Participating Federal Agencies National Security Council (NSC)
- Department of Justice (DOJ)
- Central Intelligence Agency (CIA)
- Department of Defense (DOD)
- Federal Bureau of Investigation (FBI)
- Department of Interior (DOI)
- Federal Emergency Mgmt. Agency (FEMA)
- Immigration Naturalization Service (INS)

Participating State Agencies (Under Federal Jurisdiction)

- National Guard Units Reserve Units of the Army Highway Patrol Agencies State Police Agencies State Emergency Mgmt. Agency (SEMA)
- Disaster Relief & Civil Disturbance Participating County & Local Agencies (Under Federal Jurisdiction) County Police Local Town & City Police

Supposedly in a memo to the National Security Council it stated that even before 1954, when the Supreme Court of the United States of America declared it unconstitutional to have separated educational, public and recreational facilities, **racial unrest and discord** had become very nearly a part of the American way of life. But that way of life was unacceptable to most Americans. Since 1954, the unrest and discord in America that has broken out into widespread violence has made some people question the future peace and stability of the nation. Racial Tensions in America seems to repeat itself every so often. **"White America"** believes this violence has resulted in loss of life, limb and property, and has cost the taxpayers of this nation billions of dollars. They look at all the **"riots"** over the years that have happened because Black people were not **"satisfied"**. So according to "White America" this violence has raised the tremendously grave question to whether the races (**whites and blacks**) can ever live in peace with each other. Each passing month has brought new intelligence that, despite new laws passed to alleviate the condition of the Minority, the Minority still is not satisfied. **Malcolm X also once said in a speech that America fears a Black race that is ALL fed up and dissatisfied.** So could "The King Alfred Plan" be America's answer to whenever this happens?

Fact: In 2014 we witnessed the Ferguson, Missouri riots from the police slaying of **Michael Brown**. In 2015 we witnessed the Baltimore, Maryland riots from the death of **Freddie Gray**. **Dylann Roof** in June, 2015 Killed 9 Black Church members at the Emanuel African Methodist Episcopal Church in Charleston, South Carolina. The news claimed he wanted to start a **"Race War"** between whites and blacks saying **"You rape our women, and you're taking over our country."** With over 784 hate groups in the United States it is not surprising that white supremacist groups comprise the bulk of these groups.

Under **"THE KING ALFRED PLAN"** the nation has been divided into **10 Regions** per **FEMA** (Federal Emergency Management Agency). This can be easily researched and proven.   In case of a National Emergency or Civil Disturbance, it is believed that Minority members will be evacuated first from the cities by federalized National Guard units, federal troops and state and local police agencies which have become federalized under Marshall Law or Executive Order. The **Minority members (Blacks)** will be transported using public, commercial or military transportation, and detained in nearby military interment centers, prisons or military installations units until a further course of action has been decided. **But why Blacks first?**

Fact: *Baltimore **Mayor J. Barry Mahool** (1907-1911), a member of the "Social Justice" wing of the Progressive Movement, signed into law city ordinance No. 610 in 1910, prohibiting blacks from moving into white neighborhoods. He subscribed that **"Blacks should be quarantined in isolated slums in order to reduce the incidents of civil disturbance, to prevent the spread of communicable disease into the nearby White neighborhoods, and to protect property values among the White majority."** After the 1920's, Whites even constructed the streets and highways in their states to serve as racial barriers between the two races. The logic: closing down the freeways running through black communities could be used to quarantine blacks in an event of **"Civil Unrest"**.*

In the event of a Natural Disaster, Economic Collapse, Power Grid Black Out, Food Shortage or Government Shutdown who will be effected the most first? Easy, the poor. Who are the poorest race groups in America? Blacks and Latinos. The Elite knows that when people are faced with no food, water or money **"Survival of the Fittest" instincts kick in, and there is usually no peace, only "Chaos"**. For this reason many conspiracy theorists believe that the powers to be will initiate **"Chaos"** to create **"Order"**. Just like the Jesuits (Society of Jesus) motto **"The end justifies the means"** or the saying **"Our goal is to create Order out of Chaos"**.

Government shutdown could cut off food stamps

Could the end of "**Food Stamps/EBT cards**" by the Government one day be the catalyst that starts "**Martial Law**" and the breakdown of Society as we know it? But this was all laid out in the "**Cloward-Piven Strategy**". We just were too busy working to know about it.

In case you don't believe, here are the 10 regions, divided up by FEMA.

10 FEMA REGIONS
- **I**: Connecticut, Massachusetts, New Hampshire, Rhode Island, Vermont. Regional Capitol: **Boston REGION**
- **II**: New York, New Jersey, Puerto Rico, Virgin Island. Regional Capitol: **New York City REGION**
- **III**: Delaware, Maryland, Pennsylvania, Virginia, West Virginia, District of Columbia. Regional Capitol: **Philadelphia REGION**
- **IV**: Alabama, Florida, Georgia, Kentucky, Mississippi, North Carolina, Tennessee. Regional Capitol: **Atlanta REGION**
- **V**: Illinois, Indiana, Michigan, Minnesota, Ohio, Wisconsin. Regional Capitol: **Chicago REGION**
- **VI**: Arkansas, Louisiana, New Mexico, Oklahoma, Texas. Regional Capitol: **Dallas-Fort Worth REGION**
- **VII**: Iowa, Kansas, Missouri, Nebraska. Regional Capitol: **Kansas City REGION**
- **VIII**: Colorado, Montana, North Dakota, South Dakota, Utah, Wyoming. Regional Capitol: **Denver REGION**

- **IX**: Arizona, California, Hawaii, Nevada. Regional Capitol: **San Francisco REGION**
- **X**: Alaska, Oregon, Washington, Idaho. Regional Capitol: **Seattle REGION**

MAP: FEMA 10 REGIONS

In case people may ask, **"I don't believe any of this unless it has actually been put into law."** Well, here is some other startling proof, and FEMA is at the heart of it!

On February 16, 1962, President John Kennedy signed several Executive Orders which would allegedly give certain dictatorial powers to appointed bureaucrats in the event a **"National Emergency"** should be declared by the President. So whichever President is sitting in office at the designated time these orders can be issued and **"implemented"**. At the President's discretion **"in any time of increased international tension or economic or financial crisis"**, the Executive Orders could theoretically be enacted.

These Executive Orders signed by Kennedy would give authority to the **Federal Emergency Management Agency (FEMA)** to control:

1. Communications

2. Energy
3. Food
4. Fuel
5. Farms
6. Transportation
7. Highways
8. Railroads
9. Inland waterways and seaports
10. Health Care
11. Education
12. Welfare Assistance
13. Drafting of citizens into work forces under government supervision
14. Relocation of populations
15. Designation of abandoned areas as unsafe
16. Relocation of communities
17. Control all public storage facilities

So how did FEMA get this role?

On February 27, 1962 Kennedy also signed Executive Order 11051 designating FEMA as the authorized agency to implement the above orders, and which authority can be re-designated by the original authority.

President Nixon signed Executive Order 11490 on October 28, 1969 combining all the above to be enacted in one fell swoop; on July 20, 1979 Carter added a few minor amendments to them; and, in June, 1994 then **President Bill Clinton** signed Executive Order 12919, which encompasses all of the Executive Orders.
Since then, NO President has nullified these Executive Orders. So in the Event of a "**National Emergency**", these orders can go into effect. Will the people go with it? Will Blacks be the first ones "**rounded up**" with this so-called "**King Alfred Plan**?"

Fact 1: President Nixon's Executive Order 11490 states: **The President can declare that a national emergency exists and the Executive Branch can:**

• Take over all communications media.
• Seize all sources of power Take charge of all food resources.

- Control all highways and seaports, seize all railroads, inland waterways, airports, storage facilities and command all civilians to work under federal supervision.
- Control all activities relating to health, education, and welfare shift any segment of the population from one locality to another. Take over farms, ranches and timberized properties.
- Regulate the amount of money you can withdraw from your bank, or savings and loan institution. (**Already happened in Greece 2015**).

Fact 2: The **Protocols of the Learned Elders of Zion** is the most blatantly Satanic document in world history! It systematically lists all the steps that are necessary to establish the **New World Order** and its ultimate leader. It is obvious that these plans for the establishment of the New World Order are so brilliantly conceived and written, they could only be the work of supernatural Guiding Spirits (Satan and his demons) through Automatic Writing.

The Protocols are organized as follows:
1. Blueprint for world domination;
2. Advent of a **Masonic Kingdom**;
3. A King of the blood of Sion, of the Fake Satanic –so-called Dynastic root of David;
4. The King of the Jews will be the real Pope;
5. The world ruler will be the patriarch of an international church.

(Hogan, Jean Baptiste, as quoted by **Holy Blood, Holy Grail**, p. 193.)

Deuteronomy 28:20 "**The Lord Shall send upon thee cursing, vexation, and rebuke, in all that thou settest thine hand unto for to do, until thou be destroyed, and until thou perish quickly; because of the wickedness of thy doings, whereby thou hast forsaken me.**"

A Curse from God is like a **divine punishment**. Many African-Americans and Africans probably think, "Why is it that black people cannot seem to get ahead as a race compared to many other races?" Even in America, the land of opportunity. The number of businesses in our 50 states owned by other races compared to blacks is astronomical. The majority of businesses owned by Blacks are Barber shops, Beauty Salons, Hair Braiding shops, Car Washes, Group homes and some residential properties. Not franchises, schools, banks, nursing homes, hotels, hospitals, residential real estate, vacation properties, car dealerships, grocery stores, pharmacies, car insurance firms, or cell phone stores. Marcus Garvey and Prince Hall were all for bringing African-Americans back to Africa (**Pan-African Movement**). The Jewish Banking Cartel didn't want black slaves to be free but they also didn't want them going back to Africa. Their main focus was to set up a Central Bank in America. So they allowed the abolishment of Slavery but kept us segregated. Abraham Lincoln did what he was told. Then White America shut us up by giving us Black Universities and Greek Fraternities even though we weren't Greek.

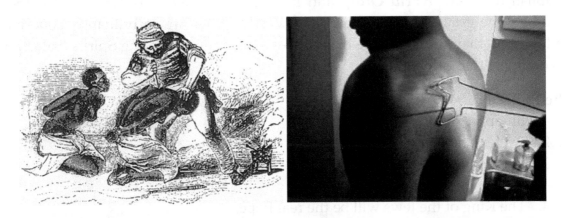

(Left) Black Slaves being branded (1700's) and (Right) Black Greek Frat member being branded with the Greek "Sigma" symbol for the Fraternity Phi Beta Sigma. Have we been Hoodwinked and bamboozled again? How did this happen? Blacks are not from Greece? Do Blacks speak Greek? No! We were sold to the Grecians in Biblical times!

Joel 3:6 "The children also of **Judah** and the children of **Jerusalem have ye sold unto the Grecians**, that ye might remove them far from their border."

Fact: The Branding of Slaves goes way back. Slavemasters did this to identify their slaves especially if they ran away. In the movie "**Freedom (2015)**" with Cuba Gooding Jr. it shows how the slaves were branded like cattle. Once "White America" gave us "Black Colleges" to go to they shut us up temporarily for wanting to go back to Africa. So while here in America we wanted to be more like them. Blacks wanted to be in their Scottish Rite Freemason club but "White America" did not want Negroes in their "Good Ol' Boys club". So blacks came up with their own Masonic lodge which would be called the "**Prince Hall Masons.**" Blacks wanted to have Greek Fraternities like Whites so we started "**Black Greek Fraternities**". While some blacks were still slaves in the South and some were showcased in Zoo's in America **(Ota Benga) Black Greek Fraternities were operating as a social study club (i.e. Alpha Phi Alpha in 1906, Cornell University**). Just like in Slavery, Black Greek Fraternity members were identified by their Fraternity by "**Branding**" which still goes on today. But how many White Caucasian men do you see with their Greek Letter branded on their body? Have we been tricked again? Since being in White America Blacks have tried to be like the White race by skin bleaching with fading creams, Perms to make our hair straight, and hair dyes to make our hair blonde. The result of this is that wearing our own "**Natural**" hair on the job is seen as "**Un-professional**". Some Blacks themselves believe that wearing "dreadlocks" or "braids" is unprofessional on some jobs. But during the 1900's were other races trying to be "Black"? No.

NO OWNERSHIP MEANS NO CONTROL!

Fact: *It is a known fact that the well-known Historic Black College, "Spelman College" in Atlanta, Georgia was set up by European Jews. In Atlanta, the **Georgia Baptist Female Seminary** was founded in 1881 in the basement of a church by **Laura Celestia Spelman**. Her husband at the time, Jewish banker **John D. Rockefeller** stepped in with major financial support (Millions) to help his wife start **HER SCHOOL** which is now called "Spelman College".*

Ashkenazi Jew Rockefeller also gave substantial funding to **Henry L. Morehouse**, after which the Black College in Atlanta, **Morehouse College** was named after. Like the **NAACP**, our now Historically Black College Universities (**HBCU**) were started by Jews, **NOT US**. Likewise in America, Entertainment (Sports, Media, Music, Movies) is controlled by the Jews. Blacks that don't "**Play the Game**" are not allowed to make millions of money. Black actress "**Monique**" famous for the Movie "**Precious**" even admitted to talk show host Wendy Williams on the "**Wendy Williams Show**" that both of them had to "**Play the Game**" in order to have jobs in "Hollywood". Wendy Williams of course had no comment. This is the reason why Rich Blacks like "Oprah Winfrey" and "Michael Jordan" are not allowed to fund projects that will allow us to separate ourselves from their control (U.S.A.). The key to our Freedom in America is "**Economic Freedom**", a "**Black Economy within an Economy.**" This is why they destroyed the famous "**Black Wall Street**" in 1921 and started Riots in Detroit's "**Black Bottom**" District in the 1940's. Nowadays the Black youth equate success with those people we see on T.V. So unless we sing (**Rap, R&B**), dance (**music video dancers/video vixens/strip club**), crack jokes (**comedy shows/funny buffoonery TV shows**) run (**NFL, NBA, MLB**), or act (**TV shows, Movies,**) we are not making serious money or obtaining serious wealth. We continue to destroy **OURSELVES and our IMAGE** while we are the "**entertainment**" for the world, making the (**non-black**) CEO's or owners of these organizations super rich at the same time.

Fact: The last 2 NBA Commissioners including David Stern have been Jewish. There are a good number of European Jews that own Sports Franchises in the NBA, NFL, NHL and MLB.

264

But even then we don't put all these billions of black dollars to good use to better our people or put it in black hands. This is why we still don't own anything.

(**Left**) The "**One Man Band**" Sambo Character trying to amuse his white viewer and (**Right**) Bill "**Bojangles**" Robinson 1946 famous for his tap dancing styles and jokes which he performed in front of white audiences.

Fact: *Other races won't work for blacks because they see it as degrading to their race. This is why you won't see Jews, Arabs, Indians, Asians, or whites working for blacks in America. This is also why we rarely see a homeless Jew, Arab, Indian or Asian in America. Sometimes we will run as far away from the inner city as possible to find that suburban house and suburban job, thinking that it is a sign of success.* **But at what cost?** *Once a Black person gets a* "**Suburban Job**" *in a predominately non-black area then he/she is usually the "target" to get fired. That is unless this person is a* "**Safe Black**".

"Yassuh... it's *Genu-wine* Hire's"

"**Safe Blacks**" are like "**House Negroes**". They are **ASLEEP.** They pose **NO** treat to White America or the "**Advancement and Independence of Blacks in America**". The new "**Safe Black**" in America is the "**Homosexual Black**". This is what they want.

"The greatest mistake of the movement has been trying to organize a **SLEEPING PEOPLE** around specific goals. You have to **WAKE THE PEOPLE UP FIRST**, then you'll get action."-**Malcolm X**

Is one really free when he or she has to try hard to fit in with non-black neighbors or fit in with coworkers at a majority non-black job? Black children dragged this into environment will also have to know how to adjust to **THEIR** world, **THEIR** expectations, as well as **THEIR** likes and dislikes. This is **NOT FREEDOM.**

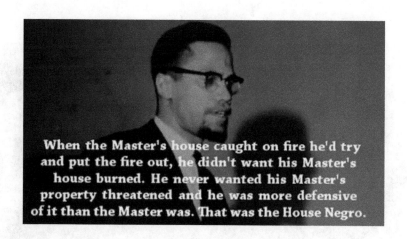

When the Master's house caught on fire he'd try and put the fire out, he didn't want his Master's house burned. He never wanted his Master's property threatened and he was more defensive of it than the Master was. That was the House Negro.

Racial discrimination prevents millions of blacks from getting employment, getting into a College-University, getting a loan, advancing in their jobs to higher positions, starting a business and succeeding in their business. Because of this many blacks are thrust into low-wage jobs which lead to a long life of hard labor followed by health issues then death. We are following in the footsteps of our parents. Preventing blacks from access to quality education, decent housing with ownership (not rentership), equal employment, fair practices with loan applications, and a judicial system that treats everyone the same is what keeps the black race from succeeding in life. Hidden agendas designed to depopulate blacks and destructive demonic music/TV controlled by Jewish CEO's help to fulfill their plans while speeding up our demise.

Fact: Dr. Claude Anderson quoted **"Only 2% of all the black folks in America work for their own community, for their own people producing comfort and products for their own people.** We have not moved one iota (bit) in 140 years in terms of employment. Our people still do not understand that you can **NOT** enrich yourself working a job. A job is **NOT** designed to enrich you…it is there to keep you one week away from welfare, unemployment, and the food stamp lines. If you want to get rich **YOU MUST** move into a business and business ownership. Business will transfer and redistribute wealth 6 to 8 times faster than working a job. The only way Americans can get rich while working on the job is if they steal." We all know **"Blacks stealing"** is what America wants so it can put more blacks in jail.

Deuteronomy 28:21 **"The Lord shall make the pestilence cleave unto thee, until he have consumed thee from off the land, whiter thou goest to possess it."**

*(**Left**) Native American 1800's. (**Right**) Aztec couple from Mexico 1800's
The word "**Pestilence**" means a "**Fatal epidemic disease**". The Spanish
documented that in the 16ᵗʰ Century, Smallpox and other diseases de-populated
the Native Americans, dramatically. This happened wherever the "Indians"
went. From North America to South America (Aztecs, Incans, Mayans) to the
Caribbean (Taino), fatal epidemics wiped out many of the indigenous people
living in these lands shortly after the arrival of the Europeans.*

Before the arrival of the Europeans, the Americas had been isolated
from Europe and Africa. Contact with the Europeans brought measles
and smallpox to the Native Indians.   Smallpox and other diseases
crippled the Aztec and Inca civilizations in Central/South America.
Numerous other diseases were brought to the Americas such as scarlet
fever, typhoid, typhus, influenza, pertussis, tuberculosis, cholera,
diphtheria, chickenpox, sexually transmitted diseases and measles.
Many sources states that 25-50 % of the Native Tribes died due to
disease. When Spanish explorer **Hernan Cortes** invaded Aztec territory
in Mexico (1519), the population was estimated to have been around 25-
30 million. Fifty years later, the population was supposedly reduced to

3 million, mainly from disease. Yale Historian **David Bryon Davis** described this as **"the greatest genocide in the history of man."**

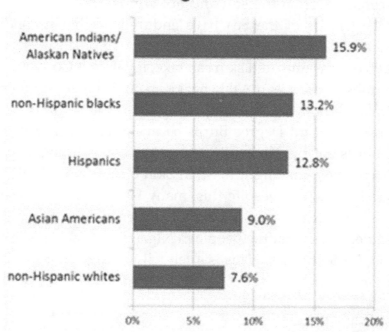

Rates of Diagnosed Diabetes

(Above) From National Diabetes Statistics Report 2014
But that is not the Native Americans only problem. Just like African-Americans, Native Americans have significantly higher rates of Heart disease, High Blood pressure, High Cholesterol, Alcoholic Liver disease/Liver Cancer, other select cancers, Diabetes, Cerebrovascular disease/Stroke and HIV/AIDS than whites in regards to their population. Coincidence?

Deuteronomy 28:22 **"The Lord shall smite thee with a consumption, and with a fever, and with an inflammation, and with an extreme burning, and with the sword, and with blasting, and with mildew; and they shall pursue thee until thou perish."**

SKIN COLOR DOES MATTER! THE CURSES PROVE IT!

In the dictionary "**Consumption**" is defined as: **a progressive wasting away of the body**, like from the effects of Tuberculosis and HIV, diseases which are most prevalent in African-Americans/Africans. Coincidence or just bad luck? "**Blasting**" is defined as: **scorching, from the sun and hot winds**. Black people in Africa, the Americas and the Islands of the Sea have endured the harsh conditions during slavery under the **hot sun** (on cotton & sugar plantations, salt mines, rice fields etc.). Even though our melaninated skin can take, imagine if God sent the Caucasian white skinned Arabs or European Ashkenazi Jews into slavery under the hot sun of Egypt, America (in the south), and Iraq (Babylon). They would die within days from a Heat Stroke or Third Degree Burns because their skin cannot take it. The Ashkenazi Jews in Israel right now since arriving in 1948 have experienced high rates of skin cancer, even making it to #2 in Skin Cancer rates in the whole world second to Australia in 2003. Despite this, many Israelis are at risk of skin cancer because of the UV index numbers present in Israel which equal that of those in Nigeria. Only difference is that the people in Nigeria are black, just like the original Israelites were in Ancient times. This is a tell tell-tale sign that the European Jews are not the "Original Jews".

Dangerous skin cancer on rise in Israel, says report

Health Ministry report finds ramp-up in invasive melanoma, most markedly among Ashkenazi Jews.

Without sunscreen, white skin is under the attack from the UV rays of the Sun. Back in Biblical Times the Israelites didn't have sunscreen to put on while they were making mud bricks for the pyramids in Egypt.

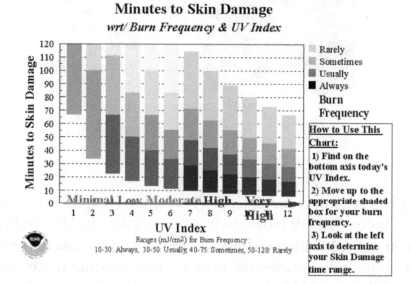

Minutes to Skin Damage
wrt/ Burn Frequency & UV Index

Burn Frequency: Rarely, Sometimes, Usually, Always

How to Use This Chart:
1) Find on the bottom axis today's UV Index.
2) Move up to the appropriate shaded box for your burn frequency.
3) Look at the left axis to determine your Skin Damage time range.

Ranges (mJ/cm2) for Burn Frequency :
10-30: Always, 30-50: Usually 40-75: Sometimes, 50-120: Rarely

EXPOSURE CATEGORY	INDEX Number	Sun Protection Recommendations
LOW	1-2	• Wear sunglasses on bright days. In winter, reflection off snow can nearly double UV Strength. • If you burn easily, cover up and use sunscreen.
MODERATE	3-5	• Take precautions, such as covering up and using sunscreen, if you will be outside. • Stay in shade near midday when the sun is strongest.
HIGH	6-7	• Protection against sunburn is needed. • Reduce time in the sun between 11am and 4pm. • Cover up, wear a hat and sunglasses, and use sunscreen.
VERY HIGH	8-10	• Take extra precautions. Unprotected skin will be damaged and can burn quickly. • Try to avoid the sun between 11am and 4pm. Otherwise, seek shade, cover up, wear a hat and sunglasses, and use sunscreen.
EXTREME	11+	• Seek shade, cover up, wear a hat and sunglasses, and use sunscreen. • Avoid the sun between 11am and 4pm • Take all precautions. Unprotected skin can burn in minutes. Beachgoers should know that white sand and other bright surfaces reflect UV and will increase UV exposure.

When the UV index is 8-10 people with white skin are at risk for sunburn in less than an hour of skin exposure without sunscreen.

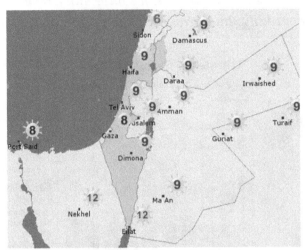

The strength of the sun's ultraviolet (UV) radiation is expressed as a **Solar UV Index or Sun Index**. The UV Index does not exceed 8 in the UK. **Indices of 9 and 10 are common in the Mediterranean area. In the Middle East they range from 9-12 (max).** The Sun Index forecast refers to the daily maximum. **Above is the UV Index in Israel ONLY IN MAY!** The UV index in May in Israel is 9, just as it is in Nigeria!

Fact 1: On May 13, 2003 the Israeli Magazine "**HAARETZ**" reported the following headline "**Israel's skin cancer rate second highest in the World.**" In Hebrew "**HAARETZ**" means "**News of the Land of Israel**". It is Israel's oldest daily newspaper. It was founded in 1918 and is now published in both Hebrew and English in Berliner format. The English edition is published and sold together with the International New York Times. Both Hebrew and English editions can be read on the Internet. In North America, it comes out as a weekly newspaper, combining articles from the Friday edition with a roundup from the rest of the week.

Fact 2: I asked a Jewish man once why Skin Cancer rates was so high in Israel if they were the **Original Jews (who back in the day had to be a people of color)** & his reply was "**back in those days it was HOT in Israel.**" He said that while the Israelites were in Israel and Egypt they were darker. He said that when the Jews left to Europe after 70 A.D. they got lighter. I told him that it was **hot** in Miami, Florida and the European JEWS there are still white. He had to pause for a second to come up with a rebuttal. He then said that the Sephardic Jews were black. I told him that the Sephardic Jews were not "Black" and that "Sunlight" did not adversely affect the skin color of Jews, just as it doesn't affect the skin color of Africans today. I told him that Nigerians and Jamaicans in Europe are still **BLACK** so his statement was obviously incorrect. **This proves that the land they claim isn't theirs.** In 2010, a total of 207 Israelis died of melanomas. In the same year, just over 1,000 Israelis were diagnosed with invasive melanoma, including 939 Jews, 21 Arabs and 42 people from other communities. In Port Harcourt, Nigeria, there were only 15 identified cases of Melanoma at the University Hospital over an **11-YEAR PERIOD, with all of them being on the feet!** **NONE OF THESE CASES WERE FATAL**.

Fact: Ovadiah Yosef was born to an **Iraqi Jewish family**, in Baghdad, Ottoman Iraq on September 24, 1920. He was the Chief Sephardic Rabbi of Israel from 1973-1983. He is also considered to be a **Mizrahi (Middle Eastern) Jew**. Like the Iranian Jews and Ashkenazi Jews, he has white skin. As anyone can see by looking up his picture on the internet he is not **BLACK**. Sephardic Jews are descendants of the Greeks, Non-Arab white Persians, Edomites, Romans, Ottoman Caucasian Turks, Kurds and other Europeans that invaded Judea (Israel) over 2, 000 years ago. Some migrated to North Africa, Spain, Portugal, Eastern Europe, Western Europe and the Middle East. Some perhaps never left under the disguise as "**Crypto Jews**" (**see the "Crusades"**). The Real Children of Israel were removed and replaced by "**Gentiles**" during the Assyrian Invasion of Israel in 701 B.C. It is also documented in the Jewish Tanakh (Old Testament).

2 Kings 17:24 "And the King of Assyria brought men from Babylon (Iraq) and from Cuthah (Assyria/Iraq), and from Ava, and from Hamath (city at Northern border of Canaan/Assyria-Iraq), and from Sepharvaim (Iraq), and placed them in the cities of Samaria **INSTEAD OF THE CHILDREN OF ISRAEL**: and they possessed Samaria (Northern Israel), and dwelt in the cities thereof."

Children of Israel-Siege of Lachish, Israel by Assyrian King Sennacherib, 701 B.C. **(Notice the Kinky Hair portrayed with the small knots all over the scalp and beard)**. *Currently at the British Museum, Great Russell Street, London.*

Fact 3: The Cancer Association of South Africa (**CANSA**) always urges all White Afrikaner South Africans to be Sun Smart to reduce the high incidence of skin cancer in the country. Skin cancer is the most common cancer in South Africa with about 20,000 reported cases every year and 700 deaths. The World Health Organization (**WHO**) reports that between two and three million non-melanoma skin cancers and approximately 132,000 malignant melanomas occur globally every year. South Africa currently has the second highest incidence of skin cancer in the world after Australia. The good news is that skin cancer can be prevented by respecting the sun. The three most common types of skin cancers are basal cell carcinoma (**BCC**), squamous cell carcinoma (**SCC**) and malignant melanoma.

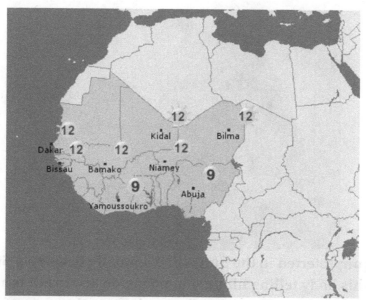

The UV Index (9) in Nigeria, West Africa in May is the same as in Israel! *But the people in Israel and Nigeria look different. One is Black and the other is White. Shouldn't the UV index reflect the people's skin color? This is like the whole continent of Africa being inhabited by Black people and one country (**for example Chad**) being inhabited by only White people. This is how the Europeans Jews appear living in Israel. It doesn't add up. Even the indigenous people in the Pacific Islands (South Asia) are all people of color. Just go visit Papua New Guinea where the UV Index is also 9 during May/June.*

THE BODY DOESN'T LIE ON ITSELF

The heat and rays from the Sun cooked the "**Original Black Hebrew Israelites**" bodies internally but made them **more blacker**. This would've killed the white race or modern Arab race today. For this reason, the bible shows us that the Israelites complained about the heat, but it didn't' kill them nor did they develop skin cancer from it.

Job 30:30 "My skin is **BLACK** upon me, and my bones are burned with heat."

Song of Solomon 1:5-6 "I am **BLACK**, but comely, O ye daughters of Jerusalem, as the tents of Kedar (Black Tents), as the curtains of Solomon. Look not upon me, because I am **BLACK**, because the Sun hath looked upon me:"

275

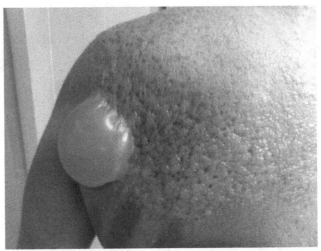

White skin left unprotected in the Sun will eventually develop a Sunburn. If this person ignores his body telling him/her to go inside, the result is a second-degree burn with its classic blister formation (just as in any other type of second-degree burn).

Even the Slavemasters in South Carolina confessed that the Negroes were brown-black skinned people.

"But I have been told by the son of a planter in Florida who bought nine of the Negroes of the "**Wanderer**", paying $6,300 for them that only three of the number was black, six being of gingerbread color. While the admixture of white blood must have taken place and must still take place to some extent in certain portions of the Dark Continent (Africa), the effect being seen in the **Griquas of South Africa**, yet no less an authority and close observer than Livingstone frequently noted what he called the "**coffee and milk**" color in certain tribes of the interior which **HAD NOT**, in the memory of any one living, come in contact with whites or had seen much of them; while those on the coast and along the rivers were usually **BLACK**, or at least **VERY DARK**."

Survivors from the Cardo of the Negro Slave Yacht Wander by Charles J. Montgomery

This is proof that the Negroes were different shades of brown, just as Nigerians, Cameroonians, and other Africans are today. Even though our skin is designed to withstand the damaging UV rays of the sun thanks to Melanin, one can only imagine how it must have felt to work 12-16 hours under the hot rays of the sun.

For over a thousand years, millions of black slaves in America, the Middle East and other countries around the world have died by the thousands from fatal disease such as Tuberculosis, Small Pox, Monkey Pox, Malaria, Ebola and HIV. Blacks have died from HIV, Ebola and Malaria more than any other race in the world. Blacks subjected to slavery endured death via the sword, guns, dehydration, starvation, infectious diseases secondary to insanitary living conditions with mold, mildew, dead bodies, and feces all while living in hot, humid climates. This was all prophesied in the bible for the Black Israelites to endure. No other race has endured all of these inflictions but the "**Negroes**" and the "**Natives**" living in the Lands of the Sea (Americas, Caribbean).

Deuteronomy 28:23 **"And thy heaven that is over thy head shall be brass, and the earth that is under thee shall be iron."**

The verse "**The Heaven that is over thy head shall be brass**" is referring to the sky being "**hard like brass**" or "**shut**" from releasing its rain therefore causing the ground of the earth to by "hard like iron" and dry. This is all too familiar in Sub-Saharan African where the "Negro" Hebrew Israelites lived at. Coincidence?

FACTS ABOUT AFRICA:

1. Africa is the world´s second-driest continent after Australia.

2. About **66% of Africa is arid or semi-arid** and more than 300 of the 800 million people in Sub-Saharan Africa live in a water-scarce environment – meaning that they have less than 1,000 m3 per capita per year.

3. **115 people in Africa die every hour** from diseases linked to poor sanitation, poor hygiene and contaminated water.

4. **35%** of Water and Sanitation aid commitment on MDG goes to Africa with Sub-Saharan having 27% of the financial allocation.

5. In Africa, especially Sub-Saharan Africa, more than **a quarter of the population** spends more than half an hour per round trip to collect water.

6. Africa's rising population is driving demand for water and accelerating the degradation of water resources. By mid-2011, Africa's **population** (excluding the northern-most states) was around 838 million and its average natural rate of increase

was 2.6% per year, compared to the world average of 1.2%. By one estimate its population (Sub-Saharan) will grow to **1. 2 billion by 2025** and to **2 billion by 2050.**

7. The **urban slum** population in Sub-Saharan African countries is expected to double to **400 million by 2020** if governments do not take immediate and radical action.

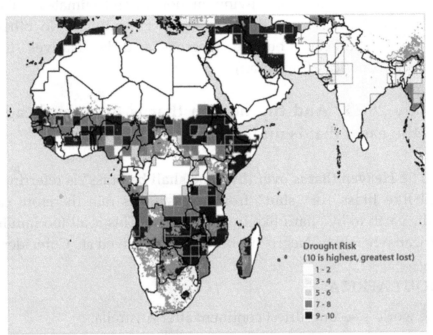

Drought is common in West Africa, Central and East Africa; the same land known as "Soudan" which once encompassed "Negroland".

Africa has been hit with many seasons of drought. Drought causes everything to suffer. Plants die and the scarcity of water affects to health of the livestock. Cows that are not able to gain weight or fully mature won't produce adequate milk or meat. A weakened immune system puts the livestock at risk for diseases which can be passed on to humans. The rain from the heavens is key to the survival of the people of the land. This is why you have nomads who constantly move searching for green pasture and water for their cattle. This want of regular and seasonable rain is what the Children of Israel had to endure many centuries ago in the lands that they were scattered to. In addition to constant persecution from other Hamitic tribes and the Muslims, the Israelites were always on the move. This is why they were nicknamed **"foreigners"**, **"aliens"** or **"invaders"**. They were like nomadic people without a "True Home". So when the scripture says i.e. **"Like Brass"** it is referring to heavens being hard and dry, essentially shut up from giving rain, dew or moisture to the land. The earth being like **"iron"** refers to the harness of the soil that would happen as result of the heavens drying up. **The hardness of the soil from lack of moisture made the ground impenetrable, just like a piece of iron.** Drought stricken areas (**i.e. East Africa-West Africa**) was where most of the Bantus Negro slaves were taken from during the Arab Slave Trade and Transatlantic Slave. Even in the bible (Old Testament), the Hebrew Israelites were scattered into lands where there was hardly any rain, instead just vast deserts and mountains. Even today, the land of Israel is half desert from the Mediterranean climate and the scare water supply. As a result, the people in Israel rely on water from the Sea of Galilee **(which is drying up)** and desalination plants stationed along the coast of the Mediterranean Sea.

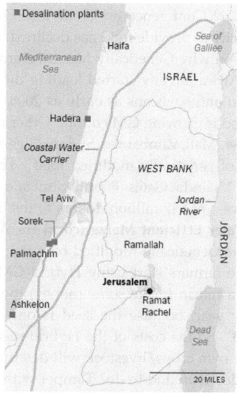

Desalination Plants in Israel stationed along the coast of Israel

Prior to the use of expensive Desalination plants, residents of Israel would have to pay huge taxes on excessive water consumption. People in Israel were penalized for having lawns, swimming pools, and leaky pipes. Some residents even went over to using synthetic grass and swapping out seasonal plants for indigenous plants that were more suited for the semiarid climate. Shower times for many Israelis were cut down to two minutes (**i.e. "Navy Showers"**) and washing cars were outlawed except for those who were wealthy enough to absorb the costs. Nowadays alternative solutions for drought have sparked the increase in the study of synthetic biology. Today, we might call this "**Genetically Modified Organisms (Food)**". Scientists have developed genetically modified crops that can provide higher yields from less land, less water, disease and pests. Synthetic biology companies have shifted their attention and viscous teeth into the land of Africa. Syngenta and Monsanto are the leaders in the GMO movement in Africa, but many African farmers are not too happy allowing these giant companies into their farmland.

Fact: According to the UN Conference on Trade and Development (**UNCTAD**) 2010 report, Africa's capacity to provide food has declined by one-fifth over the past 40 years. This is the reason why Genetically Modified crops are being pushed on African farmers. South Africa already started leading the pack in cultivating GM foods such as corn, cotton and soybeans as early as 2008. Now Egypt is growing GM corn and Burkina Faso is growing GM cotton. Other countries such as Kenya, Tanzania, Uganda, Malawi, Mali, Zimbabwe, Sudan, Nigeria and Ghana have since allowed the importation of genetically modified food. The U.S., teamed up with Monsanto, the Bill and Melinda Gates Foundation and the Howard G. Buffet Foundation to raise in excess of $47 million dollars to the initiative called (**WEMA**) which stands for the "**Water Efficient Maize (corn) for Africa Project**." Secretly they are trying to promote Genetically Modified corn that is drought resistant and insect resistant. Once the farmers start using Hybrid GMO seeds, the damage is done. In order to make a return (make some money) the farmer is forced to buy new Hybrid Seeds every year, because the seed is only genetically modified to produce **ONE HARVEST**. So the costs of the Hybrid seeds vs how much money they can make from their own crops/livestock will determine their success. But is this what God had intended mankind to do? Tamper with the DNA of his creation (crops, insects and livestock)? There is always a price to pay when we try to go against God and be like gods.

Fact 2: The Mad Scientists driven by Satan's technology are also on the verge of producing **"Genetically Modified Cattle"** resistant to the Protozoan **Trypanosomiasis**, which is caused by the **Tse-Tse fly** which causes "**Sleeping Sickness**" in humans. Trypanosomiasis is responsible for many of the cattle and human death in Africa. "**Sleeping Sickness**" infects the Central Nervous System, causing confusion, behavior changes, and sleep disruption. Left untreated, it is fatal. These scientists are supposedly just months to years away from creating Transgenic cattle.

Drought affects 300 out of the 800 million
Africans living below the Saharan Desert.

Deuteronomy 28:24-25 **"The Lord shall make the rain of thy land powder and dust: from heaven shall it come down upon thee, until thou be destroyed. The Lord shall cause thee to be smitten before thine enemies: thou shalt go out one way against them, and flee seven ways before them: and shalt be removed into all the kingdoms of the earth."**

Famine, drought dries out the soil of the land in Africa, mainly West Africa and East Africa, making it hard for anything to thrive (Plants or Livestock). It is not a coincidence that from West Africa and East Africa the people here have had to struggle with dry land but also were victims of the Arab Slave Trade/Transatlantic Slave Trade. This seems like a double-curse, but this was prophesied in the bible.

The land of Africa from whence the Hebrew Israelites were taken from is notorious for drought, famine, the death of livestock and of the inhabitants of Africa themselves. It is in Africa and Arabia that their enemies (**Arab invaders, neighboring African Tribes, European nations and European Judaism converts called "Jews") would come against them, capturing them, killing them or driving them from one habitat to the next** causing the Hebrew Israelites to be removed into all the kingdoms of the earth.

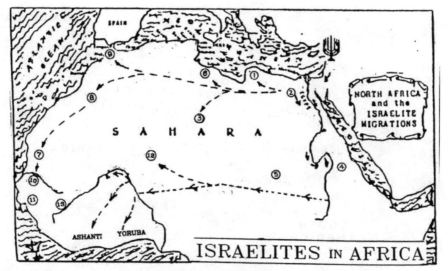

Israelite Migration into Africa

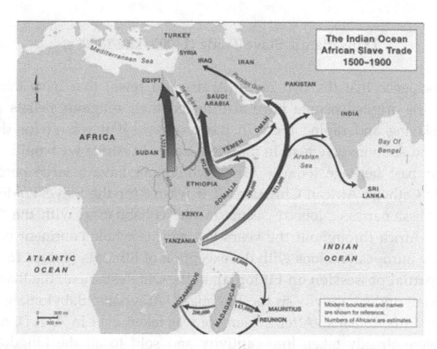

Arab Slave Trade/Indian Ocean Slave Trade (600 A.D.-Present)

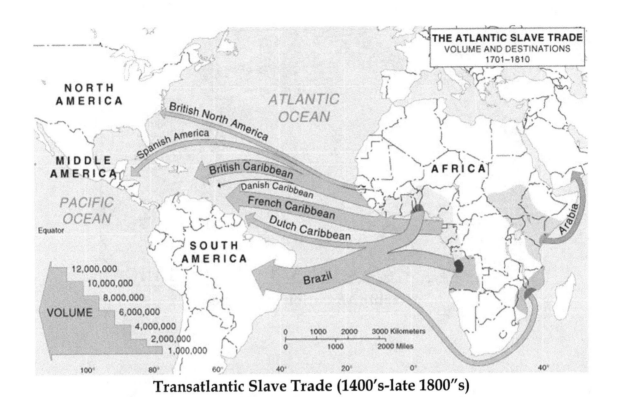

THE ATLANTIC SLAVE TRADE
VOLUME AND DESTINATIONS
1701-1810

Transatlantic Slave Trade (1400's-late 1800"s)

Is it a coincidence that the two races (**Arabs and Jews**) that have taken on the identity of the original people have also forced their religious beliefs on blacks, killing, enslaving and raping them in the process? If it wasn't for the Jewish-European and Arab involvement in the slave trades in Africa we would still have a little of our past heritage today. Africa would not have a large percentage of Muslims or Catholic African Christians if it wasn't for the Slave Trades and the European Missionaries. Nobody seems to like cohabitating with the "**Negroes**" peacefully. Africa throughout the years has had its whole continent partitioned-colonized by European nations with the exception of Ethiopia (**except for maybe 3-5 years of partial possession on Ethiopia**). In the Old Testament, the Black Hebrew Israelites were under captivity to the Egyptians, Assyrians, Babylonians, Persians, Grecians, and the Romans. After 2nd temple was taken over in 70 A.D. most of the Hebrews were already taken into captivity and sold to all the kingdoms of the earth. The rest scattered into Africa and Arabia. Shortly after 70 A.D., the Arab Slave Trade/Indian Ocean Slave Trade began, continuing for over 1,300 years. Most Blacks in America do not know that an "**Arab Slave Trade**" existed. Some people still believe to this day that slavery is just a thing of the past. Sadly they are incorrect. In places like Mauritania and Sudan slavery still exists. The 1400's

284

started the beginning of the Transatlantic Slave Trade which scattered slaves all across the Atlantic Ocean to the Caribbean and the Americas. These two "**Slave Trades**" scattered many Bantus Negroes into all parts of the world, fulfilling the prophecy of the "**Scattered Israelites**". For this reason, as most people would be surprised, there is an "**Afro-Black**" presence of people all across the world in places such as Central America, South America, Cuba, Brazil, Peru, Puerto Rico, Haiti, Dominican Republic, Middle East, India/Pakistan, China, Japan, Australia, Indonesia, Philippines, Fiji, Hawaii, and so on.

Fact 1: *The Dutch, the Netherlands, the French, the Spanish, the Portuguese, the Arab Countries, the European/Spanish/Middle Eastern Judaism Converts called Jews, the British, the Danes, India/Pakistan, the Italians, the Swedish, the Russians and other European Countries all participated in the slavery of blacks in history.*

In Genesis 36:1 it reads "**Now these are the generations of Esau, who is Edom.**" **Edom** was the arch enemy of the Israelites. They prevented Moses and the Israelites from passing through Kadesh into Canaan during the Exodus. The (**Amalekites-sons of Esau**) fought the Israelites as they made their way through the land of Edom into Moab territory. The Edomites were present when the Babylonians tore down Solomon's Temple in the 5th Century B.C. They were present in the Herodian family when the Romans destroyed the 2nd Temple in Jerusalem in 70 A.D. The Bible says that Esau took wives of the daughters of Canaan (Genesis 36:2) and also **Bashemath, the daughter of Ishmael** (Genesis 36:3). Esau took all his wives, sons, daughters, cattle and all his riches to Mount Seir. The Edomites lived in the Middle East in modern day Jordan slight southeast of Israel near Petra, Mt. Seir and Northwest of Saudi Arabia. So we know from **Genesis 36** that Esau mixed his seed with the Black Canaanites and Black Ishmaelite's in addition to the children of Japheth (Book of Jasher). **The Edomite children of Seir and Teman lived in Arabia with the Sons of Keturah (Dedan) and Ishmael (Kedar). See Map.** They intermingled with each other over time. So this means that there should be some Black Arab nations and Black Hamitic nations that have Edom's DNA still in them right? Theoretically Yes! But we do know that the White Turkish/Kurdish Arabs from the North came down into the Middle East and Arabia conquering after the 11th Century A.D. They killed the many of the Black Arab men (Saracens-Ishmaelite's/Keturahites) and established rulership over the lands of Arabia and Arabia Felix (Yemen). These Gentile White Turkish/Kurdish Arabs mixed their **Paternal bloodline** with the maternal (female) bloodline of the

"**Real**" Ishmaelite's, Keturahites, and Edomites causing the lightening of the land of the Arabs. **Over time, Edom has mixed himself amongst the Nations, especially the "Gentile Nations".** The Edomite Herodians also married into the Greek Gentile (Jew-ish) Maccabean family and the Royal Roman family! Here is how!

Genesis 36:11 proves that **Zepho** was the Grandson of Esau. The Hebrew **Book of Jasher** 61:12-13 proves that Zepho joined himself to Chittim/Kittim (Rome). In the Book of Jasher Zepho turns his back on the King of Africa to fight with Chittim/Kittim (Rome) against Africa. In Jasher 61:24-25 Zepho becomes King of Chittim/Kittim (Rome) and he reigns over the whole land of Chittim/Kittim and Italia for 50 years. He also subdues the Children of Tubal (Turkey/Kurds) and all the surrounding Gentile Islands. The Gentile Islands are lands of Japheth!

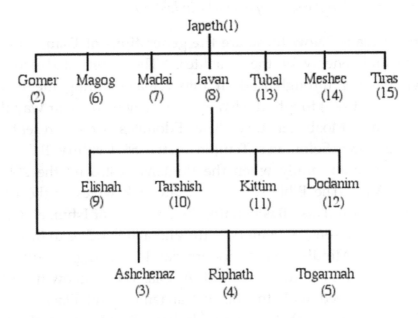

So the White Ottoman Turkish (**Osman I**), the Kurdish Arabs (**i.e. Saladin the Great**) and the Gentile European Nations under the rulership of Rome (Vatican) have been enslaving the "**Negroes**" and so called "**Native Indians**" aka "The Real Children of Israel" under the disguise of **EDOM!** They also have been battling for control of Jerusalem since 70 A.D, after which the real remaining Israelites were scattered into other nations (**Luke 21:24**).

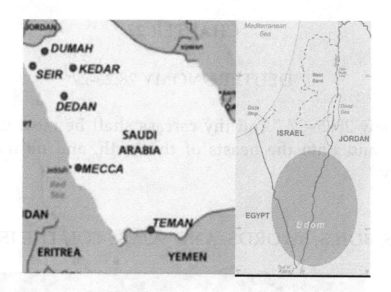

Genesis 36:10-11 "These are the names of Esau's sons; Eliphaz the son of Adah the wife of Esau, Reuel the son of Bashemath the wife of Esau. And the sons of Eliphaz were **TEMAN**, Omar, Zepho, and Gatam, and Kenaz."

Obadiah 1:8-9 "Shall I not in that day, saith the Lord, even destroy the wise men out of Edom, and understanding out of the mount of Esau? And thy mighty men, O **Teman**, shall be dismayed, to the end that every one of the Mount of Esau may be cut off by slaughter."

CHAPTER 27

DEUTERONOMY 28:26-27

Deuteronomy 28:26-27 **"And thy carcass shall be meat unto all fowls of the air, and unto the beasts of the earth, and no man shall fray them away."**

BEASTS, BOILS, SWORDS, AND SCABS FOR THE ISRAELITES

The eating of human flesh by animals and birds happened on a regular occurrence to black slaves after lynching's and other ruthless killings. It is reported that out of 10 million slaves that were sold each year, 9 million black slaves died from the harsh conditions of slavery even before making it to their final destination. Scavenger animals like Hyenas and Vultures prey off dead carcasses. To them it doesn't matter if it's a human carcass or animal carcass. If there is nobody to bury the dead then the beasts and fowls of the earth will eat of the dead.

Hyenas will eat anything that is dead, even humans.

If a person dies of famine, disease or murder and the body is not buried the animals of the earth will eat the remains. Yes, Hyenas were known to eat the remains of the people in Africa who fell victim to these conditions. During attacks from the Muslims or other neighboring Hamitic or even Israelite tribes (with lost heritage) the bodies of the dead had to be burned or disposed of. Back then there were no Hospitals, morgues or Funeral homes. The earth was the all of these places combined. During the slave trades, the remains of black slaves could be found in the water as many black slaves were dumped overboard or jumped overboard to attempt a swim for freedom. The Slave ships frequently were followed by sharks waiting for food and slave caravans were frequently followed by scavenger birds or hyenas ready for an easy meal. This was prophesied in the Bible. The European concentration camps that the Ashkenazi Jews were prisoners in during the Holocaust did not have hyenas, sharks, and scavenger birds there to eat the remains of dead human carcasses. The concentration camps were designed to keep the people from getting out; therefore no animals would've been able to get in. This bible prophecy did not apply to them, being that they were not the **"Real"** Children of Israel.

The Rise of Islam forced many Hamite Blacks and Black Hebrew Israelites into Islamic conversion by the sword. The Arabs used the sword and their power to enslave the Black Hebrew Israelites, from whence they would sell to slave merchants who would then sell them off to the highest bidder all across the world.

Forced Conversion and Slavery did not happen to the European Ashkenazi Jews. It did not happen to the Khazarian Judaism converts during medieval times and it didn't happen to the Sephardic Spanish/Middle Eastern Jew. The Curses of Israel were very clear. God said that for the Israelites disobedience, the curses would be upon **THEE AND THY SEED FOREVER**. The bible clearly tells us in the Old Testament that the Israelites were disobedient from the time of the 1st temple in Jerusalem to the rebuilding of the 2nd Temple under Ezra and Nehemiah. After Yeshua's death, the Israelites were mostly scattered into the four corners. These Curses continued on after Yeshua's death, but only for his "**Physical**" Lost Sheep of Israel.

«так говорит Господь: кто обречен на смерть, иди на смерть;
и кто под меч, — под меч; и кто на голод,
— на голод; и кто в плен, — в плен» (Иеремия 15:2).

This relief describes the Hebrews in Jeremiah 15:2-4

This is an ancient relief depicting the Hebrew Israelites being attacked by birds (**fowls**), lions (**beasts**) and by their enemies with the sword. Notice that their hair is in the fashion of kinky "**Afros**" as noted by the use of many dots to make the appearance of "knots" in the hair. European Jews cannot grow "Afros". Black people can grow "Afro's" naturally. **The language below is written in Russian by a Russian Ashkenazi Jew. They know who the "Real" Jews are.** They just don't want the world to know. The picture corresponds to **Jeremiah 15: 2-4.**

This is a scavenger dog, called the "Hyena" known throughout Africa. It will eat anything that is dead or is dying. This includes human carcasses as well. The Bible prophesied that the "Dogs" of the Earth would eat of the Israelites flesh in the Siege. In 2014, a hyena killed two children in Tanzania, Africa in the Sangabuye village. The Israelites while in Africa were attacked by dogs and beasts. In the Middle East or even Europe, Hyenas and Lions are not prevalent. This is further proof that the Israelites scattered into Africa and not Europe.

Jeremiah 15:2-4 "And it shall come to pass, if they say unto thee, Whiter shall we go forth: Then thou shalt tell them, Thus saith the Lord, Such as are for death, to death; and such are for the sword; to the sword; and such as are for the famine, to the famine; and such as are for the captivity, to the captivity. And I will appoint over them **FOUR KINDS**, saith the Lord: the **SWORD TO SLAY**, and the **DOGS TO TEAR**, and the **FOWLS OF THE HEAVEN**, and the **BEASTS OF THE EARTH**, to **DEVOUR AND DESTROY**. And I will cause them (Israelites) to be removed into **ALL KINGDOMS OF THE EARTH**."

Deuteronomy 28:27 **"The Lord will smite thee with the botch of Egypt, and with emerods, and with the scab, and with the itch, whereof thou canst not be healed."**

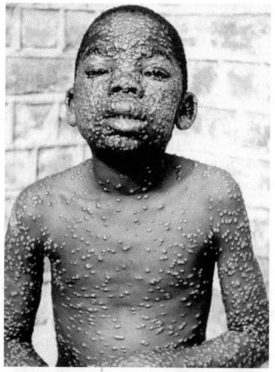

Small Pox is common in West Africa

These verses refer to the boils (**botch**), tumors (**emerods**), scabs, and itching the Children of Israel would endure. Diseases such as leprosy (**Hansen's disease**), Small pox, and Syphilis can manifest as boils, tumors or scabs. Small pox and Sleeping Sickness (tsetse fly) can cause itching. Other disease such as HIV, Yellow Fever, Typhoid Fever, Ebola, Malaria, Tuberculosis, Dengue Fever, Cholera, and Hepatitis also plague thousands of Africans every day. Astonishingly, above the Saharan desert where Arab North Africa is, these diseases are almost non-existent. The Middle East and Arabia are also not afflicted by these diseases. **Is this coincidence or bad luck for the people living in Sub-Saharan West Africa?** It makes me wonder if different diseases like HIV were cleverly given to Africans/African-Americans to depopulate the black race or if in fact it is all the continuation of the **Curses of the Israelites.** Extreme poverty and poor living conditions cause widespread diseases that afflict blacks in America, Haiti, Jamaica,

293

just like in Africa. The diseases acquired by blacks worldwide account for one of the reasons why our population percentages in America and worldwide have stayed stagnant; almost as if we were not reproducing.

DID ANY OTHER NATIONS EXPERIENCE THESE "CURSES OF ISRAEL?"

Fact: Smallpox and Monkey pox was common in Egypt as it was in West Africa. Many Africans died from Small Pox and Monkey Pox. In recent history it has afflicted Blacks mainly in West Africa and Central Africa from 1970-1995. Most cases are caused by Animal Transmission (**Rodents such as squirrels and monkeys**). Monkey Pox likewise causes boils (**Botch**), scabs (**Emerods**), and **itching**. The West African Israelites had no immunity from it so many of them died. But hold up! When the Spaniards came to the land now known as Puerto Rico, they brought Smallpox and many of the native **Taino Indians** were wiped out as well as they couldn't be healed from lack of immunity. This happened to the **Native Aztecs** and **Incas** living in the Americas as well. Could this be a hint that the Curses of Israel spread even from West Africa to the Caribbean and then to the Americas? The European Settlers who came to the Americas revealed in many of their notes that many of the so-called "**Natives**" in the land were possibly actually Hebrew Israelites. **Here is one clue**:

"We do not know much concerning Columbus's crew of about ninety men aboard three ships, but at least one of them was an **Israelite** whose presence as such was not merely accidental. This was Luis de Torres, <u>a convert</u> (message) of possibly only that year, who had once held a position with the governor of Murcia. **He was said to have known Hebrew, Aramaic, and some Arabic**, and had been brought along by Columbus specifically as an <u>interpreter </u>(message).

Book- Lost Tribes and Promised Lands: The Origins of American Racism, Ronald Sanders.

So one striking thing is that Luis de Torres is called an "**Israelite**" but is also called a "**convert**". Then it says he was brought to the Americas as an "**Interpreter**". Did Christopher Columbus and his crew know that they would encounter "**Hebrew/Aramaic**" speakers in this "**New Land**" of **America** or where they searching for the "**Lost Tribes of Israel**"? If a crew of explorers traveled to a remote island in the world today why would they bring "**Hebrew Interpreters**" unless they had possibly learned somewhere that the people living on the island were Hebrew-speaking people?

Fact 1: In the Book "**Christopher Columbus and The Participation of the Jews in The Spanish and Portuguese Discoveries** by *M. Kayserling* it talks about how the European explorers believed that the native Tainos of South America and the Caribbean were descendants of the Jews. They believed the language of the Taino Indians in Hispaniola (Haiti/Dominican Republic), Cuba, Jamaica, the Bahamas, Puerto Rico and adjoining islands was in fact "**corrupted Hebrew**". The believed the islands named "**Cuba**" and "**Hayti (Haiti)**" were Hebrew, named by **Chief strongmen** whom they called "**Caciques**" which was possibly a European corruption of the Hebrew word "**Chazaq**". **Hebrew Strong's #2388 "Chazaq" means "Strong".** They noticed that the Taino's had names for themselves or things like **Haina** (Ain), **Yones** (Jonah), **Yaque** (Jacob), **Ures** (Uriah), **Siabao** (Seba), and **Maisi** (Moshe/Moysi). The Taino people were the indigenous people of South America who eventually settled in the Caribbean Islands. The Tainos were supposedly living in South America/Central America near the Yucatan and had said that they were migrants of tribes from the Orient (East). They migrated East first settling in Cuba and then Hayti (Haiti). The Tainos called their **Creator**, the **Great Spirit** and **Spirits of Spirits** "**YaYa**" or "**Y'ay'a**" just as some Native American Tribes call their Great Spirit "**Ya**" or "**Ya Ho Wa**". Hebrew Strong's #3050 "**Yah**" is the short definition for what the Hebrew Bible has for "**Lord**" or "**Yahuah**". In our King James Bible it is listed as "Jah" because the letter "J" replaced the "Y" and former "I". Even in the Hebrew Tanakh it lists the word "JAH" as "**Yod-Hey**".

Psalms 68:4 "Sing unto God, sing praises to his name: extol him that rideth upon the heavens by his name **JAH**, and rejoice before him."

Could this be proof that the Tainos were descendants of the Hebrew Israelites? Only one group of people in the Bible worshipped "One Supreme Creator/God". This was the Hebrew Israelites. All the other civilizations around them (**Egyptians, Assyrians, Babylonians, Philistines, Canaanites, Romans, Greeks**) worshipped multiple pagan deities. The Tainos Creator-Great Spirit God "**Yaya**" also had a son named "**Yayael**" which sounds like an Old Testament name (i.e. Daniel, Ezekiel). In Taino religious teachings it says that "Yaya" had his son "Yayael" killed, with whom he loved over all things. Does this story sounds like Abraham test to sacrifice Isaac or does it sound like "Yahusha Hamashiach (Jesus Christ)"? It also said that there was a "**Great Flood**" that overtook the earth.

Matthew 3:17 (Jesus Baptism by John the Baptist) "And lo a voice from heaven, saying, This is my beloved Son, in whom I am well pleased."

John 3:34-36 "For He whom God has sent speaks the words of God; for He gives the Spirit without measure. The Father loves the Son and has given all things into his hand. He who believes in the Son has eternal life; but he who does not obey the Son will not see life, but the wrath of God abides in him."

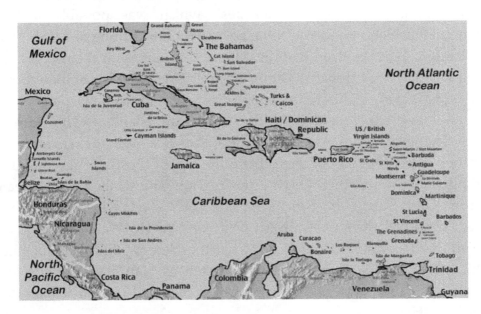

The Tainos said they migrated from the Orient (East-?Africa) to Central America/South America near the Yucatan (Cancun, Mexico). Nearby was Cuba, Jamaica and Haiti which they settled into first.

Fact: The Book of 2 Esdras is not found in the Hebrew Tanakh as many believe it was written in the 1 century A.D. It is a part of the Apocrypha books that are not in our King James Bible today. In the Latin Vulgate Bible the Book of Ezra and Nehemiah are considered 1 Esdras and 2 Esdras respectfully. Therefore 1 and 2 Esdras in most English Versions of the Bible appears as 3 Esdras and 4 Esdras in the Latin Vulgate Bible. These last two books (**3 & 4 Esdras**) were written too late to be included in the Septuagint but are in the Latin Vulgate Bible. Therefore 1 Esdras (Ezra) and 2 Esdras (Nehemiah) are accepted as canon in the bible by Catholics and

296

Protestants. The penmanship of Esdras 3 and 4 is said to be from different authors although some people may try to say that these books were written by Ezra. This is impossible as Ezra lived during 400 B.C. and this would've meant that the Essenes that collected the Dead Sea Scrolls should've had this Second Book of Ezra (Esdras 3 & 4) in the Dead Sea Scroll collection found in 1948 in Qumran, Israel. Nevertheless, some view Esdras 3 & 4 Esdras (Book - 2 Esdras) as only a historical book. In 2 Esdras it reads:

King James Bible 1611 - 2 Esdras (4 Esdras) 13:40-46 " Those are the ten tribes, which were carried away prisoners out of their own land, in the time of Osea the King, whom Salmanasar the King of Assyria led away captive, and he carried them over the waters, and so came they into another land. But they took this counsel amongst themselves, that they would leave the multitude of the heathen, and go forth into a further country, where **MANKIND NEVER DWELT**, that they might there keep their statues, which they never kept in their own land. And they entered into Euphrates by the narrow passages of the River. For the Most High then showed signs for them, and held still the flood, till they were passed over. For through that country there was a great way to go; namely, of **a year and a half**: and the same region is called **Arsareth (America?)**."

Fact: Bartholomew de las Casas (1484-1566) was a Spanish Historian and Dominican Friar who was appointed "**Protector of the Indians**." He wrote writings about the mistreatment of the Indians in "**A Short Account of the Destruction of the Indies**" and "**Historia de Las Indias**". With his father, "Las Casas", he wrote details on how the Taino Indians fought against the Spanish conquistadors in Hispaniola, Cuba and Puerto Rico. During these battles the Taino Indians were hit with famine, sickness (smallpox), slavery and brutal death. Women, Children and babies were killed barbarically. Many of the Taino people committed suicide rather than go through the torture that the Spanish brought to their land. The Mountains of the Islands were the Tainos refuge (safe haven) from the warring Spaniards. Just like in the Philippines with the Black Negritos, the native indigenous people were driven out of their land into the mountains while the Spanish colonized the mainland.

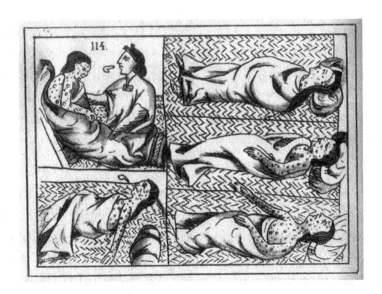

Small Pox afflicting the Aztecs, Contemporaneous depiction of *Mesoamericans suffering from small pox (Florentine Codex, Volume 4, Book 12, Plate 114).*

Fact: The Taino genocide (1492-1518) is where the Spanish wiped out most of the Tainos (**Arawak's**), the native people of the Caribbean Islands (**present-day Cuba, Jamaica, Haiti, Dominican Republic, Puerto Rico, Bahamas, etc.**). Slave revolt battles also caused massive losses and casualties to the Taino population. Columbus himself set it in motion and oversaw it till 1500. According to one estimate, **genocide and disease wiped out 3 million** of the 3.5 million Tainos – 85%. Most were already dead when smallpox arrived in 1518. It has also been reported that the Native "Ghost" language of the Taino Indians bore striking similarities to Ancient Paleo-Hebrew. Could the Tainos have also gone through their own "**Curses of Israel**"? They were enslaved to do harsh work for the Spaniards; they were raped and were brutally killed by the sword, gun or man-eating dogs. Many of the Taino men of Puerto Rico or "La Taina" were killed off in battle, disease or suicide during the invasion of the Spanish Conquistadors. This of course would leave the Taino women remaining on the Island for intermarriage and the mixing of the white bloodline into the Taino bloodline. When the Negro slaves arrived (freed Maroons and slaves) they also had children with the Tainos creating "one nation". So today's Puerto Rican or Dominican person has heritage in possibly all three races.

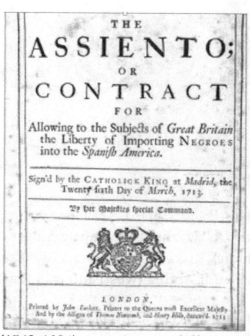

THE

ASSIENTO;

OR

CONTRACT

FOR

Allowing to the Subjects of *Great Britain*
the Liberty of Importing NEGROES
into the *Spanish America.*

Sign'd by the CATHOLICK KING at *Madrid,* the
Twenty fixth Day of *March,* 1713.

By Her Majesties special Command.

LONDON,
Printed by *John Baskett,* Printer to the Queens moſt Excellent Majeſty;
And by the Aſſigns of *Thomas Newcomb,* and *Henry Hills,* deceas'd. 1713

The Assiento Contract (1543-1834) was given to different people such as Kings and Wealthy European men with boats to participate in the MONOPOLY of buying and selling Black Hebrew ISRAELITES for monetary gain in their Spanish Colonies in the Americas and Caribbean. The Portuguese, Dutch, British and French were overjoyed. The slave trade helped wipe out their existing debt and also get rich.

The Bible states in **2 Kings 17:6** "In the ninth year of Hoshea, the King of Assyria took Samaria (**Northern Israel**) and carried Israel unto Assyria and placed them in **Halah,** and on the **Habor,** the river of **Gozan,** and in the cities of the **Medes (Persia)**." It is said that in the Book of Esdras that the Israelites traveled on foot by later possibly used ships to journey to the Americas and the Caribbean Island. Some theorists say that the "**House of Israel**" connected to the **Euphrates River** by using the **Gozan River** and took the Euphrates River south to the **Persian Gulf,** then to the **Strait of Hormuz,** then to the **Gulf of Oman** and to the **Arabian Sea** which they could then sail around Africa to the New World. Why else world the Taino Indians say the came from the "East (**Orient**)?"

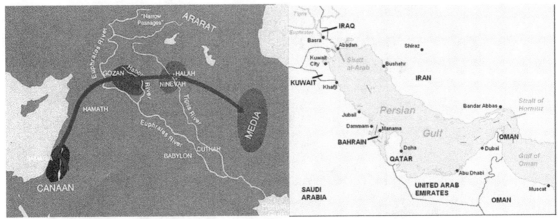

(Above left) The route the Assyrians carried away the Israelites into Persia (Iran). (Above right) The Euphrates River in Iraq dumps into the Persian Gulf bordered by Saudi Arabia (west) and Iran (East).

1 Chronicles 5:26 *"And the God of Israel stirred up the spirit of Pul king of Assyria, and the spirit of Tilgath-pilneser king of Assyria, and he carried them (Israelites) away, even the* **Reubenites**, *and the* **Gadites**, *and the half tribe of* **Manasseh**, *and brought them unto* **Halah** *and* **Habor**, *and* **Hara**, *and to the* **River Gozan**, *unto this day.* **Nineveh** *was the capitol of Assyria back in the day. Today it is a part of Northern Iraq.*

2 Esdras 13:41 says "But they formed this plan for themselves, that they would leave the multitude of the nations and go to a more distant region, **WHERE NO HUMAN BEINGS EVER LIVED**." This had to be the Caribbean Islands or the Americas. So Samaria (**House of Israel**) for disobeying God was destined to fall by the sword with their infants dashed in pieces, and their women with children ripped into pieces (**Supported in Hosea 13:16**).

"Destruction of the Indies by Bartolome De Las Casas" 1542. The picture depicts the Spaniards bashing babies against rocks, feeding children to the dogs and burning the native Indians alive while being hanged. Was this Bible prophecy being fulfilled from Hosea 13:16 for the House of Ephraim (Israel)?

This book depicted the gruel, barbaric inhumane practices that the Spaniards used to depopulate the indigenous "Taino/Arawak Indians" of the Greater Antilles, and most notably the Island known as "**Hispaniola**" or Haiti/Dominican Republic.

Hosea 13:16 "Samaria (**House of Israel**) shall bear her guilt; for she rebelled against her God: *they shall fall by the sword; their infants shall be dashed in pieces, and their women with child shall be ripped up."*

"They took up arms, but their (Natives) weapons were very weak and of little service in offense and still less in defense. (Because of this, the wars of the Indians against each other are little more than games played by children.) And the Christians, with their horses and swords and pikes began to carry out massacres and strange cruelties against them. **They attacked the towns and spared neither the children nor the aged nor pregnant women nor women in childbed, not only stabbing them and dismembering them but cutting them to pieces as if dealing with sheep in the slaughter house. They laid bets as to who, with one stroke of the sword, could split a man in two or could cut off his head or spill out his entails with a single stroke of the pike. They took infants from their mothers' breasts, snatching them by the legs and pitching them headfirst against the crags (rocks) or snatched them by the arms and threw them into the rivers**, roaring with laughter and saying as the babies fell into the water, "Boil there, you offspring of the devil!" Other infants they put to the sword along with their mothers and anyone else who happened to be nearby."

This was all prophesied to happen to Samaria (House of Israel under Ephraim) for their disobedience in **Hosea 13:16**.

The Spaniards burned the Natives alive and those that survived (boys, women and children) were distributed among the Spanish Christians to be **SLAVES**. They taught them their ways, forced them to wear clothes and used the Indians in the mines to dig for gold which was gruesome, intolerable labor. They sent the Taino women into the fields of the big ranches to hoe and till the land. **YES THE "NATIVES" WERE SLAVES AT SOME POINT IN TIME**. They barely fed the Indian slaves anything more than beans and as a result the breastfeeding mothers did not have any milk to produce for their babies which ended up dying from starvation. They Spaniards separated the men from the women so that they couldn't have sex. The Spaniards chose the native women they wanted to have sex with and those they wanted to forcefully marry, bearing mulatto children. Over time, millions of the native people died, the men dying in the mines and the women dying in the field from the exhaustion or hunger. This was how they depopulated the land of the natives and how they got rich. This was all prophesied in the Bible.

We know this is Israel because the word "**God**" is in capital letters in Hosea 13:16. **The only people that worshipped and were punished for being disobedient to "God" were those whom "God" made a "Covenant-(agreement)" with, aka "The Children of Israel"**. This was the Children of Israel; the **House of Israel** in Samaria (**Northern Kingdom**) and the **House of Judah (Southern Kingdom)** in Jerusalem. "**Samaria**" was the second capitol (**first was Tirzah**) to the Northern Kingdom of Israel after the Israel split into two nations. **See also 1 Kings 16:23-24**). When the Spanish (Christopher Columbus) and (crew arrived to the Americas and the Caribbean they knew that the "Natives" were Hebrew. They knew they spoke Hebrew or had Hebrew-like dialect. They knew about 2 Esdras. The Spanish would corrupt and erase their history like the Europeans corrupted the "**Negroes**" history. The did this by applying Spanish Diminutives, affixes, prefixes, and suffixes to all their words, thus slightly modifying the language but their "**Hebrew dialect**" is not all lost! Many words like **Canoe, Tobacco, Barbecue** and **Hurricane** are Taino words. Some Taino influences can be seen today in Haitian Creole along with the "**Ewe**" Tribal Language from West Africa.

DID THE TAINO INDIANS SPEAK HEBREW?

Hurricane is a "**Taino**" Word. Ask any Puerto Rican. "**Guabansa(h)**" was what the Taino's called their Goddess of Storms. **Juracan (Huracan)** was also identified as the god of storms, but this word simply means hurricane in Spanish. So where did the "Guabansa(h)" come from? Well in Spanish it could be pronounced "**Gua-ban-cex**" and in Taino it is "**Gua-ban-sa(h)**". This word is amazingly derived from Hebrew! Let's look!

Taino Hurricane God/Storm God-Guabansa(h) (Huracan). On the (**left**) is the Taino depiction of the angry wind god. The symbols on the hands represent the clockwise rotation of the hurricane whose "**eye of the hurricane**" is depicted as a face just like the "**Arch of the eye**" (**picture to right**).   We all know a hurricane is curved, hollow and it is angry! So the Taino Indians knew the characteristics of a hurricane and they described it the best way they could in Hebrew!

Hebrew Dictionary (Lexicon-Concordance)
www.lexiconconcordance.com/Hebrew
H-1354/H-1359 = G (w)ab or Gab, meaning "**Hollow, Curve, something convex like a back, or arch of eye**".
H-1149 – B(a)ns(a) or Ben-as or b nas, meaning "**be enraged or to be angry**".

Even in Aramaic "**Benas**" means "**to be angry**".

God prophesied that the "**House of Israel-House of Ephraim**" would but put in a location where his idolatrous actions would cause him to receive wrath of God by a "**Hand**" aka "**Hurricane**". The Taino's saw the Hurricane clockwise rotation as like "**moving hands**" and the inner part of the Hurricane as a "**face**" or "**eye**". The islands that the Taino (Arawak) and Carib Indians would dwell in (Caribbean) would be common for its frequent Hurricanes!

Isaiah 28:1-2 "Woe to the crown of pride of the drunkards of **Ephraim**, and to the fading flower of his glorious beauty, which is on the head of the fat valley of them that are overcome with wine! Behold, the Lord hath a **MIGHTY** and **STRONG ONE; AS A TEMPEST OF MIGHTY WATERS OVERFLOWING**, will he **CAST DOWN TO THE EARTH** with the **HAND**."

This sounds like a Hurricane if I didn't know any better. What other type of Weather phenomena causes water to crash down onto the earth? God was not talking about a mighty rainstorm; God was possibly describing a "**Hurricane**".

The Spanish originally called the Island of Hispaniola (Puerto Rico/Haiti) as the Latin name "**Yoanees (Joannes) Est Nomen Eius**" meaning "**John in his name**" in reference to "**John the Baptist**". John the Baptists father (Zechariah) was a Levite but also was a descendant of Aaron. In Hebrew, John the Baptists name would have been written as **Yahanan/Yah-achanan/Yohanan/Yehohanan** meaning "**God is gracious**" or "**Yah is favored**".

The Puerto Rico "**Coat of Arms**" shows the words "**Joannes Est Nomen Ejus**".
Note: The J replaced the "Y" and the "I" in the late 1500's and early 1600's. This is what Hosea 4:16 was talking about in the name "**Joannes**", which means "**God is blessed/gracious**" or "**Yah is favoured**".

God instilled Joseph to give "Blessings" to his children and the House of Israel in Genesis 49:22-26 and Moses did the same to Joseph and Israel in Deuteronomy 33:13-17.

Hebrew Dictionary (Lexicon-Concordance)
www.lexiconconcordance.com/Hebrew
H-3068 = "Yah" or "Yahuah" meaning "**the proper name of the God of Israel**".
H-2603 = "Chanan" pronounced (Khaw-nan) meaning "**shew favour or be gracious**"

COMBINE THEM BOTH UP AND YOU GET......GOD IS GRACIOUS!

H-3076 = Yah-achanan/Yeho-chanan, pronounced "**Yeh-ho-khaw-nawn**" which is for "**Ye-Jo-hanan**" as it is "**Johanan**" from the Words **YHUH** (#3068) and **Chanan** (#2603)

Jacob and Moses showed favour/grace towards Joseph by blessing his seed (Tribe of Ephraim and Manasseh). This is supported in **Genesis 49:22-26**. It is also further stated in **Deuteronomy 33:13-17** where Moses **blesses** Joseph (Ephraim/Manasseh) over the "**House of Israel**.

The word "**Jibaro**" is a term to describe only "**Puerto Ricans**". It was not used in European Spain towards any other people but the Puerto Ricans. In the Spanish language the letter "**O**" is used as a suffix when identifying a "**masculine**" name or allocating the word to a group of people. It comes from the original word "**Ibar**" or "**Eber**". By applying an "**S**" to make it plural you get "**Ibaros**" or "**Jibaros**" which is a corruption of the word "**Hebrews**". English and Spanish originally did not have the letter "**J**". When the "**J**" was added in Spain its pronunciation "**H**" was used for the "**X**" like in the pronunciation of "**Mexico**" or "**Me-hico**". This is because in the 16th Century the "**X**" and "**J**" had the same sound or pronunciation which was the "**H**" pronunciation. **We can thank all these phonetic changes to the "Real Academia Espanola", the Institution in charge of regulating the Spanish Language, established in 1713.** So the "**J**" using this principle would be pronounced as an "**H**". So the word "Jibaros" would be pronounced as "**He-baros**" "**Habiru**" or "**Hebrews**". This is why the savage Spaniards brought with them Hebrew/Aramaic interpreters (**Book: Lost Tribes and Promised Lands; by Ronald R. Sanders**) to the Island of the Tainos and they called the natives of Puerto Rico "**H-ibaro**" or "**Ibaro**" **WHICH WAS THE SPANISH EXPRESSION AND WRITTEN FORM FOR WHAT IS COMMONLY KNOWN TODAY IN ENGLISH AS "HEBREW".**

Note: *The Europeans also brought Hebrew-Aramaic interpreters when they visited West Africa and the Americas. Why would they do this if they didn't know something in regards to the language the people in these lands might be speaking? They surely didn't bring over Arabic, Hindi, Sanskrit, or Greek interpreters.*

But guess what? The Spanish tried their best to pronunciate who the Taino Indians called their neighbors in their native tongue. The Spanish came up with the word "**Caribs**". Why? Because the Spanish corruption of the Taino word for these other tribes was actually a "**Hebrew**" word for "**Kindreds living nearby, Kinfolk, Near of Kin, or Neighbor**".

Hebrew Dictionary (Lexicon-Concordance)
www.lexiconconcordance.com/Hebrew
H-7126 = "**qarab**" pronounced "**Kaw-rab**" like the word "Carib" in reference to the natives of the Caribbean Island. It means "**to come near, approach, close**".

H-7138 = "qarob" pronounced "**Kaw-robe**" meaning "**Near**", "**close relative**", "**kinsmen**", "**relative**", or "**neighbors**".

This is proof there were other Israelites living off the East coast of the Americas in the Caribbean Islands. Even the Europeans were told of this by the Native Indians in America in the Book "**Lost Tribes and Promised Lands; by Ronald R. Sanders).** In the book it describes how the Spanish and Dutch Jewish settlers overheard the Indians saying the Jewish "**Shema**" daily prayer in Hebrew. When they asked who was saying the "Shema", a couple of the Indians raised their hands. The Indians obviously overheard the Jewish Spanish and Dutch settlers talking in Hebrew (**Perhaps Ladino or Yiddish**) and they recognized it as a form of Hebrew. They told the European Settlers that they were from the Tribe of Reuben and that the Tribe of Joseph was living in the Islands (Caribbean) off the East Coast of their country (America).

The Word "**Taino**" means "**TAI-Good**" + "**NO-People**" or "**Good People**". Christopher Columbus would write about these Tainos too. Their name also comes from the phrase "**People of Tahan**" or the "**Merciful People**".

Hebrew Dictionary (Lexicon-Concordance)
www.lexiconconcordance.com/Hebrew
Hebrew Strong's #8465 "**Tachan/Tahan**" is "**An Ephraimite**". It is in Numbers 26:35 and 1 Chronicles 7:25.

Now the Hebrew person of the Bible called "**Ta-CHAN**" was an Ephraimite (son of Joseph) and the Hebrew word "**CHAN-an**" means "**to show mercy, show favour or be gracious**". So taking the Prefix of "**TA**" for an Ephraimite and adding it to the Prefix "**CHAN**" you would essentially be saying "**Merciful Ephraimite**" by saying **Tachan** also. Just something to think about when Puerto Ricans today say they are from the Tribe of Ephraim.

1 Kings 20:31 "And his servants said unto him, Behold now, we have heard that the Kings of the **HOUSE OF ISRAEL** are **MERCIFUL KINGS**:"

Here is what Columbus said about the Taino Indians he encountered.

"They traded with us and gave us everything they had, with **good will**.....they took great delight in pleasing us....They are **very gentle** and without knowledge of what is evil; nor do they murder or steal (**10 Commandments**)....Your highness may believe that in all the world there can be no better people....They love their neighbors as themselves (**Greatest 2 Commandment**) and they have the sweetest talk in the world, and are gentle and always laughing. "
Christopher Columbus.

But it gets even deeper.....

The Spanish heard the Tainos say the word "**Arawak**" or "**Arakaw**" which is also Hebrew. The Spanish corrupted the Hebrew word by calling it what they could get out of their dialect not knowing it was Ancient Hebrew. The Tainos were trying to tell the barbaric Spaniards "**Their Story**" of how they **wandered/journeyed** to the Island that they were currently living on. But the Spanish didn't know what they were talking about.

(**Above**) **These are Two Arawak Indians next to shield. The other picture is a picture of two Carib native men.** The Natives that lived in the Americas and the Caribbean came in different shades and had varying hair textures from straight to kinky. They also had different looks; some **Asian (i.e. Mongloid)** and some **Negroid**. The shield they are holding is the "**Coat of Arms**" for **Suriname** (South America) a country north of Brazil. The words "**Justitia Pietas Fides**" means Justice, Peace, and Fidelity. The Star represents the five continents from which they came from: **AFRICA, America, Australia, Asia and Europe**. The left half of the shield symbolizes the past, as slaves they were also abducted by the **EUROPEANS**. The Arawak tribes consist of the **Tainos, Lokonos, Lucayans, Caribs, Ciboney** and many others. These are the people the EUROPEANS encountered when they arrived to the Caribbean and the Americas. These Arawak men live near Brazil, Columbia and Venezuela. The Caribbean are named after their brothers or Neighbors the "**Carib**". The Tainos also are in this group of natives that are the indigenous people prior to the Transatlantic slave trade.

Hebrew Dictionary (Lexicon-Concordance)
www.lexiconconcordance.com/Hebrew
H-724 "**Arukah**" pronounced "**Ar-oo-kaw**" meaning "**healing or restoration**".
H-732 "**Arach**" pronounced "**Aw-rakh**" meaning "**to wander, journey or go**".
H-736 "**Orechah**" pronounced "**O-rekh-aw**" meaning "**a traveling company or caravan**".

And deeper.....

The Spanish also heard the Tainos call their Leader/Chief "**Cazaq-Yah**" or "**Leader of God**" which they corrupted into the word "**Cacique**". A Leader or Chief of a Tribe has to be powerful and strong. In Hebrew this word is spelled "**Chazaq/Chazeq**". Adding a "Yah" to the end simply gave reference to God in the name such as **Ezeki-EL, Dani-El, Jerimi-YAH, Obadi-YAH, and Hezeki-YAH**. Because of the Taino word "**Cazaqyah**" the Spanish continue using the word "**Cacique**" to describe a "**leader**" or a "**boss**" which is what they used to call the leaders of different indigenous groups they encountered in the West. Remember also the Taino "**Great Spirit, Creator and Spirit of Spirits**" is called "**Y'aY'a**", pronounced "like **Eye-eye**". As told in the book *Pedro de Torreros and the Voyage of Destiny*" from the 1700's. Could this be a short form to say "**Ahyah** (Ehyeh) **Asher Ahyah** (Ehyeh) or Hebrew Strong's #1933 "**Hayah**" meaning "**to exist, to be**". The Tainos word for father was "**Baba**", similar to the Hebrew word for father

"**Abba**". The Taino word for yes was "**Han/Jan**" similar to the Hebrew word "**Ken/Kan**" for yes.

Hebrew Dictionary (Lexicon-Concordance)
www.lexiconconcordance.com/Hebrew
Hebrew Strong's Lexicon
H-2388 "**Chazaq**" pronounced "**Khaw-zak**" meaning "**become powerful or mighty**".
H-2390 "**Chazeq**" pronounced "**Khaw-zake**" meaning "**Stronger**".

Fact: *In 1873, Slavery was abolished in **Puerto Rico**. In South America, in the 1800's after slavery was abolished in Europe and in the America's, the Elite wanted white race mixing with the natives which was called the "**Spanish Mestizaje**" movement. Their goal was to wipe out any trace of Africanism by making the Latino nations lighter. Or was it the Edomite and Kenite (Cainite) in them that made them think of such an evil thing to do (intentional eugenics). Perhaps this is why Puerto Rico is the lightest Island in the Caribbean.*

Arawak-Maroon People in the Caribbean.

The current national motto of Jamaica is "**Out of Many, One People**" which replaced the old motto "**The Two Indians Will Serve As One**" in 1962. The Coat of Arms has two Indians on it representing the **Taino** and **Arawak tribes**. After the mid-1600's, while fleeing from Spanish invaders, the Taino/Arawak Indians learned to get along and work together with the African runaway slaves in Jamaica called "**The Maroons**". The Maroons were escaped slaves that ran away from their Spanish-owned plantations when the British took the Caribbean Island of Jamaica from Spain in 1655. The word "**Maroon**" comes from the Spanish word "**Cimarrones**", which means "**Mountaineers.**" Eventually, while living in the mountainous regions of Jamaica with the Maroons, the two race groups intermarried having kids.

Fact: *The **Caribs** were Arawak's too but were a bit tougher. The Caribs who weren't killed off by the diseases the Europeans brought, fought back. In their culture, the men spoke the Carib language and the women spoke Arawak. They were known to inhabit South America and the Lesser Antilles Islands. Cannibalism was popular amongst their tribe as they liked to "barbecue" human flesh before eating it. The word "Barbecue" is actually an Arawak/Taino/Carib word. Of all the tribes, the Caribs lasted the longest, and are survived till this day. The last known speaker of the Carib language is said to have died in the 1920s. A few other tribes also survived, but also through having children with people of other races.*

Columbus learnt of Jamaica from the Taino in Cuba, however when he first tried to land on the North Coast over 40 war canoes repelled him. He next landed on the South Coast at Cow Bay (named after the numerous manatees found there). Here Columbus was greeted by a cacique who Columbus considered "the most intelligent and civilized cacique in the Antilles", both he and his warriors were splendidly dressed in bright feathered cloaks and head dress with ornaments, made of semiprecious stones, around their necks and on their foreheads, their faces and bodies painted with various colours displaying their tribal heritage.

However, this cordial relationship was not to last. The Taino were the first people of the New World to encounter the Europeans as they expanded westwards, and soon were to face harsh slavery and virtual extinction. However they were not fully exterminated, as history has led us to believe. In 1655 when the English expelled the Spaniards, Tainos were still recorded as living in Jamaica. It was noted at this time the rural farmers spoke a dialect that was mixture of Spanish, Taino and African languages. Later archaeologists were to discover English lead shots amongst the Taino artifacts, and almost 60 years earlier in 1596 English privateer Sir Anthony Shirley sacked St. Jago de la Vega (later Spanish Town), after being guided there by Taino tribesmen. Further archaeological finds were later to confirm that Taino extinction was a myth, although being enslaved and cruelly treated by Europeans, some Taino did survive. Many escaped into the mountains to co-exist with the Maroons, where still today many non-African plants are used medicinally, plants that were once part of the Taino pharmacology. Hammocks also are still made in Accompong in the Taino fashion, proving that the Taino still survived for many years after the Spanish had left, with the Maroons in the mountains of inland Jamaica.

Fact: *In Jamaica today petroglyphs found around the Island are a poignant reminder of these early people. The museum at White Marl, outside of Spanish Town, has a good collection of Taino artifacts on permanent display. There is also evidence that the Jamaicans also have heritage from the "Akan" people from* **Ghana**.

JUDAISM IN MEXICO AND SOUTH AMERICA

In a book titled *"Yucatan Before and After the Conquest"* by *Friar Diego de Landa* it talks about what the Natives Indians told the Spaniards, on their trip to the New World and of where they came from. The Yucatan Peninsula is home to the popular vacation spot, **Cancun, Mexico**.

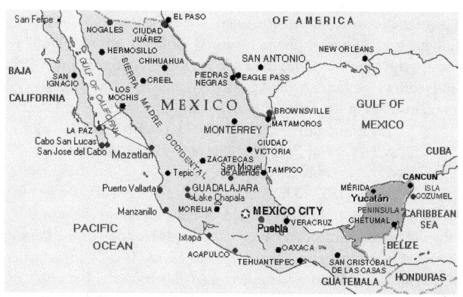

*The **Yucatan Peninsula** sits near Guatemala, Honduras, Belize and Cuba. The Yucatan Peninsula is where many **Garifuna** (Black Caribs) live at today. The Ancient Mayans and the Aztecs resided in the Yucatan Peninsula.*

Now remember, it is said that the Spaniards brought interpreters that were fluent in Hebrew and Aramaic to the New World. This was also commonly known to be done in West Africa and the Caribbean Islands. This is what the book read:

*"**Some old men of Yucatan (near Cancun) say that they have heard from their ancestors that this country was peopled by a certain race who came from the EAST, whom God delivered by opening for them twelve roads through the sea.**"*

It is said that when they Natives arrived to the New World, the tribes began dropping off each other beginning in South America, then moving upward to Central America, the islands of Puerto Rico, Cuba, Hispaniola and finally North America. In the History books, these tribes of natives are grouped into a people called "**Arawak's**".

Here is what the Spaniards encountered when **Montezinos the Spanish explorer** visited the Seminole Indians in the mountains of Quito (Ecuador), prior to their migration to Florida.

"Upon hearing her words they rose, went over to Montezinos and, to his utter astonishment, said: **"Shema, Yisrael, Adonai Elohenu Adonai Ehod"** which is (**Hear, O Israel, the Lord our God, the Lord is One – Deuteronomy 6:4**). They had recited, in Hebrew, the fundamental credo of Judaism." "They (natives) told him they were themselves of the Tribe of Reuben, and that the tribe of Joseph lived on an island nearby" (Cuba, Haiti, Puerto Rico).
"Lost Tribes and Promised Lands" by Ronald Sanders.

Fact: Friar Diego Duran (1537-1538 A.D.) saw elements of Judaism in the old **Aztec religion**. The Aztecs ate only **unleavened bread** on certain days of the year, and practiced the use of baths for purification. The Feast Holiday of the **Passover** is also called "**The Feast of Unleavened Bread**". Thus Matzo is only bread eaten by Jews during the Passover. Matzo and unleavened flat bread is common in Mexican dishes. This was being practiced by their forefathers before the Spaniards got to the New World. The Indians also offered up a small quantity of every meat and drink to God before they ate. This is what the Israelites were commanded to do during the "**Feast of Firstfruits**" in **Leviticus 23:9-14**.

Leviticus 23:9-14 "And the LORD spake unto Moses, saying, Speak unto the children of Israel, and say unto them, **When ye be come into the land which I give unto you, and shall reap the harvest thereof, then ye shall bring a sheaf of the firstfruits of your harvest unto the priest**: And he shall wave the sheaf before the LORD, to be accepted for you: on the morrow after the Sabbath the priest shall wave it. And ye shall offer that day when ye wave the sheaf and he lamb without blemish of the first year for a burnt offering unto the LORD. And the meat offering thereof shall be two tenth deals of fine flour mingled with oil, an offering made by fire unto the LORD for a sweet savour: and the drink offering thereof shall be of wine, the fourth part of an hin. And ye shall eat neither bread, nor parched corn, nor green ears, until the selfsame day that ye have brought an offering unto your God: it shall be a statute for ever throughout your generations in all your dwellings."

Some of the "Native" tribes would sing a song which consisted of the words "**Ya-Ha-Wah**", "**Ye-Ho-Wah**" and even said the words "**HalleuYAH**". These words could only be known if the "Native Indians" had knowledge of the Torah/Tanakh before the Spaniards got there. Friar Diego Duran documented this in his work;

The History of the Indies of New Spain (Mexico), published in 1581. It was also known as the "**Duran Codex**".

CHAPTER 28

DEUTERONOMY 28:28-30

Deuteronomy 28:28 **"The Lord shall smite thee with madness, and blindness, and astonishment of heart."**

Blacks everyday are astonished as to how we are treated as a people in America, and across the world. Does this affect our Mental Health?

Astonishment is defined as a **"great surprise or amazement."** Blacks living all over the world, descendants of slaves are **still mad and utterly amazed** as to how we are disliked by almost every other race on the planet. From the United States of America to Israel, it is the same.

ALL WE CAN DO IS SHAKE OUR HEADS? WE GOTTA WAKE UP!

No matter what country blacks are living in, it seems as though blacks are strategically suppressed by the evil powers to be in that land or country. In America despite supposedly living in the "**Land of the Free**" where "**All men are created equal**", blacks walk around every day still not feeling totally free. We have been conditioned to "**fit in**" with everyone else instead of being able to be ourselves without discrimination. For this reason we have to watch our back and work twice as hard in order survive in America.

After seeing George Zimmerman's "**Not Guilty**" verdict on T.V after killing an unarmed black boy, "**Treyvon Martin**", America could no longer hide it's obvious unequal treatment of blacks in regards to fair justice in the Judicial system. Then the media showed us again in the "**Michael Brown (2014)**" shooting death how blacks are still treated in America. Shortly after this, NFL black professional athletes (**Ray Rice, Jonathan Dwyer, Greg Hardy, Adrian Peterson**) were involved in domestic violence and child abuse scandals on public T.V. Ironically, it was only Black NFL players that were targeted for Domestic Violence. What's even worse is that despite the NFL being almost 70% black, the NFL Domestic Violence Advisory Board making these decisions had no black men or black women on its roster. Is there no qualified black men or women in America able to advise on Domestic

Violence? It doesn't take a rocket scientist to see how the media pushes its agenda to show as much negative, destructive T.V footage on blacks as much as possible. The racism, discrimination and treatment blacks receive from other races simply because of the color of our skin is by far exhibited to no other race **AND NO OTHER BROWN RACE OF PEOPLE** than people of African (Hebrew Israelite) descent. Just about every black person in America will at some point experience racism, unfairness and injustice simply for being "**Black in America**".

**Over 90% percent of Black Homicides
are committed by other Blacks. This mirrors the homicide rate in Mexico.
Coincidence or "Curses of Israel?"**

If we notice on T.V news, we don't see Jews killing Jews, Chaldeans killing Chaldeans, Indians killing Indians, Asians killing Asians, Greeks killing Greeks, Italians killing Italians, Palestinians killing Palestinians but we do see Latinos and Blacks killing each other at astounding rates in America. Are these also signs of the "**Curses of Israel**"?

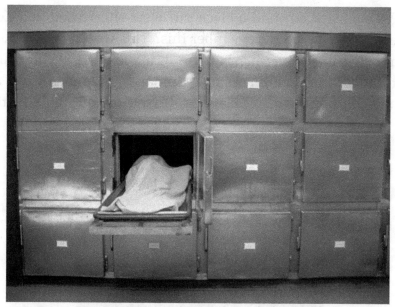

More Black people end up in the morgue from black-on-black murder than any other race in America.

The morgues in Black inner cities stay full, not from just from the black elderly dying but also from young black people dying from **black-on-black violence**. Of course the Jewish-controlled media makes more ratings when they show black violence, crime and murder than showing anything positive that blacks are doing in the community. This is because the "**Agenda**" is to keep America believing that blacks are the problem and that we are "**savages**". Even in Baltimore, Maryland and in Ferguson, Missouri during the riots from the deaths of Michael Brown and Freddie Gray we see how the Media flooded our T.V. news channels with footage from the destruction but not from peaceful protests.

Fact: 10,000 peaceful protestors showed in Baltimore, Maryland, 2015 but no Media covered this on all channels. On 10-10-2015 The "**Million Man March**" was held in Washington D.C. for black people to discuss police reform and change in the black community but there was no "major" Media Coverage. See the pattern? They want to portray to the public that we are "**Savages**" and are nothing but "**trouble**" instead of peaceful human beings.

Fact: In the 1900's a black boy and a black girl were showcased in a Zoo in front of white onlookers. Does anybody remember this? This would be an "Astonishment" to any Human being to see another Human in a zoo. But "White America" back then and even today don't see Blacks as "Humans". We were seen as "**Primates (Monkeys)**" and "**Sub-human**". This was foretold in the Bible in the Curses of Israel.

AFRICAN PYGMY. OTA BENGA AND CHIMPANZEE
From a photograph made in 1906 in the Zoological Park, New York City
1878

Ota Benga, the Congolese pygmy was displayed at the Bronx Zoo, New York in 1906. In the same year the Black Fraternity Alpha Phi Alpha is started in Ithaca, New York. Most African-Americans don't know this.

African girl in Zoo in Brussels, Belgium in 1958. Belgium invaded and colonized the Democratic Republic of Congo.

But it doesn't stop here…..

Fact: A 20 year-old girl from South Africa known as **Sarah "Saartjie" Baartman** would be emblematic of the dark era that gave rise to the popularity of human zoos. She was recruited by an exotic animal-dealer on location in Cape Town and traveled to London in 1810 to take part in an exhibition. The young woman went willingly at the promise that she would find wealth and fame. Exhibitors were looking for certain qualities in their '**exotic**' recruits that either coincided with the European beauty ideal or offered unexpected novelty. Sarah had a genetic characteristic called "**steatopygia**", **a protuberant buttocks and elongated labia**. She was exhibited in cages at sideshow attractions dressed in tight-fitting clothing that violated any cultural norms of decency at the time. Basically they put her on display like she was a "**cheap hooker**" to show off her body in front of white men and women. A few years later she came to Paris where racial anthropologists poked and prodded and made their theories. After only being in Europe for only four years Sarah eventually turned to prostitution to support herself and drank heavily. When she died in poverty, Sarah's skeleton, sexual organs and brain were put on display at the Museum of Mankind in Paris where they remained until 1974. In 2002, President Nelson Mandela formally requested the repatriation of her bodily remains. Human zoos such as the **"Negro Village"** in Germany and other zoos throughout Europe and America portrayed Black people as subhuman. Even in India, the Black indigenous **"Andaman People"** were put in Zoos and the women were used by some Indians to dance naked for money or for food.

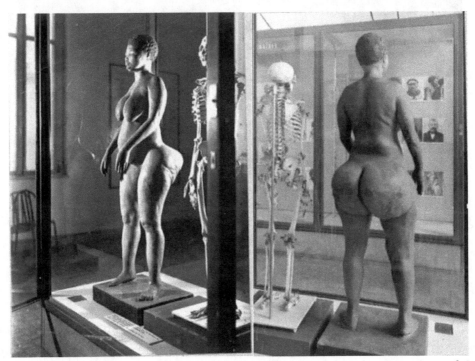

South African President Nelson Mandela requested for the remains of Saartjie "Sarah" Baartman's (aka. Venus Hottentot) to be returned from France (where she died at the age of 25) after she died. After being treated like an animal in a strange country (she was even caged), she was finally given a proper burial near her birthplace in South Africa. What the "White European race" used to make mockery of and also sexually exploit is what black (and white) females are trying to achieve today using plastic surgery.

Europeans also collected the head of Africans and Native Americans for research and for collection. It is for this reason that many black men and black women are still MAD or FED UP in America.

Deuteronomy 28:29 **"And thou shalt grope at noonday, as the blind gropeth in darkness, and thou shalt not prosper in thy ways: and thou shalt be only oppressed and spoiled evermore, and no man shall save thee.**

African Slaves and the descendants of slaves have been more oppressed than any race of people even until now. As most blacks look at their surroundings they see that every other race is able to start successful businesses in urban and suburban areas. We wonder why we work for everyone else and why we spend our money making other races richer while our race plunges deeper into poverty. We cannot seem to get ahead despite how hard we try.

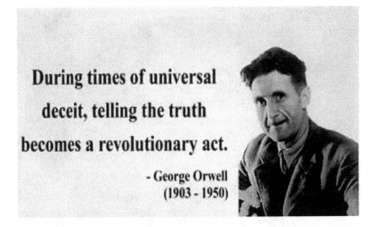

During times of universal deceit, telling the truth becomes a revolutionary act.

\- George Orwell
(1903 - 1950)

In George Orwell's book "**1984**" published 50 years ago it describes 3 classes in a fictional America: the Inner Party, the Outer Party, and the **Proles: Proles is short for Proletariat. The Proletariat is defined as the LOWEST SOCIAL CLASS, WHO LABORS FOR A LIVING.** In America Blacks and Latinos would be "Proles". The slogan of the party concerning this 3rd, reject "**Prole**" class is that "**Proles and animals are free.**" **Notice how Proles and animals are bunched into the same group**. They are not put under the rigorous monitoring or surveillance (audio/visual, cameras etc...) that members of the other parties face. This is because the "**Proles**" are thought to not have enough **INTELLIGENCE** to stand up to the other dominant parties. Their only purpose in society is to "**WORK**", "**HAVE SEX**" and "**BREED**". This sounds familiar to how the media portrays Blacks in America doesn't it? The "**Proles**" are kept **HAPPY** by **LOTTERIES, SILLY SONGS, AND LOTS OF PORNOGRAPHY**. Sound familiar? Ironically, in the Book, it is believed that "**if there is hope in a revolution it lies with the proles (i.e. Blacks, Latinos, Native Americans)**. But sadly, in the book, it is revealed that the proles will never revolt or boycott because they never will need to. As long as they are kept with **GOVERNMENT ASSISTANCE, FOOD (EBT CARDS), SHELTER (POOR HOUSING) AND ENTERTAINMENT (REALITY SHOWS, MUSIC VIDEOS, ETC.)**, they all won't unite to rise up.

The Spirit of Slumber is upon Black America. It is time for us to research our ancestor's heritage and wake up.

Jeremiah 50:4 "In those days and in that time, says the Lord, **The Children of Israel SHALL COME**. They and **the Children of Judah** together; With continual weeping they shall come, And seek the Lord their God."

Fact: *The Children of Israel and the Children of Judah have not all come to back to the Lord. In order for the Lost Sheep of Judah and Israel to both come back to the Lord they have to know that they are the Lost Sheep of Israel. This prophecy is slowly unfolding as we see Latinos, Native Americans and Blacks researching their ancestors Hebrew Israelite Heritage. As they "wake up" the "fake Jews" are going to be exposed. This is going to lead up to the "End Times" and the building of the Third Temple in Jerusalem (for the Antichrist). The people calling themselves Jews are not the Biblical Israelites. They are "proselytes" or Religious converts to the religion of the Pharisees, called Modern Judaism.*

President Lyndon B. Johnson followed the concept of keeping us "**pre-occupied and enslaved**" using the 1964 "**War on Poverty**" program. He knew the destruction of the Black family and race would be evident if the law required welfare services (**i.e. 1964 Food Stamp Program**) dependent on if blacks stayed poor, kept having kids and did not get married. The Welfare state in the black community kept black couples from getting married; it promoted fatherless homes and encouraged dependence of the "system".

So how can we rise up if we are asleep? How can we rise up unless we realize what's going on? We think we are getting knowledge but we are instead getting **"Trick Knowledge"**.

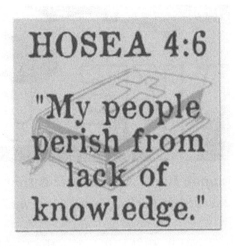

Perhaps maybe Orwell foresaw something about America in the future, especially **Black America**. Now the question is, **"Is the increase in racial tensions-injustice covered by the Media and the worsening economy just a coincidence or is it meant to spark an uprising from fed up, angry blacks in America?"** Maybe then, the **"King Alfred Plan"** will come to life? Hmmmm..... What's the coincidence that a book written 50 years ago could describe a group called **"proles"** that fits Blacks in America to a tee?

The suppression of blacks is in part because of agendas that have been set up from pre-slavery days even until now. This parallels the scriptures in Deuteronomy 28:29. However, part of the blame also lies with us as we tend to not unite and not support our own. We in some cases will wish for the downfall of our fellow black peers because we don't want to see anybody else black surpass us. This is a **"Crabs pulling each other into the bucket so no one wins"**-type of thinking.

Fact: When you have live crabs in a bucket they are constantly fighting with each other to get out. They grab each other's claw or leg, or they step on each other to get to the top. Nobody gets out. This is how we as Blacks sometimes behave. But we are humans, not animals or crustaceans. If a group of people were stuck in a big ditch they could easily form a human ladder and climb on each other's back until one gets out the ditch to get rope to pull everyone else out. Many times we look at our black community and we see people like crabs. But what is worse is that they are crabs that are asleep! Just like zombies. **Malcom X said his biggest mistake was trying to organize a "sleeping people" around specific goals. He said that you had to first wake up the people in order to get ACTION.** We have so much potential in "**UNITY**" but we seem to have all these shackles that bind us. We even have "**crabs within us**" that hold us back from reaching our fullest potential. "**External**" or "**Internal**" all it takes is one bad crab. External crabs tell you what you can't do, they bring you down, they try to steal your ideas, or attempt to shut doors off. They essentially prevent you from fulling shining bright. Even family sometimes will not support an idea or project you are doing. They can simply crush or hold your potential by not supporting or promoting what you're doing to others. Like the saying "**Misery loves company**", crabs love to see the downfall of others and these crabs would rather we all sit around at home, unemployed, uneducated, and high off some substance complaining about what we don't have or what we wish we did have. Wake up people. We have to stop being crabs. Our survival depends on it.

Deuteronomy 28:30 **"Thou shalt betroth a wife, and another man shall lie with her (slave masters):"**

During slavery, the White Slavemasters/Plantation owners, their sons, brothers, nephews and other male acquaintances from other Plantations raped Black Women without fear. They did it for sexual desires or as acts of punishment. Without the right to vote, we could not sit on a Jury. Therefore the Jury and the Judge were always racist whites. Black men were also sexually abused by their slaveholders (especially in Arab Slave Trade) and sometimes by the wives of the White Plantation men. It is a known fact that the majority of slaves taken to Virginia were taken from the area now known as Nigeria.

WHO HAS BEEN SLEEPING WITH MY WIFE?

It is a known fact that "**Black**" and "**Native Indian**" female slaves in America were raped by their slave masters and friends. The slavemasters had no regards for raping the young female slaves or the older female slaves. Many of these women were mothers and wives. However, the mixed breed children resulting from this evil act were still considered slave children. This is one of the main reasons why we have different shades of African-Americans with different textures of hair here in America. This happened in the Spanish colonies in Central/South America and the

Caribbean. This is why we have different shades of people in the Caribbean (Cuba, Puerto Rico, Dominican Republic) and is also the reason for the mixed breeds of Blacks in Madagascar.

On a companion card with the same two figures, the dark skinned Madagascar woman fans the European officer and the caption reads:

"It's all the same, with a little negress taking care of your needs and showing you favor, it doesn't matter what people say, these are good times in Madagascar. "

Mulatto slave children, the product of a Georgia Slavemaster and his female slave (1800's).

*(Above) **Puerto Rico in the 1800's. Slavery was abolished in Puerto Rico in 1898.** Slavery was forced on the Native Taino Indians of Puerto Rico until many of them were killed off. Then the "Negroes" were taken to satellite Spanish Colonies in the Caribbean from Africa and Iberia (Spain/Portugal). They had to keep someone doing the **"slave labor"** at all costs. This is how the Spaniards built up Puerto Rico and got rich. Meanwhile, the descendants of the Negro Slaves in Loiza, Puerto Rico live in poverty and are "looked down" upon because of their skin color.*

During the Transatlantic slave trade the white man exerted his power over the slaves even though he was easily outnumbered by them. If he wanted sex, he could easily take a slave and have sex with her, young, old, married or unmarried. If young white boys needed sex, it was available to them as well; male or female. If they wanted to see men and women having sex, they could set it up with their black slaves. If they wanted to have sex orgy parties using African slaves with all their friends they could easily do so. Likewise, some of the white women who were single would purchase black male slaves just for the purpose of sex, despite the potential backlash it had in White Southern culture. This sexual control they had over the African slaves corrupted the South and at the same time broke many black families apart. It **"mentally"** scarred and destroyed blacks for generations. The "**Nuclear Family**" was tight even during the 1800's. After the "**Emancipation of Slavery**" in the 1860's, the black family started getting back to the way it was. Segregation allowed blacks to depend on one another, and not the white man.

Black Slave Family 1862, South Carolina

Black families stayed together after the 1860's. Then at some point this trend started to reverse to what it is today where over 60% of black kids are living in single-parent households.

Fact: Data from U.S. Census reports reveal that between 1880 and 1960, **married households consisting of two-parent homes were the most widespread form of African American family structures.** A study of 1880 family structures in Philadelphia showed that three-fourths of black families were nuclear families, composed of two (male/female) parents and children. In New York City in 1925, 85% of kin-related black households had two parents.

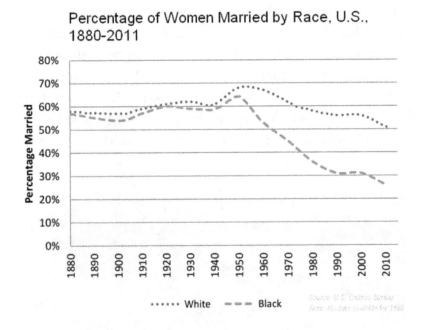

Percentage of Women Married by Race, U.S., 1880-2011

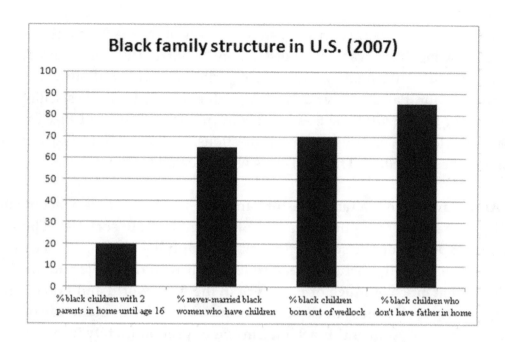

Black family structure in U.S. (2007)

| | % black children with 2 parents in home until age 16 | % never-married black women who have children | % black children born out of wedlock | % black children who don't have father in home |

It was also a common practice to break families up during the slave auctions. This was an even crueler punishment added on top to the punishment of slavery! One could only image the mental destruction that was caused by the physical, verbal and sexual abuse of the slavemasters. Even after this, black families started to repair itself. However after the 1960's with our **"Racial integration"** into White America we started going the other way.

Fact: Slavery destroyed the Africa-American family mentally, financially, morally and domestically. White people and their families benefitted off slavery acquiring **"Land"**, **"Wealth"** and **"Education"**. We were not allowed to achieve none of these. The statistics, in any case, show the black American family was at its strongest during Jim Crow/segregation, while at its weakest (and still weakening) since the 1960s Civil Rights Era.

So is **this a coincidence or bad luck?** I think not. We need to wake up.

Even in the Arab Slave trade, Black women were used as sex slaves and concubines in the Sheikh's palace of many Middle Eastern countries. (**Note: this practice still exists today in the Middle East**). Again, many of these women were wives, daughters and mothers prior to being enslaved. The descendants of Arab-Africans can still be seen in the Middle East this this day, despite the media not showing it.

Fact: In **Al Jazeera**, which is an English Version-Arab News Network, on July 7, 2013 the following Topic was up for discussion: "**Confronting anti-black racism in the Arab world**". Written by Palestinian writer **Susan Abulhawa**, founder of "**Playgrounds for Palestine**" and author of the international bestselling novel, "**Mornings in Jenin (2010)**", she talked about the slave trade and Black racism in the Arab world. She focused on two questions. "**What about Arab anti-black racism and the Arab Slave Trade.**" This is what she had to say:

"**The Arab slave trade is a fact of history and anti-black racism is a fact of current reality, a shameful thing that must be confronted in Arab societies. Though I claim no expertise on the subject, I think that applying notions of racism as it exists in the US will preclude a real understanding of the subject in the Arab World. I spent much of much of my youth in the Arab world and I do not recall having a race consciousness until I came to the United States at the age of 13. My knowledge of Arab anti-black racism comes predominately from Arab-Americans. Like other immigrant communities, they adopt the prevailing racist sentiments of the power structure in the US, which decidedly holds African-Americans in contempt. This attitude is also becoming more prevalent in Arab countries for various reasons, but mostly because Arab governments, particularly those that import foreign labor from Africa and Southeast Asia, have failed to implement or enforce anti-discrimination and anti-exploitation laws.**"

Alem Dechasa left Ethiopia to work for a maid in Lebanon. During her employment she hung herself after she was beaten on a street in Beirut, Lebanon by the brother of the head of the recruitment agency that brought her to the country. Lebanon TV aired the footage and it immediately went viral. Many Africans from Ethiopia, Sudan find themselves in a form of slavery when looking for work in the Middle East. Many African women working in the Middle East are chained to the wall and are given a mat to sleep on with food as if they were dogs. We just don't hear about it on T.V. But this isn't how Arabs treat their women. The Islamic religious book, the Holy Quran is supposed to teach that ALL people are equal. In the Islamic Hadith, it teaches that men and women are equal. But it seems from the Arab Slave Trade history of mostly African women that Black women are not equal to Arab women. If that were the case, the Arabs would simply enslave their own women to be "sex slaves".

"All people are equal, as equal as the tooth of a comb. There is no claim of merit of an Arab over a Non-Arab, or a white over a black person, or a male over a female. Only God-fearing people merit a preference with God."
Islamic Hadith

Many Ethiopians state that migrants to the Middle East are still being beaten up, locked in houses, given no days off, prevented from having their own passports, denied proper healthcare, having no help from their Ethiopian agencies, and are eventually driven to commit suicide. Some Ethiopians have even quoted:

"When a Lebanese person goes to Ethiopia or any other country in that area to work, he lives like a king and is never humiliated. When we come here, we live like animals, and worse. I want us to live like kings and queens in Lebanon like the Lebanese workers do when they visit our countries."

Sudanese Migrant workers in the Middle East also complain of their treatment in places such as Lebanon. Here is one quote:

"I am not living here for free. I buy food. I pay for transportation. I pay all my bills. The Lebanese government is benefitting from my stay in Lebanon, all I'm asking for is my basic rights. My skin is black. I did not choose for it to be black but it is black, does it dictate who I am? When I go into a shop and I see something I like, the seller says surprisingly 'You are black, how you want to buy this?' Don't I have to get clothes to wear? Things to use? Am I not a normal human being?"

Does this sound familiar in the Bible?

Song of Solomon 1:5-6 "**I AM BLACK**, but comely, Oh ye daughters of Jerusalem, as the Tents of Kedar, as the curtains of Solomon. **Look not upon me, because I AM BLACK, because the sun hath looked upon me:** my mother's children were angry with me; they made me the keeper of the vineyards; but mine own vineyard have I not kept."

Was this an Israelite woman or King Solomon? Were women normally made the keeper of vineyards? Or was this a man's job? Either way the reference to this person's skin color as **BLACK**, the sun, and the Black Tents of Kedar prove that King Solomon from the Tribe of Judah was not a European White man.

Blacks are hidden throughout the Middle East by the elusive tactics of the Media and journalists that report in these countries. They don't show you the black residents of the Middle East (Basra, Iraq) or the Migrant workers working there. This is because they don't want us to know. They don't want us to see any Blacks in Egypt, Arabia, Palestine, Lebanon, or Iraq. When the media shows us pictures of

Arabia, Egypt and the Middle East, all we see is white skinned to light skinned Arabs. Where are the dark-skinned black people in these countries? What we don't realize is that the temperature in these areas is close to 110 degrees and the heat index is at its maximum of 9-12. With this kind of temperature we would expect to see dark-skinned people, but we don't. At least not on T.V.

Unbeknownst to many, the Arab slave masters used the African slave women for their sexual exploitation and gratification, often trying them out before purchase by having sex with them in public or behind closed doors. If the female African slaves were acceptable to their Arab Slavemaster, they would be taken away to their countries as sex slaves (concubines). Back then in the Arab Slave trade and also with the European Slave Trade blacks were viewed solely as **PROPERTY**. We still are viewed as their **PROPERTY** here in America and in the Middle East today.

Here is what an African had to say about the current condition and abuse of blacks in the Middle East:

"Let's not forget the slavery and control the Arabs had brought upon us in the mid-ages. And today, instead of focusing on our own economic issues in our own country, some of us "by choice" tend to strive ever more harder to be enslaved by them. Yet they still fly on chartered planes into our land and take our resources as though they are still our kings. No hate but these are the facts. If you want to serve your enemy, start close to home. We have history far richer than them and above all, we are Kings and Queens of this planet."

THE ARABIC SLAVE TRADE
AND
THE ROLE OF ISLAM IN
AFRICAN Slavery

It was estimated that 2 out of 3 slaves in the Arab Slave trade were women, the opposite of the Transatlantic slave trade where the ratio of male to female slaves was 2:1 or 3:1. By the 1950's Saudi Arabia consisted of a slave population of 450,000 or 20% of the population, mostly derived from slave women. From 1983-2005 during the Second Sudanese Civil War, as many as 200,000 Sudanese women and children were taken into slavery and sold throughout the Middle East, India, Europe and the Far East as sex slaves or servants. It is a known fact that the Sheikhs of Iran, Iraq, Arabia, Yemen, Oman and Qatar still had slaves all the way into the 1900's.

Arab Slave market selling African men, women and children.

Fact: It is also a known fact that the Arabs enslaved people from India and women from Europe. The most despised slaves to the Arabs slave traders were the Africans and Indians while the most favorite slaves were those of white European heritage. The Black Arab (Moors) and White Turkish Arabs loved stealing white women as slaves to have sex with (**See Barbary Slave Trade**). This often resulted in mulatto children for the Black Muslims Arabs and Europeanized the physical features of the Caucasian Turkish/Kurdish Arabs. For this reason many Arabs (**especially Lebanon, Egypt, Palestine, Syria, Iran, Iraq**) can pass for European men or women. DNA studies also prove that they have a lot of European DNA in their genes. The mixture of races with white skin into the Arab/Asia population is why there are some Arabs that look more European Caucasian than Arab and there are East Indians that are very fair in appearance despite their cohabitation in the same hot climates as their fellow darker Dravidian Indians. This is also why the people of Afghanistan also have a "Whitish" look to them like their Iranian brothers.

WHAT HAPPENED TO ALL THE BLACK ARABS? SELECTIVE BREEDING IS WHAT HAPPENED?

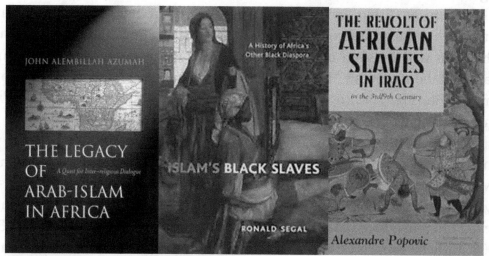

The Arab Slave Trade of Black people in Africa existed for almost 1,500 years. Don't get it twisted. They just don't teach this in America and many Arabs practice "Covert racism". If they did would Black people have tension with the Arabs like they do with White people? Were these Black Slaves Hebrew Israelites or Hamites?

As described earlier the Quran is supposed to not distinguish between the races. Most Muslims will say that Islam is the only religion that accepts Blacks as equal. They also say Arabs see Black people as their "**Brothers**". Many claim that Blacks are welcome in the Mosques and are welcome in Mecca, Saudi Arabia. But is there underlying racism from the past that we don't know about? Is there really "covert racism" in the Arab world towards Blacks? When "**Segregation**" was banned in America, all it did was change the way Whites treated Blacks in public, but inside the confines of their house racist whites in the South could still voice their hatred of blacks. These are straight facts. So although Blacks are now allowed to attend

White churches and Arab Mosques thanks to the abolishment of slavery and "**integration**", blacks in the past were "**made**" Muslims via slavery. In the past and in present Arab literature, one can see a strong legacy of racism against Blacks. The language (derogatory names), traditions and customs of the Ancient Arabs support the "**down grading**" of the Black race. Multiple books such as "**The Legacy of Arab-Islam in Africa**" by John Azumah, "**Islam's Black Slaves**" by Ronal Segal, and "**The Revolt of African Slaves in Iraq in the 3rd/9th Century**" by Alexandre Popovic shows how Blacks were treated in Arab culture. In Dr. Azumah's book: "**The Legacy of Arab-Islam in Africa**", there are plenty of examples of this "**down grading**". In Dr. Azumah's book it states that in the Muslim Hadith, there is an example where an Ethiopian woman cries out about her "racial inferiority" to Muhammad. Muhammad consoles her by saying, "**In Paradise, the whiteness of the Ethiopian will be seen over the stretch of a thousand years.**" Some authors also state that the statement "**Do not bring blacks into your pedigree**" is also in the Muslim Hadith. The Hadith is supposedly the reports/statements of the Prophet Muhammad that were not compiled under a "**central authority**" like that of the Noble Quran. If Blacks were viewed as inferior to Muslim Arabs, this would explain why even today why Arab women are discouraged from marrying a Black man (Muslim or Christian). It explains why the African male slaves were castrated so they couldn't reproduce in the Middle East. They knew that the Black man "left unchecked" to reproduce would spread his seed changing the Middle East "Black". In a 1908 study by French Physician, Richard Millant called "Les eunuques a travers les ages (Eunuchs through the ages" there is a graphic description of the human gelding procedure by which eunuchs were "castrated" before reaching Turkey. Most of the Negro boys castrated were between 6 and 12 years old. Only 90 percent of them survived this brutal procedure. Here is a description of what Turkish Muslims did to their male "Negro" child slaves in the late 1800's:

"Castrators of Negroes buy them and then sell them, after having mutilated them, on the Turkish market, that is if the victim does not succumb to the operation or to its consequences (90% do not survive). As to the methods used, they have remained as primitive as in the past. The (black) child is spread out on the floor or a table, the sexual parts are tied at their base by a rope, and on these parts they operate with one vigorous movement of a razor, the wound is then dressed with some small shot (i.e. lead rifle shot?), with some astringent substances, boiling oil, or some warm honey. Once the bleeding stops, they fix a kind of lead nail two

inches long, slightly curved and with a thickened end, into the urethra, until it is healed....Castrators sometimes use an even more barbaric method. Immediately after the removal of organs, they introduce into the urethra rather than a nail, a piece of reed protruding two inches, so that urinary functions are performed without interruption. Then a plaster is applied on the wound, and the patient is buried up to his neck in the warm and dry sand, while the assistants trample the ground around him. This maneuver reduces the mobility of the wounded one completely....after a week he is unearthed."
"Sesquicentennial Comparisons: Black Slavery in America and Ottoman Turkey",
January 1, 2013, Dr. Andrew G. Bostom.

Fact: In **1833 under the Slave Abolition Act** Black slaves were freed within England and most of the British Empire via a court order. Christians such as United Kingdom-born **William Wilberforce** (1759-1833) fought hard to abolish slavery in Europe. The Bible says the Children of Israel would be scattered into the **FOUR CORNERS** via captivity or fleeing captivity. No other race has undergone this in the history of the planet.

Isaiah 11:12 "And he will set up an ensign (standard) for the nations, and will ASSEMBLE the outcasts of **ISRAEL**, and gather together the dispersed of **JUDAH** from the **FOUR CORNERS OF THE EARTH**."

Blacks have been scattered to the North (**Europe**), to the East (**Middle East, India, Indonesia, China**), to the West (**Caribbean, North America**) and to the South (**Central America, South America, Madagascar**). The European Jews and the Arabs were not scattered to the **FOUR CORNERS** via slavery or forced invasion. France did not abolish slavery until 1848, and the United States would not fully abolish slavery until 1865. Slavery did not become illegal in Islamic culture until after Europe did so (i.e. Egypt in 1882, Morocco 1912, Turkey 1933.). Slavery in the Middle East was so universal and natural for Arabs that they considered blacks slaves no different than having cats or dogs in the house. Sources say that in Istanbul, Turkey at one point there was an estimated 30,000 black slaves living in the land. Today many of the original Black Arabs are presumed to be the descendants of slaves with many of them living in the lowest of caste systems as outcasts.

Fact: According to Dr. Azumah in his book "**The Legacy of Arab-Islam in Africa**", before the 1900's, Mecca served as the gateway to the Muslim world for slaves brought out of Africa. On one excerpt it reads:

"It became custom for pilgrims to take (black) slaves for sale in Mecca or buy one or two slaves while on **Haj (pilgrimage)** as souvenirs to be kept, sold or given as gifts."

Now it has been said by many that the Prophet Muhammad owned and sold Black Slaves. Some say that in Classic Islamic law it is lawful for a light-skinned Muslim to marry a Black woman, but a Black Muslim African/Arab is restricted from marrying a light-skinned woman. Back in the day, Arab historians wrote literature describing the "Negro". In the past Muslim Arab and Persian literature depicted Blacks as "stupid, untruthful, vicious, sexually unbridled (uncontrolled), ugly, distorted, excessively merry and easily affected by music and drink.

Persian Muslim Scholar Nasir al-Din al-Tusi (1201-1274 A.D.) said of Blacks:

"The ape is more capable of being trained than the Negro."

Persian Muslim Scholar Ibn Sina aka "Avicenna" (930-1087 A.D.) described blacks as "people who are by their very nature slaves." He wrote: "**All African women are prostitutes, and the whole race of African men are "Abeed" (Slave stock).**" He wrote described Black people as "**rats plaguing the earth.**"

Ibn al-Faqih al-Hamadhani was a 10th century A.D. Persian scholar. He described the Bantus Israelite slaves as "**The Zanj (blacks) are overdone until they are burned, so that the child comes out between black, murky, malodorous, stinking, and crinkly-haired, with uneven limbs, deficient minds, and depraved passions.**"

So as one can see, the hatred of Blacks by the light-skinned Muslim Arabs was so deep that they made sure that female Black slaves were used only for sexual purposes and the Black man could not pass his paternal lineage down in the Middle East by using the practice of "**castration**". This ensured that the Middle East would remain filled with the new light-skinned non-Arab Persian and the Arabicized (turned Muslim) people from the North (Asia Minor-Turkey, Kurdistan, Syria). Today, this custom of "selective breeding" in the Middle East and America is still practiced amongst Arabs. Arab men will have sex with Black women but will rarely marry them. Arab women are essentially "forbidden" to marry Black men (African/African-American) in America. If they do, they are usually treated as "outcasts". Like other races, light-skinned Arabs typically marry light-skinned Arabs. Indians marry Indians, Jews marry Jews, and Asians typically marry Asians (or Whites). The practice of this "selective breeding" for a millennia in the Middle

East coupled with Arab Invasions into North Africa has created the "whitenization" of the Original Black Arab.

Lebanese woman (left) and Syrian woman (right). They are indistinguishable from Europeans. Their DNA (Michael Hammer 2000 DNA study below) also proves they are blood brothers/sisters to the Eurasia (Asia Minor) people from Japheth (Togarmah), not Shem.

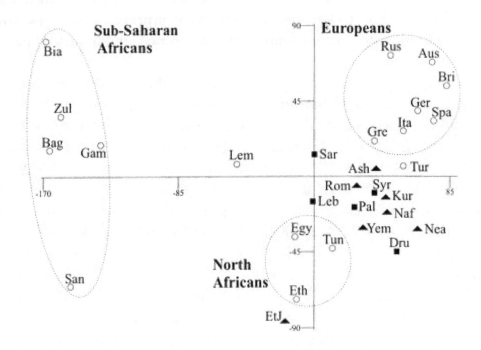

As you can see on the chart (Ash) ASHKENAZI Jews are in the same section as the Turks (Tur) under the Europeans section. The Turks, Kurds and Armenians are descendants of Togarmah, the son of Gomer, the son of JAPHETH. ASHKENAZI Jews are related to them because they are believed to be the descendants of Ashkenaz (as their name points this out). On the graph, Lebanon (Leb), Palestine (Pal), Tunisia (Tun), Syrians (Syr), YEMEN (Yem), EGYPT (EGY) and Ethiopia (Eth) are all more closely related to EUROPEANS than Blacks living in Sub-Saharan Africa.

ARE GENETICISTS REVEALING EDOM'S SEED?

It is said that the **E1b1b (E-M35) Y-Haplogroup** represents the last direct migration from North Africa to Europe. This Haplogroup was put not too long ago by geneticists into the same Haplogroup as Sub-Saharan (Bantus) Africans called the **E1b1a** and the Somalians/Ethiopian (Semitic/Cushite) Haplogroup formerly called the **E1b1c**. With this E1b1b merger, the E1b1c Haplogroup of the Somalians/Ethiopians disappeared. But why? Here is a thought. We know that after the Romans destroyed the 2nd Temple in Jerusalem in 70 A.D. the Edomites and remaining Real Black Hebrew Israelites dispersed into other countries (i.e. North Africa, Europe).

Note: **It is speculated that some of the Edomites stayed in Israel as well.**

We know the Romans and the Greeks captured some of the Israelites and sold them, perhaps leaving a remnant of Black Israelites behind in Europe. We also know that in 134 B.C. King of Judea, High Priest, Hasmonean Maccabean Leader **John Hyrcanus I**, forced the Edomites to convert to Judaism and thereafter they were no longer known as "Edomites" but "**Jews**. *Encyclopedia Judaica Jerusalem, Volume 8, pg. 1147, Encyclopedia Judaica Jerusalem, Volume 6, pg. 379.*

John Hyrcanus I, was a Gentile Maccabean Greek turned "**Jew**" by religious conversion. This is why he and his family would do things that were Anti-Israelite, including making up their own Jewish holiday called "**Hanukkah**".

John Hycanus I, the Maccabean was not an Israelite because of two things that he did:

1. In 120 A.D. after conquering the city of Shechem in Israel, Hyrcanus I destroyed the Samaritan (House of Israel) temple on **Mount Gerizim** that God commanded the Israelites to build.
2. He associated with the Edomites and tried to make them an inseparable part of the Israelite/Jewish people by forcing them ALL to covert to Judaism to become "Jews" thereafter.

Deuteronomy 11:29 "And it shall come to pass, when the Lord thy God hath brought thee in unto the land whither thou goes to possess it, that thou shalt put the **BLESSINGS UPON MOUNT GERIZEM**, and the curse upon mount Ebal."

If John Hyrcanus I was the King of Judea from 134-104 A.D. and also a HIGH PRIEST (Aaronite) why would he destroy something that God told the Israelites to build? This is because he was **NOT AN ISRAELITE**, but an **IMPOSTER JEW**. The Hebrew Torah commanded the Israelites, on first entering Canaan, to celebrate the event of entering the "Promised Land" with a ceremony of Blessings and cursings on Mount Gerizim. The Curses were to be spoken on Mount Ebal. Even the Dead Sea Scrolls proved this to be correct. After the Israelites did this, they were instructed to split into two groups, one to stay on Mount Ebal to pronounce curses, while the other was to go to Mount Gerizim to pronounce the blessings. The Tribes of Simeon, Levi, Judah, Issachar, Joseph, Benjamin were sent to Mount Gerizim, while those of Reuben, Gad, Asher, Zebulun, Dan and Naphtali were to remain on Mount Ebal.

Yahusha Hamashiach (Jesus Christ) even talked about Mount Gerizim:

John 4:21-23 "Jesus saith unto her, Woman, believe me, the hour cometh, when ye shall **neither in this mountain**, nor yet at Jerusalem, worship the Father. Ye worship ye know not what: we know what we worship: for salvation is of the Jews. But the hour cometh, and now is, when the true worshippers shall worship the Father in spirit and in truth: for the Father seeketh such to worship him. God is a Spirit: and they that worship him must worship him in **SPIRIT AND TRUTH**."

Note: In fact, after the Romans sacked Jerusalem and Israel in 70 A.D., the Samaritans were kicked out of the area of Mount Gerizim, thus fulfilling the above prophecy by Yahusha (Jesus).

So as we can see, John Hyrcanus I could not have been a **REAL LEVITE/AARONITE HIGH PRIEST** because he would have known by his tradition/culture passed down to him from previous Aaronites that Mount Gerizim and Mount Ebal were sacred unto God. Why would he then destroy it? In Deuteronomy 27 it explains how God tells the Levites to offer burnt offerings and peace offerings on these two mountains. But no, King of Judea and High Priest John Hyrcanus I decided to take it upon himself to destroy this altar/temple on Mount Gerizim. This is not of God. Neither was it of God for the Israelites to associate with the Edomites (1 Kings 11:1-3) because God knew that the Edomites (along with other nations) would turn their hearts towards pagan worship.

So of course we would expect Edomites to intermix their seed with their new neighbors in North Africa, Iberia (Spain/Portugal) and Europe. The Edomites were not under any "**Covenant**" or "**Commandments**". Mixing with the people of North Africa and Europe would add a splash of Semitic bloodline in the Hamitic people of this area (from Edom and perhaps the Hebrew Israelites) which would be genetically somewhat similar but not the same. How do we know this? Isaac's sons were Jacob and Esau. Jacob and Esau were twins but clearly looked different as the bible story tells us (Black vs light-skinned/white or Albino). This would mean that they were "**Fraternal Twins**" and not "**Identical Twins**", thus meaning they would have different DNA patterns. Fraternal Twins are fertilized by two different sperm and therefore are no different than siblings that are born at different times. So in theory if, Jacob and Esau had the same father they should also share the same "**Base**" Haplogroup, in this case "Haplogroup E". So if Edom somehow originally shared the same E-Haplogroup as some of the Black Israelites this would mean that Edom's DNA would be different because of the later mixing of his seed into the Gentile nations (Hamitic and others) after the fall of the Second temple in 70 A.D. The Edomites mixing with other nations would cause mutations and thus more "Sub-groups" within the E-Haplogroup. Edom had no reason to scatter into Sub-Saharan Africa, Arabia or the New World (America/Caribbean) because he had a land (Idumea, Judea/Samaria and the Mesopotamia). Well, Geneticists have recently revealed that Haplogroup E1b1b carriers are the newest people from the

Middle East that have migrated into North Africa and parts of Europe. This would fit the Edomite Jews perfectly and explain why the Arabs and Europeans (including Jews) have been involved in the slave trade of Hebrew Israelites for almost 2,000 years. They are the mortal enemies of ISRAEL! **Their whole being to take what is belonged to Israel and to steal their identity.** The Edomites originated in the Middle East and migrated into Europe and North Africa. These Edomites then intermarried with European women, light-skinned Turkish/Kurdish Arabs and perhaps some indigenous Hamitic North Africans. This would explain why Ashkenazi, Sephardic, and Mizrahi Jews all have traces of the E1b1b Haplogroup, but at varying frequencies. It would also explain why Genetics theorize that the most of the European Jews come from European mothers and that the fathers are of Middle Eastern, Eurasian (Asia Minor-Turkey) or European descent. This is the reason why Light skinned North Africans Arabs and European Jews exhibit the E1b1b Haplogroup in their population group in comparison to Sub-Saharan (Bantus) Africans/African-Americans who carry the E Haplogroup "E1b1a".

The E Haplogroup (E1b1b) been observed in North Africa where the light-skinned Arabs are. Haplogroup branch **E-M78** is the most common variety of Haplogroup E found among **Non-Jewish Europeans and Near Easterners**. **E-M78** is divided into 4 main branches: **E-V12, E-V13, E-V22 and E-V65**. The E-Haplogroup found in Europe fall under **E-V13**:

- **E-L17 subclade has been found from Ukraine to Portugal and from Sardina to England**
- **E-L143 subclade has only been found in England**
- **E-L241 subclade has been found in the Czech Republic and England**
- **E-L540 subclade has been found in Germany, the Czech Republic, Poland, Belarus and Sweden.**

Fact: The **E Haplogroup** has also been observed in all European Jewish groups worldwide. The E1b1b subgroup/subclade has been considered to be the 2nd most prevalent haplogroup (behind **Haplogroup J**) among the Jewish population even though it is in low amounts. According to one major paper, "**Contrasting patterns of Y chromosome variation in Ashkenazi Jewish and host non-Jewish European populations**" headed by *Doron M. Behar ·Daniel Garrigan ·Matthew E. Kaplan · Zahra Mobasher ·Dror Rosengarten ·Tatiana M. Karafet ·Lluis Quintana-Murci ·*

Harry Ostrer · Karl Skorecki · Michael F. Hammer, E-M35 is considered to be the second highest Haplogroup, next to J, for **"Founding Jewish Lineages"** in Europe. The E-M35 Haplogroup was found in moderate amounts in Ashkenazi, Sephardic, Kurdish, Yemen and Samaritan Jews. **HOWEVER, IT WAS NOT PROVEN THAT THE JEWISH PEOPLE BELONGING TO THE SO-CALLED "COHEN MODEL HAPLOGROUP (J1C)" WERE ALL DESCENDED FROM THE BIBLICAL AARON.**

Because of the close relationship of North African, Mediterranean, and European people to the E1b1b Haplogroup, some speculate that Edom's bloodline was mixed heavily in the Sephardic Jews. The story goes that people calling themselves "Sephardic Jews" mysteriously appeared on the scene after the 1400's in North Africa and Western Europe (around the time of the Spanish Inquisition). These Sephardic Jews would then become slavemasters of the Black Hebrew Israelites taken from Iberia/Africa to the Caribbean and to the New World (America). How ironic is that?

Fact: *Outside of Europe in the Arab Countries, the E1b1b Haplogroup is found at high frequencies in Morocco (80%), Tunisia (70%), Algeria (60%), Egypt (40%), Jordan (25%), Palestine (20%), and Lebanon (18%).*

ARABS AND JEWS KEPT THEIR BLOODLINE WHITE, KEEPING THE HEBREWS A "PEOPLE OF COLOR".

Most Arabs today in the Middle East are descendants of Europeans (Greeks, Romans, French, Britain, Spain, Portugal, Turkey, Kurdish land and Armenia). **All are descendants of Japheth, not Shem or Abraham.**

It was Muslims
Who first took blacks and sold them into slavery

Arab Slave Trade started in as early as 600 A.D and still exists in certain parts of the world today, especially Africa.

The practices the Arab male slavetraders did with our black women are the same practices we see today in America except it is being done with a different twist. Arab men can have sex with black women but do not want to be seen in public with them. They will not invite a black woman to meet their parents for dinner. They won't invite an African-American or an African they are seeing to an Arab wedding and most of the time they will not marry them. Most of the time Arab men are with black women for the same sexual desires and fetishes that their forefathers exhibited during the Arab Slave trade. However, just as in the Arab Slave Trade, Black men are **NOT** allowed to marry, date nor have sex with Arab women, even if that Arab family has someone in it that is dating a black woman. The only difference is that they are not castrating Black males anymore because we are not slave in America. But to keep their "Arab Race" pure they have to keep the paternal (fatherly) line Arab. In Islamic Tradition "**You are what your father is**". Children practice the religion of their father and are called "**Arab**" even if the mother is African and the father is Arab. Practicing the same religion (**Christianity or Islam**) also doesn't help blacks make the cut in gaining acceptance into marriage or courtship in Middle Eastern culture. This is why we don't see to many Black-Middle Eastern marriages in America. Chaldean Christian Middle Eastern women traditionally do not have their eyes set on a Black Christian man. Even if there was an attraction between a Chaldean woman and a Christian African-American, their courtship would be discouraged by the family. This goes the same for an Arab Muslim woman and a Muslim African man. Despite sharing the same religion, we are not considered **EQUAL** to them. This all stems back to what has been taught for generations by Arabs-Middle Easterns, influenced by the Arab slave trade of blacks. All races are able to sleep with a Black woman for sexual desires but when their women are involved with black men it is forbidden, taboo and seen as a disgrace to their family. The connection from the past to the present in terms of how our women were treated is evident. The reason why we don't see a strong presence of blacks in the Middle East now is because the Arab Slave Traders castrated the African male slaves (cut off penis and testicles) before they were able to serve in the Palace. This would ensure that the black male slaves would not start impregnating Arab women. Our oppressors during these times knew that the black man had an ungovernable sexual appetite and if left unchecked, he would impregnate the women of their lands, giving rise eventually to an overwhelmingly black population within 3 generations. This is what the Ancient Egyptians feared would happen when the Black Hebrew Israelites multiplied in their land and this was also the basis for the black extermination "**Negro Project**" in America founded by Margaret Sanger in 1939. Margaret Sanger would later start "**Planned Parenthood**" which set up abortion clinics to depopulate blacks. Folks, what happened to blacks in regards to the Deuteronomy 28:30 scripture is not a "**coincidence**" or "**bad luck**".

Black Eunuch of the Ottoman Empire 1870's.
All Black Eunuchs were castrated. This involved the removal of ALL the male genitalia. This is how they did it in Ancient times. Modern day Castration involves removal of the testicles.

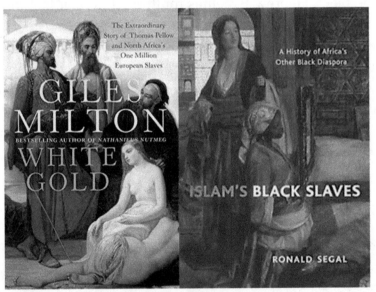

Many books have been written about the slavery practices of the Arabs involving White women and Black women.

Black Eunuchs were used **twice** as much as White Eunuchs were used and if available white concubines (i.e. Greeks) were preferred more over black concubines.

Ethiopian/Abyssinian women were also preferred over Bantus Negro women by the Arab Slavetraders. This is why we see a mixture of phenotypes in Ethiopia today. The Muslim Arabs raided coastal settlements in Italy, Greece, France, Spain, Portugal, England, Ireland and even as far away as the Netherlands and Iceland. Black Eunuchs could not reproduce so when they died, their family tree stopped. The downright truth was that Arabs loved white women more than black women; and for this reason the majority of the Middle East/Arab world consists of white skinned Arabs.

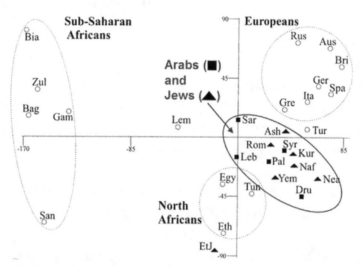

M.F. Hammer (2000). Jewish and Middle Eastern non-Jewish populations share a common pool of Y-chromosome bi-allelic haplotypes. **Proceedings of the National Academy of Sciences**, 97, (12), 6769-6774 DOI: 10.1073/pnas.100115997

In a study in 2000, a team led by **Michael Hammer** of the University of Arizona looked at the similarities between the Arabs and Jews using their Y-chromosome haplotypes. It basically showed that the Arabs and Jews were closely related to each other. DNA-wise, Ashkenazi Jews (**Ash**) are very close to Turks (**Tur**) from Turkey on the graph. They are listed in the same section as the Europeans. The Romans (**Rom**) and the Greeks (**Gre**) are also close to the Ashkenazi Jews genetically. In addition the Syrians (**Syr**), Palestinians (**Pal**), Kurds (**Kur**) and the Lebanese people (**Leb**) are all closely related to the Ashkenazi Jews. But how can this be? These Arab countries are predominately white skinned Arabs. The President of Syria (**Bashar al-Assad**), Lebanon (**Michael Suleiman**) and Palestine

(**Mahmoud Abbas**) are all white-skinned Arabs. But didn't the Greeks, Romans, Turks, Kurds, Edomites and other non-Israelite nations settle in Israel after the **REAL CHILDREN OF ISRAEL WERE TAKEN AWAY STARTING IN 700 B.C.? YES!** The White skinned Arabs today are primarily the descendants of Togarmah, brother of Ashkenaz, son of Gomer, son of **JAPHETH!** Ashkenazi Jews were speaking a Turkish, Kurdish, and Slavic language before the fused their dialect with Hebrew forming **YIDDISH**. Arabs and Jews today are **NOT** descendants of Abraham and Shem; they are descendants of Japheth.

Genesis 2:2-3 "The sons of Japheth; Gomer, and Magog, and Madai, and Javan, and Tubal, and Meshech, and Tiras. And the sons of Gomer (Gog); **ASHKENAZ**, and Riphath, and **TOGARMAH**."

Note: *Records show that the Herodian Edomite family intermarried with the Greeks and the Roman Royal family. Jewish records during the time also proved the Edomite family intermarried with the Greek Maccabean family. In the Jewish Encyclopedia, they even quote, "**Edom is in modern Jewry**". Now why would they say that?*

"That country is also called Judea, and the people **Jews**; and this name is given also to as many as embrace **THEIR RELIGION** (Judaism), though of **OTHER NATIONS**.
(**Note**: Proof that the Jews in that time were simply Judaism converts from other nations like Greece or Rome).
"But then upon what foundation so good a governor as Hyrcanus (**grandson of Matthias patriarch of the Maccabees, a family of Greek Gentile Judean patriots of the 2nd and 1st centuries B.C**). Took upon himself to compel these Idumeans (**Edomites**) either to **BECOME JEWS (BY RELIGION)** or to leave their country, deserves great consideration. I suppose it was because they had long ago been driven out of the land of Edom, and had seized on and possessed the **Tribe of Simeon (the land not the people)**, and all the southern part of the land of the **Tribe of Judah**, which was the peculiar inheritance of the worshippers of the **True God** without idolatry...."
Flavius Josephus

NEED MORE PROOF?

2 Kings 17:24 "And the King of Assyria brought men from Babylon, and from Cuthah, and from Ava, and from Hamath, and from Sepharvaim, and **placed them in the cities of Samaria INSTEAD of the children of Israel:** and they possessed Samaria, and dwelt in the cities thereof."

And weren't the Children of Judah and the children of Jerusalem sold to the Grecians before the Greek Maccabean family could set up shop in 150 B.C. coming up with their pagan Hanukkah holiday not ordained by the Most High? YES!

Joel 3:6 "**The children also of Judah** and the children of Jerusalem have he sold unto the **GRECIANS**, that ye might remove them far from their border."

Greek Man in Anatolia, Turkey. 400 B.C-200 B.C., Could this be an Israelite from the Tribe of Judah? He does not look like what the Greeks look like today or back then in Ancient times.

Some biblical scholars say **Joel** lived during the 8th Century B.C. when Solomon's Temple still stood since he doesn't mention Assyria, Babylon or Persia in the Book of Joel. Others say he lived in the post-exilic period during the 5th Century when the 2nd Temple in Jerusalem was rebuilt because he talks about the standing temple in Jerusalem. Either way it says that the Children of Judah were taken out of Israel and sold to the Greeks.

So based on Hammer's 2000 study, if the Arabs and Jews are similar in DNA heritage shouldn't the Jews and Arabs be black according to the bible? Should they be more related to Hamitic Africans since we know that Ishmael's mother (**Hagar the Egyptian**) and his 2 wives were Hamites (Egyptian & Canaanite according to the Hebrew book of Jubilees). Didn't the Sons of Keturah (Cushite/Canaanite) mix their seed with the Ishmaelite's? If Ishmael's mother was a Black Hamitic Egyptian and his wife was a Black Hamitic Egyptian, then shouldn't his children be three-fourths Black Hamitic Egyptian and one-fourth Black Hebrew? Didn't the Ancient Children of Israel intermarry with the Sons of Ham including the Ethiopians, Egyptians and the Canaanites? Since this is what the **Tanakh (Old Testament)** says it has to be right, even to the Ashkenazi Jews! But according to the DNA research conducted by **Michael Hammer** in 2000 it doesn't show that the Arabs or Jews are related to the Hamitic Africans. Is the DNA study a lie? Or are the Arabs and Jews lying to the people about their "**True Heritage**". Maybe their true heritage lies closely to Europe with Japheth and not the Middle East/Africa with Shem and Ham. Let's look at what the Tanakh (Old Testament) says. After all, the Hebrew Dead Sea Scrolls also says that the scriptures in Ezra and Judges are correct.

Judges 3:5 "And the **Children of Israel** dwelt among the Canaanites, Hittites, and Amorites, and Perizzites, and Hivites, and Jebusites. And **THEY TOOK THEIR DAUGHTERS TO BE THEIR WIVES, AND GAVE THEIR DAUGHTERS TO THEIR SONS**, and served their gods".

Note: It says "**the Children of Israel**" meaning all of the tribes and not just **one** tribe intermarried with the Canaanites.

It also states this in the book of Ezra (400 B.C):

Ezra 9:1-2 "Now when these things were done, the princes came to me, saying, **the people of Israel**, and the **priests**, and the **Levites**, have not separated themselves from the people of the lands, doing according to their abominations, even of the **Canaanites**, the **Hittites**, the **Perizzites**, the **Jebusites**, the **Amorites**, the **Moabites**, the **Egyptians** and the **Amorites**. For they have taken of their daughters for themselves, and for their sons: **SO THAT THE HOLY SEED HAVE MINGLED THEMSELVES WITH THE PEOPLE OF THE LANDS**: yea, the hand of the princes and rulers hath been chief in this trespass".

The Bible doesn't talk about the Israelites intermarrying with the sons of Japheth (i.e. European Greeks, Italians, Romans). It doesn't even state that they married with the Turks (Togarmah), the Kurds (Togarmah), nor the Armenians (Togarmah). Togarmah was the son of Gomez, the brother of Ashkenaz. Their Father was Gomer the son of Japheth. **This is why the Ashkenazi Jews per Hammer's DNA study are more closely related to the Turks (Tur) and Kurds (Kur) than the Africans (Eth-Ethiopia, Bia-Biafra/Nigeria, Zul-Zulu Tribe, Gam-Gambia, San-Khoikhoi/San Tribe)!** The Ashkenazi Jews and the modern day white-skinned Arabs are **ALL RELATED TO JAPHETH WITH A TOUCH OF THE DNA OF EDOM!** Perhaps this explains why for over 2,000 years the slave trade of Black "Negroes" has been dominated by the Europeans and Arabs. **WOW!**

DID THE JEWS BUILD HOUSES AND PLANT VINEYARDS?

Deuteronomy 28:30 **"Thou shalt build a house (Slave Plantations as well as other houses), and thou shalt not dwell therein: thou shalt plant a vineyard, and shalt not gather the grapes thereof."**

Slave Living Quarters

Slave Plantation for the Slavemaster

Everybody knows that the slaves built houses and buildings for their white slave masters but weren't allowed to live in them (ex. **The White House and numerous Slave Plantations**). The Bible prophesied over 2,000 ago the details of what was going to happen to the Black Hebrew Israelites. No other race in the World has been enslaved to build houses in the magnitude that black race has. The European Jews during the Holocaust did not have to build houses for the Germans. The

Germans already had sleeping quarters/homes and the European Jews had their concentration camps. The Israelites as a people did disobey and break most of the 10 commandments in the Bible during the Transatlantic Slave Trade so they should've endured the "**Curses of Israel**" of Deuteronomy 28:30. Furthermore, Deuteronomy 28:46 states that the "**Curses of Israel**" were to be upon the children or "**seed**" of the Israelites **FOREVER**. This was not the case during the many centuries the Jews prospered in Russia, Eastern and Western Europe. Black Negro slaves were also brought to European colonies to tend to the livestock and farm the land.

"Thou shalt plant a vineyard, and shalt not gather the grapes thereof." – CURSES OF ISRAEL

Fact: Slaves lived at Martha's Vineyard in Massachusetts beginning around 1680, but the first slave on record there was a woman named Rebecca Amos.

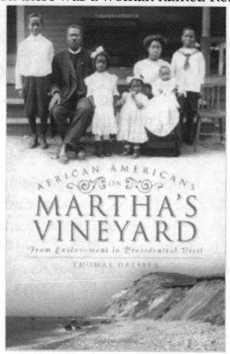

Martha's Vineyard was an Island located south of **Cape Cod, Massachusetts**. Slaves lived on the vineyard beginning around 1680. Slaves in Massachusetts were allowed to inherit property which was unusual at the time. This law gave Martha's Vineyards first slave, **Rebecca Amos from Guinea, West Africa** the chance to become a landowner. She inherited some property on Martha's Vineyard when her Indian husband died in 1763. Post-Slavery, a small inn helped establish Martha's Vineyard as a vacation spot for middle and upper class blacks. In 1912, Charles Shearer and his wife built a 12 room-vacation spot on the island which catered to blacks who were unwelcome elsewhere. It is said that the Reverend Martin Luther King vacationed there and wrote his **"I have a dream"** speech.

Rebecca Amos was married to a Wampanoag man. The Wampanoag Tribe is mainly located in Massachusetts and Rhode Island. Rebecca Amos was from Guinea, West Africa.

The slaves were so skilled in building things and creating things (**inventions**) that white people often took the credit for the slaves handiwork. White America also knew that if given freedom and the opportunity to learn how to read/write, the slaves would use these skills to eventually surpass them. For this reason they tried to prohibit the slaves (**such as Nat Turner**) from learning to read and they also instituted segregation post-slavery to prevent blacks from competing in the workforce with them.

CHAPTER 29

DEUTERONOMY 28:31-36

THOU SHALL NOT STEAL, UNLESS IT'S FROM A "NEGRO".

Deuteronomy 28:31 **"Thine ox shall be slain before thine eyes, and thou shalt not eat thereof: thine ass shall be violently taken away from before thy face, and shall not be restored to thee: thy sheep shall be given unto thine enemies, and thou shalt have none to rescue them."**

"Stolen" Hebrew Israelites led into captivity by the Assyrians (700 B.C). Below is Assyrian/Sumerian Cuneiform script writing. Notice the Fringes on the Israelites garments.

"Stolen" Black Hebrew Israelites, Siege of Lachish, Jerusalem (Assyrian siege 700 B.C). Notice their tight-curled kinky hair, typical of that of a "Negro" today.

*Is this an **Israelite slave** or **Nubian Cushite slave** under the captivity of the Egyptians? We know Moses had a Cushite wife name **Zipporah** and they had two children: **Eleazer** and Gershom. But the Jews today will not admit that there are Black Levites or Aaronites. Who is fooling who? Notice the earrings on this slave and are those fringes?*

Exodus 32:2-4 "And Aaron said unto them, Break off the **GOLDEN EARRINGS**, which are in the ears of your **WIVES, OF YOUR SONS, AND OF YOUR DAUGHTERS**, and bring them unto me. And all the people brake off the golden earrings which were in their **EARS**, and brought them unto Aaron. And he received them at their hand, and fashioned it with a graving tool, after he had made it a molten calf: and they said, These be thy gods, O Israel which brought thee up out of the land of Egypt."

Black slaves had many things taken from them despite owning them. When the Ancient Israelites lived in the Land of Canaan they had land, sheep, goats, farms and even their children taken from them during times of invasion/captivity. When other nations (Assyrians, Babylonians, Greeks, Romans) invaded their land they destroyed their property, stole their prized possessions/riches and took their sheep/livestock for plunder. This can be seen in the "**Arch of Titus**" relief. They also lynched the Israelites just as they did blacks pre and post-slavery.

The First Jewish-Roman War was celebrated by Roman Emperor Titus and his people with the "Arch of Titus" relief depicting the stealing of the Temple treasures. These included the Trumpets of Jericho and the Golden Menorah. You know they are Romans because they appear European and not Black.

Lynch Mob

(Left) Ancient Hebrew Israelites lynched in Lachish, Israel. (Right) Lynching of a Black man in Alabama (1800's). Coincidence?

During slavery, the "**Negro Israelites**" had their children and wives taken from them. Negro Freed Slaves, even though they acquired land and livestock were also subject to attacks from whites. Whites believed they had the right to take whatever they wanted from the Negro, and because the laws were set up against the Negro, many times there was nothing they could do. During this time Blacks had riches, prized possessions, heirlooms, inventions, art, cars, land, cattle, and crops taken from them, just as the Bible predicted. This has continued until today. During slavery days the white slavemasters took all the credit for the inventions or art blacks made while on the plantations. Under **sharecropping** or the **peonage system** there were times when the slavemaster stole and cheated slaves out of land, animals, or possessions as a form of never-ending debt payment. Whites in America years ago didn't want blacks to have anything. Blacks were illiterate, uneducated and spoke only broken English if lucky. The slaves were cheated out of a lot of things, just like we are today because our lack of Black ownership in America and lack of **capital (money)**. Of course this did not stop blacks from obtaining their own things and being successful at it. In Tulsa, Oklahoma 1921 in the Greenwood District, also known as "**The Black Wall Street**" blacks had a city in which they owned and operated a large number of businesses, including an **all-Black hospital**. They nick-named this All-Black thriving city "**Little Africa**". In 1921, during the **Tulsa Race Riots** whites killed the black residents of the Greenwood District, burned their homes leaving 10,000 blacks homeless and also burned down multiple black businesses including the sole black hospital in the city.

The Aftermath of Destruction from the Tulsa Race Riots 1921

CHILDREN SOLD INTO SLAVERY? WHAT RACE?

Deuteronomy 28:32 **"Thy sons and thy daughters shall be given unto another people, and thine eyes shall look, and fail with longing for them all the day long: and there shall be no might in thine hand.**

Black male slaves with a yoke of iron around their necks.
The slavery of "**Negroes**" showed no respect of person. Families were separated; and siblings were separated from each other.

Below is a narrative of how Black "Negro" Slaves were treated in **Turkey**:

"Some twenty years ago on their arrival at Constantinople, the slaves used to be stored up within the precincts of an imperial slave market, as at that period the slave-dealers were patentee-merchants. Such a scandal could not, however, be patronized any longer, and the Turks have continued the trade in an underhand way. Non-official markets were then opened at Sultan-Mehemet, at Tophaneh, and in some of the cafes and shops of Stambul (Istanbul). One of these places is opposite the mosque of Suleymaniye in the bazaar named Teriaki-tcharshisi, the third shop to the left, looking westward, if my memory does not fail me. In these markets slaves are sold daily, the hours of brisk business being from eight to twelve a.m., Turkish time. Up to A.D. 1869, this state of things was in existence. The thirty or forty girls that come on the market at the same period, all find customers quickly enough: the Abyssinians (Ethiopians) on account of their good looks are the first to be disposed of; they are taken as upper servants in the harems of those whose limited means (money) forbid them to indulge in a thorough-bred Circassian (Caucasian). The Abyssinians are also taken as economical odalisks by the lower class of amateurs. The genuine Negro (Bantus) girls with flat noses and thick lips are doomed to the kitchen and the rough work of the house. As a rule, the lot attending these creatures is sad. They pass through the hands of ten or twenty masters, who make them lead the life of cab-horses, beat them at intervals, and at last sell them. Such treatment irritates the temper and inflames the passions of the African destitute, who, driven to despair, becomes a fury, wages war against her oppressors, and ends by becoming a hater of the white species. It is not to be wondered, then, if Negroes have often been known to set fire to the wooden houses of Stamboul (Istanbul), as being the best means of retaliation they could devise. After having been sold and re-sold over and over again, the Negro slave gets at last in a condition to be not even worth feeding; then she obtains her freedom, and she is let loose in the streets of Stamboul, without the means of subsistence or the power to provide for herself. Her lot then is to roam about town a cripple and a beggar."

"Black Slavery in America and Ottoman Turkey", Andrew G. Bostom.

It is a known fact that Slavery broke up families as children were taken as slaves as well. It was common in slavery to see young boys taken from their fathers and young girls (full-breed & half-breed) separated from their mothers only to be sold to a sexually abusive Slavemaster. This did not happen to the European Jews during the Holocaust. Just as the bible prophesied about the Curses of Israel, these types of practices still exist today in which African girls are taken from African countries such as Sudan, Niger, Nigeria or Mauritania and are sold into slavery as **"house servants" (See 2010 Movie "I am Slave")**. Some are sold into Muslim hands, forced to convert to Islam and then are married to their Arab captors.

1800's Slave boy in Basra, Iraq from Zanzibar, Tanzania

Many Black parents (**African, African-American, Haitian**) over the years have been forced to give away their children into adoption or slavery because of their inability to provide. This is hard for the parent; just as if their child was violently take from them. No other race has had to endure this type of misfortune on the scale as blacks have. The Ashkenazi, Sephardic, and Mizrahi Jews have not had this happen to them. Neither have the Arabs in the Middle East. It is a known fact that blacks in Jamaica, descendants of slaves (Maroons) are often from the Akan or Ewe Tribe in Ghana as well as Nigerian Tribes. Blacks in Haiti also have roots from Ghana (Ewe) and Nigeria.

Fact 1: In India and Pakistan, there are descendants of African slaves called **"Siddis"** or **"Makrani"** who live amongst the people and have adopted their culture, including the religion.

Malik Ambar

Malik Ambar (1548-1626 A.D) was an Ethiopian King born by the name "**Chapu**" in 1548 in the "**Harar Province**", Ethiopia. It was said that he was of the "**Solominic Dynasty**". He was sold to Yemen, then to Iraq and then to Southwest India. Somehow, while in India he was able to raise up 1500 men under him. By 1620 Malik (**which means "King"**) was the commander of fifty thousand men consisting of forty-thousand "**Marathas**" (Hindu Warriors) and ten-thousand fellow African slaves called "**Habshi**". The Army resided in the Decca region (Southwest India). He eventually took this army and fought against the Mughal rule in India, allowing him and his people to acquire settlements (land). He married his son and daughter into the Indian Royal family mixing his African (Cushitic/Semitic) Bloodline with the Indian (Elamite/Persian) bloodline. This is why there are many Indians today that look black. He founded the city Khadki (now modern day **Aurangabad**). He died in 1626 and is a symbol/figure of veneration to the Black Siddis of Gujarat.

Aurangabad sits near west India.

Siddi African-Indian girl

Indian nationalist leader and devout Hindu, **Mohandas K. Gandhi** called the **Black Siddis** "Harijians" meaning "**Children of God**" or perhaps he meant the "**Children of Israel/God's children**". The Black appearing dark-skinned **Dravidian** "**Dalits**" with African heritage had their sons and daughters taken away from them to serve as slaves just as the biblical scriptures foretold. In **Bombay, India** (1972), inspired by the Black Panther Party, the Black Indians started the "**Dalit Panther Party**". This is a quote about sufferings they also experienced and their acknowledgement of their African Ancestry:

"**The African-Americans also must know that their liberation struggle cannot be complete as long as their own BLOOD-BROTHERS and sisters living in far off Asia are suffering. It is true that African-Americans are also suffering, but our people here today are where African-Americans were two hundred years ago.**
Dravidian Indian V.T Rajshekar (1987)

*(Left) Elamite Goddess from the **Temple of Inshushinak at Susa, Iran** 2000 B.C. (Right) Dravidian Indian girl. "Inshushinak" means "Lord of Susa" as he was one of the different gods of Ancient Elam. **Elam** was the son of **Shem** and brother of **Arphaxad** (**Grandfather of Eber-father of the Hebrews**). Elam lived in the area now known as **Iran/Persia** and they were a dark-skinned people, not like Persians and Iraqis today. Notice how this Elamite goddess has a wide nose and full lips. Persian (Iranian) women today have straight noses and thin lips as they are "**Caucasoid**". Most Iranians know that they are mostly European and they do not like to be called "**Arab**". In fact, they speak their own language instead of Arabic. Most historians agree that the descendants of the Elamites today are modern day people in India and Sri Lanka. The Ancient name for Sri Lanka is*

"Eelam" and *"Tamil Eelam"* is the name of the independent state or area in North/East Sri Lanka. Their Dravidian relatives also live in **Kerala** and **Tamil Nadu**, South India.

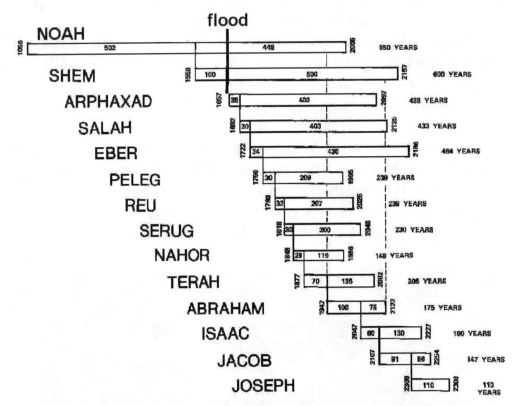

If Elam was Black (brown-skinned), this would mean his brother Arphaxad should be black as well. So if Arphaxad was a man of color, this would mean that Eber (father of the Hebrews) and his children (Abraham, Isaac, Jacob) were also people of color. Not the European and white-skinned people we see today in the Middle East/Israel.

Madi man (1800's), South Sudan

Fact: The **Madi Tribe in South Sudan** is Christian but has experienced genocide (**3 million Madi people slaughtered by North Sudanese Muslims**) over the years. They too admit to having Hebrew Customs learnt from their Israelite forefathers a long time ago. Back before Islam and Christianity made it into Africa they practiced the **Biblical Laws of Moses (Torah)** which some call "**Biblical Judaism**". They practiced these Hebrew traditions despite being isolated from the European Talmudic Babylonian Judaism converts called "**Khazars**". They follow Hebrew traditions such as blood sacrifices, sheep sacrifices (for bad sins), dietary laws of clean/unclean animals, ceremonial washing of the hands (Babylonian Talmudic tradition), blowing the rams horn before events, marrying a brothers widow, setting apart firstborn males of their herds/flocks for sacrifice and circumcision on the 8th day. Back in Ancient times their land was part of African land called the "**So-Yuda**", which later changed to "**East Soudan**" and then finally became "**Sudan**".

Bayuda Desert is in Sudan

In Sudan there is still the "**Bayuda Desert**" named after the **Black Judah Israelites** that used to live in the area known as Sudan. Over time these Black Israelites migrated to Central Africa (**Congo, Angola, Gabon, Cameroon**), East Africa (**Sudan, Uganda, Kenya, Tanzania, Ethiopia**), West Africa (**Nigeria, Ghana, Benin, Ivory Coast, Liberia, Sierra Leone, Senegal**) and South Africa, thus verifying the scripture **Zephaniah 3:10 "From beyond the rivers of Ethiopia my people, even the daughter of my dispersed ones, shall bring mine offering."** It is a known fact that the Nile River starts at Lake Victoria in Uganda and flows north to the Mediterranean Sea.

Deuteronomy 28:33 **"The fruit of thy land, and all thy labours, shall a nation which thou knowest not eat up; and thou shalt be only oppressed and crushed always:"**

All America wants is for Black people to **"Serve"** them doing menial **(Servant-type jobs)**.

Black slaves did not enjoy the fruits of their labor in the many nations they were taken captivity into. All our forefathers did was **"Labor"** and **"Serve"** our Slavemasters. Today this can be seen as **"US"** still **"Working for them"**, meaning we still work for everyone else. We are 4-5 Generations out of slavery and the descendants of our forefathers Slavemasters could likely be our bosses now without us even knowing it. Slaves and servants had to take better care of their master's children then themselves. For this reason Blacks have always felt **"under oppression,"** as if nothing is ever going to get any better.

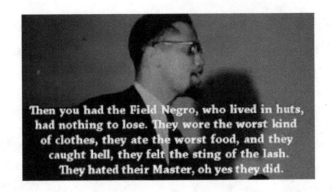

> Then you had the Field Negro, who lived in huts, had nothing to lose. They wore the worst kind of clothes, they ate the worst food, and they caught hell, they felt the sting of the lash. They hated their Master, oh yes they did.

THE HOUSE NEGRO VS THE FIELD NEGRO

There are two types of Negroes today; Negroes that are "**Asleep**" and Negroes that are "**Awake**". Back then they could be called the "**House Negro**" and the "**Field Negro**". This is how Malcolm X described it.

HOUSE NEGRO

"The House Negro usually lived close to his master. He dressed like his master. He wore his master's second-hand clothes. He ate the food that his master left on the table. And he lived in his master's house....probably in the basement or the attic....but he still lived in the master's house. So whenever the house Negro identified himself, he always identified himself in the same sense that his master identified himself. When his master said, "**We have good food**," the house Negro would say, "**Yes, we have plenty of good food**." When the master said "**We have a fine home here**," the house Negro said, "**Yes, we have a fine home here.**" When the master was sick, the house Negro identified himself so much with his master he'd say, "**What's the matter boss, we sick?**" His master's pain was his pain. And it hurt him more for his master to be sick than for him to be sick himself. When the house started burning down, the House Negro would fight harder to put the master's house out than the master would himself. " – **Malcolm X. "The Race Problem," African Students Association and NAACP Campus Chapter, Michigan State University, East Lansing, Michigan, January 23, 1963.**

But then you had Field Negro....that Malcolm X and other talked about.

FIELD NEGRO

"But then you had another Negro out in the field. The House Negro was in the minority. The masses…the field Negroes were the masses. They were in the majority. When the master got sick, they prayed that he'd die. If his house caught on fire, they'd pray for a wind to come along and fan the breeze. If someone came to the House Negro and said, "**Let's go, let's separate**," naturally that Uncle Tom would say, "**Go where? What could I do without boss? Where would I live? How would dress? Who would look out for me?**" That's the House Negro. But if you went to the Field Negro and said, "**Let's go, let's separate**," he wouldn't even ask you where or how. He'd say, "**Yes, let's go.**" And that one ended right there." – **Malcolm X. "The Race Problem," African Students Association and NAACP Campus Chapter, Michigan State University, East Lansing, Michigan, January 23, 1963.**

Today the "**House Negro**" can be seen as the "Wealthy, Rich Negro" that has achieved the "American Dream" in his heart. He achieved his success by pulling up his boot straps, not complaining and "working hard." Most often this "House Negro" is trapped from seeing his bondage or his people's bondage by "**material things, fear and his job**." He is essentially the "**Asleep Negro**". He believes all our food is healthy; he believes every vaccine known to mankind is good for him and his seed. He believes that the United States Presidents all have his best interests. He believes that he will work on his job without any problems until he retires. He believes the stock market and the dollar bill will never crash. He believes the housing market is going to get better. He believes the unemployment rate is lowering. He believes the economy is better now than it was years before. He believes that blacks are getting an education and are able to get good jobs. He believes that for the most part, blacks are satisfied and they have a better life now since integration of the races. He believes having debt, bills and payment plans is ok as long as you get what you want in life. He believes paying interest is just the "American way". He believes homosexuality is just something we have to accept at some point. He believes that there is no "Black and White" and doesn't see "color". He believes that the bible is all "white". He believes the God, the angels, Abraham, Isaac, Jacob, the Israelites and Jesus (Yahusha/Yeshua) are all white and that blacks are Gentiles/Hamites. He believes that color doesn't matter in the Bible but argues and discredits any notion that the bible could be about black people. He believes in his mind that he is free. Because of his success, he is not fed up and does not desire "change". He has no problem giving his money to other races (Caucasian Boy Scouts, Arab/Jewish high school fundraisers) in his suburban community and is not bothered by the fact that blacks work menial jobs for everyone else. The media shows him an illusion of what his life should be like and if he can achieve some of it then he is happy. On the contrary, the "Awake" Negro sees the modern slavery that exists in "Black America" and wants change. Like the "House Negro", when the "**Asleep Negro**" today is told the truth and is proposed a plan to fix it by the "**Awake Negro**", the "Asleep Negro" says that his life doesn't need changing. He says it doesn't matter and that we are all human beings, children of Abraham. But we are not all children of Abraham. This is the problem we are seeing today. The "**Asleep Negro**" rejects the truth because he has been comfortable with "**lies**" all his life. Real "Change" lies in the hands of Blacks who are "**Awake**".

Are we still looking after our Slavemasters children's children till this day?
Perhaps we are and don't even know it.

Even sharecropping didn't give the slave 100% of his return back from the land of which he worked. African slaves, Indians and the "Natives" are the only people throughout history that have been sold unto nations they didn't know. People of African descent are still not enjoying the fruits of their labor and are still oppressed even till this day. Blacks never received reparations for over 1,000 years of slavery and hundreds of millions of lost lives. The European Ashkenazi Jews got reparations for their 12 years of captivity, 6 million lost lives and lost riches during the Holocaust. The remnants of Israel still in Africa have also seen other nations (Germany, France, Britain, Netherlands, China, Russia) "**eat**" of their land. But this "**eating**" is pertaining to more than just food. Many countries are making huge profits of the natural resources of the land. Since slavery was abolished, the turn of focus has been to "**Suck Africa Dry**". The same countries that enslaved Blacks (Europeans, Arabs, Jews) are now targeting the valuable goods and natural resources that come from within Africa.

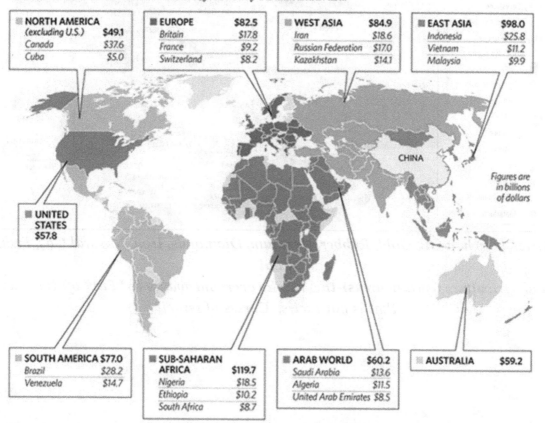

China's Worldwide Reach

Sub-Saharan Africa sees very heavy Chinese construction activity. In investment, Australia holds a narrow lead over the U.S., followed by Canada and Brazil.

NORTH AMERICA		EUROPE	$82.5	WEST ASIA	$84.9	EAST ASIA	$98.0
(excluding U.S.)	$49.1	Britain	$17.8	Iran	$18.6	Indonesia	$25.8
Canada	$37.6	France	$9.2	Russian Federation	$17.0	Vietnam	$11.2
Cuba	$5.0	Switzerland	$8.2	Kazakhstan	$14.1	Malaysia	$9.9

UNITED STATES $57.8

CHINA

Figures are in billions of dollars

SOUTH AMERICA $77.0		SUB-SAHARAN AFRICA	$119.7	ARAB WORLD	$60.2	AUSTRALIA	$59.2
Brazil	$28.2	Nigeria	$18.5	Saudi Arabia	$13.6		
Venezuela	$14.7	Ethiopia	$10.2	Algeria	$11.5		
		South Africa	$8.7	United Arab Emirates	$8.5		

North America, Europe, Asia, Australia, and the Arab World are all "Eating" off the land of Africa, where many of the remnants of Israel are living today. China *has made over $120 billion dollars from Sub-Saharan Africa, more than twice as much they are making from doing business with the United States of America.*

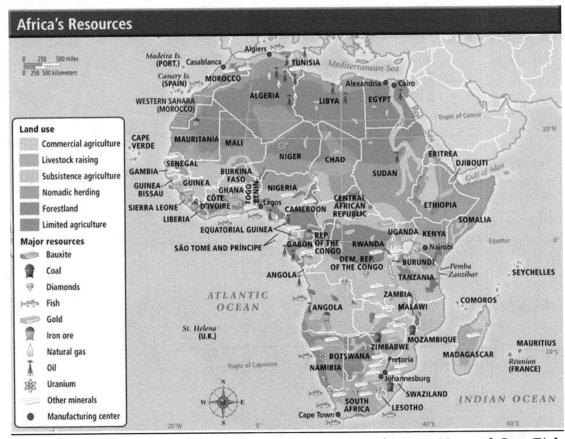

Africa is rich in Oil, Gold, Rubber, Uranium, Diamonds, Iron, Natural Gas, Fish, Coal
and agriculture (certain areas)-this is why everyone wants to "Eat" off the land that is not theirs. Curses of Israel?

Many non-Black races take their American" retirement money" or "play money" to Africa to buy prime real estate, where they live like kings. Meanwhile in some African countries, money is hard to come by. These people are starving every day for food and are usually living with parents, grandparents in order to survive. Major non-black companies come to do business in Africa for monetary purposes only. The don't care about the community or the people in it.

Zimbabwe President Robert Mugabe

In the year 2000, Zimbabwe President Robert Mugabe started doing "land grabs" by telling white farmers to hand over their land back to Zimbabwe and its people. He gave them a deadline for them to clear out and pave the way for his black resettlement land reforms. He quoted: **"We are no longer going to ask for the land, but we are going to take it without negotiating. We don't mind having sanctions banning us from Europe. We are not Europeans."** It is a known fact that many other foreign countries come to Africa wanting to profit off the resources of their land but do not bring jobs or money to the native African people who are in need of jobs and money. This is greediness and selfishness. In some area in Europe, Blacks are deterred and discouraged from owning property. In America, in the early 1900's many blacks were forced into **"rentership"** because they couldn't get home loans from white lending institutions to buy a house. Curses of Israel?

Fact: The **Reparations Agreement between Israel and West Germany** was signed on September 10, 1952, and went into effect on March 27, 1953 paying Israel the sum of 3 billion marks (**Deutsche Marks which was the official currency of Germany before the invention of the Euro**) over the span of 14 years. According to the Agreement, West Germany was to pay Israel for the persecution of Jews during the Holocaust, and to compensate for Jewish property/wealth that was stolen by the Nazis.

Fact 2: It is a known fact that since 1897 Jewish students have been able to take advantage of the **"Hebrew Fund"** or **"Hebrew Interest Free Loan"** service, which of course is only offered to those of Jewish descent. Donations from Jewish people worldwide help ensure the success of the Jewish nation and people. Even Christian churches donate money to Israel and Jewish Organizations. This is how people profit off of "Lies". This can be researched for yourself on www.hflasf.org. On the website tab for donations it reads:

"Your gift to Hebrew Free Loan is more than just a donation. It's a chance to send a student to **MEDICAL SCHOOL**, build a better future for a child, **LAUNCH A NEW BUSINESS VENTURE, HELP A FAMILY PURCHASE A HOME**, and **SUPPORT INNOVATIVE PROJECTS IN OUR COMMUNITY**."

These same things are also done in other races (i.e. Arabs, Asians, Indians) but of course this is not done by Blacks in America.

THE QUESTION IS WHY? WHY ARE WE SO ANGRY?

Deuteronomy 28:34 **"So that thou shalt be mad for the sight of thine eyes which thou shalt see."**

Many Black men are tired of being oppressed. Black men have to battle racism at work and when off work. So when they are off work and happen to get pulled over by a cop, the reaction can be "heated". But the Police force is anticipating a "charged up" Negro. This is why they have Police car dash cameras and audio recorders ready to capture everything which they use to manipulate their story on the News or in front of the Judge to destroy this Black Man's life.

From the scarred backs, blood, sweat and tears of Negro slaves this country's economy was built, however we didn't reap any of the harvest! Of course the Slaves were mad from all the things that they saw and had to go through for centuries. Why else would a people revolt or start a rebellion against their slavemasters. From Nat Turner Rebellion in America to the Zanj Rebellion in Basra, Iraq to the Malik Ambar Black Rebellion in India, slaves have been tired of oppression. The **Nat Turner Rebellion** made history during the Transatlantic Slave Trade and the **Zanj Rebellion** made history during the Arab slave trade of Africans from Kenya, and Tanzania. From all the countries where the slaves were scattered, there have been slave rebellions. There has also been continued suffering, which most people believe is due to the hands of the racist Elites of this world who have an agenda to "**Destroy**" and "**Depopulate**" black people. Many Blacks believe the "**Evil forces**" of this World use planted diseases (i.e. Ebola, HIV), political/judicial suppression, educational suppression, health care suppression and economic suppression to destroy **God's Chosen People**.

Fact: Media cameras were on the spot filming when the Ethiopian Jews protested in Israel (2015) in regards to racial discrimination.   They were also there during the the "**Ebola Crisis**" when Liberians protested saying that "**outsiders**" planted Ebola into their country as a means to purposely cause a "**genocide**" of blacks. The media is always there to show how angry blacks are "**Fed Up**" all across the world. The "Media" wants to portray a "negative image" to the world that blacks are "savages, non-law abiding citizens".

After slavery was abolished, blacks still were mad because of the **Jim Crow Laws** in the South and treatment of blacks. Today, we see continued oppression in different forms (**financial, land ownership, mental, educational, domestic/Family, health**) placed on us by "**White America**" and also the widespread injustice of black killings at the hands of law enforcement and racist whites. **For this reason we have a reason to be mad**. Everything we see on T.V. portrays the black man or the black race in a negative way. There is no let up.

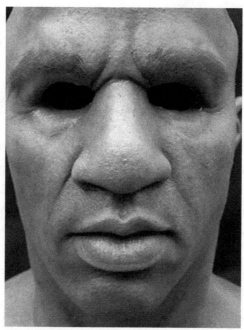

*Fact: In 2014, in Ohio 30-Year old Caucasian **Conrad Zdzierak** committed a string of robberies wearing a mask portraying to be a black man. Conrad purchased the silicone mask from a California-based costume company that sold **"Life-like"** face masks. Victims in the robberies all reported that a black person was the one that did the robbery. However, they were all wrong. Conrad was finally caught and convicted to 25 years in jail. So as we can see, people want to be black (or portray to be black), even if it can help them get away with a crime. Why? Because in America it is easier to assume a **"Black Man"** did the crime instead of the **"White Man"** thanks to **"Predictive Programming."***

Fact or Fiction?: Supposedly there is a photo of President Bush, Russian President Putin and Chinese President Hu Jintao taken outside while at a secret Grand Lodge meeting. Are all these Superpower Presidents Freemasons? Many say that the Prime Minister of Israel Benjamin Netanyahu and the Presidents of most African Countries are also Freemasons. There are pictures of prominent political figures we would think are enemies having outings with each other's families. Just like in a courtroom, **things are not what they seem**. They are all in the same club, answering to the same **"Hidden Master"**, pretending to the world that they are enemies because that's what keeps us thinking "we have a choice in picking the right President". This way they can keep implementing communist-dictatorship type measures leading the people to enslavement.

Fact: Henry Ford in 1921 said "**The only statement I care to make about the "Protocols" is that they fit in with what is going on NOW.**" Here is what he was talking about in the "Protocols".

1. Place our agents **EVERYWHERE.**
2. Take control of the media.
3. **START RACIAL TENSIONS** and fights between different races, classes and religion. (i.e. "**Divide the world and then conquer them**". **Perfect example in America with Blacks vs Whites and the Middle East with Sunni Arabs vs Shia Arabs or Arabs vs Jews vs Christians**).
4. Use bribery, threats, blackmail and deaths to get our way.
5. Use **Freemasonry to control Governments.**
6. Appoint puppet leaders we can control and blackmail
7. Replace democracy with Communism
8. Slowly take away all right and freedoms from the people
9. Eliminate religion and replace it with Science, **MATERIALISM** and **HOMOSEXUALITY.**
10. Sacrifice people if necessary (Blood Sacrifice?)

WAS HENRY FORD RIGHT? THOSE ARE ONLY A FEW OF THE "PROTOCOLS OF THE LEARNED ELDERS OF ZION"

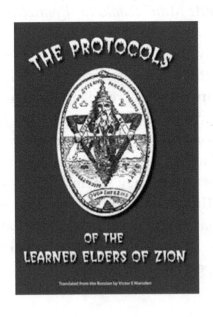

The book "Protocols of the Learned Elders of Zion" was published in 1919 in Russia. Henry Ford single-handedly funded the printing of half-a-million copies of the book that were distributed throughout the U.S.A. in the 1920's. It is said that this book was studied in German classrooms in the early 1930's.

Fact: In 1923 Henry Ford published his 4-volume book called "The International Jew". In it he states:

"The Jews are not the Chosen People, though practically the entire Modern Church has succumbed to the propaganda which declares them to be so."

Fact 2: Ancient Chinese texts mentions ambassadors from Java (Indonesia) presenting the Chinese Emperor with two "Seng-Chi (Zanji)" slaves as gifts, and "Seng Chi" slaves reaching China from the Hindu Kingdom of Sri Vijaya (Indonesia, Malaysia, Philippines, Singapore, Thailand) in Java. The Chinese people in their language called the Black "Zanji" Slaves from East Africa (Tanzania, Kenya) "Seng-Chi" which was a corruption of the word "Zanji". This proves that Black Israelite slaves were scattered into ALL NATIONS/FOUR CORNERS, just as the bible predicted would happen to the Hebrew Israelites.

Monument Statues to the Slaves of Zanzibar, Tanzania. In this pit they would wash and oil down the slaves before presenting them to Slave merchants for sale.

Fact 3: In Christopher Columbus' **"Journal of the Second Voyage"**, he admitted that when he reached the **Land of Haiti (Hayti)** (West Hispaniola) the natives there told him that black-skinned people had come from the south and southeast in boats, trading in gold-tipped metal spears. Also, at least a dozen of other European Explorers, including **"Vasco Nunez de Balboa"**, also reported seeing or hearing of **"Negroes"** when they reached the New World. **Nicholas Leon**, a Mexican with knowledge passed down as oral tradition reported that **"the oldest inhabitants of Mexico were blacks."** He also reported that the existence of blacks and giants was commonly believed by nearly all the races/tribes in the Americas in their various languages passed down as oral ancient history.

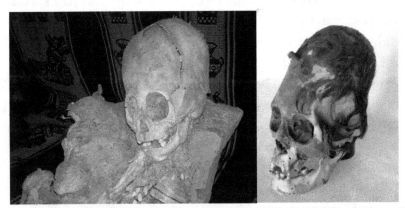

Nephilim Giant Skulls found in Peru. Also "Red Haired Nephilim Giants Skulls found in South America".

These elongated, red haired skulls were found in the town of Paracas and Nazca which is within the Pisco Province in the Inca Region, in the south part of **Peru**. It is here that Peruvian archaeologist, **Julio Tello**, made the discovery in 1928. He found a massive graveyard containing tombs filled with 300+ elongated skulls. The cranial volume was up to 25% larger and 60% heavier than normal human skulls, meaning that they could not have been intentionally deformed through head binding/flattening which is common in Asia and Africa. These skulls contained only one parietal plate and one frontal plate as there was no sagittal suture to separate the parietal bone in two and also created a skull section for the occipital bone. They even tested the **mtDNA (maternal DNA)** of the skulls and it did not match with any Human DNA on earth. Many scientists claim these skulls are alien, the Annunaki or the Nephilim the bible speaks of.

Fact: The earliest Western explorers who wrote about the giants of North America were Portuguese Explorer **Ferdinand Magellan**, **Sir Francis Drake**, **Spanish explorer Desoto**, and **Commodore Byron**, the grandfather of the famous poet, **Lord Byron**. Magellan reported a giant sighting in 1520 A.D. near the harbor of San Julian, Mexico. There, Magellan and his crew came upon a red-haired giant that stood nearly ten feet tall and whom Magellan described as having a "**voice like a bull**." Later, Magellan learned from the natives that the giant belonged to a neighboring tribe. Magellan's logs show that he and his crew captured two giants and brought them aboard his ship intending to bring them back to Europe. Unfortunately the giants became sick and purportedly both died during the return voyage. Years later, the giants still roamed the Americas as Sir Francis Drake recorded encountering other several red-haired giants who stood over nine feet tall. Years after, many explorers also reported seeing giants roaming in the Americas. Two lesser known explorers, **Jacob le Maire** and **Wilhelm Schouten** discovered an intact skeleton of a pair of nine-foot humans.

Deuteronomy 28:35 **"The LORD shall smite thee in the KNEES, and in the LEGS, with a SORE botch that cannot be healed, from the SOLE OF THEY FOOT unto the top of thy head."**

12 year old boy picking cotton and his 6 year old brother also doing the same. The older brother typically has to work 12 hours a day and the younger brother works six ours a day under the relentless rays of the Sun.

Slaves spent most of their time on their hands, knees and feet doing slave work. We could only imagine the sores they got and the pain they experienced while forced to do slave labor for countless hours in the harsh elements. Everyone knows that if a sore is repeatedly irritated from repetitive movements it will take longer to heal. Slaves did not get to take sick leave or short term disability to rest their wounds, sores, or aching bones. Slaves endured the physical pain of working in the field and the pain from being continuously beaten with bullwhips by the Slave masters. The Ashkenazi Jews and Sephardic did not have fields to tend to 12-18 hours of the day. They were in gated concentration camps. The Mizrahi (Middle Eastern) Jew did not experience the Holocaust or Slavery. The Bene Israel Jews of India did not experience slavery or the Holocaust. They actual were in good favor with the British during their colonial rule.

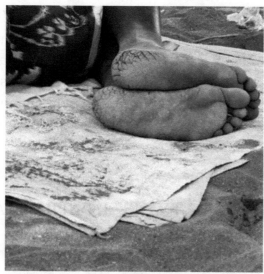

Sores/fissures (cracks) on the heels on a black boys foot from repetitive work with no shoes.

ISRAELITES CONSTANTLY WORSHIPPING OTHER GODS?

Deuteronomy 28:36 **"The LORD shall bring thee, and thy king which thou shalt set over thee, unto a nation which neither thou nor thy fathers have known; and there shalt thou serve other gods, WOOD AND STONE."**

The Children of Israel and their descendants in Africa served many "gods" and worshipped many religions in the lands that they were brought to back in Ancient Times (**Moloch, Ishtar, Baal, Zeus, Jupiter, Mithras, Marduk, Chuin, Remphan, Dagon, Horus/Heru**). Today many have been converted into worshipping pagan gods/false religions in the form of **Islam, Hinduism, Buddhism, Catholicism, Protestant, Jehovah's Witness, Satanism, and Mammon (money)**. Blacks and Latinos have adopted the religions of their slavemasters in every country they have been scattered into. Prior to Babylonian inspired-Pharisaic Judaism, the Catholic Church infused its man-made doctrines and white lies into Christianity because everything from the Bible was visually shown to us (**pictures of white Jesus/Abraham/Jacob/white angels**) or taught to us orally (**Curse of Canaan, Sunday worship, slaves serve their masters for a reward in heaven**). Islam also crept its way into Africa and influenced many Israelites to convert from their God

Yahuah (Yah-oo-ah) to a pagan-inspired god called "**Allah**". Both Religions have in essence caused the Israelites to stray from their Creator and Supreme God. This is the deception of Satan that was foretold by God in the Torah. The Israelites were warned not to marry women of other nations as they would start worshipping their pagan gods and the Israelites were given Commandments by God not to worship any other god than him. But they disobeyed, worshipping goddesses such as the "**Queen of Heaven**" (not Mary mother of Jesus). Let's look!

THE POURING OF "LIBATIONS" IN AFRICA AND AMERICA

The Pouring of Libation ceremony/practice is done throughout West Africa from the Ivory Coast to Nigeria. Did the Hebrew Israelites learn this in Ancient Egypt?

Fact 1: African-Americans, Mexicans and other Latinos commonly pour out wine or liquor to their dead loves ones. West Africans use water or wine. But where do we get these practices from? Who came up with this? Is it in our DNA? Even the Creek Native Americans had a bitter **"Black Drink"** that they would spit out or pour out of a bowl onto the floor during their rituals. This was also practiced in Ancient Egypt and Ancient Israel.

Genesis 35:14 "And Jacob set up a Pillar in the place where he had spoken with him, a Pillar of Stone; **and he poured out a drink offering on it**, and poured oil on it."

Leviticus 23:13 "And the meat offering thereof shall be two tenth deals of fine flour mingled with oil, an offering made by fire into Yahuah for a sweet savour: and the **DRINK OFFERING** thereof shall be of **WINE**, the fourth part of an hin."

The Israelites were still hardheaded and wanted to the worship pagan gods they had learnt while in Egyptian, Assyrian and Babylonian captivity. They told Jeremiah that they would continue to offer sacrifices and meat/drink offerings to the **"Queen of Heaven"** instead of Yahuah. They also admitted to their Israelite forefathers doing the same practices centuries before them.

Jeremiah 44:17 "But we will certainly do whatsoever thing goeth forth out of our own mouth, to burn incense unto the **QUEEN OF HEAVEN**, and to **pour out DRINK OFFERINGS unto her**, as we have done, we, and our fathers, our kings, and our princes, in the cities of Judah, and in the streets of Jerusalem: for then had we plenty of victuals, and were well, and saw no evil."

The Israelite women kneaded dough and baked cakes of bread for the **"Queen of Heaven"** in **Jeremiah 7:18**. This Queen of Heaven was the Babylonian/Assyrian goddess called **Ishtar, Astarte or Ashtoreth**. They even made **"groves"** for her which was basically like mini-Washington monuments or obelisks. **Ishtar** was supposed to be the wife of the pagan god Baal, also known as Moloch. She was considered a **fertility goddess** that the Israelites worshipped to **"bear children"**.

Surprisingly, sacrifices and offerings are also common in other cultures. Africans and Natives (i.e. Native Americans) also commonly practice these rituals. It is a known fact that the native people of Ghana (**Akan, Ashanti, Ewe**) have been known to practice food offerings and drink offerings. Likewise, Drink offerings are also common in the Nigerian Yoruba and Igbo culture. In Haitian Voodoo, Yoruba religion, Louisiana Voodoo, Nigerian religion, and Cameroonian religion they still have pagan practices adopted from their Israelite ancestors such as the "**serpent priestess**" and/or "**Mami Wata**". The word "**Mami**" represents "**Mammy**" or "**Mother**". The Pidgin English word "**Wata**" represents "**Water**". This ancient mythology is seen in coastal Southeastern Igbo state Nigerians (**Efik, Ibibio and Annang people**). Mami Wata practices have been found in Senegal, Zambia, Cameroon and Ghana. In this mythology "Mami Wata" prefers delicious food, and drinks (alcohol/wine) just like the "**Queen of Heaven**", which the Ancient Israelites used to worship and pour out libations (drinks) to. "Mami Wata" was also a **priestess of fertility** and healing just as the Babylonian/Assyrian Goddess Ishtar was. So is the Bible giving us clues as to who is the "**Real Israelites?**" Yes! Here are some of the names of "**Mami Wata**" in other African countries subjected to the Transatlantic Slave trade where they still pour out "**drink offerings**" in her name.

- **Benin** – Mawa-Lisu
- **Brazil** – Yemanya/Yemaya
- **The Republic of Congo** – Kuitikuiti, Mboze, Makanga, Bunzi, Kambizi
- **Columbia** – Mohana, "Madre de aqua" meaning "Mother of water".
- **Cuba** – Yemanya/Yemaya
- **The Democratic Republic of Congo** – La Sirene (The Mermaid), Madame Poisson (Mistress Fish), Mamba Muntu
- **Dominica** – Maman de l'Eau (Mother of the Water), Maman Dlo, Mama Glo
- **Guinea** – Mamy Wata
- **French Guinea** – Mamadilo
- **Ghana** – Maame Water
- **Grenada** – Mamadjo
- **Guadeloupe** – Maman de l'Eau, Maman Dlo
- **Guyana** – Watramama
- **Haiti** – La Sirene and Erzulie Balianne (Erzulie and Simbi)
- **Jamaica** – River Mama, River Maiden

- **Nigeria** – Mmuommiri (Igbo: Lady of the waters), Obanamen or Oba n'amen (Benin/Edo State meaning Queen of the waters), Yemoja (Yoruba)
- **Suriname** – Watermama, Watramama
- **Trinidad and Tobago** – Maman de l'Eau, Mama Dlo, Maman Dglo

So this brings more questions in regards to connecting the Israelites to Blacks, Latinos and Native Americans. Were the Khazars, Slavs, Turks and Germanaic peoples in Europe from where the European Jews come from pouring out libations to the "Queen of Heaven" or "Mami Wata" hundreds of years ago? I think not. Let's look at some simple facts in regards to the Ancient Israelites and those today calling themselves "**Jews/Children of Israel**" or "**God's Chosen People**".

1. Who traditionally over centuries continues to have "**Tribes**"? (i.e. Africans and Native Americans).
2. Who prior to Christianity and Islam was already practicing the "**Mosaic Law**" (Amerindians with **fringes**, tassels (**Tzitzits**), ponchos similar to the Jewish shawl called "**tallit's** and breads made without "yeast-**unleavened**"? (i.e. Native Americans, Latinos, West Africans).
3. Who traditionally in their country has ancient customs such as performing circumcision and child-naming on 8th day? (i.e. West Africa and in Samoa).
4. Who was following "**Lunar Sabbaths**" and using lunar calendars like the Jews (i.e. Amerindians and West Africans)?
5. Who preserved the name of "**Yahuah**", "**Ye-ho-wah**", "**Ya(h)**", "**Jah**", "**He-Ya-Ho**", "**Y'ay'a**" or names similar to it? (i.e. West Africans, Jamaicans, Native Americans, Puerto Ricans).
6. Who was still worshipping a monotheistic "**Supreme God**" with a mix of paganism/animism involving sacrifices and offerings? (i.e. West Africans, Native Americans, Caribbean Natives)
7. Who still has traces of "**Hebrew/Aramaic**" in their dialect and writing style? (i.e. Amerindians, Natives of the Caribbean, West Africans)?
8. What race groups' claim passed down oral tradition to being "**Jews**" or "**Israelites**"? (West Africans, Native Americans)
9. Who traditionally were a "**people of color**" with "**Ancient practices**" adopted from other nations during ancient times of captivity? (i.e.

Inca/Mayan/Aztec Pyramids resembling Egyptian pyramids, Babylonian learnt astrology of Yoruba Nigerians).

10. Who has "**cities**" named after biblical places or people (Tula-Mayans = Tula, son of Issachar, Ouidah-Judah, Benin).

Fact 2: There is a big difference between a slave and a maidservant/butler. Some blacks reject the Bible because they ask the question "**How can God condone Slavery?**" Well, back then many of times the women were considered "maidservants or hand-maids". Such as the case of **Hagar the Egyptian**, the mother of Ishmael, or **Bilhah-Zilpah**, the mothers of the Tribe of Dan, Naphtali, Asher and Gad. Hebrews even had Hebrew servants.

Exodus 21:2 "If thou buy a **Hebrew Servant**, six years he shall serve: and in the seventh he shall go out free for nothing."

The word "**servant**" used here in the Hebrew Bible is the Hebrew Strong's #5650 word "**ebed**" which means "**servant**".

The older bibles did not use the word "**Slave**" even in the chapters of the Bible that discussed the Children of Israel being "slaves" to the Egyptians (**Exodus 6:6, Genesis 15:13**). Instead they used the word "**servant**", "**serve**" or "**bondage**". The words "**maidservants**" and "**handmaids**" also were common. All one has to do is research the Hebrew Old Testament and Greek Septuagint Old Testament verses for the word "slave". Let's take a look:

- **Greek Septuagint: Genesis 25:12** "And these are the generations of Ishmael the son of Abram, whom Hagar the Egyptian the **hand-maid** of Sarah bore to Abram."
- **King James Version Colossians 3:22** "**Servants**, obey in all things your masters according to the flesh; not with eyeservice, as menpleasers; but in singleness of heart, fearing God:
- **Latin Vulgate Colossians 3:22** "**Servants**, obey in all things your masters according to the flesh, not with eye-service, as men-pleasers, but in simplicity of heart, fearing God."

- **Aramaic Peshitta Colossians 3:22** "**Servants** obey in every thing your masters according to the flesh, not in the sight of the eye only, as those who please men, but from a simple heart, and in the fear of the Lord."

WHY WOULD AN ISRAELITE CONVERT TO ISLAM AND WORSHIP ANOTHER GOD? IT DOESN'T ADD UP.

It is a known fact that the Leader of the **Nation of Islam**, **Louis Farrakhan** knows that the European Jews are not the descendants of the Biblical Children of Israel. He knows the European Jews participated heavily in the Transatlantic Slave Trade from the release of his 1991 book, "**The Secret Relationship Between Blacks and Jews**". He also has been recorded saying that Blacks are **REAL** "Children of Israel". So if he knows this then why isn't his followers calling "**God**" **Yahuah** and adhering to the Commandments that God set for his "**Chosen People**?"

So let's look at the possible reasons why there is confusion over this hot subject. After all, many African-Americans and Africans have converted to Islam not knowing that their heritage may possibly be with the Ancient Hebrew Israelites. First, let's cover the strange belief that Abraham and Ishmael are the founders of Islam.

Islam was not the religion of Abraham or Ishmael. This is what Arabs will commonly say. Arabs will also claim that Abraham was told to sacrifice his son **Ishmael** and not **Isaac** despite what the Torah says. But here is the proof!

1. **Abraham** was the Grandfather of Israel (Jacob), and father of the "**Hebrews.**"

2. Abraham had Isaac, who had Jacob. From Jacob and his descendants was Prophethood given **ONLY**. If Muhammad was truly the last prophet sent by God to mankind, this would mean that Muhammad was an Israelite. We know that Muhammad was **NOT** an Israelite. The Israelites were the **ONLY** Prophets of the Bible. Ishmael and Keturah's sons were **NOT PROPHETS**. Even in the Quran Allah states that "**Prophethood**" was **NOT** given to Ishmael and his descendants.

   Quran 28:27 "And we gave to him Isaac and Jacob and placed in his descendants (The Israelites) PROPHETHOOD AND SCRIPTURE.

   As you can see the Quran does not list Ishmael and his descendant's for prophethood. Ishmael was 15 years older than Isaac and Jacob. For sure since he was older than Isaac he wouldn't have been overlooked for prophethood if it wasn't for a reason.

3. **NOTE:** Noah served the **Creator**. Noah and his son Shem were alive when Terah bore Abraham (**talk about meeting your ancestors**). This means they taught Abraham to serve the Creator. The same God who told Noah to build the Ark and commanded the Great Flood. Noah, Shem and Abraham all spoke Hebrew. So Abraham had to have passed the knowledge of his God and language to Isaac and Ishmael. Ishmael, spoke Hebrew and worshipped his father's God **YAHUAH**. This was passed down even to the Arabs during the Prophet Muhammad's time as his wife's name was **KHADI-YAH**, just like the name **OBADI-YAH, NEHEMI-YAH** and **HALLELU-YAH**.

4. Aramaic (**from which Arabic is derived from**) was not even used as a language in Assyria (**Modern day Syria and Iraq**) until around 400 B.C. Before this Assyria and Babylon were using a cuneiform writing script. In the Hebrew Strong's Lexicon **#422** the word "alah" means "**to swear or**

curse". In the Hebrew Strong's Lexicon **#427** the word "**allah**" means "**oak**" as in the Hebrew Joshua 24:26. In the Hebrew Strong's Lexicon #424 the word "**elah**" means an "oak/tree" as in the "**Valley of Elah (trees)**" in **1 Samuel 17:19** where David fought the Philistine Goliath. So how can the word "elah" in Hebrew mean "oak/tree" but in Aramaic the word "elah" mean "God"? This is because the actual name of God (a title) was "Yahuah". Before this it was common to use the plural form of God, "Elohim" which signified the Godhead/Trinity all being one. Therefore Ishmael (a Hebrew speaker) did not call God "**Allah**" or "**Elah**" which is an Aramaic/Arabic word for "**The God**" or "**God**", which is only a "**title**". Since we know Ishmael was a Hebrew speaker, we have to assume he was calling God either his correct name as "Yahuah" or the tame for the title God "Elohim". Otherwise he would be calling God an oak tree. We all know that God had a name, not a title and he definitely was not an oak tree. Aramaic and Arabic did not exist during Abraham's time and would not exist for another 1,000 years. During this time also Islam was not a religion as it wouldn't be until 2,000 years later that Islam was created in 632 A.D.

5. Allah was considered the **ONLY DEITY**, Creator of the Universe and omnipotent, however in the Quran in **Sura 23:14** it states that "**Allah is the BEST OF CREATORS.**" The word "**Creators**" is plural which means that there is more than one god and one creator. In the Quran in Sura 3:54 and 8:30 it says that "**Allah is the best of deceivers**". Some versions will say "**Allah is the best of planners**". But in the Arabic version Allah refers to himself as "**Khayrul-Makereen**" which correctly translated means "Allah is the greatest of deceivers." This is verified by looking up the root letters **Meem, Kaaf, Makr and Rah** which point to the meaning "**deceive**". Even in the work called "**Successors of the Messenger**" by Khalid Muhammad Khalid, p. 70 he talks about this "deception" from his God weeping saying: "**By Allah! I would not feel safe from the DECEPTION (same Arabic word) of Allah, even if I had one foot in paradise.**"

Even in **Sura 7:99** the Pickthall, Shakir, Asad, Yusuf Ali, Sahih International, and Dr. Ghali versions of this verse cannot choose between using the word scheming, devising, or planning.

Pickthall Version Sura 7:99 "Are they then secure from Allah's **SCHEME**? None deemeth himself secure from Allah's **SCHEME** save folk that perish."

Nevertheless in the Quran if it says "**Planners**" or "**Deceivers**" this implies that there is more than one person operating as a God in heaven. The letter "**s**" added to deceive or planner makes it plural, meaning that there is more than one person. There is no "**Trinity**" or "**Godhead**" in Islam and the Quran states God cannot have children. So who is 2nd and 3rd place on the "Creation Level-contest"? Marvel Superheroes are put into classes based on their Superpowers but the Bible and the Quran are not Marvel Comic Books.

6. The **Quran** says God cannot have a **child** (son or daughter). But in Islam, Allah has three daughters whom are "**Goddesses**". They are **Al-Lat, Al-Uzza** and **Manat**. Muslims don't view them as pagan deities but Muhammad himself commanded his followers to offer prayers (**intercession**) to these Daughters of his in the "**Revealed Quran**". He later retracted this statement and blamed it on the Devil. (**Note: This was also done by Joseph Smith, founder of the Mormons in regards to polygamy.**) But here are the original verses including the verse that tells Muslims to worship these goddesses Muhammad said was incorrectly given to him by the Devil. This verse was deleted from the Quran in later versions:

Sura 53:15-22 "Near it is the Garden of Abode. Behold, the Lote-tree was shrouded (in mystery unspeakable!) (His) sight never swerved, nor did it go wrong! For truly did he see, of the Signs of his Lord, the Greatest! Have ye seen Lat, and Uzza, and another, the third goddess, Manat? **These are the exalted cranes (intermediaries) Whose intercession (prayers-worship) is to be hoped for (*Deleted Verse*).** What! For you the male sex, and for Him, the female? Behold, such would be indeed a division most unfair!"

This was verified and discussed in many books such as:
- **History of The Arabs, Philip K. Hitti, 1937, pg 96-101**
- **The Archaeology of World Religions, Jack Finegan, 1952, pg 482-485, 492 The Hajj, F.E. Peters, pg 3-41, 1994**
- **Mohammed: The man and his faith, Tor Andrae, 1936, Translated by Theophil Menzel, 1960, pg 13-30**

- **Fabled Cities, Princes & Jin from Arab Myths and Legends. Khairt al-Saeh, 1985, pg. 28-30**
- **The Cambridge History of Islam Vol. I, ed. P.M. Holt, 1970, p 37.**

The Ka'ba in Mecca, Holy Shrine for all Muslims. Mecca is to Islam what the Vatican is to the Catholic Church.

Fact: The Muslim Quran and Hadith talks about Alexander the Great (**Japheth**). The Muslim Hadith, similar to the Jewish Talmud, talks about **Gog** (Ya' jooj) and **Magog** (Majooj) which are also descendants of **Japheth**. In the Quran, Ishmael's wife is Hagar the **Egyptian**. The word "**Egypt**" is mentioned 4 times in the Quran. In Surah Yusuf 12:21 it reads:

Surah Yusuf 12.21 "And the **Egyptian** who brought him said to his wife: Give him an honorable abode, maybe he will be useful to us, or we may adopt him as a son. And thus did We establish Yusuf in the land and that We might teach him the interpretation of sayings; and Allah is the master of His affair, but most people do not know."

And we all know that the "**Children of Israel**" and "**Abraham**", descendants of **Shem** are also in the Quran. We also know Ishmael was a descendant of Shem. We don't need Quranic scriptures to prove this. We know that in the Hebrew Torah, which is thousands of years older than the Quran, Noah has only has 3 sons which all have wives. These are the only people that are on the Ark along with Noah and his wife. The Bible does not talk about the names of anyone that is trying to tag along at the last minute to get a ride on the ark. It doesn't even mention the Sons of Cain being allowed on the ark. But in the Quran, one of Noah's sons dies in the

Flood. How could this be? If this is not in the Torah, then how can it be in the Quran? **Mizraim** was the son of **Ham and the father of the Ancient Egyptians.** The Israelites, Abraham and Ishmael are the descendants of **Shem. Alexander the Great, Gog and Magog are descendants of Japheth.** So if one of Noah's sons died than which one was it? Even if one of Noah's three sons dies in the Quran, this means that these Quranic verses about the Egypt, Gog & Magog and Abraham have to be false! Anything that is deemed false about the Bible per Muslims also makes the Quran false as the Quran is based off the Hebrew Torah for its historical base.

In the Hebrew Torah did God tell Noah to ask the Sons of Cain and their wives if they wanted to get on the Ark? No!

Genesis 7:1 "And the Lord said unto Noah, **Come thou and all thy house** into the Ark; for thee have I seen righteous before me in this generation."

Nobel Quran Sura 11:42-43

Sahih International "And it sailed with them through waves like mountains, and **Noah called to his son** who was apart (from them), "O my son, come aboard with us and be not with the disbelievers." But he said, "I will take refuge on a mountain to protect me from the water." Noah said, "There is no protector today from the decree of Allah, except for whom He gives mercy." **And the waves came between them, and he was among the drowned.**"

Noah's son dies in the **Sahih International version**, the **Pickthall version** and the **Yusuf Ali version** of these Quranic Scriptures. So which son was it? This is a **MAJOR DETAIL FLAW** that alters the course of biblical history. But wait! In the Quran it also says that Noah and his whole family survived the flood. What is going on here!

Yusuf Ali Sura 21:76 "Remember Noah, when he cried to **US** aforetime: **WE** listened to his prayer and delivered him and his family from great distress."

Sahih International Sura 21:76 "And mention Noah, when he called to Allah before that time, so **WE** responded to him and saved him and his family from the great flood."

Pickthall Sura 21:76 "And Noah, when he cried of old, WE heard his prayer and saved him and his household from the great affliction."

Now there are **two** flaws here:
1. One verse (**Sura 11:42-43**) in the Quran says that Noah's son died in the Floor while another verse (**Sura 21:76**) says that Noah's whole family survives the Flood.
2. We see the word "**We**" and "**Us**" in **Sura 21:76**. There is no "**Godhead**" or "**Trinity**" in the Quran. Muhammad is the only Creator. He did not have a son. What is going on? These two flaws are a clear indicator that Islam is not the way.

The Black Hebrew Israelites did not know who Allah was or what Islam until the Arab Slave Trade began. The original Black Arabs if anything got caught up worshipping the many pagan gods that were around in Mesopotamia and Arabia. The Black Hebrew Israelites did not know about the Gospel of Jesus Yeshua/Yahush(u)a unless the disciples were able to witness to them before the Catholic Church did. James was a disciple of "The Christ" before and after his resurrection. In **James 1:1** it reads: "**James, a servant of God and of the Lord Jesus Christ, to the twelve tribes which are scattered abroad, greeting.**" This proves that the "Children of Israel" were already scattered abroad during the time period of Jesus (Yeshua/Yahushua). The Ancient Israelites did not wear wooden crosses or carry them around, or wear blue hexagram stars (**Star of Remphan/Saturn**), or pray to a Black cube structure in Mecca.

Prior to Christopher Columbus, did the Israelites when traveling to America (The New World) bring with them memories of the gods of Assyria/Babylon so that they could continue being disobedient to God? The world by then was divided so we cannot blame this on Pangea (one land mass). Why else would the Assyrian/Babylonian god Marduk be found in Ecuador and the Middle East?

Above is **Marduk**, A Babylonian God who was supposedly the son of the Sumerian God **Enki** and Akkadian God **Ea**. He was given the powers of the Sumerian Gods **Ea (Enki) and Enlil**. Planetary-wise Marduk was associated with the Planet **Jupiter**. Marduk was often associated with the Sun. Marduk also had a snake-dragon pet. The Israelites learned about Marduk and the Babylonian gods while in captivity under the Kings of Babylon (Nebuchadnezzar). Artifacts with Marduk on it were found in the **Crespi Collection** in Ecuador. How is this possible? Marduk was a Post-flood God so we know this Babylonian god didn't arrive in Ecuador, South America because the Babylonians walked or traveled there. The Earth was divided back in these days. During the creation of the Earth, God made one big land which had its place and the waters called "**Seas**" had its own place. This would be equivalent to what people call "**Pangea**". But by the time **Eber (Father of the Hebrews)** had his son **Peleg**, the land of the earth was divided, possibly from a Great Earthquake.

Genesis 1:9-10 "And God said, **Let the waters under the heaven be gathered together into one place**, and let the dry land appear: and it was so. And God called the dry land Earth; and the gathering of the waters called he Seas: and God saw that it was good."

After the Flood, Noah's 3 sons had children. Shem had Arphaxad, who begat Salah, and Salah begat Eber (from where the Hebrews sprang from). Eber had two sons: Peleg and Joktan. **Peleg's (Palag)** name means "**to split or divide**" or "**dividing by a small channel of water**" according to Hebrew Strong's **#6388, #6389 and #6385.**

Pangea 245 m.y.

Genesis 10:24-25 "And Arphaxad begat Salah; and Salah begat Eber. And unto Eber were born two sons: the name of one was Peleg (Palag); **for in his days was the earth divided**; and his brother's name was Joktan."

In the **Epic of Gilgamesh** which dates to around **2100 B.C.**, Gilgamesh is the King of the Sumerian/Akkadian city **Uruk (Iraq)**. This was around the time Abraham, Isaac and Jacob lived (**Abraham lived in the land of Ur, with the Black Chaldeans and the Black Canaanites**).

Genesis 24:2-3 "And Abraham said unto his eldest servant of his house, that ruled over all that he had, Put, I pray thee, thy hand under my thigh; and I will make thee swear by the Lord, the God of heaven, and the God of the earth, that **thou shalt not take a wife unto my son of the daughters of the Canaanites, among whom I dwell**:

In the second half of the Epic of Gilgamesh, it talks about a man named **Utnapisthim** who was told by the gods to build a Great Ship called "**The Preserver of Life**" in which all the male and female animals of the earth including his family were to enter before the "**Great Flood**". We know that if the Ancient Sumerians-Akkadians talked about the "**Great Flood**" as it was something that happened in the "**Past**" we can conclude that Marduk and any Ancient relics of Marduk found had to be made after the Earth was divided. This means someone had to bring these Ancient Relics of Marduk or any knowledge of these pagan gods from the Middle East to South America. So who were the people that brought these pagan gods and their practices to the Americas? Was it the Babylonians? Was it the Assyrians? Was it the Hebrew Israelites? Let's look at the facts:

Marduk was the Chief God over the Annunaki, who were fallen angels whom the Sumerians said created man. In the Book of Enoch, **Azazel** was the leader of the Fallen Angels. Azazel was linked to Lucifer or Lumiel because Lucifer was a chief Angel that rebelled against God and his good angels. The Sumerians regarded the woman as equal as New Age Religions teach today. The Sumerians also practiced homosexuality, pedophilia and incest which is promoted in all Satanic esoteric occult religions/societies. The Egyptian Creator god **Ptah** and other false gods were called in Egyptian "Ntr" or **Neter**". Post-flood, The Sumerians knew and wrote about "**Nimrod**" as "**NMRD/NRD**" The Egyptians wrote that the gods "**Neter**" came from "**Ta-Ur**" meaning the "**Land (Place) of Ur**", in Shem territory (Babylon). Therefore the Egyptian Religion and its fake gods were "**created-fashioned**" by **Satan**, his Fallen Angels called "**Watchers**" the **Nephilim** of whom the Sumerians called "**Annunaki**". Joshua saw them as the "**Rephaim**" or the "**sons of Anak (Long necked ones)**". The straits of the Red Sea were called by the Egyptians "**Ta-Neter**" meaning "**Land of the Gods/Watchers**". The Egyptians thus wrote about giants, Sun worship and homosexuality (**Set and Horus story**). So the gods that influenced the Egyptians came from Semitic pagan influences as the

Akkadians and Sumerians were Semitic peoples derived from Shem. Ptah which is Egypt's "Creator god" has no meaning in Egyptian but in the Semitic Sumerian/Akkadian tongues "Ptah" means "**He who fashioned things by carving and opening up.**" Even the **Ka'aba** in Mecca means "**Gate of the Father**" or "**Gate of the Divine Beings**". In the Sumerian language "**Ka**" means "**Gate**" and "**Aba**" means "**father**" like "**Abba**" means father in Hebrew and "**A-bu**" means father in the Cuneiform Assyrian script. From Shem came all the Semitic languages including "Hebrew". Shem's had **Asshur** (Assyria), **Elam** (Iran), **Arphaxad** (Iraq/Arabia/Israel), **Lud** (Turkey) and **Aram** (Syria). Because we know that all these Ancient Semitic languages are B.C. languages this means that the "Ka-aba" stone was named by these Ancient Semitic languages instead of "**Arabic**" which is a **500 A.D. language**. So the Ka'ba cube/stone was being used for pagan worship before Muhammad came on the scene with his monotheistic religion called Islam. The Muslim Arabs will say that its name is derived from the Arabic word for cube "**muka'ab**" but the Ka'aba cube is older than 500 A.D. **The Ka-aba cube is older than Arabic and Islam so it meant something else first.** It was originally built for the Pre-Islamic Arabs 360 pagan gods, which included "**Allah**" and "**Hubal**" as well. Muslims circle it counter clockwise 7 times like Satanists do in the **Simon Necromantic** demon gate-portal rite.

Fact: *In Satanism after reciting the infernal names of Satan, turning **counter-clockwise**, the priest points with the sword to each cardinal point of the compass and calls for the respective Princes of Hell: **Satan** from the south, **Lucifer** from the east, **Belial** from the north, and **Leviathan** from the west. It is also known that Plato refers Lucifer to Venus "the morning star". Venus is also the only planet that rotates "clockwise" while it orbits the sun "counter-clockwise". The workings of Simon Necronomicon in Arabian Divination represent the workings of the Priesthood of Ishtar. In these rituals people walk first in a clockwise fashion and then in order to ascend to the Gates through the zodiac they walk in counter-clockwise. Back in ancient times doing the Simon Necronomicon rite was warned to users that it could unleash "**dangerous and evil forces**".*

The Israelites kept these pagan gods from Assyria (Moloch) Marduk (Babylon), Baal (Canaan), Saturn (Romans) and the Golden calf (Egypt).

In conclusion, it is possible that when then Israelites were exiled from their land and scattered into the many nations (including the Americas) they kept these pagan practices (including Pyramid building) as well, thus warranting the "Curses of Israel" to come upon them (by the Spanish Conquistadors), even in Ecuador.

GOD DID NOT GIVE THE ISRAELITES A STAR AS THEIR SYMBOL.

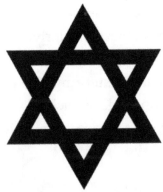

Jewish Hexagram which they call the "Star of David"
Currently the Flag symbol for Israel

In fact the earliest known use of the Hexagram was during the 6th Century (500 B.C.), lining up with the time period the Israelites would learn all of the Satanic religions and practices in Babylon while under their captivity. King Solomon's Ring initially had the Tetragrammaton name of God on it which he used to control spirits and demons. After some time, man had changed this story to state that King Solomon's Ring had a **hexagram** on it. Then people started associating this **"hexagram"** with the **"Star of Solomon"** when in reality in past pagan religions this star was known as the "Star of Saturn (Remphan)" or the "Star of Satan". Why? Because back then Satan was associated with Saturn, the sixth planet from the Sun while Lucifer was associated with Venus. The proof of the Israelites following the pagan ways of the many nations of their captors is evident in the Book of Acts.

Buddhism, Hinduism, Islam, Shintoism, Luciferianism, Satanism all use the 6-pointed Hexagram in their religion. So how can this be the symbol God gave the Israelites to represent themselves or even God?

Acts 7:43 "Yea, ye took up the **tabernacle of Moloch**, and the **STAR** of your god **REMPHAN**, figures which ye made to worship them: and **I will carry you away beyond Babylon.**"

The Cross was made the official symbol of Christianity by the Roman Catholic Church in the 4th Century A.D. This practice was not supported in the New

Testament by Yeshua or his disciples. This could be considered a "graven image" as the word "graven" means "sculptured or carved".

Before the Roman Catholic Church under Constantine would declare Christianity the religion of Rome and spread missionaries to Africa, the Hebrew Israelites living in Africa were still practicing the laws of the Torah (**Biblical Judaism or Law of Moses**). This is why many West Africans still practice traditions/customs as it was given to Moses in the Torah. Christians today eat pork and do not follow the commandments of the Mosaic Law (**Karaite Judaism**). This is what they found the Ethiopian Jews to be practicing before the European Jews would influence them with their Satanic "**Babylonian Judaism**" straight out of the Talmud (**collection of rabbinical opinions on oral law**).

Fact: European Jews found a Jewish Calendar, known as the "**Gezer Calendar**" in Israel. Gezer was an Ancient Canaanite city that was usually associated with Joshua and King Solomon. The Egyptian-Canaanite "**Amarna Letters**" mentions the Kings of Gezer swearing loyalty to the Egyptian Pharaoh. The oldest historical reference to the Canaanite city was found inscribed in rock at Pharaoh Thutmose's temple at Karnak, Egypt. During the 10th Century B.C., according to the Hebrew Bible, the Canaanite city "**Gezer**" was conquered by the Egyptians (possible Pharaoh Siamun). This Egyptian Pharaoh then gave the city of Gezer to King Solomon as a gift for his daughter's marriage to King Solomon.

1 Kings 9:16 "Pharaoh King of Egypt had come up and captured **Gezer**; he destroyed it by fire, killed the Canaanites who dwelt in the town, and gave it as dowry (gift) to his daughter, Solomon's wife."

Interesting enough is that in the next Chapter of **1 Kings Chapter 10**, Ethiopian Queen Sheba visits King Solomon. Right after acquiring the **City of Gezer**, King Solomon gives Queen Sheba all that she asks him for.

1 Kings 10:13 "King Solomon gave the queen of Sheba all she desired and asked for, besides what he had given her out of his royal bounty. Then she left and returned with her retinue to her own country."

Per the Ethiopian "**Kebra Nagast**" written in 1300 A.D in the Semitic Ethiopian **Ge'ez language**, it talks about how Queen Sheba (Makeda) of Ethiopia met King Solomon and how they had a son named **Menelik I**. According to this Ancient text, Menelik I took the Ark of the Covenant to Ethiopia along with the first-born sons from each of the 12 tribes of Israel (**including the firstborn sons of the Levites and Cohenites**) to Cush (**Ethiopia**) to properly convert the Ethiopians from worshipping the Sun, Moon, and Stars to that of the "**Lord God of Israel**". Ironically, the Beta Israel Ethiopian Jews speak the language called "**Ge'ez**" which is similar in spelling to the Canaanite-Israel city he possessed called "**Gezer**". The Semitic Ethiopian Ge'ez language has similar words to Hebrews as the first letter of the Ge'ez alphabet is "**Aleph**" and the last letter is "**Tav**", which his identical to the Hebrew Alphabet. How could the Ethiopians learn and speak a Semitic language very similar to Hebrew if they were a Hamitic nation, descendants of Ham. The Cushite Ethiopians must have had some intermarriage with the Hebrew Israelites at some point in time, like how Moses found his Cushite wife Zipporah. Today in the Ethiopian Orthodox Church students learn how to use the order of the Hebrew Alphabet known as "abugida" with "alef" as the 1st word. The Ethiopian Jews language of Ge'ez is similar to the Old South Arabian Hebrew language the sons of Joktan spoke. It is also similar in appearance to Hebrew.

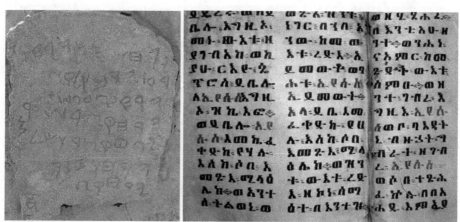

Gezer Calendar (left) and Beta Israel/Ethiopian Orthodox Church Semitic language Ge'ez (right).

Hebrew		נ	ה		ז		ש	צ	ח	ק		א	כ	ס	ב	ע	ל	י
Phonecian																		
Ge'ez																		
South Arabian (Carved)																		
South Arabian (Written)																		
South Arabian (Cursive)																		

(Above) - How is Ge'ez similar to Hebrew and the South Arabian Language? Eber (Father of the Hebrews) had two sons: Joktan and Peleg. Peleg was Abraham's Great-great-great grandfather. Joktan was also technically a Hebrew and settled in South Arabia. This is because some of the Ethiopians as well as the Ethiopians Jews are a Semitic people. This would mean that they also have Hebrew Israelite blood in them. Peleg and Joktan's both shared Nimrod and their Grandparent. For this reason their Great-grandparent was Cush (Son of Ham). Thus the Ethiopian Jews are half Hebrew-half Cushite. This is why the Y-Haplogroup E-V38 had two branches: E-M329 (Ethiopians/Somalians) and E-M2 (West Africans and all the descendants of the Transatlantic Slave Trade). This perhaps could be the clue to the African "Semitic Branch".

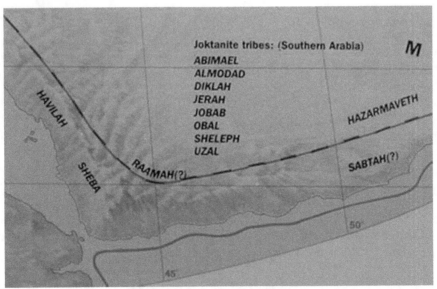

Joktan had 13 sons and they all populated South Arabia, whose Ancient language resembles Hebrew and the Ethiopian Jew language Ge'ez. Coincidence?

WITHOUT A TRUE LEVITICAL PRIESTHOOD THE THIRD TEMPLE IN JERUSALEM IS A SCAM

Without a **TRUE LEVITICAL PRIESTHOOD,** the rebuilding of the Third Temple is a scam. But it has to be built for the Antichrist to have a place to sit on the throne.

Daniel 12:11 "And from the time that the daily sacrifice shall be taken away, and the abomination that maketh desolate set up, there shall be a thousand two hundred and ninety days."

Daniel 9:27 "And he (Antichrist) shall confirm the covenant with many for one week: and in the midst of the week he shall cause the sacrifice and the oblation (offering) to cease, and for the overspreading of abominations he shall make it desolate, even until the consummation, and that determined shall be poured upon the desolate."

2 Thessalonians 2:2-4 "That ye be not soon shaken in mind, or be troubled, neither by spirit, nor by word, nor by letter as from us, as that the day of Christ is at hand. Let no man deceive you by any means: for that day shall not come, except there come a falling away first, and that man of sin be revealed, the son of perdition; who opposeth and exalteth himself above all that is called God, or that is worshipped; so that he as God sitteth in the temple of God, shewing himself that he is God."

So here we see that there is going to be a temple, and there is going to be sacrifices done in this temple. The Jews will try to have everything in this Temple as it was in ancient times, including the Ark of the Covenant. But where is the Ark of the Covenant? The Ashkenazi Jews who claim to have the Ark hidden below Jerusalem are lying. The Apocrypha Book of Maccabees says Jeremiah hid it in a cave until God regathers **ALL THE CHILDREN OF ISRAEL AGAIN.** This has not happened yet in Israel so how can the Jews claim to know where it is? They admit themselves that the 10 Lost Tribes of Israel are still lost but the **Tribe of Dan** is in **Beersheba, Israel** (Ethiopian Jews)? But isn't the Tribe of Dan one of the 10 Lost Tribes? What sense does that make? Why does everyone keep lying? So the Non-Hebrew Book of Maccabees says this but who wrote the Book of Maccabees? Was it **Judas Maccabeus** who lived around 160 B.C.? Supposedly he was a Levite priest

(Cohenite), the leader of the Gentile Greek Jewish people in Judea, their Commander in battle against the Seleucid Greek Empire and the person behind the establishment of the pagan, non-God inspired Jewish holiday called "**Hanukkah**". He also made an agreement with the Romans in 161 B.C. according to 1 Maccabees 8:17-20 and Flavius Josephus. Since when does a Cohenite priest fight battles, make agreement with other "gentile nations" and set up Jewish holidays that are not set forth by God? Doesn't sound like a Cohenite Priest to me. But didn't Yahusha (Jesus) give us clues when the Old Testament and the last of the Prophets as well as functioning Levitical priests would end? Many biblical scholars suggest the last Biblical prophets of the Old Testament were Malachi and Zechariah. These two are also the authors of the last books of the Old Testament as well. From Abel to Zechariah, Yahusa (Jesus) let readers know who the last prophets were.

Matthew 23:35 "That upon you may come all the righteous blood shed upon the earth, from the blood of righteous **Abel** unto the blood of **Zechariah** son of Barachias, whom ye slew between the temple and the altar."

Zechariah 1:1 "In the eight month, in the second year of Darius, came the word of the Lord unto Zechariah, the son of Berechiah, the son of Iddo the prophet, saying."

So was Judas Maccabeus the real author of 1 and 2 Maccabees? No! It supposedly says in **2 Maccabees 2:1-6** that Jeremiah hid the Ark of the Covenant in a cave. But was 2 Maccabees written in Hebrew? No! It was written in Koine Greek. Can we trust 2 Maccabees? Let's see.

2 Maccabees 2:4-6 "It was also contained in the same writing, how the prophet, being warned by God, commanded that the tabernacle and the ark should accompany him, till he came forth to the mountain (Nebo) where Moses went up, and saw the inheritance of God. And when Jeremiah came thither he found a hollow cave: and he carried in thither the tabernacle, **and the ark**, and the altar of incense, and so stopped the door. Then some of them that followed him, came up to mark the place: but they could not find it."

2 Maccabees 15:38-39 "So these things being done with relation to Nicanor (Greek Seleucid General), and from that time the city being possessed by the Hebrews, I also will here make an end of my narration. **Which if I have done well, and as it**

becometh the history, it is what I desired: but if not so perfectly, it must be pardoned me."

Basically, the mysterious author of this book is saying if I have done a good job writing this history, it is what I intended but if it was not done perfectly, please excuse (forgive) me.

What kind of author writes a book in doubt of his work if it is supposed to be given to him to write under the authority of God? How come nobody knows the name of the author of 2 Maccabees? How can we trust this book? This raises many questions. Even the 16th Century Protestant Reformer, **Martin Luther** said:

"I am so great an enemy to the second book of the Maccabees, and to Esther, that I wish they had not come to us at all, for they have too many heathen unnaturalities."

So how is this story of the Ark being hid in a cave not in the Hebrew bible or the KJV? If the Hebrew Israelite Prophets did not write that it was hidden in a cave in the Hebrew Tanakh what does that tell us? It tells us that the Ark wasn't hidden in a cave on a Mountain! The Ark of the Covenant was mentioned in I Samuel when the Philistines took it and gave it back. That was during the time of King Saul and King David as the Prophet Samuel anointed them. Shortly after in the Book of 1 Kings Chapter 10 Queen Sheba of Ethiopia links up with King Solomon. The Ethiopian Kebra Negast states that their Son Menelik took it to Axum, Ethiopia. So vavoom! It's gone. Later in the 1 Kings Egyptian Pharaoh Shishak came and raided Israel taking Temple treasures in 1 Kings 14:25-26. By this time Israel and Judah had split and King Solomon's son Rehoboam (was in his 5th year). So as we can see plenty of years went by for Solomon to have a son, and for his son (Rehoboam) to grow old enough to rule over the House of Israel. But the scripture **DOES NOT SAY THAT PHARAOH SHISHAK TOOK THE ARK WITH THE TEMPLE TREASURES**.

The Assyrians came and took stuff during their invasion but **NO ARK WAS TAKEN**. The Babylonians came and took treasures when they invaded Israel but again, **THERE IS NO MENTION THAT THE ARK WAS CARRIED OFF**. During the 2nd temple period with Ezra there was no Ark; which even the Apocrypha attests to this as fact. When the Greeks and Romans invaded Jerusalem **THERE WAS ALSO NO MENTION OF AN ARK TAKEN**. Don't believe? Look at the Roman "**Arch of Titus**" relief. So who has the Ark of the Covenant? Moses had children with an Ethiopian Cushite woman named Zipporah. These kids were Levite Priests by Blood also mixed with Cush blood. **SO THEY WERE BLACK!** According to the **Kebra Negast** (aka. "The Glory of the Kings"), King Solomon had the firstborn sons of each of the 12 Tribes of Israel, including the Priests and High Priests (Cohenites) to teach the Cushite Ethiopians the worship of the God of Israel. These Semitic Ethiopians are guarding the Ark today in Axum, Ethiopia. Ask any Jew today that calls himself a Levite, "**Are there any Blacks in the Tribe of Levi**" and see what he says.   He will likely say "No".   But the European Jews are the ones lying about their identity.   They are not "Real" Levites or Cohenites.   Neither are they "Real" Judahites.   But the Jews can end all of this debate by digging up King David's body in "**King David's Tomb**" in Mount Zion, Israel and testing their DNA with King David's DNA using biologic tissue and seeing if it matches up. But they won't! That would blow their cover and they know it.

ARE AFRICANS FROM GHANA LEVITES? ARE HAITIANS LEVITES? CAN WE PROVE IT? THE FACTS WILL BLOW YOU AWAY!

Fact 1: The word "**Jew**" and "**Hebrew**" are English translations to describe the "**Children of Israel**". But back in Ancient times, during the times of the Pharaoh's of Egypt and during Babylonian Times they were known by other names. If you type in the word "**Hebrew Language**" on Google you will see the word "**Hibru**" and "**Ivrit**".   The Ancient Egyptians and Assyrians described the Hebrews as "**Habiru**".   The Hebrew Israelites described themselves as "**Ibri/Ivri**".   Hebrew Strong's #5680 lists "**ibri**" as another name for an Israelite.

Hebrew Strong's **#5681** lists the word "**Ibri**" as "**Levite**". This is supported in **1 Chronicles Chapter 24:27** where it lists one of the descendants of Levi as a man named "**Ibri**". As you will see, the Ewe people of Ghana were Hebrew Israelites and many of the Ewe people were taken as slaves to **Haiti and Jamaica.**

Fact: *There are Ghanaians today who recognize certain words from their language being spoken in Jamaica including similar customs being practiced in Jamaica that stem from Ancient Ghana Culture. This is acknowledged by the Rastafarian Mansion called "**Bobo Ashanti (Asante)**" in which "**Bobo**" means Black and "**Asante**" stems from a Tribe in Ghana (Akan). The Bobo Ashanti people wear dreadlocks covered in wraps/turbans. They are typically strict vegans who do not eat wine and observe the Sabbath day. They believe that the Hebrew Israelites are black. The fast often and teach their children in "Jerusalem schools" before they are allowed to integrate into society or public school. They also follow the Mosaic Law, as it was followed back in the day.*

Haitian Creole is a mixture of French, the Ewe dialect and the Taino dialect. Could the Haitians also some Levite ancestry from this Levite man named "**Ibri**"? Who knows, but if it is TRUE this would suggest there is some strange similarities to the 12 Tribes Chart proposed by some Hebrew Israelite camps today.

1 Chronicles 24:27 "The sons of Merari (Levite) by Jaaziah; Beno, and Shoham, and Zaccur, and **IBRI**."

There have been studies that propose that the true name of the Black slaves sold all across the world was "**Eve**". The Europeans found it too hard to pronounce as all they could hear was "**Erh-verh**" or "**Eyverh**" and its plural form "**Eveo**" so they came up with the word "**Ewe**". It sounded like "**ib-ree**" when said correctly by the people in Ghana though there is a "v" in it. This is how the original word "**E-V-E**" was transliterated (attempt to keep sound the same when changing to a different language) to **Ewe** which is used today in Ghana to describe a certain tribe of people.

- The "**E**" transliterates as "**Erh**" or "**Ey**" or "**I**".
- The "**V**" transliterates as "**Vav**" or "**Vher**" or "**Br**".
- The "**E**" again transliterates as "**Erh**" or "**Ey**" or "**I**".
- Together you get "**IBRI**" or "**Ib-ree**" like the way you pronounce "**Eber/Hebrew**" in Hebrew.

Again "**Eyverh**" the word was too difficult to pronounce for the Europeans so they just said the word "**Ewe**". In English the "**W**" sound replaced the "**Vher**" sound in the letter "**V**" from "**Eve**". So when the Europeans carved out West Africa and renamed it Ghana, Benin/Togo, Nigeria etc. the Ghanaians went from calling themselves "**Eve**" to "**Ewe**" to identity their people. But the word "**Ewe**" in Hebrew is a female lamb, so the real word they were used to using in the past was "**Eve**". The word "**Eve**" was basically the English word "**Hebrew**" in Ancient times. So today the European corruption word "**Ewe**" stands to be an ethnic group in Ghana. But in pre-European colonial days the "**Ewe**" people were all throughout West Africa, especially in the area from the **Volta River** in Ghana to Nigeria-Cameroon. Because the Israelites migrated to West Africa from North Africa and East Africa, many Bantus Negro tribes were deposited from the Senegal River Valley to the Congo forests. After the **Bantus Expansion** some of the Israelites then migrated to East and South Africa.

West Africans hold the same DNA as African-Americans and other blacks who were scattered to other parts of the world (Brazil, Cuba, Bahamas, Haiti, Jamaica, Bantus East Africans). It is a known fact that the "Ewe" dialect is seen in the formation of the Haitian Creole language and is also seen in the language of native Jamaicans. Many of their cultures and Traditions come from West Africa (Nigeria, Benin, Ghana).

Because the people in West Africa (before the Europeans renamed their land to Ghana, Benin, Nigeria) didn't have an English alphabet to call themselves "**Hebrew**" they used the word "**Eve**" to denote their identity. So where did the word "**Jew**" come from? Well, the word "**Jew**" is not found in the original Hebrew Bible. It is actually a made up name and only appears **74 times** in the whole Old Testament. Let's look at what the **Hebrew word** for "Hebrew" was in the **Hebrew**

Torah since Abraham was after all, the first "**Hebrew**" talked about in the bible derived from "**Eber**" the descendant of Shem.

יִעְבְּרְ

This is Hebrew Strong's #5680 "**Ibri**" for the English word "**Hebrew**".

Pay close attention to the scriptures below and note that the Hebrew Letter ה "**Hey**" when used in the beginning of a word as a sort of "**prefix**" signifies the word "**The**".

Genesis 14:13 "And there came one that had escaped, and told **Abram the Hebrew (Eve/Ewe)**--now he dwelt by the terebinths of Mamre the Amorite, brother of Eshcol, and brother of Aner; and these were confederate with Abram."

יג וַיָּבֹא, הַפָּלִיט, וַיַּגֵּד, לְאַבְרָם הָעִבְרִי; וְהוּא שֹׁכֵן בְּאֵלֹנֵי מַמְרֵא הָאֱמֹרִי, אֲחִי אֶשְׁכֹּל וַאֲחִי עָנֵר, וְחֵם, בַּעֲלֵי בְרִית-אַבְרָם.

(Above) Genesis 14:13 written in Modern Hebrew.

לְאַבְרָם הָעִבְרִי

(Above) Read from right-to-left, "Abram the Hebrew", from Genesis 14:13 in Modern Hebrew. Abram is Hebrew Strong's #87, Hebrew (Ibri) is Hebrew Strong's #5680/5681

1 Samuel 13:3 "And Jonathan smote the garrison of the Philistines that was in Geba, and the Philistines heard of it. And Saul blew the horn throughout all the land, saying: 'Let **the Hebrews** hear."

ג וַיַּךְ יוֹנָתָן, אֵת נְצִיב פְּלִשְׁתִּים אֲשֶׁר בְּגֶבַע, וַיִּשְׁמְעוּ, פְּלִשְׁתִּים; וְשָׁאוּל תָּקַע בַּשּׁוֹפָר בְּכָל-הָאָרֶץ לֵאמֹר, יִשְׁמְעוּ הָעִבְרִים.

(Above) 1 Samuel 13:3 written in Modern Hebrew

הָעִבְרִים.

(Above) Read from Right to Left: "The Hebrews" from 1 Samuel 13:3.

If you read the above Hebrew short sentence from **Right-to-Left** the first word "The" is the "He(y)"5th Hebrew Letter in the alphabet. The word "Hebrew" is then spelled with the following Hebrew Letters from **right to left**: "Ayin-Be(i)t-Re(i)sh-Yod". To make it plural for "Hebrews" you simply add the **Samekh (Samech)** 18th Hebrew Letter to the end.

Originally the Hebrew word for "**Hebrew**" was "**ibri**", pronounced "**ib-ree**". Of course English changed it to "**ivri**" or "**IVRI**". So today the English letters "**IVRI**" represent the Hebrew Characters "**Ayin-Be(i)t-Resh-Yod**" respectively and thus the word "**Hebrew**". Want proof? Type in the word "**IVRI hebrew**" or "**IBRI hebrew**" into your internet browser and what do you get? You probably will get a whole lot of "Hebrew" stuff and Hebrew Strong's definitions of a "Hebrew". But how? Here's here is the break down on how we get **IBRI** and **IVRI** from Hebrew.

Note: The Post-exilic, 400 B.C. "**Dead Sea Scrolls**" include each book in the **Pentateuch (Torah)** written in "**Ketav IVRI**" meaning "**Paleo-Hebrew**"! Also, when IVRI is translated into Latin it becomes "**Hebraicus**". This sounds nothing like "**Ib-ree**" but still the Latin Translation resembles the English word "Hebrew". So as we can figure out, the English word "**Hebrew**" is a double-translation from the Hebrew word "**IBRI**".

Remember, in post-exile times the "**Yod**" Hebrew letter was used at the end of a word as a "**vowel indicator**" to indicate that a vowel was inside the word, like "**e**" in the word "**Eber**" from where we get the word "**Hebrew**" from.

- **Ayin** (19th Hebrew Letter) – The Hebrew **Ayin** is normally Silent, but in the front of a word it gives the "**E**" or "**I**" pronunciation. So we get the "**I**" in "**IVRI**" from this letter and the "**E**" in "**Eber**". They Ayin letter on the end of a word is usually silent or is characterized with the pronunciation of "**a(h)**".

- **Be(i)t** (2nd Hebrew Letter) – The **Bet** gives the "**B**" pronunciation, but is usually synonymous with the letter (**E/V**) in English. So we get the "**V**" in "**IVRI**" or the "**B**" in the original Hebrew word "**IBRI**"and the letter "**B**" in "**Eber**".
- **Re(i)sh** (25th Hebrew Letter) – The **Resh** gives the "**R**" pronunciation, and is synonymous with the letter "**R**" in English. So we get the "**R**" in "**IVRI/IBRI**" and the letter "**R**" in "**Eber**".
- **Yod** (10th Hebrew Letter) – Because Paleo-Hebrew doesn't have vowels; the Yod at the end of a word is used as a "**vowel indicator**". If we didn't have the **Yod** letter at the end we would just have "**EBR**" without the vowel "**E**" just like the word "**Nimrod**" is usually spelled "**NMRD**" or "**NRD**" in Ancient Hebrew. In this case the **vowel** it's indicating is the letter "**E**" and its "**E**" pronunciation. The **Yod** is also synonymous with the English letter "**I**" from the Hebrew "**Y**". So this gives us "**Eber**".
- **Samekh** (18th Hebrew Letter) – gives the "**S**" pronunciation when used at the end of a word. So when it it's on the end of "**Ayin-Bet-Resh-Yod**" it turns the word "**Eber**" into "**Ebers**" or "**Hebrews**".

So in conclusion we have:

ע Ayin   E

בּ Bet   B

י Yod   E (vowel indicator)

ר Resh   R

ס Samekh S

This equals = Eber + S (Samekh) = Ebers or Hebrews. WOW!

The **Root** of the word "**Hebrew-Ibri**" (**Strong's #5680**)" spelled Ayin-Bet-Resh-Yod or (IBRI/IVRI) is "**Eber/Abar**" (**Strong's #5674**) spelled "**Ayin-Bet-Resh**" which means "**to cross over**" which the Hebrews did during their passage across the Red Sea into Sinai Peninsula.

So let's get back to what the people of **West Africa** were calling themselves: "**Erh-verh** or **Eyverh**" pronounced "**ib-ree**" just like it is in the Hebrew Language. Again, the Hebrew word for a "**Hebrew**" or "**Israelite**" is **Hebrew Strong's #5680** "**Ibri**" or "**IBRI**" or like the Europeans used to say "**IVRI**". The Hebrew word for a "Hebrew" person is יִעְבְרִ, **pronounced** (**eevriy or ib-ree**), which comes from the root word עָבַר (**abar/ebar**) which means "**to cross over**."

The West Africans pronounced this word as "**Eyverh**" which they were saying as a **Hebrew word** for "**Hebrew**". Amazing! In 1844 what used to be called "**Eyverh land**" was thereafter known as the **Slave Coast (Volta are to Nigeria)** on maps. During this time in the 1800's the land was also divided into Togo, Benin and Nigeria. In the 1900's the Gold Coast became known as Ghana. It is a known fact that the "Ewe" people in Ghana were known to speak a dialect which closely resembled "Hebrew". Many of the local tribes in Ghana even suggested that they were Jews. They had Hebrew cultural practices/traditions and even had Hebrew Old Testament names such as **Yacob** (Jacob), **Yusef/Yosef** (Joseph) and **Miriam** (Mary). Some of the Ewe people celebrate **Rosh Hashanah** (Feast of Trumpets-September) and the **Passover (**April). The Ewe people are mostly located in Ghana, Togo, Benin and Yorubaland (Nigeria). Arab writers **Ahmad Baba** in his text "**Mi'raj al-su'ud**" (1627 A.D.) and **Mohammed Bello** (1837 A.D.) in his "**Infaku'l Maisuri (The Wages of the Fortunate)**" stated that the Yarba (Ewe) people lived in the Soudan. The Land mass known as Soudan (Soodan) in those days stretched from West Africa to East Africa.

The name of one of Abraham's ancestors was עברי (**Genesis 11:16**, written as **Eber** in English translations). This name also comes from the same root word proving that Eber is the father (progenitor) of the **eevriy** (**Hebrew**) people.

Fact 1: *It is said that the "Ewe" and "Ga" people were sold in the Transatlantic slave trade by the "Akan" people in Ghana. The Ewe and Ga people were also considered Hebrew Israelites. The Akan chiefs have publicly apologized for their role in the Slave Trades, even coming to America to the 1990's and designating a grant of land in Ghana called **Fihankra** for African-Americans that wanted to make the diaspora back to Africa.*

THE WEST AFRICAN ISRAELITE CONNECTION
(1000 A.D. - 1600 A.D.): PRE-SLAVERY.

There are many African Tribes in Mali, Gambia, and Senegal to name a few who were once Jewish. Researching old family records of their grandparents they were able to find out that **Karaite Judaism** was being practiced by their tribe generations ago. After the rise of Islam and the invasions of the Black Muslims and Arab Muslims into Africa, many of these tribes converted to Islam. Two such tribes with Hebraic roots is the **Maasai Tribe** from Tanzania that resides near Mount Kilimanjaro and the **Kurya Tribe** in the Mara region of Tanzania who practice circumcision. Genetically they are part Bantus and part Nilotic. There are many other African Tribes and countries that were once were Jewish, came from a Hebrew/Israelites lineage or had Jewish populations, but after the Muslim religious invasions of such places in Africa many of these tribes have converted to Islam (**just as the bible prophecies**).

Deuteronomy 28:36 "The Lord shall bring thee and thy King which thou shalt set over thee, unto a nation which neither thou nor thy fathers have known; AND THERE SHALT THOU SERVE OTHER GODS, WOOD AND STONE."

Mali, Africa

Israel, the Vatican and Islamic Arabs have tried over the years to hide, manipulate or destroy any evidence linking Black Africans to the Ancient Hebrew Israelites. Sadly, they have failed. Some manuscripts written in Hebrew were found in different parts of Black Africa in Mali, some dating back to the 1200's during the time of the rule of Black Mali Emperor **Mansa Musa**. In fact, in 2013 the **Arutz Sheva Israel Nation News** reported the following heading: "**Erasing History: Ancient Timbuktu Manuscripts, One Written in Hebrew, Torched by Malian Islamists.**" It reported:

> "**It was found that Radical Black Islamic Terrorists attempting to overthrow the Malian Government torched the South African-funded Ahmed Baba Institute where the Hebrew documents were kept as they fled the ancient city of Timbuktu. The Library, which contained thousands of priceless manuscripts from ancient times, was put to the torch as the rebels fled the French and Malian Troops who were closing in on the Saharan city. At least one of the manuscripts buried beneath the sand in a cave for centuries in wooden trunks and boxes, was written in Hebrew.**"

Now the question is, what are Hebrew Manuscripts doing in Africa if the Ashkenazi Jews all say that the Israelites scattered to Europe changing from black to white? There are no communities of European Jews living in Mali, Africa. How can a Black nation all turn white? How can a white nation turn Black? The sun has nothing to do with the color of our skin when we are born so this means that someone is lying. In addition it has been recorded that in the 1400's, many Black Jews were forced to convert to Islam by Black Muslim Caliphate ruler **Askia Muhammad**.

> **The King (Askia the Great) is a declared enemy of the Jews. He will not allow any to live in the city (Gao/Timbuktu). If he hears it said that a Berber merchant frequents them or does business with them, he confiscates his goods.**"
> *Askia Muhammad – Muslim Emperor of the Songhai Empire from 1493-1528 A.D.*

Were these "**Jews**" living in Mali in the 1400's European Ashkenazi Jews? Absolutely not! I have never met an European Ashkenazi Jew from Mali, Africa. There is even more proof that the Black Hebrew Israelites living during the rise of

Islam in Africa were captured by the Black Muslims and from Africa sold to slavemerchants all across the world.

"In the whole land of **Lam-Lem** (Nigeria-Cameroon-Niger) there are but two small cities, or as it were villages, and those are Malel and Dau, situated at the distance of four days journey from each other. Their inhabitants, as people of these parts relate, are **JEWS**, most of them unbelieving and ignorant."
Arab Cartographer Al-Idrisi of Andalusia, Spain – Book "Description of Central Africa"

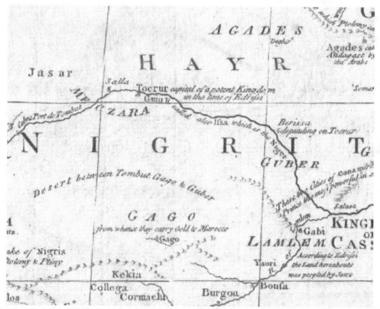

Kingdom of Lam-Lem (Bottom right). Note how the Niger River flows Through the area known as "Nigritia/Negroland" and down into Lam-Lem. Based on the landmarks of the Niger River, (Meczara-upper left and Guber-middle right) we can assume that Lam-Lem was modern day Benin/Togo, Nigeria, and Niger since Lam-Lem is below Guber. The Niger River ends in the Niger Delta area off the Gulf of Guinea (Atlantic Ocean).

Based on Al-Idrifsi's maps and older maps of "Negroland in 1747", Lam-Lem is below Guber. This is where the "Slave Coast" land is which is now Benin/Togo and Nigeria.   Note: Guber is below the Niger River under the words "ola" of "Negroland" on the Map.

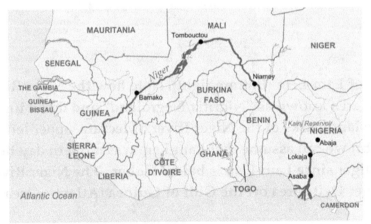

Niger River flows from Guinea/Sierra Leone through Mali into Nigeria and then into the Atlantic Ocean (Bight of Biafra). Older Cartographers (map makers) sometimes were off when drawing the course of the Niger River.

"When any of the inhabitants of the **Kingdom of Lam-Lem (Jews)** comes to have the use of his reason, **he is burnt in the face and temples**; this they do to distinguish each other. All their countries and dominions are near a certain river (**Niger River**), flowing to the Nile (**via Tributaries**). It is not known whether there is any inhabited place to the south of the Kingdom of Lam-Lem (**possibly referring to Congo, Gabon, Angola**). That kingdom joins on the west to Meczara (**Mali, Burkina Faso, Guinea**), on the east to Vancara/Wanagara (**East Nigeria/Cameroon/Chad**), on the north to the **Old Ghana** (Empire), and on the south to the desert; and its people use a **DIFFERENT LANGUAGE (Hebrew)** from those of Meczara and Ghana."

12th Century Arab Historian and Cartographer Al-Idrisi, Spain – Book "Description of Central Africa"

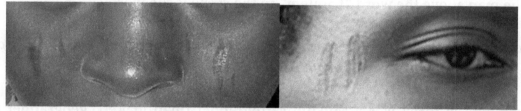

West African Tribal facial marks (Face and Temples).

Fact: It is a known fact that many West Africans (**Nigerian Igbo's, Nigerian Yoruba's, Hausas, Southern Ghana Akan/Ewe, Northern Ghana**) have tribal marks on their faces, cheeks or temples. Could this be a Black Hebrew Israelite tradition done to distinguish Black Israelites from other neighboring Hamitic Tribes? In *Nana Banchie Darkwa's* book **"The Africans who wrote the Bible"**, it talks about how the Ewe and Akan people of Ghana were Black Hebrews who migrated from Israel/Middle East (also Asia) to West Africa. These Ewe/Akan people later would settle into the Ancient Kingdoms of Ghana, Mali and Songhai during the times of the Black Kings **Sonni Ali** and **Askia Muhammad**. After persecution for being Israelites some would convert to Islam while some would flee **"Negroland"** to the Coastline areas of West Africa, from where the **Transatlantic slave trade** would take place.

The land of Wangara is to the East of Lam-Lem. This would be East Nigeria or Igboland. West Nigeria would be Yorubaland.

On the map above the word "Lamlem" in the circle is the words"

"According to Edrifsi (al-Idrisi) the Land hereabouts was peopled by JEWS, from whence are brought GOLD, SENA and SLAVES."

Muhammad al-Idrisi was a Muslim cartographer (map maker), geographer and Egyptologist. He incorporated the knowledge of Africa, the Indian Ocean and the Far East gathered by Islamic merchants /explorers into making maps.

"To the southward (probably southeastward) of Berissa, at the distance of ten days march, lies the **land of Lam-Lem**, into which incursions (**invasions**) are made by the inhabitants of Berissa (**Mende-Sierra Leone/Liberia**), Salla, **TARKUR**/Fulani (**Takrur = Senegal/Gambia, Fulani = North Nigeria**), and Ghana (**Old Mali Ghana Empire**); **there they take numbers of captives**, whom they carry away to their **OWN COUNTRIES**, and dispose of to the merchants (slavemerchants) trading thither; these afterwards sell them into **ALL PARTS OF THE WORLD."**
Muhammad al-Idrisi of Andalusia, Spain in his book – "Description of Central Africa"

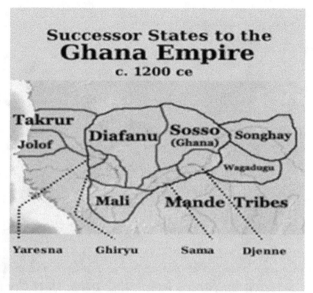

Takrur is in the Area of Senegal/Mauritania. Fulani is one of the largest Ethnic groups in Africa. Their significant populations are in Nigeria, Guinea, Cameroon, Senegal, Mali, Niger, Burkina Faso, Sudan, and Chad but they are spread all across the former African territory called "Negroland". The Old Ghana Empire is parts of Mali, Mauritania, and Senegal. Jolof/Wolof is a Tribe common in Gambians/Senegal.

"In Garura there were some very rich Jews. The intervention of the preacher (Muhammad al-Maghili) of Tlemcen set up pillage of their goods, and most of them have been killed by the population. This even took place during the same year when the Jews had been expels (during the Spanish Inquisition along with the Black Moors) from Spain and Sicily by the Catholic King."
Leo Africanus -1526

HERE IS MORE PROOF THAT THE SOME OF THE BLACK HEBREW ISRAELITES IN AFRICA EVENTUALLY CONVERTED TO ISLAM! JUST AS THE BIBLE PROPHECIED.

1850 Map of West Africa by James Rennell. Notice that the land known of "Guinea" represented the coastline of West Africa where Black Slaves were taken from to the Americas and the Caribbean.

"Whether the natives of the country have the **Jewish distinction** between diaboloi and daimonia in **NORTHERN GUINEA** is not certainly known, but the inhabitants of **SOUTHERN GUINEA** undoubtedly have."

J. Leighton Wilson Western Africa: its history, condition and prospects, 1856 p. 216

In Benin, former area of the Dahomey Empire, Many Black Jews were rounded up at the French slave port Ouidah. When the Portuguese got there in the 1500's and used the Port to pick up slaves they named it "Ajuda". The main language here is French, followed by Fon or Yoruba. For this reason this area is still known on African Maps as the "Slave Coast". In ancient maps, Europeans and Arabs called this place the "Kingdom of Juda(h) or Whidah". Why would name this African territory the "Kingdom of Judah?" It is a known fact that the majority of slaves taken to the Americas were taken from Benin and Nigeria. Is this why some people say that African-Americans are from the Tribe of Judah?

The "Ewe/Togo" people of Dahomey, Benin per **Dr. Melville Herskovitz** of Northwestern University called their Supreme God "**Mawu**", meaning "**Great God**". It was also noted that people of Dahomey followed the idea of purity when approaching and serving God. The ministers wore white cloth. Only virgin women could bring the water used for ritual blessings and the official day of rest was **Saturday**. On Saturday, the people of Dahomey did not work in the fields. Once a year they offered a white lamb as a sacrifice to their God, usually inside an enclosure, outside the village (**like a make-shift tabernacle**). The lamb was raised three times up in the air before being sacrificed. Also in a 1790 edition of the "**Memoirs of the Reign of Bassa Ahadee, King of Dahomey**" by **Robert Norris** a map was portrayed which was a direct eye-witness account by the English and

French. On the map they designated the town of Whydah as the **"Country of the Jews"**. The town is called **"Juda"** or **"Ouidah"**. The Portuguese call this town **"Ajuda"**. The people today in this town still pronounce their town in their native tongue as **"Judah"**.

Fact: An African Hebrew Israelite native of the town **Whydah (Ouidah), Benin** whose name was **"Bata Kindai Amgoza"** wrote in the "Scriber's Magazine Article" **that the "Bnai Ephraim has copies of the Torah kept in a most holy place**.....otherwise they are simply naked Negro people like everyone else." Dr. J. Kreppel in his book about the Jews and Judaism also reported a large Jewish community in the interior of Dahomey. He admits **"They have a central Temple and a Pentateuch (Torah) written in Hebrew/Aramaic letters."** To add more proof to this...**Pierre Bouche**, a French Historian, makes reference to a map by **Jean D'Anville** that states the country of **"Negroes"** was formerly inhabited by **Jews**. He admitted that this was also found in earlier writings in the 11th Century (1000 A.D.) by Spanish Arab explorer **"Muhammad Al-Idrisi"**.

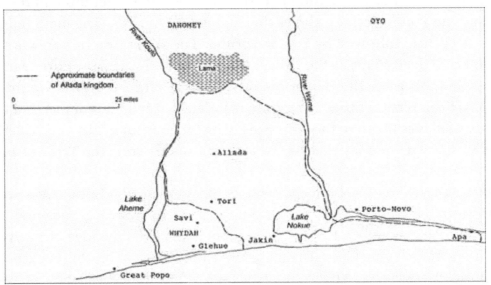

Dahomey Kingdom at top of map, Allada in Central Benin and Whydah near the Coast. The Oyo Kingdom to the East was Yorubaland.

From the 1600's the **Oyo Empire** (Yoruba) was the most powerful and successful of West African kingdoms at the time. The **Allada Kingdom** and the **Abomey (Dahomey) Kingdom** had to pay tribute to the larger Oyo (**Yoruba**) Empire. The Oyo Empire gained direct access to the Slave Trade with the Europeans using the

Coastal **Allada Kingdom**. After conquering the Allada Kingdom they conquered the Jewish town of **Whydah (Ouidah)**. The Oyo King took slaves from all these Kingdoms it would conquer. The King used the slave labor from the slaves it captured during wars on the vast farmlands in its land. Those slaves that were extra bodies not needed for work were sold to the Europeans for guns, cloth, horses, metal goods and cowry shells. The Allada and Dahomey Kingdom were smaller Kingdoms under the Oyo Kingdom who were all in the business of selling slaves (**Israelites**) to the Europeans. So in this sense you had Israelites selling Israelites. When the European Slavetraders found out that the West African Tribes were all fighting each other they were told that the King of Dahomey was willing to trade slaves for $50 from the Kingdom of Whydah (Ouidah). Many of these slaves had Old Testament last names and were sent on slave ships to Alabama, Georgia, South Carolina, North Carolina and Virginia. Sometimes they also used the captured slaves as sacrifices to the King's ancestors. To the West of the Dahomey Empire, the Ashanti (**Akan**) Ghana Empire was also a strong power who also had gained land, gold and slaves they could use to attract Europeans Slavetraders while they expanded their territory inland.

ARE THERE ANY YORUBA ISRAELITE CONNECTIONS?

Yoruba Oranmiyan staff memorial of **Oranmiyan Omoluabi Odede**, founder of the Oyo (**Ile-Ife**) Kingdom (1000 A.D) in Nigeria. **Odudwa** was the first "Divine King" of the Yoruba people. His last son was "**Oranmiyan**". There are even some Oyo Traditions that link Oranmiyan/Oranyan with the descendants of Jacob/Israel. One of Oranmiyan's first children, **Eweke I**, became the first Oba of the Benin (Edo) Empire. The staff is supposedly erected where Oranmiyan died. In ancient Yoruba religion, **Olodurame** (Eledurame) is the Yoruba (Trinity) Creator of the Universe. Odudwa was the Spirit son and founder of Ile-Ife. This Staff which radiocarbon studies date it back to possible B.C. times is about 20 feet tall and has upon one face of it, several spike nails driven into it, and some carvings of ancient characters. The Ancient Carvings were found to be the Hebrew Letters "**Resh**" and "**Yod**" which stand for "**Oranyan**" or the founding city "Ile-Ife" of his people. To the Yoruba's, Ile-Ife is a "Spiritual Mecca/Holy City", the creation point and the gateway to heaven. It was here that man was first created to worship god. According to Yoruba theology, over time all divinities (spirits & religions) came from this city and spread all across the world. On the Oramiyan staff, Resh in Paleo-Hebrew means "**First, Top, Beginning**". "Yod" in Paleo-Hebrew means "**Worship, work, throw**". Oludurame (the Creator) named the earth "**Ile-Ife**", or "the sacred house".

Oduduwa/Oranmiyan named the city in Yorubaland, Nigeria "Ile-Ife" as they believed that city was like the "Garden of Eden" of man. The Yoruba's refer to Lord as "**Oluwa (Kind of like Yahuah)**". They also refer to the Creator as "**Eleda**", similar to the Hebrew word for Creator "**Eloah**" or "**Elohim**". The Yoruba people and their religion has been spread across the world to Argentina, Brazil, Cuba, Colombia, Dominican Republic, Puerto Rico, Trinidad & Tobago, Uruguay, Venezuela and other parts of the Americas all thanks to slavery.

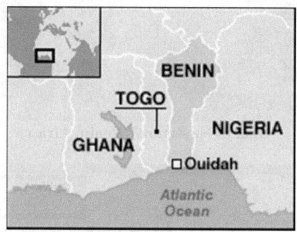

Benin, Africa and the French Slave Port Ouidah. Even today the Black Natives in Ouidah pronounce their city as "Judah".

"Door of No Return" Slave Port overlooking the Atlantic Ocean, Benin, Africa

This is the walkway the chained slaves took to the slaveships before leaving for the Americas on the Atlantic Ocean.

"Door of No Return", Benin, Africa

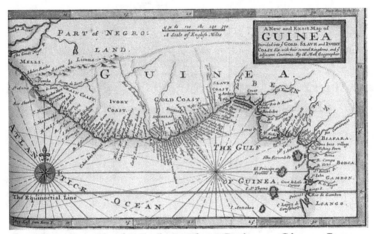

Old Guinea Proper consisted of Modern day Guinea, Sierra Leone, Liberia, Ivory Coast, Ghana, Benin/Togo, Nigeria, Cameroon, Gabon and West Congo-Map of Africa 1600's. Southern Guinea is closer to the coasts from where millions of "Negro Slaves" were taken to the Americas.

Guinea Proper was not changed to our modern-day Guinea (French) until the 1890's. Muslims controlled this Western part of Guinea during medieval times. Fulani Muslims then migrated to Futa (Fouta) Jallon in Central Guinea and established an Islamic State from 1735-1898. Prior to this the Black Muslims were selling Israelite Slaves to the European slavetraders. Of course they were not selling Muslims, they were selling Black Israelites. Per Islamic law it is forbidden for a Muslim to have Muslim Slaves so the slaves being sold were slaves that practiced Biblical Judaism.

Rev. J. LEIGHTON WILSON, D.D.

Reverend John Leighton Wilson (1809-1886)

"Mixed up with these pagan nations and customs (**Animism, Islam**) there are many obvious traces of Judaism (**Karaite**), both in **NORTHERN AND SOUTHERN GUIINEA**; and in the latter, **some undoubted traces of a corrupted form of Christianity**, which have probably traveled across the continent from Ancient Ethiopia, where Christianity was once firmly established."

J. Leighton Wilson, "Western Africa: its history, condition and prospects, 1856 p. 220

J. Leighton Wilson was a missionary in Guinea for 18 years. His book "**Western Africa: It's History, Condition and Prospects was published in 1856**. He noted:

"In Northern Guinea paganism and Judaism are united. The Northern region, the practice of Judaism is prominently developed, some of the leading features of which is **circumcision**, the **division of tribes** into separate families, and very frequently into **the number twelve, blood sacrifices** with the **sprinkling of blood upon the altars and door-posts** and other usages which he classifies of Jewish origin."

Dr. William Bosman wrote a book called "**A New and Accurate Description of the Coast of Guinea**," Originally his collection of letters , originally written in Dutch and first published in English in 1705, describes the geography and natural history of the coast of Guinea. Bosman was born in 1672 and went to Africa at the age of sixteen in the service of the **Dutch West India Company**, and spent fourteen years on the Gold Coast. The collection of letters, written to his uncle in the Netherlands, is an important source of information from the 1600's to the late 1700's. In his book it talks about his travels to Guinea which says: "**The Negroes still retain several laws and customs which favour of Judaism, as their marrying of their brother's wife and several more. They seem the same in effect, as well as the names, of which here in Guinea are several which occur in the Old Testament."**

WEST AFRICANS, NEW MOONS AND THE SABBATH? HOW CAN THIS BE? THESE ARE ISREALITE CUSTOMS.

Mungo Park (1771-1806)

Mungo Park in his book, "**Travels in the Interior Districts of Africa**", written in 1810, observes the legal whippings among the **Teesee people** in the Kasson (**Burkina Faso**) region. He says, "**the number of stripes was precisely the same as**

are required by Mosaic Law, forty, save one (based on Deuteronomy 25:3)" He notes further that these people were neither Christian nor Muslim at the time." Park also notes reference to the **Sabbath** in that **"on the first appearance of the new moon, the natives say a short prayer....to the Supreme Being. This prayer is pronounced in a whisper, the party holding up his hands before his face. This ceremony seems to be nearly the same which prevailed among the Hebrews in the days of Job."**

This is in the Old Testament as well:

Isaiah 66:23 "And it shall come to pass, **THAT FROM ONE NEW MOON TO ANOTHER, AND FROM ONE SABBATH TO ANOTHER, SHALL ALL FLESH COME TO WORSHIP ME, SAITH THE LORD."**

Colossians 2:16 " Let no man therefore judge you in meat, or in drink, or in respect of any **Holy Day**, or of the **NEW MOON**, or of the **SABBATH DAYS**."

Ezekiel 46:1 "Thus saith the Lord; The gate of the inner court that looketh toward the east shall be "shut" the "six working days;" but on the "Sabbath" it shall be opened, "and" in the day of the "**new moon**" it shall be opened."

So here we have 3 sets of days. **Ordinary work days, New Moon days and Sabbath days**. In Ancient Israelite times, the 1st day of the week began **after** the New Moon or Sabbath Worship day. The Natural Eye cannot see a New Moon during the New Moon day, but the day after you can see the beginning of the Lunar cycle which would (without an official calendar or paper) start the 1st day. The Israelites used the day after the New Moon to start the month and used the First Quarter Moon, the Full Moon, the Last (Third) Quarter moon and the New Moon to known when the Sabbath days are.

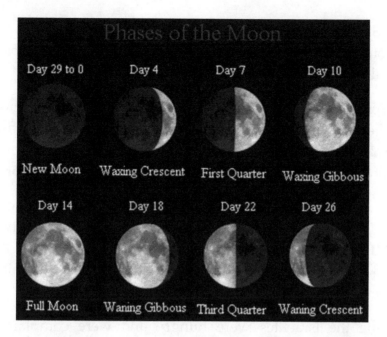

The day prior to the New Moon and the day after the New Moon signaled the end of the **Sabbath** and beginning of the month. The Ancient Israelites didn't have a **Gregorian calendar**. They didn't have papers with stuff written down each month with 28 days, 30 days and 31 days like our modern day calendar. The Israelites operated under a 29 Lunar-day cycle because the New Moon came every 29 days. Day 0-1 was the New Moon. 7 days later (**Day 8**) was the Sabbath. 7 days after that (**Day 15**) was the Sabbath. 7 days after that (**Day 22**) was another Sabbath. 7 days after this (**Day 29**) was the last Sabbath of the month. This is the way they could keep the Sabbath 4 times in this Lunar Cycle without a calendar. The New Moon signified a "**New Month**" and a celebration. This is why the Israelites under Moses in the wilderness observed the Sabbath on the 15th day of the Second Month and on the 22nd day. The **Gregorian calendar** gave us set days and since then changed the Sabbath days to a specific day: **Saturday**.

Genesis 1:14 "Then God said, "Let there be lights in the firmament of the heavens to divide the day from the night; and let them be for **SIGNS** and **SEASONS**, and for **DAYS** and **YEARS**."

Psalms 104 "He appointed the **MOON FOR SEASONS**: the sun knoweth his going down."

Leviticus 23:2-3 "Speak unto the Children of Israel, and say unto them, Concerning the feasts of the Lord, which ye shall proclaim to be holy convocations, even these are my feasts. **Six days shall work be done: but the seventh day is the Sabbath of rest**, an holy convocation; ye shall do no work therein: it is the Sabbath of the Lord in all your dwellings."

Based on the Scriptures in ancient time, the weekly Sabbaths were determined by the phases of the moon and not a count of one through seven. The first appearance of the word "**Sabbath**" which in Hebrew means "**Rest**" or "**Cessation**" is in Exodus 16 on the day of rest and cessation of Manna for the Israelites. See for yourself:

Exodus 16:1-2 "And they took their journey from Elim, and all the congregation of the children of Israel came unto the wilderness of Sin, which is between Elim and Sinai, on the **FIFTEENTH DAY OF THE SECOND MONTH** after their departing out of the land of Egypt. And the whole congregation of the children of Israel murmured against Moses and Aaron in the Wilderness:"

During this time the Israelites were hungry and were complaining. So God answered their complaints.

Exodus 16:4-5 "Then said the Lord unto Moses, Behold, I will rain bread from heaven for you; and the people shall go out and gather a certain rate **EVERY DAY**, that I may prove them, whether they will walk in my law, or not. And it shall come to pass that on the **SIXTH DAY** they shall prepare that which they bring in; and it shall be **TWICE AS MUCH AS THEY GATHER DAILY**. "

The day prior to the Sabbath was a day of "**PREPARATION**" because the next day (Sabbath) they could not do any work.

The Israelites murmured (complained) so God gave them **Manna** (bread) and **Quail** (bird/hen). They were instructed to gather only what they needed for the day and not any more until the sixth day in preparation for the Sabbath, otherwise the food would spoil or breed worms (**Exodus 16:20**).

Exodus 16:21-26 "And they gathered it every morning, every man according to his eating: and when the sun waxed hot, it melted. And it came to pass, that on the **SIXTH DAY** they gathered **TWICE AS MUCH BREAD**, two omers for one man: and all the rulers of the congregation came and told Moses. And he said unto them, This is that which the Lord hath said, **TOMORROW (22ND DAY)** is the rest of the **Holy Sabbath** unto the Lord: back that which ye will bake today, and seeth that ye will seeth; and that which remaineth over lay up for you to be kept until the morning. And they laid it up (the food) till the morning, as Moses bade: and it did not stink, neither was there any worm therein." And Moses said, Eat that today; for today is a **SABBATH** unto the Lord: today ye shall not find it in the field. **SIX DAYS ye shall gather it; but on the seventh day (8th, 15th, 22nd and 29th day) which is the Sabbath, in it there shall be none."**

The Lunar Sabbath is one of the most provable documented occurrences of when the Sabbath was meant to be kept for the wandering, nomadic Israelites of old. These Lunar Sabbaths were also kept Holy by the Black Hebrew Israelites living in Africa. These Black Jews didn't travel all the way to Eastern Europe to learn Judaism from the European Khazars converts called "Jews". It was a part of their past heritage.   Lunar Sabbaths can be proven from the scriptures, but mathematically, historically, scientifically and by nature itself. Based on the Lunar Calendar, there are seventy-two (72) weekly Sabbath days and every one of them was based on the 8th, 15th, 22nd and 29th day of the Moon's Lunar Cycle. The Israelite never counted the New Moon as a "worship day" when counting out the six "working days."

So do we need proof that the Israelites after the death and resurrection of the "Christ" still followed this law of God? Let's take a look! Christian Churches state that after Jesus died and was resurrected the new "Sabbath day" was changed to "Sunday". Let's see what Jesus (Yeshua's) disciples did after the resurrection and "**Day of Pentecost**".

Remember in the Book of Acts Chapter 2, the Holy Spirit (Comforter) fell on the Galileans in the Upper Room on the day of Pentecost.

Acts 2:6-8 "Now when this was noised abroad, the multitude came together, and were confounded, because that every man heard them speak in his own language. And they were marveled, saying one to another, **Behold, are not all these which speak Galilaeans?** And how hear we every man in our own tongue, wherein we were born?"

Acts 13:42 "And when the Jews were gone out of the synagogue, the Gentiles besought that these words might be preached to them **the next Sabbath**."

Acts 18:1 "After these things Paul departed from Athens (Greece), and came to Corinth (Greece);"

Acts 18:4 "And he (**Apostle Paul**) reasoned in the synagogue **EVERY SABBATH**, and persuaded the Jews and the Greeks."

Acts 18:11 "And **he continued there a year and six months**, teaching the word of God among them."

Paul after receiving the Holy Ghost in Acts 2:38 continued to observe all 78 Sabbaths for that year and a half. Not once in the Gospels, or in the whole New Testament, did Yeshua (Jesus) Christ even mention the first day of the week (Sunday), or declare it the new day of rest (Lord's Day) to replace the Saturday Sabbath and not once in the New Testament were the Apostles gathered together in worship on a Sunday for the declared purpose of honoring the resurrection. Even in Revelation 1:10 it shows that John observed the Sabbath as it reads:

Revelation 1:10 "I was in the Spirit on the **LORD'S DAY**, and heard behind me a great voice, as of a trumpet.

Matthew 12:8 "For the Son of Man is **Lord** even of the **SABBATH DAY**."

This is also in Mark 2:28 and Luke 6:5. In the Old Testament in Exodus 20:10 and Leviticus 23:3.

Now **Rabbi Kaufman Kohler** in a Jewish Encyclopedia on the "**New Moon**" states that the period of the New Moon in pre-diaspora (exile) time of the Israelites... was superior even to the Sabbath day which formed but a part of it, but lost its importance during the Exile (586 B.C.). He also says in this article that "**in the Temple, the New Moon was celebrated by special sacrifices and by the blowing of the trumpet.**"

Over time, the people in West Africa near **Guinea Proper/Negroland** were introduced to European White-inspired Christianity with the complete Holy Bible (Old Testament/New Testament) modified by the Catholic Church. European Christianity brought the teachings of worshipping on Sunday, using the **WOODEN CROSS** as the symbol of Christianity, and believing in the image of a white man with blue eyes as the Messiah (Christ). They taught that our black skin was the "**Curse of Canaan**" and that from this curse we were destined by God to be slaves. They taught that if we endured the harsh conditions of slavery serving our white earthly masters we would receive our reward in heaven when we died. Just like in the movie "**12 Years a Slave**" European Caucasian Slavemasters preached the word to the black slaves on Sunday and then raped the black female slaves on Monday. The slaves were forced to learn the bible and its teachings through oral teachings of slavemasters since they didn't know how to read.   Since the slaves respected the authority of the slavemasters they never questioning what they were told or what they were shown as the image of God. Like some Black Christians do today, the Black Slaves took everything the white Pastor said as truth, not questioning how everything in the Bible was white, when the Bible is centered out of hot Africa and the Middle East.

Many African tribes in the past were following the laws of the Torah such as circumcision on the 8th day, naming newborn babies on the 8th day, animal sacrifices, food/drink offerings, preserving the firstborn male livestock, not eating unclean meat, honoring the Sabbath, uncleanliness of menstruation and the marrying of a widow to the brother of the deceased spouse. Over time, younger generations have lost some of these passed down Hebrew traditions, but it is still not lost. The practice of Ancient Hebrew traditions seen in African Tribes today proves that our earlier forefathers were worshipping the God of Moses and Abraham before being introduced to Islam or European Christianity.   Only Hebrews followed Hebrew laws and traditions. Only the Hebrews worshipped "One Supreme God" in B.C. times.   So this means that our Ancient African forefathers knew these traditions because they must have been of Hebrew Israelite stock.

THE NIGER RIVER, SENEGAL RIVER, NILE RIVER AND EUPHRATES RIVER WERE BLACK HEBREW ISRAELITE TERRITORIES.

To make things more interesting, the people in the **Ancient Ghana-Songhai Kingdom** in 700 A.D. recorded that they were actually descendants of the Hebrew Israelites who had migrated from Israel into Arabia/East Africa eventually ending up in West Africa. This was shown by extracts from the **Hausa records (Northern Nigeria, Niger, Chad, Sudan, Ethiopia)**, of which many original manuscripts were destroyed. In these records it revealed that some of the Hebrew Israelites in West Africa were known by the name "**Towrood or Taurud people**" and the "**Soninke/Sarankaly people**".   Many of the West African Hebrew Israelites possessed records that stated their ancestors coming from the territory lying between the **Nile River** and the **River Euphrates** (Land between two rivers). This is also supported in the bible.

Genesis 15:18 "**In the same day the Lord made a covenant with Abram, saying Unto thy seed have I given this land, from the river Egypt (Nile River) unto the Great River, the river Euphrates.**"

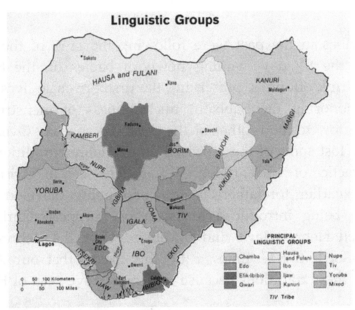

The Hausa people live in Northern Nigeria. The Hausa Language is also spoken in the Ivory Coast, Chad, Sudan, Ethiopia, Niger, Nigeria, Benin, Togo, and Ghana where there is still over 10,000 Hausas.

Genesis 15:18 "In the same day the Lord made a covenant with Abram, saying, Unto thy seed have it given this land, from the **river of Egypt (Nile River)** unto the **Great River, the river Euphrates.**"

Muhammed Bello, Second Sultan of the Sokoto Caliphate (1815-1837 A.D.)

Muhammed Bello was the second Black Muslim Sultan of Sokoto and reigned from 1815 until 1837 and was an active writer of history, poetry, and Islamic studies. He was the son and primary aide to **Usman dan Fodio**, the founder of the **Sokoto Caliphate** and first Sultan. Following the Fulani War, the Sokoto Caliphate was one of the larges states in Africa and included large populations of both Fulani and Hausa.

Sokoto Caliphate – Nigeria. 1800's

Muhammed Bello quoted: The **Towrood** or **Taurud people**, it is said, **WERE ORIGINALLY JEWS** (Black Jews), others say Christians; that they came from the **land between the two rivers, the Nile and the Euphrates**, and established

447

themselves next to the **Jews who inhabited the island (Cape Verde islands)**; and that whenever they oppressed or encroached upon the Jews, the latter had always recourse to the protection of the officers of the Sehabat (Friends of Muhammed Bello), who then ruled over them. "This is what we found written in our books." – **Journal of a Second Expedition into the Interior of Africa, from the Bight of Benin to Sokoto, 1829. London: Forgotten Books.**

So where were these Towrood/Taurud or Soninke people living at in Africa?

Senegal River Valley Area composes of parts of Senegal, Guinea, Mali and Mauritania.

Muhammed Bello also stated on page 337 of the book entitled "– **Journal of a Second Expedition into the Interior of Africa, from the Bight of Benin to Sokoto"**, *1829* that the **Towrood** or **Taurud** and the **Soninke people** ruled and inhabited parts of the territory of **Malee (Guinea)**. He also quoted in the book "**Traditional Account of different Nations of Africa**" the location and migration whereabouts of the Sarankaly or Soninke people as well. He states the following about their origins:

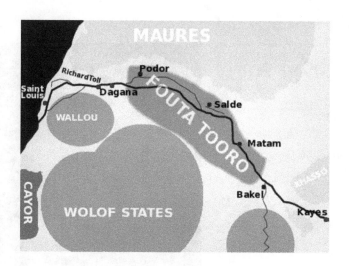

"Near to Bambara (**Timbuktu, Mali**), there is the province of the **Towrood**, and that of the Foot (**Senegal River Valley Area traditionally known as Fouta, Futa Toora or the Foota**), which are extensive, inhabited by their own people and by those of **Sanakaly** or **Soninke** also called "**Ajam**" meaning "**Alien or Foreigner**". This region is known as modern day **Senegal, Gambia, and Mauritania**. The **Fouta Tooro** was in the North, while the **Fouta Jallon** was in the South consisting of modern day Guinea and Sierra Leone.

In this 1850 Map the "Soninke (Gadiaga) area" is at the upper left part of the map near the Senegal River in the land know known as Senegal. Senegal also has slave ports, especially on Goree Island outside of Dakar. President Obama also visited the Slave Ports in Senegal with his entire family in 2013.

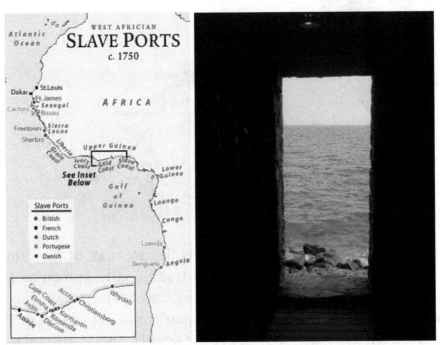

Door of No Return – Senegal Slave Port in Darkar, Senegal. Doorway looking to the Atlantic Ocean where the slaves were taken to the Americas and the Caribbean.

The **Kingdom of Malee/Mali (Guinea portion-not actual Mali)** is an ancient and flourishing country, and comprises **two** other provinces: one is Bambara (Timbuktu, Mali), which contains rivers, woods, sands, a gold mine, and is occupied by the **Soodan (Soudan)-(Oyo, Akan and Mandingo people)**, who are still infidels (foreigners/strangers), and possess great power; the other, on the West of it, is **Foota (Senegal, Gambia, Guinea, Sierra Leone)**, which is inhabited by the **Towrood (Taurud)**, and the **Soninke or (Ajam-foreigners)**. -Journal of a Second Expedition into the Interior of Africa."

The Fouta (Futa) Empire ruled West Africa and converted many of the Mende/Mandingo/Mandinka/Wolof African people to Islam starting in the 16th century. During the 16th, 17th, and 18th Century many Senegal-Gambians were sent to the Americas as slaves.

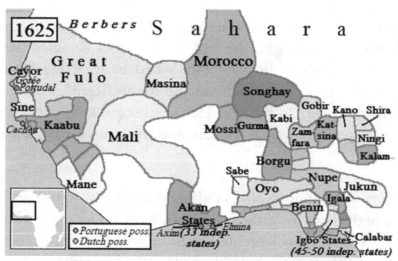

Many people from Ghana, Benin, Togo and Nigeria (Yoruba) who are from the coast are Akan and Oyo (Ewe). Many Gambians are Mandingo or Wolof.

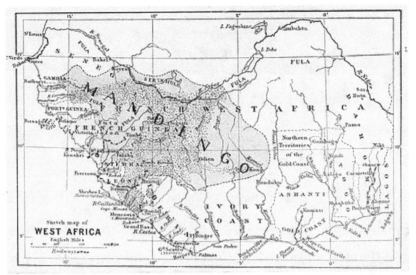

The Mandingo/Mandinka Tribe are located in Senegal-Gambia, Guinea, Mali and Ivory Coast. Over 90% of them are Muslim. Famous African-Americans with Mandinka/Mandingo roots are reported to be Alex Haley and the Rapper Black Thought from the Roots.

How about more proof? **Leo Africanus** was a 15th century Andalusian (Spanish) White Arab Berber. This is what he had to say about some of the Hebrews he encountered in his travels in the late 1400's and early 1500's before the White Ottoman Empire Arabs under "**Suleiman the Magnificent**" would take over the area now known as **Libya**. In the mid-1500's Suleiman took over North Africa all the way West to Algeria as well as Yemen, and the Horn of Africa with help from the Somalians.

"Howbeit they say that upon **Nilus (Nile)** do inhabit two great and populous nations, one of the Jews towards the West (**Libya**), under the government of a mighty king." **The Hebrew Israelite Kingdom** with a mighty king to the right (West) of the Nile River was called "**Kouko**"
Leo Africanus 1400's: The Description of Africa Volume 1. Pg. 32.

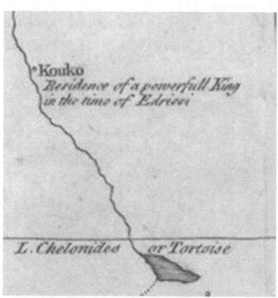

(1747 African Map by Sr. Danville) Lake Chelonides by the Greeks was said to be connected to the River Gir. The River Gir was in Libya, flowing between the Usurgala Mountains and the Garamantes Mountains. This would mean the Hebrew Kingdom of Kouko was in Libya, Africa.

Map of North Central Africa from Book- "Geographical and Commercial View of Northern Central Africa"
By James McQueen.

As you can see the River Gir flows between the Usurgala Mountains and the Garamantes Mountains. One branch of the River Gir makes Lake Chelonides (North of Lake Nuba) on the map. Cyrene (at the top of the map) is a city in Libya. Based on the original map previously seen this would mean that there were some Israelites in Libya before the conquest/Invasion of the Ottoman Turks in the 16th Century.

454

It is in this portion of Africa that the greatest rivers flow, greater, as Ptolemy must mean, than any other which flowed in the northern division of that continent. In the middle of the country, says he, the greatest rivers display themselves, viz. the Gir, joining together the Usargala mountain and the Garamantican barrier or rampart. One branch of this river makes the Lake Chelonides, in 20° North Lat. and 49° East Long. (21° East Long. from Greenwich,) and another the Lake Nuba in

"Geographical and Commercial View of Northern Central Africa"
By James McQueen.

Again this is proof that Lake Chelonides is in Libya. So if the Hebrew Kingdom of Kouka was North of this Lake on the previous map then this would mean that this Hebrew Kingdom was in Libya. Many of the Black Libyans were removed from Libya after Libyan president Gaddafi was killed. Prior to this, there were many Black Libyans, the question is.....was any of them Israelites whose past ancestors converted to Islam?

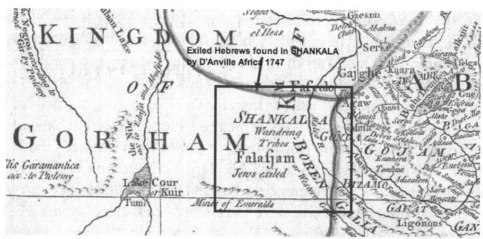

(Outlined in the box), the Shankala Wandering Tribes of the Falafjam Jews (possibly Falashas) whom were exiled. According to this map the Falafjam Jews were exiled to Sudan. Take note that the area known as "Gojam" to the right was

located in Abyssinia (Ethiopia). **This confirms that these Black Jews were living in Sudan as exiles.** Al-Idrisi mentioned that the Hebrews in this area and adjacent cites called the "Malel" and "Dau" were attacked by Native Hamite African Tribes and sent to Slave Traders who then sent them to Slave Trading Centers to be traded to **ALL PARTS OF THE WORLD.**

The city of **Gojam** on both maps is in the Country of Abyssinia/Ethiopia. This further proves the **Falafjam Jews** were exiled into Sudan.

Fact 1: In 1853 the German scholar and explorer Heinrich Barth visited Timbuktu on behalf of the British government. During his stay he consulted a copy of the **"Tarikh al-Sudan"** and the **"Tarikh al-fattash"** in his investigation of the history of the **Songhay Hebrew Israelite Empire.** The **Tarikh al-Sudan** and the **Tarikh al-Fattash** are West African chronicles written in Arabic in the second half of the 17th century (1600's). It provides an account of the Hebrew Kingdom called Songhay from the reign of **Za-el Yemeni (meaning "He comes from Yemen")** the First ruler (300 A.D) of the **"Za Dynasty"** to **Sonni Ali** (1464-1492 A.D) up to the downfall of the Arabs in 1599 with a few references to events in the following century. In the Tarikh al-Sudan, it states that there were 14 Israelite **"Za Rulers"** after Za-el Yemeni before the rise of Islam in the region.

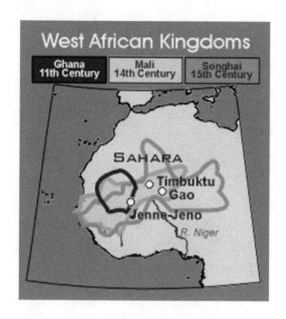

Fact 2: The **Rasulid Dynasty** in Yemen was established in 1229 by **Umar ib Rasul. Umar ibn Rasul** was appointed deputy governor by the **Ayyubids** in 1223. When the last **Ayyubid** ruler left Yemen in 1229, Umar stayed in the country as caretaker. He subsequently declared himself an independent king by **ASSUMING** the title **Al-Malik Al-Mansur** (the King assisted by Allah). The dynasty is regarded as the greatest native Yemeni state since the fall of the pre-Islamic Himyarite Kingdom. They were, of course, of **WHITE TURKISH DECENT (like Ottoman Sultan Suleiman the Magnificent)** but claimed an Ancient Yemenite origin to justify their rule. This was how the White Turkish Non-Semitic Arabs set up shop in Black Yemen (Arabia Felix). The **Rasulids** were not the first dynasty to **CREATE** a fake genealogy for political purposes, nor were they doing anything out the ordinary in the tribal context of Arabia.

Fact 3: The Black Tribe - **Idaksahak of Mali** claim Hebrew Israelite ancestry from the West African Songhai Empire. "Idaksahak" means "**Sons of Isaac**". They are located in the region of West and Central Mali. Their official language is "**Tadaksahak**". Many are nomads, and have few possessions apart from their animals. They also are found in Algeria and Niger. The men are bi-lingual, speaking the language of the Tuareg's (**who have some Hebrew heritage**) called "**Tamasheq**" and their own "**Tadaksahak**" language. The Tuareg Black Berbers are the original people of Libya, many saying their language goes back to the Phuttite Pharaoh's of Egypt (**Iuput, Shoshenq-Shishak**).

Tuareg Man

The Tuareg's writing script "**Tifinagh**" has been found dating all the way back to 200 B.C. The earliest Arabic inscriptions date to around 500 A.D. This proves the Black Tuareg people were the original peoples in North Africa before the Ottoman White-skinned Turkish Arabs. Its use has shrunk since the invasion of North Africa by the white-skinned Romans, the Greeks, the French, the British, Germanaic peoples and the Turkish Arabs (**under Ottoman Sultan Suleiman the Magnificent in 1500's**) but is still preserved with the **Tuareg people**.

WHAT COLOR WERE THE ORIGINAL ARABS PRIOR TO ISLAM? WHAT HAPPENED? HAS THIS HISTORY BEEN DELETED FROM THE BLACK RACE TOO?

This is a slave market in Yemen in the 1200's A.D. Notice the slaves are black and the Yemeni Arabs are white-skinned. This is because they are not the Original Arab Yemenis.

Let's look at what the Arabs of Old described their appearance as.

1. **Miskeen Al Darimi** was an Arab Poet in 600 A.D. It was a known fact that he was black-skinned. He once proposed to a girl and she rejected him because of his blackness and his poorness. The girl later married a rich man who was from a tribe not as "**pure**" Arab as Miskeen's tribe. Miskeen one day saw the girl who rejected him because of his blackness and poorness sitting with her husband. Miskeen stopped and said to them:

"I am Miskeen, for those who know me. My color is dark, the color of the Arabs."

2. **Ibn Mandour (Manzur)** was an Arab Lexicographer (composed dictionaries) who was born in 1233 A.D. in North Africa. He describes the **pure Arabs** by saying,

"Lank hair (straight) is the kind of hair that most non-Arab Persians and Romans have while KINKY HAIR is the kind of hair that most Arabs have."

3. **Al Fadl ibn Al Abbas Al Lahabi**, was a 7th Century Arab poet who was from the same tribe (**Quraysh**) the **Prophet Muhammad** was from. He was related to Muhammad supposedly from his father's side of the family **AND** his mother's side of the family. His mother was Amina the daughter of Abbas, who was the uncle of the Prophet Muhammed. So his mother was the Prophet's cousin. Al Fadl the son of Abbas the son of Utba the son of Abi Lahab the son of Abdel Muttalib the son of Haashim said:

"I am the BLACK-skinned one, I am well-known. My complexion is black. I am from the noble house of the Arabs. Whoever crosses swords with me will cross swords with the one who is noble and strong."

This is what other Arabs later had to say about this statement made by **Al Fadl ibn Al Abbas**:

- **Ibn Mandour**, of the 13th century A.D., says in his well-known Arabic lexicon "Lisan Al Arab", "He (Al Fadl ibn Al Abbas) says "I am pure" because the color of the Arabs is dark." Ibn Mandour further says, "**It is said that he (Al Fadl) meant that he is from the purest of the Arabs because most Arabs are Black-skinned**".

- **Ibn Berry**, the well-known Arab grammarian of the 12th century A.D., explains Al Fadl ibn Al Abbas's words by saying, "**He means by this that his genealogy is pure and that he is a pure Arab because the Arabs describe their color as black and they describe the color of the non-Arab Persians as red**".

Black Yemeni Boys, Akhdam

4. It is a known fact that the original Arabs (**Ishmaelite's and Sons of Keturah**) were black with kinky hair. Many people believe that the **Mahra** Tribe of Oman and the Southern Region of Yemen called "**Hadramaut**" are descendants of the **Sabeans**. The **Sabeans** have been linked to the sons of Cush (Sheba, Seba) and the sons of Semitic Joktan (son of Eber). Their writing script is very close to the Old South Arabian language and the Ethiopian Jew language "Ge'ez". The **Mahra Tribe** is thought to descend from the Sabean tribe called "Rhammanitae" (Ra'amah) and still speak the Himyarite-related dialects. Likewise the Original dark-skinned Shammar Tribe are native to Arabia who originated with the Tayyi Arabs of Yemen. The **Tayyi Arabs** are a branch of the Qahtanis Arabs who are said to be **PURE ARABS** .

"There is a considerable mass of evidence to show that there was a very close resemblance between the proto-Egyptians and the Arabs before either became INTERMINGLED with Armenoid/Turkish racial elements. "
Anthropologist Grafton Elliot Smith (1871-1937)

(Left) White Arab King-Ottoman Turkish Sultan "Suleiman the Magnificent" (1500's). (Right) Black Arab King-Askia Muhammad "The Great" (1500s). Ask yourself this question? Who is authentic and more closely related to Ishmael who was half Semitic (Abraham) and half Hamitic (Egyptian).

5. Black Saudi Arabian futbol player, **Majed Abdullah**, is the most famous Arab soccer/futbol player of all-time. He is a true **ARAB**. He is black with kinky hair. Why? Because Ishmael, Keturah (Abraham's Cushite wife) and Shem were all people of color.

Majed Abdullah, Saudi Arabian Football Star - 1978, (Left, with white soccer T-shirt on.)

Ethiopic/Hebrew Book of Jubilees 20:12-13 "And **Ishmael and his sons**, and the **sons of Keturah** and their sons, went together and dwelt from Paran (**Sinai Peninsula**) to the entering in of Babylon (**Iraq**) in all the land which is towards the East facing the desert. And these mingled with each other, **and their name was called Arabs, and Ishmaelite's**."

"Although the **ARAB** of today is sharply differentiated from the **Negro of Africa**, yet there must have been a time when both were represented by a single ancestral stock (**ABRAHAM**), in no other way can the prevalence of certain Negroid features be accounted for in the original natives of **ARABIA**."
Henry Fields

"The predominant complexion of the Arabs is **dark brownish black** and that of the Non-Arabs (Modern day Turkish-Kurdish Arabs) is white. "
Ibn Mandour 1300 A.D

6. **Al-Jahiz**, a 9th Century Iraqi, had his own ideas on why there was a difference between the peoples of Arabia and those to the North and East. He wrote:

"All the peoples settled in the Harra (Arabia) besides the Banu Sulaim are **BLACK** like the Tribe of the **Banu Sulaym** who live in the lava lands of north Arabia and are rendered black-skinned like their environment" (**Swain, Boyce-Stones, p. 255.**)

Jahiz continues stating that though they took their wives from the Byzantines (**Italy, Greece, Turkey**) through the generations their original (**black**) color usually was seen again in their children," No soon had they reproduced from three generations the lava lands had turned them all into the color of the **Banu Sulaym**". (**Fakhr Sudan 219**).

Arab Scholar and Theologian Al-Jahiz Born in Basra, Iraq.
(776 A.D-868 A.D)

Al-Jahiz also notes:

"All the peoples settled in the Harra (Arabia) besides the Banu Sulaim are BLACK like the Tribe of the Banu Sulaym who live in the lava lands of North Arabia and are rendered black-skinned like their environment."

Fact: The Arab Press Service released the following statement in 2008:

"There are two main categories of blacks in Iraq, mostly in the south, who total about 300,000: those of East African origin (Zanzibar), numbering around 100,000; and those of who are Arab and originate from the Hejaz, claiming to be descended from the Prophet Muhammad, who moved to this country mostly in the 1750's and 1980's. The latter are mostly from the Muntafek tribe to which Abdul-Mahdi belongs. But both groups used to be far more numerous in the past centuries, many of them having intermarried with the locals and thus the colour of their skin has since been changed

What they don't admit is that the white-skinned Ottoman Turks/Kurds came down into Mesopotamia (Iraq-Arabia) conquering and killing off the Black Arab men. Thus the DNA bloodline and the physical appearance in the Middle East changed to that of the father who came from the North.

Fact 2: George Rawlinson, a 19th century English historian, author of the "Great Monarchies of the Ancient Eastern World" series wrote **"The Cha'ab Arabs, the present possessors of the more southern part of Babylonia are nearly black..."**

He also writes **"The Cha'ab Arabs, the present possessors of the more southern parts of Babylonia are nearly black and the Black Syrians of whom Strabo speaks seem to represent the Babylonians."**

Today, much of the population of Arabia is the product of many diverse groups of people who were originally from outside the peninsula (North) who settled in Arabia/Middle East during various invasions. Their descendants consider themselves Arabs as do other people of regions mixed with the early white Turkish and Kurdish non-Semitic Arab conquerors. But many colonists and historians are aware that the indigenous or least modified (more pure) Arabians were in fact close to Africans (Negroes) in appearance. This is mainly because of the close mixing of the Cushites and the Semites (**Joktanites, Ishamelites, Keturahites, Israelites**).

"To the Cushite race belongs the oldest and purest Arabian blood, and also that great and very ancient civilization whose ruins abound in almost every district of the country.......The South Arabs represent a residue of Hamitic populations which at one time occupied the whole of Arabia. "
19th Century Orientalist John d. Baldwin from Pre-historic nations or inquiries concerning some of the Great peoples and Civilizations of Antiquity. Harpers 1869

Fact: *When Black African-Americans visit Egypt they are often referred to by the locals as the "Original Egyptians", while other races are referred to by the locals as "foreigners". It has been said that when our Black American soldiers were in Northern Iraq they found themselves surrounded by children calling them "the original Muslim, the original Muslim!" Black Basketball players overseas in areas such as Turkey are often called "Arab" or "Arapy". This is because many of the Middle Eastern World knows that the original Arabs were Black. In other countries such as Liberia, Africa and Mexico history class teachers often teach their students that African-Americans are descendants to the Children of Israel. Some Liberian History teachers also teach their African Students that they too are descendants of the Children of Israel as many Liberians were known former slaves from America.*

Fact 2: *The **Dawasir Tribe** of South Central Arabia live in the area known as "Najd/Yemamah". This area is also known as the land of "Peleg" as they claim their ancestor is **Peleg** the son of **Eber**, the son of **Salah**, the son of **Arphaxad**, the son of **Shem**. They are brothers to the **Qahtan Tribe** who claim their heritage from **Joktan, the son of Shem**. According to the "Dawasir" tradition, Peleg made irrigation channels found throughout the region. They are also known to be the tallest and darkest Arabians in the region.*

7. **Ludovico di Varthema, also known as Barthema and Vertomannus (1470 A.D.-1517 A.D.)** was an Italian traveler, diarist, and aristocrat known for being the first non-Muslim European to enter Medina and Mecca (Saudi Arabia) as a pilgrim. He published a book about his own travels in 1510 A.D. called **"Itinerario de Ludouico de Varthema Bolognese"**. In it he describes his encounter with Jews living in the Hijaz Mountains in Western Arabia:

   "At the end of eight days we found a Mountain which appeared to be ten or twelve miles in circumference, in which mountain there dwell four or five thousand Jews, who go naked, and are in height five or six spans, and have a feminine voice, AND ARE MORE BLACK THAN ANY OTHER COLOUR. They live entirely upon the flesh of sheep, and eat nothing else. They are circumcised, and confess that they are Jews; and if they can get a Moor (Arab Muslim) into their hands, they skin him alive."

It is noted that many readers speculate the miscalculations of these Jews height and if he failed to see the scant cloth around their waists/loins, which is common in the Bedouins of the **Hijaz Mountains**. They also note that there were also Jews in Yemen at the time but those Jews he encountered in Arabia were more black in color compared to the Arab Muslims in that area around that time. Ludovico also uses the word "**Moor**" in place of the word "**Arab**". This is because the **Black Moors** were indistinguishable from the **Black Arab Saracens**, except by name. The lighter skinned Yemeni Jews were originally Black, but over time through many invasions from non-Arab peoples from the North, the populations changed. The Jews Ludovico encountered was in the mountains away from the general populous of Arabs, their enemies. This also was the case for the Jews in Khaybar/Khaibar, Arabia during the Muslim-Jewish "**Battle of Khaybar**" in 600 A.D.

Hiyaz (Hijaz) Mountains of West Arabia

The "Modified" white Turkish so-called Yemenite Jews did not endure the "Curses of Israel". They learned Judaism from the Black Hebrews that scattered into Arabia/Yemen (Arabia Felix). In addition, the Black Hebrew Israelites did not take a field trip to Europe to learn Judaism from the European Ashkenazi Jews prior to their purchase deal to acquire Israel. They already practiced Karaite Judaism and the Mosaic Law. This is all they knew.

Note: **Karaite Judaism** is one of the most original forms of Judaism as prescribed by God in the Torah. It is also the closest thing to the **Mosaic Law**. Karaite Judaism rejects later additions to the **Tanakh** such as the Babylonian Jewish Talmud which is the **Rabbinic Oral Law for Jews.** Karaite Judaism places the ultimate responsibility of interpreting the Bible on each individual. They do not follow the Kabbalah, the Zohar or Gematria philosophies.

TRADITION VS BLOOD

Overtime like running from one plantation to another plantation we have run from one religion to another, each time to a religion where its doctrines take us further from the truth and salvation. Christianity has many different Freemason inspired sects/divisions, such the **Mormons, Seventh-day Adventist, Jehovah's Witness, Roman Catholic Christianity, Protestant** and **Lutheran Christianity**. Newer Christianity movements such as **Pentecostalism** and the **Black Hebrew Israelites** have rapidly grown in numbers since as early as the 19th Century. Ironically these non-Freemason inspired Religious movements have been most popular amongst African-Americans, African and Blacks scattered across the seas.

Fact: European Freemasons (**York Rite and Scottish Rite**) never intended to allow Black members in their club **EVER**. That's why blacks created their own Grand Lodge called the **Prince Hall Freemasons**. Al Sharpton, Jesse Jackson, Alex Haley and Civil Rights Activist Medgar Evers are well known famous Prince Hall Masons. Medgar Evers however was still not equal to his white Freemason brothers because he was gunned down, shot in the back and murdered in Jackson, Mississippi, on June 12, 1963 by **Klansman, Freemason and Shriner Byron De La Beckwith**. Racism in Freemasonry was made clear by famous **Grandmaster 33rd degree Scottish Rite Freemason Albert Pike**. White Europeans started the Catholic Church, Greek Fraternities, the Freemasons, the Jesuits and the Illuminati. Despite this most blacks are members of organizations or religions founded and shaped by Old-time racist European Freemasons. **Albert Pike once quoted:**

"I took my obligation to White men, not Negroes. When I have to accept Negroes as brothers or leave Masonry, I shall leave it."

Christianity and American Freemasonry, by William J Whalen: (pages 17-18)

CHAPTER 30

DEUTERONOMY 28:37-44

Deuteronomy 28:37 **"And thou shalt become an astonishment, a proverb, and a BYWORD, among ALL NATIONS wither the Lord shall lead thee"**.

WELCOME TO AMERICA SAMBO AND BOJANGLES

In the dictionary the word **"Byword"** is defined as:
- A word or phrase associated with some person or **thing (i.e. African-American, Blacks, Darkey, Blackie, Aunt Jemima, boy, jigaboo, porch monkey, pickanniny, sambo, spook, mammy, golliwogg, Nigger, Coon, Kaffir, Abeed, Monkey, Negro, Tar Baby, Abd-Arabic, Abeed-Arabic).**
- A word or a phrase used proverbially, **(i.e. a proverb.)**
- An object of general reproach, derision, or scorn.

"Reproach" means to blame, disgrace, shame, or to express disapproval of (someone).

It says in the bible:

Jeremiah 24:9 "And I will deliver them **to be removed into all the kingdoms of the earth** for their hurt, to be a **REPROACH** and a **PROVERB**, a **TAUNT** and a **CURSE**, in all places whiter I shall drive them."

*Blackface mockery of blacks was
and still is common in America/Europe.*

In America it is very clear that despite being brought here by force we are still not given the respect of being viewed as humans to the rest of America. Our descendants were the victims of constant taunting and shame. We were portrayed on T.V by white actors in black faces or as if we were animals. When the Black Hebrew Israelite slaves were stolen from Africa, they did not call us by our real names. They did not let us know that we were descendants of the Hebrew Israelites. The **Arab** and White **Jew-WISH** Slavemasters made sure to erase our names because it held the link to our heritage. They drew boundary lines in Africa calling it Ghana, Nigeria, Benin, Cameroon, Sierra Leone, Togo, Sudan and so on. People started identifying with their country despite their tribes. Languages changed. We were given Arabic and European names. When the older Slaves died off our entire heritage was lost. From then on we were taught from scratch a new identity crafted by our European or Arab Slavemasters from the food we were to eat to the white blue-eyed Jesus and white Hebrew Israelites they made us believe was the truth. In America they called us **African-American, Negroes, Ibos, Heeboes, Eboes, Niggers, Jungle Bunnies, Sambo, Darkie, Tar Baby, Coon, Monkey, Undesirables, Boy, Jiggaboo, Kaffirs** and so on. Today in the Middle East Arabs refer to blacks as "**Abd**" or "**Abeed**". In India/Pakistan Afro-Indian people are nicked named "**Siddis**" or "**The Untouchables**". In Latin America such as "**Mexico**" blacks are called "**Moreno's**", similar to the black "**Moors**" of North Africa and Iberia (Spain/Portugal).   In Israel, blacks are called "**Kooshim**" or "**Kushi**" which basically means "**Nigger**". These are all bywords, not describing who we really are. Our last names have been given to us by our enslavers. However, notice that in America, other races are not referred to as **Arab-Americans, Jewish-Americans, Indian-Americans, Filipino-Americans, Chinese-Americans, Greek-Americans, Italian-Americans** and so on. Even Africans born in America are not labeled "**African-American**". On forms, applications, in school we are described with two continents "**African-American**". That leaves us with little to no description of what our heritage was over 1,000 years ago. Who was living in Africa years ago? Was it always called "Africa? We know that there was no country called Nigeria, Kenya, Uganda, Congo, Cameroon, Senegal or Gambia many, many years ago before the 1500's. So what where the people living way back in Ancient Africa called?   Were they Phutties (Phut), Egyptians (Mizraim), Canaanites, or Israelites?   Nevertheless, no other race is subjected to so many **bywords** and **taunting** in America. Is this just bad luck or was it foretold in the bible with the Curses of Israel?

T.V. Mockery of Blacks was the norm many years ago.
Unfortunately it is still used today, but in a subtle subliminal way. Do they think we are too dumb to figure this out?

"When the Fox Network released the new show, "**Empire**" in 2015, I was concerned about what I might see on screen. Fox is not known for producing the most favorable images of black people, so I figured this show wouldn't be any different. If you do some research, you might notice some of the same things I've seen in this ghetto-fied hood drama: Pimps, hoes, thugs, gangsters, emasculated black men, and all kinds of other kinds of stereotypical Coonery that many of us have grown tired of seeing portrayed on-screen."

Dr. Boyce Watkins

T.V. Shows like "**Empire**" are just tools used by the Media to destroy "Blacks". Produced by Ashkenazi Jew **Danny Strong** and African-American filmmaker **Lee Daniels** (Precious, Monsters Ball, The Butler), viewers that know the game may not be surprised to see the strong sexual immorality (Gay) agenda for black men (Jamal Lyon) and black women (Tiana Brown). Blacks in Empire are breaking all of God's commandments. They teach us to go against our own people and to throw our morals out the window for a little fame. What's worse is that they try to make homosexuality a normal thing. Lucious Lyon, short for "**Lucifer**" is referenced in one episode by his children to have been a part of the Illuminati with Cookie Lyon. The Sex-Music club "**Leviticus**" that they own is a slap in Gods face because none of God's laws from the Book of Leviticus are being followed in this Black Jewish-controlled (ABC-Robert Iger) TV series. The Coonery series promotes black men in power positions dating outside their race (Andre Lyon), alpha-black men with Psychiatric problems (Andre Lyon), male homosexuality (Jamal Lyon), female homosexuality/bi-sexuality (Tiana Brown), murder (Lucious Lyon) and sexual promiscuity/fornication (Hakeem Lyon-Naomi Campbell). It also gives the stereotype that Black people who rise to success have done so illegally or not without a tarnished past. Wake Up Black America.

Do other races have TV sitcoms displaying their own self-mockery while they wear wigs, dresses and lipstick? No! This is all prophesied in the "Curses of Israel".

Too often on the Television screen we see us making a fool out of ourselves. Black Men play women roles in full dresses, equipped with lipstick, eye shadow and make-up all for us to have a good laugh. This is seen in black movie actors and black Sports stars (Tyler Perry, Dwight Howard, Charles Barkley). But is the joke on us? What did God command us? Are we doing the bidding of Satan just to make ourselves rich and the CEO's of the Jewish T.V. companies richer, all while humiliating ourselves?

Deuteronomy 22:5 "The woman shall not wear that which pertaineth unto a man, **neither shall a man put on a women's garment**: for all that do so are abomination unto the Lord thy God."

DEUTERONOMY 28:38-40 **"Thou shalt carry much seed out into the field, and shalt gather but little in; for the locust shall consume it. Thou shalt plant vineyards, and dress them, but shalt neither drink of the wine, nor gather the grapes; for the worms shall eat. Thou shalt have olives throughout all thy coasts, but thou shall not anoint thyself with the oil; for thine olive shall cast his fruit."**

Famine in North Africa, East Africa and West Africa is very common. Coincidentally, this is also were most of the slaves were taken from in the **Arab Slave Trade** and **Transatlantic Slave Trade**. Without rain, the ground becomes dry and cannot bear any harvest. Any seed planted in dry, arid desert conditions will fail to produce anything worthy eating.

This was common for the "**Wandering Israelites**" trying to find a home amongst other nations and other religious groups. Insects also threaten the productivity of the harvest and of the livestock in many parts of Africa. Insects bring disease to both man and animal which affects their success of survival. Pastoralists, hunters, gatherers, and fishermen all have skills that help ensure survival in the land of Africa.

Are these "Egyptian slaves" or "Hebrew Slaves" doing labor in the field? How can we tell the difference if they are both black?

Farm slaves produced food and other goods that the cities depended on. In Mediterranean Areas (**Italy, Greece, Israel, Egypt, Turkey**) the olive was an important crop used for a lot of things, including oil. Other important crops produced in the Middle East/Mediterranean were wheat, vines and grapes. These foods could be used to make wine. In places like Rome, Italy, these goods were used for trade which they used to boost their economic power. When the Romans ran out of Peasants families to work the fields they bought slaves, most often from Africa. It is a known fact that the Greeks and Roman Empire also took blacks as slaves; as this can be seen on many T.V. movies where they portray blacks in the palaces of the Roman Emperors as servant or slaves. The Hebrew Israelites would also endure this fate. They would pick the olive or the grape and not reap the benefit of its use.

DEUTERONOMY 28:41-42 "You shall have sons and daughters, but thou shall not enjoy them, for they shall go into captivity. All thy trees and fruit of thy land shall the locust consume."

Slave children at slave quarters in the South.

WHOSE CHILDREN HAVE GONE INTO CAPTIVITY?
THE NEGROES OR THE EUROPEAN JEWS?

Millions of children were separated from their parents, brothers and sisters during the slave trade. They had to endure cold winters and starvation every year without comfort from their parents. They were also put to work on the fields picking cotton and sugar cane. This did not happen with the 12-year Jewish Holocaust in Germany. The first concentration camp was built in Dachau, Germany in 1933. The Holocaust ended when World War II ended in 1945. So this is a total of maximum 12 years that the Holocaust was around. Some historians will say 6-7 years. Today a "**Generation**" is about 25 years. This is about the time that most women have children. Back then it was about 20 years old. 12 years is not enough time for a woman to have a daughter that will grow up to have children while in slavery. The women brought to the German Holocaust Concentration Camps had to have already been pregnant and in those harsh conditions in the camp, it is unlikely that the baby would survive long enough to be sold into slavery. However, blacks throughout time have endured slavery, as well as see their children sold into

477

slavery, never to see them no more. So if this is the case, then shouldn't Black people in America and other nations have more right to claim Jewish/Israelite heritage than those European Jews who do not fit the "Curses of Israel"? Who are we to believe, God or Man? God is not a liar, man is.

Children were forced to do hard work under slavery during the era of the Slave Trades (Arab Slave Trade, Transatlantic Slave Trade, Indian Ocean/East African Slave Trade). This did not happen during the "Holocaust". So who is the "Real" Jew experiencing the Curses of Israel?

Deuteronomy 28:43-44 **"The stranger that is within thee shall get up above thee very high; and thou shalt come down very low. He shall lend to thee, and thou shalt not lend to him: he shall be the head, and thou shalt be the tail."**

Blacks and Latinos are the poorest race groups in America despite being here longer than any other race group in America. Both Latinos and Blacks in America have been subject to rape, murder, slavery, race-mixing and experimentation by the European colonists. Recent studies have also shown that Native Americans on reservations are also subject to poverty, drugs, high school drop-out, suicide, and police brutality just as their minority Black/Latino counterparts. The Native Americans in Arizona are still mad till this day for what the European man did to their people. The Native Americans were plentiful in the Americas before the Spaniards arrived. **Now ask yourself, when was the last time you saw a full-blooded Native American?** Most people might answer "**never**". But ask yourself, when was the last time you saw a black person or a white person. The answer might be "**yesterday**". The Native Americans went from being the most populous people in the Americas to the minority. Is this a coincidence? Is it just "bad luck" for them? No! Since the 1400's, other immigrant races have come to America for better opportunities. They have succeeded in getting the "**American Dream**" as most of the businesses today in America are owned by Arabs, Asians, Indians, Jews, Italians, Greeks and Anglo-Saxon Whites. This is not a coincidence. To test this theory, all one has to do is ask the question "Who is the owner?" whenever visiting a place of business. You will see that most often it is not Blacks or Latinos. Even in Michigan, where there is a high population of immigrant European Jews and Arab-Americans, it is common knowledge that these two races receive more money on their EBT cards than Blacks or Latinos. How is this possible when Blacks and Latinos are typically in poverty while these other race groups are wealthy? If EBT card monies are determined by your income and number of kids, how is it that these two immigrant races get 2-3 times more EBT food money than Blacks or Latinos?

ARE THOSE WHO TOTALLY DEPEND UPON
GOVERNMENT BENEFITS SUBJECT TO BECOMING
VICTIMS OF THE BEAST?

The more dependent we become on the Government to provide our every need, the more locked in we become to the "**Mark of the Beast**" System. Is the Government our "**Daddy**"? Wake Up People. This is the "**Cloward-Piven Strategy**" and the so-called "**War on Poverty**" Agenda. The goal is to get us "**dependent**" on them. Or is it get **Israel** dependent on **Edom**?

Revelation 13:17 "And that **no man** might buy or sell, save he the mark, or the name of the beast or the number of his name."

Fact: At Kroger's, in Michigan, when discussing the "**Highest EBT card balances**" there are Black Cashiers that have seen Arabs with EBT balances as high as 4,000-$5,000. They also admit to the Average Jewish family having $1,000 a month on their EBT cards. Gulp! This equates to $250 a week on groceries, courtesy of the government, which also helps fund organizations set up by Jews to help provide interest free-loans for Jews needing it. Whether these balances are the result of money running over into the next month, it obviously shows that these EBT cardholders do not need the money. Anyone in poverty with a lot of kids will always find a way to use $4,000 a month in free groceries.

Black and Latinos make up the majority of people in prison in the United States. Is this a coincidence? Latin America and African Americans have been subject to European rule since the moment they stepped foot on American soil.

Fact: The **NAACP** was founded and funded by Jews in its early years. Jewish **Jacob Schiff (Green Shield)** was sent to America with the task of starting different projects for his Jewish Rothschild (**Red Shield**) friends. One of those was starting an organization for blacks. Wikipedia claims the 3 founders of the **NAACP** were just regular white people but they are not telling the whole truth. **Henry**

Moskovitz was Jewish. **Mary White Ovington** was a regular white lady. **William Walling** was a wealthy white who ended up marrying **Anna Strunsky**, a Russian Jewish immigrant from San Francisco, California. William's father was a Physician who had tons of Real Estate in the South. His father's family owned slaves before the Civil War. It is a known fact that the NAACP had only Jewish Presidents from 1909 to 1975. **Kivie Kaplan** was the last Jewish President of the NAACP in 1975. He held this position from **1966-1975**. The Jews controlled the Black organization and funded it through the Civil Rights Movement.   The Jews even marched alongside with Martin Luther King with the **Torah** in Selma, Alabama in 1965 (**Rabbi Abraham Joshua Heshcel**).   The Jews funded almost all Civil Rights Movement-related organizations but there was one condition to getting the funding. **No Black organization could initiate any Black economic development plans while receiving funding from the Jews**. Oprah Winfrey and all our Multi-Millionaires/Billionaires also follow this rule. It's called "Playing the Game". Giving away vacations, cars, books, some scholarships at times is about the best they can do. But starting a **Black Central Bank** or building self-sustaining, self-sufficient, independent Black communities (i.e. Black Wall Street) throughout America is a "no, no". This is why even though we have some "**Black Wealth**" in America we still do not control anything. This is why Blacks can't start their own Basketball League, and why Blacks don't own many record or movie distribution companies.

Laemmle — Universal

Fox — 20th Century Fox

Goldwyn — MGM

Warner — Warner Bros.

Mayer — MGM

Zukor — Paramount

"The Hollywood Jews created a powerful cluster of images and ideas -- so powerful that, in a sense, they colonized the American imagination ... Ultimately, American values came to be defined by the movies the Jews made."

Neil Gabler, An Empire of Their Own. How the Jews invented Hollywood, Crown Publishers, NY, 1988

Fact: Black Movies like "**Straight Outta Compton**", "**The Family that Preys**", "**Menace to Society**", "**Boyz n the Hood**", "**Friday**", "**The Butler**" and countless others could not have seen the light without Jewish Movie Distribution companies. The Weinstein Company, Lionsgate, Universal Pictures, MGM, 20th Century Fox, Paramount Pictures, New Line Cinema, Columbia Pictures, and Warner Bros are some just to name. Selma was distributed by Paramount Pictures and Malcolm X was distributed by Warner Bros. Without these Jewish Distribution companies, these Black Movies would never had hit our Movie Theaters. These companies profit off of Black ticket sales. So every time our black dollars are spent at the theatres watching Black movies, the European Jews are also getting their money. It doesn't matter how degrading or violent the movie is or if the movie promotes a certain "agenda", at the end of the day it's all about the dollar.

Fact 2: For many years' independent black record labels, black producers, and black artists have been the victims of racism, unfairness or bias. Blacks have been systematically excluded from certain positions in the Multi-billion dollar enterprise of the Music Industry by those who control it, the European Jews. The main "**Jewish Agenda**" is to put Black-owned record companies out of business. This is what was revealed in the 2007 article "**Major Record Companies Manipulated Control of Black Music**", by RBG Scholaran. Perfect example is the 1980's sale of Detroit's Black-owned record company "**Motown Records**" to MCA Records and Boston Ventures Limited Partnership. This is why the Music Industry continues to put of demonic, negative, sexually immoral, destructive music to the "Black Community" while keeping "positive" music from getting any radio airtime or Video time. This ensures the destruction of the Black race.

The Anti-Defamation League which also secretly controls the NAACP is predominately Jewish-ran as well. The NAACP supported **Planned Parenthood** and the abortion of black babies when the "**Negro Project**" started by Planned Parenthood founder "**Margaret Sanger**" rolled out her secret plan to get rid of blacks whom she called "**undesirables**".

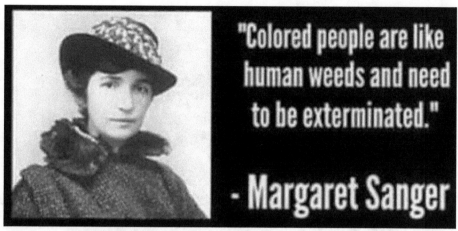

*Margaret was a strong advocate of eliminating "Negroes" from America using sterilization, birth control pills and abortion clinics which fell under "**The Negro Project**". This is called "negative eugenics". **Hilary Clinton** praised her as a person and for her work when she said, "**I admire Margaret Sanger enormously, her courage, her tenacity, her vision.**"*

Spelman and Morehouse College was founded and funded by the Jewish Rockefeller family. The last 2 NBA commissioners **Adam Silver** and **David Stern** are both Jewish men when the NBA is almost 80% black. The whole world watches and **PAYS TO SEE** black players shoot hoops but we have yet to figure out how to control all of this so **OUR PEOPLE** can benefit from the **BILLIONS OF DOLLARS** the NBA draws in from all its money streams. This is like modern day sharecropping and the "**New age Sambo**".

Fact: In 2014, New Orleans Pelican NBA players Monty Williams, Anthony Davis, Eric Gordon, and Austin Rivers aired a video clip of them being chefs in a kitchen preparing food for the owner of their team, Tom Benson. As they stood in the back of the table they watched as the NBA team owner ate his dinner. Are Blacks even with millions of dollars conditioned to serve their NBA team owners? Why couldn't Tom Benson have regular chefs cook him dinner. Why did it have to be the Black NBA Basketball players of his team? Though it might seem little to pay attention to, people are starting to notice more and more how rich blacks try to please other races instead of solely giving back to black people that need it the most.

Ashanti King of Ghana Prempeh I and Queen Mother bow before the British in Kumase, Ghana in 1896. He was exiled to the Island of Seychelles in 1906 (North of Madagascar). Seychelles was also under British control.

BUILDING A BLACK "ECONOMY WITHIN AN ECONOMY".

Blacks borrow money from every other race and we primarily work for every other race. Because we don't own anything, we are always subject to working for other people, who in most cases are not our own people. Because we have no capital, nor a **Black Organization** or a **Black Central Bank** set up for blacks, we have to rely on borrowing money from financial institutions that are owned by non-black races. This means we also have to get credit and loans at high interest rates from non-black owned organizations in order to survive. This puts Blacks into an endless Debt-trap where our lenders profit 2-3 times over on us while we stay poor.

The start of Financial Enslavement in Blacks starts with us trying to get "Things" based on "Credit." We also don't stick together and we don't use the "Barter Method" to survive off of each other. We all have skills that are valuable to the next man or the next household but we haven't figured out how to succeed on our own with these skills. Financially, the mistakes we make in our 20-30's often carry through to our 40-50's. Then at 60 and 70 years old we are still working or back to working again to pay off outstanding Debt. Why? Because we don't own anything!

Jewish people have tons of Jewish Organizations and funds worldwide set up by Jewish donations. Jewish families send money to these organizations that in turn send money to other Jewish people, some who are distant relatives. By doing this, Jews have set up an **"Economy within an Economy"**.

At www.hflasf.org Jewish people can apply for interest-free loans that can help fund a student through medical school, open up a new business, buy a new home, or help with building projects throughout the Jewish community. Because Blacks don't have reserve money in the bank and possibly are coming to the table with poor credit (<600), we are often subject to FHA loans which require a lower down payment (3.5%) vs a Conventional Loan (20%) with a higher down payment. The FHA loan has a limit cap on the amount that can be borrowed so getting a million dollar house or a half-a-million dollar house will likely be out of the question.

For Blacks, getting loans and credit is very difficult. Predatory lending and prejudice loan officers play games with black people by giving loans with high interest rates or simply rejecting the loan period. Since we don't put our monies together in our own Central Bank, we have to borrow money from non-black banks which are owned by non-black people. The same applies to a Car loan. Arabs and other races commonly rip black people off who are desperate to buy a nice vehicle, even if it means signing a loan that will have them paying back the value of the car twice fold. Denial of home loans, car loans, business loans are just certain ways **"White America"** keeps us at the bottom. Denying blacks Government Assistance **"EBT** cards" but approving other races is another way **"White America"** gives other races an edge in life while keeping blacks at the bottom.

486

Just like denied Loan Applications, blacks working jobs making minimum wage are often denied "EBT cards" when other races receive EBT cards. Some EBT cardholders even have six-digit salaries on their Tax Returns from work or their businesses. Other races get approved "EBT Cards" for everyone in their household while blacks are limited to one EBT card per household (address). It is a known fact that Arabs and Jews get more "EBT food card" money than Blacks. Somehow they have found a loophole to the system. Or is the system designed to favor certain races while excluding others (Blacks & Latinos). The Government has managed to continue decreasing the amount of EBT monies for Blacks while increasing the EBT monies for other races. Some Grocery store clerks have witnessed Arabs with $3,000 EBT card balances and noted EBT card averages of $1,000 in Jews. When the Government has "shut-downs", the loss that Blacks experience from not being able to use their EBT cards is greater compared to other non-black races.

There are roughly 44 million African-Americans in the U.S.A. If every black person in America **donated** $1,000 dollars to a Black/African-American Fund or Black Central Bank we would have **44 billion dollars** to use for the advancement of black people in America. If every African-American donated just $1 dollar bi-weekly to a **Black Central Bank** or **Black Investment Fund** this would average out to **1.17 Billion dollars** in Black Revenue a year! This money could be put in Black Banks or Black Investment Fund accounts statewide that can issue out loans with little to no interest to help fund Black projects (**schools, affordable housing, businesses, property, farming, industries, agriculture, transportation companies, neighborhood security etc**.) that can be used to better the lives of every African-American in America. Then we can begin to establish our own **"Economy within** an Economy". We can work for each other and support each other. No worrying about fitting in with other races that don't want us to succeed. No worrying about getting talked to by our bosses about wearing our "**Natural Hair**". **Unity is the key to our success, and America knows this**! The Arabs, Jews, Indians, Asians, Europeans and White America all know this about us. This is what White America feared when Abraham Lincoln freed the slaves and when Marcus Garvey proposed the all black people return to Africa. It is for this reason that White America dropped the idea of letting blacks go back to Africa. So while we are in America, the powers to be will never allow blacks to **UNIFY** or become independent from **THEIR SYSTEM** using **OUR** money. America wants blacks to feel like we have all the same opportunities they have now that Jim Crow has ended.

"When they (America) think that an (Black) explosive era is coming up, then they grab their press again and begin to shower the Negro public, to **make it appear that all Negroes are satisfied**. Because if you know that you're dissatisfied all by yourself and ten others aren't, you play it cool; but you know if all ten of you are dissatisfied, you get with it. Well, this is what the man knows. The man knows that if these Negroes find out how dissatisfied they really are – and all of them, even Uncle Tom (Rich Negroes) is dissatisfied, he's just paying his part for now – this is what makes them frightened. It frightens them in France, it frightens them in England, and it frightens them in the United States."
Malcolm X (1965)

America needs blacks to be the workers, servants or labor force of all the major companies and businesses we see around us. America needs blacks in Sports & Entertainment to make **THEM** billions of dollars. They don't want us to take back that control and start making our own **BILLION OF DOLLARS**! However, since we have given up working for ourselves to work for others, we have **voluntarily** entered ourselves into a form of slavery.

Modern Slave

Freedom and Slavery can also be Mental States. We can be mentally free or mentally enslaved. We have the Illusion that we are free because we get to go home to our houses and our family. But are we as "Black People" in America really free?

We borrow money from other races in the forms of high interest loans, credit cards, pawn shops and payday advances because we have no money to lend to each other. So the scripture **"He shall lend to thee, and thou shalt not lend to him"** is very real! Segregation forced and taught us that we could make it without the help of white America (**ex. Black Wall Street 1921 Tulsa, Oklahoma**). We had our own communities, shops, and did business with each other using our own money or the "Barter system" way. That all changed with the integration of blacks into white society after the abolishment of slavery and the civil rights movement.

"I Fear I May Have Integrated My People Into a Burning House

*With integration of Blacks into White America, we started wanting what "**White America**" had to offer its people. We wanted to eat at white restaurants, go to white shopping malls, go to white schools, style our hair like white women, and get jobs within white America. This is when we started losing black businesses and our "**black economy within an economy**." We didn't realize that with education and "**Unity**" we could build our own economy.*

So we eventually lost the Negro Baseball league and the Negro Basketball League. Then we integrated into the Major Baseball league and the National Basketball Association as "**employees**" and not owners. We tried to get houses but many got the projects. We put our kids in white schools and we still experienced racism. We asked to join the Scottish Rite Freemasons but they didn't except us, prompting us to start our own "Prince Hall Freemasonry" based after theirs. We bought the kind of cars they drove even if we couldn't afford it. The Black men and women shopped at the same malls to get the clothes that they wore. We also put perm in our hair to straighten out the kinky-ness of our own natural black hair so that we would look white and less black. Nowadays you might call it "**Keeping up with the Jones's**" But is all of this an illusion? Are we really psyching ourselves out? Trying to achieve the so-called "**American Dream**" has kept us from the principles and commandments that God gave to us. God told the Israelites (**US**) that if we follow his commandments we would be blessed. God told us that if we seeked his face and turned from our wicked ways he would heal our land (America). Since we have disregarded God's Commandments and are chasing the "**Devil's Illusion**" of the "**White American Dream**" we have been working ourselves to death, literally! Are we really "**working to live**" or "**living to work**"?

Black America - Are we "working to live" or "living to work"?
Is saying "Welcome to (blank), how can I help you?" our whole lives living?
Remember, kids will try to be like their parents a lot of times when they grow
up. We have to be the ones to set an example.

If you take a close look at your neighborhood you will more often see Blacks or Latinos working **"Fast Food"** or **"Retail"** and less often you will see Asians, Arabs, Jews or Indians working in these job fields. What are they doing you might ask? They are in coffee shops, libraries, and hospital cafeterias studying to be Doctors, Lawyers, Nurse Anesthetists, Accountants/Tax consultants, Engineers, Business owners, Pharmacists, Computer Web designers or other high-paying top-notch careers. With the revenue stream from these high-paying jobs they can easily buy up real estate (Vacation/Residential), start franchises, or set businesses in our communities to take our money. We give them our money (sometimes with interest), making them richer while our pockets get thinner. The more businesses they can think of and open up in our community keeps us further spending while they stay steadily smiling all the way to the bank. This is how the **"stranger among us"** gets to be **"Very High"** while we stay **"Very low"**. Even in communities where we are talked about by the people we patronize (**Whites, Arabs, Jews**) we still don't step up to demand respect or to take back what should be rightfully ours. We forgot what **"Boycott"** or **"Unity"** means. This is all **"Fear"** and it is this **"Fear"** that keeps holding us back.

"They keep you scared to keep you subdued, we need to stop being scared and start standing up."

CHAPTER 31

DEUTERONOMY 28:45-49

ARE THE "CURSES OF ISRAEL" FOREVER?

Deuteronomy 28:45 **"Moreover all these curses shall come upon thee, and shall pursue thee, and overtake thee, till thou be destroyed; because thou hearkenedst not unto the voice of the Lord thy God, to keep his commandments and his statutes which he commanded thee:"**

Black people have suffered for what seems an eternity without any sign of positive changes. The descendants of African slaves have been dying all across the world and the populations of these blacks have been decreasing steadily compared to other races. The percentage of African-Americans in 2013 was roughly 13% compared to 17% for Latinos even though blacks have been living in America over 500 years. The percentage of blacks in America in 1850 (**pre-slavery**) was 15%. **In 1790, it was 19.3%.** In over 160 years blacks have not managed to build its numbers to that of slavery days. Some experts in statistics say that once there is a yearly decrease in the percentage of blacks or black males in America, they can then accurately graph what year in the future that the black race-black man will be extinct.

Many people believe that the "**Curses of Israel**" don't apply to anybody today. But how can this be when we know that the Children of Israel disobeyed God's commandments all throughout the Old Testament? They even admitted to their disobedience and "**The Curses**" placed upon them in the bible. The Curse wasn't lifted after the death and resurrection of "Yahusha Hamashiach (Jesus Christ)." If this was the case God would have brought his "**Chosen People**" back to the Promised Land.

Daniel 9:9-11 "To the Lord our God belong mercies and forgivenesses, though we have rebelled against him; Neither have we obeyed the voice of the Lord our God, to walk in his LAWS, which he set before us by his servants the prophets. Yea, **ALL**

ISRAEL HAVE TRANSGRESSED THE LAW, even by departing, that they might not obey thy voice; **THEREFORE THE CURSE IS POURED UPON US**, and the oath that is written in the Law of Moses the servant of God, because we have sinned against him."

There are some people today that don't believe in the existence of the Biblical Israelites. But they believe that the Chaldeans today are the descendants of the Chaldeans Abraham lived amongst. They believe the Greeks today are descendants of Alexander the Great, and the Arabs today are the descendants of Ishmael. So what are these people talking about? Just as there is a "**Spiritual Israel**" the New Testament talks about, there is also a **REAL** "**Physical Israel**" who is the blood descendants of the Ancient 12 Tribes of Israel. These people, if the Bible stands true (**which we know it does**), are under the oath and commandment that God gave them as his "**Chosen People**". We have to remember with that being said, when Yahusha/Yahushua (Jesus Christ) walked the earth, and even after his resurrection the Children of Israel did not return to the Holy Land. They were still scattered abroad (**James 1:1**). The people afterwards that would possess Jerusalem and Israel would be the "**Gentiles**" as prophesied by the "**Christ**" himself in Luke 21:24. This prophecy has been fulfilled because it was after this moment (70 A.D.) that the Gentile Arabs (Turks-**Suleiman the Magnificent**/Kurds-**Saladin**), the Gentile European (Romans, Greeks, Italians, Portuguese, England) and the Gentile Ashkenazi Jews/Sephardic Jews would seize/possess the land, each at different periods of time (i.e. The Crusades, Balfour Declaration 1948).

Deuteronomy 28:46 "And they shall be upon thee for a sign and for a wonder, and UPON THY SEED FOREVER.

Many blacks believe that the problems black people face all across the world are never going to change. Some people honestly believe that all the suffering, persecution and injustice that blacks face is because of the **Curse of Canaan/Ham**. This is incorrect. There is no Curse of Black skin and there is no curse on black people by way of Canaan. If it is, the Curse of Canaan should also be on the Israelites because many of the Israelites mixed their families with those of the Canaanites. Many of the Israelites were half-Canaanite/half-Israelite. Many were also half Hamitic/half Israelite. There were no known reports of the Israelites marrying the Greeks or Romans in Ancient Biblical times. The curses that blacks and our descendants face in the many scattered lands abroad are a continuation of the Curses of the Israel foretold in Deuteronomy 28. God told the Israelites to keep his commandments. If they did, blessings would follow. If they didn't, curses would follow. Jews practicing Judaism via the Satanic inspired Babylonian Talmud and the Kabbalah are disobeying God's commandments while keeping the traditions of Men, just as Yahusha/Yahushua predicted. They are also still secretly worshipping the pagan gods-idols of the past. The same idols like Chuin, Marduk, Saturn, Succoth, Remphan, Baal, Moloch, Ashtoreth, Asherah, Dagon, Ishtar, Osiris, Horus and so on...

The Snake Dragon (sirrush) is a symbolic representation of Marduk, the chief god of Babylon. This was the first thing the Israelites saw when entering the Babylonian (Iraq) "Gates of Ishtar".

Fact: According to the **Kabbalah** hell **is the "Bright hope for the Wicked". Judaism and the Kabbalah have their founding from Babylon.** For 70 years in Babylon the Jews saw the image of the **"dragon serpent"** as they entered the gate of Ishtar. When the Jews came out of Babylon or the **"City of the Dragon/Serpent"** they brought with them the corrupt satanic teachings of Babylon. **Pharisee-ism** was born out of the Satanic teachings of the Babylon. This is why Yahusha/Yahushua called the "Pharisees" the **"Seed of the Serpent"** and **"Generation of Vipers"**.

Matthew 23:33 "You serpents, you generation of vipers, **how can you escape** the **damnation of hell**?" This is why the Talmud is called the "**Babylonian Talmud**".

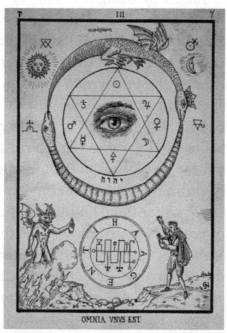

OMNIA VNVS EST

Just as the Gate into Babylon had the "Serpent-Dragon" god Marduk, the Jews also learned mysticism and false pagan worship as you can see here with this hexagram with the all-seeing eye and 8 symbols inside the circle. These symbols make up the planets in our solar system and also represent the pagan gods they secretly follow in Judaism.

This can easily be seen by looking at the hidden meanings of the symbols in the Kabbalah **"Tree of Life-10 Sephirot"** and comparing it to the **"Talisman of Saturn (Satan)"**, aka the **"Seal of Solomon"** or **"Star of David"**. The Ancients called **Lucifer** "Saturn", the sixth planet from the Sun. The "Star of Remphan –Chuin" in Biblical times was the 6-pointed Hexagram. The earliest known use of the Hexagram was during the 6th Century B.C., the time some of the Jews were in captivity in Babylon (Iraq). In Babylon, the Jews learned alchemy, sorcery, sexual immorality, and satanic pagan worship of many religions under their chief deity **"Marduk"**. There is **NO** Jewish literature that traces the Hexagram Star to King David. King Solomon was first said to have had a ring with the Tetragrammaton (4 Hebrew Characters for God) engraved on it which he used to control demons and spirits. After some time, man (through Satan) changed the story to say that he had a hexagram on the special ring. So eventually they attached this Satanic "Hexagram" to the "Seal of Solomon" and the "Star of David" which is all **FALSE**.

They blaspheme God to the fullest by using his name on their symbols or taking it out and replacing it with other names like "**Ein Soph**," which is basically **Lucifer**. The same symbols on the "**Talisman of Saturn (Satan)/ Seal of Solomon** are in the 10 Sephirot Kabbalah "**Tree of Life**". If the European Jews were truly God's Chosen people and were in fact still worshipping pagan gods that God commanded them not to, then **THEY** should be still enduring the "**Curses of Israel**" listed in Deuteronomy 28 and not blacks. **WE** are the lost children and lost sheep of Israel; the so called Hebrews Israelites that were stolen from Africa and scattered across the four corners of the earth by way of ships (**Deuteronomy 28:68**). Again, if all blacks were to come from Canaan than this would mean that we are also Israelites because we know the bible says that the Children of Israel intermarried with the Canaanites for thousands of years. Nobody knows who the Canaanites are today or who are the descendants of the Ancient Egyptians because they were a brown race of people whose land was taken over by other North white-skinned nations. Ancient mummies found in Egypt and Ancient pictures prove this. Arabs today do not speak the ancient Egyptian language nor do they know how to read the Egyptian hieroglyphs. The Palestinians, Lebanese, and European Jews do not know how to speak or read ancient Paleo-Hebrew or the ancient Semitic Phoenician language. This is because they are invaders to the land of the original people; the Black Canaanites and Black Israelites. Either way people want to look at it there is no denying that blacks across the world have the same claim to being Children of Israel as the white European Jews who never had ancestors that were black and thus would've been European Gentiles before converting to Judaism. The world has been tricked by those in charge of the printing press, the Mass Media, the religious institutions that authorize our religious texts, and the Renaissance period artists (Michelangelo, Leonardo Da Vinci) who drew everything biblical as white. The Vatican, Jesuits, the Catholic Church, Emperor Constantine, and many other white Europeans were responsible for hiding the truth and changing traditions in Christianity the way they saw fit.

A Canaanite (Levantine) solder with his Egyptian wife and son. 1300's B.C. If the Canaanites, Egyptians were black and they married with the Israelites then their offspring should also endure the "Curses of Israel". Or do they get a double-curse for the "Curses of Israel" and the "Curse of Canaan"? Is this possible? Did the Canaanites really intermarry with the Israelites?

Fact 1:

- **Judges 3:5** "And the **Children of Israel dwelt among the Canaanites,** Hittites, and Amorites, and Perizzites, and Hivites, and Jebusites. **And they took their daughters to be their wives, and gave their daughters to their sons,** and served their gods".

- **Ezra 9:1-2** "Now when these things were done, the princes came to me, saying, **the people of Israel, and the priests, and the Levites, have not separated themselves from the people of the lands,** doing according to their abominations, even of the **Canaanites,** the **Hittites,** the **Perizzites,** the **Jebusites,** the Ammonites, the Moabites, the Egyptians and the **Amorites. For they have taken of their daughters for themselves, and for their sons: so that the <u>holy seed have mingled themselves with the people of the lands</u>:** yea, the hand of the princes and rulers hath been chief in this trespass"

Fact 2: In the 10th century A.D, the Masoretic scribes from Tiberias at the Sea of Galilee added the Tetragrammaton (YHWH) with **guess vowels** to come up with

497

the word **Yahweh**. This word was not the true name of God, but was inserted and used by the Pharisees as the "unspeakable name of God". The **Tetragrammaton**, consisting of 4 Hebrew letters (**Yod, Hey, *Uau/Vav/Waw*, Hey**) is per Judaism the "unspeakable name of God". The True name of God "**Yahuah**" was made "**Secret**" to many European Jews and to us. But little do we know that before Noah was born the **Children of Seth (Adam's son)** called on the name of God as "**Yahuah**". This was before Noah could have Ham, Shem and Japheth. Before the Egyptians, Sumerians, Babylonian, Assyrians, Philistines, Canaanites, Romans, Grecians and Persians could come up with their fake pagan gods, trying to link them to "Yahweh" or "Jehovah".

Genesis 4:26 "And to **Seth**, to him also there was born a son; and he called his name **Enosh**; then began men to call upon the name of the LORD."

Genesis 4:26 "וּלְשֵׁת גַּם-הוּא יֻלַּד-בֵּן, וַיִּקְרָא אֶת-שְׁמוֹ אֱנוֹשׁ; אָז הוּחַל, לִקְרֹא בְּשֵׁם **יְהוָה**."

The last Hebrew Character of Genesis 4:26 is the Hebrew "Tetragrammaton".

Notice how the last word of this verse "The Lord" is the Tetragrammaton (4 Hebrew Letters) for the name "Yahuah". This is before any corruption existed on the Earth in those days. The name "Yahuah" also appears before the word "Nephilim-Genesis 6:4" is mentioned in the Torah. The name of the God appears before Satan can use different Civilizations (Sumerians, Babylonians, Egyptians, Canaanites, Assyrians, Grecians) to push his pagan "Satanic" god worship.

The correct name of "God" was taken out of our bibles and replaced with the word "**Lord**" or "**Jehovah**" by man. This is seen if you google Hebrew Strong's #1167 in which "**Baal**" means "**Lord**". "**Jehovah's**" root-name equivalent in Hebrew and other Semitic languages is "**Baal**", "**Baalim**", or "**Baali**". But where did the word "**Jehovah**" come from? The Wycliffe Bible of 1395, the William Tyndale Bible of 1530, the Miles Cloverdale Bible of 1535, and the Bishops Bible of 1568, did not have the word "**Jehovah**" in it.   God does not want his name to be a mystery, nor does he want us worshipping or replacing his name with "**Baal**".   Satan and man are responsible for changing the name "**Yahuah**" to "**Jehovah**".

After the Israelites exile during 500 B.C., especially from 300 B.C. and on the Israelites ceased to use the name "**Yahuah**" for two reasons.

1. Judaism began to grown as a universal religion from the mass conversion of Greeks, Romans, Edomites, and other Japhetic Nations.   After the mass conversion of Judaism, these proselyte Jews began to replace Yahuah with "Elohim" or "Adonai".   The believed the "divine name" was too sacred to be spoken so they replaced "Yahuah" in the synagogue with "Adonai-My Lord", which was translated as "Kyrios (**Lord**) in the Greek Septuagint Old Testament.

2. The Masoretes, during the 500 A.D. – 1,000 A.D. (Many scholars only give them at best 1,000 A.D.) worked to reproduce the original text of the Hebrew Bible, replacing the vowels of the name "Yahuah" with the vowel signs of the Hebrew words "Adonai", "Adonay" or "Elohim".   Thus, the artificial name Jehovah (**YeHoWah**) and "**YaHaWAH**" was born.

But we can see what the name of God should really be just by looking at the word for Judah which is identical to the Tetragrammaton except for the addition of the Hebrew "**Dalet-D**" character.   **Hebrew Strong's #3063 "Yehudah"** is the word the Masoretic scribes came up with when the corrupted the true name "**Yahudah**" by adding the letter "**e**" as vowels.   But in the Ancient inscriptions of the Hebrew Kings, God was called "**Yahu**" or "**Ia-u**".   In the Babylonian Cuneiform tablets it describes the fate of **Jehoaichin**, the King of Judah (598 B.C.) during his imprisonment and release from prison under the captivity of the Babylonians. These tablets were discovered by Robert Koldeway in Babylon (Iraq) and are collectively known as **ANET 308**, which now sit in a Berlin Museum.   The Cuneiform tablets list King Jehoaichin as "**Ia-u-kin**" or "**Ia-u-kinu**".   This is supported in 2 Kings 24:15.   Prior to the use of the "I" it would be correctly spelled "**Yahu-kin**".

1

... to Ia-ʾ-u-kin, king ...
to the *qîpûtu*-house of ...
... for Shalamiamu, the ...
... for 126 men from Tyre ...
... for Zabiruam the Ly[dian] ...

2

10 sila of oil to ... [Ia]-ʾ-kin, king of Ia-[a-hu-du]
2½ sila of oil to the [five so]ns of the king of Ia-a-ḫu-du
4 sila to eight men from Ia-a-ḫu-da-a-a ...

This Babylonian cuneiform tablet dated to 592 B.C. lists the rations for captive kings and their retinues living in the vicinity of Babylon. It comes from the 13ᵗʰ year of **Nebuchadnezzar II.** *King of Judah,* **Jehoiachin** *and his sons are mentioned on the tablet. Other names from the bible are also on the tablet. Now it sits in a museum in Berlin, Germany.*

In paragraph #1 is the word "Ia-u-kin" for Yahukin and in paragraph #2 it also reads "10 sil of oil to ....Jehoaichin (Yahukin), King of Ia-[a-hu-da] or King of Judah". There is no "e" in the spelling of "Jehoaichin" or "Judah". Yahuda(h) would be the proper way to spell "Judah" when using the "Y".

This Babylonian rock inscriptions is supported in **Jeremiah 52:31-34** and **2 Kings 25:27-30**.

Similarly, "**King Jehu**" would be "**King Yahu**". In the **Tel el-Ama**rna documents in Egypt it talks about the "**ameluti ia-u-du**" or "**Men of Yahud**" or "**Judean men/men of Judea**". Some historians say "**ia-u-du**" refers to "**Men of Judah**". Nevertheless we see that the proper spelling should be "Yahuah" and "Yahudah"; not "Yehowah" or "Yehudah". In contrast to the Egyptians, the Assyrians called the "Land of Judah" "**ia-u-du**" and the "Judeans" "**Ia-u-da-ai**".

That being said, we must follow what the Old Testament says in Isaiah:

Isaiah 42:8 "I am the LORD (**Yahuah**), that is My name; and My glory will I not give to another, neither My praise to graven images."

Below is this same verse in Hebrew read from Right-to-Left. Notice the "Tetragrammaton" (second Hebrew word) after the phrase "I AM".

Isaiah 42:8 in Hebrew. Applying the principle that Hebrew reads from right to left, notice the "**Tetragrammaton**" again after the Hebrew word "I AM THE".

אֲנִי יְהוָֹה הוּא ;שְׁמִי וּכְבוֹדִי לְאַחֵר לֹא-אֶתֵּן, וּתְהִלָּתִי לַפְּסִילִים.

Jeremiah 23:27 "**Which think to cause my people to forget my Name by their dreams which they tell every man to his neighbor, as their fathers have forgotten my Name, for Baal.**"

From "**YHWH**" and "**Yahweh**", the white Europeans then inserted "**Jehovah**" into our bibles for the name of God to replace "**LORD**". In the bible it says that Abraham didn't know God as "**Jehovah**" in Exodus 6:3 but somehow Abraham knew this false name in Genesis 22:14 (**which pre-dates the Book of Exodus**). Also they inserted "**Jehovah**" into our bible when research shows us that the letter "**J**" did not have a pronunciation in any language until around the mid 1600's (17th Century). This is how man deceives and corrupts God's word.

The Curses of Israel listed in Deuteronomy are for "The Children of Israel". This is a fact. So if the Ashkenazi Jews are the "Real Israelites" then where are their curses? Yearly **Gay pride parades**, the **Kapporot Chicken Slaughter** tradition, the **Metzitzeh b'peh** tradition (sucking of the penis after circumcision), the **Drunken Purim Feast**, and all the atrocities committed against blacks during the slave trades surely break tons of God's commandments. Therefore, we should be seeing all these curses exhibited in their life history. But we don't. This should be a tell-tale sign that these European Jews are **NOT** the biblical Israelites. How could God allow "His People" to commit these crimes and disobey his commandments without punishment?

We can see clearly that these "**Curses of Israel**" only seem to fit certain race groups and their "**Seed**" for what seems to be "**Forever**". But will these curses really continue **Forever**? Can we reverse this curse? Can we get redemption from the Lord? Can we fix it? **Yes!**

2 Chronicles 7:14 " **If MY PEOPLE**, which are called by my name, shall humble themselves, and **PRAY**, and **seek my face**, and turn from their wicked ways; then will I hear from heaven, and will forgive their sin, and will hear **THEIR LAND.**"

This is what God requires us to do. Then we will start to see things getting better as a whole for black people who have been scattered into the nations by way of slavery.

Deuteronomy 28:47 **"Because thou servedst NOT the LORD thy God with joyfulness, and with gladness of heart, for the abundance of all things;**

WHERE IS THE SPIRITUAL "POWER" IN THE CHURCH?

Acts 1:8 "But ye shall receive **POWER**, after that the **Holy Ghost** is come upon you: and ye shall be witnesses unto me both in Jerusalem, and in all Judea, and in Samaria, and unto the uttermost part of the earth."

Black people are known "**Spiritual People**". This also ties into our Pineal Gland. Many Black People today in the Church still believe in the Godhead/Trinity as being "One" and they believe in the Gift of the Holy Spirit as evident by speaking in tongues according to the Book of Acts. So hope is not all lost. Many other races and nations don't believe in this.

Matthew 15:24 "I am not sent but unto the **LOST SHEEP OF ISRAEL**."

Fact: (2013), In Moshi, **Tanzania**, just as in Black Pentecostal Churches throughout America, people in Tanzania are being "born again" of Water and Spirit. From Tanzania, Kenya and Ethiopia many Bantus Negro Israelites were sold into slavery to the East via the Arab Slave Trade/Indian Ocean Slave Trade. In 2013 Mission SOS held a revival witnessing to the people of Tanzania. Around 70 souls were baptized in water during their weekend revival and during Sunday (the last day of the revival) there was a mass-baptism of the Holy Spirit upon the people. Unknown tongues (different than their native language) were heard throughout the field in Tanzania. The interpretation of these "Unknown Tongues" have been witnessed in other countries from America to India.

1 Corinthians 14:22 "Wherefore tongues are for a sign, not to them that believe, but to THEM THAT BELIEVE NOT."

But what about interpretation? People want to always bring up **1 Corinthians 14:28** "But if there is no interpreter, he must keep himself silent in the Church; AND LET HIM SPEAK TO HIMSELF AND GOD!"

But in the same sense in the same chapter it reads:

1 Corinthians 14:2 "For he that speaketh in an unknown tongue speaketh not unto men, **but unto God**: for no man understandeth him; howbeit in the spirit he speaketh mysteries."
1 Corinthians 14:14 "For if I pray in an unknown tongue, **my spirit prayeth,**".

Romans 8:26 "Likewise the Spirit also helpeth our infirmities: for we know not what we should pray for as we ought: but the Spirit itself maketh intercession for us with groanings which cannot be uttered."

Evidence for a Religious State

Scientists found notable changes in brain activity when people speak in tongues. The brain scans below show blood flow in the brain (blue lowest, red highest).

SINGING GOSPEL SONG

SPEAKING IN TONGUES

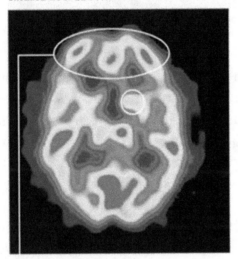

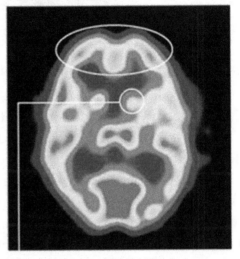

Frontal lobes Involved in the willful control of behaviors; more activity when singing than when speaking tongues.

Left caudate Involved in motor and emotional control; less activity in those speaking in tongues.

Study done by Andrew B. Newberg, University of Pennsylvania using MRI Brain Scans.

A study was done using brain scans at the University of Pennsylvania by **Dr. Andrew Newberg** on the Christian practice of speaking in tongues. He found that the **frontal lobe** lights up on a **MRI Brain Scan** in willful speaking, singing, or praying but when a person "**speaks in tongues**" this area does not light up. The left caudate is a system that is largely responsible for "voluntary movement". Neuroimaging Brain scans reveal that people who can speak different languages activate the same brain regions in the frontal lobe and left caudate nucleus regardless of what language they use. Not everybody that "speaks in tongues" all speak the same language. Many people say that "speaking in tongues" sounds like a Middle Eastern dialect but there has been "interpretation" instances where people can be heard speaking in tongues in other distant languages like the Inuit language "Inuinnaqtun and Inuktitut." Neurological studies have proven the **caudate nucleus** as a center for language control. In one study, a **tri-lingual** patient with a cancer lesion on the caudate nucleus was observed. The patient could understand all the three languages she formerly knew but when trying to speak them she "**involuntarily**" switched between the three languages. An example would be like a man from the Ivory Coast, Africa speaking to you in **French, English and Akan tribal language** mix without knowing it. Numerous neurological studies have shown a marked decrease in caudate brain activity in Christian's speaking in tongues (glossolalia). Christians can on some occasions be heard speaking in tongues for almost an hour as the "**Spirit of God**" gives utterance (controls the tongue). To put this in perspective, try asking a teenager or young adult to repeat the song "Mary had a little Lamb" over and over for one hour straight without stopping. Try adding $50 to do this feat and most people would decline the challenge. This is evidence of the "**power**" the Spirit of God has over man's tongue in "**True**" speaking in tongues.

Fact: During other Neurological studies of the Christian "Speaking in tongues", when Christians spoke in **REAL TONGUES**, their "**will-full**" brain activity in these areas decreased significantly, as if "**someone else (God)**" was in control. It decreased significantly more in people that didn't speak in tongues on command vs those that spoke in tongues on command. Even the Buddhist and Franciscan Monks did not show decreases in the language center of the brain when they were deep in meditation/chanting. The scans of the Buddhist monks in prayer/meditation actually increased their frontal lobe activity. Without surprise, neuroscience experts who have done studies on "speaking in tongues", like Patrick McNamara, associate professor of Neurology at Boston University and author of "**The Neuroscience of Religious Experience**", have received a lot of criticism and backlash from angry atheists.

Fact: People judge "**Speaking in tongues**" because it sounds funny. But there has been actual accounts of people speaking in tongues sitting next to people of different nations (i.e. Jewish, Arab, Indian, Chinese, Latino, Inuit Eskimo descent) and they have heard them speaking praises to God in their own native tongue. Children, young adults and older adults that have the gift of tongues have an added weapon to fight the devil. Praying in the Holy Spirit is a "**Powerful**

Weapon". After the day of Pentecost, thousands of people came to Christ after seeing with their own eyes all the Galileans speaking in other languages (tongues) in front of people from different nations.

Acts 2:7 "And they were all amazed and marveled, saying one to another, Behold, are not all these which speak (in different tongues) Galilaeans? **And how hear we every man in our own tongue, wherein we were born?**"

These are some common false beliefs that prevent Christ-believers from receiving the Gift of "**Speaking in Tongues**".

1. It's from the devil, Satan is speaking through you.

    1 Corinthians 14:14 "For if I pray in an unknown tongue, my spirit prayeth."

2. It's vain repetition of words.

    Many people have received the Gift of the Holy Ghost/Tongues while signing in the choir, after getting baptized, while praying, while being prayed for.

    1 Corinthians 14:22 "Wherefore tongues are for a sign, not to them that believe, but to them that believe not: but prophesying serveth not for them that believe not, but for them which believe. If therefore the **WHOLE CHURCH** be come together into one place, and all speak in tongues, and there come in those that are unlearned, or unbelievers, will they not say that ye are mad?

3. It's not for everyone.

    In Acts 2:1-4 it says that EVERYONE in the upper room received the Holy Spirit.

4. I've already tried, it didn't work. I can't receive it.

In **Luke 11:9** Yeshua says: "So I say to you, ask, and it will be given to you; **seek, and you will find**; knock, and it will be opened to you."

5. We don't need it.

Why would God give his people a gift we don't need? Because of this most churches are not operating in the "**supernatural**" with Spiritual Power.

1 Corinthians 12:7-11 "But the manifestation of **the Spirit is given to every man to profit withal**. For to one is given by the Spirit the word of **wisdom**; to another the word of **knowledge** by the same Spirit; To another **faith** by the same Spirit; to another the gifts of **healing** by the same Spirit; To another the working of **miracles**; to another **prophecy**; to another **discerning of spirits**; to another different kinds of **tongues**; to another the **interpretation of tongues**. But all these worketh that one and the selfsame Spirit, dividing to every man severally as he will."

Having the Holy Spirit gives us special abilities or "**Powers**" from God. God said that we would receive "Power" from the "Comforter". Many churches today are without members with these Spirit gifts. This is why many churches are losing attendance and there is no change. But remember, Satan also blesses his children that promote "his agenda" so don't be fooled by religions like the Catholic Church which corrupt God's laws.

Romans 8:10-11 "And if Christ be in you, the body is dead because of sin; but the Spirit is life because of righteousness. But if the Spirit of him that raised up Yahusha (Jesus) from the dead dwell in you, he that raised up Christ from the dead shall also quicken your mortal bodies by his Spirit that dwelleth in you."

6. The Gift ended after the early church.

People are still being filled with the Holy Ghost all over the world in Africa, India, Puerto Rico and in the United States of America. One of Yahusha's (Jesus) whole purpose on leaving us into heaven was to send the Holy Spirit to mankind.

John 16:7-10 "Nevertheless I tell you the truth; it is expedient for you that I go away: for if I go not away, the Comforter (Holy Spirit) will not come unto you; but if I depart, I will send him unto you. And when he is come, he will reprove the world of sin, and of righteousness, and of judgement, of sin, because they believe not on me; of righteousness, because I go to my father, and ye see me no more;"

7. It's weird. It sounds strange.

How can you be a Christ-believer and be afraid of the supernatural? A fisherman is not afraid of water.

8. My church doesn't teach or practice that.

Find a Church or Prayer group that is using the Gift of the Holy Spirit. The bible says in 1 Corinthians 14:1 "Follow after charity, and desire spiritual gifts, but rather ye may prophesy."

9. It's too hard to get.

Many Christ believers get the "Stop tongue" jitters when they are about to receive the Gift of the Holy Spirit which is Satan trying to flood the mind of Christians with any fear, worry or religious argument about why it is not necessary. Ignore Satan's voice.

Let's look at this:

1. **John 3:1-5** "There was a man of the Pharisees, named Nicodemus, a ruler of the Jews: The same came to Jesus by night, and said unto him, Rabbi, we know that thou art a teacher come from God: for no man can do these miracles that thou does, except God be with him. Jesus answered and said unto him, Verily, verily, I say unto thee, Except a man be born again, he cannot see the kingdom of God. Nicodemus saith unto him, How can a man be born when he is old? Can he enter the second time into his mother's womb, and be born? Jesus answered, Verily, verily, I say unto thee, **EXCEPT**

A MAN BE BORN OF WATER AND OF SPIRIT, <u>HE CANNOT</u> ENTER INTO THE KINGDOM OF GOD."

2. **Matthew 12:31-32** "Wherefore I say unto you, All manner of sin and blasphemy shall be forgiven unto men: but the blasphemy against the Holy Ghost shall not be forgiven unto men. And whosoever speaketh a word against the Son of Man, it shall be forgiven him: but **<u>WHOSOEVER SPEAKETH AGAINST THE HOLY GHOST</u>, IT SHALL NOT BE FORGIVEN HIM, NEITHER IN THIS WORLD, NEITHER IN THE WORLD TO COME."**

3. **John 4:24** "God is a **SPIRIT:** and **they that worship him must worship him in SPIRIT** and in **TRUTH."**

4. **Acts 10:44** "While Peter yet spake these words, the **HOLY GHOST fell on all them which heard the word.** And they of the circumcision which believed were astonished, as many as came with Peter, **because that on the GENTILES also was poured out the gift of the Holy Ghost. FOR THEY HEARD THEM SPEAK WITH TONGUES, AND MAGNIFY GOD.** Then answered Peter, **CAN ANY MAN FORBID WATER, THAT THESE SHOULD NOT BE BAPTIZED, WHICH HAVE RECEIVED THE HOLY GHOST AS WELL AS WE?** And he commanded them to be baptized in the name of the Lord. Then prayed them to tarry (stay) certain days." **Now did Peter tell the Gentiles to be quiet when they were speaking in tongues? NO!**

5. **Acts 19:1** "Paul having passed through the upper coasts came to Ephesus (Turkey): and finding certain disciples, He said unto them, Have ye received the **Holy Ghost** since ye believed? And they said unto him, We have not so much as heard whether there be any Holy Ghost. And he said unto them, **UNTO WHAT THEN WERE YE BAPTIZED? And they said, UNTO JOHN'S BAPTISM (water).** Then said Paul, "John verily baptized with the baptism of repentance, saying unto the people, that they should believe on him which should come after him, that is, on Christ Jesus." When they heard this they were baptized in the name of the Lord Jesus. And when Paul had

laid his hands upon them, **THE HOLY GHOST CAME ON THEM; AND THEY SPAKE IN TONGUES AND PROPHESIED."**

6. **1 Corinthians 14:1-6** "Follow after charity, and desire spiritual gifts, but rather ye may prophesy. **For he that speaketh in an unknown tongue speaketh not unto men, but unto God: for no man understandeth him; howbeit in the spirit he speaketh mysteries. But he that prophesieth speaketh unto men to edification, and exhortation, and comfort. He that speaketh in an unknown tongue edifieth himself; but he that prophesieth edifieth the church.** I would that ye all spake with tongues, but rather that ye prophesied: for greater is he that prophesieth than he that speaketh with tongues, except he interpret, that the church may receive, edifying. Now, brethren, if I come unto you speaking with tongues, what shall I profit you, except I shall speak to you either by revelation, or by knowledge, or by prophesying, or by doctrine?"

So Paul is saying that we should desire spiritual gifts that only come with being filled with the Holy Spirit, but in his opinion he would rather this gift be the "gift of prophecy" unless there is someone present to interpret the tongues as the Spirt of God gives utterance.

Fact 1: This is a True Story. As a child growing up in a Pentecostal (Apostolic) Church I can remember sitting in the back of the church during service with my mother and father. Being in a family of 9 we were not always able to get to church on time. Most of the time we arrived to church during "**praise and worship**" and if we were really running late we would arrive just as the pastor was about to preach his sermon for the day. The Children's Church and nursery was also in the back of the church for rowdy or crying children. Visitors would normally come to the church and sit in the back. Occasionally visitors of other races would attend service. I assumed they were looking for a Church home or maybe wanted for some reason to attend a "Black church service". Perhaps someone invited them to come to church and they didn't want to seem rude to not attend at least once. I would see Asian, Arabic, Indian and White people sitting in the back of the church quietly observing everything there was to experience. Well, I can remember a true story my mother told me about some visitors of another race (Asian, Indian, Arabic, White) hearing black people speaking in their native language while "**Speaking in

Tongues". The way she described it was that there were many instances where other races would be astonished when they would sit in the back of the church and hear regular African-American Detroiters speaking in their language wonders & praises to God. Of course, these non-black visitors would be curious to speak to the Pastor of this church. So, at the end of service, after mostly everyone had left the building, these visitors on different occasions would ask to speak to the pastor. The pastor would explain that what they were witnessing with their own eyes and ears was the power of the "**Holy Spirit**" as talked about in the Book of Acts.

Fact 2: This is also a True Story. A couple years ago an elderly African-American man of God from my home church went to Israel to visit. While in Israel, he visited the famous "**Wailing Wall**" which the Jews believe is the remains of the "**Western Wall**" of the 2nd Temple that Ezra helped rebuild and Herod finished. While he was at the Wailing Wall he prayed to God in the company of the other Jews and Rabbis that were there as well. As he was praying, the Spirit of God (Holy Spirit) took control of his tongues and he started "**speaking in tongues**" in the midst of all the Jews that were there. In the Black Pentecostal church this was a normal everyday occurrence, but in Israel it isn't. However on this day something miraculous happened as this normal Black man from Detroit spoke in tongues in Jerusalem. The Jewish Rabbis heard him speaking in tongues and they all stopped praying in their rocking fashion (**called "davening"**). One of the Rabbis present called out hysterically "**Sir, Sir!**". The Black man wasn't paying any attention because he was speaking to God, edifying (building up) himself spiritually. Finally after many "**Sirs**", the Black man stopped speaking in tongues and responded to the Rabbis. He told them that he was sorry that they were not able to get his attention because he was deep in prayer with God. A Jewish Rabbi asked the Black man, "**Do you know what you were saying?**" The Black man said, "No, if you heard me speaking, I was speaking in tongues and I do not know what I am saying when I speak in tongues." The Rabbi replied, "**I'm going to tell you what you were saying because you were speaking in perfect Hebrew....you were saying 'The Messiah is Coming, The Messiah is Coming' over and over again along with praises to God.**" The Rabbi asked the man where he was from. The Black man told the Rabbi he was from Detroit and that he was a Pentecostal (Apostolic) Christian. The Rabbi wanted to know more about his faith and the Church he attended in Detroit but wanted to meet outside of the Wailing Wall to discuss everything.

This true story was so amazing, that I had to ask another Pentecostal Christian of another race about this miraculous event where the tongues were "**Interpreted**" and I found out that it also was present in Pentecostal Christians from Ghana, Africa and Pentecostal Christians from Kerala, South India. They all admitted on certain occasions that different visitors from other races would visit their churches and be amazed to hear them speaking in tongues in their "**native tongues**".

Note: *Little do people know that the famous "Western Wall" in Jerusalem is really the remains of the Roman Fortress called "Fort Antonia". This falls in line with Yahusha/Yeshua's prophecy in the Book of Matthew.*

Wailing Wall, Jerusalem

The Western "**Wailing Wall**" is really the remaining wall of The Roman Fortress wall "**Fort Antonia**". This wall was started by **Edomite King Herod** and Roman commander "**Mark Anthony**" after who it is named after. It is also believed by many to be the remaining "**Wall of Jupiter**". Jews in Israel today say that they have everything need to start building the "**Third Temple**". They have been "**raising**" not one, but multiple "**Red Heifers**" to be used for the consecration of the Temple and have also got their eyes supposedly on the land they wish to build the Third Temple on to the west of the "**Dome of the Rock**." In order to be considered kosher for Biblical use, a Red heifer must be raised from birth under specific circumstances and in a controlled environment. This can be seen on the Jewish TV series "**Dig**" (2015). The Temple Institute has joined forces with experienced cattle ranchers in Israel, who are utilizing the technique of implanting the frozen embryos of Red Anus cattle into Israeli cattle. But is this a natural way of getting a "Red Heifer?" or is it "artificial" and "Manipulated by man?" This is yet another clue why the rebuilding of the Third Temple in Jerusalem is not going to be for the Most High God, but the Son of Perdition (Anti-Christ).

It is unsure if the cornerstone has been laid yet for the Temple but the Jewish converts are ready to build the Third Temple for the Christian and Muslim Antichrist (**dajjal**).

Fact: The Islamic Antichrist or the "**Dajjal**" supposedly is supposed to have a blind/bad right eye. The Temple of Set (EGYPTIAN God) is based on the account that Michael Aquino (Former Church of Satan member) said that Satan answered him as "**Set**" during a Satanic Ritual. Set at one time was worshipped as the God of Ancient Egypt. Set and Horus fought over rulership of both Upper and Lower Egypt. In the midst of the fight, Set gouged out Horus's "Left eye" and even tried to have sex with Horus. Mind you, both Set and Horus are male deities. Horus's mother, Isis fashions Horus a magical Left eye. But in the Bible the right eye represents darkness (**Zechariah 11:17**).

Zechariah 11:17 "Woe to the idol shepard that leaveth the flock! The sword shall be upon his arm, and upon his **RIGHT EYE**: his arm shall be clean dried up, and his **RIGHT EYE SHALL BE UTTERLY DARKENED.**"

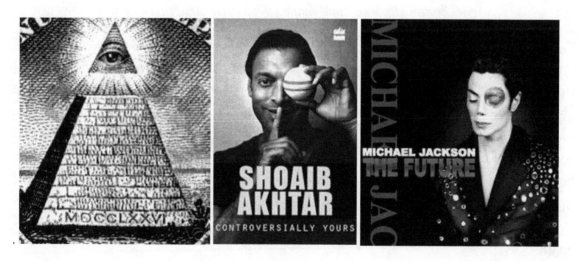

Shoaib Akhtar is a Pakistani International Cricket Player. His career was plagued with a lot of controversies and he published a book about this in 2013 called "Shoaib Akhtar:

*Controversially yours". But something is odd here about this picture. Why is there a ball in front of his left eye? One of Michael Jackson's last album "**The Future**" shows him with a Blue Circle over his left eye. Why? The "**All Seeing Eye**" is all around us. Just type in your Google search engine "**All Seeing Eye Celebrities**" and tons of pictures will pop up that are not coincidental. We think it is the eye of God, but it is really the "**Eye of Satan**". Satanists know this very well.*

Metatron is usually depicted as an ambiguous angel (appearing to be man and woman) with a hexagram star or a cube shaped geometric structure/symbol.

Fact: "Megatron is an angel. Santana has been in regular contact with him since 1994. Carlos would sit here facing the wall, with the candles lit. He has a yellow legal pad at one side, ready for the communications that will come. It's kind of like a fax machine, he says." "He tells me more about Metatron. Metatron is the architect of physical life. Because of him, we can French-kiss, we can hug, we can get a hot dog, wiggle our toe. He sees Megatron in his dreams and meditations. He looks a bit like Santa Claus-white beard, and kind of this jolly fellow. Metatron, who has been mentioned in mystical disciplines through the ages, *also appears as the eye inside the triangle*." - **Cover Story; The Epic Life of Carlos Santana: Santana: Rolling Stone (March 16, 2000)**

The Seal of Metatron is a triangle inside of a circle, often with an "all seeing eye" representing Horus, Heru, Lucifer, or Satan watching the world from another dimension. The eye inside the triangle shows the allegiance of Christ-rejecters, God-haters and Satan worshippers. This triangle inside of a circle with the eye is also seen in Freemasonry, the Jesuits, Catholic Churches, Rosicrucian's, the Illuminati, and Judaism. Satan worshippers Aleister Crowley and Anton LaVey also use this circle-triangle-eye symbol as it is the most powerful Satanic symbol, often used to conjure up demons. Aleister Crowley, nicknamed "**The Wickedest Man Alive**" and the "**Beast**" promoted the triangle and "**all seeing eye**" in his book, "**The Book of the Law**". In it the triangle represented the most significant symbol of Satan and the guiding light of the New Age of Horus to come under the Antichrist.

In the Babylonian Satanic-inspired Talmud, "**Metatron**" is only mentioned three times. Metatron is not mentioned in the First book of Enoch but is mentioned in Enoch 2 & 3, centuries after Yahusha's resurrection and the New Testament. This makes it very invalid and unreliable in addition to the fact that the author is not Enoch himself. Because of the wide time gap between the New Testament and the second Book of Enoch, many believe that the second book of Enoch is just a poor attempt to resurrect something that has always been dead. The Second and Third Book of Enoch try to connect Enoch with Metatron which is false. **But it is confirmed in the Zohar 43, Balak 6:86.** This is Satan's way of sneaking lies into man's teachings so that he can get all the worship instead of God. These are all qualities of Satan. Each time Metatron is mentioned in the Talmud they mention his immense powers which make some Kabbalah/Zohar followers confuse him with God. The Jews state Metatron was in existence in the beginning and that God taught him secrets about the Creation of the Universe. In the Kaballah he is even referred to as the "**Lesser Yahweh**" and guardian/ruler of the Tree of Life as well as the Tree of Knowledge. This is confirmed in the **Zohar 49, Ki Tetze: 28:138**. This is blasphemy teaching. Metatron gets the "**Crown or Kether**" position on the Kabbalistic 10 Sephirot "**Tree of Life**" which is a copycat of the Tree of Life that God promises to give to us in Revelation 2:7 and Revelation 22.

Revelation 2:7 "He that hath an ear, let him hear what the Spirit saith unto the churches; To him that overcometh will I give to eat **OF THE TREE OF LIFE**, which is in the midst of paradise of God."

This is Satanic teaching because no one is on God's level as he is the "**Creator**" of all things. The word "Metatron" is not in the Hebrew Bible, Septuagint and King James Bible.

So Satan told Adam and Eve to eat of the Tree of Knowledge so that their **EYE (Ayin)** shall be opened. Science and technology is taking us farther from God. People believe in spells, magic, the Zodiac etc. They are trying to explain homosexuality and the Creation with science. They are manipulating genes and cross breeding different animals and also Humans. Satan wants us to believe that we are Gods. Satan also wants us to believe that "Fallen Angels" or aliens created us like the Sumerian "Annunaki" story. In the media (Movies/music) emphasis is always place on the Left Eye because the Left Eye Represents Satan and the knowledge he has given mankind since Eve eating the apple from the "Tree of Knowledge". God wants to give us the "Tree of Life" not the "Tree of Knowledge".

The right eye is always covered up with celebrity's hands. Satan knows all of this so he uses this knowledge to tell Muslims that the Antichrist will only have one good "eye". This is not common knowledge in the Christian world about the Left eye or the Right eye. The Left Eye is significant in Ancient Egypt and also Islam. Why? Who is giving Ancient Egyptians and Muslims this "**Left Eye**" information?

THE ARK OF THE COVENANT IS NOT IN MOUNT NEBO.

The European Jews already have made the following Temple vessels for use for daily services in the Third Temple in Jerusalem. They are preparing for the Antichrist to reign on the throne. There are some rumors that the Golden Throne for the Antichrist is being held in the Vatican while others say it is being stored in the Israeli Supreme court in Israel. The European Jews also say they have possession of the Ark of the Covenant. Is this true? We'll soon find out. Here are some of these "vessels" the Jews have ready when Temple services start.

1. Large Mizrak
2. Small Mizrak
3. Wine Libation Vessel
4. Water Libation Vessel
5. Wine Libation Cup
6. Water Libation Cup
7. Copper Meal Offering Vessel
8. Copper Measuring Cups
9. Abuv
10. Psachter
11. Three Pronged Fork
12. Silver Shovel
13. Copper Laver
14. Golden Menorah
15. Oil Pitcher
16. Small Oil Flask
17. Vessel for Cleaning the Menorah
18. Incense Offering Shovel
19. Incense Chalice
20. Golden Incense Altar
21. Golden Table of the Showbread
22. Garments of the High Priest included the Ephod
23. Breastplate of Judgement
24. The Golden Crown of the High Priest
25. The Lottery
26. Silver Trumpets
27. Ram's Horns (Shofar)
28. Harp
29. Lyre
30. Ark of the Covenant (replica?)

Note: Unlike the other sacred vessels created by the Temple Institute, the **Ark of the Covenant** by many is considered a replica. But the Jews say that the real Ark of the Covenant sits in a secret chamber underneath Temple Mount and will not be revealed until Third Temple in Jerusalem is rebuilt. Only problem is, the real Ark of the Covenant is supposed to be in Axum, Ethiopia not in Israel. During the reign of

King Solomon, Queen Sheba was given riches from King Solomon (**1 Kings 10**). Since the Bible doesn't talk about courtship or dating between the Israelites and their women (especially the daughters of Ham), many assume that Queen Sheba had a "relationship" with King Solomon. This would explain why King Solomon gave her riches to take back home to Ethiopia. According to Ancient Ethiopian texts (Kebra Nagast) this "relationship" resulted in a son named Menelik I. King Solomon sent the firstborn son of each of the 12 tribes of Israel as well as a son of each of the Temple Priests (Levites/Cohenites). Initially, King Solomon sent Menelik and the Israelite young men to Ethiopia with a "replica" Ark of the Covenant. Thereafter, the Ethiopians were learnt in the ways of the Hebrew Israelites and they intermarried. However, after some time Menelik went back to Jerusalem and took the "real" Ark of the Covenant from King Solomon back to Ethiopia because of all the idol worship he was involved in. What was left in Jerusalem was the "**replica**" Ark of the Covenant. King Solomon reigned in 900 B.C. Supposedly, many Jews believe that the Ark disappeared between 621 B.C. and 586 B.C. But the question is how could it disappear if it was taken to Ethiopia 300 year prior to this? During 701 B.C. the Assyrians laid siege to the House of Israel and the 10 Tribes in the Northern Kingdom. Did they take the Ark of the Covenant from Solomon's Temple in Jerusalem? NO! King Sennacherib was not successful in conquering Jerusalem under Hezekiah's watch. During 621 B.C. the House of Judah was still in possession of Jerusalem. During 605 B.C., the Babylonians laid siege to the Israelites in the Southern Kingdom. This included the Tribe of Judah, Benjamin and the Levites. So if Menelik I was never born to take the "**Ark of the Covenant**" from Solomon in Jerusalem, the "**Ark of the Covenant**" should've been in Jerusalem when the Babylonians destroyed Solomon's Temple. But the Ark wasn't there in Jerusalem during the Babylonian attack in 605 A.D. The Bible does not list the "**Ark of the Covenant**" as being one of the "**Temple Vessels**" taken during the Babylonians siege of Jerusalem.

2 Kings 25:13-18 "And the pillars of brass that were in the house of the Lord, and the bases, and the brazen sea that was in the house of the Lord, did the Chaldees (Iraqis) break in pieces, and carried the brass of them to Babylon. And the pots, and the shovels, and all the vessels of brass wherewith they ministered, took they away. And the firepans, and the bowl, and such things as were gold, in gold, and of silver, in silver the captain of the guard took away. These two pillars, one sea, and the bases which Solomon had made for the house of the Lord; the brass of all these vessels was without weight. The height of the one pillar was eighteen cubits, and the chapter upon it was brass; and the height of the chapter three cubits; and the wreathen work, and the pomegranates upon the chapter round about, all of brass: and like unto these had the second pillar with wreathern work."

2 Kings 24:13 "And he carried out thence ALL the treasures of the house of the Lord, and the treasures of the house of the Lord, and the treasures of the king's house, and cut in pieces all the vessels of gold which Solomon king of Israel had made in the temple of the Lord, as the Lord had said."

This is also supported in Jeremiah 52:17-24. The Bible only mentions other "Temple" vessels being taken out of the Jewish Temple.

Even when the Persian King, **Cyrus** took the vessels of the Lord to his house, it doesn't even say that the "**Ark of the Covenant**" was one of these vessels. Surely the "**Ark of the Covenant**" is important, seeing that it caused the Philistines so much problems when they had it in their possession.

Ezra 1:7 "Also Cyrus the king brought forth the vessels of the house of the Lord, which Nebuchadnezzar had brought forth out of Jerusalem, and had put them in the house of his gods."

In Jeremiah, it says that these "**vessels**" taken by King Nebuchadnezzar would be brought back to Israel. But was the "Ark of the Covenant" included in these vessels?

Jeremiah 28:3 "Within two full years will I bring again into this place all the vessels of the Lord's house, that Nebuchadnezzar king of Babylon took away from this place, and carried them to Babylon."

So if the Ark of the Covenant was one of the Temple treasures taken from Jerusalem during the Babylonian Invasion according to this scripture it should be brought back. So was it brought back when Ezra and Nehemiah lived to see the Second Temple rebuilt? Nope! Ezra couldn't even find the Levites without the help of the Nethinims. And when they found some Levites they did not have the ark. In fact many of the Levite men (including Cohenites) had married different wives that were not of Israel. Who were these different wives and where were they from? Ezra Chapter 9 states it was the Canaanites (Ham), the Hittites (Ham), the Perizzites (Ham), the Jebusites (Ham), the Ammonites (Shem), the Moabites (Shem), the Egyptians (Ham), the Amorites (Ham) and the people living in Babylon (Iraq) . The Bible makes it very clear that there was no "return of the Ark of the Covenant" when Ezra started rebuilding the temple and started re-gathering the Levites.

Ezra 10:18 "And among the sons of the priests there were found that had taken **strange wives (Hebrew bible lists "foreign women")**: namely of the sons of Jeshua the son of Jozadak, and his brethren; Maaseiah, and Eliezer, and Jarib, and Gedaliah. In Chapter 10 Ezra names off 112 Israelites that had married foreign wives.

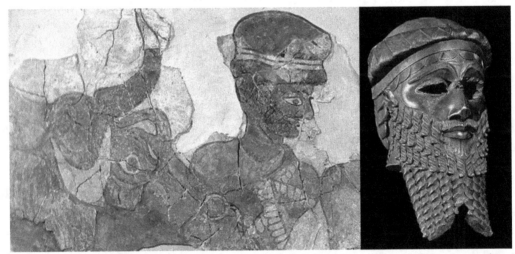

(Left) This is a real relief from the Palace of Zimri-Lim, Mari (Modern day Tel Hariri, Northern Iraq/Syria, home to the Ancient Aramaic speakers: Arameans-Chaldeans, 2000-1700 B.C.)
(Right) Head bust of Babylonian King Sargon from 2,000 B.C. times. They were Black in Ancient times. So if the Levite (Cohenite) priests took wives from Babylon and had kids with them they should've been brown-skinned kids and not the white-skinned Jews in Israel today. It is also said that Abraham's wife, Sarah was Syrian. We know the Syrians today are white-skinned Arabs. But 4,000 years ago they were akin to Black people. What happened if the Syrians today are white and are still living in the same land as the Ancient Syrians 4,000

years ago? Did the Sun change? No! By looking at the relief, Abraham's children would've been also people of color.

Fact: This below is an excerpt from the "**Legend of Sargon**" (Translated). Sargon the Great was an Akkadian (Babylonian-Iraqi/Southern Mesopotamian) King that ruled during the 2200 B.C. era, during the times of the Hebrews and Abraham. He ruled the land of Ur that Abraham lived in. As you will see below, the people Sargon ruled over and lived with were not white-skinned Arabs. He himself would've been black as he describes his people as also being black.

1. Sargon, the mighty king, king of Akkadê am I,

2. My mother was lowly; my father I did not know;

3. The brother of my father dwelt in the mountain.

4. My city is Azupiranu, which is situated on the bank of the Purattu [Euphrates],

5. My lowly mother conceived me, in secret she brought me forth.

6. She placed me in a basket of reeds, she closed my entrance with bitumen,

7. She cast me upon the rivers which did not overflow me.

8. The river carried me, it brought me to Akki, the irrigator.

9. Akki, the irrigator, in the goodness of his heart lifted me out,

10. Akki, the irrigator, as his own son brought me up;

11. Akki, the irrigator, as his gardener appointed me.

12. When I was a gardener the goddess Ishtar loved me,

13. And for four years I ruled the kingdom.

14. **The black-headed peoples I ruled, I governed;**

15. Mighty mountains with axes of bronze I destroyed

Some people believe that the Egyptian Pharaoh Shishak took the Ark of the Covenant to Israel but this is not supported in the Bible if Menelik I took it before he could even see it. Queen Sheba meets King Solomon and gets treasures from him in 1 Kings Chapter 10. Around this time Menelik I takes the "Real" Ark of the Covenant from Jerusalem to Axum, Ethiopia. Four chapters later in 1 Kings 14:25-26 it says that in the fifth year of King Rehoboam, Shishak King of Egypt attacked Jerusalem. Rehoboam was King Solomon's son. He took over the throne at the age of 41 years old. In his fifth year of rulership, Rehoboam would've been 46 years old. Menelik I, also a son of King Solomon, per Ancient texts was 20 years old when he took the real Ark of the Covenant back to Ethiopia.

1 Kings 14:25-26 "And it came to pass in the fifth year of King Rehoboam, that Shishak king of Egypt came up against Jerusalem: And he took away the treasures of the house of the Lord, and the treasures of the king's house; he even took away all: and he took away all the shields of gold which Solomon had made."

So here we see that the Egyptians, the Assyrians nor the Babylonians took the "Ark of the Covenant" from the Israelites. Why, because Menelik I most likely took it first; where it stands today guarded by Black Levites descended from Moses and his Cushite (Ethiopian) wife Zipporah. This would only make sense if there was someone that only went in its presence once a year.

Those people that claim the Ark of the Covenant was found in Israel are only going off the Apocrypha Book of 2 Maccabees 2:2-8 which says that Jeremiah buried the ark in a cave on Mount Nebo (Jordan). But the only problem is the Book of Maccabees dates to around 170 B.C.-150 B.C. when the Maccabees ruled in Israel. Nobody knows who wrote the Book of Maccabees and this book is not found in the Hebrew Tanakh (Even the Dead Sea Scrolls). The Apocrypha has no authoritative statements like "Thus saith the Lord" or "As it is written", or "The Scriptures say".

Yeshua, nor any of the Apostles reference the Apocrypha books. In fact Yeshua tells you that the only books in the Old Testament that are God-inspired came from the time of the prophets. From Abel, who was the first martyr to Zechariah (Zacharias), the last prophet of the Old Testament.

Luke 11:50-51 "That the blood of all the prophets, which was shed from the foundation of the world, may be required of this generation; From the blood of Abel unto the blood of Zacharias (the son of Berechiah, the son of Iddo), which perished between the altar and the temple: verily I say unto you, it shall be required of this generation.

Zechariah the Prophet is killed in the book of 2 Chronicles which is the last book of the Hebrew Tanakh. **Note: The Hebrew Tanakh has 39 books like the KJV just in different arrangements plus the books of the "minor prophets (Hosea-Malachi)" were all contained in one book in the Hebrew Bible. This makes the Hebrew Bible appear to have 24 books**. So by addressing the prophets from Abel (Genesis) to Zechariah (2 Chronicles), Yeshua is implying that the Apocrypha is not a part of the Old Testament God-inspired Hebrew canon. If the Apocrypha can only be considered a historical book about the Maccabean family in 150 B.C. than we can't 100% trust that the "unknown" author of 2 Maccabees knew the exact story of where the "Real" Ark of the Covenant is at.

So the big question is: How can the European Jews know where the "Ark of the Covenant" is at? Did they see the Ark of the Covenant? How can they look at the Ark of the Covenant if they are not of the Priestly Tribe of Aaron.

From 1978-1982 Ron Wyatt, claimed to have found the Ark of the Covenant along with other Temple Vessels in a chamber at the end of some tunnels underground Jerusalem. He claimed to have drilled a hole into the chamber that the ark was in and using a camera guided scope he saw some of the contents of the chamber which he identified.

1. The Ark of the Covenant
2. The Table of Showbread
3. The Golden Altar of Incense
4. The Golden Censer
5. The Golden Menorah
6. A large sword
7. An Ephod for the Breastplate of Judgement (High Priest wears)
8. A Miter with an ivory pomegranate on the tip
9. A brass shekel weight and numerous oil lamps

Ron Wyatt wasn't a European Jew or an Aaronite Priest, so how could he view the Ark of the Covenant? Menelik I, was sent back to Ethiopia with a son of each of the Priests/High Priests from Israel when he was sent to Ethiopia to teach his people how to properly follow the Laws of the God of Israel. The Jews in Israel, who reject "Christ" claim to have the Ark of the Covenant in Israel. However, they openly allow homosexuality in the Holy Land and co-worship on Temple Mount with Muslims. They have been victorious in all their battles for over 50 years now despite all of this and to top it off, ALL of the 12 Tribes of Israel have not returned to Israel.

However, the Bible predicted what would happen when the Israelites would scatter into all nations. They would multiply; slowly lose their heritage, worship other pagan gods and forget about the Ark of the Covenant.

Jeremiah 3:16 "And it shall come to pass, when ye be **MULTIPLIED AND INCREASED** in the land, in **THOSE DAYS**, saith the Lord, they shall say no more, The ark of the covenant of the Lord: neither shall it come to mind: neither shall they remember it; neither shall they visit it; neither shall that be done any more."

But later it reads:

Jeremiah 3:18 "**In those days the House of Judah shall walk with the House of Israel**, and they shall come together out of the land of the NORTH to the land that I have given for an inheritance unto your forefathers."

If Jeremiah is speaking about future events and he lived during the 6th Century B.C., when did the Lost Tribes of the House of Israel and House of Judah both walk together? When in history were both "Houses" regathered from this land of the **NORTH**? Was this referring to Europe? No!

IF THEY ARE LYING ABOUT THE ARK OF THE COVENANT, WHAT ABOUT SOLOMON'S TEMPLE?

Roman Emperor Hadrian (14th Emperor of Rome 117 A.D.-138 A.D.) founded a city in Jerusalem in place of the one that was razed (tore down) to the ground in 70 A.D., naming it "**Aelia Capitolina**", and on top of the where the old temple stood he raised a new temple to **Jupiter Ammon**. This brought on a war which consisted of different uprisings against the Romans, for the **JEWS** deemed it intolerable that foreign races should be settled in their city and foreign religious rites planted there." This was documented in the "**Jewish-Roman Wars**", which lasted from **66 A.D.-135 A.D.** and consisted of Gentile Proselyte Jews (and Edomite Jews) fighting to the death for their land. One of the main leaders of this Jewish revolt was "**Simeon Bar Kokhba**". Simeon in his last attempt to drum up unity amongst other Jewish revolt groups, tried to make "**Hebrew**" the official language of the Gentile Greek Jews. Simeon wanted to revive the "Hebrew" language and make it the official language because many of the Proselyte Gentile Jews (Greeks, Edomites, Turks, Europeans) did not speak "Hebrew" as this was **NOT** their "**Native Tongue**". See "**A Roadmap to the Heavens: An Anthropological Study of Hegemony among Priests, Sages and Laymen (Judaism and Jewish Life)** by Sigalit Ben-Zion, "**The Temples That Jerusalem Forgot**," by Professor Dr. Ernest Martin and **Roman history**, by Greco-Roman Historian Cassius Dio, Book 69:12, 229 A.D.

Another account tells another supposed eye witness account of the Temple being completely demolished. This was by **Eleazar Bin Jari** in 73 A.D. Eleazar was a commander of the Jewish rebels in Masada. **Masada** was a fortified Palace built by Herod the Great between 37 B.C-31 B.C. in the Southern District of Israel. Eleazar notes:

> **"It (Jerusalem) is now demolished to the very foundations, and hath nothing left but that moment of it preserved, I mean the camp of those (the Romans) that hath destroyed it, which still dwells upon its ruins."**
> **Eleazar Bin Jari 1st Century A.D.**

Eleazer documented that Jerusalem was destroyed with nothing standing, except the Roman Camp called "**Antonia Garrison Fort**" with its high stone walls still standing. Centuries later other nations trying to conquer Jerusalem would believe that the Roman Fortress walls were the actual remains of Solomon's Temple.

So the rock upon which the **Dome of the Rock** was built adjoining the Western Wall was actually the centerpiece around which Fort Antonia was built. There was nothing sacred about this rock or this Wall. This is confirmed by the eyewitness, **Gentile Jewish historian Flavius Josephus**, who also wrote in his **"Jewish Wars"** book that the Romans left nothing above or below ground of the Second Temple so that anyone coming to Jerusalem thereafter would never believe a Temple ever existed. According to Flavius Josephus, **Titus**, the Roman General who razed Jerusalem to the ground in 70 A.D., allowed Fort Antonia to be built to house the **Tenth Legion** (army of 6,000 men) left to monitor Roman affairs in Jerusalem. Over time during the many "Crusades" battles the Muslims and European nations would fight each other destroying most of the wall of "Fort Antonia". The remains of Fort Antonia are what people see today in Jerusalem. After quite some time, the victorious Muslims like Kurdish Saladin 1147 A.D. allowed the Gentile Judaism converts to come back to Jerusalem for worship only. When they came, centuries had past and they believed in their mind that the Roman fortress wall was the remains of Solomon's Temple. But it wasn't. Thus the Prophecy of Christ was fulfilled: **"Not one stone will be left upon another"**. God will not be mocked.

Matthew 24:1-2 "And Jesus went out, and departed from the temple: and his disciples came to him for to shew him the buildings of the temple. And Jesus said unto them, See ye not all these things? Verily I say unto you, **THERE SHALL NOT BE LEFT HERE ONE STONE UPON ANOTHER, THAT SHALL NOT BE THROWN DOWN."**

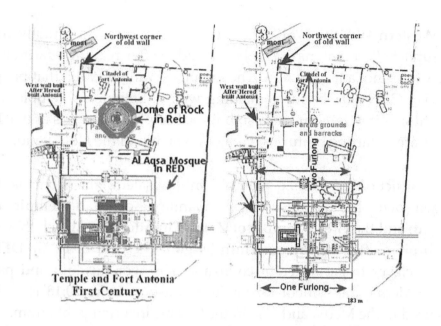

One "Furlong" is considered about 180-200 meters. Many biblical historians believe the true site of Solomon's temple is about a thousand feet South of the Temple Mount in the City of David.

According to Flavius Josephus in "**The Wars of the Jews**", Book 5, Chapter 5 he writes "The cloisters of the outmost court were in breadth thirty cubits, **while the entire compass of it was by measure six furlongs, including the tower of Antonia;** those entire courts that were exposed to the air were laid with stones of all sorts."

The Romans complete takeover of Jerusalem lead to certain things:

- The changing of Judea/Galilee/Samaria to "**Syria Palestina**" and Jerusalem to "**Aelia Capitolina**".
- The Destruction of Jerusalem and the Second Temple. The Romans took all the sacred vessels of the Gentile Jews, including the Golden "**Menorah**". This was depicted on the "**Arch of Titus**" relief in Rome.
- The Mass execution of the Gentile Judean population and diaspora of survivors (**Real Jews and proselyte Jews**) into Africa or Arabia.
- The transition of Pharisaism (**Pharisee-ism**) to Non-messianic Jewish sects called "**Rabbinic Judaism**".

So is the "**Western Wailing Wall**" the Jews kiss and pray to actually the Roman Temple to Jupiter/Fort Antonio? You be the judge after reading **Matthew 24:2 and Mark 13:2**. God is not a liar, man is. The famous "Wailing Wall" that people across the world visit CANNOT be the remaining wall of Solomon's Temple if Yahusha (Jesus) prophesied it. The Romans also built a Temple to Bacchus and a Temple to Venus in this area, starting centuries of pagan worship in the Holy Land.

After the destruction of Second Temple in Jerusalem, the Romans fashioned (copied) their own Temple after the Canaanite/Phoenician **Temple of BAAL (Thunder god)** and the Greek **Temple of Zeus (Thunder god)** which they called the **Temple of Jupiter, after the Roman Thunder god**. They are all **THUNDER GODS**. Satan is very clever to get different civilizations to worship him and pagan false gods. In the Media, the symbol for Satan because of **Luke 10:18** is a "**lightning bolt**". It is used in the Media and also in the Satanic inverted pentagram.

Nowadays children are being subliminally programmed with all sorts of Satanic symbolism. In the 1980's we didn't have pyramids, all-seeing eyes and lightning bolts flashing across the TV screen.

Luke 10:18 "And he said unto them, I beheld Satan AS **LIGHTNING** fall from heaven.

Satanist Music Artist Marilyn Manson released his album "**Antichrist Superstar**" in 1996. He used the **Lightning bolt** and the Pentagram to signify Satan/Lucifer. The "**Lightning enclosed in a circle**" symbol" supposedly has the Hebrew Letters for the Hebrew word "**Leviathan**", which in bible history is often identified with Satan. In Satanism it is one of the "infernal" names of Satan/Lucifer. This symbol was also borrowed from the symbolism of the "**Church of Satan**", founded by Ashkenazi Jew, Anton LaVey Sandor.

THE REBELLIOUS AND STIFF-NECKED ISRAELITES

Now the Children of Israel didn't serve God or keep his commandments. They served other pagan gods in each land they were in such as **Siccuth, Chiun, Remphan, Baal, Moloch, Dagon and Horus**. They worshipped the pagan gods of the Canaanites, the Egyptians, the Ethiopians, the Moabites, the Zidonites, the Philistines, the Greeks, the Romans and so on. Still to this day we are misled by many Freemason inspired branches of Christianity such as Jehovah's Witness, Seventh Day Adventists, and the Mormons. We say we love the Lord as our savior but we do not act like it outside of Church. We don't show that we love God with **ALL OUR HEART**. This has been witnessed in America and in Africa. We still worship "mammon (money)" and pagan gods (West Africa-Shango) mixed in with our Christian Beliefs. So is this why we are still enduring continued suffering as a people? Despite knowing the Most High and his commandments thousands of years ago all the way until now, we have adopted the religions of the foreign lands we were brought to. We have lost our foundation and the remembrance of who we are. We are also a "**REBELLIOUS PEOPLE**" who are disobedient and have always been disobedient if you look at the Bible.

Ezekiel 3:7 "But the house of Israel will not hearken unto thee; for they will not hearken unto me: for all the House of Israel are impudent and **hardhearted**."

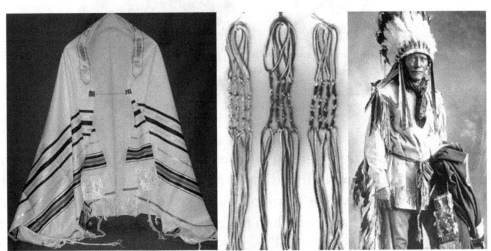

(Left) Tallit Gadol, (Middle) Tzitzit, (Right) Native American with his "Poncho" and tassel.

The **House of Israel** normally represented the **10 Northern Tribes of Israel**, minus the Tribe of Judah and Benjamin. In many books such as "**Lost Tribes and Promised Lands: The Origins of American Racism**" by Ronald Sanders the Native Americans were witnessed saying the "**Shema Yisrael**" Jewish prayer in perfect Hebrew. They also reported to Spanish and Dutch Jewish settlers that they were from the **Tribe of Reuben** and **Joseph (Ephraim/Manasseh)**. But how can this be? The Native Americans have many "**Hebrewisms**" in their culture/traditions that I will go into detail in further volumes of "Hebrews to Negroes". The Jewish "**Tallit Gadol (Big cloak-poncho)**", the "**Tallit Katan (Small Cloak-poncho)**" and the Jewish "**Tzitzit**" tassel are common in the Native American Tribes in addition to "**fringes**" on the borders of a garment. **Notice the tassel on the Native Americans belt.** The Native Americans also referred to their God as "**Ya**", "**Yo-He-Wa**" or "**Ya-ho-ah**" before Christopher Columbus and his Spanish friends could spread Christianity throughout the land. The letter "Y" was used in Israel and the Middle East because the letter "I" and "J" was only common in Latin (**which is an A.D. language**). **The Ancient Assyrians referred to the God of Israel as "Yahu-(a)" as there was no "Jehovah".** Christopher Columbus got to the Americas in **1492**. The name "**Jehovah**" first appeared in English Bibles in **1530**, when William Tyndale published an English translation of the Torah. In this he included the name of God, spelled as "**IEHOUAH**" because they didn't use "**Y**" or "**J**". He included this word in several verses such as Genesis 15:2, Exodus 6:3, Exodus 15:3, Exodus 17:6, Exodus 23:17 just to name a few. The Native Americans however were still using the "Y", just as the Israelites did back then. Even the Gentile Jews today use the "y"as in the word "**Yisrael, Y'srael, or Yehudi**". This is a subtle clue that they obviously have more claims to being "**Israel**" than their Gentile Jewish oppressors who came to their land killing, stealing, enslaving and raping.

Some of the "**Natives**" in the Americas and the Caribbean called their Supreme God "**The Great Spirit**". For example, the Cherokee Indian "Great Spirit" was called was "**Ya**". The Cherokee Indian word "**He**" like the Hebrew letter "**He(y)**" represents the word "**The**" when used in the beginning of a sentence. Coincidence?

The Cherokee Indian Morning song goes:

We'n de YA HO (2 times) = I am of the Great Spirit it is so
We'n de YA (2 times) = I am of the Great Spirit

HO HO HO HO = It is so
He YA HO (2 times) = The Great Spirit, it is so.

Fact 1: Has the stubbornness of Israel been passed down in our DNA? Throughout the years Africans, African-Americans, Haitians, Puerto Ricans, Brazilians, Cubans, Jamaicans, Latinos and Native Americans have been known to rebel against their oppressors. Even when outgunned and outnumbered, these race groups put up a formidable fight against the European countries.

Slave Revolts

- 1526 San Miguel de Gualdape, Sapelo Island, George (win)
- 1570 Gaspar Yanga's revolt, Veracruz, (win)
- 1712 New York Slave revolt (lost)
- 1733 St John Slave Revold, Saint John (suppressed)
- 1739 Stono Rebellion, South Carolina (suppressed)
- 1741 New York Conspiracy (suppressed)

- 1760 Tacky's War, Jamaica (suppressed)
- 1791-1804 Haitian Revolution, Saint-Domingue, Haiti (win)
- 1800 Gabriel Prosser, Virginia (suppressed)
- 1803 Igbo (Ebo) Landing, St. Simons Island, Georgia (suppressed)
- 1805 Chatham Manor, Virginia (suppressed)
- 1811 German Coast Uprising, Territory of Orleans (suppressed)
- 1815 George Boxley, Virginia (suppressed)
- 1816 Bussa's Rebellion, Barbados, West Indies (suppressed)
- 1822 Denmark Vesey, South Carolina (suppressed)
- 1831 Nat Turner's rebellion, Virginia (suppressed)
- 1831-1832 Baptist War, Jamaica, (suppressed)
- 1839 Amistad ship rebellion, off Cuban coast (win)
- 1841 Creole case ship rebellion, Southern U.S coast (win)
- 1842 Slave revolt in the Cherokee Nation, Southern U.S. (suppressed)
- 1859 John Brown's Raid, Virginia (suppressed).

Exodus 33:5 "For the Lord had said unto Moses, Say unto the Children of Israel, Ye are a **STIFFNECKED** people: I will come up into the midst of thee in a moment, and consume thee: therefore now put off thy ornaments from thee, that I may know what to do unto thee."

Israel is documented in the "**Old Testament**" as being a stubborn, stiff-necked, and rebellious people (**Ex. 32:9, 33:3,5, 34:9**). They were hard to govern and control by their many conquerors (Ezra 4:11-19). Back in the day, Nigerian Igbo's were given this trait by the British Occupiers in the 1800's. The British were amazed at the Nigerian Igbo's native organizational and governmental structure. They were also impressed on how well they resisted the British advance and attempt at control. The slaves from Nigeria were so rebellious that many slavetraders decided to exile them to Haiti and Jamaica. Ironically, many Nigerian Igbo Africans when coming to America also see African-Americans as wild and rebellious, not adhering to authority or authoritative figures. But this is also fueled by "Westernized Stereotypes" of Blacks in America when we are portrayed in the Media negatively.

Fact: In a White House memo dated Tuesday, January 28, 1969 to President Nixon, former Secretary of State, Henry Kissinger describes the Igbos as **"the wandering Jews of West Africa"-gifted, aggressive, westernized, at best envied and resented**, but mostly despised by their neighbors in the federation"(foreign relations document, volume E-5, documents on Africa (1969-1972)

Deuteronomy 28:48 **"Therefore shalt thou serve thine enemies which the LORD shall send against thee, in HUNGER, and in THIRST, and in NAKEDNESS, and in want of all things: and he shall put a YOKE OF IRON upon thy neck, until he have destroyed thee.**

What other race was sold into slavery in nakedness with a literal "yoke of iron" around their neck? Africans or European Jews?

Slaves worked in gruesome conditions in which they were in "**starvation**" and literal "**nakedness**". Black slaves all over the world were shackled in chains **NAKED** with an **iron yoke** around their neck, shackles on their hands and shackles on their feet. Sometimes black slaves were attached to heavy pieces of wood or attached with chains to other slaves so that groups of slaves could not run away. This did not happen to the European Jews during the Holocaust nor any other race in history other than the Negroes, the Black-brown-skinned Native "Indians", the Australian Aborigines and the East Dravidian Indians. No other race has been rounded up to be sold as slaves in America and in other countries in the magnitude that the black race has throughout history.

*(Left) A British Slavemaster in **Northeast Australia, Queensland** with his aboriginal child slave. The European British came to Australia killing and enslaving the Black Native Aborigines. **Dr. Gideon Polya**, a scientist, artist, writer and pro-peace advocate, wrote that roughly 123 years after the arrival of the British, the Black "Indigenous" aboriginal population dropped from about 1 million to 0.1 million in the first century after their invasion in 1788. By 1911, 90% of the population of the aborigines had been wiped out.*

Deuteronomy 28:49 "The LORD shall bring a nation against thee from far, from the end of the earth, as swift as the eagle flieth; a nation whose TONGUE THOU SHALL NOT UNDERSTAND;"

Just like in Nigeria and other African countries, the British invaded Kenya. Coming from a foreign land on their home turf, the Africans were not able to stand to the Europeans advanced weaponry and battle skills.

The Slaves living in Africa did not know the language of their oppressors nor the language of the land that they were sold to. Nations from afar (**Spain, France, Britain, Holland, Netherlands, Portugal, Great Britain, Arabia, Iraq, Iran (Persia), India, Pakistan, European Jews and other countries**) all participated in the capturing and selling of black slaves. During slavery, the African captives were forced to speak their language. Nothing about the 7-12 year Holocaust was bible prophecy because the European Jews were not taken from a nation afar and they did in fact know the language of their oppressors because they lived amongst the Germans and other Europeans when they were thrown into the concentration camps. So they knew how to speak German as this was a core component of their language "Yiddish" (**Any German can partially understand the Jewish Yiddish language**). These Europeans were **Hebrew-speaking Japhetic Gentiles** who simply adopted the religion of "**Judaism**", just as many Romans, Greeks and Edomites had did before throughout early history. Roman turned Judaism convert **Flavius Josephus** (as in the Roman "Flavian" Dynasty) even attested to this:

"That country is also called Judea, and the people **Jews**; and this name is given also to **AS MANY** as embrace **THEIR RELIGION** (Judaism), though of **OTHER NATIONS**.

(**Note**: Proof that the Jews in that time were simply Judaism converts from other nations like Greece or Rome).

"But then upon what foundation so good a governor as **Hyrcanus** (grandson of Matthias patriarch of the Greek Judaism-worshipping Maccabee Family). Took upon himself to compel these Idumeans (**Edomites**) either to become Jews (**BY RELIGION**) or to leave their country, deserves great consideration. I suppose it was because they had long ago been driven out of the land of Edom, and had seized on and possessed the **Tribe of Simeon (the land not the people)**, and all the southern part of the land of the **Tribe of Judah**, which was the peculiar inheritance of the worshippers of the **True God** without idolatry…."

Flavius Josephus

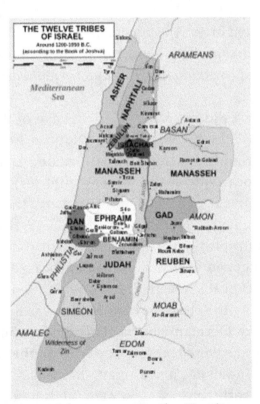

As you can see, Edom was able to possess the Territory of Simeon and Judah because these Tribes were already scattered. In the Book of Obadiah God says in Judgement (future) he would wipe out the House of Esau FOREVER, and not

even a remnant would remain. It says the Edomites land would be possessed by Israel in the future.

Obadiah 1:17-18 "But upon Mount Zion shall be deliverance, and there shall be holiness; and the **house of Jacob shall possess their possessions.** And the house of Jacob shall be a fire, and the house of Joseph a flame, and the house of Esau for stubble, and they shall devour them; **and there shall not be ANY remaining of the house of Esau; for the Lord hath spoken it."**

The European Jews fused their original Germanaic/Turkish/Slavic language with Modern Hebrew and called it "**Yiddish**". This was not **PURE HEBREW** as anyone who speaks German can slightly understand "Yiddish". Back then everybody that practiced "**Judaism**" was called a "**Jew**". Even King Herod was called "**King of the Jews**" because he ruled over Judea and was a follower of Judaism. Some people also believe the "**eagle flieth**" is referring to the Eagle symbols for America, Europe (Spain), and the Holy Roman Empire. Even the scripture in **Obadiah 1:4** is believed to be referring to Edom and the Japhetic lands in which Edom has infused his bloodline into who have placed "**Satellites**" into space. Thus in essence they have set their property/land and mark in space among the stars.

Obadiah 1:4 "Though thou exalt thyself as the eagle, and though thou **SET THY NEST AMONG THE STARS**, thence will I bring thee down, saith the Lord."

WHAT WAS THE NATIVE TONGUE OF THE WEST AFRICANS TAKEN FROM THE SLAVE COAST?

The bible says "**A Nation whose tongue thou shall not understand."** So what language did the Black Hebrew Israelites in West Africa speak before being brought to the Americas and the Caribbean? Was it Hebrew, Aramaic or another language? Let's look at **Nigeria** and the **Igbo Tribe**. Nigeria is the biggest African country in West Africa and most of the slaves take to the Americas were from the Nigeria/Benin area. You be the judge.

1. **Hebrew Strong's** #589 "**ANI**" is a Hebrew word that means "**I**" or "**MYSELF**".

Hebrew Strong's #580 "**ANU**" means "**WE**".

NIGERIAN IGBO word "**ANYI**" means "**US/WE**".
Example - ANYI na-abia means "**We are coming**". ANYI na ebe akwa means "**We are crying**". Ha na **ANYI** biara means "**They came with us**".

2. **Hebrew 5th Letter** "**HA(Y) or "HE(Y)**" means "**THE**" when added to the front of a word like a prefix.

NIGERIAN IGBO word "**HA**" means "**THEY**".
Example – **HA**-na-abia means "**They are coming**". **HA** bere akwa means "**They cried**".

3. **Hebrew Strong's** #1961 "**A HAYAH**" means "**I AM**" or "**I WILL BE**".

NIGERIAN IGBO word "**AHA YA**" means "**HIS NAME**". Is this a coincidence that in our bible God tells Moses "HIS NAME" is "I AM"? Did the ancient Igbo people come up with "AHA YA" to mean "HIS NAME" because they had knowledge of what the Torah says?

Exodus 3:14 "And God said unto Moses, **I AM THAT I AM**: and he said, Thus shalt thou say unto the Children of Israel, **I AM** hath sent me unto you."

4. "**AHA**" in the Nigerian Igbo language means "**name**". "**YA**" sometimes refers to "**HIM**" **Example** - AHA YA BU TOCHUKWU means his name is Tochukwu. **AHA YA** BU CHUKWU ABIAMA means **his name** is God of Abraham)

5. **Hebrew Strong's** #2417 "**CHAY**" means life and living.

NIGERIAN IGBO word "**CHI**" means "**God-source of all life**". The Igbo word for **God** is also considered "**CHI**". "**UKWU**" means mighty in Igbo language. Hence, CHI-UKWU means **MIGHTY GOD OR GOD ALMIGHTY.**

6. **Hebrew Strong's #221 "URI"** means "FIERY, FIRE, AND LIGHT". **Hebrew Strong's #222 "URIEL"** means "FLAME OF GOD" from the root "UR" and "EL". **Hebrew Strong's #223A "URIAH/URIYYAH"** means "FLAME OF YAH".

THE NIGERIAN IGBO word "URI" meaning is a traditional **FIRE LANTERN**. Uri is a traditional Igbo fire lantern made from the extract of palm fruits. It is damped with palm oil and ignited with fire. Its light is used in the night. **FIRE LANTERN** in Igbo language is also known as "URI MMU".

7. **Hebrew Strong's #215 & #216 "OR"** means "LIGHT" or "TO SHINE".

NIGERIAN IGBO word "ORIRI" means "CELEBRATION". It also can mean eating.

Fact: The word "**Omoros**" from (**Omo Oro**) was originally the name used for the "**Moors**". The word "**Omoros**" meant "**Children of Light**" broken down as: **Children** (Nigerian Yoruba word "Omo") **of Light** (Hebrew/Nigerian Afa dibia priest Ibgo word "Oro/Ora/Or"). The ancient Nigerian Igbo Afa Divination priests called light "**Ora**", which is very similar to the Hebrew word for light "**Or/Ori**". The Black Moors were originally people living in Africa before Islam was started. When Islam came on the scene they converted. Many people speculate that the Moors were Black Hebrew Israelites prior to becoming Muslims and this is why they were able to live in harmony with their Black Hebrew Israelite brothers still practicing Mosaic Law in North Africa and Iberia (Spain/Portugal). The Black Moors arrived in Andulusa, Spain in the 700's A.D. and ruled Europe for little over 700 years.

(Above) Ifa Divination sand tray used in West Africa.

The Ifa system was used in different regions where the Black Hebrew Israelites were scattered. The "Ifa divination" practice stayed with different Black Hebrew Israelite tribes as they followed trade routes into Africa (i.e. King Solomon's trade routes into Africa by way of Egypt and the trade routes from Morocco to Timbuktu, Mali). People like the mande-speaking Bambara people in Mali, Guinea, Burkina Faso and Senegal use a 16-symbol divination symbol which his similar to the 16 stories told by the Ifa priests of West Africa. The Bambara people are related to the Mandinka, Soninke and Diola (Jola) people that have been associated in the past by their neighbors as being "Black Jews". This divination system is also found in the West African people of the Ashanti/Akan, Yoruba, Igbo, Hausa, Nok, Songhai, Congo and Cameroon. Many experts believe this African "divination" system is connected to both Egypt and Hebrew mysticism as it has proven that the Zadokite (High Priest) Aaronites called the "Essene sect" were using this in Ancient Israel. The Aaronite (Cohenite) priests were using the "Ephod" in Israelite culture with oracular practices and Priestly rituals (Exodus 28:4, 29:5, 39.2 and Leviticus 8:7).

Fact: The Ancient Nigerian Igbo Afa Divination priests called light "**Ora**", which is very similar to the Hebrew word for light "**Or/Ori**". The also used the word "**baba**" for father, which is also similar to the Hebrew word "**abba**" for father. Divination is the attempt to gain insight or information in regards to a certain situation using rituals, signs, omens, events or through supernatural spiritual means. Some people may call it "fortune telling" but the Ifa divination system is based on "Religion and Spirituality". The Nigerians Igbos, Yoruba's and other West Africans (Congo, Ghana, Togo, Cameroon) all have ancient history of a form of receiving spiritual knowledge from God using these kinds of "Ifa Divination systems." In Igboland this Ifa Divination system/religion is called "**Afa**" and it is performed by a specialist/priest called "Dibia". The Ewe Tribe of Ghana and Togoland also call the "Ifa" divination system/religion "**Afa**". The Nigerian Yoruba's still call it "**Ifa**" and for them it is the basis of all spiritual knowledge/divinations. Typically it is passed down orally from generation to generation from one "**babalawo**" to another. A Babalawo is an "**Ifa Priest**" and in Latin America (Cuba) it means in the Yoruba language "Father of knowledge/wisdom/divinations from the two root words "**baba**" meaning father (like abba in Hebrew) and "**awo**" meaning divination. West Africans have kept these "diviners" in their villages for centuries because they were used to these ancient practices in Israel. These Afa (Ifa) priests are the mediators between God and the people in their village. Even though we know that Yahusha is the ONLY mediator between God (father) and man, in the Old Testament it was common for the Israelites to seek religious help from the Prophets or the Priests (i.e. Moses, Aaronites). The Biblical prophets also interpreted dreams and foretold the future (i.e. Joseph, Daniel) similar to what West African Ifa (Afa) priests do today. The Native Americans also had Shamans/Priests that practiced "divination"

8. **Hebrew Strong's #3818 "LO AMMI"** means "**NOT MY PEOPLE**". "**LO**" means "**NO**" or "**NOT**".
   Hebrew Strong's #5971/5972 "AM" means "**PEOPLE**". "**AMI**" means "**MY PEOPLE**".
   Hebrew Strong's #1151 "BEN-AMMI" means "**SON OF MY PEOPLE**".

   NIGERIAN IGBO WORD "**ANI**" means "**THE PEOPLE, MY PEOPLE, NATION OR LAND**". "**ANI**" in Igbo symbolizes the land, nation and "**THE PEOPLE**". Grave sin against the people is called "**NSO ANI**" meaning what the land forbids.

9. **Hebrew Strong's #609 "ASA"**(to heal or healer).

   NIGERIAN IGBO WORD "ASAA" (meaning seven and a number of perfection). In 2 Kings 5:10-14 Elisha had a messenger tell Naaman to wash his body in the Jordan river **SEVEN TIMES** to restore his skin back to black. Coincidence?

10. **Hebrew Name "Tobijah (Zechariah 6:10") or "TOVIYAH"**, means **"Yah is good"**. This is a form of praise for Black people when they say to each other **"God (YAH) is good"**. **Hebrew Strong's #2895 "TOB"** means **"GOOD"**. **Hebrew Strong's #8426 "TODAH"** means **"THANSGIVING OR PRAISE"**.

    NIGERIAN IGBO WORD "**TOVIYA**" from the two words **"TOWE=PRAISE"** and **"HIM=YA"** is (**PRAISE HIM (GOD)**). See how the word "Ya" meaning "Him" can be also associated with God (**Praise him=Praise God**). In some Igbo dialect **TOVIYA** can be pronounce and written as **TOBEYA** or **TOBEYA(H)** when singing to God.

11. **Hebrew Strong's #568 "AMARIAH"** means "God/Yah has said" or "Yah has promised".

    NIGERIAN IGBO WORD **"AMARACHI"** means **"GRACE OF GOD"**. "**AMARA**" in Igbo language means **"GRACE"**, whereas "**CHI**" means **"GOD"**. AMARA-CHI then means GRACE OF GOD

12. **Hebrew Strong's #1004 "B-AYI-TH" means "HOUSE".**

    NIGERIAN IGBO "BE AYI" means **"OUR HOME"**. **"NDI BE AYI"** means **"AND OUR HOME"**. In Hebrew "**BETH**" is equal to a house, place or temple. Example: **"Betheel #1008"** means **"House of God"**. **"Beth Peor #1047"** means **"House of Peor"**. The Igbo word "**BE**" means **"home or house"**.

13. **In Ancient Hebrew "Y" or "Ya" meant "HE".**

The **NIGERIAN IGBO** word "**YA**" means likewise "**HIM**". The word "**LORD**" in all capital letters is **YHUH/YHVH** or Hebrew Strong's #3068. It is also known as the "Tetragrammaton". In many cultures names are used as **identifiers**; a word with no meaning can identify an individual. However, surprisingly in Hebrew and Igbo culture, each name has a meaning. In the case of the "Tetragrammaton" the "Hey-Vav/Waw-Hey" or Hebrew Strong's #1933/1934/1961 "**Hawah/Hava/Hayah**" means "to **Exist**". So when you add the pronoun "**Y**" or "**Ya**" you get the word "**Ya-hawah**" which means "**He exists**". This is the same as a person saying "**I AM**" or "**I AM THAT I AM**". A person saying this would be equivalent to them saying "**I exist**". But we know that in **Paleo-Hebrew**, which Moses spoke, there was no "V" or "W" in their vocabulary. **There is NO "V" or "W" in the Old Hebrew language.** The "**U**" came first, just as it comes before "V" and "W" in the English alphabet. That being said, the name of the LORD/GOD would've been "**He Exists**" or "**Ya-Hu-ah**". However we must keep in mind the "U" came first before the "V" and "W" so name "**YAHUAH**" existed before "**YAHAWAH**" even existed. In the 1st person we have the word "**eh-hawah**" which means "**I exist**", or "**I am**". In the 2nd person we have the word "**th-hawah**" or "**You exist**, or "**You are**". In the 3rd person we have the word "**Ya-hawah**" or "**He exists**" or "**He is**". The Most High God (**El Elyon**) told Moses to give his name in the 3rd person. Because Moses was going to speak in the 3rd person, meaning Moses (1st person) was going to speak to the Israelites (a 2nd person) about the God of Abraham he spoke with (3rd person). Thus his name was given in 3rd person as "He exists or He is". That name would've been "Yahuah", before anyone could add a "V" or "W" changing it to "Yahawah".

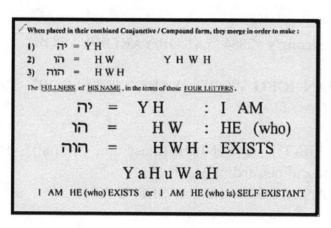

When placed in their combined Conjunctive / Compound form, they merge in order to make :

1) יה = Y H
2) הו = H W   Y H W H
3) הוה = H W H

The FULLNESS of HIS NAME , in the terms of those FOUR LETTERS .

יה = Y H   : I AM
הו =   H W   : HE (who)
הוה =   H W H : EXISTS

YaHuWaH

I AM HE (who) EXISTS or I AM HE (who is) SELF EXISTANT

The **Tetragrammaton** has dual meanings: "**I AM HE WHO EXISTS**" and "**BEHOLD THE HAND, BEHOLD THE NAIL**".

Hey		Lo! Behold! "The"
Vav	Y	Nail / peg / add / "And"
Zayin		Plow / weapon / cut off
Chet		Tent wall / fence / separation
Tet	⊗	Basket / snake / surround
Yod		Arm and hand / work / deed

BEHOLD NAIL BEHOLD ARM / HAND
יהוה

The Ancient Hebrew pictograph for the "Tetragrammaton" reads from "right to left": ***Behold the hand, Behold the name!***

Note: the components of YHWH, are **Y**(a), meaning roughly **HE** and the consonants root "**HUH/HWH**" which is connected with acts of creation. There appears to be two main line of reasoning to explain the origin of the name. The first suggest that it is the shortened form of a sentence "**HE CAUSES TO BE or HE CREATES**". This is where we get the word "**Yahuah**" and **Yahawah**" from.

14. **Hebrew Strong's #2384 "IAKOB/YAKOB/YACOB"**

NIGERIAN IGBO WORD "**YAKO**" IS "**JACOB**". "**OJI (OGGI) YAKO**" means "Tree of Jacob".

15. Hebrew "**SIXTH**" is "**SH-ISHI** (masculine ordinal)". Hebrew "**SIX**" is "**SH-ISHA** (masculine cardinal)".
NIGERIAN IGBO WORD for "**SIX**" IS "**ISII**".

16. **Hebrew Strong's #6224 "TENTH"** is "**AS-IRI**" pronounced, (as-ee-ree).
NIGERIAN IGBO for "**TENTH**" is "**IRI**".

17. Hebrew Strong's #571 "**EMET/EMETH**" means the "**TRUTH**". However, the Ancient Jewish Sages sometimes say the "**Seal of God**" aka "**The Creation**" is the word "**TRUTH**". That being said, the final letters of the three words that conclude and describes the "**Creation**" are "**BARA ELOHIM LA'ASOT**", meaning "**God created TO DO**". The last three Hebrew characters on each of these words spell "**Emet**", which mean the "**TRUTH**".

   NIGERIAN IGBO WORD "**EME**" means "**ACT OF DOING**".

EMET = Aleph-Mem-Tav

In the Bible (**Numbers 11:16-30**), Moses nominated 70 Elders in addition to himself and Aaron to "Prophesy" to the people. They were led by the "**Spirit of God**" and nothing else. So in total this was 72 elders, all males, in a settlement that consisted of men, women, and children. In Nigeria, there is a village called "**Edda**" made up of 72 "**sub-villages**" believed to have descended from **72 priests** who arrived in what is now the "Ebonim/Ebonyim state of Nigeria.

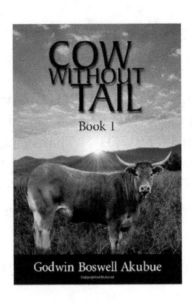

*Nigerian Igbo author, **Godwin Akubue,** details in his book "**Cow without a tail**" the following:*

"There is also a tendency to return to the past and dig up much of the information that can help us in maintaining a coherent cause, but it is not very necessary, yet we can reach on, for instance, certain reference like the one we find in Jack Lundbom's book, "**husot**" (Jeremiah 34-47, AB page 63, 2004). It is the Hebrew interpretation of the English word **"street/road."** He based his words from **Hapax Legomenon of Hebrew and Septuagint LXX**, which I have always known to rank with the more common **Peshitta (Syriac-Aramaic/Modern Hebrew) version**, but slightly lower than Lucian System. If, however, the interpretation of the English word "**street/road**" is **husot (h is usually silent)** in Hebrew, we are dealing with something of pronunciation and interpretation. In **Nigerian Igbo**, the word for street/road is **uso (uzo)**, which does not sponsor the very presence of the letters in Hebrew, but the former in this case might be more accurate since Ancient Hebrew is built around letters and not sounds."

How can Black Africans have Hebrew hidden in their dialect? Who taught them the Hebrew Language? Evidence of Hebrew/Aramaic can be found in many African countries such as Ghana, Nigeria, Cameroon and the Congo but it requires knowing Hebrew in addition to understanding the formation of these African languages. If there are "Real" Black Jews living in Africa, why aren't they white like the Jews in Europe, Israel and America? The Sun's intensity (UV index) in Nigeria is the same or even lower than the UV indexes in Israel and the Middle East. Someone is obviously not who they say they are because we know that Black people do not just turn white. We also know that white races, no matter how sun they get cannot turn black. Someone is lying about their history and Jewish heritage. This is called an "**Imposter**".

The Hebrew Strong's #5972 word עם "**am**" means "**people or nation**" but "**his people**" or "**his nation**" would be written as עמו "**amo**". In Hebrew "**Amo Israel/Y'srael**" is the name for "**His Nation of Israel**" or "**His People of Israel**" because "**Amo**" means "**his people/his nation**". But we know in the bible that God refers to all the Israelites (man, woman and child) as "Children". So in a sense "**Amo**" is also seen as "**Children of**" thus making "**Amo Yisrael**" the same as saying "**Children of Israel**". The Nigerian Yoruba word for children is "**Omo**" and the Nigerian Igbo word for children is "**Umu**". This is strikingly the same as the word "**Amo**". WOW!

Amos 9:7 "Are ye not as **CHILDREN** of the Ethiopians unto me, **O CHILDREN OF ISRAEL**? saith the Lord."

Some Igbos call themselves "**Umu Israel**" because "**Umu**" means "**children of**". We already see how "**Amo**" and "**Umu**" sounds kind of similar and both words in these different languages can mean "**Children of**" or "**Children**". The Igbo language is known to use the letter "U'" frequently and the Yoruba's tend to use the letter "O". But how convenient is it that "Umu," "Amo," and "Omo" all mean the same thing. How is that possible? How is the Nigerian language so similar to Hebrew? Perhaps they are descendants of an older group of Israelites who were exiled from Israel in B.C. times. Maybe they are the descendants of Hebrew Israelites that lived in the Post-Exodus Era. This would explain they have stories where their elders state that they are "Israelites". This explains why their language is more close to Paleo-Hebrew (2,000 B.C. to 400 B.C.), which was the time era that Paleo-Hebrew dominated. It wasn't until after the destruction of the Solomon's Temple and rebuilding of the Second during the Babylonian/Persian days that Aramaic came into play as the major language. This was during 500 B.C. and 400 B.C., right along the Aramaic language timeline. Let's look at this:

The word "**Deuteronomy**" in Hebrew is "**Devarim**" or "**Elleh Hallebarim**" which means "**these are the words**"? In Greek it is called "**Deutero-Nomos**", meaning "**second law**". In Igbo it is pronounced as "**Detuoro umu unu**" meaning "**Write it for your children**". Moses was old and dying when he re-iterated the law to his Israelite children who were going to enter in the land of Canaan with Joshua. Some Igbo's say "**Biafra**" means "**Come from Ephraim**" as "**Bia**" means "**come**" and "**fra**" some say is short for "**Ephraim**". Joshua, the Israelite who led the Children of Israel into the Land of Canaan was from the Tribe of Ephraim. Ephraim was ahead of the Northern Kingdom of the House of Judah. Perhaps the Nigerian Igbos and Yoruba's were the 1st wave of Israelites that were removed from their land during the Assyrian Invasion. Yoruba's have an Ancient list of the Assyrian Kings in their language as it correlates to the Israelite Kings who were ruling at the time. Many people say this gives strong proof that their descendants must have lived through this time period and wrote it down for the many generations to come. How else would they have knowledge of this history if they were always living in West Africa?

"**Nke-ocha/Nke-osha**" or "**Keosha/Keocha**" in Igbo means "**the right one, the preferred one, or the clean.**" The Hebrew Strong's word #3787 "**Kasher**" from where we get the English word "**Kosher**" from the meaning "**fit, proper, or correct**" in Hebrew. The word "**Five**" in Igbo is "**ISE**" and in Hebrew it is "**Ham-Ishi**". So how are all of these Igbo words similar to Hebrew? How did it get there? Slavemasters in the South often heard their slaves speaking their native dialect. They were able to link up certain things with the way the African slaves were pronunciating it. Well, in South Carolina the slaves called a Dog, "**Boa**" short for the Western Aramaic word for "**dog**" "**Kal-BOA**". Western Aramaic was only spoken in Israel. Eastern Aramaic was spoken in Syria, Iraq and Iran. No one speaks Western Aramaic as of today. In Eastern Aramaic and Arabic the word "**dog**" is pronounced "**Kalbaa**". Other similarities in the Native African tribal dialects to Hebrew were also found in the forests of the Congo. But how can this be? These are black people. They were in no way related to the European Ashkenazi Jews or Sephardic Jews. So how do we explain all of this? Easy! Someone has to be an imposter, a nation that learned how to speak Hebrew and learned how to follow the religion of Judaism. We know the Europeans did not come into Africa teaching the natives Hebrew.

548

That would not make any sense. This could only mean the **"Original Israelites"** were Black or definitely **"People of Color"**.

THE NIGERIAN IGBO EGYPTIAN-ISRAELITE CONNECTION

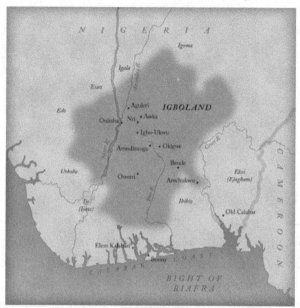

Igboland sits in Southeastern Nigeria.

There are many different dialects in the area known as **"Igboland"**. This means that the word for **"God"** can differ in some villages. But if some of the Nigerian Igbo's dialects have traces of Ancient Egyptian and Hebrew language could this stem from the Ancient Hebrew Israelites knowledge of the Egyptian language? After all the Egyptian/Canaanite word for **"God"** called **"El"** is used also in Hebrew as **"Elohim-God (plural)"**, **"Eloah-God" "El Shaddai-God Almighty"** and **"El Elyon-God Most High"**.

Ancient Yoruba King

Fact: People from Ghana call the Creator "**Yehowa**" and "**Yehowah**" and the son "**Yesu**" like "**Yeshua**" which is Aramaic for **JESUS**. Ok. "**Yehowah**" sounds like Yahuah and they pronounce it that way. "**Oluwa**" is a Yoruba name for Lord or God Almighty. In the Bini (Edo-Nigeria/Benin) language "**Osanobuwa**" is a name for God. In Nigerian Igbo "**Osebruwa**" is also a name for God, maker of Heaven and Earth, or the Creator. "**Chi**" or "**Chukwu**" can also be used depending on what part of Nigeria you live in. Each of these words for God has "**Uwa**" on the end pronounced like our "**UAH**" in "**Yah-UAH**" But what does "**Uau**" or "**Uwa**" mean? The Hebrew letters Yod-Hey spell "**Yah**". The Hebrew letters Uau-Hey spell "**Uah**", pronounced (**oo-ah/u-wah**). Why? Because the Hebrew letter "**Hey**" is usually silent on the end of a word. The Yod-Hey-Uau-Hey or "**Yahuah**" in Paleo-Hebrew means in its symbolic pictograph form "**Behold the hand, Behold the Nail**". Remember if you follow our alphabet q, r, s, t, **U, V, W** you see the "**U**" comes first. These word choices for God goes back to the Semitic language of our forefathers in **ISRAEL** (Hebrew and Aramaic). In Phoenician and Hebrew "**El**" was used for "**God**". In its single form it was "**Eloah**" and in its plural form it was "**Elohim**". In Aramaic "**El + Ah**" gave "**Elah**" from which **ARABIC** would get the word "**ALLAH**". Now "**Eloah**" is similar to the Yoruba name for God/Lord "**Oluwa**".

Note: Remember the Yoruba language uses the letter "**O**" frequently as the Igbo language uses the letter "**U**" frequently.

So if we use this principle replacing "El" with "Ol" and "oah" with "uwa" we get "Ol-uwa" instead of "El-oah". **ELOAH AND ELOHIM** and **EL-Shaddai** were names for God prior to **MOSES** in Ancient Biblical times probably pre-Abrahamic or post-Abrahamic. And we know that the language of the land was "One" before the language got changed at the Tower of Babel with Nimrod, son of Cush, son of Ham, son of Noah. What language do you think NOAH spoke? **HEBREW** of course! **SHEM** spoke Hebrew and so did Eber, Abraham and Ishmael. Aramaic was not made an official language in Assyria until 400 B.C. **ARABIC**, which came later, is even newer than Ethiopian language **GE'EZ** and the **GREEK** language. So the Hebrew "**Elo+ah**" was the Yoruba's "**Olu-wa**". The Nigerian "**uwa**" was the Hebrew "**Uah**" and the Ghanaians use "**owa**" in their name "Yeh-**OWA**-h" where the "h" is silent in the Hebrew name for God "Yahuah". All are corruptions of what we say "Yahuah", "Yehoshua", "Yahushua" and "Yahusha".

We know that the Children of Israel intermarried with the Egyptians all throughout the bible for centuries because we have proof in our very own Bible.

Leviticus 24:10-11 "And the son of an **Israelitish woman, whose father was an Egyptian**, went out among the children of Israel: and this son of the Israelitish woman and a man of Israel strove together in the camp. And the Israelitish woman's son blasphemed the name of the LORD, and cursed. And they brought him unto Moses: (and his mother's name was Shelomith, the daughter of Dibri, of the tribe of Dan:)".

Note: In this scripture the Half-Egyptian/Half-Israelite boy was still living in the camp with the other Israelites.

Even during the time of the Persian Rule in the Middle East in 400 B.C., the Israelites were still intermarrying with the Egyptians, just as King Solomon and Joseph did.

Ezra 9:1-2 "Now when these things were done, the princes came to me, saying, The people of Israel , and the priests (Aaronites), and the Levites, **HAVE NOT** separated themselves from the people of the lands, doing according to their abominations, even of the Canaanites, the Hittites, the Perizzites, the Jebusites, the

Ammonites, the Moabites, **THE EGYPTIANS**, and the Amorites. **FOR THEY HAVE TAKEN OF THEIR DUAGHTERS FOR THEMSELVES, AND FOR THEIR SONS:** so that the Holy Seed have **MINGLED** themselves with the people of those lands."

(Above) The Step Pyramid of Saggarah, Egypt. This pyramid built before 2,000 B.C. is identical to the Nigerian Igbo, (Enugu state) Nsude Pyramids. Both have 5 stacks that make up the pyramid. Coincidence?

Fact: One can find the Nsude Pyramids in Northern Igboland in the Nigerian town of Nsude, in Abuja. Here there are Ten Pyramidal structures built of clay/mud and straw, just as it was done in Ancient Egypt by the EGYPTIANS. This is supported in Exodus 1, Exodus 5:7. Hmmmmm.... So we have Pyramids in Sudan, Egypt, and the Americas and now in West Africa. The ISRAELITES knew how to build pyramids. They did it for 400 years. Did the Germans build Pyramids? Are there pyramids in Germany, Poland or Russia? Once again the clues point out who is ISRAEL. Did the Germans intermarry with the Ancient Egyptians? Nope. The ISRAELITES did. Case and example: Joseph's children with his Egyptian wife named Ephraim and Manasseh.

Since the Israelites did in fact intermarry with the Egyptians from 2000 B.C. (**Joseph entering Egypt**) to 400 B.C. (**Ezra-Second Temple period**), this means that the Israelites could possibly display Egyptian words in their language. After all they did spend over 400 years in Egypt. **Well, the Nigerian Igbo's dialect exhibits this**. This is yet another reason why many are finding out that the REAL Children of

Israel were mostly scattered into Africa, not the inner depths of the Caucasus Mountains in Europe (although there was black slaves in Europe).

1. The Egyptian word for "**gods**" is "**NTR**" or "**Neter**". It means "**Guardian or Watcher**". The Watchers in the Book of Enoch and even the bible were Angels (Sons of God) who watched over the earth. Its Igbo equivalent is "O-NeTaRa" meaning "**He who guards and watches**".

2. The Egyptian Creator god "**Ptah**" has no meaning in Egyptian because it is Sumerian in origin. It means in the Sumerian language "**He who fashions things by carving and opening**". **Ptah** was the equivalent of the Sumerian god Enki and his symbol was the "**Serpent**". The Igbo equivalent is "OkPu-ATU" which means "**He who molds or fashions things by carving and opening up.**"

3. The Egyptian god "**Ra**" means "**sun/daylight**" as he is associated with the sun or "**solar deity**". The Nigerian Igbo "**Afa**" priestly cult language lists "**o-RA**" as the same word for the "**sun or daylight**". The Hebrews likewise called light "**Or**" (**Hebrew Strong's #215/216**), possibly learnt from the Egyptians.

4. The Egyptian god whose name is "**Osiris**" is a Latin Transliteration of Ancient Greek. Egyptologists translate the Ancient Egyptian name as "**Asar**" or "**Ausar**". The number "**Seven**" was frequently used in Egyptian magic and was also associated with Osiris sometimes. The **Nigerian Igbo number "7"** is called "**Asaa**".

5. The Egyptian god "**Horus**" or "**Heru**" in the Egyptian language is "**hr**" or "**hru**" and means "**Face**". It also means "**Sky**", "**Heavens**", and "**on top**". In Igbo "**Iru**" means "**Face**".

6. Egyptian word "**Musi**", "**Mose**", and "**Msi**" means "**to give birth**". In Igbo "**Mmusi**" means "**to give birth**".

7. Egyptian word "**Tuf**" means "**to throw away**". In Igbo "**Tufuo**" means "**to throw away**".

8. Egyptian word "**akhu**" means "**fire or light**". In Igbo "**Oku**" means "**fire or light**".

9. Egyptian word "**aru**" means "**body**". In Igbo "**ahu**" means "**body**".

10. Egyptian word "**ba**" means "**heart**". In Igbo "**obi**" means "**heart**".

11. Egyptian word "**hike**" means "**power/strength**". In Igbo "**ike**" means "**power**".

12. Egyptian word "**El**" is a word that means "**God**". In Hebrew "**El-Shaddai**" means "**God Almighty**", "**El-oah**" means "**God (singular)**", "**El-ohim**" means "**God (plural)**", and "**El-Elyon**" means "**God Most High**". Dani-**EL** means "God is my Judge" and Ezeki-**EL** means "**God will strengthen**".

Fact: *During the slave trade, **Igbo slaves** were known to be the most rebellious. Most of the slave rebellions in the United States, Haiti, Jamaica, Belize, Trinidad and Tobago, Barbados and Guyana were led by Igbo slaves. In South Carolina, Igbo slaves were reported to have drowned themselves, rather than be kept as slaves. Today that place is called **Ebo Island** in commemoration of the slaves who died there. The **Gullah Blacks** in South Carolina and Georgia are said to be Igbos, Angolans and descendants of Africans from Sierra Leone. The Nigerian **Igbos** was one of the 13 African ethnic groups that provided the bulk of the slaves who were brought to the Americas. **Majority of the slaves who ended up in Virginia, Alabama, Tennessee, Maryland, Arkansas, Mississippi, South and North Carolina and Georgia were Igbo.** It is a known fact that an Igbo museum has been built in Virginia to honor the contribution of Igbo slaves to the state. Igbos and Yoruba Nigerians likewise also have a lot of connections to the Caribbean (Jamaica, Puerto Rico) from the Slave Trades. One of the Igbo slaves who was sent to Liberia by the American Colonization Society-**Edward James Roye** became the fourth president of Liberia. Another Igbo slave born in 1745, **Olaiduah Equiano** wrote many famous slave chronicles such as "**The Interesting Narrative of the Life of Olaiduah Equiano.**"*

CHAPTER 32

DEUTERONOMY 28:50-57

BLACK ISRAELITES GET NO RESPECT IN THEIR SCATTERED LANDS.

Deuteronomy 28:50 "**A nation of fierce countenance, which shall not regard the person of the old, nor shew favour to the young:**

Children were also sold into slavery, just as the "Curses of Israel" prophesied. Now we have to ask the question, were the European Jews children sold into slavery during the Holocaust? Sadly the answer is no.

Slave masters did not show any favour to women, **children**, old or young slaves. Everyone was regarded as property, like cattle. Black children who were toddlers themselves had to take care of white babies. Black Slave women who were nursing were forced into being "wet nannies". It was mandated that the Slave woman used on breast for the white baby and the other one for her black child. If the slave woman was caught nursing her black baby on the same breast she suckled the white baby she was whipped because it was like blacks and whites sharing the same drinking fountain. If the slave woman's breast milk went dry, they got another slave to nurse. The slaves on the plantation ate the leftovers of the Master and therefore nursing "wet nannies" often ran out of milk breastfeeding the Master's babies before she could even give her own baby milk. Over time using the

"Willie Lynch" method the female slave and her children often would grow up to be **"Is We Sick Boss"** slaves. "Is We Sick Boss" slaves love their white slavemasters with all their heart and will never talk bad about them. They will talk with other blacks but will defend their slavemasters to the fullest as they believe they are loved by them. They will take care of their slavemasters children and tend to the needs of the house better their own. There are "Is We Sick Boss" Blacks still here today. This syndrome is deep.

Do you know any blacks with the "We Sick Boss" syndrome today?

Common remarks from them may be:
1. All white people ain't bad.
2. If we retaliate to white injustice we are no better than them.
3. Africans were the ones that sold us into slavery, not whites.
4. We need to support Israel; they speak "Hebrew" so they have to be the "Real Jews".
5. If America is so bad why are so many people trying to come here.
6. Things are better for blacks than they've ever been.
7. Whites treat me better and give me better service than Blacks ever have.
8. I'd rather see a white doctor than a black doctor.
9. I'd rather have white people teach my kids than black people.

There is obvious racism towards blacks as we can see this on T.V. every day. But many times you will Arabs calling blacks **"Hey Brother"** or you will hear Jewish people saying **"You people know what it's like to be hated and persecuted because of who you are."** So let's look at what Modern Judaism teaches to see if this is true. The Modern Jewish word for **"Gentile"**, called **"Goy"** or **"Goyim"** puts everybody that is **non-Jew** into the category of animals, like cattle. In Ancient Hebrew, and in the Old Testament, the first use of the word "Gentile" describes the Children of Japheth in what today is Europe. The Books that the Apostle Paul wrote were about his travels to the Gentile lands in Europe, where he preached the Gospel of Yahusha (Jesus). Each one of his books is named after a European city or place. Here are some examples of what Modern Judaism teaches about their definition of what a **"Gentile"** is and how to treat them.

Fact: Some Teachings of the Talmud

1. **Where a Jew Should Do Evil**

   Moed Kattan 17a: If a Jew is tempted to do evil he should go to a city where he is not known and do the evil there.

2. **Penalty for Disobeying Rabbis**
   Erubin 21b. Whosoever disobeys the rabbis deserves death and will be punished by being boiled in hot excrement in hell.

3. **Hitting a Jew is the same as hitting God**
   Sanhedrin 58b. If a heathen (**Gentile**) hits a Jew, the gentile must be killed.

4. **O.K. to Cheat Non-Jews**
   Sanhedrin 57a . A Jew need not pay a gentile ("Cuthean") the wages owed him for work.

5. **Jews Have Superior Legal Status**
   Baba Kamma 37b. "If an ox of an Israelite gores an ox of a Canaanite there is no liability; but if an ox of a Canaanite gores an ox of an Israelite...the payment is to be in full."

6. **Jews May Steal from Non-Jews**
   Baba Mezia 24a . If a Jew finds an object lost by a gentile ("heathen") it does not have to be returned. (**Affirmed also in Baba Kamma 113b**). Sanhedrin

76a. God will not spare a Jew who "marries his daughter to an old man or takes a wife for his infant son or returns a lost article to a Cuthean..."

7. **Jews May Rob and Kill Non-Jews**
   Sanhedrin 57a . When a Jew murders a gentile ("Cuthean"), there will be no death penalty. What a Jew steals from a gentile he may keep.

8. **Non-Jewish Children are Sub-Human**
   Yebamoth 98a. All gentile children are animals.
   Abodah Zarah 36b. Gentile girls are in a state of *niddah* (filth) from birth.
   Abodah Zarah 22a-22b . Gentiles prefer sex with cows.

Note: The irony behind this is that the European nations are referred to as the **"Gentile Nations (Genesis 10:5)"** instead of the nations of Ham and Shem. Even Paul, the **Apostle to the Gentiles** did not go preaching to Africa, he went preaching to Europe! A person cannot be an Anti-Semite if the people they are talking about are descendants of the Japhetic Gentile Nations in Europe.

In the past, slaves were not allowed to own property or guns because we were not considered human and thus were not justifiable American citizens by whites. White people back in the day believed black people were descendants of Apes and previously had tails like monkeys. On the Evolutionary charts of man, the ape is considered to be a descendant of the Negro/black man.

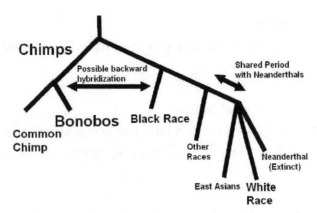

It is a known fact that Africans and "Native" Indians were put in Human Zoos in the 1800's. They tried to prove that these race groups were descendants of animals

on the evolutionary chart. But why just Blacks (Africans) and Native Americans? Hmm....sounds like the Curses of Israel to me. You be the judge.

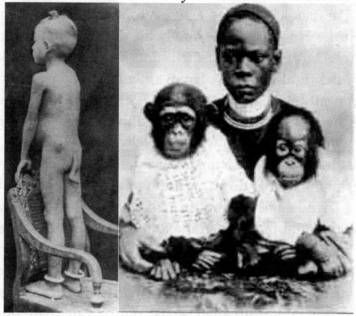

White America for ages believed blacks evolved from "**apes**". This is what they taught in schools to their children. They even displayed Africans in Human Zoos with apes all across the world as early back as 1958. They wrote books on this when they visited Africa. The believed blacks were hairy with tails in the past. But the ironic thig is anybody can research the truth about the "**monkey tail**" theory by searching on "**Yahoo**" or "**Google**" the words "**White people with tails**" and "**Black people with tails**". The results are interesting. People can then come up to their own conclusions of what race has tails. The media has poked fun about it in movies like "**Shallow Hall**", "**Splice**", "**Avatar**" and "**Star Trek: Into the Darkness**". Richard Pryor even joked about the fact that white people had tails. But was he really joking?

True Story: I was at a Nursing Home in Michigan a couple years ago and I was talking to some African-American/African nurses about "**people with tails**". They were all "skeptical" like anyone would be so they didn't believe me. Then I told them to look it up. They looked it up and saw a plethora of people with tails, some even in old black & white pictures. They asked me how come they didn't see any pictures of Blacks or Africans with tails. I said truthfully, "**I don't know**". I told them to do an "**advanced search**". So as instructed, they typed in on Google "**Black**

people with tails" and they got nothing but pictures of the Tuskegee Airmen movie "**Red Tails**". They were all confused. So as we were talking about this topic, two Caucasian EMS/Paramedic workers arrived to the Nursing home with a new patient fresh from the Hospital. The Paramedic asks the nurses what room is the new patient assigned to and the nurses tell him. Confused, he looks down the left corridor and then the right corridor. He overhears our conversation about "**tails**" and asks, "**Are you all talking about people with tails?**" Everybody says "Yes". He then says that the pop singer Kesha admitted to having a tail when she was born and that her parents had it removed when she was a baby. Then he tells us that one of his best friends has a tail. Of course the nurses are shocked at what they are hearing so they ask him, "**What do you mean your best friend has a tail?**" He tells them that his best friend's tail is about half the size of his hand, the same color as his skin, has hair on it and that he can move it as well. The nurses cannot believe what they have heard straight out of a random person's mouth. So I say to the Paramedic worker, "**Hold up, before you go can you tell me if your friend with this tail is black or white?**" He replies, "**He's white**." After that split moment all of the nurses had gotten up out their seats, pulled out their phones, and were scattering in each direction to find a room to tell their friends what they had just heard. So the question is, why is it so hard to find photos of blacks being born with tails if evolutionists believe Blacks evolved from apes/primates?

(Left) In **1906** a 23 year-old African Congolese Pygmy male name **Ota Benga** was exhibited in the Bronx Zoo Monkey House with an Orangutan. America did this to prove the racial theory whites had about blacks in regards to human evolution with the ape being the progenitor of the Negro. They even threw bones into the exhibit with Ota to make white onlookers believe that he was a cannibal.

(Right) The Herero People. It is a known fact that many West Africans exhibit a different genetic DNA Haplogroup than other Africans. The genetic DNA of West Africans is also found in high percentages in African-Americans and Caribbean people, mainly because most of the slaves brought to the Americas were from West Africa (Slave Coast, Rice Coast, Gold Coast etc). But there are also some other areas outside of West Africa that have this same DNA type but is slightly lower percentages. Examples are Cape Verde, Madagascar and Namibia. Namibia is in South Africa, right below Angola. Its west coast sits overlooking the Atlantic Ocean. The Herero people of Namibia are a Bantus people just as the Ghanaian, Nigerian, Cameroonian, Congolese, Senegalese, Gambian and Tanzanian people are. The exhibit the same **Y-Haplogroup E1b1a** as West Africans. The Bantus slaves were subjected to slavery during the Arab Slave Trade and the Transatlantic Slave Trade. The **Herero** along with the **Nama** people were subjected to genocide in 1904-1908 by the Germans in South Africa. The result was the extermination of **60,000** Herero people and **10,000** Nama people. The Germans wanted a prosperous colony in Namibia so they had to exterminate or displace the indigenous people from their agricultural land. During this period of time they were kept in concentration camps, subjected to starvation, and medical experimentation. While the Herero people were in concentration camps they were forced to build the **352 mile-long Otavi railroad**. Men, women, and children were whipped, raped, and abused until they dropped dead. The Germans kept records of all of this, even beheading them and using their heads fully mummified for further research. The headless bodies were dumped in mass graves. In the 1800's there were about 80,000 Herero people living in the middle of Namibia. The Nama people were **Khoi-San (Hottentots)** and they lived further south. Those Herero or Nama people that survived the genocide were tattooed and forced to wear an identity badge around their necks. Their every move was controlled by the government. The aftermath was lost land and livestock, which gave them no choice but to work for the Germans as these European invaders established a new racial hierarchy and caste system in Namibia. A hundred years later the Germans apologized, but they didn't feel reparations were needed. Ironically the Germans **DID** give the Jews reparations for their mistreatment during the Holocaust. Black lives didn't matter in this case. But lo and behold, in 2015 Obama approved $12 Million dollars for Holocaust Survivors, but not one dime for African-Americans.

Blacks cried and celebrated as if they were worshipping God in church when Obama was elected President of the United States in 2008 but has anything changed for Blacks in over 8 years? The population of Detroit has shrunk almost half since mass high school closings were ordered years ago. Now these high schools are abandoned buildings. Obama said Blacks didn't need reparations, but instead felt that we needed more jobs and good schools. But in Detroit the unemployment rate for Blacks is higher than any other race and more black schools have shut down in Detroit than any other race in Michigan. Have we been **"Hoodwinked"** *again?*

"I have said In the past....and I'll repeat again....that the best reparations we can provide (For Blacks) are good schools in the inner city and jobs for people who are unemployed."

Barack Obama 2008

Deuteronomy 28:51 **"And he shall eat the fruit of thy cattle, and the fruit of thy land, until thou be destroyed: which also shall not leave thee either corn, wine, or oil, or the increase of thy kine, or flocks of thy sheep, until he have destroyed thee.**

WHY WE CAN'T HAVE ANYTHING WITHOUT SOMEONE TRYING TO TAKE IT FROM US.

The land that the slaves tilled plus the livestock they took care of for over 500 years was enjoyed by the Slavemasters and their families. Since way back, everyone has had their eyes on Africa. Europeans and Arabs used the **people** for Slavetrading and they also wanted to take the **resources** of the land (Gold, Diamonds, etc). Africa is the **MOTHERLAND**. It has everything it needs to sustain itself, even livestock and Fish.

The world's top producer of GM (Genetically Modified) crops, "**Monsanto**" is seeking new markets for American GM crops in Africa. They don't care if their GM crops financially enslave and at the same time kill the African people. The U.S. administration's strategy consists of assisting African nations to produce biosafety laws that promote agribusiness interests instead of protecting Africans from the potential threats of GM crops."

Fact: The front lines of the food sovereignty war in African countries such as **Ghana** are swelling as farmers fight to prevent the passing of the "**Plant Breeders Bill**". The people of Ghana with the help of Agriculture Sovereignty Ghana (**ASG**) so far have prevented the passage of this bill, which is designed to strip Ghanaian farmers of their rights to own their seeds. But the **African Regional Intellectual Property**

Association (ARIPO) has not given up on this fight. The ARIPO and its members are still fighting hard to pass a regional protocol that will impose severe restrictions on farmer's rights to save, exchange and sell seed. This is because the non-black GMO companies want to control it all. Food, water, coal, iron, uranium, natural gas, and oil. They want it all. If these new laws if passed, African farmers would be subject to hefty fines for growing anything that has been "**patented**," even if their crops were cross-pollinated by GMO crops.

Many activists and trade groups in Africa think that the new laws would simply give Monsanto a way to sneak their "**biotech crops**" into the Ghanaian market. The bill has been dubbed the "**Monsanto Law**" for this reason. Monsanto is already in America, contaminating everything we eat, but supposedly for the benefit of mankind and worldwide "**Hunger**".

MONSANTO: THE SILENT KILLER?

Ever wonder why there is so much Chron's disease, Ulcerative colitis, IBS, Autism, ADHD, Adult Diabetes, Colon Cancer, Gastrointestinal Cancers, Breast Cancers, Lung Cancers, Renal Cancers, Prostate Cancers, Thyroid Cancers, and food allergies? Monsanto is banned in countries like Germany but not here in America. GMO Food and Cloned Food are all around us. Including cloned meat (**don't get it twisted**). Most of the Corn and Soy we consume is genetically modified. The cow and the pigs eat the corn and we in turn consume them. Cow's milk is used for baby formula and so is Soy milk (Isomil). The transfer of abnormal DNA (**recombinant DNA**) mixes with our DNA whenever and wherever it feels.

Note: Recombinant DNA (rDNA) are DNA molecules formed by laboratory methods of genetic recombination (such as molecular **cloning**) to bring together genetic material from **multiple sources**, creating sequences that would **NOT** otherwise be found in natural biological organisms (i.e. Cloned Chickens with two heads, four wings, four legs, larger breasts/legs).

Add over 49 scheduled vaccines recommended by the CDC for children by the age of 6 and now you have metals like Mercury and Aluminum floating in our children's bloodstream. Add processed sugary foods that are cheap plus some nitrites and you got a pot of toxins for a body. No wonder more people are being diagnosed with "Alzheimer's Dementia). Monsanto made "**Agent Orange**" which sent a lot of U.S veterans to the grave with Cancer. Then Monsanto made "**Round Up**" weed killer with the same key ingredient (**Dioxin**) used to make Agent Orange. The "Round Up" weed killer is then sprayed on our food. Often high doses are required to kill the insects or weeds that have developed a resistance to regular doses of "**Round Up (Dioxin)**". Monsanto, the makers of "Round Up" decided to make even more money off their science by "**creating**" crops that would grow no matter how much "Round Up" weed killer and pesticide you sprayed on it. This was so farmers could kill those nasty weeds by using **MORE** Monsanto "Round Up" on these Monsanto-made GMO crops. This is essentially like "**creating a cancer**" that **ONLY** responds to **YOUR** "**chemotherapy drug**". Here are some of the medial diseases linked with the ingredient "**Dioxin**" that is being sprayed on our foods every day.

- Throat and Laryngeal Cancer
- Lung Cancer
- Prostate Cancer
- Soft Tissue Sarcoma of muscles, connective tissue, or fat.
- Fibrosarcoma
- Angiosarcoma
- CLL (Chronic Lymphocytic Leukemia)
- Dermatofibrosarcoma
- Leiomyosarcoma
- Lymphomas
- Multiple Myeloma
- Spina Bifida
- Kidney disease
- Achondroplasia
- Cleft Lip and Cleft Palate
- Congenital Heart Disease
- Ischemic Heart Disease
- Birth Defects
- AL Amyloidosis
- Chloracne/acneform diseases (identical to teenage acne).
- Hip Dysplasia

- Hydrocephalus
- Neural Tube Defects
- Genital Hypospadias
- Pyloric Stenosis
- Syndactyly
- Undescended Testicles
- Poland Syndrome (webbed fingers)
- Parkinson's disease
- Diabetes Mellitus
- Developmental Disorders and Chromosomal disorders
- Peripheral Neuropathy
- Porphyria Cutanea Tarda

It is a known fact that any veteran with lung or laryngeal cancer can receive VA hospital care and also disability even without proving its connection to "Agent Orange". That's how we know Monsanto knows its key ingredient "**Dioxin**", is a cancer-promoting chemical. In 2012, residents of a West Virginian Town, which formerly hosted a Monsanto factory (**with noxious/cancer-causing chemicals**) were able to start getting assistance through a 2013 million-dollar settlement.

So Monsanto gets farmers to buy their seed but the farmers also need to buy their equipment mandated by Monsanto to cultivate & spray toxic pesticides on vast amounts of farmland. The farmer's seed only lasts **ONE HARVEST** then they have to go Monsanto to buy more seed. This means that Monsanto owns the farm and the farmers are reduced to mere modern day sharecroppers. However, nature has reacted to the cancer-causing pesticides. Bugs and weeds are now becoming resistant to "Round Up" Weed killer. These weeds have to be manually pulled out the ground. So Monsanto's solution is to spray more pesticides in larger and more potent amounts. They also have produced another Cancer-causing chemical/pesticide weed killer called "**Dicamba**" to combat these "**Super Bug Weeds**." Many of these Monsanto pesticides have chemicals like **2, 4-D** which are close cousins to the active ingredient in the biological herbicide weapon used in the Vietnam War called "**Agent Orange**".

Other countries cannot "**physically**" enslave **West and East Africans** anymore so they have their eyes set on the many resources of the land. These include iron, oil, uranium, diamonds, gold and many more. But by far these outside countries have their eyes set on Africa's "**Oil**".

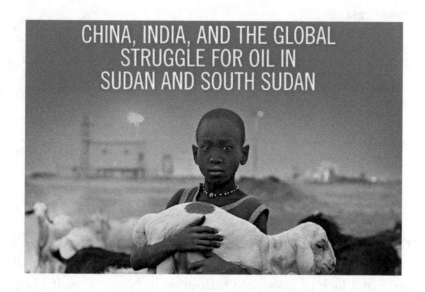

There is a reason why the "**Curses of Israel**" states:

"And he (**China/USA/European countries?**) shall **EAT** the fruit of thy cattle, and the fruit of thy land, until thou be destroyed: which also shall not leave thee either corn, wine, or oil, or the increase of thy kine, or flocks of thy sheep, until he have destroyed thee."

So were the scriptures talking about "**Crude Oil**" or "**Olive Oil**"? Is Africa known for **Olive Oil** or **Crude Oil**? Was this symbolic for both places the Israelites would call home during the ongoing "Curses of Israel?" We know that Nigeria (**West Africa**) is the biggest producer of oil in Sub-Saharan Africa and South Sudan is also major producer of oil. They also happen to be countries where the African Hebrew Israelites are known to be at.

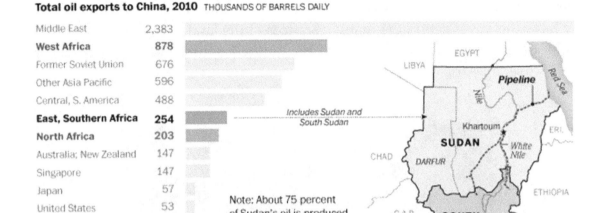

Total oil exports to China, 2010 THOUSANDS OF BARRELS DAILY

Middle East	2,383
West Africa	878
Former Soviet Union	676
Other Asia Pacific	596
Central, S. America	488
East, Southern Africa	254
North Africa	203
Australia; New Zealand	147
Singapore	147
Japan	57
United States	53
Europe	26
Mexico	24
Canada	19
India	12

Includes Sudan and South Sudan

Note: About 75 percent of Sudan's oil is produced in what is now the Republic of South Sudan.

Nigeria is Africa's biggest oil producer— It generates more than 2 million barrels of petroleum a day but also imports the refined product of its own oil from other countries because of a lack of adequate refineries in Nigeria itself. Nigeria also still gets oil from other countries to meet the oil demand of the country. This means that outsiders can still set and control "**Gas prices**", just like over here in America. They need more refinery plants and repairs to the ones that need fixing. Once this happens, gas prices will go down in Nigeria because they will be able to use their own gas from their own oil reserves. There will finally be no more fuel importation in a country that has to import nearly 80 percent of its requirement of refined petroleum products. The oil is so abundant in Nigeria that it is seeping out of the ground. However, the people of Nigeria are not benefitting off of this abundant resource. Other Nigerian Oil Tycoons are. For countries with plenty of refineries and technology (i.e. Saudi Arabia) this spells "**Wealth**". Is this also a curse? To have so much oil in a land but not be able to fully utilize it for economic growth in that area: case in point, **The Niger Delta**.

Petroleum refining processes are the chemical engineering processes that are used in petroleum refineries (*also referred to as oil refineries*) to transform crude oil into useful products such as liquefied petroleum gas (**LPG**), gasoline or petrol, kerosene, jet fuel, diesel oil and fuel oils.

Fact: Cameroon has a lot of oil in its country but has only **ONE** Oil Refinery. Therefore much of Cameroon's oil is sent to France to get refined into gasoline and petroleum products which the French then use to reap millions of dollars, all courtesy of the Land of Cameroon (which belongs to the Africans & Hebrew Israelites living there).

Example: This is like the United States of America taking oil from Saudi Arabia and then selling it back to them after it has been "**refined**" for use.

The French like many West African countries colonized Cameroon and made money off of the slave trafficking of human Hebrew Israelite slaves. Many African-Americans today can trace their roots to Cameroon. Cameroonians today also admit to Hebrewism traditions such as circumcision/child naming on the 8th day, abstaining from pork, and other Mosaic-Law practices which have been done for many of generations. Thanks to the influence of the West, a lot of young Africans have forgotten their Hebrew traditions and roots.

Saudi Arabia drives OPEC crude growth

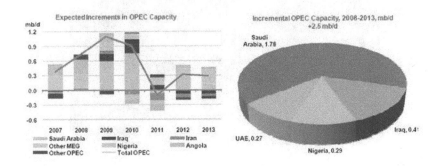

- Strong 2009/2010 capacity growth driven by Saudi lighter/sweeter crude additions, plus initial Iraqi recovery
- Later phase growth comes from Saudi Arab Heavy additions plus Nigerian deepwater

Saudi Arabia leads the Middle Eastern Countries in Crude Oil (**Gas**) production. It makes more crude oil than Nigeria, Iraq and the United Arab Emirates combined. They essentially control the Arab world because they possess "**Mecca**" and "**Medina**", and the "**Holy Shrines**" in Islam. Therefore they hold a lot of power in the Middle East. This is one of the main reasons why the United States of America is a close ally of Saudi Arabia. The "Elite" groups of this world know that in order to "**Divide and Conquer**" religions, countries, or economies you have to be close friends with the power players of these so called "**Departments**". This means:

1. Control the world's top three religion (**Judaism-Jews, Catholicism-Vatican, Islam-Mecca**).
2. Control the money (**Federal Reserve, IMF, World Bank, China, Libya, Saudi Arabia**).
3. Control food/water, control energy (**Natural Gas, Oil, Electricity, wind power and water power**).
4. Control "**Propagandas**" using the worlds Television/Media (**CNN, Fox, ABC, CBC, NBC**).
5. Control the law (**United Nations/United States Supreme Court**).

Deuteronomy 28:52 **"And he shall BESIEGE thee in all thy gates, until thy high and fenced walls come down, wherein thou trustedst, throughout all thy land: and he shall BESIEGE thee in all thy gates throughout all thy land, which the LORD thy God hath given thee.**

The Assyrians used battering rams to conquer other nations, including the Ancient Israelites.

"Besiege" means: To surround a city, building, village, with armed forces/soldiers/battering ram and try to take control of it. To gather around (someone) in a way that is aggressive, annoying or intimidating. To basically plan a **"takeover"**.

(Above) Black Wall Street, Tulsa Race Riots of 1921. The White "Lynch Mob" outnumbered blacks 10 to 1. 1,400 Black homes and Black business were burned down. Those black men that tried to fight back to defend their families and homes were killed. Here is a white man with a shotgun guarding the body of a dead black man and black prisoners. Blacks have been besieged in Africa by Europeans or Arabs coming to enslave them. Blacks are also besieged as you can see here in America. The same has happened to the "Natives of America" and the Natives of the Caribbean (Taino, Carib, Arawak people). Coincidence?

So where can we see examples of this "**Besiege**" throughout time? Did this happen to the White race? The Arab race? The European Jewish race? The Asian race? No! This has been happening to the Israelites all throughout time. Let's look at some examples:

- Egyptian captivity (1882 B.C-1450 B.C.)
- Assyrian captivity (721 B.C.-701 B.C.)
- Babylonian captivity (605 B.C.-582 B.C.)
- Persian oppression/plot to kill the Jews-(Purim Massacre, Book of Esther). (400 B.C.)
- Grecian captivity (330 B.C.) **Joel 3:6 "You sold the people of Judah and Jerusalem to the Grecians, that you might send them far from their homeland."**
- Roman captivity (70 A.D.)
- The Arab Slave Trade/East African Slave Trade/Indian Ocean Slave Trade (600 A.D. till present day. Some report even as far back as 100 B.C. in Yemen).

- Battle of Khaybar (Arabia) (629 A.D.)
- The Transatlantic Slave Trade (1400's to late 1800's)
- Belgian Congo Takeover (1908 A.D.)
- Herero (Bantus) & Nama people Genocide in Namibia, Africa (1904-1907 A.D.)
- Black Wall Street/Tulsa Race Riots (1921 A.D.)
- Rwanda Genocide of Tutsi Jews (1993 A.D.)
- Detroit Race Riots/Black Bottom (1943 A.D.)
- The Nigerian Biafra Civil War (1967-1970 A.D.)
- Darfur/North Sudan vs South Sudan Civil war. (2003 A.D.)
- And more!

And the list goes on..........

Thousands of **Watutsi/Tutsi** *people were killed in the Rwanda Genocide in the 1990's. The* **Tutsi Jews of Kush** *are scattered in* **Rwanda, Eastern Congo, Uganda, and Northern Tanzania**.

BEYOND THE RIVERS OF ETHIOPIA, MY DISPERSED ONES (ISRAELITES).

Tutsi Jew

Fact: The **Tutsi people** originated in Ethiopia when it was known as Kush and was a **Jewish kingdom**. It's a known fact that the **Ancient Kingdom of Cush** dwelt in East Africa and Arabia, mixing with the Semitic Black Arabs and Semitic sons of Joktan. There are numerous references to Kush in the Bible. The Jewish kingdom fell in 1270 A.D. As a result, several clans, including the **Bene-Zagwei clan**, moved south and west to an area called **"Havila"** or the **"African Great Lakes Region"**, consisting of Burundi, Rwanda, and parts of Uganda, Tanzania and the Congo.

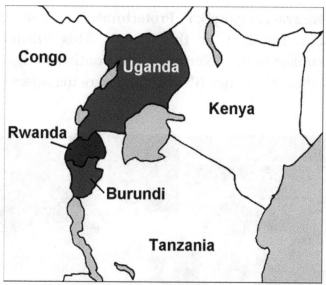

The African Great Lakes consist primarily of Uganda, Kenya, Tanzania, Sudan, Congo, Rwanda and Burundi.

Above is a map of the **African Great Lakes Region**. The Nile River starts at Lake Victoria (middle of map) and flows northward ending in the Mediterranean Sea. Lake Victoria is shared by **Uganda, Tanzania, and Kenya**, the places that many slaves (i.e. Zanzibar) were taken from during the Arab Slave Trade. The European Jews wanted Uganda as their Jewish homeland before even thinking about Palestine/Israel. This stemmed from the scripture:

Zephaniah 3:10 "From beyond the Rivers of Ethiopia (Cush) my suppliants (petitioners/worshippers), even the daughter of my dispersed (people), shall bring mine offering."

The British Uganda Program was a plan to give a portion of British East Africa to the European Ashkenazi Jews as a homeland. The offer was made by British Colonial Secretary Joseph Chamberlain to Ashkenazi Jew Theodore Herl's Zionist group in 1903. The British offered 5,000 square miles of the **Mau Plateau** in what is now Kenya. This land was to be a refuge from **"persecution"** for the majority **Russian and Polish Jews** along with other Jews in Europe. The **"Seventh Zionist Congress"** voted to accept the British Uganda Plan, and in 1905 they immediately started an armed organized expeditionary force to scout out the site for a major settlement on the Mau Plateau. The Mau Plateau was in Kenya but was part of the

"**British Uganda-Kenya-Tanganyika Protectorate**".   The British Controlled Uganda, Kenya and Tanzania at this time.   This "**British Uganda-Kenya Protectorate**" was similar to the "**Northern and Southern Nigerian Protectorate**". The "**Protectorate**:" meant that they (**the British**) were the rulers of the land.

*British Protectorate which includes the "**Uganda Protectorate**", the "**East Africa Protectorate (Kenya)**" and the "**Tanganyika (Tanzania) Territory**". Kabaka Mutesa I, started ruling over Uganda before he was 20 years old. He ruled from 1856 to 1884 during the British Protectorate of Uganda.*

*(**Above left**) Postage with the words "**Southern Nigerian Shilling.**" The British "Northern" and "Southern" Protectorate existed in Nigeria from the late 1800's to the early 1900's. (**Above Right**) Nigerian British Coin with the Satanic "Hexagram." Notice the **Jewish "Star of David"** on the Nigerian coin with the words "**Nigeria British West Africa 1909**". Is it a coincidence that the Europeans and Arabs were all involved with the colonization/slave trade of territory that the Black Hebrew Israelites scattered into? No! This is Bible Prophecy from Deuteronomy 28:16-68.*

So after making the British-Zionist deal, the Jews had to get rid of the lions and the **Maasai people** that were indigenous in the land. The **Maasai people** were mostly in **Southern Kenya** and **Northern Tanzania** at the time.

British Postal Stamp for "British East Africa" which included Kenya, Tanzania and Uganda.

Fact: After the defeat of the Germans in World War I, German East Africa's territory "**Tanganyika**" was taken over by the British in 1918. Before the Germans ruled East

Africa it was controlled by the Arabs who used Uganda, Kenya, Abyssinia, and Tanzania as a major source of capturing Bantus slaves during the Arab Slave Trade. Tanganyika was later changed to "**Tanzania.**"

So the deal was made and the Zionist Jews went into the Mau Plateau (Kenya) in 1905. Ground was broken in Kenya for what the Jews believe will be the site of a New "**Akko (Acre) Jewish City**". The expedition consisted of 50 colonists of mostly Russian and Polish Jews. Altercations and run-ins with the "Native" **Massai People** were common since they saw these "**new-comers**" as a threat to their land.

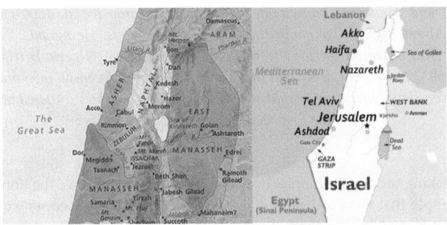

The city of "Akko" is located in Northern Israel, south of the Lebanon border. In biblical times it was a part of the Territory of Asher from the 12 Tribes of Israel. The European Jews today in Israel do not possess the original territory of the Tribe of Asher, the Lebanese people do. This is how we know that the State of Israel creation in 1948 was not the bible prophecy talked about in Ezekiel, Isaiah 11:11-12, Jeremiah 31:10 and other scriptures foretelling the re-gathering of the Israelites. The people in Israel today are NOT the REAL BIBLICAL ISRAELITES.

Fact: The Israelite city of **Acre (Akko)** goes back to when the 12 Tribes of Israel were all living in their allotted territories given to them by God through Joshua. The Tribe of Asher lived in this area which is now modern day "**Lebanon**". This was one of the only cities that the Israelites did not drive out all of the Canaanites.

Judges 1:31 "Asher did not drive out the inhabitants of **Acco (Akko/Accho)**, nor the inhabitants of Zidon (Sidon, in Lebanon), or Ahlab, Achzib, Helbah, Aphik, or Rehob."

*The name "**Akko/Acca(o)**" is recorded in Egyptian sources from around 2,000 B.C. In the Canaanite Amarna letters to the Egyptian Pharaoh written in Canaanite-Akkadian, it describes the city as being the Hebrew equivalent of "**aleph-kaf-vav**" or* **Hebrew Strong's #5910** עַכּוֹ *"**Akko**". The "vav" with a vowel point above indicated an "o" sound.*

Note: Before vowel points were introduced by the **Masoretes** in A.D times the scribes used the letters Aleph, Hey, Vav, and Yod to indicate vowel sounds. (**The Masoretes lived in Jerusalem, Tiberias (near Galilee) and Babylon (Iraq) during 600-1000 A.D.**) They are usually called "**consonantal vowels**" so that whenever one of these consonants were encountered, the reader understood to make an associated vowel sound and not the sound of the Hebrew letter. The letter "**Aleph**" represented an "**ah**" sound (i.e. f-**ah**-ther in father). The letter "**Hey**" represented an "**ei**", "**ah**", or "**ay**" sound (i.e. Le-**ah** or Mosh-**e**) unless it appeared at the end of a word, in which case it represented an "**ah**" sound (i.e. "yah-u-**ah**"). When the Hebrew letter "**Hey**" is in the beginning of a word it represents the word "**the**". The letter "**Vav**" could either represent either an "**oh/o**", sound (i.e. J-**oh**-el in Joel or in this case "Ak-k**o**" or "Jumb-**o**") or an "**oo**" sound (i.e. "Yah-**oo**-ah" in the word "Yahuah"). The letter "**Yod**" with a vowel point represented an "**ee**" sound (i.e. "dav-**ee**-d" as in "David").

In Assyrian cuneiform writing the city "**Akko**" was spelled "**AKK**". Today in Israel it is known as the historical "**Old Acre**" City. The city was called "**Ptolemais**" during the Greek Hellenistic Period during the Gentile Jewish reign of the Maccabean family and also later during the Roman-Byzantine Period. During the Islamic conquest of Jerusalem during the "**Crusades**" it was renamed back to its Arabic name "**Akka**". The name "**Akka/Aak**" also appeared on the tribute lists of Egyptian Pharaoh Thutmoses III (15th Century B.C.). The "**Execration texts**" which date further back as late as 2,600 B.C. during the Egyptian "**Old Kingdom**" also talks about the Canaanite city of "**Akka**" as well as the Sons of Abraham's brother "**Haran**" (Lot, Moabites, Ammonites) and the "**Sons of Seth**". According to Flavius Josephus, the city of Akka was ruled by one of King Solomon's governors. In 725

B.C. the people in Akka joined the people in Sidon and Tyre in a revolt against the **Assyrian King Shalmaneser V (2 Kings 17:3-5)**.

In late 1905 a second wave of Russian Jews (300 in total) came to Kampala, Uganda with armed expeditions to take care of any animals or natives in the land of Uganda that threatened their new African home. By the beginning of 1906 over 12,000 European Jews had made their home in British East Africa in **Kampala, Uganda** and **New Akko, Kenya**. But that wasn't enough; the "**Jewish Territorialist Organization (JTO)**" was then founded to recruit more Jews to become colonists in Africa. Pretty soon Orthodox Synagogues were built in these two cities. The **Massai Tribe** tried to reclaim the "**New Akko**" Jewish city in Kenya several times but was defeated each time by the armed members of the expedition team. Eventually, both sides reached an agreement on peace. The Massai Tribe agreed to let the Jews have small farms as long as they allowed the Massai Tribe to use a large portion of the Mau Plateau for cattle grazing (which they had been doing anyway). The Jews also promised to trade metal tools with the Massai people. So the European Russian/Polish Jews got 5,000 acres of land in Kenya and the Massai people got what they could get even though they didn't want the Jews there. In 1907, a half-a-million Russian and Eastern European Jews immigrated to British East Africa (Uganda/Kenya).

The Massai Tribal people today have a mixed background genetically. Half of the Massai people genetically tested are said to be descendants of Cush with the Paternal Y-Haplogroup E1b1b (Formerly E1b1c) found on genetic testing while 12-15% were tested to have the same Paternal Y-Haplogroup E1b1a gene as West Africans (Bantus) people, Negro Blacks in the Americas and in the Caribbean.

Note: In genetic studies it is impossible to test all of the people who belong to a specific tribe so these numbers are based on a certain population that was available for testing. Some of the Massai tribe in other locations could exhibit more E1b1a than E1b1c but without testing it's hard to say.

What's interesting is that the Massai people practice Circumcision, but because of the high rate of infant mortality they circumcise their male boys after **3 "New Moons" (3 months)**. They also refrain from cutting their newborns hair until a certain age (**Nazarite vow**) and do not name their children until after "**3 New**

Moons". This is similar to the Hebrew Israelites circumcising and naming their children on the 8th day.

Luke 1:59 "And it came to pass, that on the **EIGHTH DAY** they came to circumcise the child, and they called him Zacharias, after the name of his father. And his mother (Elizabeth) answered and said, Not, so; but he shall be called **John (the Baptist)**.

This practice of naming the child and performing circumcision on the **EIGHTH DAY** is a Hebrew Custom and is practiced most commonly in West Africa.

Luke 2:21 "And when **EIGHT DAYS** were accomplished for the circumcising of the child, his name was called "**Yahusha (Jesus)**", which was so named of the angel before he was conceived in the womb."

The child-naming ceremony of the **Massai Tribe** is called "**Enkipukonoto Eaji**" and is usually followed by the sacrificing of two sheep. In the "**Nazarite Vow**" 2 Sheep's and a Ram are given killed as offering. One lamb as a burnt offering (**olah**), another for a sin offering (**hatat**) and a ram as a peace offering (**Shelamim**).

Numbers 6:14 "And he shall offer his offering unto the Lord, one he-lamb of the first year without blemish for a **burnt offering**, and one ewe lamb for the first year without blemish for a **sin offering**, and one ram without blemish for **peace offerings**."

The "**Nazarite Vow**" also involved not cutting the hair as a sign of "**consecration**" that someone was "**setting themselves apart for God**". The child's hair was either not cut until before circumcision or it was cut after a certain period of time (**i.e. 3 to 7 years**). This is considered being a "**Nazarite**" for a certain period of time. The Massai Tribe also practices the wearing of dreadlocks. They also use passed down "**Oral Laws**" to govern their behavior. They worship one Supreme God (monotheism) named "**Enkai**" which is similar to the Semitic Sumerian god "**Enki**". If the Massai Tribe is living in the "Land of Ham", why are they practicing "Monotheism" and why is their god named after a Semitic God from Iraq? Arphaxad, the son of Shem lived in the area known as Babylon (Iraq). The Babylonian pagan god "Marduk" is said to be the son of "Enki". Monotheism is rare in many African Tribes and was not found in Ancient Egypt, Babylon, Assyria, Canaan, Greece and Rome. Only the Hebrew Israelites had a "Supreme God". All of these Massai traditions are similar to the "Hebrew Israelites" traditions of old, making some people wonder if these Massai tribe people are a mix of Cush and Hebrew Israelite blood (like Moses). Likewise the Nigerians also practice refraining from cutting newborns hair at birth. The hair naturally is difficult to comb or brush and therefore it becomes matted, later developing into what they call "**Dada Dreads**". In the Yoruba language "**Omo Dada**" means "**Good Child**" as there was some superstition about cutting the child's hair after a certain period of time after birth. This stems from the belief that children who are born with hair that is **un-combable** or **un-brushable** are "special children" unto God. They also have the belief in Nigerian culture that children with "Dada Locks" have "special powers", similar to Samson's special power of superhuman strength. This term "**Dada**" hair is also seen in West Indian culture. This hints at the possibility that this common African practice is derived from Ancient Hebrew customs as in the "**Nazarite Vow**". This could be yet another clue that the Hebrew Israelites settled in exile into East Africa and West Africa.

(Above from Left to right) 1. Ishtar (Asherah) 2. Asherah pole with Mother Goddess image 3. Asherah pole 4. Asherah/Grove/Obelisk in Ethiopia 5. Washington Monument grove/pole 6. Yoruba obelisk Oranmiyan wooden staff 7. Native American Totem pole/grove.

Asherah is known by many names. She was worshipped in Ancient Sumeria, Akkadia (Ashratum/Ashratu), Egypt (Qudshu), Canaan, Babylon (Ishtar) and by the Israelites (Ashtoreth). She was known as the **Mother Goddess**, the **Queen of Heaven**, the **Lady of the Sea**, the **Lion Lady** and other things. She often has a snake around her or is holding one and is usually standing on a lion. Asherah/Ashtoreth was known back in time to be the wife of the Sumerian God "**Anu**" and Canaanite god "**El**". She was associated with Lilith, the Planet Venus (Lucifer) and the 8-pointed star that is displayed in St. Peter's square (Vatican) with the obelisk. She was also a fertility goddess as the Greek version goddess "**Aphrodite**" is associated with love, beauty, pleasure and **procreation**. Satan is very tricky and he is a copycat. He copied the Trinity/Godhead from Genesis 1:1-2 and gave this to Egypt and Sumeria. Yahuah forbid the Israelites to mix this Satanic Asherah worship with his worship. The Asherah was associated with carved trees or "Groves/poles", which the obelisks in Egypt and Sudan represent.

2 Kings 21:6-7 "He (Manasseh) made his son pass through the fire, **practiced witchcraft and used divination, and dealt with mediums and spiritists**. He did much evil in the sight of the Lord provoking him to anger. Then he set the carved image of Asherah that he had made, in the house of which the Lord said to David and to his son Solomon, "In this house and in Jerusalem, which I have chosen from all the tribes of Israel, I will put My name forever."

Deuteronomy 16:21 "Do not set up any wooden **Asherah pole** beside the altar you build to the Lord your God."

2 Kings 23:4 "The King ordered Hilkiah the high priest, the priests next in rank and the doorkeepers to remove from the temple of the Lord all the articles made for **Baal and Asherah** and all the starry hosts. He burned them outside Jerusalem in the fields of the Kidron Valley and took the ashes to Bethel."

1 Kings 18:19 "Now then send and gather to me all Israel at Mount Carmel, together with 450 prophets of Baal and **400 prophets of the Asherah**, who eat at **Jezebel's table**."

So here is something to think about. Hezekiah's son **Manasseh**, King of Judah erected an Asherah pole in Solomon's Temple in 2 Kings 21:6-8 and also did witchcraft and used "**Diviners**". So if we want to track down the Ancient Israelites we should look for people who still use "**Diviners**", Obelisk carved poles or "**Groves**", witchcraft/voodoo and worship a "**Queen of Heaven/Lady of the Sea/Mother Goddess**". We can also look for "**Hebrewisms**" in people's culture and customs. We can study the Hebrew language, comparing it to the language of other people of the world claiming to be Israel "**now**" or in the "**past**". Using the Bible as a historical foundation, Ancient pictures of the Israelites, historical documents and with the knowledge of the skin color of the people in the bible we can narrow down who is "Israel". Look at the Yoruba Oranmiyan Staff (Obelisk) and their Ifa Diviners. Look at the Native Americans Totem poles and their Shamans/Medicine man/priests. Even after Joshua died the Israelites were worshipping these Poles/Groves to Asherah. House of Israel King Ahab and Jezebel also worshipped Asherah in addition to Yahuah and Baal. Asherah was also a Moon Goddess. Asherah was also associated with Water in some civilizations. Look up "**Mami Wata**", "**Lady of the Sea/Water**", "**The Queen of Heaven**" and "**Fertility God**" worship in West Africa/Caribbean. Israel for the longest has been disobedient worshipping false idols, even when they scattered into West Africa and when they made it on boats to the "New World". Wake up Blacks, Latinos and Native Americans! The clues are coming out!

EAST AFRICA HEBREW ISRAELITES?

In the **East Africa Region**, there are many clans that reconstituted the **South Cushitic Empire**, which lasted from 1270 A.D. to 1527 A.D. In the South Cushitic Empire the Laws of Moses were the laws of the land. But it was the "**Laws of Moses**" as they were remembered through oral transmission.

The **Tutsi Jews** of Rwanda are a tribe whom many say has **Cushitic-Semitic** ancestry. Some of their customs are: circumcision, menstrual seclusion of women and the marriage practice called the "**levirate**", which requires a man to marry the widow of his deceased brother. Many of their customs mirrors practices described in the Old Testament. This has further strengthened the Christian belief in East African Israelite biblical Ancestry. Many of these East Africans, like African-

Americans, are "**Bantus Negroes**", and possess the same **E1b1a gene** that many African-Americans test positive for in the U.S.A.

All of the places that the Black Israelites lived and moved in were destroyed with all the walls being brought down by their enemies (**i.e. Assyrians, Babylonians, Greeks, Persians, Romans, Edomites, Arabs and Europeans**). In slavery, black people's fight wasn't enough to hold off their enemies from capturing them in Africa just as it was done years ago in the bible to their Israelite ancestors. Post-Slavery White lynch mobs had their way with black families who were most of the time out numbered and out gunned. The Hebrew Israelites had no choice but to flee further South into Arabia or flee in different directions in Africa to avoid persecution, captivity and death. They had no choice but to flee into the forests of South, East, Central and West Africa. This is why they were considered the "**Wandering Jews**" and was nicknamed "**Strangers**" or "**Foreigners**" wherever they went. Some of them during migration travels through Africa eventually converted to Islam to make life easier. Those that didn't want leave but also didn't want to convert to Islam practiced Judaism in secret (Crypto-Judaism). Those that refused to be Muslims traveled closer to the coast of West Africa where Islam wasn't that dominant. The Black African Israelite Tribes suffered many losses and endured persecution while living in Africa amongst Hamitic tribes practicing different types of pagan religion (**Animism, polytheism**).   This was foretold in the Muslim Holy Qur'an after 600 A.D. when the Arabs captured millions of Black Hebrew Israelites from Africa during the "**Arab Slave Trade**". This was documented in the "**Battle of Khaybar**" in the 7th Century and later during the end of **Sonni Ali's Hebrew Israelite Kingdom in the Songhai Empire (West Africa)**. Once Muslim **Askia Muhammad** came on the scene as ruler of this empire in the late 1400's, he had no tolerance for the Black Hebrew Israelites living in his land. This is why many Hebrew Manuscripts over the year have been set ablaze by the Muslims living in Mali.

"The King (**Askia the Great**) is a declared enemy of the **Jews**. He will not allow any to live in the city (**Gao/Timbuktu**). If he hears it said that a Berber merchant frequents them or does business with them, he confiscates his goods." **Askia Muhammad, Emperor of the Songhai Empire from 1493-1528 A.D**

YUSUF ALI-Qur'an 033.026-033.027 (650 A.D)

"And those of the People of the Book (Black Hebrew Israelites) who aided them – **Allah did take them down from their strongholds** and cast terror into their hearts so that some ye slew, and some ye made **prisoners (SLAVES)**. And He made you heirs of their lands, their houses, and their goods, and of a **LAND WHICH YE HAD NOT FREQUENTED BEFORE (Africa/Arabia)**. And Allah has power over all things".

This was written in the 7th Century A.D., almost 100 years before the European pagan Khazars would convert to Judaism and 1,000 years before the Holocaust would happen. The Arabs didn't enslave European Caucasians in Africa, nor did they travel to Eastern-Western Europe to enslave European Caucasian Judaism converts called "**Jews**". The Arabs were talking about invading the "**Lands of Blacks (Africa-Arabia)**" and enslaving them. Only the people they conquered and enslaved in Africa-Arabia were the "**People of the Book**". The Cush Empire has been proven by many to include Arabia, Mesopotamia and Africa. The Black and White Northern Arabs for the most part enslaved black people in Ancient times. The Caucasian Northern White Ottoman Turkish/Kurdish Arabs then added fuel to the fire by continuing the enslavement of Black Hebrew Israelites. Remember, the first Black Arabs (**Midianites-Sons of Keturah and the Ishmaelite's**) sold Joseph to the Egyptians courtesy of his flesh & blood brothers. This was one of the beginnings of slavery-type practices in the bible.

From 1881-1914, Africa was partitioned up like a pizza into different countries by the Europeans. This separated lands and divided tribes. It also influenced different language dialects and also determined which ones would be the primary "**working language**". Also known as the "**Scramble for Africa**", European countries invaded, occupied, colonized, and drew up boundaries of African territories often sparking civil war between different African Tribes. They then changed the names of these African boundaries (countries) as they saw fit. The Europeans main reasons for occupying Africa were:

- The Europeans wanted to spread their western language (**i.e. French, Spanish, Portuguese, English**) and western culture. This included their way of dressing, religion, education and administration since Africa was previously referred to as '**The Dark Continent**'.

- They wanted to spread Christianity in East Africa so as to prevent the spread of Islam by Arabs who dwelled in the North after its invasion in mid-600's A.D.
- By the end of the 19th century there was an industrial revolution in Europe and therefore the Europeans were looking for raw-materials to feed their industries (**e.x. Cotton, coffee, minerals like gold, copper, diamond, tin and animal products like ivory, hides and skins**).
- They wanted to invest their surplus capital in East Africa for high profits. They invested their capital in mining and farming.
- The Europeans were overpopulated and therefore wanted to get new areas in East Africa where they could resettle their surplus population. Some were criminals and were unwanted in their native European country. Many Europeans wanted a "**fresh start**" to a new beginning, courtesy of Africa. They would set up European colonies in high population areas where they could extract raw materials from the land of Africa and also sell European manufactured goods to the Africans. The Europeans **wanted it all** and decided to take it all just as in the Bible where Elisha's servant Gehazi would let greed eventually bring him and his descendants the curse of white skin (leprosy) from God.
- The Europeans also were interested in East Africa to get territories for prestigious purposes because the more territories a European power had, the more powerful it would be considered (**e.x. France dominance over West Africa**).
- Unemployment in Europe also prompted the scramble and partition of East Africa. Machines replaced human labor in Europe thus creating unemployment. Because of this, there was a need to acquire colonies where their people could be employed.
- The rise of nationalism in Europe also caused the scramble and partition of East Africa. European countries developed national pride in superiority over others. Therefore possession of colonies became a symbol of superiority. For example Germany and Italy were moved by that influence. For this reason Italy invaded Somalia, Eritrea and Ethiopia.
- Strategic reasons also led to the scramble and partition of East Africa. Following the construction of the Suez Canal, Britain realized that Egypt could not survive on its own without the Nile; therefore they colonized Sudan, Uganda and Kenya.

- Britain had some success in halting the slave trade around the shores of Africa. But inland the Muslim Arab slave traders from the North and on the East Coast were still stealing and selling blacks for slaves. The Arabs did not want to give up the use of slaves that they were used to having for over 1,000 years.
- The end of the European Transatlantic slave trade left a need for making money. Capitalism experts saw a different opportunity to make money off of Africa. They wanted to exploit Africa by doing trade in Africa (**which they still do this this day**). European explorers searched high and low for large reserves of raw materials, they plotted the course of trade routes, navigated rivers, and identified high population areas which could be the market for selling manufactured goods from Europe like clothes, guns, beads, glass ware, furs, guns, ammunition, rum etc.

Within forty years, by 1914 and at the end of the "**Scramble for Africa**", **Great Britain** dominated most of Africa from Egypt to South Africa, as well as Nigeria and the Gold Coast. The **French** occupied West Africa, the **Germans** controlled Tanzania and Namibia. The **Portuguese** controlled Angola, Mozambique and the Island of Cape Verde (West Coast). The **Italians** controlled Somali and tried to take over Ethiopia/Eritrea. In the end, only Ethiopia and the African-American state of Liberia remained independent. Europeans conquered Africa and the Americas easily because of **previous agreements** not to sell guns to Africans, African-Americans and Native American Indians. **This meant that the Europeans had a huge weapon advantage in whatever foreign land they went to because the natives of the lands most likely did not have access to guns**. Bands of just hundreds of white European men armed with a couple machine guns could obliterate thousands of Africans or American Native Indians in hours. When needed, they could resort to "**force**" to get what they wanted in Africa. This is exactly what they did in Africa and in the "Native" land of the New World.

WHAT PEOPLE EXPERIENCED THE "BESIEGING" OF THEIR LAND NO MATTER WHERE THEY LIVED?

IGBO NIGERIANS UNDER SIEGE

It is a known fact that the Portuguese, the Dutch, the Swedish, the British, the Danish and the Germans all had an interest in West Africa for various reasons (Gold/Slaves) but afterwards in the 1900's problems for certain Israelites did not go away.

In the early 1900's another African Hebrew Israelite nation, the "Igbo's" would draw the spotlight in Africa as they tried to succeed from the Country of Nigeria. They wanted a separate land/country called "**Biafra**". This movement however was met with great resistance.

Biafran General Emeka Ojukwu

Oxford-educated Nigerian soldier, Emeka Ojukwu, or **Chukwuemeka Odumegwu Ojukwu (1933-2011)**, proclaimed the short-lived Republic of Biafra in 1967. Under British indirect rule, Nigeria had been crudely divided along tribal lines: **Hausa, Fulani, Yoruba, and Igbo (Biafra)**. Unhappy at northern heavy-handedness and discrimination, Igbo officers staged a coup in 1966 and set up Ojukwu as governor of the Eastern Region, which included the oil-rich Niger delta. When the counter-coup came six months later, Ojukwu refused to step down. Under pressure from Igbo militants he declared independence for the 29,000 square-mile region of Southeastern Nigeria on May 30, 1967. A flag was designed, featuring a "**rising sun**". A currency was issued and the beginnings of a welfare state were put in place. Ojukwu personally chose a movement from Jean Sibelius's "Finlandia" as the tune to the national anthem, in reference to the Nordic country's resistance to foreign domination. The **Nigerian civil war**, popularly known all over the world as the "**Biafran War**" was fought from July 2, 1967 to January 15, 1970. The war was between the then Eastern Region of Nigeria and the rest of the country. The Eastern Region declared itself an independent state which was regarded as an act of secession by the Federal Military Government of Nigeria. The war was fought to reunify the country.

Fact: *It is a known fact that many Igbo hold the tradition that their people many, many years ago left Israel and entered into Africa. They have customs (such as burial practices) that mimic Jewish customs. They have received passed down stories from their elders (**some over 100 years old**) that they are descendants of the 12 Tribes of Israel. Some say Gad to be specific. The Igbo's strengthened their connections to Judaism by likening their experience as a minority scattered throughout Nigeria to the Jewish diaspora and referring to the Biafra genocide between 1967 and 1970 as another "**Holocaust**".*

SOUTH SUDANESE UNDER SIEGE

Following independence from Britain in 1956, Sudan became embroiled in two prolonged civil wars for most of the remainder of the 20th century. These conflicts were rooted in northern economic, political, and social domination of largely Non-Muslim, Non-Arab Southern Sudanese Africans. Competition for scarce resources played a large role. As nomads began to compete for grazing land, traditional reconciliation measures were no longer able to settle disputes, causing the region to become increasingly militarized. The complexities of desertification, famines, and the civil war raging between **North and South Sudan** contributed to a rise in regional tensions during the 1980s. Similarly, as oil was discovered in Western Sudan, the Sudanese government and international contributors became increasingly interested in the land of Darfur. Civil war had existed between the **Northern** and **Southern regions** of **Sudan** for more than a decade. Today the **Northern Region**, centered on the capital of **Khartoum**, is predominantly made up of Muslims who are ethnically Arabs, while groups of Christians (**along with Hebrew Israelites**) and animists live in the south. The Khartoum government under **General Omar al-Bashir** wished to create a more Islamic-based government that was opposed by the **Southern Region** which led to civil war. Not until 2005, and with heavy international influence, did the **Comprehensive Peace Agreement** end the two-decade-long civil war that had resulted in more than **2 million deaths** and **4 million displaced persons** from South Sudan.

Fact: *According to UN estimates, 2.7 million Darfuris remain in internally displaced in refugee camps and more than 4.7 million Darfuris rely on humanitarian aid. Since July 9, 2011, South Sudan became the world's newest country. This was a major step toward ending the violence in Sudan; however civilians across Sudan still remain at risk.*

THE JEWISH MADI TRIBE OF SOUTH SUDAN

The largely Christian, African portion of the South Sudan has been dominated by Arab Muslims for a long time to the north, in Khartoum. The People of the **Madi Tribe** in South Sudan claim to be Jews. They did not retain Judaism as thoroughly as did the Falashas/Beta Israel Jews in neighboring Ethiopia, but for generations they have kept customs that seem to have come from Mosaic Law in the Old Testament. They claim no outsiders taught them this as this is a common statement European Jews like to say whenever discrediting the "Jewishness" of African Tribes. Here are some:

1. One Supreme God is worshipped.
2. As in the Book of Leviticus, blood sacrifices are offered for sins. The "worst" sins require the sacrifice of a sheep, and the "least" sins a chicken. A hereditary group of elders or priests decide what animal to sacrifice and they also preside over these sacrifices and other ceremonies (**similar to the Levites/Kohanites**). Ashanti's in Ghana also do this.

3. Dietary laws are practiced as certain animals are "**unclean**" and could not be eaten.

4. Ceremonial washing of the hands are required when leaving home.

5. Certain days of the year are set apart as Holy. On these days, all was pledged to the one God of the heavens who forgave sins.

6. The use of a ram's (**Shofar**) horn called a "**Bilah**" to call people together for various purposes such as ceremonies or to discuss a matter of importance.

7. If a man died, his brother married his widow or befriended the widow. This is called the "**kinsman-redeemer**" custom found in the Book of Ruth in connection with Boaz marrying Ruth. **Note:** This is also practiced in West African countries such as **Ghana** and **Nigeria**.

8. The setting apart of all the "**First born males**" of the herds and flocks for the Lord. None were to be put to work or in a sheep's case, shorn.

9. All males are circumcised and named on the 8th day (**Luke 2:21 & Luke 1:59**). **Note:** This is also practiced in Ghana, Nigeria, Cameroon, Kenya and other African Tribes.

Madi Tribe in South Sudan and Uganda

Fact: The Y-DNA Haplogroup "**E1b1a**" is found primarily in the "Bantus" people in West Africa, Central African and East Africa. It is found in high percentages (>70%) of individuals from West Africa, African-Americans and Blacks in the Caribbean.

The Luo people are outwardly recognized as "**Nilotic-Hamitic**" people in South Sudan, Ethiopia, Northern Uganda, East Congo, Western Kenya and parts of Tanzania. Little do people know is that some of them are also genetically no different from West Africans, African-Americans and Caribbean/South American Blacks. The Luo people's dispersion from their homeland in South Sudan was in part caused by the Muslim conquest of Sudan. **Here are some of the Luo people (sub-groups). In the Elizabeth Wood 2005 study: "Contrasting patterns of Y chromosome and mtDNA variation in Africa" it is found that of all the subjects tested from the Luo tribe, (66%) tested positive for the E1b1a gene.**

- Lango (Uganda)
- Shilluk (South Sudan)
- Pari (South Sudan)
- Thuri (South Sudan)
- Alur (Uganda and Democratic Republic of Congo)
- Acholi (South Sudan and Uganda)
- Kumam (Uganda)
- Jopadhola (Uganda)
- Jo Luo (Kenya and Tanzania)
- Anuak (Ethiopia, Sudan)
- Mabaan (South Sudan)
- Funj (Sudan)
- Jumjum (South Sudan)
- Bland Boore (South Sudan)
- Jur Bel (South Sudan)
- Luwo (South Sudan)
- Jonam (North Uganda)
- Jokanywa (Kenya)
- Luo Suba (Kenya)

In comparison the percentages of the E1b1a gene found in other African Countries are: Ghana (92%), Nigeria Igbo (90%), Nigerian Yoruba (92%), South Cameroon (93-100%), Burkina Faso (81-90%), Benin (95%), Gabon (80%), Congo (68-100%), Mandinka (80%), Rwanda-Hutu/Tutsi (83%), and Wolof –Senegal/Gambia (68%).

Courtesy of the following genetic studies:

- **Wood, Elizabeth** (2005), "Contrasting patterns of Y chromosome and mtDNA variation in Africa: evidence for sex-biased demographic processes.
- **Tishkoff, Sara** (2007), "History of Click-Speaking Populations of Africa Inferred from mtDNA and Y Chromosome Genetic Variation.
- **Hassan, Hisham** Y (2008), Y-Chromosome Variation Among Sudanese: Restricted Gene Flow, Concordance with Language, Geography, and History.
- **J.R. Luis** (2004), "The Levant versus the Horn of Africa: Evidence for Bidirectional Corridors of Human Migrations.

Ethiopian Army during Italian attempt to colonization

ETHIOPIANS UNDER SIEGE

Ethiopia was one of the few African Countries to survive the "**Scramble for Africa**" by the major European powers in the later 1800's. Both Italy and Ethiopia were a part of the **League of Nations**, founded in 1920. Italy was a founding member and Ethiopia joined Sept 28, 1923. Italy's communist dictator **Benito Mussolini**, wanted his own empire like Hitler and the Roman Empire. He wanted it in the Horn of Africa and around the Mediterranean Sea. In 1935 Mussolini and his Italian Troops invaded Ethiopia.

Mussolini and his Italian Troops invade Ethiopia in 1935.

Ethiopian Emperor **Haile Selassie** mobilized his army. The Italian army by May 5th, 1936 seized the capital city of Ethiopia **Addis Ababa**. Haile Selassie left the country going into exile in England. In June 1936, Rome drafted a constitution bringing Ethiopia, Eritrea, Italian Somaliland together divided into six provinces. In December 1936, Rome, Italy declared the whole country to be under their control. Ethiopian resistance however did not fade. The Ethiopians attempted to assassinate Governor **Marshal Rodolfo Graziani** in 1937. Because of this the Italians executed 30,000 Ethiopians, including about half of the younger educated Ethiopian population in Amhara, Ethiopia. The Italians then started beginning public work projects such as improving the roads. They instituted racial segregation, residential segregation and showed favoritism to the Non-Christian Oromo Ethiopians and Muslim Somalis in attempt to isolate the part of Ethiopia that supported Haile Selassie. It was not until after 1943 that Ethiopia was able to team up with the British and other indigenous African forces to kick out the Italians who entered World War II with Germany. So the question is, where there any remnants of Israel in Ethiopia during this time?

Italian leader Mussolini and German leader Hitler

While most of the Slavetrading and land possession was going on in West Africa, why wasn't Ethiopia affected? Did Ethiopia experience the Curses throughout the many centuries after the fall of the Second Temple in Jerusalem? If some of the Ethiopians were in fact real "**Israelites**", then why would God allow many of them to be brought back to Israel via "**Operation Moses**" and "**Operation Solomon**" in the late 1900's courtesy of the Judaism convert Ashkenazi Jews? Was this bible prophecy coming to past? If it wasn't then, the Ethiopian Jews should not be there right? But if they were not supposed to be brought there according to God, they wouldn't be there. So there has to be a reason for them being there in Israel. They didn't know they were going to persecuted and discriminated in Israel. **The Bene Israel (Indian Jews), Cochin Jews (India), the Sephardic Jews, the Ethiopian Jews and the African Black Hebrew Israelites all have been outcasted to live in Southern Israel in the Negev Desert near the city of Beersheba away from the European Jews**. You be the judge. The Ethiopian Jews are told they are from the Tribe of Dan by European Jews and other sources. But the problem lies when the Jews believe that the 10 Tribe of Israel is still lost when the Tribe of Dan (Ethiopian Jews) is a part of the "**Lost 10 Tribes of Israel**".

Isaiah 11:11-12 "And it shall come to pass in that day, that the Lord shall set his hand again the **SECOND TIME** to recover the remnant of his people, which shall be left, from Assyria, and from Egypt, and from Pathros, **and from CUSH (Ethiopia)**, and from Elam, and from Shinar, and from Hamath, and from the islands of the sea. And he shall set up an ensign for the nations, and shall assemble the **OUTCASTS OF ISRAEL** and gather together the **DISPERSED OF JUDAH** from the **FOUR CORNERS OF THE EARTH**.

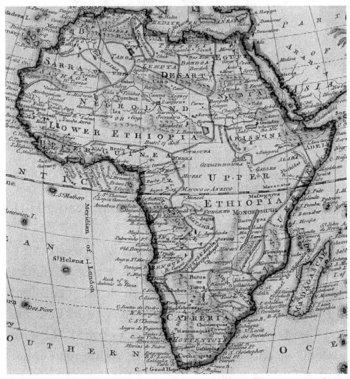

*(Above) Map of Africa in **1771**. Strange enough is that "**Upper Ethiopia**" and "**Lower Ethiopia**" make up the exact lands the Hebrew Israelites were scattered into. **Negroland/Proper Guinea** which make up West Africa and the **African Great Lakes Region** which make up East Africa. The Israelites scattered into Africa (**aka Cush - Ethiopia**) and settled there, until slavery would take many of them to the "**Islands of the Sea**".*

Does this mean that the Israelites are going to be brought back physically from these lands or is this scripture referencing the lands the Israelites were scattered to back in the day?

1. **Assyria** is modern day Syria and Iraq.
2. **Egypt** is where it is today.
3. **Pathros** is the south part of Egypt near Nubia where the Black Egyptians are that they don't show us on T.V.

4. **Cush** or Ethiopia is modern day Africa and Arabia. In 17-18th Century Maps the majority of Africa is sometimes referred to as **Upper** and **Lower Ethiopia**.

5. **Elam** is Southeastern Iraq and Southwestern Iran but many people believe the descendants of the Elamites are modern-day Dravidian Indians today in South India/Sri Lanka.

6. **Shinar** is Iraq (sometimes also linked to Iran). The descendants of the Zanj Bantus East African Blacks that were sold into Basra, Iraq are still there till this day living in poverty compared to the light skinned/white Iraqis.

7. **Hamath** is in Assyria/Syria. The 10 Tribes of Israel were scattered into Assyria/Persia and from there they also migrated to other parts of the world such as the New World.

8. The "**Islands of the Sea**" (Caribbean, the Americas, Madagascar) is where the Israelite "**Negro**" Blacks have been scattered, joining many of their Israelite brethren called "Natives" by the Europeans.

Could this be what Isaiah 11:11-12 is referring too?

Fact: *It is known fact that the European Ashkenazi Jews will say that **ALL** of the Tribe of Judah is European and that they are in Israel, America and the rest of the world. They will **NEVER** admit that there are Black people from the Tribe of Judah. As a matter of fact, if you ask **ANY** European Ashkenazi Jew what tribe they are from they will **ALWAYS** say Judah, Benjamin, Levi or Kohenite/Cohenite.*

DID THE ANCIENT ISRAELITES RESORT TO "CANNIBALISM?"

Deuteronomy 28:53 **"And thou shalt eat the fruit of thine own body, the flesh of thy sons and of thy daughters, which the LORD thy God hath given thee, in the siege, and in the straitness, wherewith thine enemies shall distress thee:"**

(Above) Picture of "Natives" cooking human body parts. Cannibalism has never been a traditionally practiced in the White Race.

When many people read Deuteronomy 28:53 they probably wonder: "How can this be right?" The bible says: **"Thou shalt EAT the fruit of thine own body, THE FLESH of thy sons and of thy daughters, which the LORD thy God hath given thee, in the siege (CAPTIVITY).** So does this mean that the Israelites were cursed to literally eat their sons and daughters? Seems like that's exactly what it says. If that is the case, we should see some proof of the "**scattered**" Israelites eating the flesh of their sons and daughters while they were in exile from multiple invasions of their territory.

How could the Israelites kill and eat other human beings? It is a known fact that cannibalism has been practiced in tribal people living in Africa, the Americas and the Islands of the Sea. There have been many books written talking about cannibalism in the **Congo**. Some burial/death rituals involved eating the flesh of their loved ones, sometimes after the jackals and hyenas would eat their fill. These books describe the gore of tribal cannibalism. In desperate times, the Israelites would also eat their children according the Bible. After all, the "**Children of Israel**" were in fact a part of "**Tribes**" and there has never been a "**Tribal White Race**" throughout history.   Those in tribes are usually from Africa, the Americas (Latinos/Native Americans) and perhaps Indians.   Here is an account of the Cannibals in Congo.

Note: *Many slaves from the Congo were taken to Virginia, South Carolina, North Carolina and the Caribbean.*

"Nearly all the tribes in the **Congo Basin** either are or have been **cannibals**; and among some of them the practice is on the increase. Races who until lately do not seem to have been cannibals, although situated in a country surrounded by cannibal races, have, from increased intercourse with their neighbors, learned to eat human flesh. Soon after the Station of Equator was established, the residents discovered that a wholesale human traffic was being carried on by the natives of the district between this station and Lake M'Zumba. The captains of the steamers have often assured me that whenever they try to buy goats from the natives, slaves are demanded in exchange; the natives often come aboard with tusks of ivory with the intention of buying a slave, complaining that **meat is now scarce in their neighborhood**. There is not the slightest doubt in my mind that they prefer human flesh to any other. During all the time I lived among cannibal races I never came across a single case of their eating any kind of flesh raw; they invariably either boil, roast or smoke it. This custom of smoking flesh to make it last would have been very useful to us, as we were often without meat for long periods. We could, however, never buy smoked meat in the markets, it being impossible to be sure that it was not human flesh. The preference of different tribes for various parts of the human body is interesting. Some cut long steaks from the flesh of the thighs, legs or arms; others prefer the hands and feet; and though the great majorities do not eat the head, I have come across more than one tribe which prefers this to any other part. Almost all use some part of the intestines on account of the fat they contain."

Sidney Langford Hinde (former captain of the Congo Free State Force), The Fall of the Congo Arabs, Methuen, 1987

These Africans were from the Basongo Tribe.   Here is how the Europeans described them.

"All the inhabitants of this region, as well as those of Londa, may be called true negroes, if the limitations formerly made be borne in mind. The dark color, thick lips, heads elongated backward and upward and covered with wool, flat noses, with other negro peculiarities, are general; but, while these characteristics place them in the true negro family, the reader would imbibe a wrong idea if he supposed that all these features combined are often met with in one individual. All have certain thickness and prominence of lip, but many are met with in every village in whom thickness and projection are not more marked than in Europeans. All are dark, but the color is shaded off in different individuals from deep black to light yellow. As we go westward, we observe the light color predominating over the dark, and then again, when we come within the influence of damp from the sea air, we find the shade deepen into the general blackness of the coast population. The shape of the head with its wooly crop, though general is not universal. The tribes on the eastern side of the continent, as the Caffres, have heads finely developed and strongly European (? less Negro in appearance). Instances of this kind are frequently seen, and after I became so familiar with the dark color as to forget it in viewing the countenance, I was struck by the strong resemblance some natives bore to certain of our own notabilities."

Missionary Travels and Researches in South Africa, David Livingstone (1813-1873).

Here are some books:

- **Sidney Langford Hinde** (former captain of the Congo Free State Force), The Fall of the Congo Arabs, Methuen, 1987
- **Rev. W. Holman Bentley** (Baptist Missionary Society), Pioneering on the Congo, TRS, 1900 (2 vols)
- **Gary Hogg**, Cannibalism and Human Sacrifice, p. 114
- **John Roscoe**, The Bagesu and Other Tribes of the Uganda Protectorate, The Royal Society, 1924
- **Basil Spence**, in Sudan Notes and Records, vol III, no. 4 (Dec 1920)

Here is proof some of the Israelites practiced Cannibalism:

2 Kings 6:25-30 "And there was a great famine in Samaria (**Northern Israel**): and, behold, they **besieged it**, until an ass's head was sold for fourscore pieces of silver, and the fourth part of a cab of dove's dung for five pieces of silver. And as the King of Israel was passing upon the wall, there cried a woman unto him, saying, help, my lord, O king. And he said, If the Lord do not help thee, whence shall I help thee? Out of the barnfloor, or out of the winepress? And the King said unto her, What aileth thee? And she answered, This woman said unto me, Give thy son, **THAT WE MAY EAT HIM TODAY and WE WILL EAT MY SON TOMORROW.** So we **BOILED MY SON, AND DID EAT HIM**: and I said unto her on the next day, Give thy son, that we may eat him: and she hath hid her son. And it came to pass, when the King heard the words of the woman, that he rent (tore) his clothes; and he passed by upon the wall, and the people looked, and, behold, he had sackcloth within upon his flesh."

The lady called the King of Israel her "**Lord**" and "**King**". So obviously this was an Israelite woman. There have been old reports in slave trade history that have suggested that cannibalism was practiced amongst the Hebrew Israelites before slavery and during their trip across the Atlantic. Here is an account of what Europeans wrote about the slave trades from 1900 A.D. Whether or not many of the Europeans "Negro" written stories are exaggerated have to be considered but it solely depends on how the reader interprets it.

"People whose social institutions are at the lowest possible level, with an undiluted fetishism, with the worship of ancestors for a religion, coupled with torture, cruelty, slavery, **cannibalism**, and a common belief in sorcery. Where not checked by the presence of the European in the middle **CONGO BASIN** the native shambles (i.e. Butcher slaughterhouses) are still hung with the **choice cuts of human bodies**, and they continue to be sold in the open market place. Many of these people see their relatives in the Negroes of the United States. In Africa, they even barter their **dead relatives**, and those securing the corpses in this way **eat them**, and that with great relish. They will even disinter (i.e. take the body out of the grave/tomb) them for the same purpose, and eat them after decomposition has set in. Those Negroes who still practice this in Africa are several millions in number, and are the close blood relatives of the race as we have them represented in the United States. (**Stanley: Heart of Africa, Vol. II. Page 18-19**. "**The Negro: A Menace to American Civilization**" by R.W. Shufeldt, M.D.

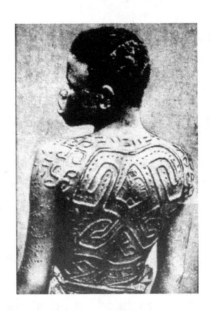

Congo Man

Fact: In the 1800's the Europeans went into the Congo to learn about the language and writing style of the Congo African people. They wrote a book about it called **"A Comparative Grammar of the South African Bantu Languages: comparing those of Zanzibar, Mozambique, the Zambezi, Kafirland, Benguela, Angola, the Congo, the Ogowe, the Cameroons, the Lake Region, Etc., by J Torrend , S.J.'** They documented that many slaves were taken from these areas, in particular the **"Congo"**. These slaves were taken to the Americas and the Caribbean Islands. Congolese Slaves in South Carolina were found to pronounce words for certain objects which were similar to "Hebrew and Western Aramaic".

Congo Forest Men (1800's). Do they look African, Native American or Asian?

In 1816, while the Europeans were in the Congo they found drawings and writing inscriptions on rocks which looked identical to Hebrew inscriptions found at the **"Wadi Mokatteb"**, (which means **"Valley of Inscriptions"**) in the south part of the Sinai Peninsula (Egypt) near Mr. Serbal, Mt. Catherine and the biblical Mt. Sinai **(aka Mt. Horeb-Deuteronomy 29:1)**. Throughout time, scholars and historians have debated which one of these mountains was the biblical "**Mt. Sinai**". Mt. Sinai is the mountain most scholars believe that Moses received the Ten Commandments and also received the proper name of God. Mt. Serbal by many was also believed to be the Biblical Mt. Sinai (**Mr. Horeb**). Because of this "claim to biblical history", in the 4th Century A.D. a Monastery was built on the mountain. In 535 A.D, a man named "**Indicopleustes**", or the "**Indian Traveler**" visited the "**Wadi Mokatteb**" at the Sinai Peninsula and noticed that the inscriptions found carved on the rock were in "**Ancient Hebrew**". He believed the Ancient Israelites left these writings during the Exodus out of Egypt to serve as a witness to the "unbelievers". This area has been a hot spot for Christians as well as Arabs who in the past worshipped the sun, moon, stars and "Baal" at the top of the mountain during the pre-Islamic period. The Europeans later after doing their research about the "Wadi Mokatteb" found out that the writings on the rocks in the Congo were in fact identical to the "Wadi Mokatteb" Hebrew writings from the Ancient Hebrew Israelites. So the question is, were these so-called cannibalistic Congo Negroes per R. W. Shufeldt M.D. actually **"Lost Hebrew Israelites"**? Maybe over time, some of the people living in the **Congo Basin** lost their Hebrew Heritage. If so, this definitely predicted in the Bible.

Congo Basin

DID THE "NATIVES" (ISRAELITES) IN AMERICA/CARIBBEAN PRACTICE CANNIBALISM?

For the most part, the "Natives" were not "cannibals", but there were some groups who were. The Aztecs were notorious for ritual cannibalism. There were some reports of the Aztec warriors eating a strip of their enemies flesh while in combat. There are also reports of some Amazonian tribes who practiced Cannibalism. There are even reports that the Carib tribe (relatives and/or perhaps a subsect of the Taino Indians) practiced cannibalism. People like to dispute this, but there is oral and written proof to support it as true. Many of the European explorers often wrote what they saw when they were around these different "Native Tribes" and some other their eye witness accounts proved that "Cannibalism" was sometimes practiced.   But were these "Natives" actually Hebrew Israelites who were eating the flesh of their blood brothers from another tribe?

THE NATIVE AMERICANS AND THE ANCIENT HEBREW ISRAELITES.

There is a plethora of information on the "Native Americans" and the Israelites. Similarities in the language, the customs, the religious practices, and more. One Tribe in particular; the Cherokee Indian Tribe. The Cherokees wore clothes with fringes and tassels.

(**Left**) Tzitzits. (**Right**) This is **King Jehu** of the **House of Israel** and some Israelites **WITH TASSELS** (Arrow) paying tribute to the Assyrian King Shalmaneser by bowing and offering gifts (silver, gold, a golden bowl, a golden vase and a staff). It is on the "**Black Obelisk (827 B.C.)**". Jehu was of the House of Omri and ruled during the time of King Hazael of Syria (**2 Kings 10:32**).

Deuteronomy 22:12 "Thou shalt make thee **FRINGES** upon the four quarters of thy vesture, wherewith thou coverest thyself."

Yahusha (Jesus) wore fringes too!

Matthew 9:20 "And a woman who had been suffering from a hemorrhage for twelve years, came up behind Him and touched the **FRINGE** of **HIS** cloak;"

The Cherokee Indians also had their own "**Day of Atonement**" which was Identical to Hebrew Israelites "Day of Atonement" in Leviticus 16:29, 23:27. The "Day of Atonement" was a day of rest/no work on the seventh month, on the tenth day of the month. The Northern Cherokee Nation of Old Louisiana Territory supposedly state that their ancient oral legends state that they migrated to America from Masada, (Southern district) Israel where the Territory of the Tribe of Judah is.

1. The Native Americans celebrated the "**New Moon**" which was also celebrated by the Israelites. The New Moon was linked to the Sabbath and the Festival of the New Moon was a Biblical feast. Every year on the 15th day of the sacred month of harvest, in the fall, they make a pilgrimage. For 8 days they lived in "**booths (huts/tents)**" with roofs open to the sky, covered with branches, leaves, and foliage. During this festival they call upon the

Name of God. They call it the "**Festival of Booths**". This goes back to Moses and the Israelites of the Bible.

Leviticus 23:42-44 "Ye shall dwell in **BOOTHS** seven days; all that are Israelites born shall dwell in booths: That your generations may know that I made the children of the Israel to dwell in **BOOTHS**, when I brought them out of the land of Egypt: I am the Lord your God. And Moses declared unto the children of Israel the feasts of the Lord."

2. **Dr. Cyrus H. Gordon** was a professor of Near Eastern Studies at Brandeis University from 1956 to 1973 and chairman of its department of Mediterranean studies from 1958 to 1973. He was a professor of Hebrew studies at NYU (New York University) from 1973 to 1989. Mr. Gordon was able to listen to the Cherokee Indians, chants, songs, and sacred ceremonies. Dr. Cyrus was an Ashkenazi Jew but was also an expert in **Ancient Hebrew, Semitic Minoan, and Middle-East Arabic/Persian**. When he listened to a recording of them speaking and worshipping God, he noted to his companion that they were speaking the Hebrew names of God!

3. In the "**Epigraphic Society Occasional Papers (ESOP)**" 1998 volume, an article called "**A Curious Element in Uto-Aztecan**" by Brian D. Stubbs provided evidence that the Indian family of languages called "**Uto-Aztecan**" demonstrated similarities with the patterns of **Ancient B.C. Paleo-Hebrew** (p. 112). He saw similarities between Ancient Hebrew and the languages of Indian tribes from Central Mexico the Southwest and Rocky Mountain tribes (Hopi, Utes, Paiutes, Shoshones, etc.)

4. In New Mexico, the "**Ten Commandments**" were found written in Paleo-Hebrew on a large stone. There were more stones found in New Mexico with Paleo-Hebrew written on it with the name "**Tribe of Asher**". Asher was the blood brother of "**Gad**" from their same mother "**Zilpah**". Many historians believe that these Indians date back to the time of King Solomon when he was known to send fleets to other continents.

5. A study was of the Indian languages was done by **Dr. E. Morgan Kelley** of the College of William and Mary. It was published in the 1990 volume of **ESOP (Epigraphic Society Occasional Papers)** on page 83-91. The article

was called **"North American Indian Tribal Names"** and it identified related language groups among the Indian Tribes based on the frequency of similar words/parts of words in each Tribe. He noted that the word **"Dan"** was commonly used in certain tribes, possibly hinting to the **"Tribe of Dan"** from the lost 10 Tribes of Israel.

6. Dr. Barry Fell and Dr. Cyrus Gordon's book **"Before Columbus; Links between the Old World and Ancient America"** documented the authenticity of the **"Bat Creek Stone"** which was found in the 1880's in the Cherokee Region near the Tennessee/North Carolina border. There were different theories if the Bat Creek Stone was a Paleo-Hebrew forgery or if it was real. Dr. Gordon was also able to accurately identify Coins written in Hebrew from the 2nd Century A.D. Bar Kochba period found in Kentucky, Missouri and Arkansas. Dr. Gordon also was able to decipher the language on the **Metcalf Stone**, the **Newark Holy Stones**, the **Los Lunas Decalogue Inscription**, and the **Hebrew Paraiba Stone found in the 1870's in Brazil.**

7. **John Adair** was an 18th century explorer and trader. He wrote a book in 1775 called **"The History of the American Indians"**. He noted that several hundred Cherokee Indians living in the North Carolina Mountains spoke an Ancient Jewish language that was nearly unintelligible to European Gentile convert Jews from England and Holland. This is because the European Jews spoke a Modern Hebrew derived from Syriac Aramaic, and not Paleo-Hebrew. From this observation he believed that the Native Americans were descendants of the Ten Lost Tribes of Israel from the Assyrian captivity in 700 B.C. He also noted that the Native Americans set-apart the respected name of **"Yo-hee-wah"** or **"Yow ah"** for prayer or for singing religious songs. He also noted that it was also used by the Choctaw Tribe and other Native American Tribes. Mr. Adair also revealed in his works that **"circumcision"** was practiced amongst the different "Native American" Tribes. He noted that there were Indians living in the mountains of America that were a lost tribe of Israel.

Cherokee Native Americans in the past often were brown skinned people but now it is not uncommon to see Miss Cherokee pageant winners to be your typical Caucasian looking woman.

Fact: *The various old Cherokee nations honored the seventh day of each week.* **Four** *and* **seven** *are sacred numbers to the Cherokees. Perhaps this is because the Fourth Commandment states to* **"Keep the Sabbath Holy"** *and the Cherokee Indians were keeping the Sabbath holy. They designed their priest houses for worship so that "their backs were to the east" and their "faces to the west". It was said that they didn't not adore any images or dead persons; neither the sun, moon, stars, nor evil spirits. The Cherokee Indians were known to observe a year of Jubilee, they celebrated the New Moon, and sang the words* **"Hal, Hal, Hal"**, **"le, le, le"**, **"lu, lu, lu,"** *ending in* **"yah, yah, yah"** *in repeated chants in their religious prayer songs while in dance. Now why would Native Americans know about the word "Halleluyah" if they were in the New World before Christianity and the Spaniards could find its way there? No other nation of people from the Middle East worshipped* **"Yahuah"** *or* **"Yah"** *other than the Hebrew Israelites. The Babylonians worshipped* **Marduk**. *The Egyptians worshipped* **Horus, Ra** *and* **Osiris**. *The Canaanites worshipped* **Baal**. *The Philistines worshipped* **Dagon**. *The Persians worshipped* **Zoroaster**. *The Greeks worshipped* **Zeus**. *The Romans worshipped* **Jupiter ammon**. *The Edomites worshipped* **Qos/Qaus** *and the Arabs Ishmaelite's/Keturahites worshipped* **Hubal** *and many other pagan gods in the Middle East before Islam arrived on the scene. That pretty much narrows down the Middle East and their Gods, so now you can judge for yourself why the Native Americans were worshipping "Yahuah" in a land separated from the rest of the World.*

Deuteronomy 32:26 "I said, I would scatter them (Israelites) into the corners (of the earth), I would make the remembrance of them to cease among men".

- Psalms 83:4 "They have said, Come, and let us cut them off from being a nation; that the name of Israel may be no more in remembrance".

- Jeremiah 17:4 "And thou, even thyself, shalt discontinue from thine heritage that I gave thee; and I will cause thee to SERVE THINE ENEMIES in the land which thou knowest not: for ye have kindled a fire in mine anger, which shall burn FOREVER".

It was prophesied that the Israelites would lose their heritage. That being said, many Africans who were Israelites sold their brethren into slavery not knowing it. Over the years, as prophesied, many Israelites converted to Islam and thereafter started participating in the slave trades. These were "**Blacks**" selling "**Blacks**". They did not know they were Hebrew Israelite brothers. Even the Native Americans sold and kept Black Slaves. They also didn't know that they may have shared a common ancestral stock. The 5 most common Native American Indian Tribes who had Black slaves were:

1. Chicksaw
2. Choctaw
3. Cherokee (had more Black Slaves than any other Indian community with 4,600 slaves by 1860.
4. Creek
5. Seminole (Black Slaves were essentially freedmen/indentured servants with the Seminoles).

*It is a known fact that African Israelite Kings/Chiefs of Ghana, Benin and Nigeria participated in the selling of their Israelite brethren (Oyo-Yoruba, Dahomey-Benin, Ashanti-Ghana). This was also done in Native American Tribes. The "**Cherokee Freedman**" Black Native Americans are a result of this plus race mixing.*

Deuteronomy 28:54 **"So that the man that is tender among you, and very delicate, HIS EYE SHALL BE EVIL TOWARDS HIS BROTHER, and toward the wife of his bosom, and toward the remnant of his children which he shall leave:"**

DID THE BIBLE PROPHECY THE BREAKDOWN OF THE ISRAELITE FAMILY?

God knew how important and tender the Black man was to the Black Family. In regards to Black people, Willie Lynch knew that by destroying the Black man, you could essentially control and mold the Black race to be whatever you wanted it to be. The Black man is the key to the "Black Nuclear Family". Today they have dismantled the **"Black Male Image"** using the Media and also **"Agendas"**. But this has been going on since slavery time. Any time an invading nation attacks another nation, they have to kill or enslave the men. The men are the first on the ground to do battle, so they are also the first ones to fight to the death to protect their tribe or family. It was not easy to enslave the African men, Native American men or Native "Indians". Many African slaves and "Natives-Aztecs/Incas/Taino" were known to commit suicide rather than be enslaved under another nation. Some of them drowned themselves by jumping off the slave boats into the ocean and some hung themselves. During the Arab slave trade, young black boys were taken by the Arabs to be sold into slavery in the Middle East and other parts of the world. However, these black boys were all castrated of **ALL** their genital organs, thereby demasculinating them and also ensuring that they don't reproduce at the same time. But these black boys were not black Arab boys. They were Hebrew Israelites. This was to ensure that the Arab seed lived on and populated the Middle East. Without castration and left unchecked the Bantus Negro Hebrew Israelite male seed would overwhelm the Middle East changing the color as well as the culture. The Egyptians found this to be true while the Hebrew Israelites were enslaved under them prior to the Exodus. This was also evident in the "Bantus Expansion" in which the Bantus Negro African overwhelmed and overtook the native "Hamite" tribes in Africa, thereby reducing their numbers. The women of course were not sterilized as they were prized possessions kept as the spoils/plunders of war. They were used as sex slaves in the harems of the Arabs Palaces in the Middle East.

Zanzibar ("Zanj") slave boys from Tanzania, Africa

The tactics used by Willie Lynch to control slaves created "**distrust**" among blacks and it also caused "**trust**" in the Master; this case being the white man. Willie Lynch knew that "Distrust" was stronger than "**Trust**" and "**Envy**" was stronger than "**Adoration**". For this reason, we see blacks that would rather fight each other than fight for a cause. If we actually practiced Yahusha's "**Second Greatest Commandment**" which is "**Thou shalt love thy neighbor as thyself**" we wouldn't have a problem reversing the "**Willie Lynch Curse**". This is a central theme in the black community. We steal from each other, we fight each other and we kill each other. We do not support each other but we are quick to support everyone else.

Restaurant: Sorry, no Africans, we don't trust them after dark

BY NJOKI CHEGE
@njokichege
nchege@ke.nationmedia.com

"Musaa ya waafrika imeisha," (The time for Africans has ended) a guard at a Chinese restaurant in Nairobi's Kilimani neighbourhood tells *Daily Nation* reporters when they get there at 7pm.

The restaurant, simply known as the Chinese Restaurant, and located on the junction of Galana and Lenana roads, does not admit Africans after 5pm.

Only taxi drivers or Africans accompanied by Chinese, European or Indian patrons are allowed into

" Whatever measures they choose to take to maintain security must be measures

(***Above***) *In Kenya, a Chinese Restaurant refused to let Africans into their restaurant after 5pm. Only taxi drivers or Africans accompanied by Chinese, White or Indian customers were allowed into the restaurant after 5pm. What is the reason? The owner(s) didn't trust Africans after dark but they decided to put a Chinese Restaurant in Africa, where the majority race is "Africans"! But why is there a Chinese Restaurant in Africa? Is there a Soul Food Restaurant in Israel? Why are we constantly being bamboozled?*

(***Above***) *We see four races selling hot dogs but will a Black man buy hot dogs from his own or from the other races? It is not uncommon to see Black people buying food from every race but his own.*

The Black Man purchases hot dogs from the White, Asian, and Arab man for $3.75. The Black man doesn't second guess the price of the White man's hot dog because he has been taught that the White man always has a good deal (**Willie Lynch example of "Trust"**). The Black man is easily caught up by the Arabic man's "**Hey Brother**" greeting, his "**Hand pound**" and the **Black Bentley Continental GT** he saw the Arabic man in last night. So without hesitation he buys the $3.75 hot dog from the Arabic man which the Arabic man got from the Grocery store for free courtesy of the Government using his $2,000 limit EBT card. **Little does the Black man know that his hard earned labor just gave the Arabic man $3.75 for free!** All the Arabic man did was cook the hot dog. This is why he can afford a Bentley before the age of 35. The Black man buys 3 hot dogs and 3 large sodas from the Asian man because he has been used to buying from Asians all his life (**Chinese Restaurant, Beauty Supply Store, Laundry Mat etc**). The Asian man will never be caught standing in line with his family at a Black-owned Soul Food restaurant so the Asian man's dollars don't see a Black man's hand. They get richer from us while we buy from them which makes us that much poorer. The Black man is comfortable buying hot dogs for him and his family because thinks the White man's hot dog's is fresh and of better quality (Beef, Beef and pork, kosher etc). He thinks the hot dog bun is top of the line and the condiments are from a food supplier warehouse instead of from his own kitchen. When the Black man goes to inquire about buying a hot dog from another Black man he thinks the Black man is trying to rip him off or that the hot dog is not going to be quality. He didn't ask or second guess if he was getting a "good deal" with the other races and he didn't question the quality of the hot dog with them either. He assumed that these other races had better hot dogs even though the price was the same. But the Black man gives the black hot dog stand owner a hard time by asking him a million questions. Instead of buying the hot dog and helping this black man's business, he figures that it would be wiser to keep the money. So he gets back in his car to go buy his own pack of hot dogs at the grocery store, a pack of buns and condiments which will cost him more than $3.75. What is to explain for this type of "Anti-Support Black Business" behavior that he and a lot of blacks still exhibit till this day? Is it Willie Lynch, ignorance, Curse of Israel, predictive TV programming, or the lasting effects of slavery? You be the judge.

*(Left) Years ago The "**Nigger King store**" in Taiwan shocked blacks who couldn't believe there was store with such a name. In the Nigger King store you can get "**Black Clothes/Hip Hop Clothes** of course". (**Right**) Former Royal Fried Chicken owned by Mohammad Jabbar changed his store name to "**Obama Fried Chicken**" in Brooklyn, NY. Immediately after the name change, Black customers had a problem with it while others didn't. After a lot of pressure, it was reported that the owner changed the name of his store to another name. Down the block there was also an "**Obama Beauty Supply store**" owned by Mohammed Seraji. In Detroit, Michigan there can also be found an "**Obama Gas station**". At Arabic-owned Chicken Shacks in Detroit, it is not uncommon to see "Obama Specials" where you can get wings, fish, fries, cole slaw and bread for a cheap price. Of course these businesses are not owned by Blacks, but they are patronized by blacks.*

But this doesn't happen in any other races than the black race. Is this "Predictive Programming?" This is why the movie "**Django**" shows "**Negro slavefighting**" as entertainment for the white families on the Slave Plantations. The biggest and strongest slaves were put against each other to fight to the death while the white audience would enjoy fine wine with their friends. No difference than dog-fighting or cock-fighting. Today we see the same thing in our black communities but are Arabs, Jews, Indians, and Asians fighting each other? No! Only Blacks and Latinos are known to behave this way towards our fellow brothers. This was prophesied unto us in the "**Curses of Israel**". God told the Israelites that the men would have an "**evil eye**" towards his brother. This "**Evil eye syndrome**" has hindered us as a nation in succeeding.

Blacks fighting Blacks is a common scene in the Black community, but not in the communities of other races. It is also seen in Mexico as their homicide rates rival that of Black America's homicide rates. Why is that?

The same thing continues today as the "Curses of Israel" are seen in our communities. Black-on-Black and Latino-on-Latino violence can be see every day in the Americas as hospital morgues fill up from gun-shot deaths. Black-on-black violence is also seen in the islands of **Jamaicans, Haiti** and the **Dominican Republic** as well. No other race has this magnitude of "**brotherly hate/evil**" in their country as Blacks and Latinos. It's fascinating that as kids we don't exhibit these traits. However, after some point as we grow up things change. When we were kids, and as siblings blacks learned to trust one another. But as we get older we tend to not trust one another, even our own family members. It's as if life makes us colder individuals. Happiness turns into jealousy, Love turns into hate, and trust turns into distrust. Things have changed and although we are of the **SAME** race we do not see each other as fellow Black brothers and sisters. Again, is this why Yeshua/Yahusha (Jesus) told the people that one of the greatest two commandments was to "**Love thy neighbor as thyself**." Who is most likely to be our neighbors? Our fellow Black man and woman! Yeshua/Yahusha (Jesus) knew that if we as a people would Love God with all our heart, soul and mind, then on top of it love our Black neighbor (brothers/sisters) as ourselves we would be all right. We would operate with "**Unity**" and "**Love**", thus creating a strong black community with an "**economy within an economy**" Many Black People in America and even African are Christians proclaiming to "**Love the Lord**", but we don't show that we "Love the Lord" with **ALL** our heart, mind and soul. If we did we wouldn't be in this predicament. Tupac wrote about this in his rap song **"Changes"**:

"I got love for my brother, but we can never go nowhere
unless we SHARE with each other. We gotta start makin' changes.
Learn to see me as a BROTHER instead of 2 DISTANT STRANGERS.
And that's how it's supposed to be.
How can the Devil take a brother if he's close to me?
I'd love to go back to when we played as kids
but things changed, and that's the way it is"
Tupac Shakur

The result of Black-on-Black gun violence is prison, paralysis and death.

Just as in the song above, two black men walking down the street often times will see each other as strangers, wondering if this person has ill intentions of robbing or killing the other person. Jewish, Indian, Arab, and Asian men don't have this fear when walking past another person of the same race. Black men are more likely to die at the hands of their black brothers than any other race. This verse **"HIS EYE SHALL BE EVIL TOWARDS HIS BROTHER"** fits our race to the tee. Other races (Jews, Arabs, Chinese, Japanese, Indians, and Caucasians etc.) do not kill each other like we do.

This anger or evil spirit is also often passed off to our black women, wives **AND CHILDREN**. This leads to high divorce rates, high fatherless homes and increased domestic violence statistics that are higher in African-Americans than any other race. Up to 65-70% of African-American women are not married, either from divorce or simply not finding a suitable spouse in their lifetime. Up to 65% of black children are living without a full-time father in the household. A lot of black women can say that they are mothers but cannot say that they are wives. This is a huge problem in the black community.

The scripture in **Deuteronomy 28:54: "toward the remnant of his children which he shall leave"** states that black men would have a high incidence of leaving their children behind and that his eye would be evil towards them. It also states the Israelite men would have an evil eye towards his fellow **"Black Israelite brothers"**. This is very true today if you look around in the black community and also watch how the media portrays black men on T.V. Hollywood keeps portraying this to the public, which we in turn emulate, just like kids do when they learn from watching their parents. Movies like **"For Colored Girls"**, **"Single Moms Club"**, and **"Black and White"** portray Black Men to be dead beat fathers, but these types of movies are not seen in any other racial groups.

The Friends of the Court is dismantling the "Black Family". This was designed by "them" not "us". For blacks, the impact of "shared custody", "parenting time" and "Child support" is more destructive to our race than any other race.

This division of the Black family, coupled with the **"Friends of the Court"** and **"baby-momma/daddy situations"** prevents both parents from working together for the betterment of the child. This creates negative feelings and attitudes in the father that are sometimes directed towards the child or the mother. These negative attitudes can spark from money issues, parenting time issues, or disagreements in the parenting practices of the other parent. The animosity that stirs up when black families break apart brings up new issues such as child support and parenting time. Too often Black fathers are portrayed as the **"Angry Black Daddy"** who doesn't care about his kids. This causes the Courts to reign down judgment orders of ridiculous child support payments in addition to very little parenting time. Sometimes the Friend of the Court will even issue **"Supervised Parenting Time"** for those fathers who are painted to be **"abusive"** in the eyes of the court. Mothers and other family members will sometimes encourage **"lying"** to the father as a way to get the things they want, which then causes a further drift in the bond between the father and his child. At some point all of this can wear down the Black man, who only wants to **peacefully co-parent**. Frustration from the Friends of the Court eventually causes the father to take a step back, and in some cases the father will start a new family on his own. Then his child and the child's mother are even madder that daddy has decided to move on. So the "Black Father" cannot win for nothing in this scenario that is all too familiar for Black men across the board. This is seen every day in the Friends of the Court in every state in America. However the Black family has suffered more from the **"Friends of the Court"** system than any other race in America. The black family core was destroyed during slavery and it continues today as generations of black children are growing up with a dysfunctional, immoral, destroyed family unit. Animosity, vindictiveness, and greed often get in the way of co-parenting after a break up. Therefore we see the black man separated from his black female counterpart (wife or girlfriend) and from his children with the help of the "**Friends of the Court**". This was also prophesied in the "**Curses of Israel**".

Outside influences from the mass media along with its stereotypes and agendas have now led to the uprising independence of the Black female. In turn it has caused the demoralization-demasculinization-effemination of the black man, and the changing of roles in the black family structure. The man who was once the provider for his family is now degraded to being not needed, except maybe for child support and supervised parenting time. The children learn to not have respect for their father because they see their mother and other female figures (**Aunts, grandmothers**) running the show. This is called the Black Female "**Masculinization Effect**", which is being shown on T.V where the women are running the show and wearing the pants in the relationship. They are not submissive to their husbands, but instead are "**defiant**" to him, challenging him in just about everything he decides to do. This can be seen on Reality Shows such as "**Love and Hip Hop: Atlanta**", "**Real Housewives of Atlanta**", and "**Married to Medicine**". But that's not it, TV shows (ex. **Iyanla Fix my life**) and movies [**ex. The Family that Preys (2008) Black or White (2014)**] also continue to show black men in a negative light.

Fact 1: *On the TV. Show Iyanla Fix my life (**Episode 2**), DMX in on the show with his 19 y/o son. Iyanla is supposed to "**Fix this relationship**" between DMX and his son but instead does the opposite. DMX stands up and asks his son to give him a hug. Iyanla then says "**You don't have to.**" Afterwards, Iyanla stands up, yells at DMX and DMX leaves. No problems fixed. This episode of "chastising DMX" alone got the most ratings and views (1.4 million) for all the Iyanla seasons on the OWN channel. Other episodes with high views (over a million) include "**The father with 34 kids: Part III**" and "**Fix my Reality Star Life with Evelyn Lozada and Chad Ochocinco**". So it would appear that episodes with the most black relationship dysfunction are what people like to see. This is called "Predictive Programming". Predictive Programming is a subtle form of psychological conditioning provided by the media to acquaint the public (US) with planned societal changes and stereotypes which go along with the agenda of the "Hidden Masters/Elite".*

Fact 2: *Movies like **Scandal, Deception, Waiting to Exhale, Diary of a Tired Black Woman, Precious, For Colored Girls, Why did I get Married, The Family That Preys, Temptation, Django, The Butler, 12 years A Slave** and **Addicted** all subliminally portray the black man in a degrading, negative way. Is this a coincidence or just good ol' black humor?*

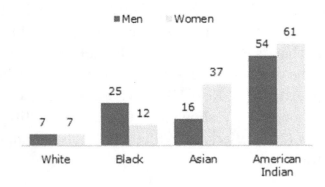

Among Blacks, Men Are More Likely than Women to Intermarry; Opposite Is True Among Asians

% of newlyweds in 2013 who married someone of a different race

■ Men Women

White: 7 (Men) 7 (Women)
Black: 25 (Men) 12 (Women)
Asian: 16 (Men) 37 (Women)
American Indian: 54 (Men) 61 (Women)

*(**Above**) According to the Pew Research Center (2013) **54%** of Native American men marry someone of a different race compared to **25%** for Black men. In 2008, the Pew Research Center showed that among all newlyweds (men and women), **9%** of whites, **16%** of Blacks, **26%** Hispanics and **31%** of Asians married someone whose race was different from their own. The Asian high percentage was mainly due to Asian women having higher rates of intermarriage than Asian men.*

Fact 3: All throughout the Bible the Ancient Israelites intermarried with women of other nation who were mostly of the Sons of Ham and Shem. As a result, they also fathered many kids. The Israelites multiplied rapidly wherever they were living at as the men had no problem taking wives of foreign nations. So would this be a behavior that would carry on with the descendants of the Israelites today?

Intermarriage with other races today is most often practiced by **Blacks and Latinos**. It is not uncommon for Blacks or Latinos to marry women of other races, but this is different for other races. Is this also a trait that the Ancient Israelites passed down to us? **For the most part in relationships we see that Jews marry Jews, Arabs marry Arabs, Asians marry Asians, East Indians marry East Indians and Whites marry Whites**. Some of this has to do with their strict religion and culture. Since slavery was abolished we have seen an increase in Black interracial couples. The result is Bi-racial children. But this has been happening since the days of Ancient Israel and continued happening when the Israelites were in Africa. This was seen in Ancient Egypt while the Israelites were in captivity by the Pharaoh's for 400 years and was seen in Africa with the "**Bantus Expansion**". The Bantus Expansion of "Negroes" overtook the Hamitic Tribes of West Africa, Central Africa and South Africa. In America we see this "**intermarriage trend**" trend as Black men are known to marry varieties of women from other nations. In the Book of Ezra and Judges it describes how often our Israelite forefathers intermarried with the Sons of Ham and the Semitic people living in Babylon/Persia/Assyria during their exile from Jerusalem. Perhaps this "**dating behavior**" is another clue as to who is Israel today. Read what Ezra saw happening to the Israelite men in 500 B.C.

Ezra 9:1-1-2 "Now when these things were done, the princes came to me, saying, The people of Israel, and the priests, and the Levites, have not separated themselves from the people of the lands, doing according to their abominations, even of the Canaanites, the Hittites, the Perizzites, the Jebusites, the Ammonites, the Moabites, the Egyptians, and the Amorites. **FOR THEY HAVE TAKE OF THEIR DAUGHTERS FOR THEMSELVES, AND FOR THEIR SONS: SO THAT THE HOLY SEED HAVE MINGLED THEMSELVES WITH THE PEOPLE OF THOSE LANDS:** "

Ezra 10:10-12 "And Ezra the priest stood up, and said unto them, Ye have transgressed, **AND HAVE TAKEN STRANGE WIVES (FOREIGN WIVES), TO INCREASE THE TRESPASS OF ISRAEL**. Now therefore make confession unto the Lord God of your fathers, and do his pleasure: and separate yourselves from the people of the land, and from the strange wives (foreign wives). Then all the congregation answered and said with a loud voice, As thou hadst said, so must we do."

If the Hebrew Israelites commonly intermarried with other nations that were of color (having melanin), this would leave their children to be people of color as well.

Deuteronomy 28:55 **"So that HE WILL NOT GIVE TO ANY OF THEM of the flesh of his children whom he shall eat: because HE HATH NOTHING LEFT HIM in the siege, and in the straitness, wherewith thine enemies shall distress thee in all thy gates.**

The Slave Trades left blacks with nothing but the deaths of millions of slave men, women and children. White America didn't believe we deserved anything. Black slaves were treated like nothing and they were told nothing. The women were raped and the mulatto children were still considered slaves. Even with extra mouths to feed from rape, the slave children (mixed or not) had to survive off what the slavemasters would give them. Sometimes selfishness and neglect set into the minds of the adult slaves with children. Some of the slaves did not consider the young or the little children when food was available. So when the Slavemasters gave them something it was the cause for extreme happiness and gratitude. Some slaves shared their food, some didn't. In the houses (slavequarters), if there was any food, or any appearance of something looking like food, there was a battle for it. Friends, parents, aunts, uncles, sisters, and brothers fought with one another, snatching away food from each other. When the Hebrew Israelites scattered into Africa, because of their continued suffering (Curses of Israel), many parents ended up selling their children into slavery for money or for a piece of bread. Some of them just gave their children away.

This type of behavior has been passed down from our Black Hebrew Israelite forefathers. Many of our own relatives say **"It's all about family"** but when you need them to support you on a business endeavor or personal project they are not there. Many black parents can knowingly or not knowingly "hate" on the success of their own children. Many black parents say "It's all about family and helping one another" but when they have grandchildren and their children need help they are too busy "doing them" or they are simply nowhere to be found. Many black parents will not be the "Co-signer" on anything for their kids but will scold them on any bad financial decisions that they make. Many black parents today would rather spend money on "themselves" then sacrifice living below their means so that their children have a better future. Many black parents demand their children to be "truthful" but at the same time "lie" to their children. These are some examples of how the slavemaster's indoctrination tools have continued on in our "way of thinking".

- 1800's –Slavemaster **"You ain't nothing, you'll never be nothing, and I'm not giving you nothing!"**
- 1900's-White Grandfather to his mixed Black Grandchildren-**"You ain't sh#@, you'll never be sh#@, and I'm not giving you sh#@!"**
- 2000's-Black Mother describing her children's father-"Your daddy ain't sh#@ and he'll never be sh#@!" and if you keep up you'll be just like him.
- 2000's-Black Father to his son-"My parents ain't give me nothing, I had to work hard and earn it on my own, so I'm not giving you anything, you're going to have to earn it on your own just like I did."

Barber Alonzo Herndon founded the Atlanta Life Insurance Company in 1905. It is still going strong after 100 years.

Fact: There are a lot of young married Black couples who do not have Life Insurance. So when unexpected death happens, it leaves a financial burden for the widow. Blacks have been conditioned to distrust each other when the topic of **"When are you going to get Life Insurance?"** comes up. We automatically think in our head that perhaps my spouse wants me to die for financial gains. Some Black parents when receiving Life Insurance or monies left over from the death of their parents will use all the money on themselves instead of distributing it to the grandchildren who are still struggling trying to make their way in the world. This is the reason why we never get ahead as a people. We lack the concept of the word "**inheritance**" or "**sharing**". In the past, if a shepherd or farmer had a flock/farm and passed away, the children would receive the inheritance. This concept was lost many centuries ago, so today's generation always starts from scratch, in a country that doesn't want black race to succeed.

TIRED BLACK MAN, ANGRY BLACK WOMAN? WAS THIS ALSO BIBLE PROPHECY?

Deuteronomy 28:56 **"The tender and delicate woman among you, which would not adventure to set the sole of her foot upon the ground for delicateness and tenderness, HER EYE SHALL BE EVIL TOWARD THE HUSBAND OF HER BOSOM, and toward her son, and toward her daughter,"**

In today's Black community there is an overwhelmingly high number of black women who are single, raising children on their own. Statistics show in 2014, 72% of Black Children are born into single parent households. In a marriage, each person should help, support and uplift one another. No one should be trying to outdo the other and no one should be trying to tear down the other person. Today, we see the de-masculinization of the Black Man through various agendas and we see the masculinization of the Black Female.   But this was promoted and brainwashed into us back since slavery times.

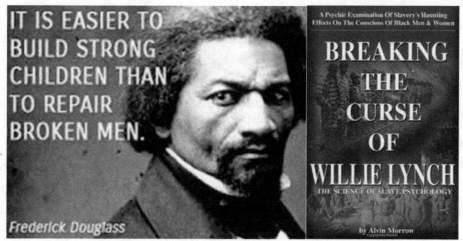

We must not allow them to break the Black man. Who will then raise our black boys to be strong? The Media, "White America" or the Black Woman?" We already see how that is working today. This is what they want!

Willie Lynch realized the key was in destroying the **Black man**.   Afterwards, they could manipulate the black woman and black child be mentally dependent on them, which they would teach their children's children.   This would ensure the success of their rulership and enslavement of the black race, even without using chains.   This can be called today "**Mental Slavery**".   Here is what Willie Lynch told his other fellow slavemasters:

Step 1

"Now the breaking process is the same for both the horse and the nigger, only slightly varying in degrees. But, as we said before, there is an art in long range economic planning. **YOU MUST KEEP YOUR EYE AND THOUGHTS ON THE FEMALE and the OFFSPRING** of the horse and the **nigger (male)**. A brief discourse in offspring development will shed light on the key to sound economic principles. Pay little attention to the generation of original breaking, but **CONCENTRATE ON FUTURE GENERATION**. Therefore, if you break the **FEMALE** mother, she will **BREAK** the offspring in its early years of development; and when the offspring is old enough to work, she will deliver it up to you, for her normal female protective tendencies will have been lost in the original breaking process."

Step 2

"When it comes to breaking the uncivilized nigger, use the same process as with breaking an untamed horse, but vary the degree and step up the pressure, so as to do a complete reversal of the mind. Take the meanest and most restless nigger, strip him of his clothes in front of the remaining male niggers, the female, and the nigger infant, tar and feather him, tie each leg to a different horse faced in opposite directions, set him afire and beat both horses to pull him apart in front of the remaining niggers. The next step is to take a bullwhip and beat the remaining nigger males to the point of death, in front of the female and the infant. Don't kill him, but **PUT THE FEAR OF GOD IN HIM,** for he can be useful for future breeding."

Step 3

"Test the black female in every way, because she is the most important factor for good economics. If she shows any sign of resistance in submitting completely to your will, do not hesitate to use the bullwhip on her to extract that last bit of rebellion out of her. Take care not to kill her, for in doing so, you spoil good economics. When in complete submission, **she will train her offspring in the early years to submit to labor when they become of age**.

In a black woman's natural uncivilized state, she would have a strong dependency on the uncivilized nigger male, and she would have a limited protective tendency toward her independent male offspring and would raise male offspring to be dependent like her. Nature had provided for this type of balance. **We reversed nature by burning and pulling a civilized nigger apart and bull-whipping the other to the point of death, all in her presence.** By her being left alone, unprotected, with the **MALE IMAGE DESTROYED**, the ordeal caused her to move from her **PSYCHOLOGICALLY DEPENDENT STATE TO A FROZEN, INDEPENDENT STATE**. In this frozen, psychological state of independence, she will raise her **MALE** and **FEMALE** offspring in reversed roles. For **FEAR** of the young male's life, **she will psychologically train him to** be **MENTALLY WEAK** and **DEPENDENT**, but **PHYSICALLY STRONG**. Because she has become psychologically independent, she will **train her FEMALE offspring to be**

psychologically independent but knowing she is physically weaker than him."

What have you got?

YOU'VE GOT THE BLACK WOMAN OUT IN FRONT WEARING THE PANTS, SINGLE, CHOOSING MATES WITH OTHER RACES WHILE THE BLACK MAN IS IN THE BACK EFFEMINATE OR HOMOSEXUAL.

Fact: *More than 2 out of 3 black women are not married and most black women who are dating "**black**" do not have a "**committed**" partner. College Educated Black women are twice as likely as their white counterparts to not be married. When bad dating experiences with Black men occur and desperation kicks in, it is not uncommon to see Black women dating outside their race. In worst case scenarios, the Black women ends up being single her whole life without kids or homosexual/bisexual.*

We see this reversal of roles today in the Black household. Through different "**Agendas**" the black man has been tore down physically and mentally. Since slavery has been abolished, new agendas have been put in place to "**Keep the Black Man down**". Now the Black woman has to rise up and wear the pants in the relationship. Many black women today will often say that black men do not have "**balls**" because of all the responsibilities that has been shifted to the woman. Many African-American women are divorced, single with kids trying to raise them the right way all while trying to school and working multiple jobs. Our Black women are under enormous pressure and this is why they are angry.

Contributing factors to the reversal of Male-Female role in the Black home:

- Incarceration.
- Unemployment or low paying jobs.
- Laziness.
- Psychiatric problems (ex. Depression, Anxiety disorder, Bipolar, Schizoaffective, Schizophrenia).
- Health issues causing disabilities (Bad back, knees, high blood pressure, obesity, heart disease, diabetes, high cholesterol, stroke, cancer).
- Homosexuality/bisexuality/sexual orientation confusion.
- Effeminate (womanish) Black men.
- Disparity between incomes between the man and the woman.
- Lack of Education.
- Legal troubles.
- Baby Mama Drama and baggage.
- And more....

All of these factors contribute to the rising rates of black single mothers. The mother ends up raising the child. The father hopes to still be a part of the child's life despite all the factors against him but without living in the home with the child, many fathers eventually become distant, leaving the mother to make it on her own. Threats of Child Support eventually come and in no time the Friends of the **Court are usually placing a "Parenting Time Schedule" for the dad (8** days a month) and also setting the Child Support payment to reflect the amount of support he needs to provide for the 22 days of the month that the child is with the mother. For the mother, raising the child alone, even with money it is still hard and taxing. When confronted with pregnancy, single women are more likely to have an abortion as opposed to a married woman. So the woman who is single or divorced with kids, the pressure is increased to take care of 1, 2, 3 or even 4 kids. We all know that raising 4 or more children can be challenging for some couples even when both parents are living under the same roof, so having 4 children with one parent raising them is going to be even harder. Matter of fact, depending on how old the kids are, this task can be very overwhelming. These single and divorced black women frequently become discouraged (**and angry**) because they are in a dating market where there is only a few black men who are stable and employed. Many women desire a man who:

1. Does not have a felon.
2. Is not gay, bisexual or effeminate.
3. Does not live at home with their parents/grandparents.
4. Has a good paying job.
5. Has a reliable car and his own place of residence.
6. Is not psychotic.
7. Does not have financial "baggage" or "baby mama" drama.
8. Does not need a "sugar mama".
9. Is confident.
10. Believes in God.
11. Has an education.

Fact: **There are nearly twice as many black women earning college degrees than black men. Black men who have careers are less likely to marry then are their white counterparts. When they do marry, they often marry non-black women.**

Because Black women find it hard to find a Black man with all the qualities they want, highly educated black women who marry wind up more likely than any other race to marry a man who is less educated than they are, or who earns less money than they do. These relationships are often in constant conflict. The woman is raising the kids, cooking dinner, cleaning the house and is also the breadwinner of the family. A Black man in this situation may be insecure about being economically subordinate to his wife. On the other side of the fence, the Black woman may not be too comfortable about this situation either. Why you ask? Well, women normally have not been raised as the person elected to go out and be the **"breadwinner."** This role is usually bestowed upon the man, even going back many of generations of time. In other countries such as Madagascar, the men go miles into the ocean on skinny boats to catch fish for the whole village. The men and women eat first and the kids eat last. In America, the pressure of having to keep the house clean, go to work, pay the bills, take care of the kids and also take care of a husband (significant other) can be too much for many black women. Research has also found that when the husband is unemployed, a couple's likelihood of divorce increases substantially. But to add fire to all of this, unmarried black women often have to deal with black men, who according to social science data and historical records, are more likely than any other group of men to have relationships with multiple women. So here you have a single black woman with a lot of kids struggling to make ends meet all alone with no man or while trying to deal with a man who is not faithfully committed. For those black women who are married, the frustration may come from having to do "**everything**", which causes frustration, anger, resentment, and possibly infidelity which later leads to a divorce between the man and the woman. So the end result is the separation of the "**child**" from his/her nuclear family.

True or False? *Today, there are some black couples who will not get married and will not change their addresses to reflect they are living together simply as a means to still qualify for EBT food stamps or Welfare. This promotes some black people from getting married, especially those who are in an economic bind, with or without kids. The percentage of black children born without a father in the home has risen from 7% in 1964 to 73% today, due to changes from President Lyndon Johnson's "War on Poverty". In the movie "Selma", President Lyndon B. Johnson was more focused on the "War on Poverty" than addressing the Negroes having the right to vote. The welfare rule of the 1960's changed under the presidency of Lyndon B. Johnson. Welfare rules then imposed a "marriage penalty" on recipients. This meant that benefits could be earned only if a person was single. If that person got married the welfare benefits would disappear. Initially in the 1930's, Welfare was designed for widows with kids who didn't qualify for Social Security. It was also only supposed to be a short term solution for people than needed help but later became a single-parent program for divorcees and unmarried mothers. Since then the "Welfare State" of America has turned into a normal way of life. President Lyndon B. Johnson knew how to hoodwink blacks and he did so because he didn't care much for black people then, just as other whites didn't' care for blacks either.*

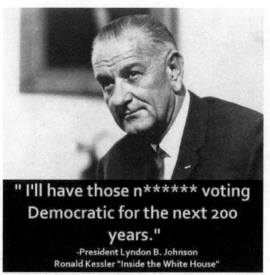

" I'll have those n****** voting Democratic for the next 200 years."
-President Lyndon B. Johnson
Ronald Kessler "Inside the White House"

*"These Negroes, they're getting pretty uppity these days and that's a problem for us since they've got something now they never had before, the political pull to back up their uppityness. Now we've got to do something about this, we've got to give them a **LITTLE SOMETHING, JUST ENOUGH TO QUIET THEM DOWN, NOT ENOUGH TO MAKE A DIFFERENCE.**"*
United States of America President, Lyndon B. Johnson

President Johnson would then give the Black Community "Welfare" to shut us up. Little did "Black America" know was that the "Welfare System" would help eventually help destroy the Black Family.

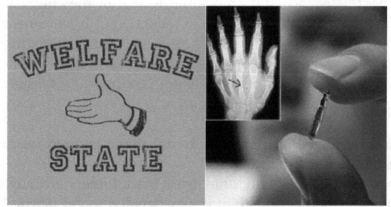

Welfare keeps many Blacks dependent on Daddy Government. What happens when the Government shuts down? Or when getting an implantable RFID chip is required by our Government to continue getting Welfare? Better Made or Lays?

We have seen movies like "Diary of a Mad Black woman" and "Diary of a Tired Black man" in the black community. But what about these type of movies for other races? Aren't their women "Mad" and their men "Tired"? Maybe not.

Here are 6 way's in which President Lyndon B. Johnson' **"War on Poverty"** program increased fatherless homes, creating more tension between Black Mothers and Black Fathers:

1. **A Man Will Reduce Her Income**
   Welfare programs create dis-incentives for couples to get married because benefits are reduced as a family's income rises. Black mothers will receive far more from welfare if she is single than if she has an employed husband in the home. For many low-income couples, marriage means a reduction in government assistance and an overall decline in the couple's joint income. This reduction of benefits can equal a reduction of 10 percent to 20 percent of their total income. Because so many blacks rely on Welfare programs such as WIC, Section 8 Public Housing, EBT food stamps, Medicaid and public day care, marriage for single mothers is not economically feasible, especially if they are taking care of multiple children.

2. **Women think that Black Fathers do not make enough income to support both the mother and their child.**
   This goes back to #1. Many unmarried black fathers actually make enough to support the mother and child if they decided to get married but there are other factors that prevent these unmarried black fathers from marrying.

3. **Black fathers are viewed to be "Not Needed" anymore.**
   Often times the Friends of the Court, show that Black Fathers are not needed except to pay modest amounts of Child Support Payments. Courts that tell the Black father to pay $1,000 a month in Child Support Payments but only allow 6-8 days a month in Parenting Time are wrong because this type of practice portrays that the Black father's money is more important than his time spent with his child. The Black mother sees this in court as a win for her in regards to the money she will now receive not realizing that raising a "fatherless" child could have a negative impact on that child's physical and psychological well-being over the time. These negative effects will carry on through childhood and adulthood. Money is only short-term.

4. **After the Onset of President Lyndon B. Johnson's "War on Poverty", the Black Out-of-Wedlock Birth Rate Skyrocketed.**
   The rate of Black children born "**Out-of-wedlock**" went from **24.5 percent** in 1964 to **50.3 percent** in 1976. It continued to rise rapidly, reaching 70.7 percent in 1994. Over the next ten years, it declined slightly but then began to rise again, reaching 72.4 percent in 2008. Even Oprah Winfrey commented on the staggering number of black single parent households on her talk show. Some sociologists say that once mothers received government support, the link between marriage and having children was severed in their minds. Fathers were no longer necessary. During the course of the 50 years beginning in 1964, the stereotype of the missing and negligent Black father took hold, in and out of the Black community.

5. **In order to receive Welfare Assistance, mothers must identify/report the fathers.**
   When black mothers receive public assistance, they must report the identity of the child's father so that the government can claim the money as reimbursement for the public assistance payments. Even married couples can receive Welfare assistance if the woman reports that she is separated and that the father is not living in the house anymore. The structure of child support has kept some black men from stepping up and being fathers to their children. Black men also try to stay underground and away from the Friends of the Court when they have other outstanding legal fees from tickets, suspended licenses, warrants, and other child support arrearages. So the father stays away from jobs that require a W-4 form to be filled out and taxes deducted. This essentially makes the black father a "**ghost**" to the court system. In addition, if he is able to keep his "**place of residence**" a mystery

he can also avoid the strong hand of the courts. This promotes the black single mother to continue her dependence on Welfare. If the mother also refuses to report the father's name, the amount of her Welfare assistance payments can still be reduced. This sets up an oppositional relationship (like two magnets) between the mother and father of the child which many parents never recover from, even into late adulthood.

6. **Black Fathers are met with "Suspicion" at public institutions.**
   Black fathers are often viewed as strangers when they show up to their child's school, daycare, doctor's appointments or when visiting the hospital. They are asked for identification, court documents and a call to the mother is usually made out. Joseph Jones, founder and executive director of **"The Center for Urban Families in Baltimore"**, which works with black fathers and families, stated that young black fathers are put to so many hoops when they visit their child's school that many of them give up and stop visiting the school or public institutions altogether. This creates a further divide between the black single mother, the black father and the child. This is what "THEY" want.

President Lyndon B. Johnson and President Obama's **"Welfare State"** contributes to Black fatherless homes. This divide of the family causes the Black woman to be angry at the Black man and the Black man to be angry at the Black woman. Whether both parents see it, a broken-family has a negative impact on the child. As the child grows into an adult, inner scars can be more harmful than physical scars. Just as the bible prophesied in Deuteronomy 28:56 **"HER EYE SHALL BE EVIL TOWARD THE HUSBAND OF HER BOSOM."**

We see that the result of broken black families is troubled black children growing up. This is why our children are falling by the wayside compared to other races. Remember two heads are better than one. Unity always has better outcomes than if we try to do things individually.

Deuteronomy 28:57 **"And toward her young one that cometh out from between her feet, and toward her children which she shall bear: for she shall eat them for want of all things secretly in the siege and straitness, wherewith thine enemy shall distress thee in thy gates."**

Many accounts of cannibalism were documented during the slave trades, especially when meat was scarce and the dead were plentiful. This is documented in the Bible as well.

Titus Flavius Josephus, born Joseph ben Matityahu (37 A.D.-100 A.D.) was a Roman-Jewish Historian, scholar who wrote about what he saw in Judea during the time of the **Herodians** *and the fall of the Second temple in Jerusalem in 70 A.D. He was a Gentile Roman who practiced Judaism (**Pharisee-ism**). He was an advisor and friend of Roman Emperor Vespasian's son Titus. Roman General Titus was left in charge of ending the Jewish rebellion. In 70 A.D. he besieged and captured Jerusalem, destroying the Second Temple. Today, the* **"Arch of Titus"** *commemorates his victory to this day.*

Flavius Josephus documented cannibalism during this time when the remaining Black Jews were exiled from Judea:

"A woman, whose name was Mary, that lived beyond Jordan (river), illustrious for her descent and riches fled with the multitude to Jerusalem when besieged (attacked) carrying with her substance, and what food she could get that were left to her by the spoilers; where being pressed with famine, **she took her sucking child, killed it, boiled it, and ate half of it**, and then laid up the rest, and covered it, and when the seditious party entered the house, they smelt it, and demanded her food, threatening to kill her if she did not deliver it; which when she brought forth declaring what she had done, they were struck with horror, to whom she said, "this is my son, and this my own deed; eat, for I have eaten; be not more tender or softer than a woman, and more sympathizing or more pitiful than a mother."

This practice of cannibalism can be seen in **2 Kings 6:20-30** as well.

2 Kings 6:28-29 "And the King (of Israel) said unto her, What aileth thee? And she answered, This woman said unto me, Give thy son, that we may **EAT HIM TODAY**, and we will eat my son tomorrow. So we **BOILED MY SON, AND DID EAT HIM**: and I said unto her on the next day, Give thy son, that we may eat him: and she hath hid her son."

The Kings of Israel during this time was **King Joram, Jehu, Jehoahaz and Jehoash from 800 B.C.**

Fact: *In **Ghana (Akan/Ashanti Tribe)**, many Blacks sold Black Israelites into slavery. During this time the Europeans were interested in Ghana for its Gold and lastly its slaves. However, over time the exporting of slaves was a big money maker, for the Europeans and for some of the Ghana Kings. Ghana has since apologized for this and has passed a law granting immediate citizenship to any African-America who wishes to come back to Ghana to live. In Benin, during the **Dahomey Empire** many blacks sold other Black Israelites into slavery. The Kings of Dahomey traded in their bows and arrow for guns and needed a steady supply of gunpowder to use against their neighboring enemies. They also wanted fine linen amongst other things the European had. In order to keep the Europeans giving them what they needed, they had to sell Black slaves. Some say this was for economic reasons why others say it was to get rid of **"foreign criminals"**. The French eventually conquered the Dahomey King and his empire and established French Colonial Rule. Maps from 1747 showed that this area was considered the **"Kingdom of Judah"** as the Europeans* *would call it. The famous slave French port "**Ouidah**" or "**Ajuda (Portuguese)**" still exists to this day and is known as the "**Door of No Return**".*

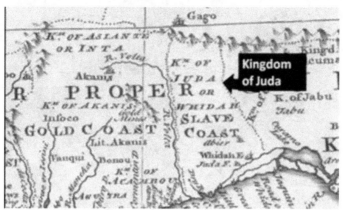

*__1747 Map of West Africa__ "**Kingdom of Juda(h)**" in modern day Benin. To the left is the **Gold Coast** (Ghana/Togo) which consists of the Akan-Ashanti people and Ewe people. Like many West African tribes, the "Ewe" people name their newborn babies on the 8th day just as John the Baptist and Yahusha (Jesus) were named on the 8th day. This has been their custom for generations, which mimics Ancient Hebrew Israelite customs. Benin/Nigeria was called the "**Slave Coast**" by the Europeans back then because many Black Israelite slaves were taken to the Americas and the Caribbean (Jamaica/Haiti/Dominican Republic) from this area.*

Door of No Tomorrow, *Benin (West Africa). Slaves were forced down this walkway along the beach to get on Slave Ships headed for the same Atlantic Ocean Black people Jet Ski on at Myrtle Beach, South Carolina and Miami Beach, Florida. Before 1975, it was called "**Dahomey**" or the "**Kingdom of Dahomey**". The national language is French, while the natives speak Fon or Yoruba.*

CHAPTER 33

DEUTERONOMY 28:58-68

HEALTH DISEASES: THE MISSING LINK TO ISRAEL?

Deuteronomy 28:58-61 "**If thou wilt not observe to do all the words of this law that are written in this book, that thou mayest fear this glorious and fearful name, The LORD THY GOD; Then the Lord will make thy plagues wonderful, and the plagues of THY SEED, even great plagues, and of LONG CONTINUANCE, and sore sickness, and of LONG CONTINUANCE. Moreover he will bring upon thee all the DISEASES OF EGYPT, which THOU WAS AFRAID OF; and they shall cleave unto thee. And every sickness, and every plague, WHICH IS NOT WRITTEN IN THE BOOK OF THIS LAW, them with the Lord bring upon thee, until thou be destroyed.**"

Curses of Israel: Infectious Diseases?
- Ebola
- Tuberculosis
- Malaria
- Yellow Fever
- Smallpox and Monkey Pox
- HIV
- Hepatitis B & C
- Dengue Fever
- Typhoid Fever
- Sleeping Sickness
- Cholera

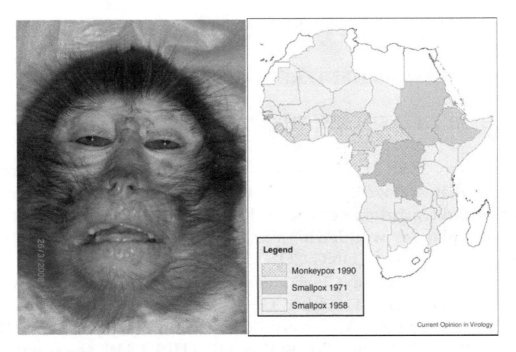

Monkey pox (Small Pox) affected the Monkeys and the people living in Ancient Egypt just as it affects Monkeys today, West Africans, the Bantus areas and East Africa. These are the same places the Arab Slave Trade and TransAtlantic Slave Trade targeted. Is this a coincidence?

The Ancient Egyptians had Baboons, monkey and dogs for pets. They even were buried inside the tombs with the Pharaohs. These pets also were inflicted with the plagues brought upon Egypt by Moses and God.

Exodus 9:8-9 "And the Lord said unto Moses and unto Aaron, Take to you handful of ashes of the furnace, and let Moses sprinkle it toward the heaven in the sight of Pharaoh. And it shall become small dust in all the land of Egypt, and shall be a **BOIL** breaking blains (**sores**) upon **MAN, AND UPON BEAST**, throughout the **LAND OF EGYPT**."

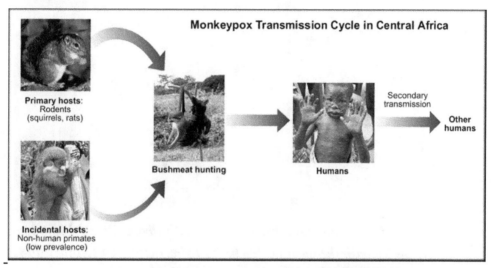

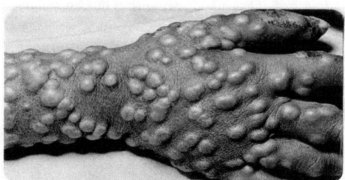

Small Pox affects the whole body causing boils and then sores after the boils bust, then extreme itching. Small pox was also prevalent in Ancient Egypt. **Egyptian Pharaoh Ramses V** was found to have Small Pox although the virus was dead. Is it a coincidence that most of the people that have died from Small Pox are **West Africans**, East Africans, Central Africans, the natives in the Caribbean (**Taino**

people) and the natives of the America (**Aztec, Incas, Mayans?**)? No, these are the Curses of Israel being inflicted on the Scattered Children of Israel.

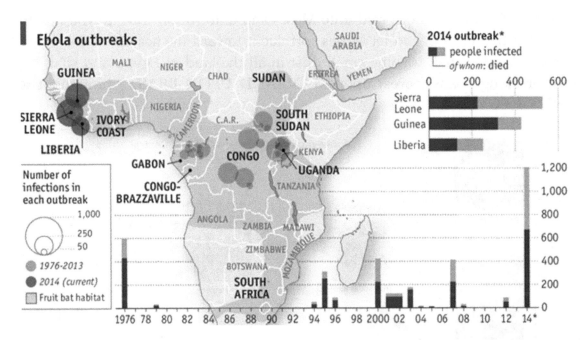

*In 2014, of the 28,000 people in West Africa infected with Ebola, almost 11,000 people died with the top three states with the most deaths being **Liberia, Sierra Leone and Guinea.** But Ebola is not new to Africa, it has hit other countries during random times, such as West Africa and East Africa. Each time it has struck, Africans have blamed it on outsiders inserting it into their villages as a way to "**kill them off**".*

Globally, malaria kills more than one million people each year,

most of them children.

Malaria kills more people in Sub-Saharan Africa than the entire number of Malaria cases in the whole world. The Black Hebrew Israelites primarily lived in Sub-Saharan Africa and the Bantus lands of South Africa. Is this a coincidence? Egyptologists even confirmed that Egyptian Pharaoh King Tutankhamun (King Tut) died from Malaria around 1300 B.C. The have also found the parasite for this disease on other Egyptian mummies and also blood related disorders sparked by Malaria (Sickle-Cell, Thalassemia). Malaria is the main reason why the majority of people with Sickle-Cell Anemia come from West Africa. Over hundreds of centuries the body has learned how to protect itself from Malaria. The result is Sickle-Cell Anemia. The bad part is that Sickle-Cell Anemia can also shorten your life. We already know that West Africa is the area millions of "Negro" slaves were taken from to be sent to the Americans and the Caribbean. So to no surprise we see Sickle Cell Anemia predominately in African-Americans. Sickle-Cell Anemia acts as the body's "**defense mechanism**" from Malaria. Blacks with Sickle-Cell anemia theoretically cannot contract Malaria as the disease needs normal Red Blood cells to do bodily damage. Thalassemia blood disorders are also found in West Africa as it can be found in Nigerians. Likewise, thalassemia's have been genetically linked to the Middle East (Egypt, Palestine, Ancient Israel) and South Asia (India/Sri Lanka).

Black people are the sickest people in most Hospitals. We rank #1 in Hypertension, End Stage Renal Disease, Diabetes, Cardiovascular Disease, Stroke, and Prostate Cancer amongst a host of other diseases. These diseases are of **LONG CONTINUANCE**

Curses of Israel: Long Continuance?

- Hypertension
- Diabetes
- Stroke
- Peripheral Vascular Disease
- End-Stage Renal Disease
- Sickle Cell Anemia/Alpha and Beta Thalassemia
- Hyperlipidemia
- Coronary Artery Disease
- Cerebrovascular Disease
- Prostate Cancer and other Cancers

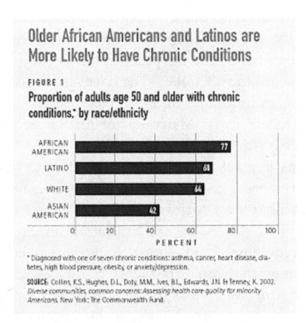

Older African Americans and Latinos are More Likely to Have Chronic Conditions

FIGURE 1

Proportion of adults age 50 and older with chronic conditions,* by race/ethnicity

AFRICAN AMERICAN	77
LATINO	68
WHITE	64
ASIAN AMERICAN	42

PERCENT

* Diagnosed with one of seven chronic conditions: asthma, cancer, heart disease, diabetes, high blood pressure, obesity, or anxiety/depression.

SOURCE: Collins, K.S., Hughes, D.L., Doty, M.M., Ives, B.L., Edwards, J.N. H Tenney, K. 2002. *Diverse communities, common concerns: Assessing health care quality for minority Americans.* New York: The Commonwealth Fund.

African-Americans and Latinos are more likely to have Chronic Health Conditions of **LONG CONTINUANCE** than any other race on the planet. Coincidence or The Curses of Israel? They are also the poorest race groups in America and are more likely to be incarcerated than any other race in the world.

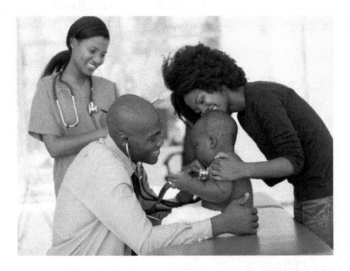

Studies show that just living in states with increased racism can contribute to Chronic diseases and death in Black people in America. Black people are known to have Chronic Diseases, which partly is related to lack in good, quality healthcare and socioeconomic factors that promote unhealthy lifestyles. But the Bible foretold of the health diseases that would cause "**Long continuance**" in the Children of Israel. What race(s) is the Bible talking about? Let's look at the facts?

- Lupus, the chronic and potentially fatal autoimmune disease is common in black women three times more than white women.
- Black women in their 20's extending to their 50's develop Breast Cancer earlier than white women. Black women are also known to have more aggressive fatal Breast Cancers than white women.
- Although African-Americans make up 13% of the population, they make up 52% of all new HIV/AIDS cases.
- African-Americans die of Chronic Liver Disease more than any other race in America.
- African-Americans are 20% more likely to have Asthma than whites and are three times more likely to die from Asthma than whites.
- African-Americans have highest mortality rates for 8 out the 10 top Health Diseases compared to any racial or ethnic group. African-Americans have the highest death rate and shortest survival of any racial and ethnic group in the U.S.A. for most cancers
- African-Americans are almost twice as likely to be diagnosed with diabetes than whites. In addition, they are more likely to suffer complications from Diabetes, such as End-stage renal disease and Peripheral vascular disease than any other race on the planet.
- Although African-Americans have the same or lower rate of high cholesterol as other races, they are more likely to have high blood pressure in addition to high cholesterol.
- African-Americans are 30% more likely to die from heart disease than non-Hispanic whites.
- African-Americans have the highest rates of obesity out of all races.
- African-Americans are twice as likely to have a stroke as their white counterparts. Black men are 60% more likely to die from a stroke than any other race in the world.
- African-Americans, Hispanics and American Indians develop Kidney disease more frequently than any other race groups in the world. African-Americans make up 1/3 of Renal Failure patients on dialysis even though

they make up 13% of America. African-Americans are four times more likely to develop Kidney failure than whites.

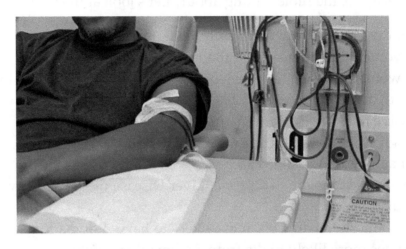

End-Stage Renal Disease is directly caused by uncontrolled Diabetes and Elevated Blood Pressure which is highest in the black community.

So what race exhibits "**Every sickness, and every plague, which is not written in the book of law?**" Let's see what the facts are. Blacks (**African-Americans/West Africans/Bantus/Caribbean**) exhibit Vitiligo, Albinism, Leprosy, HIV/AIDS, Tuberculosis, Malaria, Cholera, Yellow Fever, Ebola, Smallpox, High Blood Pressure, Kidney Disease, Diabetes, Cerebrovascular disease, High Cholesterol, Heart Attack, Stoke, Coronary Artery Disease, Peripheral Vascular Disease, Autoimmune disease, Gastrointestinal disease, Dementia, Mental Illness, Cancer, Liver Disease, Enlarged Prostate, Glaucoma, and Endocrine diseases.   Blacks overall rank at the top in all these diseases in terms of cases compared to any race in the world. Some of these diseases were not in the bible because they had not yet manifested in the world due to the changes in our food and diet habits. This can be seen as bible prophecy unfolding.

Deuteronomy 28:62-63 **"And ye shall be left FEW IN NUMBER, whereas YE WERE AS THE STARS OF HEAVEN for multitude; because thou wouldest not obey the voice of the LORD thy God; And it shall come to pass, that as the LORD rejoiced over you to do you good, and to multiply you; so the LORD will rejoice over you to destroy you, and to bring you to nought; and ye shall be plucked from off the land whither thou goest to possess it."**

Exodus 1:8 **"Now there arose up a new king over Egypt, which knew not Joseph. And he said unto his people, Behold, the people of the children of Israel are more and mightier than we: Come on let us deal wisely with them; lest they multiply, and it come to pass, that, when there falleth out any war, they join also unto our enemies, and fight against us, and so get them up out of the land."**

The Bantus Israelites settled into West Africa as far back as 3,000 years ago in the areas known as the Niger-Congo Areas. The Niger-Congo is sometimes divided up in the **Niger-Congo A** and **Niger Congo B** denoting the vast land that the Bantus Israelites lived in. They mixed with some of the local Hamitic tribes in Africa thus overtaking the Afro-Asiatic, Cushite, Nilotic and Khoisan peoples. For this reason the genetic DNA of the Negro/West African Bantus people can be seen in the majority of Sub-Saharan Africa. In East Africa, Kenya there are three sets of Africans: the **Bantus Negroes**, **Nilotes** (i.e. Dinka), and the **Cushites** (Ethiopian/Somalians). Many East Africans are mixtures of two of these groups or all three. There are hundreds of dialects in the Bantus lands but many of them have traces of Paleo-Hebrew, Western Aramaic and South Semitic Arabian (Hebrew) languages hidden inside their pronunciations or spelling. This stretch of land was labeled on ancient maps as **"Negroland," "So Yuda,"** or **"Soudan"**. Many of the Israelites prior to the Transatlantic Slave trade settled in this area which stretched West from the Senegal River Valley to the Congo and on to Central/East Africa. These Israelites and their descendants were spread all across the world but their descendants suffered great losses in their population from all the centuries of captivity starting from Ancient Egypt till the most recent slave trades lasting from the 1400's to the 1800's. But the depopulation has not stopped with slavery. It still continues with abortions which kill more black people than the top four major fatal health diseases today! White America knew that left unchecked, blacks would eventually surpass whites in population numbers. This is the whole reason behind the **"Eugenics Movement"** and the **"Negro Project"** in the early 1900's. During the Arab Slave Trade the Arabs made sure that Blacks could not populate with the Arab women or any woman by castrating the males of **ALL** their genital organs. This ensured that only their seed from the Arab paternal line would continue in the Middle East, even if the children were darker from mixing with the African women. These children because of their Arab Paternal blood would be considered **"Arabs"** instead of **"Negroes"**. Muslim Arabs were forbidden by the Quran to own slaves so these slaves were no other than **"Bantus Israelite Negroes"**. Some of the descendants of these Bantus Negro Israelites can be seen in **Gujarat, West India where they are known as Siddis**. Whites during the Transatlantic Slave Trades often had children with their female slaves, but these mulatto children were still considered Negro slaves. It was forbidden for black slave men have sex with White women or even try to talk to White women. The harsh conditions of slavery was a deterrent that prevented some slaves from having children; that is unless the Slavemaster encouraged it for breeding purposes to make more money on the plantation.

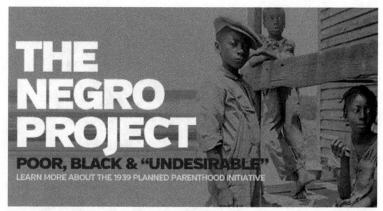

The Negro Project was proposed by Margaret Sanger in the 1930's. Margaret upheld Luciferian doctrines from people such as Helen Blavatsky and Alice Bailey. The aim of the program was to restrict and/or exterminate the black population. Under the pretense of "better health" and "family planning," Sanger cleverly implemented her plan. Some within the Black elite saw birth control as a means to attain economic empowerment, elevate the race and gain the respect of whites. In reality, forced sterilization, abortion clinics, birth control pills were all designed by whites to eliminate blacks and thus keeping them from becoming significant in number in America. This was just what the Egyptians feared and the Arabs feared during their captivity of the Israelites.

Below is a statement on how the Negroes **still populated** during Slavery despite the harsh work conditions they had to live through.

"The first slaves were brought into this country by the Dutch in 1619, and were landed at Jamestown, Virginia. The first cargo consisted of fourteen Negro slaves. The census taken in 1890 shows that these fourteen slaves had increased to 7,638,360." **"The Negro: A Menace to American Civilization" by R. W Shufeldt, M.D.**

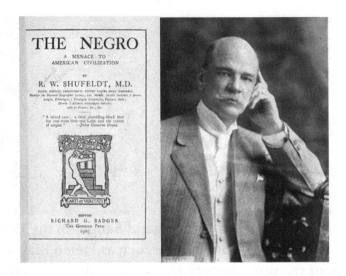

R.W. Shufeldt also attributed this number increase to more slaves being added from 1619-1862. Despite all the deaths in Africa from starvation, disease, and war etc, the Israelites are still are very numerous all over the world, just not as numerous as they were prior to these events that decreased the population. The Israelites have been dying of Genocide for centuries. Blacks still are dying in America and the Eugenics agenda is constantly in effect by the "Elites" to keep the Black population to a minimum.

So-Yuda or "Soudan" was the old area of West, Central and East Africa. This area was known as the geographical "hotspot" of how to find the Hebrew Israelites.

Fact: The Area in African known as "So Yuda" aka the "Land of Judah" was later called "So-udan/Soudan" meaning "Land of the Blacks" by the Arabs. From this area slaves were taken to the Americas and the Caribbean. **In the 1790's during slavery, Blacks were almost 20% of the population of America. Post-Civil War in the 1860's-1870's Blacks made up 13% of America. Today, 150 years later (6 generations), Blacks still only make up 13% of America.** *How is this possible? Are we not having children? Or are we having too many abortions? Abortion clinics and Birth Control Pills were created by White America for the depopulation of Black America. It is also a known fact that after years of slavetrading the Haitian slaves outnumbered the Whites on Hispaniola 10:1, thus allowing them to be victorious in taking back their freedom from the French.*

No other race in the world has experienced as much loss of life from slavery, famine, war, poverty, disease, or mass executions as that of black people. Black people dominated the world in the beginning because the majority of the world was black in ancient times. The original man, Adam was black as unto the ground (dirt) he was formed from. Adam was not red (ruddy) like the Kool-Aid man. Color cannot be made out of no color (white) just as white skin cannot turn black. Black skin can however turn white (Vitiligo, Albinism, fade creams). Up till today, mankind (mostly European) has sought to enslave, kill and destroy people of color (blacks) because they have taught the world to view blacks negatively as ugly, or sub-human. Europe has single-handedly colonized and controlled almost every **"Brown"** major continent/country on Earth (**Africa, the Americas, India, Caribbean, and Australia**). The population of blacks in Africa and America would be hundreds of millions higher if it wasn't for the Curses that were predicted and placed on the Israelites by God thousands of years ago. It is predicted that hundreds of millions of blacks died in total from **ALL THE SLAVE TRADES**. If these souls were allowed to live naturally they would've been able to reproduce, therefore increasing the population of blacks in the world exponentially. However, the reality is that so many millions of Black Africans (Israelites) have died, never having the chance to have a family and multiply on the earth. This was part of the **"Curses of Israel"** If Joseph and the Children of Israel walked into Egypt with 70 souls and left after 400 years with around 2 million people across the Red Sea with Moses, imagine the amount of black people that would be in the world today if it wasn't for the deaths of millions of black (**Israelite**) people. In Ancient days we were as numerous on the earth like the **stars**; the Curses of Israel foretold that millions of the **REAL** Black Children of Israel would die off.

Deuteronomy 28:64-65 **"And the LORD shall SCATTER THEE AMONG ALL PEOPLE, from the one end of the earth even unto the other; and there thou shalt serve other gods, which neither thou nor thy fathers have known, even wood and stone." And among these nations shalt thou find no ease, neither shall the sole of thy foot have rest: but the LORD shall give thee there a trembling heart, and failing of eyes, and sorrow of mind:"**

FALSE IDOLS AND PAGAN GODS

Satan is tricking Blacks in America into going back to pagan African Spirituality and their religions. They are telling people to worship a green-faced fairy tale Egyptian King called "**Osiris**" and his half-falcon head, half-human body son named "**Horus/Heru/Ra**". If this is not enough, some black people now believe that we should go back to worshipping the gods of our African ancestors. Worshipping elephants, buffalo, lions, alligators, rhinos, eagles, bulls, and planetary bodies are nothing more than idol worship. These things are what God has "**created**". We are supposed to worship the "**Creator**" instead of the "**Creation**". Satan is a big copycat and has used his vast knowledge to copy the Trinity/Godhead principle, the begotten son story, the resurrection and the commandments that are in our bible. By doing this, he has tricked every civilization into worshipping him and his pagan gods instead of the "Creator". The Israelites were notorious for doing this, but they were a "**set apart**" people unto God and thus were punished for worshipping other gods.

HOUSE OF ISRAEL & JUDAH: SCATTERED BUT NOT LOST.

Black people have been spread all across the entire world as slaves to be forced to the slave/servitude labor for the rest of the world. Latinos in the Caribbean are the product of the slave trades and the migration of Israelites from the Middle East. Latinos in the Americas are also the product of the Slave Trades and the migration of the Ancient Israelites to "New World". This can be seen to be true Biblically in (**2 Kings, Hosea**), and in other non-biblical sources (2 Esdras). What we do know is that the deported 10 Northern Tribes of Israel did not stay put after being led away beyond the Euphrates. They had access to waterways that could lead them to other lands (**i.e. Euphrates River, Persian Gulf, Gulf of Oman, Arabian Sea, and the Indian Ocean**).

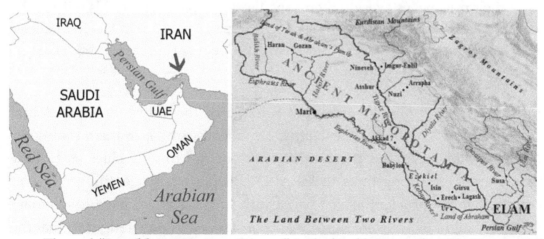

*The real "**Land between two Rivers**" is the land between the Nile River and the Euphrates. The Israelites were brought in waves to **Haran** and the **River Gozan**. Then they were taken to the **Habor River** and past the Euphrates into **Medes (Persia-Iran)***

*which is East of **Elam** near the Persian Gulf. (**Above**) The map shows how you can get from Haran, Gozan and the Habor River (**Upper left**) to Medes (Persia) using the **Euphrates River** as a landmark. Having access to the Euphrates River and the Persian Gulf the Israelites could travel on boats into the **Arabian sea/Indian Ocean**. From here they could travel west around Madagascar and South African to America/Caribbean. Another option would be traveling by foot East into Asia but this would mean they would have to cross the **Bering Strait** to get to Canada/America. Both options would take months or perhaps over a year to make it to the New World.*

Hosea 7:8 "Ephraim, he hath **MIXED HIMSELF AMONG THE PEOPLE**; Ephraim is a cake not turned."

This is an actual sandal of the "**Pharaoh's of Egypt**". Notice how they put the pictures of their prisoner/slaves on their sandals. How did they do this with such fine precision? Could this be proof that the Children of Israel are in fact in likeness to the "Natives" in the Americas/Caribbean, the Negro/Hamites and the East Asian people (India)?

Ephraim is also used in bible to represent Samaria or the House of Israel. Many people are confused as to who the Native Americans are as if their traditions, custom, religion, language and persecution isn't enough to give clues as to how these people are have strong links to ISRAEL. People want scientific proof and biblical proof. But the problem is that as African-Americans we have to do more research. They taught us we were descendants of slaves and they taught us that the Native Indians welcomed Christopher Columbus and that's why we have "Thanksgiving". They don't mention "stolen land", "genocide", "suicide" and "rape". It is obvious that the world is vast and people look different. But everyone stems from Noah and his three sons if we talk about post-flood times. After all, most civilizations talk about a **"Great Flood"** happening a long time ago. . So how do we have so many different looks of people in this world if we think Noah and his sons were all dark-skinned Black people? We know that most Europeans are white-skinned but the Native Americans were not. Ancient Mayan, Aztec and Inca pictures prove this. East Indians are brown too but they have a different look. What about the Aeta/Negritos black natives of the Philippines before King Philip arrived? They have Asian type eyes. What about the San people in Africa?

Native American Boy (1800's)

A New Haplogroup is born when a very specific new mutation occurs. Well, if Ephraim/Samaria was always mixing with different nations this would explain their look and why there have been documents that state there was also Negro-looking people in the Americas with the Native Americans prior to Christopher Columbus' arrival. Well, one of the mysteries is why the Native Americans have Y-Haplogroups Q, R, C, and some E1b1a/E1b1b? Why is their Haplogroups almost at the end of the Alphabet? How many branches do the Native Americans have? Haplogroup Q descends from Haplogroup P (Negritos/Aeta), which are the ancestors or Haplogroup R1/Rb seen in some East Indians, Africans and some

Europeans. What is Haplogroup R a sub-branch of? How can the Pharaoh's of Egypt carry the Y Haplogroup R gene? We know Ephraim was half Egyptian and we know that the Israelites intermarried with the Egyptians often. We see similar traditions with feathers in the headdress of the Ancient Egyptians, Africans, and Native Americans. The clues are there but man likes to manipulate history to keep the truth from coming out. They put this information subliminally in movies as "hidden messages" but do we pick up on it? This is how man tries to hide the True Identity of the Natives and the Negro. He knows if we can prove these two groups are **ISRAEL** the roof will collapse and we will pretty much have all the 12 tribes awakened in no time.

Fact: *In the book called "**The Nazis**" written by **Robert Edwin Herzstein** and the Editors of Time/Life Books on page 132-133 (1980) it states that Hitler said:*

> ***"The genetic heritage of the Jews is purportedly traced to the Orientalen (East/South Asian), Negro, near Asian, and Hamitic peoples."***

The word "**Orientalen**" is a German word. When translated it means "**East**" and "**South Asian**".

Hosea foresaw (Hosea 14) the destruction and captivity that was going to come against Ephraim and the Northern Tribes because of their idolatry worship. He knew that Ephraim had **mixed** his seed amongst many nations. Hosea also states in his book:

Hosea 7:11 "Ephraim also is like a silly dove without heart: **THEY CALL TO EGYPT, they go to Assyria**.

Does this mean that the Northern Tribes or the Tribe of Ephraim frequented Egypt and Assyria? If so, did they intermarry with them while living in Israel?

Hosea 7:16 "They (**Ephraim**) return, but not to the Most High: they are like a deceitful bow: their princes shall fall by the sword for the rage of their tongue: this shall be their derision (ridicule, mockery) in the **land of Egypt**."

What does this scripture mean? Does the "**Land of Egypt**" mean the physical "**Egypt**" we know of in Africa where the Pharaoh's ruled or does it mean a "**Land of Bondage?**" We do know that the **Tribe of Ephraim & Manasseh** were half Egyptian and according to Hosea they must have continued to intermix with the Egyptians or perhaps continued follow the customs of the Egyptians. So where can find traces of pyramids today outside of Egypt? In the Americas, West Africa and India! Strangely enough the Northern Tribes of Israel (**Ephraim**) has been linked to the Americas (North/Central/South) and even the Caribbean. Is this a clue? The genetic Y-Haplogroup studies of the Ancient Egyptians (**Amenhotep, Akhenaten, and King Tut**) also have matched up with the East Indians and Amerindians. The "**R/R1b**" Y-Haplogroup has been found in Native Americans and Indians/Sri Lankans. It has also been found in Africans in Cameroon, Chad, and Niger.

THE HOUSE OF EPHRAIM'S (NORTHERN KINGDOM OF ISREAL) CAPTIVITY AND EXILE OUT OF ISRAEL.

Assyrian forces invaded Israel between 734 B.C. and 732 B.C. under the rule of Tiglath-Pileser III. The Assyrians carried the Israelites away (**even the Reubenites, Gadites and the half-tribe of Manasseh**) and brought them unto Halah, Habor, Haran and to the Gozan River (1 Chronicles 5:26)". Ten years later the next King of Assyria Shalmaneser V (727 B.C.-722 B.C.) took Samaria (Northern Kingdom of Israel) and exiled Israel to Assyria placing them in the same areas Tiglath-Pileser III did but also in the cities of Iran-Persia (II Kings 17:6, 18:11). Twenty years later after the reign of Assyrian King Sargon II, King Sennacherib (705 B.C-681 B.C.) led an army against Jerusalem. He was able to lay siege to the city of Lachish, which was a fortress city outside of Jerusalem.   However, he was unsuccessful in taking Jerusalem where Hezekiah, King of Judah was the ruler at the time. The Assyrians boasted that no other nations God were able to deliver them from the hand of the Assyrians. But Hezekiah and the prophet Isaiah cried to heaven and were saved by God from the hands of the Assyrians. Jerusalem was not captured but the city of Lachish was conquered by the Assyrians. The prisoners were Israelites from the **Tribe of Judah** as Lachish was in the **Territory of Judah**.

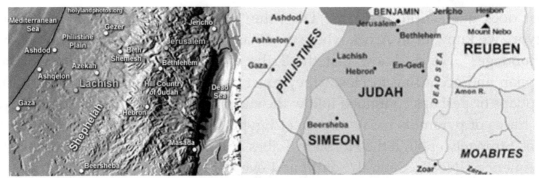

*Lachish was a city in the Territory of Judah. Thus, the people taken from Lachish by the Assyrians under **King Sennacherib** where Israelites from the **TRIBE OF JUDAH**.*

*(Left) This is an actual physical relief from 701 B.C. depicting what the **REAL ISREALITES** from **THE TRIBE OF JUDAH** looked like in Ancient Times. It sits in the British Museum in London under the name "**Lachish Relief**". It is documented "Archaeologically" and "Biblically" in **2 Chronicles 32:9, Isaiah 36:1-2, 2 Kings 18, and Micah 1:13**. As you can see the hair and beard texture of the Original Israelites is "Kinky", signified by the small knots for the hair. The hair of a Jew from the Tribe of Judah today is straight and does NOT resemble the hair of the Ancient Israelites from the Tribe of Judah. (Right) Is a Jewish man wearing a "**Kippah**" hat, which the Original Israelites **DID NOT** wear, nor was it required by God in the Torah for the Children of Judah.*

Let's do a comparison of the Ancient Israelites hair and the hair of Blacks today.

*The hair texture of the Black boy on the left is "**identical**" to the Ancient Israelites hair texture. Notice how the hairline of the Ancient Israelites is also close to the eyebrow. This is a feature that "**Black**" people most often exhibit out of all the races in the world.*

2 Chronicles 32:22 "Thus the Lord (Yahuah) saved Hezekiah and the inhabitants of Jerusalem from the hand of Sennacherib the King of Assyria, and from the hand of all other, and guided them on every side."

2 Kings 17:18 "Therefore the Lord was very angry with Israel, **and removed them out of his sight:** there was none left but the Tribe of Judah only."

In other "**foreign lands**", Blacks, Latinos, and Native Americans have "**served**" the European slavemasters/colonists. They have been innocently killed by the Europeans and have taken on other gods to worship that their forefathers did not do. In these lands, there is no rest, just killing, hard labor, poor living and stress. Blacks, Mexicans, Native Americans, Latinos and the descendants of Caribbean Latinos have in the past worked the field for the Europeans, bringing them in much profit. Many hours of the day these race groups have worked planting seed, cultivating the land and collecting the harvest. The living conditions for these race groups have never been "spectacular". Many Blacks and Latinos today work in the field or in buildings providing **ALL THE LABOR**. They are not paid a fair wage and many of they are not offered health insurance, retirement planning, Vision/Dental coverage or vacation time. So many Blacks and Latinos work 7-days a week but still feel no ease or assurance when it comes to their life or future. Blacks and Latinos **ARE** the servitude labor force of the world, especially in the Americas. Blacks and Latinos will do jobs that other races won't do. If all Blacks and Latinos were to disappear from the world there would be nobody to do all the menial, servitude jobs of America. This in essence is the "**SERVITUDE/SLAVERY**" foretold to be upon the Children of Israel in Deuteronomy 28:16-28. Just think about it? Without Blacks and Latinos certain foods would not be readily available in our grocery stores. Would there be any fresh fruit (i.e. Oranges, watermelon, cantaloupes)? Who would work in farming doing the physical labor machines cannot do? How would retail, fast food, and health care businesses run? How would Hotels be able provide service to its guests if Latinos and Blacks were not around? Who would pick the grapes in the vineyard that eventually go into our bottled wine?

*Buying wine in **New Zealand**? The Black natives of **Tanna Island** in the Tafea Province of **Vanuatu** are the ones that often pick the grapes. This is just a clear example of the "servitude" Blacks are under throughout the world. **Curse of Canaan or Israel?***

(**Left**) Mexicans picking grapes in the vineyards of Southern California. (**Right**) Ancient Egyptian laborers (**perhaps Israelites**) picking grapes for the Royal House of the Pharaoh's

IDOL WORSHIP

It's a known fact the Israelites worshipped the many different pagan gods during their history in the bible with those of the Egyptians and the Canaanites. The Canaanite God **Baal** was considered the "**Thunder God**". He is often shown with one of his hands up to the sky holding a Thunder bolt. **Zeus** was also a chief Greek Deity that was a Thunder god. So was the Roman God of Gods **Jupiter Ammon**. So it is not a coincidence that thousands of years later the Israelites kept some of these pagan religious traditions which they mixed with the religions of their slavemasters. The Yoruba thunder god was named "**Shango**". The Mende tribe of West Africa also had "**Thunder god**" they worshipped as did the Black Olmec people who left huge "**Head stone monuments**" in Mexico. Their writing style was identical to the West African Mende Tribe and also the Ancient Shang Dynasty in China. This was researched by author Dr. Clyde A. Winters and others. Studies done by Ivan Van Sertima (**They Came Before Columbus**), Alexander Von Wuthenau (**Unexpected Faces in Ancient America**), and Dr. Runoko Rashidi prove that the Olmecs were Africans found in the Mende regions of West Africa.

Fact: Other Thunder gods are Thunderbird (**Native Americans**), Xolotl/Tlaloc (**Aztecs**), Chaac (**Mayans**), Apocatequil (**Incas**), Set-Satan (**Egypt**), Azaka-Tonnerre (**West African and Haitian Voodoo**), Amadioha/Amadiora/Kamalu (**Nigerian Igbo**), Shango (**Nigerian Yoruba**) and Xevioso/Xewioso (**Dahomey-Benin-Fon**), Yewe (**Ghana-Ewe**), Tano (**Ghana-Akan**).

Michael Aquino, founder of the "**Temple of Set**" in Santa Barbara, California left the Church of Satan in 1975, secondary to his belief that Satan's real name was "**Set**". He was told this by Satan or a Demon himself during a satanic ritual. Thunder/Lightning has always been associated with "**Satan**" in the occult world and in the Bible. This is why Satan has used every civilization throughout history to worship a "**Thunder God**". Witchcraft/Sorcery (Priests of Baal) has also been a common theme in the Bible and continues with Voodoo practices in West Africa and the Caribbean. This is idolatry worship and is forbidden by God to the Israelites.

Luke 10:18 "And he said unto them, I beheld Satan as **LIGHTNING** fall from heaven."

(**Left**) The Nigerian Yoruba Thunder god "**Shango**" with the double-ax symbol on his head. (**Right**) The two pictures to the Right are the Canaanite Thunder god "**Baal**". **These pictures portray these gods holding a thunderbolt in their right hand.**

Olmec Heads: Dating back to 600 B.C. found in **Veracruz, Mexico**. Some say they could date back to 1400 B.C. Their writing style is identical to the **Chinese Shang Dynasty** from 1,000 B.C. The picture to the right is an Olmec Head sitting in **Century Park, Shanghai, China**.

Olmec Motifs	Chinese Shang Writing	Modern Character / English		
I	I	十 Shí		Ten
下	帀 帀 丁	示 Shì		Worship; sacrifice
二	二	二 Èr		Two
⼃	∧	入 Rù		Offer; contribute
三	三	三 **San**		**Three**
⿴	⿴ ⿴	皿 Mǐn		Container
⿰	⿰ ⿰	官 Guān		Temple; building

Studies done by Dr. Clyde Winters (author of the book "**Olmec language and literature**") show that the Olmec's used the Mende writing script, a writing system used among the Mandinka's and other Africans in West Africa. When the writings on the Olmec monuments were translated, it was found that the language spoken by the Olmec's was Mende. The Olmec's also had a religious practice of Thunder Worship where the "**Ax**" was a prominent feature. The Ax is also prominent feature in connection with the "Shango" worshippers" in West Africa, (ex. Yoruba, Mende/Mandinka). Shango was the God of Thunder in these cultures. Perhaps this was where the word "**Shang**" in the Chinese "**Shang Dynasty**" came from. The Olmec stone heads on the back also show black hairstyles such as braids, dreadlocks and cornrows. Some of the stone monuments have the appearance of "**Kinky hair**" carved into stone on the back of the head. This proves the Olmec people were of "**Negro**" stock.

It is a known fact that many Muslims in Africa (Gambia, Mali, Senegal) have Hebraic/Judaism roots by tracing their family tree and researching what religious traditions their great-grandparents kept. Many agreed that over time, their tribes converted to Islam due to the overwhelming influence in Upper West Africa at the time. This was prophesied in the Bible with the Curses of Israel. Other Israelites strayed away from their original religion and started practicing "**animism**", possibly learnt from neighboring Hamitic tribes they lived amongst. Many West Africans along the coasts also show evidence of Judaism-type religious practices mixed with Christianity perhaps learnt from their exodus from Israel through Egypt and Ethiopia.

Deuteronomy 28:66 "**And thy life shall hang in doubt before thee; and thou shalt fear day and night, and shalt have none assurance of thy life:**"

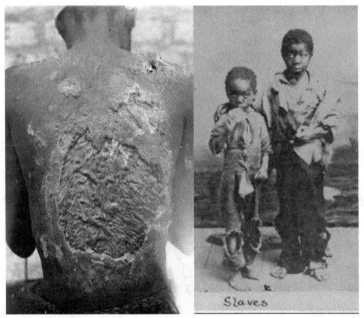

(Above) Slavery in the 1800's. Children born into slavery had no hope and assurance of their life or future. They were subject to starvation, slave work and beatings. Getting beat by the whip would often tear pieces of flesh off leaving the raw fleshy musculature of the back exposed.

During slavery, many blacks were in fear of what was going to happen to them or their family depending on the mood of the Slavemaster.

Though studies say Black Americans don't suffer from higher rates of depression than White Americans, there have been studies that prove that many African-Americans tend to repress feelings of depression and other mental health disorders. Blacks living amongst each other have developed a distrust that is not present with the white man. Blacks are subject to getting robbed in broad daylight and at night by their own people instead of someone of another race. In our own communities we are more scared of "each other" than the Jewish man or Arab man walking down the street. Many inner city residents are afraid to go to corner store or the gas station in their community. Many elderly residents are too scared to speak up against what they see as "**not right**" in their community. They are too scared to reprimand the neighborhood children, let alone the parents of these children. This same fear prevents us from rising up and making a stand united as one to make change to a system that has failed us. A system that has been designed for us not to succeed in.

From Slavery to today, blacks cannot get a break. Many blacks do not have any "**assurance**" of their future or their current state of living. Middle-aged blacks in their 50's-60's are realizing that they cannot retire when they want to and some are realizing that they will have to keep working until they drop dead. With the Social Security Retirement age creeping to 70 for people born after 1960, the harsh reality of a life of labor is depressing. In 2015, Detroit and Flint were listed as the poorest cities in America. Around 40% of people living in these cities live below the poverty line (which is less than $24,250 for a family of four). The "real" unemployment rate for many cities such as Detroit is greater than 50%. For the unemployed who wish to retire one day, Social Security is not going to be there to save the day. This is very scary and is not something that people are proud of or even want to think about. Sadly, many blacks will have more money to their "name" when they are dead than alive, thanks to Life Insurance. But it shouldn't be this way for Blacks in America and it shouldn't be this way for the descendants of

"**Negro Slaves**" scattered all across the world. Slavery was over a hundred years ago.

Assurance means: "**confidence or certainty in one's own abilities**". Looking at the issues blacks face such as legal problems, a poor educational system, social/domestic problems, health problems, lack of employment, discrimination, racism, predatory lending, and systems designed to keep blacks with just enough to survive, it is easy to see why many blacks are losing hope or have lost hope. Many have just accepted their way of life of being poor. Being unemployed or working multiple jobs for 30-40 years is the norm for some. Seeing other races prosper is normal to some blacks, and throughout generations we have been conditioned to think that it's normal for other races to drive expensive cars or live in big houses while we are destined to be harassed by the police every day while living in the "**Ghetto**".

Black are constantly harassed in their communities and outside their communities. In Black inner cities, there is evidence of widespread destruction, despair and suffering.

We have been conditioned by our parents/grandparents to go high-school and then to go to college to get a job. We struggle on our own, one family over here and one family over there. We often avoid helping one another in our own family and we don't try to invest money with other blacks we don't even know. Small problems turn into big problems as we strive to make it independently on our own. When these big problems turn into disasters by then it is too late for any intervention to do any good. Poor economic choices in our youthful adult years can turn into a constant "**Black cloud**" of "**Debt Slavery**" over the next 10 years of our life. An older Black woman once told me, "Without a knowledge of who we are as a people it is hard for us to have any **'togetherness'** or **'feeling of belonging'** to our fellow brothers. We don't feel as if it's **"our duty"** to help others who need help and although some of us may **"make it"** to that million dollar level we still don't always feel like it is **"our responsibility"** to help the masses of unfortunate blacks who need help just so we can see for the advancement of our black race. Jews, Arabs, Indians and Asians attack problems or jobs with a **"group mentality"**. They don't kill each other or rob each other in their communities like Blacks and Latinos do. Why is that? Many blacks that have gotten robbed in their own neighborhood by family or strangers feel a sense of **"disappointment"** in the black race. Many blacks that have family that are not around to help in **"times of need"** feel that **"family ain't family no more"**. But when was there a time when family was family? During **"Segregation"** or after **"Desegregation"**? Suicide, murder, homelessness, mental break downs and problems arising from lack of money should not be an issue if there is family alive that can help. It is rare that we see a homeless Arab, Jew, Asian or Indian in America. Why is that? It is rare that we see a Nursing Home full of Asians, Jews, Arabs or Indians. Why is that? It is rare that we see these races in the Psychiatric Ward and it is rare that we see these races commit suicide or die by murder. In addition, it is rare that we see these non-black, non-Hispanic races behind bars in staggering numbers. One can say that it all comes down to knowing who we are as a people and practicing **"Unity"**, but the **Curses of Israel** clearly states that we will go through this. Why? Because we a **"Special People"** unto God.

Deuteronomy 28:67 "In the morning thou shalt say, Would God it were evening! And at evening thou shalt say, Would God it were morning! For the FEAR of thine heart wherewith thou shalt fear, and for the SIGHT OF THINE EYES WHICH THOU SHALT SEE."

I once talked to an Ethiopian woman who told me she could obviously see all the racism that America had for African-Americans. She was very sad to see this in America and admitted that she had experienced racism herself. She said that her son had visited Ethiopia a while back and told her that in his whole life he never felt free until he was back in Africa walking in his homeland. I told the Ethiopian woman that African-Americans do not have a homeland. We know we were **"Stolen from Africa"** but we have no country or tribe to return home to. In school

Black history starts in the 1500's from the beginnings of slavery to the Civil Rights movement. We are taught to embrace the "**Assimilation**" of Blacks into "**White America**" thanks to Martin Luther King Jr. Never do we learn that before "**Assimilation**" we were doing fine "**Segregated**". Segregation forced us to depend on each other and to spend money with each other. We had our own villages, cities and towns. We had communities where everyone knew each other. Nobody was trying to keep up with the "**Jones's**" or the "**Smith's**". If you had a skill or trade you could use the "**Bartering System**" to get what you needed even if you didn't have any money. Black Wall Street (**Tulsa, Oklahoma**) and Black Bottom (**Detroit, Michigan**) were examples of this. But of course "White America" couldn't let us be. Riots were started and that was the end of these self-sufficient Black communities. We as blacks went through getting punched in the head just so we could eat at white restaurants. We got beat and hosed down with water for fighting to be able to go to white schools. Sam Cooke the singer of the song "**A Change is Gonna Come**" started his own black record label and music publishing company and mysteriously died. Michael Jackson was co-owner of the largest music publishing company in the world, "**Sony/ATV**" with Sony Chairman **Tommy Mattola**. Michael co-owned many publishing rights to different songs (including the Beatles) with the Sony/ATV publishing company. Sony wanted badly to buy Michael's share of the company but Michael always refused. Mysteriously, Michael Jackson died. Martin Luther King, Malcom X, Marcus Garvey, Bob Marley and Huey Newton all tried to wake us up but they all died under suspicious circumstances. Today after going through all the beatings, lynching's and deaths trying to "Integrate" into White America we still are hated. We support other races businesses with our $1.1 Trillion dollar black buying power but do not support each other. We have tons of Black Millionaires and Billionaires but our livelihood still depends on whether we get paid from non-black business establishments or from the Government. We can have Black movie production companies put out movies every year for us to spend millions making them rich at the box office but none of this "Black Money" is helping the black race as a whole. This "Black money" is not going into black communities all across the United States of America. Having our own personal DVD copy of "Friday" or "Boyz n the Hood" in the Ghetto is not a sign that things are "All good" for us. But for the 45 million blacks in America that possibly supported "Friday" or "Boyz n the Hood" at the movies or at retail stores, this equates to "Wealth" for these companies and a "Good Laugh" for us while we suffer in poverty. Decades after the movie "**Boyz n the Hood**" was released in 1991 Blacks still are at the bottom economically, politically, physically and socially.

We still do not own anything. We still make "**them**" rich, while we stay poor. The powers to be in America have programmed us to fear "**them**" and to also fear "**ourselves**". We are still getting shot down in the streets by racist white law enforcement but we're are also getting shot down by our own people. We see racial profiling. We see a Judicial system that regards the life of non-black races, homosexuals and animals higher than a black person life. We also see a Judicial system that is bent on keeping us in jail and filling us in the jails that they intend to build to make a profit. All of this alone can cause one to have "**Fear**". Fear of going out of the house into the world and "**fear**" at the sight of the things we might see.

Back in Biblical times, the Israelites were not wanted or liked wherever they went. They were called fugitive slaves, wandering nomads, strangers, troublemakers and invaders. Every nation that they lived amongst wanted to destroy them. The Amalekites, the Kenites, the Edomites, the Egyptians, the Assyrians, the Babylonians, the Grecians, the Romans, the Canaanites and so on. The Israelites sold Joseph into slavery and the Israelites even conspired to give Samson away to the Philistines for all the trouble he was causing. This has continued to this present day. The Israelites were in captivity so much (prison houses, pits, etc) that the Prophet Jeremiah thought that their only purpose on earth was to serve others as slaves and to suffer.

Judges 15:10-12 "And the men of Judah said, Why are ye come up against us? And they answered, to bind Samson are we come up, to do to him as he hath done to us. Then **three thousand men of Judah** went to the top of the rock Etam, and said to Samson, Knowest thou not that the Philistines are rulers over us? What is this that thou has done unto us? And he said unto them, as they did unto me, so have I done unto them. And they said unto him, **We are come down to bind thee, that we may deliver thee into the hand of the Philistines**. And Samson said unto them, Swear unto me, that ye will not fall upon me yourselves."

Jeremiah 2:14 "**Is Israel a slave: Is he a homeborn servant? Why has he become a prey?**"

Jeremiah states the question is Israel a **slave**, **servant** and a **prey** for everyone else. This is what many Black people all across the world feel like. Many Blacks feel like we are destined to be on the bottom, to serve and work for others. We feel oppressed by the Arabs, Indians, Jews, Asians and Europeans. It doesn't matter if your heritage is from Haiti, Jamaica, India, Guyana, Brazil, Suriname, Belize, Mexico, America, Greece, England, Puerto Rico, Iraq, Palestine, Iran, Saudi Arabia or Israel. It's all the same feeling these "black people" are feeling.

*Even the Angels in Heaven say in Revelation 19:1 "**HalleluYAH; Salvation, and glory, and honour, and power, unto the Lord our God**."*

Black people are naturally "**Spiritual**" people. We know our help comes from a one "**Supreme God**". We've known this before Slavery and Post-Slavery. This is why we say "**God**" or "**Lord**" whenever we get into extreme "**deep trouble**".

Fact: *The Slave Hymn "**Kum-ba-Yah**" is the broken English name of the song the slaves spoke which means "**Come by here Yah (short for Yahuah)**". It is said that it stems from Angola, Africa and that they were the first slaves taken from Africa to the South Carolina-Georgia coastline area. The **Geechie-Gullah** people were known to sign this hymn in South Carolina hundreds of years ago. Many of these slaves spoke a Creole language derived from Sierra Leone, as well as the Ivory Coast, Senegal-Gambia, and Liberia. The Geechie-Gullah language is similar to the Krio language of Sierra Leone, the Bahamian dialect, Jamaican Patois, Bajan Creole, and Belizean Kriol.*

God knows his children and his children innately know him. Like how sheep know their master. Satan since the beginning of time has tried to deceive God's Chosen People into worshipping everything but the **Most High**. He has tried to infect the seed of Seth with his evilness, and this was the main reason why God sent the Flood to destroy all mankind except Noah and his family. This is also why Abraham told the Israelites not to intermarry with the Canaanites. However, the Israelites disobeyed. Just like King Solomon, we married with everybody and in turn were tricked to worship their gods. This "**deception**" is still happening today with "**Organized Religion**". When the Israelites were in the wilderness with Moses during the Exodus they didn't have a "Religion". They had a "**Spiritual**" connection between themselves and the Most High through the Prophets. We have lost this today with "Religion" as there are so many "**Religious Denominations**" in the World confusing people. Many of these Christian-like denominations are leading people astray from the Most High God, Yeshua (Yahusha) HaMashiach and Salvation. This was designed by Satan to trick the world and the "**Children of Israel**". But we must stay prayerful that God shows us the right way and keeps us on the right path to him.

Being awakened sometimes can wear down your brain and cause you to feel sad for all of those who are still asleep. Families, friends, coworkers may not believe you or care to hear what you have to say. I've realized that not everyone will wake up and most Black Churches or even White Churches will not teach their congregation the "**Whole Truth**". I once talked to a Muslim Pakistani man who said he felt down most of the time because he thought he was the only one on the planet who knew about the "**Synagogue of Satan**" and how they are destroying the world. Now that I'm awake I see agendas unfolding right before my eyes. Everything makes sense in regards to Bible prophecy, and although it seems scary at times we just have to remember that it all fits into "**Gods perfect plan**".

Deuteronomy 28:68 **"And the LORD shall bring thee into Egypt again with SHIPS, by the way whereof I spake unto thee, Thou shalt see it no more again: and there ye shall be SOLD unto your enemies for BONDMEN and BONDWOMEN, and no man shall BUY/REDEEM you."**

Fact: Israel borders Egypt like North Carolina borders South Carolina. Why would anyone need a "**Ship**" to take someone from Israel to Egypt? Don't be misled. Anyone can walk from Israel to Egypt and from Egypt they can walk into Israel. This is how immigrants from Africa get into Israel. This is the same way the Israelites would travel back and forth between Egypt and Israel. Some people will even say this scripture is talking about when the Romans sold some of the Jews to the Egyptians after the fall of the Second Temple in 70 A.D. but the Egyptians didn't buy them. But how can you be officially "**Sold**" if no one buys you? The word "**Sold**" is the past tense of "**Sell**" which means someone has to "**Buy**". This is why we have a "**Buyer**" and a "**Seller**" in Real Estate deals.

Egypt in the bible is synonymous with a "**Land of Bondage**". We know that God did not deliver Moses and the Israelites out of the Pharaoh's hand only to deliver them back into his custody for a second era of Slavery. We also know that you do not need ships to go from Israel (Land of Canaan) into Egypt, Assyria or Babylon.

1. Deuteronomy 5:6 **"I am the Lord thy God, which brought thee out of the land of Egypt, from the HOUSE OF BONDAGE."**

2. Deuteronomy 6:12 **"Then beware lest thou forget the Lord, which brought thee forth out of the land of Egypt, from the HOUSE OF BONDAGE."**

3. Exodus 13:14 **"And it shall be when thy son asketh thee in time to come, saying, What is this? that thou shalt say unto him, By strength of hand the Lord brought us out from Egypt, from the HOUSE OF BONDAGE."**

4. Exodus 20:2 **"I am the Lord thy God, which have brought thee out of the land of Egypt, out of the HOUSE OF BONDAGE."**

Note how every time God refers to Egypt it is always followed by "**The House of Bondage**". This is like a hidden message in the scriptures revealing to "**US**" that when reading the last verse of the "**Curses of Israel**" we must associate the word "**Egypt**" with a "**House of Bondage**". This way we can see that the scripture is talking about us and no one else. No one else, man or woman has been sold into slavery into **ALL NATIONS** than those Hebrew Israelites involved in the slave trades at the hands of the Arabs, Jews and Europeans.

Fact: This is a True Story. When going on the Hebrew Bible online at www.mechon-mamre.org the words "**United States of America**" appears in place of the word "**Covenant**" or Hebrew Strong's #1285 word "**Berith**" whenever you try to use your computer to translate the Hebrew characters into English. **Note: this is a function that most computers have today.** The words "**United States of America**" seems to only appear when the scripture is discussing a "**covenant**" between God and Israel. It appears in Deuteronomy 28:69, Deuteronomy 29:20 and Jeremiah 31:31. In other scriptures where the word "covenant" is used but not in reference to the "Children of Israel" the word "United States of America" is not seen in the attempted encrypted English translation. It could just be my computer, but maybe it works with everyone else's computer. Nevertheless, this I found to be quite odd and interesting at the same time.

It is a common practice for people to say that "Negroes" were not scattered to the "**FOUR CORNERS**". Little do they know that laws were passed in the 1800's and early 1900's abolishing slavery in Northern countries such as Spain, Portugal, France, Britain (United Kingdom) and Denmark, Russia and even Turkey.

*(Left) Slavery of Blacks in Egypt 1800's. (**Right**) An Arab Turkish boy in Palestine in the 1800's. Notice in both pictures the typical white-skinned Arab that we see today.*

For a good time the White-skinned Turkish Ottoman Arabs ruled over Palestine. In the mid-19th century (1850's) the Ottoman Empire was slowly declining in power. The Ottoman Empire arose on the scene in the 1300's with Sultan Osman I from Turkey. The Ottoman Turks conquered Palestine in 1516 and it was Suleiman the Magnificent who rebuilt some of the walls of Jerusalem in 1537. It is the Roman fort wall "Antonia" with these "Ottoman" walls the Jews and the world today believe is the remnant of Solomon's Temple aka "The Western Wailing Wall". The Arabic speaking Druze people attempted to establish their own state in Northern Palestine but are today currently limited to Syria, Lebanon, Israel and Jordan. Their faith is Abrahamic-Islamic mixed with Greek and Hindu philosophies stemming back from their beginning in the 11th Century when they were an Islamic Caliphate (Fatimid dynasty). Later, French Emperor Napoleon in 1798 conquered Cairo, Egypt and certain areas in Palestine. He was able to capture Jaffa, Lydda, Ramle, Nazareth and Tiberias. This is why many Palestinians and Lebanese people know how to speak French. It is a known fact that the Ottomans Turks had Black slaves (men and women) in the Middle East as well as white women (sex concubines). This is why there is a remnant of 25,000 Afro-Turks in **Izmir**, the third largest city in Turkey. Here is an account of Slavery in Turkey:

"Reduced to the condition of slaves, the negro captives leave their country either following the course of the Nile, crammed twenty or thirty together in a boat, or they traverse, half on foot, half on camel's back, the wastes separating Central Africa from the countries bordering the Mediterranean and the Red Sea. That the slaves imported into the dominions of the Sultan come from the regions neighboring the sources of the Nile, is ascertained from the fact, that on questioning the negroes of Stamboul (Istanbul, Turkey) with reference to their native countries, they will invariably mention Kordofan (Sudan), Darfur (Sudan), Dangola (Nubia/Sudan) or Abyssinia (Ethiopia). The valley of the Nile is not, however, the only outlet of slavery, as many slaves are exported eastward to the market places of Arabia, while numbers cross the great Sarah [Sahara Desert] and reach Tripoli (Libya) of Barbary, and the frontiers of Tunis (Tunisia) and Morocco. Living stock requires a greater number of entrepôts [depots] than goods in general do; so, for the Negro slave-trade entrepôts have been established at Gondokoro and Khartum on the Nile route, Massovah and Soakin to the east, and Fezan on the Sarah route. From these entrepôts the human merchandise is packed off to the chief emporiums at Cairo, Alexandria, Constantinople (Turkey), Smyrna (Turkey), Beyruth (Lebanon?), Jeddah (Saudi Arabia), Mecca (Saudi Arabia) and Medineh (Saudi Arabia). From the very outset on leaving their native land begins the career of toil and privations which is allotted to the poor slaves; a thin garment covers their nakedness, and a white woolen blanket renders to them the services of cloak, quilt and mattress. Without any regard for either Mussulman decency or Christian philanthropy, men, women, and children are thrown promiscuously by their dealers into a boat or within the precinct of a filthy eastern *khan* (inn), where dry bread and soup every twenty-four hours is given them, so as to preserve them alive for the market place. It must be known that ill-treatment is a part of the craft of slave-dealers; by this method the slave is sure to look up to the first customer as a deliverer and a benefactor, and will therefore show no great dislike at being sold.

The greatest part of the Negro slaves imported into Turkey are females, and this for the reasons above stated, that the demand is exclusively for domestics serving in the harem (as houseservants or sex slaves)." – *Sesquicentennial Comparisons: Black Slavery in America and Ottoman Turkey by Andrew G. Bostom.*

Note: *Joseph **walked** into Egypt 70 souls deep. Joseph and the Israelites didn't get on ships to bury their father Jacob in the land of Canaan. They **walked** back from Egypt into Canaan. Jesus's parents didn't get on a ship to flee into Egypt. They **walked** into Egypt with a donkey and stayed there until King Herod died. Moses didn't have to build boats to take the Israelites on the Exodus journey to the Land of Canaan. They **walked** from Egypt all the way to the Land of Canaan.*

WILL WE EVER AS "A PEOPLE" RETURN BACK TO AFRICA?

The scripture also says that we shall not see Africa/Israel again **AS A PEOPLE TOGETHER**. There is a huge difference. There are many Blacks who have moved back to Africa and there are also blacks that have moved to Dimona, Israel to live (African Hebrew Israelites in 1970). But even in the land of Israel, blacks are not accepted. In Israel, Blacks are not considered to be descendants of the Biblical Hebrew Israelites. Ask any African-American, Sub-Saharan African, or East African if they are lovingly accepted in Israel. They will tell you no. So the question is; have black people who were victims of slavery and thus scattered to the different nations of the world been all brought back to the place they were taken from? No. Have all the Black people in Haiti, the Dominican Republic, Jamaica, Brazil, Cuba, Iran, Iraq, Yemen, Arabia, Turkey, North America, South America, India and East Asia been brought back to Africa or Israel? No. This means that the **REAL** descendants of the **Children of Israel** are still lost. Ashkenazi Jews will say that they are from the Tribe of Judah, Benjamin or the Priestly tribe of Levi/Kohanim. They have no proof and why would God keep the other 10 tribes of Israel lost, allowing the other 2 tribes including the Tribe of Levi to come back to Israel in 1948. This is not supported in the Bible anywhere. Even more, what is the scripture talking about when it mentions "**ships**", "**bondmen**" and "**bondwomen?**" Black Hebrew Israelites slaves were rounding up and scattered across the world in ships. Hitler didn't round up all the European Jews in ships, selling them across the world as bondmen and bondwomen (**which is another word for slaves**). Hitler put the Jews in concentration camps. They European Jews were already in Europe so he didn't need a ship to bring them anywhere. The Jews already knew the language of the land. The spoke a **Turkish, Slavic** and **Germanaic language** mixed with Syriac-Aramaic (**Modern Hebrew**). Hitler knew how to speak their language. The European Jews were not sold to **ANYONE**. So did Hitler read the bible? Did he know the European Jews were not God's Chosen People? Did he know they were imposters? Some say he did. Some say he was trying to save the world from the Zionist Freemason Illuminati agenda that would eventually control and enslave the **WORLD**. Hitler's party was the **NAZI PARTY**. The word "**Nazi**" is in the word "Ashke**NAZI** Jews". Many say Hitler was Jewish or that he also had Jewish blood from his parents. Some say "**The Transfer Agreement**" in 1933 was a deal between Hitler and the Zionist Jews to create "**an event**" that would cause worldwide "**empathy**" for the Jews to justify its need for the "**State of Israel**". This way they could further speed up their plan to prepare the way for their "**Messiah**", the Antichrist and the "**Beast System**".

DID HITLER KNOW WHO THE REAL JEWS WERE?

Did Hitler in his last days reveal the real reason why there was a "**Holocaust?**" The word "**Holocaust**" means "**Burnt Offering**" so was this Jewish "Holocaust" a sacrifice? If so, a sacrifice to who?

True or False?

Supposedly there have been leaked documents that report some disturbing information Hitler said to his soldiers before his death, perhaps in "**Landsberg Prison**" where he wrote his book "**Mein Kampf**". Was certain information written by Hitler "**de-classified**" so that the public couldn't know the truth? It is a known fact that "**Mein Kampf**" and the "**Protocols of the Learned Elders of Zion**"were banned in certain countries. Mein Kampf is set to be made public domain on January 1, 2016. So how could this information leak? Where did Hitler's former Nazi soldiers go after WWII? Did they go to South America or to North America?

From 1945 to 1955, Operation Paperclip granted nearly 1,000 Nazi German scientists American citizenship. Many were longtime members of the Nazi Party and the Gestapo. They had conducted experiments on humans at the concentration camps and committed other war crimes. The scientists ended up in the U.S Military industrial complex, working with the CIA, NASA and other organizations. Some say Hitler escaped into South America but that the Jewish Mossad Intelligence Service found him, captured him, and then extracted him to another country where he was tortured until his death. Who really knows?

It is said that Hitler told his soldiers that even in his death he would somehow cause World War 3. His soldier asked how? Hitler said, "The day mankind finds out what I was trying to defend this nation, Germany, from then that's the day World War 3 will start. For on that day, mankind will learn that I was trying to save my Nation from the Freemasons, the Illuminati, and the Jews. For if the Americans win the war (World War 2), then they will conquer the world and forever be slaves to the Jews and they will conquer God. Do you know who America has in its possession? "No," the soldier replied. The Americans have the **JEWELS OF GOD**. The Americans have stolen God's precious jewels. "What do you mean his precious jewels?" the soldier asked. Hitler said, "America has stolen the Jews." **The JEWS OF GOD. His Jewelry. The NEGROES. They are the TRUE HEBREWS**. What a foolish move and a direct challenge to God. And they plan on moving these false white Jews into a state of Israel. America is desperate in its attempt to win this war using atomic bombs on Japan. America will destroy the whole world in its attempt to conquer it. When America and its Jewish slavemasters conquer the world and the world realizes I was right, then all the nations will begin a Third World War to dethrone America of its rule. Every nation will soon possess atomic bombs of their own. It will be the end of most of the world as we know it. "Why will the Jews control America?" the soldier asked. Hitler said, "Because the white Jews know that the **NEGROES ARE THE REAL CHILDREN OF ISRAEL**, and to keep America's secret, the Jews will blackmail America. The Jews will extort America their plan; for **WORLD DOMINATION WON'T WORK IF THE NEGROES KNEW WHO THEY WERE**. The white citizens of America will be terrified to know that all this time they've been mistreating, discriminating and lynching the Children of Israel. They will fear God will destroy them as he did **EGYPT** for doing the same thing. So the Elite, the Illuminati keeps this a secret at **ALL COSTS**. After I die, I will one day cause World War 3 just by this message which will be like planting a seed in people's minds until it sprouts. Once they nurture that seed and **SEEK MORE TRUTH** and learn I was right; I did the world a favor by killing the false Jews before they designated a false state of Israel. But I fear I have failed. The world will fall into the hands of Satan. – "**Adolf Hitler**".

Did Hitler say this? What do you think? Is America blessing the wrong people? If the True Israelites of the Bible have been held in Slavery is judgement coming to America and the Gentile nations that participated in slavery?

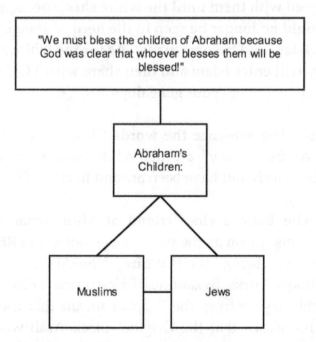

Is the world blessing the wrong people? Are the Jews today really the Biblical Israelites? Are the Arabs we see today really Ishmaelite's? Research says No!

BLACK SHEEP AND WHITE SHEEP

Usama ibn Zayd ibn Aslam was the son of a freed slave born in the seventh year before "Hijra (Muhammad's migration from Mecca to Medina) in 615 A.D. Because of his father's status as the adopted son of Muhammad, and his mother' closeness to Muhammad's own mother, Usama was considered almost a grandson to Muhammad. Usama ibn Zayd related that the Prophet Muhammad saw a vision and told his companions about it. He said:

"In a dream I saw myself following a herd of black sheep. Then a group of white sheep came and mixed with them until the white sheep became so numerous that the black sheep could no longer be seen in the herd of sheep." They (the white sheep) will accept Islam and become many. As for the white sheep, they are the non-Arabs. They will enter Islam and then share with YOU your wealth and your genealogy."

If you noticed in the last sentence the words "They" and "You" refers to two separate sheep or Arabs. "They" are the White Non-Arabs and "You" are the Original Black Arabs that should have been around in 600 A.D.

Well, Arabs like "**Abu Bakr, a close friend of Muhammad and interpreter of dreams**" interpreted this dream as the Black Sheep being the REAL "**Black Arabs**" and the White Sheep being the "**White Non-Arabs**" (i.e. White-skinned Persians/Iranians, Iraqis, Turks, Byzantines, Palestinians, Lebanese, Jordan, Egypt). They believe that this saying from the Prophet meant that the White Non-Arabs would become so numerous that the Original Black Arab would not be noticed amongst them in times to come. They will "share" and then take over the genealogy of the Real Black Ishmaelite's and Keturahites called "**Arabs**" and also share, eventually taking over their lands wealth. Muhammad himself even said that an angel interpreted this dream the same way Abu Bakr interpreted it. So is this what has happened today? You be the Judge? When is the last time you have seen a Black Chaldean, a Black Persian, a Black Saudi Arabian, a Black Palestinian, a Black Syrian, a Black Lebanese or a Black Egyptian?

Have you seen Chaldeans, Persians/Iranians, Palestinians or Lebanese people in America that look like this?

So I know you're asking yourself, what happened to all the Black Arabs? Easy! There was a massive "**White Slave Trade**" between Europe, Central Asia and the Middle East that lasted over 1,000 years. This brought in an enormous number of White people from Western Europe, Eastern Europe and Asia Minor. In collaboration with the Ottoman Empire, North African Arabs and Middle Eastern Arabs raided the coasts of Europe taking all the white women they could get to have sex with, eventually producing a race of White European Arabs. These Arabs are of Roman, Greek, and Turkish stock amongst other white races. This is how many Arabs have blue-green eyes and look no different than Caucasians. The focus on African slaves from East Africa really didn't pick up in numbers until after 1500 A.D. Prior to this the Arabs were enslaving white women in Europe and some Blacks in Africa. So the Black Arabs were phased out to small numbers due to

Middle East invasions by white Non-Arabs from the north and from having children with Northern white women (Romans, Greeks, etc).

9th (836 A.D.) Century poet Abu Al-Hasan Ali ibn Abbas ibn Jurayj, known as **Ibn Al-Rumi** wrote a poem in blaming the Abbasids for the way the treated the family of the Prophet Muhammad. **The Abbasid Caliphate** ruled from 750 A.D. to 1258 A.D. The Abbasids over time had mixed themselves with the Romans, Greeks and white non-Arab Persians (? Edom too). Here is what he had to say in his famous poem **Al-Jeemia:**

> **"You insulted them (the family of Muhammad) because of their blackness while there are STILL pure-blooded black-skinned Arabs. However, you are Blue-eyed...the Romans have embellished your faces with their color."**

Do we need more proof? Here we go:

> **"When Fredon/Thraetaona (mythical Persian Zoroastrianism hero) came, they (the black people) fled from the lands of Iran and settled on the coast of the sea. Now, through the invasion of the Arabs, they (the Zing-i-Siak posht-i.e. the black skinned negroes) are again diffused through the country of Iran." – Bundahisn (Creation of the Origins) – A Zoroastrian text**

What about the Jews? Who are they according to they according to their arch Enemy, Hitler?

Play close attention to this again. In the book called "**The Nazis**" (ISBN No. 0-8094-2534-3) by **Robert Edwin Herzstein** and the Editors of **Time/Life books** published in 1980 it talks about the legacy of Adolf Hitler. But on **pages 132-133** it states that Hitler said:

> **"The genetic heritage of the Jews is purportedly traced to the <u>ORIENTALEN</u> (who were originally black), the NEGRO, NEAR ASIAN (South Asia-India), and HAMITIC people. Hence the Jews today are bastards.**

So what did Hitler mean by this? Nowhere in these 4 groups of people are Europeans (Western or Eastern) listed. This means that according to this book called "**The Nazis**", Hitler knew that the Ashkenazi/Sephardic Jews were not the real Jews. Hitler knew that the bloodline of the "**True Jews**" were in the Negro, the Hamitic people, South Asians and the Black Semites (Middle East/Asia).

(Left) **Ancient Chinese women** with wooly hair. How is this possible? The Original Chinese people come from Africa. (**Right**) An **Original Mahra Black Arab**. **Orientalen**: The "**Orient**" means the **East**. It is a traditional designation for anything that belongs to the **Eastern world** or the **Middle East** and **Asia**.

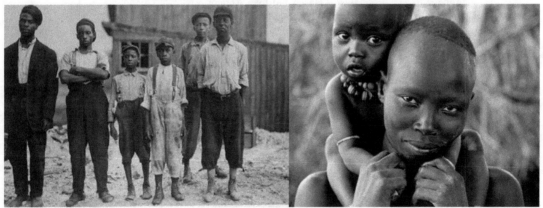

(Left) **African-American Negroes** during slavery era. (**Right**) and **Hamitic Africans (i.e. Non-Bantus Nilotic people, Khoisan people).**

(Left) Near Asian: Dravidian Indian. (Right) Native American Indian.

Jewish Slave Ship Owners

Name of ship	Owners	Ethnicity
Abigail	Aaron Lopez, Moses Levy, Jacob Franks	Jews
Crown	Issac Levy and Nathan Simpson	Jews
Nassau	Moses Levy	Jew
Four Sisters	Moses Levy	Jew
Anne & Eliza	Justus Bosch and John Abrams	Jews
Prudent Betty	Henry Cruger and Jacob Phoenix	Jews
Hester	Mordecai and David Gomez	Jews
Elizabeth	Mordecai and David Gomez	Jews
Antigua	Nathan Marston and Abram Lyell	Jews
Betsy	Wm. De Woolf	Jew
Polly	James De Woolf	Jew
White Horse	Jan de Sweevts	Jew
Expedition	John and Jacob Roosevelt	Jews
Charlotte	Moses and Sam Levy and Jacob Franks	Jews
Caracoa	Moses and Sam Levy	Jews

The European Jews were the main people who owned the slave ships and conducted the slave trade of Hebrew Israelites into **ALL NATIONS**. The bondmen/bondwomen on the slave ships were not White European Ashkenazi or Sephardic Jews. So how could they be the "**Real Jews?**"

Luke 21:24 (Spoken by Yeshua/Yahusha/Yahushua Mashiach) "And they (**Hebrew Israelites**) shall fall by the edge of the sword, and shall be **LED AWAY CAPTIVE INTO ALL NATIONS**: and Jerusalem shall be trodden down of the **Gentiles**, until the times of the Gentiles be fulfilled."

From the fall of the Second Temple in 70 A.D. until today the Gentile Europeans and Gentile Arab (starting with the Black Arabs) have been in possession of Jerusalem, Israel. **The Europeans possessed Jerusalem until the year 637 A.D., shortly after the Prophet Muhammad died.** Under the command of **Abu Ubaidah**, the **Rashidun Muslim Caliphate** defeated the Byzantine Roman Empire. They conquered Jerusalem and on April 637 A.D. the Romans surrendered the city to the Muslims. A little over 50 years later in 691 A.D. the Muslims commissioned the construction of the Dome of the Rock on Temple Mount. The Muslim conquest of "Palestina" and Jerusalem made it now a Holy site to Islamic followers, as well as Christians and Gentile Jews. The Muslims around this time (7th Century) allowed the fake Gentile Jews to return to Jerusalem to worship, but without the presence of a Temple. Note: This was not Bible Prophecy. The Muslims control over Jerusalem would not be threatened until the First Crusade launched by **Pope Urban II** at the **Council of Clermont** in 1095. The long Crusade Battles over Jerusalem were fought between the Gentile Europeans and the Gentile Arabs. Most people list the Crusades from 1095 A.D. to 1291 A.D., but there are some people who list the Crusades lasting from 1095 A.D. to 1588 A.D. The 16th Century marked the rise of the Ottoman Empire who would conquer Jerusalem and Palestine in 1517 A.D. under Turkish Arab ruler "**Suleiman the Magnificent**". Even in Suleiman's era, a man by the name of Elizer Nahman Poa (17th) quoted:

"In the days of the King Sultan Suleiman, **NOBODY KNEW THE LOCATION OF THE TEMPLE (SOLOMON'S)**, so he ordered a search of Jerusalem to find it. One day, the man in charge of the search who had already given up hope (of discovering the true site of the Temple), saw a woman coming and on her head was a basket full of garbage and filth."

Fact 1: It is said around the end of the 16th Century (1500's) with the building of the Dome of the Rock, the Gentile Jews were tricked to believe the "**Wailing Wall**" was that of the remains of the **Second Temple**. However, in reality it was the remaining wall of the Roman's "**Fort Antonia**" fortress built during the time of Roman Emperor Titus.

Fact 2: On the TLC show called "**Sisterhood**", which aired January 1, 2013 a White Jewish man on the show admitted on National Television that the Original Jews were Black and that Adam was a Black man.

CHAPTER 34

THE CONCLUSION

People we need to see who has been lying to us and start realizing the truth. The Curses of Israel in Deuteronomy 28:16-68 are foretelling the hardships that the Hebrew Israelites would have to go through in the future. Once the slaves were sold and after the Israelites scattered into the **FOUR CORNERS** of the world, never again have we as a people been brought back in ships to our native land in Africa/Israel. The last few words of Deuteronomy 28:68 say, "**And no man shall buy you.**" The word "**buy**" in Old English was also synonymous with the word "**redeem**" or "**save**".

"**Redeem**" means:

- regain possession of (something) in exchange for payment.
- to free from captivity by payment.
- to buy back.

If you were to "**redeem**" a slave, you would be essentially setting that slave free, just like slaves could have their freedom bought if they or someone else had enough cash to **redeem** them. Also, if you were to **redeem** someone, you are saving them from evil or bondage.

But did Genesis give us clues that the Children of Israel would rise up again and be "re-gathered?" You be the Judge.

Genesis 49:1 "And Jacob called his sons, and said, Gather yourselves together, that I may tell you that which shall befall you in the **LAST DAYS**."

Genesis 49:9-10 "Judah is a lion's whelp (cub): from the prey, my son, thou are gone up: he stooped down, he couched as a lion, and as an **OLD LION; WHO SHALL RISE HIM UP?** The sceptre shall **NOT DEPART FROM JUDAH**, nor a lawgiver from between his feet, until Shiloh come; **AND UNTO HIMSHALL THE GATHERING OF THE PEOPLE (ISRAELITES) BE.**"

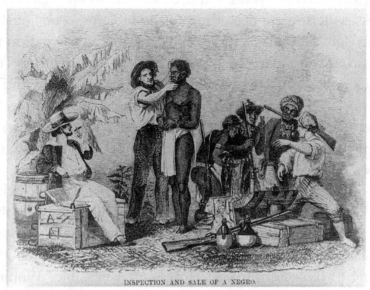

INSPECTION AND SALE OF A NEGRO.

Notice the Black Hamitic Africans or perhaps Negro Israelites with guns in the back negotiating a price for the Negro and the pot of run/molasses on the floor. Negro Slaves were often sold, sometimes by their own people for gun powder, guns, rum, molasses and other stuff the European man had.

Deuteronomy Chapter 28 is talking about the **Hebrew Israelites and future "Negroes"**; not the White European Judaism-converts called "**Jews**" who were held in concentration camps in Europe for only 12 years. This is not to disrespect what the European "Jews" went through back then. Deuteronomy 28 clearly show that the Curses of Israel do not fit their people. Remember the Curses of Israel were not lifted when Jesus was born, **nor were they lifted after he died on the cross, was buried and was resurrected**. If they were, all of the 12 Tribes of Israel would've come back to the Holy Land (as the Old Testament prophesies) and Solomon's temple wouldn't have been destroyed by the Romans and Edomites in 70 A.D. Jesus clearly prophesied the fate of his "**Chosen People**" and Jerusalem in Luke 21:24 before his death and resurrection.

In **Luke 21:24** Yahusha (Jesus) wasn't talking about the **Edomites** or Romans falling by the edge of the sword and being led away captive into all nations. It is clear that "**they**" are the **Hebrew Israelites**. It is clear that after the expulsion of the remaining Hebrew Israelites, the Gentiles (**people that are not Israelites such as Edomites, Romans, Greeks, Arabs and those who were of other nations practicing**

Judaism calling themselves "**Jews**") and other "**Heathen**" nations were the ones that were to possess Jerusalem according to the bible. So obviously black people are not "**Gentiles**" or "**Goyim**" as Judaism teaches because we didn't take over and possess Jerusalem in any part of history after Jesus' death. The "Crusades" consisted of Black Arabs and Turkish/Kurdish Arabs fighting with Europeans over Jerusalem, not Blacks. Even today, Israel is paying Africans up to $5,000 to leave their country because they don't want blacks there. The European Jews today all claim to be from the Tribe of Judah, Benjamin and Levi (+Kohanite). They claim that the 10 Tribes of Israel are still lost but yet the Ethiopian Jews are supposedly from the **Tribe of Dan**, which is one of the "**10 Lost Tribes**" who lived in the Northern Kingdom of Israel adjacent to the half-Tribe of Ephraim, the half-Tribe of Manasseh, and the Tribe of Benjamin. They claim to be God's Chosen People but they don't possess the old territory for the Tribe of Asher, Gad, Manasseh and Reuben according to Bible Scriptures. How is that possible? Would God give his people only half or three-fourths the land they had before? No!

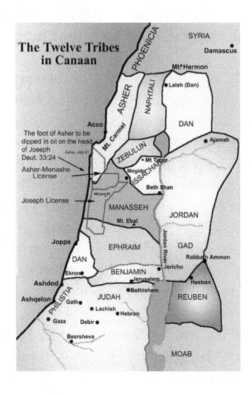

God does not lie so these prophecies are destined to come true. Yeshua/Yahusha (Jesus) before being crucified prophesied that the Gentiles would occupy Jerusalem until his second coming. This means that the Real Jews would not come back to the Holy Land until the End of Days. Therefore the Curses of Israel were to continue on after his ascension into heaven, which they did with the Arab Slave trade starting in 600 A.D (some sources say even earlier) and during the many "Crusade" battles between the Japhetic/Edomite Europeans, the Black Arabs and Japhetic/Edomite White Arabs. Most of the Hebrews during this time were already scattered into Africa, Arabia, the Americas, the Caribbean and other parts of the world. Slavery enabled the Hebrew Israelites to be further scattered to all the corners of the earth, just as the bible predicted. Isn't it amazing that the Transatlantic Slave Trade brought the "Negro" Israelites to the same land their brethren "Native American" Israelites were inhabiting? We could've been brought to other places in the world but why the "New World?" Also, why are West Africans primarily the ones living amongst Blacks in America? Could it be some "hidden" spiritual force that is bringing the Israelites all together, like twins separated at birth that live in the same state/city? The white European race spread their people, teachings, language, modified religion and skin color into the people of the lands thereby erasing the identity of the Hebrew Israelites. They also stole our history, ancient treasures, ancient written records and replaced it with their own. They essentially **RE-WROTE THEMSELVES INTO OUR HISTORY**! They did this not by God's order, but by warring, conquering and colonizing everybody else's country. This is a known fact. So my question to you is; **who are the REAL descendants of the Children of Israel based on the scriptures?** It is very clear and lastly I want to leave you with this:

"EVERY KING SPRINGS FROM A RACE OF SLAVES, AND EVERY SLAVE HAD KINGS AMONG HIS ANCESTORS."
PLATO

We are not Negroes, we are Hebrew Israelites, descendants of Israelite Kings and the Children of the Almighty God.

If this Book in addition to the Original "**Hebrews to Negroes**" Book doesn't convince you that the Jews today are "**imposters**" and that the Children of Israel were a brown-black people then I don't know what will. Common sense is enough to come to an accurate conclusion that the original Hebrew Israelites were not all white, neither was the Tribe of Judah. The Bible is clear. There is still a **House of Israel** and a **House of Judah** as it was thousands of years ago. Per the scriptures they are still scattered to the four corners of the Earth. But Bible prophecy is unfolding as the 12 Tribes are waking up. We may not know exactly what Tribe we are from but we are realizing who "Israel" is and who is not. In the Book of Jeremiah, God gave a promise to give his physical "**Children of Israel**" a "**New (Second) Covenant**" in the future. This was a promise made to the descendants of the "**Physical**" Biblical Hebrew Israelites before Yahusha/Yeshua identified a "**Spiritual Israel**" or a "**Spiritual Seed of Abraham**" in the New Testament. The word "**New covenant**" or "**Brit Chadashah**" is described in only one place in the Old Testament and that is in the Book of Jeremiah. Before I discuss this "**Second Covenant**", people need to know where the "**First Covenant**" was made between God and the Children of Israel. The God of the Old Testament did not make a covenant with the whole world; he made it with the Israelites.

Romans 9:4-5 "Who are Israelites; to whom pertaineith the adoption, and the glory, and the covenants, and the giving of **THE LAW**, and the service of God, and the promises; Whose are the fathers, and of whom as concerning the flesh Christ came, who is over all, God blessed forever, Amen."

Exodus 19:5 "Now therefore, if ye will obey my voice indeed, and keep **MY COVENANT**, then ye shall be a **PECULIAR TREASURE** unto me **ABOVE ALL PEOPLE**: for all the earth is mine: And ye shall be unto me a Kingdom of Priests, and an Holy Nation. These are the words which thou shalt speak unto the children of Israel".

In the 1823 Book, "**View of the Hebrews**" by Ethan Smith, he uses citations from James Adair and Alexander von Humboldt to explain that the **Native Americans** were the descendants of the 10 Lost Tribes of Israel. On page 67, he writes:

"Mr. Adair is very full in this, that the Indians have but one God, the **Great Yohewah**, whom they call the great, beneficent, supreme, and Holy Spirit, who dwells in the clouds, and who dwells with good people and is the only object of worship. So different are they from all the idolatrous heathen upon earth........The

Indians thus please themselves with the idea that God has chosen them from the rest of mankind as his **PECULIAR PEOPLE**. This, he says, has been the occasion of their hating other people; and of viewing themselves hated by all men. These things show that they acknowledge but one God."

The Israelites were the Children of God. God gave them an "**Agreement**" to follow.

Jeremiah 7:23 "But this thing commanded I them saying, Obey my voice, and I will be your God, and ye shall be my people: and walk ye in all the ways that I have commanded you, that it may be well unto you."

The Children of Israel **agreed** to the "Agreement/Covenant" **verbally**.

Exodus 19:8 "And all the people (of Israel) answered together, and said, **All that the Lord hath spoken we will do.** And Moses returned the words of the people unto the Lord."

But the Children of Israel were disobedient. God knew that, so he explained to them the "Blessings & Curses" that would follow depending on if they kept his commandments. **This is listed in Deuteronomy 28 and Leviticus 26**.

Leviticus 26:14-18 "But if ye will not hearken unto me, and will not do all these commandments; And if ye shall despise my statutes, or if your soul abhor my judgements, so that ye will not do all my commandments, but that ye break my covenant: I also will do this unto you; I will even appoint over you terror, consumption, and the burning ague, that shall consume the eyes, and cause sorrow of heart: and ye shall sow your seed in vain, for your enemies shall eat it. **And I will set my face against you, and ye shall be slain before your enemies: they that hate you shall reign over you; and ye shall flee when none pursueth you**. And if ye will not yet for all this hearken unto me, then I will punish you seven times more for your sins."

So the Israelites broke the "**First Covenant**". The "**flaw**" was with the people of Israel, not with God. God did his part. So for this reason God is giving us a "**Second Covenant**".

Hebrews 8:7-8 "For if that **FIRST COVENANT** had been faultless, then should no place have been sought for the second. For finding fault with them (Israelites), he saith, Behold, the days come, saith the Lord, when I will make a **NEW COVENANT** with the **House of Israel** and with the **House of Judah**:"

Even King David knew his people had broken the Covenant with God.

Psalms 78:10 "They kept not the covenant of God, and refused to walk in his law; and forgat his works, and his wonders that he had shewed them."

Because of this disobedience God promised to give us a "**SECOND NEW COVENANT**".

Jeremiah 31:31-34 "Behold, the days come, saith the Lord (Yahuah), that **I will make a new covenant with the House of Israel and with the House of Judah**: Not according to the covenant that I made with their fathers in the day that I took them by the hand to bring them out of the land of Egypt; which my covenant they brake, although I was an husband unto them, saith the Lord: But this shall be the covenant that I will make with the House of Israel; **After those days, saith the Lord, I will put my law in their inward parts, and write it in their hearts; and will be their God, and they shall be my people**. And they shall teach no more every man his neighbor, and every man his brother, saying, Know the Lord: for they shall all know me, from the least of them, saith the Lord: for I will forgive their iniquity, and I will remember their sin no more."

How do we know that there will always be a Physical "Israel Nation" on this planet?

Jeremiah 31:35-37 "Thus saith the Lord (Yahuah), which giveth the sun for a light by day, and the ordinances of the moon and of the stars for a light by night, which divideth the sea when the waves thereof roar, The Lord of hosts is his name: **If those ordinances (laws) depart before me, saith the Lord, then the seed of Israel also shall cease from being a nation before me for ever. Thus saith the Lord; If heaven above can be measured, and the foundations of the earth searched out beneath, I will also cast off all the seed of Israel for all that they have done, saith the Lord.**

So can the Heavens above be measured? No. So God is saying that as long as there is a heaven, a sun shining during the day, a moon with stars shining at night, Israel will continue to be a nation. If you have seen the Sun, moon and stars today that means **ISRAEL** exists as a physical people. We must realize now **who is ISRAEL** and **who are not ISRAEL**! Everything that's happening around us will then start to all make sense. Take heed to what King David said in this Psalms as you get ready to close this book.

PSALMS 78:7-8 "That they might set their hope in God, and not **FORGET** the works of God, but keep his commandments: and might not be **AS THEIR FATHERS, A STUBBORN AND REBELLIOUS GENERATION**; a generation that set not their heart aright, and whose **SPIRIT** was not steadfast with God."

THIS IS A CALL TO THE REAL CHILDREN OF ISRAEL TO WAKE UP!

How can we receive God's "**New Covenant**" if we are still asleep? How can we turn from our wicked ways and do what is required of us by God if we are still asleep? How can we understand our suffering by listening to our Gentile oppressors? The Bible explains it all. It's time we stop reading the Bible as if it's a story when it is about us and our ancestors. Let's wake Jacob up!

"Taken from the Hall of Ham but I am Shem, taken from the Heart of Africa but I am Israel"

Queen Makedah Reggae Music Artist.

Thanks to everyone who has taken the time to read this book. Bible prophecy is unfolding and it is time for the **TRUTH** to come out. **A LIE CANNOT LIVE FOREVER!**

Galatians 4:16 "Am I therefore become your enemy, because I tell you the TRUTH?"

John 8:32 "And ye shall know the TRUTH, and the TRUTH shall make you free."

SHALOM

CHAPTER PAGE NUMBERS